America's
TEST KITCHEN

THE BEST OF

America's

TEST KITCHEN

THE YEAR'S BEST RECIPES, EQUIPMENT
REVIEWS, AND TASTINGS

2010

BY THE EDITORS AT
AMERICA'S TEST KITCHEN

PHOTOGRAPHY BY
CARL TREMBLAY, KELLER + KELLER, AND DANIEL J. VAN ACKERE

AMERICA'S TEST KITCHEN
17 Station Street, Brookline, MA 02445

Library of Congress Cataloging-in-Publication Data
The Editors at America's Test Kitchen

THE BEST OF AMERICA'S TEST KITCHEN 2010
The Year's Best Recipes, Equipment Reviews, and Tastings

1st Edition

Hardcover: $35 US
ISBN-13: 978-1-933615-54-7   ISBN-10: 1-933615-54-0
1. Cooking. 1. Title
2009

Manufactured in the United States of America

10 9 8 7 6 5 4 3 2 1

Distributed by America's Test Kitchen
17 Station Street, Brookline, MA 02445

EDITORIAL DIRECTOR: Jack Bishop
EXECUTIVE EDITOR: Elizabeth Carduff
EDITOR: Elizabeth Wray Emery
DESIGN DIRECTOR: Amy Klee
ART DIRECTOR: Greg Galvan
DESIGNERS: Erica Lee and Tiffani Beckwith
FRONT COVER PHOTOGRAPH: Carl Tremblay
STAFF PHOTOGRAPHER: Daniel J. van Ackere
ADDITIONAL PHOTOGRAPHERS: Keller + Keller and Peter Tannenbaum
FOOD STYLING: Marie Piraino and Mary Jane Sawyer
ILLUSTRATOR: John Burgoyne
PRODUCTION DIRECTOR: Guy Rochford
SENIOR PRODUCTION MANAGER: Jessica Quirk
SENIOR PROJECT MANAGER: Alice Carpenter
PRODUCTION AND TRAFFIC COORDINATOR: Laura Collins
COLOR AND IMAGING SPECIALIST: Andrew Mannone
PRODUCTION AND IMAGING SPECIALISTS: Judy Blomquist and Lauren Pettapiece
COPYEDITOR: Jeffrey Schier
PROOFREADER: Karen Fraley
INDEXER: Elizabeth Parson

PICTURED ON THE FRONT COVER: Triple-Chocolate Mousse Cake (page 270)

CONTENTS

INTRODUCTION   1

STARTERS & SALADS   2

SOUPS & STEWS   20

VEGETABLES & SIDE DISHES   42

BREAKFAST & BREADS   70

PASTA   108

MEAT   126

POULTRY   178

SEAFOOD   206

DESSERTS   224

TEST KITCHEN RESOURCES   272

INDEX   316

INTRODUCTION

THIS HAS BEEN OUR BUSIEST AND MOST PRODUCTIVE year ever, and to think that, for years, I worried about running out of recipes to test and perfect. Well, it seems that we are still up to our ears with new projects, new recipes, and new challenges.

One of our most difficult endeavors is going back to a recipe that we have done before, thinking that we can make it even better. This year at *Cook's Illustrated,* we did just that with Chicken Noodle Soup and discovered that ground chicken made a much better broth than parts or bones and required only 30 minutes of simmering. Hmm. So much for the "all day on the back of the stove" approach used for centuries. We also found a way to make a terrific cassoulet in a slow cooker, developed a make-ahead green bean casserole, vastly improved au gratin potatoes by cutting the heavy cream with chicken broth and using a mix of cheeses, completely reinvented the omelet by using small pieces of frozen butter in the egg mixture (the science is fascinating), finally figured out how to make the world's best blueberry muffin using a quick-cook blueberry swirl, took a fresh look at our quick tomato sauce in an effort to perfect it (grated onions did the trick), and revisited, yet again, the notion of roast turkey and hit it out of the ballpark using a covering of salt pork, which made the meat extra juicy and incredibly flavorful.

We also seem to be having a bit more fun recently, discovering recipes that have been overlooked in the food world's rush to find whatever is new. That list includes Wisconsin Cheddar Beer Soup, a legendary Garlic and Cheese Mashed Potatoes dish from France, St. Louis Gooey Butter Cake, Green Chile Cheeseburgers, both Cornell and Huli Huli Chicken, Spiedies (fabulous grilled and marinated chicken sandwiches), New Orleans Barbecue Shrimp, French Silk Chocolate Pie, and 7UP Pound Cake.

Plus, this book also provides the best of our tastings and testings, including full page charts summarizing our findings on, to name a few, supermarket olive oil, black peppercorns, vanilla extract, and chocolate chips, as well as answers to which skillet, automatic drip coffeemaker, silicone spatula, plastic wrap, cookware set, and blender (and many more) one should buy.

I look back over the last year of life in Vermont and feel equally exhausted with all the projects we have undertaken, from building a greenhouse, to boiling 350 gallons of maple syrup, to expanding our root cellar garden, to constructing a bear-proof bee house (the bears destroyed our hives this spring), to planting feedlots for deer. But, at the end of the day, I know that the food will be good, whether a winter dinner in front of the fire or a summer supper out the back door of the kitchen. This book contains our best work from the year, the "best of the best," if you will, and you should feel confident that the recipes will work the first time and every time.

Calvin Coolidge once said about gardening that "it is extremely practical on the one hand, and lends itself to the artistic on the other." The same is true, of course, of cooking—it is the perfect marriage between necessity and aspiration, of satisfying hands-on heavy lifting and the song of the muse. Over the years, I have noticed that Vermonters rarely tip their hats to creativity but they instinctively appreciate the fine art of handling a team of workhorses or the perfect pitch of hay, as a bale sails up to the top of the pile. This book is about putting food on the table but it is also about the fine art of cooking, pursuing the perfect recipe and the best technique. Yes, you can do one without considering the other, but it lessens the pleasure of cooking, the moment when the ultimate French omelet slides onto a plate and then onto a fork to be savored by a family member or neighbor. That's the true joy of cooking, and we hope we offer it here in the pages of *The Best of America's Test Kitchen 2010.*

CHRISTOPHER KIMBALL
Founder and Editor,
Cook's Illustrated and *Cook's Country*
Host, *America's Test Kitchen* and
Cook's Country from America's Test Kitchen

CHAPTER 1

STARTERS & SALADS

Caponata   4

Crispy Bacon-Cheddar Potato Skins   7

Boneless Buffalo Chicken with Blue Cheese Dressing   9

Cherry Tomato Salads   10

    Greek Cherry Tomato Salad

    Cherry Tomato Salad with Basil and Fresh Mozzarella

    Cherry Tomato Salad with Tarragon and Blue Cheese

    Cherry Tomato and Watermelon Salad

    Cherry Tomato Salad with Mango and Lime Curry Vinaigrette

Baked Goat Cheese Salads   12

    Herbed Baked Goat Cheese Salad

    Honey-Raisin Baked Goat Cheese Salad

    Sun-Dried Tomato Baked Goat Cheese Salad

Waldorf Salad   14

    Waldorf Salad with Red Grapes and Almonds

    Waldorf Salad with Dried Cranberries and Pecans

    Curried Waldorf Salad with Green Grapes and Peanuts

German Potato Salad   17

CAPONATA

EVERY SICILIAN VILLAGE HAS ITS OWN SPIN on caponata—a dish revered in Italy for hundreds of years, but far less well known in other parts of the world. If you've never encountered caponata, imagine a soft mélange of stewed vegetables—typically eggplant, celery, onion, red pepper, and tomato—augmented by the bolder flavors and textures of such Mediterranean stalwarts as capers, anchovies, olives, raisins, and pine nuts. The mixture is enriched by the viscous, deeply flavorful cooking liquid from the vegetables, and enhanced by sugar and a splash of wine vinegar. This relish is typically used as a topping for bruschetta or as an accompaniment to grilled meat or fish—but I find it so addicting I can simply eat spoonfuls from a bowl. It is always served warm or at room temperature, never cold.

Although its ingredients may vary, caponata's preparation is usually the same: The vegetables are first sautéed, then simmered in liquid with the other components to meld the flavors. While the method sounded simple enough, a first trial of recipes revealed that it wasn't foolproof. I found that the problems almost always stemmed from caponata's star ingredient: eggplant.

Eggplant is essentially a sponge, consisting of a maze of tiny air pockets ready to absorb anything, especially the medium it's cooked in. It's also packed with water. I knew from experience that both properties make eggplant troublesome to cook. When it is sautéed, for example, the air pockets will suck up any oil in the pan, forcing the cook to keep adding oil to prevent sticking or burning. Meanwhile, the moisture inside turns to steam. This one-two punch transforms the eggplant into oil-soaked mush before it has a chance to caramelize.

In the test kitchen, we get around these problems by salting and pressing the eggplant—the salt draws out moisture and pressing eliminates air pockets. But after this treatment, the eggplant was still too greasy for my liking. What about dehydrating the eggplant in the microwave? After all, this appliance works by causing the water molecules in food to oscillate rapidly and generate steam. Food left in the microwave long enough will eventually transition from merely heating up to actually dehydrating.

I placed the cubed, salted eggplant in a single layer on a plate and nuked it for 10 minutes. Lots of water leached out, all right—but it also pooled on the plate, poaching the eggplant into a soupy mess. A few coffee filters placed under the eggplant absorbed moisture so well that the eggplant shriveled to one-third its size, eliminating any need for pressing. I was able to sauté the dried eggplant in the smallest amount of oil yet (1 tablespoon versus the nearly ½ cup I had been using). I then removed it from the pan while I sautéed some onion, celery, and bell pepper, returning it when I was ready to stew them all together. Once I added liquid to the pan, the eggplant plumped back up, absorbing the flavors of the other ingredients instead of just oil.

Tomatoes are almost as integral to the dish as eggplant, providing a rich, fruity sweetness that nothing else can replicate. The question was, when should I add them? If I added them too early, they lost their fresh taste; if I added them just before taking the pan off the heat, they gave the dish the texture of fresh salsa rather than blending into a harmonious medley. I struck the perfect balance by gently simmering the tomatoes with the browned eggplant and other ingredients at the very end of cooking.

Adding canned tomatoes to deepen the tomato flavor seemed like a good idea, but while tasters praised their concentrated flavor, they didn't care for their pulpy texture. Tomato paste also proved problematic, contributing intensity but camouflaging the delicate flavor of the fresh tomatoes. Running out of options, I gave V8 juice a try. A small amount was just enough to provide another layer of tomato flavor, while still allowing the fresh tomatoes to shine.

With the major problems solved, I needed to focus on the sweet and sour finish that is essential to traditional caponata. Honey, molasses, and maple syrup all overpowered the other flavors in the dish; brown sugar was the winner for the sweet component, lending more complexity than white. As for the sour note, red wine vinegar provided just the right bracing degree of tartness.

Tasters agreed that the customary inclusion of raisins and olives was a must. After trying a dozen different olive varieties, I made the happy discovery that almost any olive would work. A few anchovy fillets deepened the overall flavor of the dish, and a sprinkle of toasted pine nuts provided an aromatic crunch. At last I had a simple, well-balanced recipe for an authentic caponata that tasted great as an appetizer, as a relish, or just straight from the bowl.

—FRANCISCO J. ROBERT, *Cook's Illustrated*

CAPONATA

Caponata

MAKES 3 CUPS

Serve caponata spooned over slices of toasted baguette or alongside grilled meat or fish. If coffee filters are not available, food-safe, undyed paper towels can be substituted when microwaving the eggplant. To allow the steam released by the eggplant to escape, remove the plate from the microwave immediately. Although the test kitchen prefers the complex flavor of V8 vegetable juice, tomato juice can be substituted. Caponata is best made in advance and can be refrigerated in an airtight container for up to 1 week.

- 1 large eggplant (about 1½ pounds), cut into ½-inch cubes (about 7 cups)
- ¾ teaspoon kosher salt
- ¾ cup V8 vegetable juice (see note)
- ¼ cup red wine vinegar, plus extra for seasoning
- 2 tablespoons brown sugar
- ¼ cup chopped fresh parsley
- 1½ teaspoons minced anchovy fillets (2 to 3 fillets)
- 8 ounces ripe tomato (about 1 large), cored, seeded, and chopped medium (about 1 cup)
- ¼ cup raisins
- 2 tablespoons minced black olives
- 2 tablespoons extra-virgin olive oil
- 1 celery rib, chopped fine (about ½ cup)
- 1 red bell pepper, stemmed, seeded, and chopped fine (about ½ cup)
- 1 small onion, minced (about ½ cup)
- ¼ cup pine nuts, toasted (see page 16)

1. Toss the eggplant and salt together in a medium bowl. Line the entire surface of a large microwave-safe plate with a double layer of coffee filters and lightly spray with vegetable oil spray. Spread the eggplant in an even layer over the coffee filters. Microwave on high power until the eggplant is dry and shriveled to one-third of its original size, 8 to 15 minutes (the eggplant should not brown). (If the microwave has no turntable, rotate the plate after 5 minutes.) Remove the eggplant from the microwave and immediately transfer it to a paper towel–lined plate.

2. Meanwhile, whisk the vegetable juice, vinegar, brown sugar, parsley, and anchovies together in a medium bowl. Stir in the tomato, raisins, and olives.

3. Heat 1 tablespoon of the oil in a 12-inch nonstick skillet over medium-high heat until shimmering. Add the eggplant and cook, stirring occasionally, until the edges are browned, 4 to 8 minutes, adding 1 teaspoon more oil if the pan appears dry. Transfer to a bowl and set aside.

4. Add the remaining oil (you should have 2 to 3 teaspoons left) to the now-empty skillet and heat until shimmering. Add the celery, bell pepper, and onion; cook, stirring occasionally, until softened and the edges are spotty brown, 6 to 8 minutes.

NOTES FROM THE TEST KITCHEN

CAPONATA'S SUPPORTING PLAYERS

V8 JUICE
Though not traditional, a little V8 juice enhances caponata's tomato flavor.

RED WINE VINEGAR
Red wine vinegar brings the right degree of acidity.

ANCHOVY
A few minced fillets add dimension without imparting an overtly fishy taste.

BROWN SUGAR
Brown sugar adds more complexity than white sugar.

OLIVES
Black olives lend fruitiness and bump up the robust flavors of the relish.

A CURE FOR WHAT AILS EGGPLANT

To rid the eggplant of excess moisture and collapse the air pockets that make it soak up oil like a sponge, we came up with a novel solution: salting it and then heating it in the microwave. The salt pulls out liquid from inside the eggplant at the same time the microwave causes it to steam. In addition, the microwave helps to compress the eggplant, making it less spongy. To keep the eggplant from poaching in the liquid it released, we set it on a layer of coffee filters.

RAW
Without pretreatment, the raw eggplant looks good but cooks up oily and mushy.

MICROWAVED
Salted, microwaved eggplant isn't as pretty, but the shrunken cubes soak up far less oil.

5. Reduce the heat to medium-low; stir in the eggplant and vegetable juice mixture. Bring to a simmer and cook until the vegetable juice is thickened and coats the vegetables, 4 to 7 minutes. Transfer to a serving bowl and cool to room temperature. Season with up to 1 teaspoon additional vinegar to taste. Sprinkle with the pine nuts before serving.

POTATO SKINS

WITH TASTY HITS OF SALT, CHEESE, AND BACON, potato skins have an obvious appeal. But if your house isn't a restaurant or sports bar with a preheated deep-fat fryer at the ready, it can be hard to get them perfectly crisp. Most recipes I found instruct the home cook to bake the potatoes, scoop out and discard the flesh, top the shells with cheese and bacon, and then bake again. One and all, these failed to produce satisfying crunch.

Right off the bat, I opted to save time by microwaving the potatoes. (Russets were the obvious choice for our potato skins; they have a high starch/low-moisture content that makes them ideal for baking—or, in this case, microwaving—and their sturdy skins hold up well once the flesh is scooped out.) Although they were a little soggy coming out of the microwave, I dutifully scooped out the flesh, filled the skins with cooked bacon and plenty of cheese, and hoped that baking them in a really hot (475-degree) oven would crisp them up. It didn't. For my next test, I tried brushing the skin side of the shells with rendered bacon fat. This added flavor and dialed up the crispness, but not enough. A colleague happened to be baking crisp-crust pizza on a hot pizza stone, and, following course, I preheated a baking sheet and put the filled skins directly on the hot pan. The louder crunch of these skins showed I was making progress.

Up to now, I'd been using hollowed-out potato halves. I cut the shells in quarters on the theory that increasing the surface area that made contact with the hot sheet would mean more crispy bits. It did, but I still wasn't satisfied. Then I remembered a test kitchen recipe for twice-baked potatoes that bakes the shells before they are filled. I microwaved the potatoes, scooped out the flesh, baked the shells for 15 minutes to cook out excess moisture, filled them, and returned them to the oven to melt the cheese. I held my breath while colleagues chomped. Touchdown!

—MEGHAN ERWIN, *Cook's Country*

Crispy Bacon-Cheddar Potato Skins
MAKES 16 POTATO SKINS

Serve with sour cream and sliced scallions, if you like.

- 4 russet potatoes (about 8 ounces each), scrubbed
- 6 slices bacon, chopped
  Salt and pepper
- 4 ounces sharp cheddar cheese, shredded (about 1 cup)
- 4 ounces Monterey Jack cheese, shredded (about 1 cup)
- 1 tablespoon cornstarch

1. Adjust an oven rack to the upper-middle position and heat the oven to 475 degrees. Set a foil-lined rimmed baking sheet on the rack. Prick the potatoes all over with a fork, place them on a paper towel, and microwave until tender, 10 to 15 minutes, turning the potatoes over after 5 minutes.

2. Meanwhile, cook the bacon in a large skillet over medium heat until crisp, about 8 minutes. Reserve 2 teaspoons of the bacon fat, then transfer the bacon to a paper towel–lined plate. Blot the bacon with paper towels to remove excess grease.

3. Quarter the potatoes lengthwise, let cool for 5 minutes, and then scoop out most of the flesh (reserve for another use), leaving a ¼-inch layer of potato flesh. (The potatoes can be refrigerated in an airtight container for up to 2 days.) Brush the exterior of the potatoes with the reserved bacon fat and season with salt and pepper. Transfer the potatoes, skin-side down, to the preheated baking sheet and bake until golden brown and crisp, 15 to 20 minutes.

4. Combine the cheeses, cornstarch, half of the bacon, ½ teaspoon salt, and ¼ teaspoon pepper in a bowl. Remove the potato shells from the oven and top with the cheese mixture. Return to the oven and bake until the cheese melts, 2 to 4 minutes. Transfer the skins to a paper towel–lined plate and sprinkle with the remaining bacon. Serve.

NOTES FROM THE TEST KITCHEN

PIERCING PAYS OFF
We have found that it's important to pierce the potatoes thoroughly with a fork before they go into the microwave. Piercing the skin ensures that moisture will escape from the potatoes during cooking, yielding crisp, sturdy shells.

BONELESS BUFFALO CHICKEN WITH BLUE CHEESE DRESSING

BONELESS BUFFALO CHICKEN

ANYONE WHO'S BEEN TO A SPORTS BAR knows Buffalo wings, and these days deep-fried nuggets of boneless chicken breasts are likely to get the same treatment. Maybe it's because we don't want the hassle of prying small amounts of meat from messy bones. More likely, it's because every inch of every nugget gets a crunchy fried-chicken coating. To finish, the nuggets are tossed in a blend of hot sauce and butter. Its blaze-orange color is as hot as its burn, which only a cold beer can douse.

But with so many steps—marinating the chicken, dredging it in a flour-based coating, frying, and tossing with Buffalo sauce—there's plenty of room for error, as I found out to my dismay early in my testing. I was stymied by recipes that produced dry, tough chicken with crusts that turned soggy and greasy the minute they hit the sauce.

I hoped I could ensure moist chicken meat by soaking it in a marinade before dredging in flour and frying. One recipe I'd seen called for marinating the meat right in the Buffalo sauce, which I had assumed would add moisture and another layer of flavor. The cooked chicken was indeed moist, but the extra sauce made it too hot to eat. The oil-based marinade I turned to next was greasy. But a fried chicken–style marinade of buttermilk and salt kept the delicate white meat juicy and moist, and helped season it as well.

To prevent the fried crust from getting soggy when sauced, I knew I'd have to create a coating more substantial than the seasoned flour in the failed recipes. I turned to a technique we use in the test kitchen for an extra-crunchy coating on fried chicken: dipping the chicken in beaten egg whites, then dredging it in a mixture of cornstarch, flour, and baking soda (for browning) that turns moist and lumpy with the addition of a little buttermilk. The idea is that this pebbly coating fries up craggy and extra-crisp, and it worked beautifully. Since the quantity of liquid is so small, swapping out the buttermilk for a little of the hot sauce mixture added flavor without too much heat.

I had been using the standard sauce of equal parts melted butter and hot sauce, but with the fried coating the dish was too greasy. Cutting the butter way back (to just 1 tablespoon) solved that problem. Unfortunately, without butter to thicken the sauce and soften its burn, the sauce slid off the nuggets in a scorching puddle.

Attempting to solve the first problem, I went back to that box of cornstarch. Admittedly, it was an unusual approach to Buffalo sauce, but I wasn't going to be a stickler if the method worked. I was pleased to see that 2 teaspoons cornstarch yielded a thick, glazy sauce that coated the nuggets without undoing their crunch. I turned my attention to the heat level. A simple fix—cutting the hot sauce with some water—reduced the burn.

Served with a side of creamy blue cheese dressing for dipping, my boneless Buffalo chicken hit every mark: crunchy, juicy, fiery, and tender. Best of all, I could enjoy it in the comfort of my own kitchen.

—LYNN CLARK, *Cook's Country*

Boneless Buffalo Chicken with Blue Cheese Dressing

SERVES 4 TO 6

Stilton is an English blue cheese with a pungent, slightly sweet flavor. A relatively mild cayenne pepper–based hot sauce, such as Frank's, is essential; avoid hotter sauces like Tabasco.

BLUE CHEESE DRESSING

- 3 ounces Stilton cheese, crumbled (about ¾ cup) (see note)
- ¾ cup mayonnaise
- 6 tablespoons sour cream
- 1½ tablespoons cider vinegar
- ¼ teaspoon pepper
- ⅛ teaspoon garlic powder

CHICKEN

- 1½ pounds boneless, skinless chicken breasts, trimmed and cut into 1½-inch chunks
- ½ cup buttermilk
- 1 teaspoon salt
- ¾ cup hot sauce (see note)
- ¼ cup water
- ¼ teaspoon sugar
- 1 tablespoon unsalted butter
- 1½ cups plus 2 teaspoons cornstarch
- 4 large egg whites
- ½ cup unbleached all-purpose flour
- ½ teaspoon baking soda
- 4 cups vegetable oil

1. FOR THE DRESSING: Combine all of the ingredients in a food processor and process until smooth, about

30 seconds, scraping down the sides of the bowl as necessary. (The dressing can be refrigerated in an airtight container for up to 1 week.)

2. FOR THE CHICKEN: Combine the chicken, buttermilk, and salt in a large zipper-lock bag and refrigerate for 30 minutes or up to 2 hours. Combine the hot sauce, water, sugar, butter, and 2 teaspoons of the cornstarch in a saucepan. Whisk over medium heat until thickened, about 5 minutes.

3. Whisk the egg whites in a shallow dish until foamy. Stir the flour, baking soda, remaining 1½ cups cornstarch, and 6 tablespoons of the hot sauce mixture in a second shallow dish until the mixture resembles coarse cornmeal. Remove the chicken from the marinade and pat dry with paper towels. Toss half of the chicken with the egg whites until well coated, then dredge the chicken in the cornstarch mixture, pressing to adhere. Transfer the coated chicken to a plate and repeat with the remaining chicken.

4. Heat the oil in a Dutch oven over medium-high heat until the oil registers 350 degrees. Fry half of the chicken until golden brown, about 4 minutes, turning each piece halfway through cooking. Transfer the chicken to a paper towel–lined plate. Return the oil to 350 degrees and repeat with the remaining chicken. (The fried chicken can be held in a 200-degree oven for 30 minutes before being tossed with the sauce.)

5. Warm the remaining hot sauce mixture over medium-low heat until simmering. Combine the chicken and the hot sauce mixture in a large bowl and toss to coat. Serve with the blue cheese dressing.

NOTES FROM THE TEST KITCHEN

OUR FAVORITE DRY MEASURING CUPS
Dry measuring cups vary in material, weight, shape, and price. To test accuracy, we filled cups to the brim with water and checked whether they fell within 5 percent of the target weight. (We have found that this yields a more precise measurement than filling them with a dry ingredient like flour, where the amount can vary.) We discovered we preferred stainless steel over plastic for its heft and durability. We also liked long handles that extend straight out; angled or raised handles obstructed our ability to level off the ingredient. Our favorite cups, **Amco Stainless Steel 4-Piece Measuring Cup Set,** $9.95, have it all: accuracy, good weight balance, and long, level, well-marked handles.

CHERRY TOMATO SALADS

CHERRY TOMATOES ARE OFTEN CONSIDERED a support player in salad. But when summertime cherry tomatoes are especially sweet and juicy, they are more than worthy of taking center stage. I knew from experience, however, that I couldn't merely slice them in half, toss them with vinaigrette, and call it a salad. Like bigger, meatier beefsteak and plum varieties, cherry tomatoes exude lots of liquid when cut, quickly turning a salad into soup.

In the test kitchen we often slice larger tomatoes, sprinkle them with salt, and allow them to drain to remove liquid and concentrate flavors. Following suit, I tossed 2 pints of halved cherry tomatoes with ¼ teaspoon salt (plus a pinch of sugar to accentuate sweetness) and let them drain in a colander. After 30 minutes, only a paltry 2 tablespoons of liquid had leached out. What if I exposed even more of the tomatoes' surface area to salt? I tried again with a fresh batch of tomatoes, cutting each one along the equator and then in half again. Progress: The salted, quartered tomatoes netted ¼ cup of liquid. But even this wasn't enough to prevent the salad from turning soggy when I tossed the tomatoes with oil and vinegar.

Some tomato salad recipes call for removing the watery seed pockets of the tomatoes, thus eliminating a major source of liquid. I wasn't about to cut open 40 or so cherry tomatoes and painstakingly push out the jelly and seeds with my thumb; I needed a more efficient method. That's when I thought of a salad spinner. The centrifugal force of the whirling bowl spins water off lettuce and herbs. Why wouldn't it have the same effect on tomatoes? It did—spinning salted and drained tomatoes resulted in the release of ½ cup of liquid.

My tomatoes were no longer liquidy, but when I tossed them with dressing, I noticed they tasted a little dull. This was not too surprising, as the jelly is the most flavorful part of the tomato, and I had stripped it away. If I added the jelly to the oil and vinegar I was using to dress the tomatoes, I'd be putting the liquid I'd taken such pains to remove right back in. But how about reducing the jelly to concentrate its flavor? I strained the seeds from the jelly and then boiled it in a small saucepan with a chopped shallot and a little vinegar. After cooling the mixture and combining it with olive oil, I tossed it with the cherry tomatoes. This time I nailed it, with every bite of the salad delivering sweet tomato flavor.

—DAVID PAZMIÑO, *Cook's Illustrated*

Greek Cherry Tomato Salad

SERVES 4 TO 6

If in-season cherry tomatoes are unavailable, substitute vine-ripened cherry tomatoes or grape tomatoes from the supermarket. Cut grape tomatoes in half along the equator (rather than quartering them). If you don't have a salad spinner, use plastic wrap to tightly cover the bowl of salted tomatoes that have stood for 30 minutes and gently shake to remove seeds and excess liquid. Strain the liquid and proceed with the recipe as directed. The amount of liquid given off by the tomatoes will depend on their ripeness. If you have less than ½ cup of juice after spinning, proceed with the recipe using the entire amount of juice and reduce it to 3 tablespoons as directed (the cooking time will be shorter).

    2   pints ripe cherry tomatoes (about 24 ounces),
        quartered (see note)
        Salt
    ½   teaspoon sugar
    2   garlic cloves, minced
    ½   teaspoon dried oregano
    1   shallot, minced (about 3 tablespoons)
    1   tablespoon red wine vinegar
    2   tablespoons extra-virgin olive oil
        Pepper
    1   small cucumber, peeled, seeded, and
        chopped medium
    ½   cup chopped pitted kalamata olives
    4   ounces feta cheese, crumbled (about 1 cup)
    3   tablespoons chopped fresh parsley

1. Toss the tomatoes, ¼ teaspoon salt, and sugar in a medium bowl; let stand for 30 minutes. Transfer the tomatoes to a salad spinner and spin until the seeds and excess liquid have been removed, 45 to 60 seconds, stirring to redistribute the tomatoes several times during spinning. Return the tomatoes to a bowl and set aside. Strain the tomato liquid through a fine-mesh strainer into a liquid measuring cup, pressing on the solids to extract as much liquid as possible.

2. Bring ½ cup of the tomato liquid (discard any extra), garlic, oregano, shallot, and vinegar to a simmer in a small saucepan over medium heat. Simmer until reduced to 3 tablespoons, 6 to 8 minutes. Transfer the mixture to a small bowl and cool to room temperature, about

5 minutes. Whisk in the oil and pepper to taste until combined. Season with up to ⅛ teaspoon salt to taste.

3. Add the cucumber, olives, feta, dressing, and parsley to the bowl with the tomatoes; toss gently and serve.

VARIATIONS

Cherry Tomato Salad with Basil and Fresh Mozzarella

Follow the recipe for Greek Cherry Tomato Salad, substituting balsamic vinegar for the red wine vinegar and omitting the garlic and oregano in step 2. Substitute 1½ cups lightly packed fresh basil, roughly torn, and 8 ounces fresh mozzarella, cut into ½-inch cubes and patted dry with paper towels, for the cucumber, olives, feta, and parsley in step 3.

Cherry Tomato Salad with Tarragon and Blue Cheese

Follow the recipe for Greek Cherry Tomato Salad, substituting cider vinegar for the red wine vinegar, omitting the garlic and oregano, and adding 2 teaspoons Dijon mustard and 4 teaspoons honey to the tomato liquid in step 2. Substitute ½ cup roughly chopped toasted pecans, 2 ounces crumbled blue cheese (about ½ cup), and 1½ tablespoons chopped fresh tarragon for the cucumber, olives, feta, and parsley in step 3.

Cherry Tomato and Watermelon Salad

Sweet watermelon and salty feta taste surprisingly good together.

Follow the recipe for Greek Cherry Tomato Salad, substituting white wine vinegar for the red wine

---

NOTES FROM THE TEST KITCHEN

SHOPPING FOR SHALLOTS
When shopping, avoid shallots packaged in cardboard and cellophane boxes, which prevent you from checking out each shallot. Instead, go for loose shallots or the ones packed in plastic netting. They should feel firm and heavy and have no soft spots. Since most of our recipes call for less than 3 tablespoons of minced shallot, in the test kitchen we use only medium shallots (which yield about 3 tablespoons minced) or small shallots (which yield 2 tablespoons or less). A medium shallot should be about 1½ to 2 inches wide.

vinegar and omitting the garlic and oregano in step 2. Substitute 1 cup watermelon, cut into ½-inch cubes, for the cucumber and olives, and 3 tablespoons roughly chopped fresh mint for the parsley in step 3.

Cherry Tomato Salad with Mango and Lime Curry Vinaigrette

Follow the recipe for Greek Cherry Tomato Salad, substituting 4 teaspoons lime juice for the red wine vinegar, omitting the garlic and oregano, and adding ¼ teaspoon curry powder in step 2. Substitute 1 mango, pitted and cut into ½-inch dice (about 2 cups), ½ cup toasted slivered almonds (see page 16), and 3 tablespoons chopped fresh cilantro for the cucumber, olives, feta, and parsley in step 3.

BAKED GOAT CHEESE SALADS

WHEN DONE RIGHT, baked goat cheese salad is an irresistible blend of flavors and textures: warm, creamy, and tangy cheese rounds enveloped by crisp golden breading set atop lightly dressed greens. Coating and heating the cheese are clearly the major challenges of this recipe, as all too often an insubstantial coating and the high heat of pan frying lead to oozing rounds of cheese.

Fortunately the test kitchen has found solutions to both of these problems: A coating of herbs, eggs, and ground Melba toasts (rather than bread crumbs) provides a sturdy, flavorful coating that forms a cohesive, shell-like barrier around the goat cheese. And rather than pan frying the cheese rounds, we have found that freezing the breaded rounds for a couple of hours and then baking them at a high temperature (475 degrees) gives us the best of both worlds—a crisp, well-browned exterior and warm, gooey—but not oozing—cheese.

For the holiday season, I wanted to go further and add a variety of flavors to the cheese. A nut coating seemed apt for a holiday first course, and it was easy to replace the Melba toast crumbs with pecans ground in the food processor (like Melba toast, nuts are sturdy enough to protect the cheese from the high heat of the oven and prevent leaking). Since I already had the machine out, I experimented with giving the cheese a whirl in the bowl,

which allowed me to incorporate herbs such as chives and thyme throughout the cheese instead of just coating the outer layer with them. The technique was easy to vary: An almond-coated variation in which the goat cheese is studded with raisins and honey provides a pleasing contrast of sweet and tangy flavors, while a walnut-coated version pairs the cheese with bold sun-dried tomatoes and fragrant basil. I set my dolled-up rounds on a bed of greens tossed with a classic red wine vinaigrette. Now I had three salads worthy of any holiday table.

—KRIS WIDICAN, *Cook's Country*

Herbed Baked Goat Cheese Salad

SERVES 6

For a sweet counterpoint to the herb flavor, add 1 cup dried cherries, golden raisins, or dried cranberries to the salad just before tossing it.

VINAIGRETTE
- ¼ cup extra-virgin olive oil
- 1½ tablespoons red wine vinegar
- 2 teaspoons Dijon mustard
- 1 small shallot, minced (about 1 tablespoon)
- ⅛ teaspoon salt

SALAD
- 1½ cups pecans
- 12 ounces goat cheese, softened
- 2 tablespoons chopped fresh chives
- 1 teaspoon minced fresh thyme
- 2 large eggs
- Vegetable oil spray
- 12 cups hearty salad greens

1. FOR THE VINAIGRETTE: Combine all of the ingredients in a jar, seal the lid, and shake vigorously until emulsified.

2. FOR THE SALAD: Pulse the pecans in a food processor until finely chopped, about 10 pulses; transfer to a medium bowl. Add the cheese, chives, and thyme to the food processor and process until smooth, about 30 seconds. Refrigerate the cheese mixture in a covered bowl until firm, at least 1 hour or up to 2 days.

3. Using your hands, take 2 tablespoons of the chilled cheese mixture at a time and roll into twelve

HERBED BAKED GOAT CHEESE SALAD

1½-inch balls. Beat the eggs in a medium bowl. One at a time, dip the balls in the egg, allow the excess to run off, then roll them in the nuts, pressing gently to adhere. Place the balls 2 inches apart on a rimmed baking sheet. Press the balls into 2-inch disks with a greased measuring cup. Cover with plastic wrap and freeze until completely firm, at least 2 hours or up to 1 week.

4. Adjust an oven rack to the upper position and heat the oven to 475 degrees. Remove the plastic and spray the cheese lightly with vegetable oil spray. Bake until the nuts are golden brown and the cheese is warmed through, 7 to 10 minutes. Let cool for 3 minutes. Toss the greens with the vinaigrette and serve the warm cheese rounds over the dressed salad.

NOTES FROM THE TEST KITCHEN

THE PERILS OF TEMPERATURE
Cheese rounds that aren't frozen lose their shape when baked.

NOT FROZEN
A runny mess

THE BEST GOAT CHEESE
Just like cow's or sheep's milk cheeses, goat cheese can be aged or fresh, soft or firm, domestic or imported, musky or mild, etc. That said, most of what you can buy in supermarkets is relatively young cheese packaged in a log shape; it has a creamy, slightly grainy texture and a tangy, milky flavor. When shopping for goat cheese, avoid precrumbled cheeses—they tend to be dry and chalky—and be sure to take a close look at the label, as many supermarket goat cheeses include herbs and spices that could affect how you use them. Our favorite brand, **Vermont Butter & Cheese Chèvre**, has a distinct—but not overpowering—tang that works well in recipes or on its own. Once opened, goat cheese can be wrapped in parchment or wax paper and stored in the refrigerator for up to 2 weeks.

VARIATIONS
Honey-Raisin Baked Goat Cheese Salad
For crunch, add 2 thinly sliced apples or firm pears.

Follow the recipe for Herbed Baked Goat Cheese Salad, substituting almonds for the pecans. Omit the chives and thyme and add 1 tablespoon golden raisins and 1 teaspoon honey to the cheese in step 2. Continue with the recipe as directed.

Sun-Dried Tomato Baked Goat Cheese Salad
To bring out the brightness of the tomatoes, toss a cup or so of roughly torn basil leaves in with the salad greens.

Follow the recipe for Herbed Baked Goat Cheese Salad, substituting walnuts for the pecans. Omit the chives and thyme and add 1 tablespoon sun-dried tomatoes packed in oil, rinsed and patted dry, and 1 tablespoon chopped fresh basil with the cheese in step 2. Continue with the recipe as directed.

WALDORF SALAD

WALDORF SALAD WAS CREATED IN 1893 at New York's posh Waldorf Hotel by maître d'hôtel Oscar Tschirky for a charity fund-raiser hosted by the equally posh Mrs. William Vanderbilt. The recipe, which appeared in the *Oscar of the Waldorf* cookbook three years later, was little more than peeled apples, celery, and mayonnaise. To this day, it remains the most requested recipe at the hotel's restaurant.

In the 1970s, many Americans dressed up the salad with raisins, walnuts, and sometimes even Mandarin orange segments. While we love the underlying combination of the original, today it is one of those throwback dishes that make us nostalgic even when the reality falls short.

I wanted to wake up the flavors of the early version and develop new variations, but certainly not get as fancy as the executive chef, John Doherty. His recipe in the 2006 *Waldorf-Astoria Cookbook* calls for homemade mayonnaise, crème fraîche (a rich, thickened cream from France), apples cut in perfect matchstick slices (only a chef with a large staff and sharp knives could bother), homemade candied walnuts, microgreens, and black truffles.

WALDORF SALAD

Many of the recipes I tried call for diced Granny Smith apples, but my tasters preferred the salad when I balanced the tart Grannies with sweet Braeburn or Gala apples; I left the peel on for color. Tasters preferred diced celery to larger slices, as the latter made the salad cumbersome to eat. I toasted the walnuts—usually tossed in raw—to enhance their flavor. We also liked golden raisins, plumped in a little water, for sweetness.

Dressed with mayonnaise alone, the salad was gloppy and greasy. Adding lemon juice helped, but tasters preferred cider vinegar, which subtly reinforced the taste of the apple. A spoonful of honey and a healthy shake of salt and pepper helped unite the flavors. Among several variations I developed, tasters liked best one that paired red grapes with toasted almonds, another that featured dried cherries and pecans, and a third that went out on more of a limb, using peanut butter, curry powder, and grapes. These Waldorf salads are more than good memories—they are good eating.

—DIANE UNGER, *Cook's Country*

Waldorf Salad

SERVES 4 TO 6

You can use reduced-fat mayonnaise here, and regular raisins will work in place of the golden raisins.

- ¾ cup golden raisins (see note)
- ¼ cup water
- ⅓ cup mayonnaise (see note)
- 3 tablespoons cider vinegar
- 1 tablespoon honey
- 3 Granny Smith apples, cored and cut into ½-inch pieces (see photos)
- 3 Gala or Braeburn apples, cored and cut into ½-inch pieces (see photos)
- 3 celery ribs, chopped fine, (about 2¼ cups)
- ¾ cup walnuts, toasted and chopped
  Salt and pepper

1. Combine the raisins and water in a bowl. Cover the bowl tightly with plastic wrap and microwave until the water begins to boil, about 1 minute. Let stand until the raisins are soft and the liquid has been absorbed, about 5 minutes.

2. Whisk the mayonnaise, vinegar, and honey in a large bowl. Add the apples, celery, walnuts, and plumped raisins to the bowl and toss until well coated.

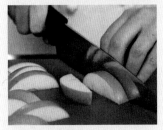

Refrigerate, covered, for 30 minutes. Season with salt and pepper to taste and serve. (The salad can be stored in an airtight container for up to 2 days.)

VARIATIONS

Waldorf Salad with Red Grapes and Almonds

Follow the recipe for Waldorf Salad, omitting step 1. In step 2, substitute 1 cup seedless red grapes, halved, for the plumped raisins and ¾ cup toasted sliced almonds for the walnuts.

Waldorf Salad with Dried Cherries and Pecans

Follow the recipe for Waldorf Salad, substituting ¾ cup dried cherries for the raisins and ¾ cup toasted, chopped pecans for the walnuts.

Curried Waldorf Salad with Green Grapes and Peanuts

Follow the recipe for Waldorf Salad, omitting step 1. In step 2, whisk 2 tablespoons peanut butter and 1 teaspoon curry powder into the mayonnaise mixture, and substitute 1 cup seedless green grapes, halved, for the plumped raisins and ¾ cup dry-roasted peanuts for the walnuts.

GERMAN POTATO SALAD

SLICED NEW POTATOES AND SAUTÉED ONIONS tossed in a pungent, mustardy, bacon-based dressing and served warm is nothing new to most Americans. German potato salad hitched a ride with immigrants, acquiring new fans along with the "German" in its name. (Germans call it *kartoffelsalat,* which is simply "potato salad" in English). The felicitous combination of flavors gives it popularity, but it suffers in many translations. Recipes I tested tended to be waterlogged and heavy instead of the tart-sweet, vinegary potato salad that I love. Surely I could fix that.

I started at the very beginning with the potatoes. Tasters preferred the taste of mild, waxy red potatoes over Yukon golds. Also, the red potatoes held up better when boiled, which is how most recipes suggest cooking them. Just to be sure, I also tried steaming them, thinking it would lock in more potato flavor. But steaming produced unevenly cooked slices, which were alternately crunchy or mushy depending on where the

potatoes had landed in the steamer basket. I went back to boiling. Still, even with careful attention, it was hard not to overcook the thin slices (slicing the potatoes prior to cooking avoids the awkward task of having to slice them hot). Resigned to watching the clock carefully, I moved on to the question of flavor.

In hopes of getting a jump start on seasoning the potatoes, I added vinegar to the potato cooking water. It worked, and along the way I made an interesting discovery. The vinegar had mysteriously extended the cooking time, yet the potatoes emerged both tender and structurally sound (now I could relax a little!). A call to our science editor helped me figure out what was going on. It turns out that cells in vegetables are held together by pectin, which acts like glue. When vegetables are heated in water, the pectin slowly dissolves, cell walls break down, and starch is released. Acidic vinegar slows pectin's dissolving, letting the potatoes stay firmer longer and simplifying the timing.

I turned to the dressing, starting by frying four slices of chopped bacon. Tasters demanded more, and more again. I kept going—all the way up to eight slices—before they were happy. I transferred the cooked bacon to a plate, leaving 2 tablespoons of rendered fat in my skillet, just enough to flavor the dressing but not so much that the fat would turn waxy as it cooled. To that I added olive oil; untraditional, but I found it cut the heaviness of the bacon fat. Next I added onion, which is traditional, sautéing it until softened and lightly browned.

For the acid component—key to German potato salad—I tested cider, distilled white, and both red and white wine vinegars. Tasters liked white vinegar best for its clean, sharp flavor. They also preferred coarse-grain mustard to creamy. I stirred in a little sugar to get the salad's characteristic sweet-sour flavor. Finally, I coated the warm potatoes in warm dressing, folded in the cooked bacon and chopped parsley, and tasted. The bacon flavor had permeated the potatoes, and the dressing was nicely balanced, but overall tasters thought the salad still needed some excitement.

I dusted off some old German cookbooks and found some interesting additions to this recipe, among them chopped pickles, sauerkraut, and sliced cucumber. The cucumber added crunch and freshness; the pickles and sauerkraut added welcome brininess. All at once, however, they were overkill. It occurred to me I could

GERMAN POTATO SALAD

streamline their attractions by making a quick pickle of my own. I sliced and marinated a cucumber in a mixture of vinegar, sugar, salt, and fresh dill. Twenty minutes later, I had a fresh "pickle" whose tang, crunch, and vibrancy beautifully offset the tender potato slices. At the same time, I revisited my dressing, ultimately eliminating the vinegar and sugar and replacing them with the cucumber marinade. Now the dressing had a fresher, brighter flavor, as did the entire dish.

—DIANE UNGER, *Cook's Country*

German Potato Salad

SERVES 8

Unlike a nonstick skillet, a traditional skillet will allow the bacon to form caramelized bits on the skillet bottom. This will result in a richer tasting dressing and a more flavorful salad.

- 2 tablespoons sugar
- 1 cucumber, peeled, quartered, seeded, and cut into ¼-inch slices
- 1 cup distilled white vinegar
- 1 teaspoon chopped fresh dill
  Salt
- 3 pounds small red potatoes (about 18), scrubbed and sliced ¼ inch thick
- 8 slices bacon, sliced thin
- ¼ cup olive oil
- 1 onion, minced (about 1 cup)
- ¼ cup coarse-grain mustard
  Pepper
- ¼ cup chopped fresh parsley

1. Stir the sugar, cucumber, ½ cup of the vinegar, dill, and ½ teaspoon salt together in a bowl.

2. Bring the potatoes, remaining ½ cup vinegar, 1 tablespoon salt, and 8 cups water to a boil in a large pot. Reduce the heat to medium and simmer until the potatoes are just tender, 10 to 15 minutes. Drain the potatoes and return them to the pot.

3. Meanwhile, cook the bacon in a large skillet over medium heat, stirring occasionally, until brown and crisp, 5 to 7 minutes. With a slotted spoon, transfer the bacon to a paper towel–lined plate; pour off and discard all but 2 tablespoons of the bacon grease. Add the oil to the skillet and heat over medium heat until shimmering. Add the onion and cook, stirring occasionally, until softened and beginning to brown, 5 to 7 minutes.

4. Drain the cucumbers and reserve the juice. Whisk the cucumber juice, mustard, and 1 teaspoon pepper into the skillet; bring to a simmer. Pour the dressing over the warm potatoes, stir to combine, and let sit until slightly cooled and the potatoes have absorbed the dressing, about 10 minutes.

5. Stir the parsley, drained cucumbers, and bacon into the potatoes to combine. Season with salt and pepper to taste. Transfer to a serving bowl and serve. (The salad can be refrigerated in an airtight container for 1 day and served at room temperature.)

NOTES FROM THE TEST KITCHEN

COARSE-GRAIN MUSTARD
Mustard aficionados argue that the coarse-grained condiment improves sandwiches and sausages; it's also an essential component of German-style potato salads. After sampling 11 mustards, tasters appreciated spiciness, tanginess, and the pleasant pop of seeds. They disliked mustards with superfluous ingredients such as xanthan gum, artificial flavors, and garlic and onion powders. But the most noteworthy factor turned out to be salt; our winners, **Grey Poupon Harvest Coarse-Ground Mustard** and **Grey Poupon Country Dijon,** contained nearly twice as much of this flavor amplifier as the lowest ranking mustards.

CUCUMBERS: WHICH KIND SHOULD YOU BUY?
Supermarkets carry two kinds of slicing cucumbers: seedless English and standard American. To assess which we prefer, we tasted them grated in yogurt sauce, salted in a salad, and plain. The American cucumbers had the crispest texture and more concentrated flavor, while the English were much milder and more watery.

It turns out that cucumbers contain a "softening" enzyme that breaks down cell walls when the vegetable is cut open. Due to genetic differences between the English and American varieties as well as differences in how they are grown (English cucumbers are almost exclusively raised in greenhouses, while most American kinds are grown outdoors), English cucumbers have weaker cell walls that are more easily broken down by the enzyme. Weak cells lead to less-than-crisp texture and flavor that leaks out.

CHAPTER 2

SOUPS & STEWS

Creamless Creamy Tomato Soup   22

Corn Chowder   23

Wisconsin Cheddar Beer Soup   26

Hearty Root Vegetable and Mushroom Stew   28

Hearty Chicken Noodle Soup   31

Hungarian Beef Stew   33

Kentucky Burgoo   35

Carne Adovada (New Mexico Pork Chili)   38

Slow-Cooker Cassoulet   40

CREAMLESS CREAMY TOMATO SOUP

TOMATO SOUP SHOULD HAVE IT ALL: good looks, velvety smoothness, and a bright, tomatoey taste balanced by the fruit's natural sweetness. But poor versions are the norm, featuring either an acidic, watery broth or an overdose of cream. Though the cream is meant to tame tartness and lend body, I've always found that adding any amount goes hand in hand with muting flavor. I wanted soup with rich tomato flavor and a satisfying texture. Could I get there without the cream?

The first step in the process was to pass over fresh tomatoes for canned, which are almost always far better than your average supermarket tomato, boasting more consistently rich and concentrated flavor. Plus they're already peeled—a big timesaver for soup. I opted for whole tomatoes rather than diced or crushed; the latter two types often contain calcium chloride, an additive that prevents them from breaking down completely, compromising texture. I then developed a simple working recipe, sautéing onions and garlic in butter, stirring in the tomatoes and some chicken broth, and then giving the whole thing a quick spin in the blender. The results were decent, but dull.

If cream subdues tomato flavor, could the milk solids in the butter be tamping it down as well? I substituted extra-virgin olive oil for the butter and found that the soup brightened as a result. A few more small changes—a bay leaf and a pinch of red pepper flakes sautéed with the onions—upped the flavor significantly. To compensate for the flavor the oil lost as it cooked, I drizzled a little more over the soup before it went into the blender. Most tasters also welcomed a couple tablespoons of brandy.

Now that I had my flavor profile nailed down, I was on to bigger problems: tartness and thin texture. Sugar is often used as a means to combat tartness. We preferred brown sugar to one-dimensional white sugar and corn syrup, but sugar could take us only so far—add enough to tone down tartness, and the soup becomes unpalatably sweet.

I needed a thickener that would also help temper the acid. Flavor-dulling dairy ingredients were definitely out, but what about a starch? Cooking flour along with the onions to form a roux made for a thicker soup, but the texture turned slimy instead of creamy, and it did nothing for flavor. Cornstarch produced similar results.

I scoured our cookbook library before I found inspiration in another tomato-based soup: gazpacho. This Spanish classic is made from tomatoes, olive oil, and garlic, along with an unusual element for thickening: bread. But gazpacho is served cold. Would bread work as a thickener for hot soup?

I tore several slices of sandwich bread into pieces and stirred them into the pot with the tomatoes and chicken broth as they simmered. When I processed the mixture in the blender, I ended up with bread chunks that swam in a sea of broth and resisted being sucked down into the blender's spinning blades. To cut back on the liquid in the blender, I decided to try leaving out the broth until the very end. With my next batch of soup, I pureed the tomatoes with the aromatics and bread before returning the mixture to the pan and whisking in the broth. One taste and I knew I'd hit on just the right solution. My tomato soup had the same velvety texture as the creamy kind, but with bright, fresh flavor. None of my tasters even guessed that my soup contained a secret ingredient. Only after the pot was empty did I divulge it.

—J. KENJI ALT, *Cook's Illustrated*

NOTES FROM THE TEST KITCHEN

A BETTER BLENDER

A blender has one basic job—to blend food into a uniform consistency, whether it's crushing ice or producing lump-free purees for smoothies, soups, or hummus. And just two things matter for success at this basic job: the configuration of the blender blades and a V-shaped jar that keeps food close to the blade edges. We gathered 9 models of blenders, including basic machines as well as those that boasted fancy new features (such as "dual-wave action" and "reversible motion" blade design), to find out which brand is best. After crushing hundreds of ice cubes and pureeing our way through countless soups and smoothies, we found two winners. The **KitchenAid 5-Speed Blender** (left), $149.99, impressed us with its brute strength and efficiency, while the **Kalorik BL Blender** (right), $49.99, though noticeably slower than our winner, performed nearly as well and was also the quietest of the bunch, making it our best buy. (See page 308 for more information about our testing results.)

Creamless Creamy Tomato Soup

SERVES 6 TO 8

Be sure to buy canned whole tomatoes that are packed in juice. If half of the soup fills your blender by more than two-thirds, process the soup in three batches. You can also use an immersion blender to process the soup directly in the pot. For an even smoother soup, pass the pureed mixture through a fine-mesh strainer before stirring in the chicken broth in step 2.

- ¼ **cup extra-virgin olive oil, plus extra for drizzling**
- 1 **onion, chopped medium (about 1 cup)**
- 3 **garlic cloves, minced**
  Pinch red pepper flakes (optional)
- 1 **bay leaf**
- 2 **(28-ounce) cans whole tomatoes (see note)**
- 1 **tablespoon brown sugar**
- 3 **slices high-quality white sandwich bread, crusts removed, torn into 1-inch pieces**
- 2 **cups low-sodium chicken broth**
- 2 **tablespoons brandy (optional)**
  Salt and pepper
- ¼ **cup chopped fresh chives**

1. Heat 2 tablespoons of the oil in a Dutch oven over medium-high heat until shimmering. Add the onion, garlic, pepper flakes (if using), and bay leaf. Cook, stirring frequently, until the onion is translucent, 3 to 5 minutes. Stir in the tomatoes and their juice. Using a potato masher, mash until no pieces bigger than 2 inches remain. Stir in the sugar and bread; bring the soup to a boil. Reduce the heat to medium and cook, stirring occasionally, until the bread is completely saturated and starts to break down, about 5 minutes. Remove and discard the bay leaf.

2. Transfer half of the soup to a blender. Add 1 tablespoon more oil and process until the soup is smooth and creamy, 2 to 3 minutes. Transfer to a large bowl and repeat with the remaining soup and remaining 1 tablespoon oil. Rinse out the Dutch oven and return the soup to the pot. Stir in the chicken broth and brandy (if using). Return the soup to a boil and season with salt and pepper to taste. Serve the soup in individual bowls. Sprinkle each portion with pepper and chives and drizzle with additional olive oil.

CORN CHOWDER

CHOWDERS WERE ORIGINALLY MADE FROM FISH, and linguists trace the word chowder to "jowter," Old English for fishmonger, or "chaudière," French for the cauldron used by 18th-century seafarers to cook robust stews from their catch. At some point chowder came ashore and made its way inland, where its character was shaped in the new land. Farmhouse ingredients began to dominate some versions. Chowder recipes emerged that called for chicken, veal, cream, potatoes, and a real American original: corn.

Poring over corn chowder recipes, I saw that the list of ingredients had made its way through history almost unchanged: corn, salt pork or bacon, chopped onions, broth, cubed potatoes, and milk or cream. The cooking method hadn't changed, either: Chopped onions are sautéed in salt pork or bacon fat. Everything else is added and simmered together until the vegetables are tender. So I was surprised when five recipes I tried (including the first ever to appear in print, from Mrs. Lincoln's *Boston Cook Book* of 1884) produced noticeably different chowders. Not one delivered everything we sought from ours namely, velvety texture; unambiguous corn flavor; plentiful, plump kernels; and, since it was summer, delicacy.

I combined the best features from the two recipes we liked the most and was about to start my testing when I happened to find a *Good Housekeeping* recipe from 1888 that used a dozen ears of corn (most recipes called for three to six ears). Aha! Use more corn, get more corn flavor. Hopeful, I made the recipe, scraping 12 ears into my soup. The chowder was packed with kernels. Unfortunately, it lacked the silken, full-flavored base I sought.

To start building that base, I returned to my combined working recipe and tested salt pork versus bacon. Tasters preferred the sweet smokiness of the bacon. Next, to add depth of flavor to the chowder, I sautéed the fresh kernels (with the chopped onions) in the bacon fat. Tasters preferred red potatoes over other types, as they retained their shape in the chowder and added a pretty gleam of pink.

To thicken the chowder, I tried the standard roux, a paste of cooked flour and butter. It was a little heavy for summer but it worked, as did cornstarch. I thickened a third pot of chowder with pureed potatoes. That was also acceptable, though my chowder was veering into potato soup territory.

Amid these possibilities, I couldn't let go of the idea that I had to use the corn to both thicken the chowder and intensify its flavor. I blended a few cups of fresh kernels with some chicken broth (the base of my soup). Even when I let the blender run for almost 10 minutes, the tough outer hulls never completely broke down. I tried the same with cooked kernels and broth, stirring them back into the chowder. Better—the soup was thick and robustly flavored, but it was still far from silky.

I drew up a list of ingredients that might work and ticked them off one by one. Frozen corn was as raggedy as fresh. Cornmeal and polenta were grainy. Corn muffin mix produced chowder with an artificial aftertaste. Hominy (dried corn kernels that have been soaked in lye to remove the hulls) yielded the smoothest puree of all, but its distinctive savory flavor was all wrong for sweet, creamy chowder.

I'd saved canned corn for last. Truthfully, I wasn't all that keen on using it, certain it would taste tinny. A Fannie Merritt Farmer recipe from 1896 made me reconsider. Though the process of canning was far from new at the turn of the century, canned foods still had a certain cachet; also, fresh corn was unavailable for most of the year. I made a pot of chowder with two 15-ounce cans and was delighted to discover that the corn broke down beautifully, yielding a golden, satiny chowder base with a vibrant, fresh corn taste. The cream I was using underlined its velvety texture.

Reading through my file of recipes one last time, I was reminded that Mrs. Lincoln's *Boston Cook Book* based its version on a corn stock made with the shucked cobs. I streamlined this approach, simply tossing the cobs into my simmering chowder and then fishing them out before I served it. It was a subtle but significant difference that pushed my chowder from excellent to exceptional.

—MARÍA DEL MAR SACASA, *Cook's Country*

Corn Chowder

SERVES 6 TO 8

Be sure to reserve the cobs for the chowder. They add an extra layer of corn flavor.

- 6 ears corn
- 2 (15-ounce) cans whole kernel corn, drained
- 5 cups low-sodium chicken broth
- 3 slices bacon, chopped fine
- 1 onion, chopped medium (about 1 cup)
  Salt and pepper
- 1 pound red potatoes (about 3), scrubbed and cut into ½-inch cubes
- 1 cup heavy cream
- 4 scallions, sliced thin

1. Cut the kernels from the ears of corn (see page 54); reserve the kernels and cobs separately. Puree the canned corn and 2 cups of the broth in a blender until smooth.

2. Cook the bacon in a Dutch oven over medium heat until crisp, about 8 minutes. Using a slotted spoon, transfer the bacon to a paper towel–lined plate and reserve. Cook the onion, corn kernels, ½ teaspoon salt, and ¼ teaspoon pepper in the bacon fat until the vegetables soften and turn golden brown, 8 to 10 minutes.

3. Add the potatoes, corn puree, remaining 3 cups broth, and reserved corncobs to the Dutch oven and bring to a boil. Reduce the heat to medium-low and simmer until the potatoes are tender, about 15 minutes. Discard the cobs and stir in the cream, scallions, and reserved bacon. Season with salt and pepper to taste and serve. (The soup can be refrigerated in an airtight container for up to 3 days.)

NOTES FROM THE TEST KITCHEN

THE BEST CANNED CORN

We usually substitute frozen corn for fresh, but when you plan to puree corn into velvety smoothness in a chowder, canned corn is a better choice because the softer kernels break down more readily. We tasted five nationally available brands, both plain and in chowder. Manufacturers add water, salt, and sometimes sugar to canned corn, but our top brand, **Libby's Organic Whole Kernel Sweet Corn,** had no added sugar—the sweetness came from the corn itself.

CORN CHOWDER

WISCONSIN CHEDDAR BEER SOUP

WISCONSIN IS KNOWN FOR ITS CHEESE and its beer, so it's no surprise that cheddar beer soup—complete with the traditional popcorn garnish—is a standard item on local menus. This hearty soup is simple to make: Carrots, onion, and celery are sautéed in butter, flour is added to make a roux, and then chicken broth, dairy, and beer are whisked in. Shredded sharp cheddar cheese is added at the end and melts to a velvety smooth consistency. Or at least that's the idea. But just as often the cheese clumps together or breaks, leaving the soup streaked with pools of fat.

I started according to custom by sautéing onion, carrot, and celery, but my tasters found the celery bitter, so I omitted it. Cream and half-and-half were both too heavy, even when cut with the chicken broth—milk worked better. Thinking I'd want an intensely flavored beer, I tested robust ales like Bass and Samuel Adams (and even a few Wisconsin microbrews), but tasters were keen on the milder, less bitter flavor of American lagers. Some recipes keep the soup chunky, but my tasters preferred the texture of a pureed soup.

NOTES FROM THE TEST KITCHEN

SECRETS TO SMOOTHNESS
Because cheddar—and especially sharp cheddar—is a poor melting cheese, most recipes for cheddar beer soup end up grainy. To make a smooth soup with intense cheddar flavor, we added 1 cup of shredded American cheese (which contains emulsifiers that promote even melting) to the flavorful cheddar, resulting in a smooth texture. A couple of teaspoons of cornstarch tossed in with the shredded cheese ensured thorough, efficient melting, which kept the soup silky and free from clumps.

WHICH BEER IS BEST?
Although any domestic lager will work in this soup, it just didn't seem authentic without a Wisconsin beer. We tasted five widely available Wisconsin brands—Miller, Miller High Life, Miller Genuine Draft, Schlitz, and Pabst Blue Ribbon—both in soup and on their own. After some heated debate, tasters selected **Miller High Life** for its hoppy character and balanced flavor, praising it as the "perfect complement to the tanginess of the cheddar."

It was time to focus on the big problem—the cheese. All that aging gives sharp cheddar plenty of flavor, but an aged cheese has very little moisture. (That's why aged cheddars crumble.) It turns out that low-moisture cheeses are much more likely to break when melted. The result is a grainy, greasy soup. Milder cheddar (which is aged less) wasn't much of an improvement. Even colby—a mild Wisconsin cheese similar to Monterey Jack—was grainy in the soup. Knowing that American cheese is made with emulsifiers to promote melting, I tried using equal amounts of sharp cheddar and American; this ratio resulted in smooth melting but bland taste. One cup of American to three cups of sharp cheddar was the best mix for nongrainy melting and rich flavor.

While most of the soup was melting smoothly, it was studded with hard little clumps of cheese. I was adding the shredded cheese off the heat, but it still clumped when I tried stirring in the cheese over low heat—and using high heat caused the soup to separate. Although shredded cheese melts faster than larger pieces, a bit of research helped me understand that the surface of the shredded cheese melts so quickly that pieces can fuse together, creating a mass that becomes harder to melt. To keep the shredded cheese from fusing, I tried packaged shredded cheese, which includes cornstarch to prevent clumping. Finally the soup was smooth! Adding my own cornstarch to hand-shredded block cheese worked just as well and let me use any good sharp cheddar.

—LYNN CLARK, *Cook's Country*

Wisconsin Cheddar Beer Soup
SERVES 6

You will need one 4-ounce chunk of American cheese from the deli counter for this recipe; do not use presliced or packaged shredded cheese here. Freeze the American cheese for 15 minutes to make shredding easier.

- 4 tablespoons (½ stick) unsalted butter
- 1 onion, minced (about 1 cup)
- 2 carrots, peeled and chopped fine (about 1 cup)
- 2 garlic cloves, minced
- ⅓ cup unbleached all-purpose flour
- 1¾ cups low-sodium chicken broth
- 1 (12-ounce) bottle beer
- 2 cups whole or low-fat milk
- 12 ounces sharp cheddar cheese, shredded (about 3 cups)

WISCONSIN CHEDDAR BEER SOUP

4 ounces American cheese, shredded (about 1 cup)
(see note)

2 teaspoons cornstarch
Salt and pepper

1. Melt the butter in a large Dutch oven over medium heat. Add the onion and carrots and cook until lightly browned, 8 to 10 minutes. Add the garlic and cook until fragrant, about 30 seconds. Stir in the flour and cook until golden, about 1 minute. Slowly whisk in the broth, beer, and milk. Bring the mixture to a simmer, then reduce the heat to low and simmer gently (do not boil) until the carrots are very soft, 20 to 25 minutes.

2. Meanwhile, toss the shredded cheeses and cornstarch in a large bowl until well combined. Puree the soup in a blender in two batches until completely smooth, return to the pot, and simmer over medium-low heat. Whisk in the cheese mixture, one handful at a time, until smooth. Season with salt and pepper to taste and serve. (The soup can be refrigerated in an airtight container for up to 3 days.)

HEARTY ROOT VEGETABLE AND MUSHROOM STEW

GREAT VEGETABLE STEWS marry hearty vegetables with a richly flavored broth and herbs or spices that complement the vegetables. But all too often they are little more than a jumble of soggy vegetables devoid of color and flavor. I was after a hearty vegetable stew, one that could be as soul satisfying in the dead of winter as a beef stew. And although I love fiery Indian and Thai curries, I was looking for vegetable stew at its simplest, where the flavor of the vegetables, not the spices, takes center stage.

With this in mind, I began my first order of business: selecting the veggies. Hearty root vegetables, an integral part of many meat stews, would be key, both for their earthy flavor and for their thickening properties (root vegetables are quite starchy). Tasters really liked the flavor of parsnips, turnips, and rutabaga, as well as the more traditional carrots and potatoes. While I found that any combination of two to three root vegetables produced a flavorful, balanced stew, it was important to include potatoes, which helped balance the sweetness of the other vegetables.

Next I looked for other vegetables to serve as a contrast to the starchy ones. I wanted a hearty stew, not a soup, so delicate spring vegetables like asparagus and zucchini were immediately ruled out. Mushrooms, with their meaty flavor and texture, were an ideal choice.

Looking for the meatiest mushroom I could find, I began with portobello caps, which I halved and sliced. Tasters loved the pairing of mushrooms and root vegetables but were turned off by the portobellos' texture, which was spongy no matter how long they cooked. Simple white mushrooms cut into chunks provided just the right texture.

The main components of my stew decided on, I turned to the cooking liquid. Chicken broth would no doubt make a rich base, but I wanted a true vegetable stew. So I chose vegetable broth as my liquid.

Meat stews typically begin by browning the meat, and I began similarly, sautéing the mushrooms in oil. A little thyme and garlic deepened their flavor. Next I deglazed the pot with white wine to add flavor and some acidity. After the broth was added to the pot I tossed in the root vegetables and some bay leaves. While other stews are cooked covered, I chose to cover the pot only partially to ensure a gentle simmer; otherwise, the vegetables had a tendency to disintegrate.

After an hour of simmering the vegetables were tender and had released enough starch to thicken the sauce somewhat without falling apart, but the sauce had a disappointing canned flavor that was simply not rich enough. Clearly the store-bought vegetable broth wasn't working. Hoping to avoid the arduous route of making stock from scratch, I decided to try a hybrid technique. I tossed cubed mushrooms, onions, carrots, celery, and garlic heads in tomato paste and roasted them in the oven. I then threw them in a pot with some dried porcinis, store-bought broth, and water and simmered the mixture on the stove for 30 minutes before straining out the solids.

The stew made with this stock was definitely good; however, it was only slightly easier than making stock from scratch. I wondered if I could incorporate some of the ingredients that had been used to fortify the broth into the stew itself—building flavor without a separate simmering step and without discarding any vegetables.

I made the stew again, sautéing a traditional mirepoix of minced celery, onion, and carrot along with some dried porcini (in butter, instead of oil, for more richness) before adding the fresh mushrooms. Additionally, I browned some tomato paste with the garlic and thyme before adding the liquid. Now I was getting somewhere. Tasters were impressed by its hearty flavor and thick texture, but still wanted a richer taste.

Not wanting to lengthen my shopping list, I looked more closely at my existing ingredients to see if I couldn't eke out more flavor from them. In meat stew, much of the flavor comes from fond, the browned bits that cling to the bottom of the pan when browning the meat. In my vegetable stew, I was getting the fond from browning the mirepoix and mushrooms. I had sautéed them until they were just beginning to brown; but if browning was the key to flavor, how could I go wrong with more of a good thing? I extended the cooking time, sautéing the aromatics until they were well browned—a full 15 minutes. I then added the mushrooms and cooked them over medium-high heat until they released their liquid. Once the pot was dry I lowered the heat and continued cooking. Since mushrooms begin browning only after their liquid has evaporated, lowering the heat at this point gave me more control at the critical juncture. I was able to cook them until a dark brown fond coated the bottom of the pan, which took about 15 minutes, without burning them.

This increased stovetop time for both the aromatics and the mushrooms turned out to be the key—the stew now had the deep, rich flavor that I had been looking for. I finished the stew with some lemon juice and parsley for brightness, and tasters agreed—no one missed the meat.

—ADELAIDE PARKER, *America's Test Kitchen Books*

NOTES FROM THE TEST KITCHEN

PURCHASING AND STORING DRIED MUSHROOMS

When purchasing dried mushrooms, avoid packages filled with small, dusty pieces or those labeled "wild mushroom mix"—they are often older and of lesser quality. Dried mushrooms should have an earthy (not musty or stale) aroma. Store dried mushrooms in an airtight container in a cool, dry place for up to one year.

Hearty Root Vegetable and Mushroom Stew
SERVES 6

We think this stew tastes best with a combination of two or three types of root vegetables, including carrot, parsnip, turnip, rutabaga, celery root, or parsley root.

- 4 tablespoons (½ stick) unsalted butter
- 2 medium onions, minced (about 2 cups)
- 1 celery rib, minced (about ½ cup)
- 1 carrot, peeled and minced (about ½ cup)
- 1 ounce dried porcini mushrooms, rinsed and minced
  Salt
- 1½ pounds white mushrooms, quartered
- 6 garlic cloves, minced
- 1 tablespoon tomato paste
- 2 teaspoons minced fresh thyme, or ½ teaspoon dried
- ½ cup dry white wine
- 3 cups low-sodium vegetable broth
- 2½ cups water
- 1½ pounds root vegetables, peeled and cut into 1-inch pieces (see note)
- 1 pound red potatoes (about 3), scrubbed and cut into 1-inch pieces
- 2 bay leaves
- ¼ cup chopped fresh parsley
- 1 tablespoon fresh lemon juice
  Pepper

1. Melt 2 tablespoons of the butter in a large Dutch oven over medium heat. Add the onions, celery, carrot, porcini mushrooms, and 1 teaspoon salt and cook, stirring often, until the vegetables are well browned, about 15 minutes.

2. Add the remaining 2 tablespoons butter and white mushrooms, increase the heat to medium-high, and cook, stirring often, until their liquid is released and evaporates, about 10 minutes. Reduce the heat to medium and cook, stirring often, until a dark, thick fond forms on the bottom of the pot, 5 to 8 minutes.

3. Stir in the garlic, tomato paste, and thyme and cook until fragrant, about 30 seconds. Stir in the wine, scraping up the browned bits. Stir in the broth, water, root vegetables, potatoes, and bay leaves and bring to a simmer.

4. Reduce the heat to medium-low, cover the pot partially (the lid should be just off center to leave about 1 inch exposed), and cook until the stew is thickened and the vegetables are tender, about 1 hour. Off the heat, remove and discard the bay leaves and stir in the parsley and lemon juice. Season with salt and pepper to taste and serve.

HEARTY CHICKEN NOODLE SOUP

A SMOOTH SPICE SOLUTION

The large quantity of paprika in authentic Hungarian goulash can turn it gritty. Here are two solutions.

COMMERCIAL CONVENIENCE
Hard-to-find Hungarian paprika cream is a smooth blend of paprika and red bell peppers.

HOMEMADE SOLUTION
We created our own quick version by pureeing dried paprika with roasted red peppers and a little tomato paste and vinegar.

SKIPPING THE SEAR, BUT NOT THE FLAVOR

Most stews begin by browning meat on the stovetop to boost flavor. They also call for lots of added liquid. Our recipe skips the sear and goes into a moderate 325-degree oven. Though this relatively low temperature can't compare with the sizzling heat of a 500-degree skillet, over time the dry top layer of meat will reach 300 degrees—the temperature at which the meat begins to brown, forming thousands of new flavor compounds.

Even at a relatively low oven temperature, our method still triggers browning—but only on the "dry" part of the meat above the liquid.

CHOOSING SWEET PAPRIKA

Some cooks think of paprika as merely a coloring agent. But the best versions of this sweet Hungarian spice (made from a different variety of red pepper than hot or smoked paprika) pack a punch that goes beyond pigment. We sampled six brands, two from the supermarket and four ordered online. Our findings? It pays to mail-order your paprika—the supermarket brands had little flavor and even less aroma. Our favorite was **The Spice House Hungarian Sweet Paprika.** This paprika outshone the competition with the complexity of its "earthy," "fruity" flavors and "toasty" aroma.

KENTUCKY BURGOO

TODAY, BURGOO IS A CHUNKY STEW of tomatoes, corn, potatoes, chicken, and mutton (mature lamb), but I'd heard that it began as a way to make use of whatever was hunted or ready to harvest: cabbage, lima beans, squirrel, opossum, and deer. It goes without saying that I was curious, so I traveled to Kentucky to sample one of its best-kept secrets.

Reddish orange and nearly as thick as oatmeal, the burgoo set before me at one restaurant was too murky for me to discern individual ingredients. I nudged my spoon in, doubtful. Before I knew it, I'd polished it off. Heady and meaty, this burgoo had a warming, slow heat, a strangely compelling, tangy quality, and a familiar taste I liked but couldn't quite place. I was a convert.

Back in the test kitchen, my work was cut out for me. I had tasted burgoo at all the barbecue restaurants in Owensboro and gathered a half-dozen recipes, but how would I ever squeeze the long list of ingredients into even my largest pot? Burgoo is traditionally cooked in an enormous cauldron over an open flame. It's stirred with something that looks like an oar. The cook boils whole chickens (and sometimes beef or pork stewing meat) to make broth; uses a second pot to boil mutton until tender (to tame the funky smell and taste); removes the meat from both pots; shreds it; chops vegetables; then cooks everything together until the flavors meld and the broth concentrates.

I peeled, chopped, shredded, and reduced, hoping to re-create a reasonable approximation. Many hours later, I had many gallons of burgoo. Some tasted pretty good, too, but it had been a project and a half to make. For this recipe to work at home, I needed to streamline the ingredients, cut back the cooking time, and find new ways to build flavor.

The test kitchen has a few "rules" for making stew: Brown the meat first. Add aromatic vegetables. Sprinkle in flour as a thickener. Deglaze the pan and simmer everything with broth, herbs, and spices until tender. If you're adding more vegetables, do it in stages so that the delicate ones don't overcook. I thought if I followed these rules, I might get away with using store-bought broth, precut frozen or canned for some of the vegetables, and small pieces of chicken and mutton for a tasty, reasonably quick burgoo.

KENTUCKY BURGOO

I hit my first stumbling block while shopping. The supermarket didn't carry mutton—ever. My butcher suggested substituting a more common cut of stewing meat from lamb. Shank made the burgoo greasy. Leg of lamb was labor-intensive, requiring that I bone and then cube it. Lamb shoulder chops, however, became tender in less than 1½ hours and tasted wonderful. The bones added flavor and body. Tasters preferred chicken thigh meat to breasts, which dried out and got lost in the busy stew. As for vegetables, the ease of using canned tomatoes, frozen corn, and frozen lima beans made up for the onions, garlic, and potatoes I had to chop by hand.

The burgoo was now thick and tasted pretty good, but it lacked the rich meatiness and heat I remembered. Adding more meat to my already full pot was not an option. I thought long and hard and realized that the flavor that had eluded me in the burgoos I'd tasted must be my missing ingredient. I went back to the recipes I'd collected, and a light went on—Worcestershire sauce! Astonishingly, it took a full ¼ cup to give the stew the richness it lacked. Adding ¾ teaspoon of black pepper at the end of cooking rather than at the beginning restored a pleasant, spicy heat. To brighten the burgoo, I tried both vinegar and lemon juice. Lemon won hands-down.

"Insulting a man's burgoo is on par with insulting his mama," a colleague from that part of the country had told me. No worries, this version guarantees compliments.

—KRIS WIDICAN, *Cook's Country*

NOTES FROM THE TEST KITCHEN

BUTCHER SHOP LAMB CHOPS

Our recipe relies on inexpensive lamb shoulder blade chops for deep, meaty flavor. If you think all lamb chops are expensive, think again. Lamb rib chops and loin chops are indeed pricey (about $13 and $10 per pound, respectively); they're also relatively lean and best cooked to medium-rare. But inexpensive shoulder blade chops (about $5 per pound) are an excellent value. Cooked slow and low in order to break down their connective tissue, the chops become moist, flavorful, and tender. We used the silky shredded meat from shoulder blade chops in our burgoo. The stew also benefited from the bones, which added both body and deep meaty savor.

CHEAP, FLAVORFUL CHOP

Kentucky Burgoo

SERVES 6 TO 8

If you can't find lamb shoulder chops, substitute 1½ pounds of lamb stew meat or beef chuck stew meat.

- 2 pounds bone-in, skin-on chicken thighs
- 6 (6 to 8-ounce) lamb shoulder blade chops, about ½ inch thick (see note)
  Salt and pepper
- 1 tablespoon vegetable oil
- 2 onions, chopped medium (about 2 cups)
- 2 garlic cloves, minced
- 2 tablespoons unbleached all-purpose flour
- 6 cups low-sodium chicken broth
- 1 (14.5-ounce) can diced tomatoes
- ¼ cup Worcestershire sauce
- 1 pound Yukon gold potatoes (about 2), peeled and cut into ½-inch chunks
- 1½ cups frozen corn
- 1½ cups frozen baby lima beans
- ¼ cup fresh lemon juice from 2 lemons

1. Pat the chicken and lamb dry with paper towels and season with salt and pepper. Heat the oil in a large Dutch oven over medium-high heat until just smoking. Brown the chicken, about 5 minutes per side; transfer to a plate. Pour off the fat from the pan and reserve. (You should have about 3 tablespoons of fat; if you have less, supplement it with vegetable oil.) Add 1 tablespoon of the reserved fat to the Dutch oven and heat until just smoking. Brown half of the chops, about 5 minutes per side; transfer to a plate. Repeat with 1 tablespoon more fat and the remaining chops.

2. Add the remaining 1 tablespoon fat and onions to the now-empty pot and cook until softened, about 5 minutes. Add the garlic and flour and cook until fragrant, about 1 minute. Stir in the broth, tomatoes with their juice, and Worcestershire, scraping up any browned bits with a wooden spoon. Return the chicken and lamb to the pot and bring to a boil.

3. Reduce the heat to medium-low and simmer, covered, until the chicken is tender, about 30 minutes. Transfer the chicken to a plate. When cool enough to handle, pull the chicken into bite-sized pieces and refrigerate; discard the bones and skin. Continue to simmer the stew until the lamb is tender, about 40 minutes longer. Transfer the lamb to a plate. When cool enough to handle, pull the lamb into bite-sized pieces and refrigerate; discard the bones.

4. Add the potatoes to the pot and simmer until tender, about 15 minutes. Add the corn, lima beans, reserved chicken, and reserved lamb and simmer until heated through, about 5 minutes. Stir in the lemon juice and ¾ teaspoon pepper. Season with salt to taste. Skim any fat, if necessary, and serve.

CARNE ADOVADA

WHEN IT COMES TO CHILI, Texans like to grab the lime-light—with raucous world chili cook-offs and official state dishes (chili con carne). But cross the state line into New Mexico and you'll find a little-known chile-based dish that deserves a Texas-size reputation: *carne adovada,* literally "marinated meat." Like many New Mexican dishes, it's headlined by local chiles. Meltingly tender chunks of pork butt are braised in an intense, soulful red chile sauce with hints of cumin, oregano, onion, and garlic. It's at once smoky yet bright, spicy yet sweet.

It's easy to find recipes for carne adovada. If you don't live in the Southwest, however, it may not be so easy to find the requisite chiles. I tested several recipes, and the one that emerged as most promising required toasting, seeding, and grinding nearly two dozen dried New Mexico chiles (commonly Anaheims left to ripen until red). Tasters loved the toasty, fruity notes added by all those chiles, which also thickened the sauce nicely. But I wanted to reproduce those rich and complex flavors using ingredients available in any supermarket.

I began by reaching for a jar of chili powder, typically a combination of dried ground chiles, cumin, oregano, and garlic—the same spices used in traditional recipes for carne adovada. I browned cubed pork shoulder in oil and then set it aside. After softening onion and garlic in the residual fat, I added ½ cup supermarket chili powder, about the same amount as carne adovada recipes usually specify for freshly roasted and ground dried New Mexico chiles. Then I stirred in chicken broth, pureed the mixture, added back the reserved meat, and put the pot in the oven. After two hours, the meat was tender and the sauce was an attractive rust-red, but the dish tasted utterly flat, and the meat juices had made the sauce runny.

In the test kitchen, we often use canned chipotle chiles in adobo to provide smoky depth. I tried various

quantities before deciding that a tablespoon brought the right amount of complexity and heat. Wondering how to replicate the fruity quality of dried chiles, it occurred to me that I could use actual fruit. Since the flavor of chiles is sometimes described as raisin-y, I hoped raisins might supply that nuance, but tasters rejected the dots of dried fruit in the sauce. I tried soaking the raisins in hot water to soften them, then made a puree and stirred it in. Tasters liked the agreeably subtle flavor it contributed. To replicate the bitter quality of freshly ground dried chiles, I borrowed an idea from some Mexican mole sauces and stirred in both cocoa and unsweetened chocolate. In carne adovada, however, they tasted wrong. A colleague suggested I soak the raisins in coffee instead of water, and indeed, a half-cup of joe brought the flavors into robust, bittersweet balance.

To thicken the sauce, I stirred in flour with the spices, which gave it the necessary heft. I also tried a dash of cinnamon—a classic carne adovada seasoning—but just as quickly removed it; it bullied the sauce. Tasters couldn't detect the miniscule amount of oregano included in the chili powder blend. This herb is a must in carne adovada, so I added a full teaspoon. At the last minute, I stirred in lime juice, lime zest, and cilantro to brighten the otherwise earthy dish. These aren't traditional ingredients, but my tasters insisted that flavor trumps authenticity. At last, using ordinary off-the-shelf ingredients, I'd developed an easy version that rivals the original and brought carne adovada a la casa.

—KELLEY BAKER, *Cook's Country*

Carne Adovada (New Mexico Pork Chili)
SERVES 6 TO 8

Pork shoulder—usually labeled pork butt or Boston butt—comes either boneless or on the bone. If using bone-in pork shoulder, buy a 6 to 6½-pound roast. Serve the finished dish over rice or with warm corn tortillas.

- ¼ **cup raisins**
- ½ **cup brewed coffee**
- 1 **(4 to 5-pound) boneless pork shoulder roast, fat trimmed to ⅛-inch thickness and cut into 1½-inch chunks (see note)**
- **Salt and pepper**
- 1 **tablespoon vegetable oil**
- 2 **onions, chopped medium (about 2 cups)**
- ¼ **cup unbleached all-purpose flour**

CARNE ADOVADA (NEW MEXICO PORK CHILI)

½ cup chili powder

1 teaspoon dried oregano

1 tablespoon minced canned chipotle chile in adobo sauce

6 garlic cloves, minced

2½ cups low-sodium chicken broth

1 teaspoon grated lime zest plus 1 tablespoon fresh lime juice

¼ cup chopped fresh cilantro

1. Adjust an oven rack to the lower-middle position and heat the oven to 350 degrees. Combine the raisins and coffee in a small bowl. Cover tightly with plastic wrap and microwave until the liquid begins to boil, 1 to 3 minutes; let stand for 5 minutes, until the raisins are plump.

2. Pat the pork dry with paper towels and season with salt and pepper. Heat the oil in a Dutch oven over medium-high heat until just smoking. Brown half of the pork, about 10 minutes. Transfer to a plate and repeat with the remaining pork.

3. Pour off all but 1 tablespoon of the fat from the Dutch oven. Add the onions and cook until softened, 5 to 7 minutes. Add the flour, chili powder, oregano, chipotle, and garlic and cook until fragrant, about 1 minute. Add the broth and the raisin mixture, scraping up any browned bits, and bring to a boil. Working in 2 batches, transfer the mixture to a blender or food processor and puree until smooth. Return the sauce to the pot.

4. Add the browned pork to the sauce in the pot and transfer to the oven. Cook, covered, until the pork is fork-tender, about 2 hours. Skim the sauce, then stir in the lime zest, lime juice, and cilantro. Season with salt and pepper to taste and serve. (The chili can be refrigerated in an airtight container for up to 3 days.)

SLOW-COOKER CASSOULET

CLASSIC CASSOULET IS A PROJECT RECIPE. There's the overnight soaking and long cooking of the white beans, the half-week needed to make confit (goose or duck cooked in its own fat), and the slow simmering of pork and sausages—and that's before all the ingredients are simmered together so that their flavors can meld. Most recipes I found for slow-cooker cassoulet dump canned white beans, cubed pork loin, sausage, chicken parts (in lieu of confit), broth, wine, and tomatoes into the cooker; six hours later, you're left with a washed-out mess of gray meats and blown-out beans. There had to be a better way.

I wanted to replace the lean pork loin with something that wouldn't dry out during long cooking. Cubes of well-marbled pork shoulder worked, but a big shoulder roast provided more meat than I needed. Boneless country-style ribs gave me more control over how much I bought. To enhance their meatiness, I browned the ribs before adding them to the slow cooker.

Chicken breasts became dry and stringy with long cooking; my tasters preferred the moist texture and richer flavor of bone-in thighs. Unfortunately, six hours of cooking (the time the pork needed, even when cut into small chunks) were too much for the thighs. To slow down their cooking, I wrapped the thighs in a foil packet and cooked them on top of (rather than in) the stew; after six hours, the thigh meat was moist and ready to be shredded. Pork sausages are traditional for cassoulet, but my tasters found andouille and chorizo (common additions to slow-cooker recipes) too distinctly flavored. They preferred garlicky kielbasa, especially when I browned it first and added it to the stew just before serving (to prevent it from drying out).

I knew that I wanted to use dried white beans; great Northern beans are similar to traditional French flageolets yet easier to find. Added raw, however, the beans didn't soften fully in six hours of slow cooking. Hoping to avoid an overnight soak, I tried a common trick of boiling the beans and then letting them sit for an hour off-heat. This worked, but not fast enough for me. Simmering the beans for 20 minutes before adding them to the cooker gave them just enough of a head start so that they were tender and creamy by the time the stew was done.

For the broth base, I sautéed chopped onion in the flavorful drippings left from browning the meats, then added plenty of garlic and thyme, as well as tomato paste for richness and body. Next, I stirred in chicken broth and brandy (my tasters preferred the complexity of brandy to the more traditional white wine), along with canned tomatoes, and added this mixture to the cooker. To thicken the stew, I removed a cup of the cooked beans, mashed them to a paste, and returned them to the broth. A buttery bread-crumb topping provided the classic crowning touch to this rich, meaty cassoulet.

—CALI RICH, *Cook's Country*

Slow-Cooker Cassoulet

SERVES 6 TO 8

An equal amount of boneless pork shoulder roast can be substituted for country-style ribs. We prefer great Northern beans here.

- 1 pound (about 2½ cups) dried medium-sized white beans, rinsed and picked over (see note)
- 2 pounds boneless country-style pork ribs, cut into 1-inch chunks (see note)
  Salt and pepper
- 1 tablespoon vegetable oil
- 8 ounces kielbasa sausage, halved lengthwise and sliced thin
- 2 onions, minced (about 2 cups)
- 6 garlic cloves, minced
- 1 tablespoon minced fresh thyme
- 1 tablespoon tomato paste
- 3½ cups low-sodium chicken broth
- ½ cup brandy
- 1 (14.5-ounce) can diced tomatoes, drained
- 2 pounds bone-in, skin-on chicken thighs, trimmed
- 2 slices high-quality white sandwich bread, torn into pieces
- 2 tablespoons unsalted butter, melted

1. Bring the beans and 8 cups water to a boil in a medium saucepan over medium-high heat. Reduce the heat to low and simmer, covered, until just beginning to soften, about 20 minutes. Drain the beans and transfer to a slow cooker.

2. Pat the pork dry with paper towels and season with salt and pepper. Heat the oil in a Dutch oven over medium-high heat until just smoking. Cook the pork until well browned, about 10 minutes; transfer to the slow cooker. Brown the kielbasa in the empty pan, about 5 minutes; using a slotted spoon, transfer to a paper towel–lined plate and refrigerate. Add the onions to the fat in the pan and cook until softened, 5 to 7 minutes. Stir in the garlic, thyme, and tomato paste and cook until fragrant, about 30 seconds. Add the broth, brandy, and tomatoes, scraping up any browned bits with a wooden spoon. Bring the broth mixture to a boil, then transfer to the slow cooker.

3. Season the chicken with salt and pepper and wrap in foil (see photo). Place the foil packet on top of the stew in the slow cooker. Cover and cook on low until the pork and chicken are tender, 6 to 7 hours.

4. Remove the foil packet from the slow cooker and transfer to a plate. When the chicken is cool enough to handle, pull the meat from the bones in large chunks, discarding the skin, bones, and excess fat. Transfer 1 cup of the beans from the slow cooker to a bowl and mash until smooth. Stir the mashed beans, chicken meat, and reserved kielbasa into the slow cooker. Cook, covered, until heated through, about 10 minutes.

5. Meanwhile, pulse the bread, butter, and ¼ teaspoon salt in a food processor until coarsely ground, about 10 pulses. Toast the crumbs in a large skillet over medium-high heat until golden, about 5 minutes. Season the cassoulet with salt and pepper to taste. Serve, passing the bread crumbs at the table. (The finished cassoulet can be refrigerated in an airtight container for up to 3 days. When ready to serve, bring the cassoulet to a simmer over medium heat, thinning the broth with water as necessary. The crispy bread crumbs can be stored in an airtight container for up to 1 day.)

NOTES FROM THE TEST KITCHEN

SECRETS TO SLOW-COOKER CASSOULET

1. Placing the chicken in a foil packet that will fit into the slow cooker helps protect the chicken from overcooking.

2. Simmering the dried beans for 20 minutes before adding them to the slow cooker gives them the head start they need.

A FLAVORFUL KIELBASA

With so many brands of kielbasa on the market, which is best? We tested five national supermarket brands and found our favorite: **Smithfield Naturally Hickory Smoked Polska Kielbasa.** It has a smoky, complex flavor profile and hearty texture.

CHAPTER 3

VEGETABLES & SIDE DISHES

Garlic Mashed Potatoes   44

Aligot (Garlic and Cheese Mashed Potatoes)   45

Au Gratin Potatoes   48

Sautéed Green Beans   51

Sautéed Green Beans
with Garlic and Herbs

Sautéed Green Beans
with Smoked Paprika and Almonds

Spicy Sautéed Green Beans
with Ginger and Sesame

Sautéed Green Beans
with Roasted Red Peppers and Basil

Sweet Corn Spoonbread   52

Individual Spoonbreads

Beer-Battered Onion Rings   55

Skillet Ratatouille   56

Summer Vegetable Gratin   58

Summer Vegetable Gratin with
Roasted Peppers and Smoked Mozzarella

Summer Squash Casserole   61

Make-Ahead Green Bean Casserole   62

Stuffed Cabbage Rolls   64

Cheesy Broccoli and Rice Casserole   67

GARLIC MASHED POTATOES

REGULAR MASHED POTATOES ARE GREAT, but flavor them with sweet, nutty-tasting roasted garlic and you might make me forget the entrée is even on the plate. But mashed potatoes with roasted garlic do not have the makings of a quick side dish. First you have to roast a head of garlic for an hour and wait for it to cool so you can squeeze the garlic out of its skins, and then you have to puree the roasted garlic—all before making the mashed potatoes. I wanted to find a faster, easier way to infuse mashed potatoes with the addictive flavor of roasted garlic.

For fluffy mashed potatoes, the test kitchen has determined that russet potatoes (a high-starch spud) mashed with butter and half-and-half are best. As for "quick" roasted garlic substitutes, I tested recipes that called for pan-roasting unpeeled cloves and microwaving peeled cloves in oil. The pan-roasted garlic took almost as long as actual roasting and required much more attention. The cloves quickly microwaved in oil had pleasantly mellow garlic flavor. But when pureed and added to my mashed potatoes, the microwaved garlic and the boiled potatoes tasted like separate elements—it was obvious that they hadn't been cooked together. Minced garlic sautéed in butter and added to the cooked potatoes had the same problem.

If the garlic and potatoes needed to be cooked together to integrate their flavors, I needed to reexamine my cooking method. The test kitchen has a recipe for mashed sweet potatoes where the cut potatoes aren't cooked in a big pot of boiling water; instead they're simmered, covered, on the stovetop with butter and a small amount of cream. This technique avoids the "washing away" of flavor that can come from boiling. I decided to give it a shot.

I began by mincing 12 cloves of garlic and sautéing them in plenty of butter to mellow their bite. Sprinkling in just a teaspoon of sugar helped to mimic the sweet flavor of roasted garlic. I cut the potatoes in small pieces to allow more surface area to soak up garlic flavor and promote even cooking and then tossed them in the pot to coat them with the garlic butter. My tests revealed that I needed about 1¾ cups of liquid to prevent the potatoes from scorching. Using only half-and-half muted the garlic flavor, so I replaced some of it with water.

After 25 minutes of occasional stirring, the potatoes were perfectly tender and infused with plenty of garlic flavor. I mashed them right in the pot, adding more butter and half-and-half to give the mash a smoother consistency, and they tasted great, but they were a bit on the gluey side. The problem was the russets' excess starch, which is usually rinsed away by traditional boiling. The fix was a matter of giving the raw, cut russets a good rinse under running water before adding them to the pot. This quick recipe for roasted-garlic mashed potatoes is so easy and satisfying, you may never go back to the old method again.

—DIANE UNGER, *Cook's Country*

Garlic Mashed Potatoes

SERVES 8 TO 10

Cutting the potatoes into ½-inch pieces ensures that maximum surface area is exposed to soak up garlicky flavor.

- 4 **pounds russet potatoes (about 8), peeled, quartered, and cut into ½-inch pieces**
- 12 **tablespoons (1½ sticks) unsalted butter, cut into 12 pieces**
- 12 **garlic cloves, minced**
- 1 **teaspoon sugar**
- 1½ **cups half-and-half**
- ½ **cup water**
   Salt and pepper

1. Place the cut potatoes in a colander and rinse under cold running water until the water runs clear. Drain thoroughly.

2. Melt 4 tablespoons of the butter in a Dutch oven over medium heat. Add the garlic and sugar and cook, stirring often, until sticky and straw-colored, 3 to 4 minutes. Add the rinsed potatoes, 1¼ cups of the half-and-half, water, and 1 teaspoon salt to the pot and stir to combine. Bring to a boil, then reduce the heat to low and simmer, covered, stirring occasionally, until the potatoes are tender and most of the liquid is absorbed, 25 to 30 minutes.

3. Off the heat, add the remaining 8 tablespoons butter to the pot and mash with a potato masher until smooth. Using a rubber spatula, fold in the remaining ¼ cup half-and-half until the liquid is absorbed and the potatoes are creamy. Season with salt and pepper to taste and serve.

GETTING ROASTED GARLIC FLAVOR

1. Cook the minced garlic (and a little sugar) in butter until the garlic is sticky and straw-colored; this blooms the garlic's sweet flavor and tempers its harshness.

2. For deeply integrated garlic flavor, toss the raw potatoes with the garlic-butter mixture, add the half-and-half and water directly to the pot, cover, and gently cook until tender.

THE BEST POTATO MASHER

Flimsy or poorly designed potato mashers can make an easy task overly arduous. Our favorite potato masher, the **WMF Profi Plus 11¼-inch Masher,** $20, features sturdy construction and an oval mashing disk that produces soft and silky spuds with a minimum of effort.

ALIGOT

LEAVE IT TO THE FRENCH TO TAKE A CONCEPT as simple as throwing cheese and garlic into mashed potatoes and elevate it into something far more interesting than, well, mashed potatoes with cheese and garlic. The dish, called *aligot,* comes from the Auvergne region of south-central France, where it is so revered that an entire festival is devoted each year to celebrating it.

I first encountered aligot at a Boston bistro, where the taciturn waiter billed it merely as "French" mashed potatoes. That didn't prepare me for the dish that arrived at my table. Instead of a fluffy mound of spuds, this mash pooled on the plate. And when I lifted my fork to take a bite, the potatoes stretched and pulled like taffy. Was that a good thing? One intensely garlicky, cheesy bite and I knew it was a superb thing.

I did a little research when I got home and learned that aligot gets this uniquely elastic, satiny texture through prolonged, vigorous stirring. Now I was really intrigued. Here in the test kitchen, we've confirmed time and again that a light touch is the secret to great mashed potatoes. How could a heavy-handed technique create such a velvety puree without any trace of glueyness or stickiness?

Most aligot recipes combine pureed boiled potatoes with butter and crème fraîche, then energetically beat in handfuls of cheese until the mixture achieves its signature stretch and lifts in long, elastic ribbons. This hearty side dish is traditionally served with equally rib-sticking fare such as sausages or grilled meat. When I looked closely at a few of the recipes, one thing became clear. Aligot calls for so much butter, cheese, and crème fraîche that if I planned to serve it for anything but a really special meal, a little lightening up would be in order.

The next pressing issue: choosing a potato. Red Bliss were too dense and their flavor all but undetectable in aligot. Russets did far better on flavor, lending a nice earthiness, but their high starch content wasn't quite right for this dish. The medium-starch Yukon Golds were the clear winner, yielding a puree with a mild, buttery flavor and a light, creamy consistency.

In the test kitchen, we've found that how you cook potatoes for a regular mash is critical to their final texture. To avoid glueyness, we've gone so far as to steam as well as rinse the spuds midway through cooking to rid them of excess amylose, the "bad" starch in potatoes that turns them tacky. But if the potatoes were to be stirred so vigorously later (rough handling also bursts the granules that contain amylose, releasing the starch into the mix), would such treatment even matter? As it turned out, no. When I compared a batch of aligot made with steamed and rinsed potatoes to one made with simple boiled potatoes (the method advocated by virtually every recipe I came across), tasters could detect no difference.

Now, what about mashing? The French turn to a tool called a tamis, a metal sieve mounted over a shallow drum. Food is pressed through the screen to create a super-smooth puree free of even the tiniest lumps. Both a ricer and a food mill seemed like close cousins to the tamis, but neither gave me the velvety texture I was looking for. Normally I wouldn't dream of "mashing" potatoes in a food processor—its metal blade would surely burst every starch granule in the mix. But since glueyness wasn't an issue in aligot, I brought the processor out and found that it worked beautifully.

ALIGOT (GARLIC AND CHEESE MASHED POTATOES)

Next up: creaminess. Traditional aligot uses butter and crème fraîche to add flavor and loosen the potato puree's texture before mixing in the cheese. Since crème fraîche isn't always easy to find, I decided to try making aligot with sour cream (a common substitute) as well as with heavy cream and milk. Sour cream and heavy cream both produced results that were certainly creamy but also way too rich. Whole milk proved best, providing depth without going overboard.

At last, I could concentrate on selecting the cheese. *Tomme fraîche*—a soft, mild cheese made from fresh curds—is the authentic choice, but given the U.S. government ban on the sale of raw (unpasteurized) cow's milk cheese aged less than 60 days, this cheese is out of reach for most Americans. I'd been using Cantal, which seemed like a good bet given that it's a semihard version of tomme fraîche with a flavor similar to mild cheddar. But adding handfuls of this shredded cheese thickened my potatoes so much that I needed brute force to stir them. Plus, the dish lacked the stretchiness I remembered from my bistro meal. Searching for a more elastic substitute, I tried cheddar and then Swiss, with similarly unsatisfactory results. Grabbing a quick piece of pizza one day and watching how ribbons of gooey mozzarella stretched between two slices, it came to me: Why not try typical pizza cheese, the prepackaged mozzarella from the supermarket dairy section?

This was a stretch in the very best way—after adding a generous 3 cups, I could lift my wooden spoon and entertain my colleagues with the aligot's incredible expansion. Yet its taste fell flat: The mozzarella was just too mild. Stirring and lifting, I tested versions in which I replaced some of the mozzarella with slightly stronger tasting Cantal (in smaller portions, it didn't lessen elasticity), sharp cheddar, and nutty Gruyère. Gruyère turned out to be the top choice. But with 3 cups of cheese and 2 pounds of potatoes (a lesser proportion of cheese than most recipes called for), tasters thought the aligot was still overly rich. Cutting back to just a cup of mozzarella and a cup of Gruyère reduced the stretch slightly, but kept richness in check.

As for the stirring, at this point my arm was going around in circles in my sleep. Testing proved that stirring was key to the aligot equation: Too much and the aligot turned so rubbery that it reminded me of chewing gum; too little and the cheese didn't truly marry with the potatoes for that essential elasticity. I eventually concluded that five minutes was the right workout. But I still didn't understand why the stirring worked so well, since the vigorous motion (like that of the food processor) releases amylose, the pesky starch molecule that turns good potatoes gluey. After consulting with our science editor, I learned that, in this case, amylose was an asset—the sticky molecules were binding with the proteins from the melted cheese, enhancing its stretch without causing glueyness.

Thus informed, I could focus on the remaining element: garlic. Adding two minced cloves to the potatoes as I pureed them in the food processor yielded just the right amount of garlic punch.

At last my aligot was so rich, garlicky, and stretchy, I was willing to bet it would pass muster even in Auvergne.

—CHARLES KELSEY, *Cook's Illustrated*

Aligot (Garlic and Cheese Mashed Potatoes)

SERVES 6

The finished potatoes should have a smooth and slightly elastic texture. White cheddar can be substituted for the Gruyère. For richer, stretchier aligot, double the mozzarella.

- **2 pounds Yukon Gold potatoes (about 4), peeled and cut into ½-inch-thick slices**
- **Salt**
- **6 tablespoons (¾ stick) unsalted butter, cut into ½-inch pieces**
- **2 garlic cloves, minced**
- **1–1½ cups whole milk**
- **4 ounces mozzarella cheese, shredded (about 1 cup) (see note)**
- **4 ounces Gruyère cheese, shredded (about 1 cup) (see note)**
- **Pepper**

1. Place the cut potatoes in a colander and rinse under cold running water until the water runs clear. Drain thoroughly. Place the potatoes in a large saucepan; add water to cover by 1 inch and add 1 tablespoon salt. Partially cover the saucepan with a lid and bring the potatoes to a boil over high heat. Reduce the heat to medium-low and simmer until the potatoes are tender and just break apart when poked with a fork, 12 to 17 minutes. Drain the potatoes and dry the saucepan.

2. Transfer the potatoes to a food processor; add the butter, garlic, and 1½ teaspoons salt. Pulse until the butter is melted and incorporated into the potatoes, about 10 pulses. Add 1 cup of the milk and continue to process until the potatoes are smooth and creamy, about 20 seconds, scraping down the sides halfway through.

3. Return the potato mixture to the saucepan and set over medium heat. Stir in the cheeses, 1 cup at a time, until incorporated. Continue to cook the potatoes, stirring vigorously, until the cheese is fully melted and the mixture is smooth and elastic, 3 to 5 minutes. If the mixture is difficult to stir and seems thick, stir in the remaining milk, 2 tablespoons at a time, until the potatoes are loose and creamy. Season with salt and pepper to taste. Serve immediately.

NOTES FROM THE TEST KITCHEN

THE SCIENCE OF STRETCH

Normally we wouldn't dream of mashing potatoes in a food processor, let alone whipping them by hand for a protracted period. Such rough handling causes the release of amylose, the tacky gel-like starch found in potatoes that spells the end of light, fluffy texture. But in these cheesy, garlicky French mashed potatoes, the release of amylose is actually a good thing—when combined with the cheese in the recipe, it helps produce aligot's signature stretch. When cheese is stirred vigorously into the hot boiled potatoes, this rough treatment causes the waterlogged starch granules in the spuds to burst, releasing sticky, gluey amylose. At the same time, the protein molecules in the melting cheese are uncoiling and stretching out. When amylose released from the potatoes comes into contact with the uncoiled proteins, it links them together into long, elastic fibers that give aligot its stretch.

AU GRATIN POTATOES

WELL-MADE AU GRATIN POTATOES TRANSFORM humble ingredients into something almost ethereal. To my mind, perfection would be layers of paper-thin, tender potatoes; a crunchy, browned crust; lots of cheese; and the cohesiveness to be sliced into neat, elegant squares. What you actually get can range from curdled cream and unevenly cooked potatoes to cheese that's barely there and slices that fall into sloppy heaps. We tested and tasted half a dozen recipes, picked the version that came closest to my ideal, and continued testing.

The choice of potato was critical. Yukon golds and red potatoes produced loose, wobbly gratins, so I decided on starchy russets. Test kitchen experience had taught me that the starch would help the casserole firm up. I came across many recipes that warned cooks not to rinse the potato slices: Rinse them and you rinse away the starch. Thick potato slices took forever to cook and never fused. But short of hiring a surgeon, how could I cut the potatoes to an even thinness? Happily, an inexpensive mandoline made short work of slicing 3 pounds of potatoes to an even, near-translucent thinness. I tested one more technique to help the gratin bind (which, by happy coincidence, intensified the cheese flavor): Rather than sprinkling all the cheese on top, I used half of it in the center. This gratin sliced into attractive, cohesive squares.

My working recipe called for milk and cream, but the dairy kept curdling in the oven. I'd seen a recipe that suggested baking the gratin at a low temperature (300 degrees), then cranking up the heat at the finish to brown the top. Alas, the gentle temperature meant a longer cooking time without any payoff—the dairy curdled regardless. Next, I made the gratin with just heavy cream; with less protein than milk, cream is less apt to curdle. This time it didn't curdle, but tasters found it one-dimensional and excessively rich. I tried cutting the cream with chicken broth. This both lightened the dish and let the potatoes be the star.

I'd been using 1 cup of grated sharp cheddar cheese, standard in American versions of the dish. From the start, tasters demanded, "More cheese!" I tripled the amount before they were satisfied. Unfortunately, like most aged cheeses, sharp cheddar separates and becomes greasy when melted. Looking for better melting, I replaced some of the cheddar with an unconventional choice: Monterey Jack, which melts well. Unfortunately, it was so mild that we could barely taste it. By replacing some of the Monterey Jack with ½ cup Parmesan, I achieved an acceptable balance of good melting and flavor. For extra insurance, I tossed the shredded cheeses with 2 teaspoons cornstarch, which helped prevent the cheeses from clumping when melted.

Delicious as it finally was, my gratin dawdled in the oven. Some recipes call for warming the liquids before pouring them over the potatoes—might that trim the oven time? Sad to say, it shaved just two minutes—minus the minute and a half needed to heat the liquid in the first place. I'd just have to accept that good things come to those who wait.

—LYNN CLARK, *Cook's Country*

AU GRATIN POTATOES

Au Gratin Potatoes

SERVES 6

Slicing the potatoes ⅛ inch thick is crucial for the success of this dish. Use a mandoline, V-slicer, or food processor fitted with a ⅛-inch slicing blade. You do not need to grease the baking dish. You will need a 2 to 3-quart gratin dish.

- 5 ounces sharp cheddar cheese, shredded (about 1¼ cups)
- 5 ounces Monterey Jack cheese, shredded (about 1¼ cups)
- 1 ounce Parmesan cheese, grated (about ½ cup)
- 2 teaspoons cornstarch
- 3 pounds russet potatoes (about 6), peeled and sliced ⅛ inch thick (see note)
- Salt and pepper
- ¾ cup heavy cream
- ½ cup low-sodium chicken broth

1. Adjust an oven rack to the middle position and heat the oven to 350 degrees. Toss the cheeses and cornstarch in a large bowl until evenly coated.

2. Shingle half of the potatoes in a large gratin dish, sprinkle evenly with 1 cup of the cheese mixture, ¾ teaspoon salt, and ¼ teaspoon pepper. Top with the remaining potatoes, ¾ teaspoon more salt, and ¼ teaspoon more pepper.

3. Combine the cream and broth in a large measuring cup and pour over the potatoes. Top with the remaining 2 cups cheese mixture and bake until golden brown and a fork inserted into the center meets little resistance, 75 to 90 minutes. Let cool for 10 minutes and serve.

NOTES FROM THE TEST KITCHEN

THE IMPORTANCE OF THIN SLICES

Don't try to slice the potatoes for this recipe by hand. Even the professional cooks in our test kitchen struggled to get the slices consistently thin enough. Thin slices aren't merely aesthetics; they meld into a cohesive, uniform casserole that cuts into neat squares. More important, though, thick slices won't become meltingly tender in the oven because there's not enough liquid in a gratin to cook them evenly. If you don't have a mandoline, a V-slicer, or the slicing disk on a food processor is a better option than cutting by hand. The slices might not be quite as perfect (and they won't shingle as nicely), but the gratin will taste fine.

TOO THICK AND UNDERCOOKED

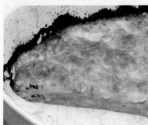

THIN AND COOKED JUST RIGHT

THE SECRETS TO AU GRATIN POTATOES

1. Thick, uneven hand-sliced potatoes won't lie flat in the dish or cook evenly. To get perfectly sliced potatoes easily and efficiently, use a mandoline slicer.

2. Most recipes call for sprinkling a little cheese over the top of the casserole. For a cheesier gratin, use a combination of sharp cheddar, tangy Parmesan, and easy-melting Monterey Jack not only on top of the spuds, but also in between.

3. Heavy cream won't separate when it's cooked, but too much makes the gratin heavy and overwhelms the potatoes. Cut the cream with chicken broth.

SAUTÉED GREEN BEANS

THE STANDARD TECHNIQUE IN MOST RECIPES for sautéed green beans goes something like this: parboil, shock in ice water, dry with towels, and, finally, sauté. While the method has advantages—it allows you to do most of the prep work in advance—sometimes I want things a little more streamlined. Could I achieve tender, lightly browned, fresh-tasting beans, without all the fuss and in just one pan?

First, I tried simply sautéing the raw beans in a skillet in oil—big mistake. The dry heat took so long to penetrate the beans that their exteriors blackened before the interiors cooked through. Water was clearly going to be necessary. My next thought was to do a variation on parboiling. I threw beans and a small amount of water into a cold pan, covered it, and brought it to a simmer. Once the beans were almost cooked, I removed the lid and waited for the water to evaporate. I then added a little oil and sautéed the beans until browned. While promising, the method wasn't foolproof. If the water took too long to evaporate, the beans turned limp before they could brown. And even when I achieved lightly browned and properly cooked beans, the caramelized flavor seemed superficial.

Why not reverse the process and sauté the beans first? Following this line of thinking, I briefly sautéed the beans until they were spotty brown but not yet cooked through, then added ¼ cup water to the pan. As soon as the water hit the skillet it turned to steam, and I quickly covered the pan. Once the beans were almost cooked (an efficient process in this steamy environment), I removed the lid and let the excess moisture evaporate. This produced just the right crisp-tender texture I was looking for and, at least initially, the caramelized flavor was deeper. But once I added water to the skillet, it seemed to wash off some of that intensified flavor, making my veggies taste more like ordinary steamed green beans.

The solution: I simply steamed the beans for a minute or so less so they remained slightly undercooked, then blasted the heat once the lid was removed. This quickly evaporated what little water was left in the pan and allowed me to promote additional browning before the beans fully cooked through. I also found that adding a little softened butter to the skillet once the water had evaporated (softened butter was quicker to melt and faster to brown than cold) provided some welcome richness and further aided browning.

As far as additional flavors, I decided to limit extras to herbs, spices, and a few pantry items. Mixed into the butter (or, in some cases, oil), combinations such as garlic and herbs, smoked paprika and almonds, and ginger and sesame added complexity without tampering with the dish's one-pan simplicity.

—KEITH DRESSER, *Cook's Illustrated*

Sautéed Green Beans with Garlic and Herbs
SERVES 4

This recipe yields crisp-tender beans. If you prefer a slightly more tender texture (or if you are using large, tough beans), increase the water by a tablespoon and increase the covered cooking time by 1 minute. To serve 6, increase all of the ingredients by half and increase the covered cooking time by 1 to 2 minutes. Do not attempt to cook more than 1½ pounds of green beans with this method.

- 1 **tablespoon unsalted butter, softened**
- 3 **garlic cloves, minced**
- 1 **teaspoon minced fresh thyme**
- 1 **teaspoon olive oil**
- 1 **pound green beans, trimmed and cut into 2-inch pieces**
-   **Salt and pepper**
- ¼ **cup water**
- 2 **teaspoons fresh lemon juice**
- 1 **tablespoon chopped fresh parsley**

1. Combine the butter, garlic, and thyme in a small bowl; set aside. Heat the oil in a 12-inch nonstick skillet over medium heat until just smoking. Add the beans, ¼ teaspoon salt, and ⅛ teaspoon pepper; cook, stirring occasionally, until spotty brown, 4 to 6 minutes.

2. Add the water, cover, and cook until the beans are bright green and still crisp, about 2 minutes. Remove the cover, increase the heat to high, and cook until the water evaporates, 30 to 60 seconds. Add the butter mixture and continue to cook, stirring frequently, until the beans are crisp-tender, lightly browned, and beginning to wrinkle, 1 to 3 minutes longer. Transfer the beans to a serving bowl and toss with the lemon juice and parsley; season with salt and pepper to taste and serve.

Sautéed Green Beans with Smoked Paprika and Almonds

Follow the recipe for Sautéed Green Beans with Garlic and Herbs, omitting the thyme and parsley. Stir ¼ teaspoon smoked paprika into the softened butter with the garlic in step 1. Sprinkle the cooked beans with ¼ cup toasted slivered almonds before serving.

Spicy Sautéed Green Beans with Ginger and Sesame

Combine 1 teaspoon toasted sesame oil, 1 teaspoon grated fresh ginger, and 1 tablespoon chili-garlic paste in a small bowl. Follow the recipe for Sautéed Green Beans with Garlic and Herbs, substituting vegetable oil for the olive oil and increasing the amount to 2 teaspoons. Cook as directed, replacing the butter mixture with the sesame oil mixture and omitting the lemon juice and parsley. Sprinkle the cooked beans with 2 teaspoons toasted sesame seeds before serving.

Sautéed Green Beans with Roasted Red Peppers and Basil

Combine 2 teaspoons olive oil, 1 shallot, minced, and ⅛ teaspoon red pepper flakes in a small bowl. Follow the recipe for Sautéed Green Beans with Garlic and Herbs, replacing the butter mixture with the oil-shallot mixture. Add ⅓ cup roasted red peppers, cut into ½-inch pieces, to the pan with the oil-shallot mixture. Substitute 1 teaspoon red wine vinegar for the lemon juice and 2 tablespoons chopped fresh basil for the parsley.

NOTES FROM THE TEST KITCHEN

CHOOSING A NONSCRATCH SCRUBBER

Heavy-duty copper and steel wool pads are best at cutting through messes on stainless steel pans, but what should you use on delicate nonstick surfaces? To find out, we rounded up eight brands of nonscratch scrubbers. Every scrubber passed the nonscratch test, but some were more effective than others. Our two favorite scrubbers, the **Chore Boy Scratch-Free Scrubber,** $1.19 (left) and the **Chore Boy Soap Filled Scrubber,** $1.69 (right) have ribbonlike nylon strands which form a mesh of sharp, raised edges that are still gentle. Conversely, models with thicker abrasive scrubbing surfaces didn't dig as deeply into grime. (See page 311 for more information about our testing results.)

SWEET CORN SPOONBREAD

THE IDEAL SPOONBREAD SHOULD BE A TALL, creamy custard packed with sweet corn. But more often than not, the results are squat, gritty, and bland. What's the secret to really great spoonbread? To appreciate spoonbread, it helps to know its history. In the 19th century, batters of cornmeal and water were baked, fried, or griddled to make humble dishes like johnnycakes and corn dodgers. With the addition of milk and eggs, these dishes evolved into rich, "spoon-able" corn custards called spoonbreads. Some later versions elevated the dish (literally) with baking soda, but the most refined recipes folded beaten egg whites into the batter, turning spoonbread into a fluffy cornmeal soufflé with a golden crust and a silky interior.

Hoping to replicate this soufflé-style spoonbread, I rounded up half a dozen recipes and tried them out. I chose recipes that used both classic cornmeal and fresh corn kernels—a modern addition to many spoonbreads. My tasters and I were disappointed by the poor texture (gritty from cornmeal, with unappealing chunks of chewy corn kernels) and weak flavor of each one.

This style of spoonbread is made by cooking cornmeal in milk, cooling the mixture, stirring in egg yolks, and then folding in beaten egg whites and baking. After playing with the ratios, I found that 1 cup of cornmeal, 2¾ cups of milk, and 3 eggs were the right amount for my 1½-quart soufflé dish. But even though I was simmering the cornmeal in milk, it remained gritty; I tried soaking the cornmeal in milk for a few minutes before simmering, and this successfully eliminated the grit. Beating the egg whites with cream of tartar made for a more stable foam and higher rise.

The raw corn, however, was too bland and chewy. Sautéing the kernels in butter helped to intensify their flavor, as did adding a little sugar, salt, and cayenne pepper. Steeping the cooked corn in milk before adding it to the cornmeal mixture spread the deep, sweet flavor of sautéed corn throughout the spoonbread. To remedy the chewy texture, I turned to my blender and pureed the corn and milk. The silky mixture that came out of the blender tasted like cream of corn soup—good enough to eat on its own. Incorporated into the spoonbread, my "corn milk" produced a light, creamy texture and sweet corn taste that set this spoonbread far apart from its workaday ancestors.

—KELLEY BAKER, *Cook's Country*

SWEET CORN SPOONBREAD

Sweet Corn Spoonbread

SERVES 6

You will need 2 cups of corn kernels for this recipe. Frozen corn can be substituted for the fresh, provided it is thawed and well drained.

> 1 cup cornmeal
> 2¾ cups whole milk
> 3–4 ears fresh corn, husks and silks removed (see note)
> 4 tablespoons (½ stick) unsalted butter
> 1 teaspoon sugar
> 1 teaspoon salt
> ⅛ teaspoon cayenne pepper
> 3 large eggs, separated
> ¼ teaspoon cream of tartar

1. Adjust an oven rack to the middle position and heat the oven to 400 degrees. Grease a 1½-quart soufflé dish or 8-inch square baking dish. Whisk the cornmeal and ¾ cup of the milk together in a bowl; set aside.

2. Cut the kernels from the ears of corn (see photo). Melt the butter in a Dutch oven over medium-high heat. Add the corn and cook until beginning to brown, about 3 minutes. Stir in the remaining 2 cups milk, sugar, salt, and cayenne and bring to a boil. Remove from the heat, cover, and let the mixture steep for 15 minutes.

3. Transfer the warm corn mixture to a blender or food processor and puree until smooth. Return the corn mixture to the pot and bring to a boil over medium-high heat. Reduce the heat to low and add the cornmeal mixture, whisking constantly, until thickened, 2 to 3 minutes; transfer to a large bowl and cool to room temperature, about 20 minutes. Once the mixture is cool, whisk in the egg yolks until combined.

4. With an electric mixer on medium-low speed, beat the egg whites and cream of tartar until frothy, about 1 minute. Increase the speed to medium-high and beat until stiff peaks form, about 3 minutes. Whisk one-third of the whites into the corn mixture, then gently fold in the remaining whites until combined. Scrape the mixture into the prepared dish and transfer to the oven. Reduce the oven temperature to 350 degrees and bake until the spoonbread is golden brown and has risen above the rim of the dish, about 45 minutes. Serve immediately.

VARIATION

Individual Spoonbreads

Follow the recipe for Sweet Corn Spoonbread, dividing the batter among 6 greased 7-ounce ramekins. Arrange the ramekins on a rimmed baking sheet and bake as directed, reducing the cooking time to 30 to 35 minutes.

NOTES FROM THE TEST KITCHEN

EGG WHITES 101
Egg whites are most easily whipped in a clean metal bowl with a pinch of cream of tartar, which promotes stabilization.

SOFT PEAKS
Soft peaks will droop slightly downward from the whisk or beater.

STIFF PEAKS
Stiff peaks will stand up tall on their own.

OVERWHIPPED
Overwhipped egg whites will look curdled and separated; if you reach this point, you'll need to start over with new whites and a clean bowl.

CUTTING THE KERNELS
Cutting the kernels off ears of corn can be tricky, as the cobs can roll around on the cutting board. Here's how we do it.

Use a chef's knife to cut the cobs in half. Stabilize the cobs by standing them on their cut ends, then slice the kernels from the cob.

BEER-BATTERED ONION RINGS

ON A RECENT NIGHT OUT WITH FRIENDS, I ordered beer-battered onion rings and hoped that for once I'd avoid disappointment. (In my experience, good onion rings are as rare and as welcome as a parking space in downtown Boston.) Several minutes later, eight fat, golden onion rings stacked high on a wooden dowel arrived at the table to "oohs" and "ahhs." To my surprise, these tasted as good as they looked. The coating had maximum crunch with the barest trace of bitterness; the onions were tender and sweet. Sprinkled generously with salt, the rings were hard to stop eating. I was inspired to head into the test kitchen to make some myself.

What a disaster! Not a single recipe produced rings nearly as good as those I'd eaten. They offered up a litany of frying flaws: soggy, doughy, heavy, raw—and where had that distinctively yeasty and malty undertone gone?

I started my tweaking by stirring together a basic batter of flour, Budweiser, and salt. I'd finesse it later; first I wanted to figure out which onion to use. I coated the onions in batter and fried them for about five minutes in 350-degree peanut oil. Sweet onions creamed the competition; tasters preferred their gentle flavor to basic yellow onions. That settled, I turned my attention back to the batter, reconsidering each component.

Beer is meant to provide flavor and lift in batter. Flavor was an easy matter: I experimented with full-bodied ales and lagers like Bass and Samuel Adams in place of milder Budweiser. These brews lent welcome hoppy, toasty flavors to the coating.

Lift was trickier. The carbonation in beer creates gas bubbles that lighten beer batters, but with just beer my rings were doughy. Clearly, I'd need a second leavener. Recipes are split on whether to use eggs or baking powder. Eggs did little, but baking powder yielded a coating that was thick and substantial, yet light. Finally, to add crunch to the coating, I used cornstarch, a technique I knew from test kitchen experience would work. I gradually substituted cornstarch for flour until I had a 1 to 1 ratio. Now my rings shattered when I bit into them.

Unfortunately, part of that crunch came from the onions, and while crunchy coating appealed, crunchy onions definitely did not. Some recipes call for soaking the onions in water, milk, or buttermilk to tenderize them. They all worked, but I wondered if I could use the soak to build flavor, too. Since these were beer-battered onion rings, I soaked them in beer for an hour before proceeding with my recipe. At last, I had nicely flavored rings with crisp coating encasing tender slices of onion. But did I really have to wait an hour?

To shorten the soaking time, a colleague suggested adding salt, which works by breaking down and softening the exterior cell walls of the onion. That shaved only 10 minutes off the time; for the next round, I added 2 teaspoons of white vinegar as well (the acid works in a similar manner). A mere 30 minutes later, I had soft, tender onions. In one final test, I tried malt vinegar, which is made from beer. As I'd hoped, it subtly echoed the caramel beer notes of the batter.

—LYNN CLARK, *Cook's Country*

Beer-Battered Onion Rings

SERVES 4 TO 6

You will need two 12-ounce beers, preferably full-flavored ales or lagers like Bass or Samuel Adams. In step 1, do not soak the onions longer than 2 hours or they will turn mushy. Cider vinegar can be used in place of malt vinegar.

- 2 **sweet onions, such as Vidalia, sliced into ½-inch-thick rounds**
- 3 **cups beer (see note)**
- 2 **teaspoons malt vinegar (see note)**
  Salt and pepper
- 2 **quarts peanut or vegetable oil**
- ¾ **cup unbleached all-purpose flour**
- ¾ **cup cornstarch**
- 1 **teaspoon baking powder**

1. Place the onion rounds, 2 cups of the beer, vinegar, ½ teaspoon salt, and ½ teaspoon pepper in a large zipper-lock bag; refrigerate 30 minutes or up to 2 hours.

2. Heat the oil in a large Dutch oven over medium-high heat to 350 degrees. (Use an instant-read thermometer that registers high temperatures, or clip a candy/deep-fat thermometer onto the side of the pot.) While the oil is heating, combine the flour, cornstarch, baking powder, ½ teaspoon salt, and ¼ teaspoon pepper in a large bowl. Slowly whisk in ¾ cup more beer until just combined (some lumps will remain). Whisk in the remaining ¼ cup beer as needed, 1 tablespoon at a time, until the batter falls from the whisk in a steady stream and leaves a faint trail across the surface of the batter (see page 56).

ENSURING CRUNCHY ONION RINGS

1. Soak the rings in a combination of beer, vinegar, salt, and pepper.

2. Add the beer to the batter gradually until the batter falls from a whisk to form a ribbon trail.

3. Fry the battered onion rings in small batches and transfer them one at a time to the hot oil.

CHOOSE SWEET ONIONS

We found that tasters preferred milder sweet onions to harsher yellow storage onions. Sweet onions come in many varieties, including Vidalia from Georgia, Walla Walla from Washington state, and Maui from Hawaii. All have low sulfur and high sugar content; the sulfur compounds account for onions' pungency. Because they're sugary, sweet onions nicely counterpoint the slight bitterness of the beer batter.

MALT VINEGAR ENHANCES BEER FLAVOR

We softened raw onions in a mix of beer, vinegar, salt, and pepper before we battered and fried them. Both the salt and the acidic vinegar shorten the necessary soaking time by breaking down the cell walls of the onions. We like malt vinegar, which is made by fermenting malted barley ale, because it contributes another dimension of toasty beer flavor. But cider vinegar will get the job done in a pinch.

3. Adjust an oven rack to the middle position and heat the oven to 200 degrees. Remove the onions from the refrigerator and pour off the liquid. Pat the onion rounds dry with paper towels and separate into rings. Transfer one-third of the rings to the batter. One at a time, carefully transfer the battered rings to the oil. Fry until the rings are golden brown and crisp, about 5 minutes, flipping halfway through frying. Drain the rings on a paper towel–lined baking sheet, season with salt and pepper to taste, and transfer to the oven. Return the oil to 350 degrees and repeat twice more with the remaining rings and batter. Serve.

SKILLET RATATOUILLE

RATATOUILLE, featuring eggplant, zucchini, pepper, tomatoes, and fresh herbs, may be a rustic dish, but that doesn't mean it's simple to prepare. Bad versions are a soggy mess of vegetables indistinguishable in taste and texture, often sitting in a watery tomato bath. But the good ones more than make up the difference—the flavors of a well-made ratatouille are light and multilayered; each vegetable can be tasted independently, its flavor heightened by the presence of the others.

The name ratatouille is derived from the French *touiller*, meaning "to stir"—a possible warning of the work involved in the classical French preparation, where each vegetable is sautéed separately and combined at the last minute. This method, although time-consuming, lends itself perfectly to skillet cookery. But considering all the chopping and prep work involved in making this dish, I thought I could at least simplify and speed up the cooking process. I've seen recipes that make ratatouille by tossing all the ingredients together in one pot, slowly stewing them till tender. I was skeptical that these vegetables would retain their individual character, but there was only one way to find out.

Before I began cooking, I prepared the vegetables. I kept the usual main ingredients—eggplant, zucchini, onion, bell peppers, and tomatoes—in my recipe. To keep some contrast in texture, I sliced the onions and peppers into strips and cut the zucchini and eggplant into 1-inch cubes, leaving the skin on. Fresh, ripe tomatoes would be ideal, but outside the peak summer months they have little flavor and poor texture. Because they are picked at the height of the season, canned diced tomatoes are guaranteed to be ripe and sweet.

With the key players in place, I could now address cooking technique. Despite my skepticism, I thought it made sense to start with the simplest method first— the one-pot version that stewed everything together. I sweated the onions and peppers, then tossed in the rest of the vegetables and simmered them on the stove until tender. My low expectations were fulfilled: The resulting product was mushy, soupy, and one-dimensional. I knew the eggplant and zucchini were the two parties guilty for releasing much of the liquid that led to this dish's soupiness. Browning them before the vegetables were combined, I thought, would help reduce this liquid and, at the same time, help develop additional flavor in the pan.

Returning to the stove, I sautéed the eggplant and zucchini, separately, in a large skillet with olive oil. Eggplant is often salted and set aside to release liquid before cooking, but the prospect of tacking an extra half-hour onto our overall cooking time wasn't really appealing. Instead, I thought that using relatively high heat to brown the eggplant and the zucchini on the stovetop could both evaporate the juices and concentrate the vegetables' flavor. Since I wasn't looking to cook them through but just sear the outside, it only took about 5 minutes each on medium-high heat to get a good browning.

My next step was to sauté the onions and peppers together until golden brown. I covered them for the first 10 minutes so they would release excess liquid, then cooked them another five minutes uncovered. Garlic and fresh thyme were added to the skillet for flavor. Then I gently folded in the tomatoes, zucchini, and eggplant, turned down the heat, and let the vegetables simmer together, covered, until just saucy. I found that uncovering the skillet for the final 10 minutes of cooking allowed the juices to reduce and thicken to just the right consistency.

The vegetables were cooked through but still retained their shape.

This ratatouille was a vast improvement on the soupy mess I'd made earlier. And despite the etymology of the dish, very little stirring was actually required; in fact, the less I stirred, the better. I had finally achieved a medley of vegetables with distinct textures and flavors that were in harmony but still retained their own voice.

—ADELAIDE PARKER, *America's Test Kitchen Books*

Skillet Ratatouille

SERVES 4 TO 6

Minced fresh rosemary can be substituted for the thyme. Do not peel the eggplant as the skin helps it hold together during cooking. It is important to cook the eggplant and zucchini until they are brown, but to stir them as little as possible to prevent them from turning mushy.

- ¼ cup olive oil
- 1 eggplant (about 1 pound), cut into 1-inch pieces (see note)
- 2 zucchini (about 1 pound), cut into 1-inch pieces (see note)
- 1 onion, halved and sliced ¼ inch thick
- 1 red bell pepper, stemmed, seeded, and sliced into ¼-inch strips
  Salt
- 2 garlic cloves, minced
- 2 teaspoons minced fresh thyme (see note)
- 1 (14.5-ounce) can diced tomatoes
- 2 tablespoons chopped fresh basil or parsley
  Pepper

1. Heat 1 tablespoon of the oil in a 12-inch non-stick skillet over medium-high heat until shimmering. Add the eggplant and cook, stirring occasionally, until browned, 5 to 7 minutes. Transfer the eggplant to a medium bowl. Repeat with 1 tablespoon more oil and the zucchini; transfer to the bowl with the eggplant.

2. Heat the remaining 2 tablespoons oil in the skillet over medium-low heat until shimmering. Add the onion, bell pepper, and ½ teaspoon salt, cover, and cook, stirring occasionally, until the vegetables are softened and have released their liquid, about 10 minutes. Uncover, increase the heat to medium, and cook, stirring occasionally, until the onion is golden brown, 5 to 10 minutes longer.

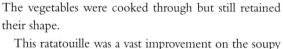

3. Stir in the garlic and thyme and cook until fragrant, about 30 seconds. Add the tomatoes with their juice, scraping up any browned bits. Gently stir in the browned eggplant and zucchini and bring to a simmer. Cover, turn the heat to medium-low, and cook for 5 minutes until saucy.

4. Uncover and continue to cook until the ratatouille is thickened but the vegetables still retain their shape, about 10 minutes longer. Gently stir in the basil and season with salt and pepper to taste. Transfer to a dish and serve.

SUMMER VEGETABLE GRATIN

WHEN SUMMER YIELDS A BUMPER CROP of zucchini and tomatoes, I often consider making a simple, Provençal-style vegetable gratin. I imagine a crisp, golden, bread-crumb and cheese topping providing a pleasing contrast to the fresh, bright flavor of the vegetables. Then reality interrupts: As they cook, juicy vegetables exude a torrent of liquid that washes away flavors, turning my idyllic side dish into a squishy, soggy mistake.

There are plenty of vegetable gratin recipes out there, and I spent a day in the test kitchen trying a few, hoping to find the one of my dreams. But it wasn't meant to be—most were so flooded that I had to serve them with a slotted spoon. One even called for half of a loaf of sourdough bread to be layered among the vegetables, presumably to soak up some of the juices. But it didn't work. Even with 4 cups of spongy bread cubes, a deluge of liquid still ruined the dish. And with the release of juices, along went the flavor—the gratins were hopelessly bland and watery.

Before I could outline a dehydration plan, I had to determine exactly which vegetables to include. After some experimentation, I decided to stick with a fairly typical combination of tomatoes, zucchini, and yellow summer squash (another common addition, eggplant, was simply too mushy and spongy).

My first move was to bake the casserole uncovered. The practice of covering the gratin with foil during baking (recommended by most recipes to speed cooking) was keeping too much moisture in. This was a step in the right direction, but my gratin was still waterlogged. To rid the zucchini and squash of some of their liquid, precooking methods such as grilling, broiling, or sautéing came to mind. While these methods were workable, I didn't want to spend all day at the grill, oven, or stove just to make a mere side dish. Salting, a technique frequently used to draw moisture from vegetables, made more sense. This method worked like a charm on the zucchini and summer squash, drying them out and thoroughly seasoning them as well. The tomatoes, however, were still exuding more liquid than I wanted. Should I go one step further and remove their watery jelly and seeds before salting them?

SUMMER VEGETABLE GRATIN

To my surprise, when I tried this, the gratin lacked deep tomato flavor. I wanted to make sure my results weren't a fluke, so I prepared two gratins—one with salted seedless tomatoes and one with salted tomatoes with the seeds and jelly intact—and tasted them side by side. The gratin made with tomatoes that had jelly and seeds was significantly richer and fuller in flavor than the one without them. After some research, I learned why: These two components contain far more flavorful glutamate compounds than the tomato flesh. If I wanted a gratin with intense tomato flavor, it was actually in my best interest to leave the jelly and seeds in, even if it meant a little extra liquid in the dish.

In my testing, I discovered that the spots where the edges of the tomatoes peeked through the layers of zucchini were particularly good, having taken on the appealing qualities of oven-roasted tomatoes. To capitalize on this effect, I remodeled the architecture of the casserole, moving the tomatoes to a single top layer where they could really roast and caramelize. This worked well, especially when I drizzled the tomatoes with an aromatic garlic-thyme oil. The fragrant oil was so good that I decided to toss the zucchini and squash in it as well.

To add complexity, I inserted a layer of caramelized onions between the zucchini/squash and tomato layers and sprinkled the gratin with Parmesan bread crumbs. When my gratin came out of the oven leaking very little juice, I knew my rescue mission was a success.

—REBECCA HAYS, *Cook's Illustrated*

Summer Vegetable Gratin

SERVES 6 TO 8

The success of this recipe depends on good-quality produce. Buy zucchini and summer squash of roughly the same diameter. While we like the visual contrast zucchini and summer squash bring to the dish, you can also use just one or the other. A similarly sized broiler-safe gratin dish can be substituted for the 13 by 9-inch baking dish. Serve the gratin alongside grilled fish or meat and accompanied by bread to soak up any flavorful juices.

- 6 tablespoons extra-virgin olive oil
- 2 zucchini (about 1 pound), ends trimmed and sliced crosswise into ¼-inch-thick slices (see note)
- 2 yellow summer squash (about 1 pound), ends trimmed and sliced crosswise into ¼-inch-thick slices (see note)
  Salt
- 1½ pounds ripe tomatoes (about 3 large), sliced ¼ inch thick
- 2 onions, halved lengthwise and sliced thin, pole to pole (about 3 cups)
  Pepper
- 2 garlic cloves, minced
- 1 tablespoon minced fresh thyme
- 1 slice high-quality white sandwich bread, torn into quarters
- 2 ounces Parmesan cheese, grated (about 1 cup)
- 1 large shallot, minced (about ¼ cup)
- ¼ cup chopped fresh basil

1. Adjust an oven rack to the upper-middle position and heat the oven to 400 degrees. Brush a 13 by 9-inch baking dish with 1 tablespoon of the oil; set aside.

2. Toss the zucchini and summer squash slices with 1 teaspoon salt in a large bowl; transfer to a colander set over a bowl. Let stand until the zucchini and squash release at least 3 tablespoons of liquid, about 45 minutes. Arrange the slices on a triple layer of paper towels; cover with another triple layer of paper towels. Firmly press each slice to remove as much liquid as possible.

3. Place the tomato slices in a single layer on a double layer of paper towels and sprinkle evenly with ½ teaspoon salt; let stand for 30 minutes. Place a second double layer of paper towels on top of the tomatoes and press firmly to dry the tomatoes.

4. Meanwhile, heat 1 tablespoon more oil in a 12-inch nonstick skillet over medium heat until shimmering. Add the onions, ½ teaspoon salt, and ¼ teaspoon pepper; cook, stirring occasionally, until the onions are softened and dark golden brown, 20 to 25 minutes. Set the onions aside.

5. Combine the garlic, 3 tablespoons more oil, ½ teaspoon pepper, and thyme in a small bowl. In a large bowl, toss the zucchini and summer squash in half of the oil mixture, then following the photos on page 61, arrange in the greased baking dish. Arrange the caramelized onions in an even layer over the squash. Slightly overlap the tomato slices in a single layer on top of the onions. Spoon the remaining oil mixture evenly over the tomatoes. Bake until the vegetables are tender and the tomatoes are starting to brown on the edges, 40 to 45 minutes.

6. Meanwhile, process the bread in a food processor until finely ground, about 10 seconds. (You should have about 1 cup crumbs.) Combine the bread crumbs, remaining 1 tablespoon oil, Parmesan, and shallot in a medium bowl. Remove the baking dish from the oven and increase the heat to 450 degrees. Sprinkle the bread-crumb mixture evenly on top of the tomatoes. Bake the gratin until bubbling and the cheese is lightly browned, 5 to 10 minutes. Sprinkle with the basil and let sit at room temperature for 10 minutes before serving.

NOTES FROM THE TEST KITCHEN

ASSEMBLING THE GRATIN

1. Toss the salted zucchini and squash in half of the garlic-thyme oil, then arrange the slices in a greased baking dish.

2. Spread the caramelized onions in an even layer on top of the zucchini and squash.

3. Slightly overlap the salted tomatoes in a single layer on top of the onions, then top with the remaining garlic-thyme oil.

4. When the vegetables are tender, sprinkle the gratin with the bread-crumb mixture, then bake until golden brown.

VARIATION

Summer Vegetable Gratin with Roasted Peppers and Smoked Mozzarella

Follow the recipe for Summer Vegetable Gratin, substituting 4 ounces shredded smoked mozzarella (about 1 cup) for the Parmesan, and 8 ounces jarred roasted red peppers for the summer squash (do not salt the roasted peppers).

SUMMER SQUASH CASSEROLE

AT ITS BEST, squash casserole is everything a casserole should be: homey, rich, and satisfying. It's also easy to prepare, appeals to almost everyone, and goes well with nearly anything off the grill. It seems everyone has a claim on what the best summer squash casserole should be, but most of the recipes I tried ended up being less appealing than the savory, comforting promises they touted. And they certainly didn't showcase the freshness of the squash. But I didn't want to oust this option just yet. Pairing the appealing aspects of a casserole—warm, hearty, and comforting—with one of the season's best vegetables could amount to a flavorful, satisfying side dish if done well. I set out to see what I could do.

Many of the recipes I tried were a confusing mix of extra vegetables with excessive amounts of butter and cheese that distracted from the real purpose of the dish: to highlight the squash. After dumping the extras and upping the main ingredient to four squash, a full 2 pounds, I was finally looking at a casserole that didn't skimp. I did hold on to the onion found in several recipes, which tasters felt added flavor without being distracting.

The richness of casseroles comes from some combination of dairy products, and I decided to keep things simple. Sour cream, popular among most of the recipes I tested, helped add creaminess without making the dish too heavy. Cheddar cheese was another common choice; I settled on extra-sharp for its stronger flavor.

All the recipes called for precooking the squash in some way—steaming, boiling, or roasting, to name a few—to remove moisture from the watery vegetable prior to baking. I opted to sauté the squash over high heat because this method would hold on to the most squash flavor. Furthermore, recipes that required steaming, boiling, or roasting necessitated cooking the squash separately from the accompanying ingredients (such as the onion). By sautéing, I could add the squash right to the skillet after I had the softened the onions. Opinions on how to slice the squash were numerous; I settled on ½-inch chunks that gave me big, tender pieces that stayed firm through baking.

Last I addressed the topping. I tried everything from homemade bread crumbs to crushed Melba toasts, but crumbled Ritz crackers were the sure favorite among tasters for their buttery rich flavor and crunch. This was a summer squash casserole that lived up to its promises.

—DAN ZUCCARELLO, *America's Test Kitchen Books*

Summer Squash Casserole

SERVES 6 TO 8

Be sure to use at least a 12-inch skillet for this recipe; otherwise, the skillet will be too full.

- 4 **tablespoons (½ stick) unsalted butter**
- 1 **onion, minced (about 1 cup)**
- ½ **teaspoon salt**
- 3 **garlic cloves, minced**
- 1 **teaspoon minced fresh thyme**
- ⅛ **teaspoon pepper**
- 4 **yellow summer squash (about 2 pounds), trimmed and cut into ½-inch pieces**
- 4 **ounces extra-sharp cheddar cheese, shredded (about 1 cup)**
- ½ **cup sour cream**
- 20 **Ritz crackers, crushed to coarse crumbs (about 1 cup)**

1. Adjust an oven rack to the middle position and heat the oven to 450 degrees.

2. Melt the butter in a large skillet over medium heat. Add the onion and salt and cook, stirring occasionally, until softened, 5 to 7 minutes. Stir in the garlic, thyme, and pepper and cook until fragrant, about 30 seconds. Add the squash, increase the heat to high, and cook, stirring occasionally, until just tender, 6 to 8 minutes.

3. Stir in the cheese and sour cream, then transfer the mixture to an 8-inch square baking dish. Sprinkle the top evenly with the cracker crumbs and bake until the sauce is bubbling around the edges and the Ritz crumbs are golden brown, 20 to 25 minutes. Serve.

MAKE-AHEAD GREEN BEAN CASSEROLE

I AM A BIG FAN OF GREEN BEAN CASSEROLE, but with the pressure of cooking the roast, making the gravy, mashing the potatoes, and all the other preparations for a holiday dinner, having one side dish ready to go would make life much easier. But you can't just freeze and bake a regular green bean casserole: I tried it with several recipes, including the "back of the can" version, and all were incredibly bland (the freezer notoriously dulls flavor) and watery (the freezing and thawing breaks down the beans, causing them to purge liquid into the sauce). Recipes touted as "freezer-to-oven" were just as bad.

Starting over with the test kitchen's recipe for dressed-up green bean casserole, I sautéed mushrooms in melted butter, added some garlic, and then flour to thicken the sauce. Into the pan went 1½ cups each of chicken broth and cream, which are simmered for 10 minutes to reduce. I poured this mixture over blanched green beans and topped the casserole with our combination of canned fried onions and buttery bread crumbs (we have found that canned onions are too greasy on their own). After a few days in the freezer, even this version baked up lacking flavor, with spent beans and a dull, watery sauce.

To boost the flavor of the casserole so it could stand up to freezing and baking, I doubled the amount of garlic and added a healthy dose of white wine and fragrant thyme to the sauce. Correcting the texture of the beans and sauce was not so easy. Tackling the beans first, I wondered if the blanching was contributing to their dull color and bland flavor. I tried roasting, sautéing, steaming, and even microwaving the beans, but nothing helped. Out of desperation, I prepared a casserole using raw beans and was amazed that they came out perfectly, with a nice green color and surprisingly firm texture (not to mention brighter flavor). Apparently the long oven time required to defrost and bake the casserole gave the raw beans plenty of time to cook through.

But the beans were still giving up too much liquid to the sauce, which was unpalatably watery. If I couldn't prevent the beans from expelling liquid, maybe I could find something to thicken it. I tried tossing the beans with flour, but that made the casserole too pasty. Tapioca worked OK, but I had to take the extra step of pureeing the pearls in order to fully coat the beans.

MAKE-AHEAD GREEN BEAN CASSEROLE

Cornstarch was the best option here; tossing my two pounds of beans with ¼ cup of cornstarch (before adding the sauce) thickened the liquid shed by the beans and produced a perfect sauce. I now had a green bean casserole that could be made weeks in advance and still taste like it had been made an hour before the big holiday meal.

—MEREDITH BUTCHER, *Cook's Country*

Make-Ahead Green Bean Casserole

SERVES 10 TO 12

Covering the casserole with both plastic wrap and foil protects it from freezer burn.

TOPPING

- 2 **slices high-quality white sandwich bread, torn into pieces**
- 2 **tablespoons unsalted butter, melted**
- ¼ **teaspoon salt**
- 2 **cups canned fried onions**

CASSEROLE

- 3 **tablespoons unsalted butter**
- 10 **ounces white mushrooms, sliced thin**
- 1 **teaspoon salt**
- ½ **teaspoon pepper**
- 6 **garlic cloves, minced**
- ½ **teaspoon dried thyme**
- ¼ **cup unbleached all-purpose flour**
- ½ **cup white wine**
- 1½ **cups low-sodium chicken broth**
- 1½ **cups heavy cream**
- 2 **pounds green beans, trimmed and cut into 1-inch pieces**
- ¼ **cup cornstarch**

1. FOR THE TOPPING: Pulse the bread, butter, and salt in a food processor until coarsely ground, about 10 pulses. Combine the bread mixture and onions in a bowl, transfer to a large zipper-lock freezer bag, and freeze for up to 2 months.

2. FOR THE CASSEROLE: Melt the butter in a large skillet over medium heat. Add the mushrooms, salt, and pepper and cook until the mushrooms release their liquid, about 5 minutes. Increase the heat to medium-high and cook until the liquid has evaporated, about 5 minutes. Add the garlic and thyme and cook until fragrant,

about 30 seconds. Stir in the flour and cook until golden, about 1 minute. Slowly whisk in the wine, broth, and cream and bring to a boil. Reduce the heat to medium and simmer, stirring occasionally, until the sauce is thickened, about 10 minutes.

3. Toss the green beans with the cornstarch in a large bowl and transfer to a 13 by 9-inch baking dish. Pour the warm mushroom mixture evenly over the beans. Let cool completely, cover with plastic wrap, cover with foil, and freeze for up to 2 months.

4. TO SERVE: Adjust an oven rack to the middle position and heat the oven to 400 degrees. Remove the plastic from the baking dish and replace the foil. Bake until the sauce is bubbling and the beans are tender, about 80 minutes, stirring the beans thoroughly after 50 minutes. Remove the foil and spread the topping mixture over the beans. Bake until golden brown, about 8 minutes. Serve.

NOTES FROM THE TEST KITCHEN

THE SECRET TO A SILKY SAUCE

Tossing the beans with cornstarch before assembling and freezing the casserole helps absorb excess liquid, leaving the sauce thick and silky.

STUFFED CABBAGE ROLLS

RECIPES FOR STUFFED CABBAGE ROLLS have a reputation for being temperamental; indeed, my own grandmother always said her recipe for stuffed cabbage was fussy—but well worth the trouble. She would boil a head of cabbage and wrap the softened leaves around a filling of seasoned ground meat and white rice, then simmer the rolls in a smooth tomato sauce flavored with warm spices, sugar, and vinegar. But after hours of testing recipes, I was left with pots of blown-out rolls filled with chewy, flavorless meat and bland rice swimming in a sugary sauce. This wasn't the dish I remembered.

I started with the easiest fix: the tomatoes. Crushed tomatoes were too watery, and diced tomatoes were distractingly chunky. Tasters liked the smooth texture of tomato puree, but it was too thick and pasty. Canned tomato sauce had the same smooth texture and was thin enough to properly coat the rolls without becoming pasty. Sautéed onions and garlic provided a savory foundation, and ground ginger, cinnamon, and nutmeg provided the requisite warm spice flavor to the sauce. Brown sugar was preferred to white for its more complex flavor, and red wine vinegar was chosen over white for its bite.

Tasters found the traditional filling of ground beef and white rice bland and tough. Since I was already sautéing onions and garlic for the sauce, I upped the amount and added some to the filling. In search of more meaty flavor, I tried adding Italian sausage, but the Italian seasonings were off-putting here. Kielbasa was too smoky, but bratwurst, a mild German sausage, boosted the meaty flavor perfectly. My tasters had never been fans of the rice in the filling—they found it distracting and bland. Since the rice's main function is as filler, I decided to omit it. In its place, I added a panade of milk and bread to help keep the filling soft and moist. A quick whirl in the food processor ensured that the filling was evenly combined.

Cooking the stuffed rolls on the stovetop, even over low heat, caused the cabbage to blow apart. Instead I tried cooking them in the oven; this allowed the rolls to cook more evenly and gently, thus keeping them intact. But the cabbage itself was still a little mushy. I had been precooking the cabbage in the traditional way by blanching the head in boiling water and peeling off the hot leaves with tongs. But the inner leaves were overcooked and soggy by the time they were released. Freezing the head of cabbage, which softened the leaves and allowed them to peel off one at a time, required a day of advance planning. Instead I turned to the microwave. After a quick turn (in a bowl covered with plastic wrap), all of the leaves were easily removed from the cabbage head and, best of all, were soft enough for filling and rolling—and not waterlogged at all.

To be sure, these aren't the cabbage rolls my grandmother made, but I'd like to think they might even be better.

—LYNN CLARK, *Cook's Country*

Stuffed Cabbage Rolls

SERVES 6

If the tops of the cabbage rolls appear dry after the foil is removed in step 4, spoon some of the sauce over them before returning to the oven.

- 1 **head green cabbage (about 2 pounds), cored**
- 1 **tablespoon vegetable oil**
- 1 **onion, minced (about 1 cup)**
- 3 **garlic cloves, minced**
- 1 **teaspoon ground ginger**
- ½ **teaspoon ground cinnamon**
- ¼ **teaspoon ground nutmeg**
- 1 **(28-ounce) can tomato sauce**
- ¼ **cup packed light brown sugar**
- 3 **tablespoons red wine vinegar**
  Salt and pepper
- 2 **slices high-quality white sandwich bread, torn into pieces**
- ½ **cup milk**
- ¾ **pound 85 percent lean ground beef**
- ¾ **pound uncooked bratwurst, casings removed**

1. Adjust an oven rack to the middle position and heat the oven to 375 degrees. Place the cabbage in a large microwave-safe bowl, wrap tightly with plastic wrap, and microwave on high power until the outer leaves of the cabbage are pliable and translucent, 3 to 6 minutes. Using tongs, carefully remove the wilted outer leaves; set aside. Replace the plastic and repeat until you have 15 to 17 large, intact leaves.

2. Heat the oil in a Dutch oven over medium-high heat until shimmering. Add the onion and cook until softened and lightly browned, 5 to 7 minutes. Add the garlic, ginger, cinnamon, and nutmeg and cook until fragrant, about 30 seconds. Transfer half of the onion mixture to a small bowl and reserve. Off the heat, stir the tomato sauce, sugar, vinegar, ½ teaspoon salt, and ¼ teaspoon pepper into the pot with the remaining onion mixture until the sugar dissolves.

3. Pulse the bread and milk in a food processor to form a smooth paste, about 10 pulses. Add the reserved onion mixture, beef, bratwurst, ½ teaspoon salt, and ¼ teaspoon pepper and pulse until well combined, about 10 pulses.

4. Following the photos on page 67, trim the tough ribs from the cabbage leaves, roll 2 heaping tablespoons

STUFFED CABBAGE ROLLS

ASSEMBLING CABBAGE ROLLS

1. Remove the thick rib from the base of the cabbage leaves by cutting along both sides of the rib to form a narrow triangle. Continue cutting up the center about 1 inch above the triangle.

2. Overlap the cut ends of the cabbage to prevent any filling from spilling out.

3. Place 2 tablespoons of the filling ½ inch from the bottom of the leaf where the cut ends overlap. Fold the bottom of the leaf over the filling and fold in the sides. Roll the leaf tightly around the filling to create a tidy roll.

ADD BRATWURST FOR BETTER FLAVOR

Cabbage rolls stuffed with the traditional filling of ground beef and rice were bland, so we lost the rice and supplemented the beef with an equal amount of bratwurst. Not only did this German-style pork and veal-based sausage add flavor (it's seasoned with ginger, nutmeg, and caraway seeds), but it also kept the filling tender and moist.

MICROWAVE, DON'T BOIL

Removing leaves from a tightly packed head of cabbage is no easy feat. The most common method is to float the whole head in a vat of boiling water—a messy, cumbersome project with mixed results at best. We found the microwave a much better tool. Microwaving makes the cabbage leaves soft and pliable, not soggy and overcooked.

To prepare the cabbage, cut out the core, place the head in a large microwave-safe bowl, cover with plastic wrap, and cook on high power until the leaves become pliable and can be easily removed.

of the meat mixture into each leaf, and arrange the rolls, seam-side down, in a 13 by 9-inch baking dish. Pour the sauce over the cabbage rolls, cover with foil, and bake until the sauce is bubbling and the rolls are heated through, about 45 minutes. Remove the foil and bake, uncovered, until the sauce is slightly thickened and the cabbage is tender, about 15 minutes. Serve. (The cabbage rolls can be made 1 day in advance. After spooning the meat into the cabbage and arranging the rolls, cover the dish with plastic wrap and refrigerate. Cover and refrigerate the sauce separately. Proceed with the recipe as directed.)

CHEESY BROCCOLI AND RICE CASSEROLE

CLOSE YOUR EYES AND TAKE A BITE of the typical back-of-the-can recipe for cheesy broccoli and rice casserole. Bet you wouldn't know what you were eating. Gloppy canned soup, shelf-stable "cheese food," and lifeless frozen broccoli combine into a stodgy mass of weak, muddled flavors. I wanted a lively casserole with tender rice, fresh broccoli flavor, and sharp cheddar bite.

I started with a half-dozen recipes that skipped the canned soup and made the casserole from scratch. They all worked similarly: Butter and flour were stirred together on the stovetop to make a roux; heavy cream was poured in and simmered until reduced; and cheese, fresh broccoli florets, and cooked rice were folded in before baking. These casseroles put the canned soup–frozen broccoli version to shame, but they were still weak on flavor and couldn't seem to get the broccoli (too crunchy) or rice (overcooked and blown out) cooked right.

Addressing the flavor first, I suspected that the heavy cream was masking the other ingredients, so I tested versions that replaced it with either milk or half-and-half. Milk was a little too lean and thin, but half-and-half was an improvement, especially when I cut it with chicken broth to add flavor. While some recipes call for American cheese, my tasters much preferred the bold bite of extra-sharp cheddar paired with nutty Parmesan.

Fresh broccoli was definitely better than frozen, but I knew I'd need finesse to get the most out of it. In the test kitchen, we've learned that broccoli stalks have just as much flavor as the florets, but they take longer to cook. This time I started my sauce by sautéing chopped broccoli stalks in butter with onion, then adding the flour, the liquids, and finally, broccoli florets that I'd precooked in the microwave to ensure they'd be tender in the baked casserole. With twice as much broccoli as most recipes, my casserole now had plenty of fresh broccoli flavor.

To avoid overcooked rice, I tried adding raw rice to the simmering cream sauce (instead of stirring in cooked rice just before baking). Unfortunately, the starch that released from the rice as it cooked over-thickened the sauce and produced a heavy, dense casserole. I was discouraged and almost out of ideas when a colleague suggested I try making the starch from the rice work to my advantage. I reduced the flour (I had been using 4 tablespoons) 1 tablespoon at a time, and ultimately discovered I could eliminate the flour altogether; the natural starch from the rice was enough of a thickener.

Some recipes simply top this style of casserole with more cheese, while recipes closer to the back-of-the-can version sometimes opt for canned fried onions. Wanting something fresher and more substantial, I made garlicky fresh bread crumbs enriched with a little extra Parmesan. This topping baked up brown and crisp, adding a final layer of flavor and texture to my casserole.

—MEGHAN ERWIN, *Cook's Country*

NOTES FROM THE TEST KITCHEN

MAXIMIZING BROCCOLI FLAVOR
Broccoli stems are full of broccoli flavor, but because they're tough they require longer cooking than the florets. We sauté the chopped broccoli stems with onion to create a savory base of vegetable flavor. We microwave the quicker-cooking broccoli florets and stir them into the casserole right before baking.

SAVE THE STEMS

Cheesy Broccoli and Rice Casserole
SERVES 8 TO 10

Take care not to overcook the broccoli florets in step 2.

- 2 slices high-quality white sandwich bread, torn into pieces
- 1½ ounces Parmesan cheese, grated (about ¾ cup)
- 4 tablespoons (½ stick) unsalted butter, melted; plus 2 tablespoons, chilled
- 1 garlic clove, minced
- 1 large bunch broccoli (about 2 pounds), florets cut into 1-inch pieces, stems trimmed and chopped
- 1 onion, minced (about 1 cup)
- 1¼ cups long-grain white rice
- 4 cups low-sodium chicken broth
- 1¼ cups half-and-half
- 1 teaspoon salt
- 8 ounces extra-sharp cheddar cheese, shredded (about 2 cups)
- ⅛ teaspoon cayenne pepper

1. Adjust an oven rack to the middle position and heat the oven to 400 degrees. Grease a 13 by 9-inch baking dish. Pulse the bread, ¼ cup of the Parmesan, melted butter, and garlic in a food processor until coarsely ground, about 10 pulses. Set aside.

2. Place the broccoli florets in a large microwave-safe bowl, cover tightly with plastic wrap, and cook on high power until bright green and tender, 2 to 4 minutes; set aside. Melt the remaining 2 tablespoons butter in a Dutch oven over medium heat. Add the onion and broccoli stems and cook until softened, 8 to 10 minutes. Add the rice and cook, stirring constantly, until the rice is translucent, about 1 minute. Stir in the broth, half-and-half, and salt and bring to a boil. Reduce the heat to medium-low and cook, stirring often, until the rice is tender, 20 to 25 minutes. Off the heat, stir in the cheddar, cayenne, remaining ½ cup Parmesan, and broccoli florets.

3. Pour the mixture into the prepared baking dish and top with the bread crumb mixture. Bake until the sauce is bubbling around the edges and the top is golden brown, about 15 minutes. Cool for 5 minutes and serve. (The filling can be prepared, placed in the greased baking dish, covered with plastic wrap, and refrigerated for up to 1 day. Refrigerate the topping separately. Bring the filling to room temperature before adding the bread crumbs and baking as directed.)

CHEESY BROCCOLI AND RICE CASSEROLE

CHAPTER 4

BREAKFAST & BREADS

Eggs Benedict 72

French Omelets 75

Eggs en Cocotte 77

Eggs en Cocotte
with Parmesan Cream

Eggs en Cocotte
with Mushroom Cream

Quiche Lorraine 79

Quiche with Bacon,
Scallions, and Cheddar

Savory Bread Pudding 82

Savory Bread Pudding
with Spinach and Feta

Savory Bread Pudding
with Bacon and Onion

Blueberry Muffins 85

Blueberry Muffins
with Frozen Blueberries

Blueberry Muffins
with Orange Glaze

Blueberry Muffins with
Almond Crunch Topping

Homemade Pancake Mix 87

Ultimate Cinnamon Buns 88

St. Louis Gooey Butter Cake 91

Butterscotch Gooey Butter Cake

Chocolate Gooey Butter Cake

Cornmeal Biscuits 94

Popovers 96

Rustic Dinner Rolls 99

Pizza Bianca 101

Pizza Bianca with Tomatoes
and Mozzarella

Pizza Bianca with Tomatoes,
Sausage, and Fontina

Skillet Pizza 105

Skillet Cheese Pizza

Skillet Pizza with Fontina,
Arugula, and Prosciutto

Skillet Pizza with Goat Cheese,
Olives, and Spicy Garlic Oil

Skillet Pizza with Ricotta,
Bacon, and Scallions

EGGS BENEDICT

EVEN SEASONED COOKS GROW ANXIOUS at the idea of tackling a multicomponent dish such as eggs Benedict—the hollandaise sauce, poached eggs, Canadian bacon, and toasted English muffins all require precise timing to come together. After a few stabs at eggs Benedict, I shared their anxieties. My first attempts turned out poached eggs that spun into skeins of congealed egg white, barely holding on to overcooked yolks. The hollandaise sauce came together as recipes promised, but would suddenly separate beyond repair with one moment too long on the stove. Finally, the English muffins and Canadian bacon were stone cold by the time I was ready to assemble my first serving.

I started with the notoriously unstable hollandaise, hoping to solve my biggest challenge first. Like mayonnaise, hollandaise is an emulsified sauce (egg yolks do the emulsifying) that depends on the proper suspension of fat in liquid. If the balance goes out of whack, or if the mixture overheats, the sauce breaks into a puddle of oily melted butter and scrambled egg. The classic preparation is to whisk yolks with lemon juice and a small amount of water over a double boiler until thickened. You slowly drizzle in melted butter, whisking briskly all the while, and finish it with more lemon juice. If all goes well—a big if, I quickly realized—a thick, smooth emulsion forms. After a few frustrating attempts, I sought a more reliable method.

Newer recipes I tested make hollandaise in a food processor or blender by pouring hot melted butter onto the yolks to ensure an emulsified sauce without the tedious whisking. These methods usually worked, but only if I served the sauce immediately—not very

---

NOTES FROM THE TEST KITCHEN

POACHING EGGS BY THE DOZEN
Getting 12 eggs into, and then out of, a skillet at precisely the right degree of doneness is no easy feat. Unless, that is, you follow these simple steps.

1. Crack the eggs into four teacups (three eggs per cup) and tip the cups simultaneously into the simmering water.

2. Cover the pan and remove it from the heat. The residual heat of the water will poach the eggs in about five minutes.

3. Use a slotted spoon to move the eggs from the pan to a paper towel-lined plate.

PREVENTING FEATHERY WHITES
One of the least appealing characteristics of poorly poached eggs is uneven, feathery whites instead of a beautifully round, domed egg. We've found that we can solve the problem by adding a couple of tablespoons of vinegar to the poaching water. The vinegar lowers the water's pH, which ensures that the egg whites will stay intact during cooking.

| POACHED WITHOUT VINEGAR | POACHED WITH VINEGAR |

THE BEST ENGLISH MUFFINS
Are there real differences among brands of English muffins? To find out, we got busy toasting four different brands and invited our tasters to the table. We were looking for slightly yeasty, slightly sweet flavor and a texture—once toasted—that was crisp and craggy on top and soft and chewy inside. Although we liked all the muffins, **Bays English Muffins** were our favorite. Interestingly, this brand had more salt than the competition, which brought out the sweetness of the muffins.

practical if you're also trying to poach eggs, toast English muffins, and crisp Canadian bacon. In the test kitchen library, I uncovered an intriguing unconventional method. Far from some newfangled technique that required yet another kitchen appliance, it was a recipe from the *Toll House Tried and True Recipes* cookbook, printed in 1944! It called for softened butter in place of melted butter, and for a lot more water than is in the standard recipes.

I whisked one stick of butter with four egg yolks and slowly poured in half a cup of boiling water (conventional hollandaise recipes call for 1 or 2 tablespoons water). At first, the mixture was a watery, lumpy mess, but I pressed on, cooking it over a double boiler "until thick," as directed. I added the lemon juice off of the heat and was happily surprised with the result. The sauce was foamier than a classic hollandaise, and it tasted a little lean, yet it held without breaking for as long as an hour. In further tests, I tweaked the amounts of butter and yolks to bring back the classic richness (it took 4 more tablespoons of butter and two additional yolks). Satisfied with the sauce, I turned to the eggs.

Cookbooks suggest several classic methods for poaching eggs. I cracked them into a vat of boiling water, but they sank and were tough to remove without breaking. I tried cooking the eggs in simmering water, but the temperature wasn't constant, and the agitating water threatened to break the yolks. In the end I had success "cooking" them off of the heat. First, I added water, salt, and vinegar to a large skillet and brought it to a simmer. While it was heating, I cracked the eggs into teacups, with each cup holding three eggs. I then slipped the eggs into the pan and removed it from the heat. I covered the skillet and waited about five minutes before I removed the eggs with a slotted spoon. The method consistently produced restaurant-worthy poached eggs with soft, runny yolks and perfectly formed, round whites.

To avoid toasting 12 muffin halves in my toaster while poaching eggs and whisking hollandaise, I lined up the muffins on a baking sheet and tried broiling them. This worked great, and I wondered if I could use the same technique for the Canadian bacon. (I had been frying it in a skillet.) I laid the bacon on the toasted muffins and slid the tray back under the broiler. Because Canadian bacon is precooked, all I needed to do was warm it through.

Before hanging up my apron, I reread the recipe for hollandaise and noticed something I'd overlooked: The sauce could be served cold, which implied it could be made ahead. I made one final batch and refrigerated it. The next day, I gently reheated it in the microwave, and then spooned it over poached eggs. It looked, tasted, and stayed together as though I had taken it off the stove only moments earlier. Not one taster could tell it was a day old, nor did anyone believe such a thing was even possible!

—DIANE UNGER, *Cook's Country*

Eggs Benedict
SERVES 6

Make sure the bowl does not touch the simmering water in step 1.

HOLLANDAISE
- 12 tablespoons (1½ sticks) unsalted butter, softened
- 6 large egg yolks
- ½ cup boiling water
- 2 teaspoons fresh lemon juice
- ⅛ teaspoon cayenne pepper
  Salt

EGGS
- 2 tablespoons white vinegar
- 1 teaspoon salt
- 12 large eggs
- 6 English muffins, split
- 12 slices Canadian bacon

1. FOR THE HOLLANDAISE: Whisk the butter and egg yolks in a large heat-resistant bowl set over a medium saucepan filled with ½ inch of barely simmering water (don't let the bowl touch the water). Slowly add the boiling water and cook, whisking constantly, until thickened and the sauce registers 160 degrees on an instant-read thermometer, 7 to 10 minutes. Off the heat, stir in the lemon juice and cayenne. Season with salt to taste. Leave the bowl over the pan of water to keep warm, whisking occasionally. (The hollandaise can be refrigerated in an airtight container for up to 3 days. Reheat in the microwave on 50 percent power, stirring every 10 seconds, until heated through, about 1 minute.)

FRENCH OMELET

2. FOR THE EGGS: Adjust an oven rack to be 6 inches from the broiler element and heat the broiler. Fill a large skillet nearly to the rim with water. Add the vinegar and salt and bring to a simmer over high heat. Following the photos on page 72, crack 3 eggs into each of 4 teacups and carefully pour the eggs into the skillet. Cover the pan, remove from the heat, and poach the eggs until the whites are set but the yolks are still slightly runny, 5 to 7 minutes. Using a slotted spoon, transfer the eggs to a paper towel–lined plate.

3. While the eggs are poaching, arrange the English muffins, split-side up, on a baking sheet and broil until golden brown, 2 to 4 minutes. Place 1 slice of bacon on each English muffin and broil until beginning to brown, about 1 minute. (If you like, you can toast the English muffins and warm the bacon 20 minutes in advance. Reheat them in a 200-degree oven just before serving.)

4. Arrange 1 poached egg on top of each English muffin. Spoon 1 to 2 tablespoons hollandaise over each egg. Serve, passing the remaining hollandaise at the table.

FRENCH OMELETS

IN CONTRAST TO LACY BROWN HALF-MOON omelets stuffed to the seams with filling that any short-order cook can get right, the French omelet is a pristine affair. The ideal specimen is unblemished golden yellow with an ultra-creamy texture and minimal filling. The method for making it, penned more than a century ago by legendary chef Auguste Escoffier, sounds simple enough: Melt butter in a blazing hot omelet pan, add beaten eggs, scramble vigorously with a fork until the omelet starts to set, roll it out onto a plate, and—voilà!—breakfast.

That's the idea, at any rate. In reality, success is maddeningly elusive. The temperature of the pan must be just right, the eggs beaten just so, and your hand movements as swift as your ability to gauge the exact second the omelet is done. With everything happening at lightning speed, even a few extra seconds of cooking can spell disaster.

I'm all in favor of tradition—when it works. But surely it was high time to figure out a different approach to making this creamy style of omelet, one that even an inexperienced cook could get right the first time around.

I began by examining the equipment. The classic method calls for an omelet pan made of high-quality black

carbon steel—preferably reserved exclusively for eggs and seasoned over a period of years—and a fork. Modern concessions allow for a nonstick skillet and a heatproof spatula. Certainly, an 8-inch nonstick pan seemed like a fine idea. I wasn't so sure about a bulky spatula.

In the kitchen, I first tested two omelets side by side: one using a spatula, the other using a fork. (Forks usually scratch nonstick pans, but I figured I could sacrifice one pan for testing.) I used three eggs per omelet, along with salt and pepper and butter as the cooking fat. I started as instructed by many classic tomes: I preheated the pan for several minutes over high heat to get it good and hot, added the butter and waited for it to melt, then poured in the seasoned egg mixture and got busy stirring. The difference was clear: The fork did a better job than the spatula, scrambling the eggs into smaller curds with silkier texture. I eventually achieved the same results using bamboo skewers and wooden chopsticks—without scraping my pan.

But there was a problem. The omelets were turning out brown and splotchy instead of evenly golden. This was due to hot spots over the pan's bottom, which I was able to eliminate when I preheated the pan for a full 10 minutes over low heat.

Typically, to achieve a creamy omelet, you pull the eggs off the heat at just the right moment, but it's nearly impossible to know when that occurs. What if I cheated and used creamy ingredients instead? In my next tests, I made omelets with heavy cream and half-and-half. The results were richer, but tougher.

I recalled an intriguing recipe I'd found in my research: It called for adding diced butter (about 1 tablespoon) to the beaten eggs right before cooking. I heated up a pan and in went the butter-studded egg mixture. Sure enough, the butter made the omelet richer and creamier! As it turned out, very cold butter (I popped it into the freezer for a few minutes before cooking) melted less quickly than merely chilled butter, allowing it to disperse more thoroughly throughout the eggs (melted butter clumped in one place), producing the creamiest results. There was one hitch: Some tasters thought the butter made the omelet a little too rich. I removed some protein—one egg white—and cut the butter to just half a tablespoon, which satisfied everyone.

I had creaminess. Now what about lightness? I knew that the way I beat the raw eggs would be a big factor. A little air helps, but excessive beating with a whisk unravels the egg proteins, causing them to cross-link,

HOW TO MAKE A FRENCH OMELET

1. Add the eggs to the skillet and stir with chopsticks to produce small curds.

2. Turn off the heat while the eggs are still runny and smooth them with a spatula into an even layer.

3. Sprinkle with the cheese and chives. Cover and allow the residual heat to gently finish cooking the omelet.

4. Slide the omelet onto a paper towel-lined plate. Use the paper towel to lift the omelet and roll it up.

THE BEST INEXPENSIVE OMELET PAN

Most brands of cookware offer an 8-inch nonstick "omelet" pan, but these are usually just small versions of their skillets, with upright sides that make it difficult to turn and roll out a perfect omelet. We tested four pans with gently sloped sides, all under $25, and found a great buy: the **KitchenAid Gourmet Essentials Hard Anodized Nonstick Open French Skillet**, $19.99. Although this pan does not have quite the steady, long-lasting heat of heavier, more expensive pans, its hard anodized material heated quickly and evenly, and the gently sloped sides allowed easy rolling.

leading to denser eggs. After some arm-numbing testing, I concluded that 80 strokes with a fork was enough to achieve a viscous, emulsified consistency for the lightest eggs.

At this point, I was still using high heat, which gave me only a tiny window for perfection. I tried a range of different heat levels but found that anything lower than medium-high heat wouldn't trigger the rapid vaporization of the eggs' water that causes them to puff up with steam before solidifying. But even at medium heat, the omelet cooked so quickly it was still vexingly difficult to judge when it was done on both sides. To solve this problem, I turned to a test kitchen technique we've used in the past. I cooked an omelet until just formed but slightly runny on top, took it off the heat, smoothed the egg into an even layer, covered the pan, and let it sit for a minute or two. The skillet's gentle residual heat finished cooking the omelet without turning it tough, a brilliant solution.

Now I just needed to get the darn thing out of the pan. The traditional way is to give the skillet a quick jerk to fold the omelet over. You then slide it out of the pan, tilting the skillet so that the remaining flap of eggs rolls over neatly—or not. I've spent hours cleaning dried egg off my stove trying to master this "jerk" technique. For an easier approach, I tried slipping the omelet onto a plate, then using my fingers to roll it. Too hot. I tried again, this time sliding the omelet onto a paper towel and using the towel to help roll the omelet into the sought-after cylinder. Voilà! Not only did I have a perfect French omelet, it was perfectly easy to make.

—CHARLES KELSEY, *Cook's Illustrated*

French Omelets

MAKES 2

Because making omelets is such a quick process, make sure to have all your ingredients and equipment at the ready. If you don't have skewers or chopsticks to stir the eggs in step 3, use the handle of a wooden spoon. Warm the plates in a 200-degree oven.

- 2 **tablespoons unsalted butter, cut into 2 pieces**
- ½ **teaspoon vegetable oil**
- 6 **large eggs, cold**
  Salt and pepper
- 2 **tablespoons shredded Gruyère cheese**
- 4 **teaspoons chopped fresh chives**

1. Cut 1 tablespoon of the butter in half again. Cube the remaining 1 tablespoon butter into small dice, transfer to a small bowl, and place in the freezer while preparing the eggs and skillet, at least 10 minutes. Meanwhile, heat the oil in an 8-inch nonstick skillet over low heat for 10 minutes.

2. Crack 2 of the eggs into a medium bowl and separate a third egg; reserve the white for another use and add the yolk to the bowl. Add ⅛ teaspoon salt and a pinch of pepper. Break the yolks with a fork, then beat the eggs at a moderate pace, about 80 strokes, until the yolks and whites are well combined. Stir in half of the frozen butter cubes.

3. When the skillet is fully heated, use paper towels to wipe out the oil, leaving a thin film on the bottom and sides of the skillet. Add ½ tablespoon of the reserved butter piece to the skillet and heat until the foaming subsides, 45 to 90 seconds. Swirl the butter to coat the skillet, add the egg mixture, and increase the heat to medium-high. Following the photos on page 76, use 2 chopsticks or wooden skewers to scramble the eggs using a quick circular motion to move around the skillet, scraping cooked egg from the side of the skillet as you go, until the eggs are almost cooked but still slightly runny, 45 to 90 seconds. Turn off the heat (remove the skillet from the heat if using an electric burner) and smooth the eggs into an even layer using a rubber spatula. Sprinkle the omelet with 1 tablespoon of the cheese and 2 teaspoons of the chives. Cover the skillet with a tight-fitting lid and let sit 1 minute for a runnier omelet or 2 minutes for a firmer omelet.

4. Heat the skillet over low heat for 20 seconds, uncover, and, using a rubber spatula, loosen the edges of the omelet from the skillet. Place a folded square of paper towel onto a warmed plate and slide the omelet out of the skillet onto the paper towel so that the omelet lies flat on the plate and hangs about 1 inch off the paper towel. Use the paper towel to lift and roll the omelet into a neat cylinder and set aside. Return the skillet to low heat and heat for 2 minutes before repeating the instructions for the second omelet, starting with step 2. Serve.

EGGS EN COCOTTE

OEUFS EN COCOTTE IS A CLASSIC FRENCH DISH of eggs cooked in individual ramekins that are usually placed in a water bath in the oven. I envisioned the ideal eggs en cocotte to have perfectly set whites with soft, runny yolks, enriched with a splash of cream. Most of the recipes I found for this dish followed the same basic formula: Crack one or two eggs into a buttered ramekin, season with salt and pepper, add some cream, place the ramekins in a water bath, and bake until set. Simple enough, right? Wrong. After cooking my way through dozens of eggs, I was faced with the same problem time and again: whites that were not cooked all the way through and yolks that were hard and overcooked—a far cry from the eggs en cocotte I imagined. Determined to find a way to make this recipe work, I decided to take a closer look at the method.

The gentle heat and humidity created by the water bath is supposed to keep the eggs from overcooking at the edges or drying out. To see if the water bath was necessary, I compared a batch of eggs en cocotte cooked in a water bath against a batch cooked simply on a baking sheet. While both batches of eggs suffered the same issues—soupy, transparent whites and overcooked yolks—the eggs cooked on the baking sheet had notably harder edges. So the water bath was indeed creating a gentler cooking environment for the eggs. I pressed on to solve what was clearly my fundamental problem: getting the whites to cook through without overcooking the yolks.

Up to this point I had been putting two eggs in each ramekin. I wondered if using only one egg per ramekin would ensure more even cooking. I quickly determined there was no difference between one and two eggs, and since two eggs are a typical serving, I decided to develop my recipe with two eggs in each ramekin.

I then tested a number of different variables: oven temperature; room-temperature eggs versus cold eggs; preheating the ramekins; and resting the eggs in the water bath after cooking. No luck. Almost ready to throw in the towel, I gave the water bath some more thought. It was definitely providing a gentle cooking environment, but maybe it was too gentle. What about covering the pan with foil to trap some of the steam created by the water?

I loaded up another batch of ramekins with eggs and cream, placed them in a water bath in the oven, and covered them with foil. This was definitely an improvement, but the whites were still too soupy to eat. Having watched me cook my way through literally hundreds of eggs, a fellow test cook turned to me and said, "Why not steam the eggs on the stovetop?" Intrigued by the possibility, I quickly cracked another dozen eggs into ramekins, placed them in a roasting pan of simmering water on the stovetop, and covered them with foil. Now I was getting somewhere—these egg whites were the most thoroughly cooked yet.

To eliminate boiling water splashing onto the eggs and the task of checking eggs under foil, I switched from the roasting pan to a large Dutch oven. I filled it with about an inch of water, placed a rack in the bottom of the pan, and brought it to a boil. I gently placed four ramekins, each with two eggs, on the rack, covered the pot with a tight-fitting lid, and then reduced the heat to medium. The rack allowed me to create a hotter steaming environment and all but eliminated the risk of splashing the eggs. In less than seven minutes, the eggs emerged with the whites creamy and set and the yolks soft and runny.

Now that I had achieved perfectly cooked eggs en cocotte, I turned my attention to the cream and some flavorings. Most recipes called for adding a tablespoon or two of cream to the eggs. During my testing I realized the pooling cream on top was obscuring any visual clue I might have that the whites were properly cooked—and since timing was essential in this dish, not having that visual clue was a real hindrance. Why not simply spoon some hot cream over the eggs when they had finished cooking? This worked wonders and enabled me to cook my eggs en cocotte consistently and perfectly time and again.

To add a bit of flavor, I sautéed a minced shallot in a little butter, poured in the cream, reduced it slightly to thicken it, and stirred in a pinch of fresh thyme. I spooned this over my next batch of eggs en cocotte— I had arrived. These were the simple yet elegant eggs I had hoped for. A bit untraditional, yes, as my recipe steams the eggs rather than bakes them in a water bath. But I think this divergence is justified by every perfectly cooked bite.

—SUZANNAH MCFERRAN, *America's Test Kitchen Books*

Eggs en Cocotte
SERVES 4

You will need a rack that fits inside your Dutch oven. If you do not have a rack, see the photo showing how to make your own foil rack. We find it easiest to use tongs and a sturdy, flat spatula to transfer the ramekins into and out of the pot. The eggs can overcook quickly, so check them often after 5 minutes of cooking. If you are serving this dish for company, you may want to practice once or twice to get your timing down.

2 tablespoons unsalted butter
1 shallot, minced (about 3 tablespoons)
½ cup heavy cream
½ teaspoon minced fresh thyme
  Salt and pepper
8 large eggs

1. Melt 1 tablespoon of the butter in a small saucepan over medium heat. Add the shallot and cook until softened, about 3 minutes. Stir in the cream and simmer, stirring occasionally, until thickened, 3 to 5 minutes. Stir in the thyme and season with salt and pepper to taste. Remove the cream mixture from the heat and cover to keep warm.

2. Meanwhile, place a rack in the bottom of a large Dutch oven and fill with water to just below the surface of the rack. Cover the pot and bring to a boil over high heat. Rub the inside of four 4 to 5-ounce ramekins with the remaining 1 tablespoon butter. Crack 2 eggs into each ramekin and season with salt and pepper.

3. When the water is boiling, gently place the ramekins on the rack in the pot and cover. Reduce the heat

---

NOTES FROM THE TEST KITCHEN

MAKING A FOIL RACK

Fold a 12- to 14-foot sheet of aluminum foil in half lengthwise and then in half lengthwise again; gently roll and scrunch it into a narrow tube. Coil the foil tube into a tight disk about 6 inches across, and flatten slightly.

to medium and cook the eggs until the whites are set but the center jiggles slightly when shaken, and the yolks are pale yellow and covered with a light film, 5 to 7 minutes, checking the eggs every 30 seconds after 5 minutes of cooking.

4. Spoon 1 tablespoon of the warm cream mixture into each ramekin and serve immediately.

VARIATIONS

Eggs en Cocotte with Parmesan Cream

Follow the recipe for Eggs en Cocotte, stirring 1 ounce grated Parmesan cheese (½ cup) into the cream mixture with the thyme in step 1.

Eggs en Cocotte with Mushroom Cream

Be sure that the porcini mushrooms are thoroughly rehydrated and softened before using here.

Follow the recipe for Eggs en Cocotte, adding ¼ ounce dried porcini mushrooms, rehydrated and minced (soaking liquid discarded), to the saucepan with the shallot in step 1.

QUICHE LORRAINE

QUICHE MAY HAVE ORIGINATED IN 16th-century Europe, but we'd argue that it's practically become an American citizen in the past 50 years. More specifically, any American who has eaten brunch in the last 40 years has encountered quiche Lorraine—and probably has been smitten by the combination of creamy custard, salty bacon, and nutty Gruyère cheese. But making it from scratch—yes, including the crust—can be intimidating. To begin with, the pie dough requires a meticulous mixing technique, long chilling, gentle rolling, careful shaping, and parbaking. Even if you manage that, achieving the custard's beautifully silken texture, and keeping it from breaking, let alone under- or overcooking, requires lots of hands-on attention. I sought a recipe that would take the fear out of making quiche.

In the test kitchen, we've had success with a pat-in-the-pan sweet pie crust that resembles basic shortbread cookie dough. I attempted a savory version, beating softened butter and cream cheese (the acidic cheese acts as a tenderizer) in a mixer, adding flour and salt, and beating for another minute. Traditional pie dough demands hours of chilling before rolling; after 30 minutes of chilling, I simply pressed my dough onto the bottom and up the sides of a pie plate. I rolled a bit that I'd reserved into coils, which I laid around the rim of the pie plate and crimped for a decorative edge. After the crust chilled for 30 minutes, I baked it empty (called blind- or parbaking). It emerged as light and flaky as traditional crust, but with far less anxiety and effort.

I tested several custard recipes and got results that ranged from soupy to extra-firm. I decided to work from a recipe that called for 2 cups half-and-half and two whole eggs, plus two yolks; tasters liked this custard but found it a little loose. After testing a series of ratios, I ultimately eliminated ½ cup of the half-and-half as well as one of the yolks. Now the quiche was setting up nicely, but it tasted a tad lean. I baked quiches with heavy cream, and with a combination of heavy cream and half-and-half. I also baked one with a mixture of sour cream and half-and-half, an idea that isn't as farfetched as it sounds; French cooks often use crème fraîche, their version of sour cream, in quiche. As soon as I tasted the quiche made with sour cream, I knew I'd turned the corner. The custard had a faint but appealing tang. It set firmly yet had an astoundingly silken texture.

Classic quiche Lorraine recipes in Alsace-Lorraine (the region in northeast France where the dish originated) omit cheese. Try explaining that to an American quiche fan! Here recipes typically instruct the cook to sprinkle 1 cup Gruyère over the parbaked crust before gently pouring in the custard and baking. Each time I tried this, the custard set before the cheese fully melted. I tried a more complicated technique—stirring the cheese into a custard I'd warmed on the stovetop—to no avail. The mixture separated in the oven.

In the end, I achieved success by combining several techniques: I cut the amount of cheese in the recipe in half, shredded it quite fine, and stirred it into room-temperature custard. I poured the mixture into a warm pie shell to give it a small head start heating up. After about 30 minutes in the oven, the custard had melded into a harmonious whole. Unfortunately, my solution came at a price: meager cheese flavor.

It occurred to me that I might be able to incorporate

QUICHE LORRAINE

extra cheese into the crust. I whisked ½ cup Gruyère in with the flour. It barely registered. I upped the amount, but the crust turned greasy. When I tried the same idea with ½ cup Parmesan, that version got the thumbs-up for its more intense cheese flavor.

The quiche was nearly perfect and was as easy as I'd hoped, but I couldn't help noticing that the chopped bacon (which I'd been stirring into the custard) kept sinking to the bottom of my pie. The next time I baked the quiche, I set some of the bacon aside. After the quiche had baked about 25 minutes and the custard was beginning to firm at the edges, I sprinkled the bacon over the quiche. Bon appétit!

—CALI RICH, *Cook's Country*

Quiche Lorraine

SERVES 8

Shred the Gruyère on the small holes of a box grater for the best texture.

CRUST

- 1 **cup (5 ounces) unbleached all-purpose flour**
- 1 **ounce Parmesan cheese, grated (about ½ cup)**
- ¼ **teaspoon salt**
- 6 **tablespoons (¾ stick) unsalted butter, softened**
- 2 **ounces cream cheese, softened**

CUSTARD AND TOPPING

- 5 **slices bacon, chopped fine**
- ¾ **cup half-and-half**
- ¾ **cup sour cream**
- 2 **large eggs plus 1 large yolk**
- ¼ **teaspoon salt**
- ¼ **teaspoon pepper**
  Pinch nutmeg
- 2 **ounces Gruyère, shredded (about ½ cup; see note)**

1. FOR THE CRUST: Adjust an oven rack to the lower-middle position and heat the oven to 375 degrees. Whisk the flour, Parmesan, and salt together in a bowl. In a large bowl, beat the butter and cream cheese with an electric mixer on medium-high speed until smooth and creamy, about 1 minute. Reduce the speed to low, add the flour mixture, and mix until the dough forms large clumps, about 1 minute. Reserve 3 tablespoons of the dough. Flatten the remaining dough into a 6-inch disk and transfer to the center of a 9-inch pie plate.

2. Following the photos on page 81, press the dough evenly into the bottom and sides of the pie plate and use the reserved dough to form a crimped rim. Refrigerate the dough for 20 minutes, then transfer to the freezer until firm, about 10 minutes. (Once the dough is pressed into the pie plate, it can be covered with plastic wrap and refrigerated for up to 2 days.)

3. Spray two 12-inch square pieces of foil lightly with vegetable oil spray and place greased-side down in the chilled pie shell. Fill with pie weights and fold the excess foil over the edges of the dough. Bake until the surface of the dough no longer looks wet, 15 to 20 minutes. Carefully remove the foil and weights and continue to bake until the crust just begins to brown, about 5 minutes. Transfer to a wire rack and let cool until just warm, about 15 minutes. Reduce the oven temperature to 350 degrees. (After it has baked and cooled, the shell can be wrapped in plastic and held at room temperature for 1 day. If making ahead, heat the pie shell in a 350-degree oven for 5 minutes before adding the custard in step 5.)

4. FOR THE CUSTARD AND TOPPING: While the crust cools, cook the bacon in a large skillet over medium heat until crisp, about 8 minutes; use a slotted spoon to transfer the bacon to a paper towel–lined plate. Whisk the half-and-half, sour cream, eggs, yolk, salt, pepper, nutmeg, Gruyère, and three-quarters of the bacon together in a large bowl.

5. Pour the custard mixture into the warm pie shell and bake until the crust is golden and the custard is set around the edges, about 25 minutes. Sprinkle the remaining bacon over the surface of the quiche and continue to bake until the center of the quiche is barely set, 5 to 10 minutes. Cool on a wire rack for 15 minutes and serve. (The quiche can be refrigerated in an airtight container or covered in plastic wrap for up to 3 days.)

VARIATION

Quiche with Bacon, Scallions, and Cheddar

Follow the recipe for Quiche Lorraine, substituting sharp cheddar for the Gruyère. Add 1 minced scallion to the custard with the bacon in step 4. Sprinkle 1 thinly sliced scallion along with the remaining bacon over the quiche after it has baked for 25 minutes.

SAVORY BREAD PUDDING

WHAT COMBINES THE BEST QUALITIES of quiche, soufflé, and strata and is easy to make? The answer is savory bread pudding. The best savory bread puddings have a rich, scoopable custard and enough of the bread sticking out for some of the edges to crisp up during cooking. Made properly, savory bread pudding offers a crunchy toasted bread topping that perfectly contrasts the rich, cheesy custard beneath.

But bread pudding is not without its issues. First, it is easy to go overboard and add too much of a good thing. Many of the savory bread puddings we sampled in the test kitchen were simply too rich, with a belly-busting overabundance of custard. A good bread pudding should have a restrained filling with a few additional components chosen to accent the bread and custard.

Naturally, bread is the foundation of bread pudding and was a logical place for us to begin. Though sliced white sandwich bread was the type specified in many recipes, I also saw some that called for other breads such as Italian, French, sourdough, multigrain, rye, pumpernickel, challah, and focaccia, and even hamburger and hot dog buns. I tried them all, and in the end tasters preferred French baguettes for their strong crumb and neutral flavor. Tasters thought that the crust gave the bread pudding a better texture, so I left it on.

Some recipes cube the bread and stale it overnight, but these bread puddings looked more like the cobblestone streets in the French Quarter than something I'd like to eat. I wanted a more rustic look and had much better results tearing the baguette into ragged pieces. Toasting the torn pieces to a deep golden brown enriched their flavor and gave the bread a crispness that helped to prevent the finished dish from turning soggy.

I then turned my attention to the custard that binds the pieces of bread together. Recipes commonly call for low-fat milk, whole milk, or half-and-half, and sometimes even heavy cream (the last option usually in combination with another dairy liquid). I tried each one of these alone as well as in every conceivable combination, and most tasters preferred a mixture of 3 parts cream to 2 parts milk. It was rich but not over the top.

Though the question of the liquid was settled, I still had some egg testing to do—my custard kept curdling. I tested whole eggs, yolks only, whites only, and various combinations. Because whites set faster than yolks, I found that replacing the traditional whole eggs with just

SAVORY BREAD PUDDING WITH SPINACH AND FETA

egg yolks (eight of them) helped stave off curdling. Plus, it yielded a flavorful custard that tasters favored.

Though my basic bread pudding was very good, I knew the flavorings and fillings would be the ingredients to catapult it to glory. I added garlic, fresh thyme, and a healthy dose of Parmesan cheese, all of which added dimensions of flavor without taking over. As for salt and pepper, I learned that a heavy hand is best; a teaspoon of salt and ¾ teaspoon pepper brought the flavors into focus.

For baking my casserole, I found that a wide, shallow baking dish allowed the bread pudding to bake much more evenly than the deep soufflé dish recommended in many recipes. (A standard 13 by 9-inch Pyrex dish works great.) Lowering the baking temperature from the frequently recommended 375 degrees to 350 degrees was another tactic I adopted to even out the cooking and to help curdle-proof my pudding. The result was a savory and versatile dish—perfect for brunch, but also great served alongside roast pork or chicken or as a light dinner when served with a salad.

—MEGAN WYCOFF, *America's Test Kitchen Books*

Savory Bread Pudding

SERVES 6 TO 8

We prefer the flavor and texture of a high-quality French baguette here, but a conventional supermarket baguette will also work.

- 1 (18 to 20-inch) French baguette, torn into 1-inch pieces (about 10 cups) (see note)
- 1 tablespoon unsalted butter
- 8 large egg yolks
- 3 cups heavy cream
- 2 cups whole milk
- 2 ounces Parmesan cheese, grated (about 1 cup)
- 2 teaspoons minced fresh thyme
- 2 garlic cloves, minced
- 1 teaspoon salt
- ¾ teaspoon pepper

1. Adjust an oven rack to the middle position and heat the oven to 450 degrees. Arrange the bread in a single layer on a baking sheet and bake until crisp and browned, about 12 minutes, turning the pieces over halfway through the baking time. Remove the bread from the oven and let cool.

2. Reduce the oven temperature to 350 degrees. Grease a 13 by 9-inch baking dish with the butter.

3. Whisk the yolks, cream, milk, ½ cup of the Parmesan, thyme, garlic, salt, and pepper together in a large bowl. Add the toasted bread and toss until evenly coated. Let the mixture sit until the bread softens and begins to absorb the custard, about 30 minutes, tossing occasionally. (If the majority of the bread is still too hard after 30 minutes, let it soak for another 15 to 20 minutes.)

4. Pour half of the bread mixture into the prepared baking dish and sprinkle with ¼ cup more Parmesan. Pour the remaining bread mixture into the dish and sprinkle with the remaining ¼ cup Parmesan. Bake until the custard is just set, about 60 minutes, rotating the dish halfway through the baking time.

5. Remove the bread pudding from the oven and let rest for 10 minutes before serving.

VARIATIONS

Savory Bread Pudding with Spinach and Feta
Follow the recipe for Savory Bread Pudding, omitting the Parmesan cheese. Stir 1 (10-ounce) package frozen chopped spinach, thawed and squeezed dry, and 4 ounces feta cheese, crumbled (about 1 cup), into the yolk mixture in step 3.

Savory Bread Pudding with Bacon and Onion
Cook 6 slices bacon, cut into ¼-inch pieces, in a 12-inch nonstick skillet over medium heat until well browned, about 10 minutes. Use a slotted spoon to transfer the bacon to a paper towel–lined plate, leaving the fat in the skillet. Stir 1 onion, halved and sliced thin, and ½ teaspoon salt into the fat left in the skillet, cover, and cook over medium heat, stirring occasionally, until the onion softens and releases its juice, about 10 minutes. Uncover and continue to cook, stirring often, until the onion begins to brown, about 6 minutes. Follow the recipe for Savory Bread Pudding, sprinkling the bacon and onion slices over the first layer of bread with the Parmesan in step 4.

BLUEBERRY MUFFINS

IF YOU'VE EVER HAD A MUFFIN made with locally grown, freshly picked wild blueberries, you know that the intense, sweet-tart fruitiness of the berries is what makes a blueberry muffin so good. Supermarket blueberries can be great if they're in season but tend to be watery and lackluster otherwise. I wanted to make blueberry muffins that would taste great with any blueberries, any time of year. They would be packed with blueberry flavor and have a moist crumb, one sturdy enough to hold up under the weight of a substantial helping of fruit.

Without a doubt, intense, fruity flavor was my top priority. Starting with a basic blueberry muffin recipe, I decided to see how many supermarket berries the batter could hold, and then I'd try to work some magic on their flavor. The recipe called for the creaming method, which incorporates a lot of air into the batter by beating butter and sugar, adding eggs and then milk, and finally folding in flour, salt, and baking powder. I did a test run by folding 1 cup of blueberries into this creamed batter before baking the muffins. As soon as I broke into the first one, I could see that 1 cup of fruit wasn't enough. Doubling the amount of berries only weighed the crumb down with heavy pockets of weak, watery fruit. I moved on, scouring the test kitchen pantry for ingredients to bolster the blueberry flavor. The two most promising were dried blueberries and blueberry jam.

I started by swapping out the fresh berries for dried, only to find that they yielded muffins with chewy, raisin-like blueberry bits. The dehydrated blueberries also greedily soaked up moisture from the muffins, making the crumb dry. Rehydrating the berries before incorporating them into the batter wasn't the answer; while the dried berries did plump up and lend a likable zing, they still weren't juicy or fresh-tasting.

Next, I cracked open a jar of blueberry jam. After dividing up the batter, I swirled a spoonful of jam into each filled cup. The muffins baked up with a pretty blue filling, but tasters unanimously agreed that the sugary jam had made them too sweet. What if I made my own fresh, low-sugar berry jam to swirl into the muffins? I simmered 1 cup of fresh blueberries on the stovetop to concentrate flavor and evaporate excess juices, adding a mere teaspoon of sugar for a touch of sweetness. After about six minutes, I had ¼ cup of thick, potent, deep-indigo jam that was chock-full of moist, tart blueberries. I used a chopstick to swirl a teaspoon

of it into each of the batter-filled cups, then baked. Success! The flavor was pure blueberry, very close to that of a wild-berry muffin.

There was just one thing missing: the juicy texture of fresh berries. This was easily solved; I just added 1 cup of fresh, uncooked berries to the batter before swirling in the jam. The muffins now contained the best of both worlds: intense blueberry flavor and the liquid burst that only fresh berries can provide.

At this point, I had conquered blueberry flavor. Now all I needed was a great muffin base to show it off. While the creaming method works fine for muffins filled with tiny wild blueberries, it yielded a texture that was too cakelike and tender to properly support the heavy jam and plump berries in these muffins. Giving the quickbread method a shot, I whisked together the eggs and sugar, added milk and melted butter, and then gently folded in flour, baking powder, and salt. Tasters agreed that this method was ideal, producing a hearty, substantial crumb that could support a generous amount of fruit.

To achieve the supremely moist muffins I sought, I examined the fat in the recipe. While the butter was contributing tons of flavor, I knew that oil has a propensity for making baked goods moist and tender. Unlike butter, oil contains no water and is able to completely coat flour proteins and restrict them from absorbing liquid to develop gluten. Using small increments, I gradually replaced some of the butter with oil and found that an equal amount of each (4 tablespoons melted butter, 4 tablespoons oil) produced just the right combination of buttery flavor and moist, tender texture.

Almost there, I wondered if I could make the muffins even richer. I felt confident that something other than the whole milk I'd been using could deliver more flavor. Rich and tangy sour cream, a popular choice for quickbread batters, made these muffins somewhat dense and heavy. Buttermilk, however, was just the ticket. It provided appealing richness but was light enough to keep the muffins from turning into heavyweights. As a bonus, its slight tang also nicely complemented the blueberries.

Baking the muffins at 425 degrees on the upper-middle rack gave them a golden brown crust. And, as a crowning jewel, I sprinkled lemon-scented sugar on top of the batter just before baking. The hot oven melted the sugar slightly, which then hardened as it baked to create an irresistibly crunchy shell. I now had truly great blueberry muffins I could make any time of the year.

—YVONNE RUPERTI, *Cook's Illustrated*

Blueberry Muffins

MAKES 12 MUFFINS

If buttermilk is unavailable, substitute ¾ cup plain whole-milk or low-fat yogurt thinned with ¼ cup milk.

TOPPING

- ⅓ cup (2⅓ ounces) sugar
- 1½ teaspoons grated lemon zest

MUFFINS

- 2 cups (about 10 ounces) fresh blueberries, picked over
- 1⅛ cups (8 ounces) plus 1 teaspoon sugar
- 2½ cups (12½ ounces) unbleached all-purpose flour
- 2½ teaspoons baking powder
- 1 teaspoon salt
- 2 large eggs
- 4 tablespoons (½ stick) unsalted butter, melted and cooled slightly
- ¼ cup vegetable oil
- 1 cup buttermilk (see note)
- 1½ teaspoons vanilla extract

1. FOR THE TOPPING: Stir the sugar and lemon zest together in a small bowl until combined; set aside.

2. FOR THE MUFFINS: Adjust an oven rack to the upper-middle position and heat the oven to 425 degrees. Spray a standard muffin tin with vegetable oil spray. Bring 1 cup of the blueberries and 1 teaspoon of the sugar to a simmer in a small saucepan over medium heat. Cook, mashing the berries with a spoon several times and stirring frequently, until the berries have broken down and the mixture is thickened and reduced to ¼ cup, about 6 minutes. Transfer to a small bowl and cool to room temperature, 10 to 15 minutes.

3. Whisk the flour, baking powder, and salt together in a large bowl. Whisk the remaining 1⅛ cups sugar and eggs together in a medium bowl until thick and homogeneous, about 45 seconds. Slowly whisk in the butter and oil until combined. Whisk in the buttermilk and vanilla until combined. Using a rubber spatula, fold the egg mixture and the remaining 1 cup blueberries into the flour mixture until just moistened. (The batter will be very lumpy with a few spots of dry flour; do not overmix.)

4. Following the photos on page 87, use an ice cream scoop or large spoon to divide the batter equally among the prepared muffin cups (the batter should completely fill the cups and mound slightly). Spoon 1 teaspoon of the cooked berry mixture into the center of each mound of batter. Using a chopstick or skewer, gently swirl the berry filling into the batter using a figure-eight motion. Sprinkle the lemon sugar evenly over the muffins.

5. Bake until the muffin tops are golden and just firm, 17 to 19 minutes, rotating the muffin tin halfway through the baking time. Cool the muffins in the muffin tin for 5 minutes, then remove them and transfer to a wire rack and let cool for 5 minutes before serving.

VARIATIONS

Blueberry Muffins with Frozen Blueberries
Follow the recipe for Blueberry Muffins, substituting 2 cups frozen berries for the fresh. Cook 1 cup of the berries as directed in step 2. Rinse the remaining 1 cup berries under cold water and dry well. In step 3, toss the dried berries in the flour mixture before adding the egg mixture. Proceed with the recipe from step 4 as directed.

Blueberry Muffins with Orange Glaze
Follow the recipe for Blueberry Muffins, omitting the lemon-sugar topping. Add 2 teaspoons grated orange zest to the egg mixture in step 3. Proceed with the recipe as directed, sprinkling 4 teaspoons turbinado sugar over the muffins before baking. While the muffins cool, whisk together 1 cup confectioners' sugar and 1½ tablespoons orange juice until smooth. Drizzle each cooled muffin with 2 teaspoons of the glaze before serving.

Blueberry Muffins with Almond Crunch Topping
Follow the recipe for Blueberry Muffins, omitting the lemon-sugar topping. In step 1, combine ⅓ cup finely ground almonds and 4 teaspoons turbinado sugar; set aside. In step 3, add ⅓ cup finely ground almonds to the flour mixture. Proceed with the recipe as directed, adding 1 teaspoon almond extract with the vanilla extract in step 3 and sprinkling the almond topping over the muffins before baking.

GETTING THE MOST BLUEBERRY FLAVOR

1. Cook half of the fresh blueberries into a thick jam to concentrate their flavor and eliminate any excess moisture.

2. Stir 1 cup of the fresh blueberries into the batter to provide juicy bursts in every bite.

3. Scoop the batter into the muffin pans, completely filling the cups.

4. Place 1 teaspoon of cooled berry jam in the center of each batter-filled cup, pushing it below the surface.

5. Using a chopstick or skewer, swirl the jam to spread the berry flavor throughout.

HOMEMADE PANCAKE MIX

ON BUSY MORNINGS I can barely make a cup of coffee, much less follow a recipe for pancakes. That's why boxed pancake mix is so handy. Throw a scoop of mix into a bowl, add eggs and milk, and ladle the batter into a hot pan, and soft, fluffy pancakes are on the table in no time. But boxed mixes, designed to last for months, often taste of the preservatives that ensure their long shelf life. Also, manufacturers include extra baking powder to guarantee high-rising pancakes, with the unintended consequence of bitter flavor.

Plenty of recipes for homemade pancake mix exist. Most use a food processor to cut vegetable shortening into a blend of flour (4 cups makes a manageable amount of mix), baking powder, baking soda, sugar, and salt. When you're ready to get cooking, you add eggs and milk and grab your skillet. But the homemade mixes I tried produced heavy, bland pancakes.

My first discovery was that all-purpose flour made pancakes that were too tough. It turns out that the preservatives in a boxed mix also promote tenderness. A switch to lower-protein cake flour didn't fix the problem; I got flat, dry pancakes. But replacing half the all-purpose flour with cake flour yielded the sturdy yet tender cakes I was after.

Some recipes fortify the dry mix with powdered milk or powdered buttermilk; since my tasters couldn't tell much difference, I opted for the powdered milk, which is easier to find. Beyond salt and sugar, I attempted to build flavor with vanilla, cinnamon, even ground oatmeal; none impressed my tasters. Then I tried an unusual ingredient I had spied in the supermarket near the powdered milk: malt powder. My tasters loved the sweet, nutty flavor it brought to the pancakes.

Not surprisingly, they also preferred the flavor of butter to the vegetable shortening that homemade mixes typically call for. While many recipes use only 8 tablespoons of fat (for 4 cups of flour), I found that 12 tablespoons delivered moister, more flavorful pancakes. Using butter meant that the mix needed to be stored in the refrigerator or freezer (for up to 2 months), but this seemed like a minor inconvenience for such a big improvement in flavor. For the leavener, my tasters stopped me at 2 tablespoons of baking powder—any more and they could detect its bitter, chemical flavor.

Now my pancakes tasted good and were plenty soft, but they lacked stature. Dried buttermilk powder hadn't made the grade in the mix, but I wondered if I could get higher-rising pancakes by using fresh buttermilk instead of milk when I mixed up the batter. For that to work, I'd need to add some baking soda to my mix—one teaspoon was plenty. Sure enough, the acid in the buttermilk reacted with the baking soda right away, causing the batter to bubble and the pancakes to rise higher in the skillet. With a mile-high stack of pancakes on my plate, I had finally beaten the box.

—DIANE UNGER, *Cook's Country*

Homemade Pancake Mix

MAKES ABOUT 6 CUPS OF MIX

This mix will make enough for 3 batches of 8 pancakes each.

- 2 **cups (10 ounces) unbleached all-purpose flour**
- 2 **cups (8 ounces) cake flour**
- 1 **cup nonfat (2.5 ounces) dry milk powder**
- ¾ **cup (3⅓ ounces) malted milk powder**
- ⅓ **cup (2⅓ ounces) sugar**
- 2 **tablespoons baking powder**
- 1 **teaspoon baking soda**
- 1 **tablespoon salt**
- 12 **tablespoons (1½ sticks) unsalted butter, cut into ½-inch pieces**

Process all of the ingredients in a food processor until no lumps remain and the mixture is the texture of wet sand, about 2 minutes. Freeze in an airtight container for up to 2 months.

To Make 8 Pancakes:

If you don't have buttermilk, make clabbered milk by whisking ½ tablespoon white vinegar or lemon juice into ½ cup whole or low-fat milk and letting the mixture thicken for 10 minutes.

Whisk 2 cups of the mix, 2 lightly beaten large eggs, and ½ cup buttermilk in a large bowl until smooth. Lightly oil a large nonstick skillet or nonstick griddle and heat over medium-low heat for 3 to 5 minutes. Pour ¼-cup portions of the pancake batter onto the skillet or griddle and cook until golden brown, about 2 minutes per side. Repeat with the remaining batter as desired. Serve.

ULTIMATE CINNAMON BUNS

WHETHER THEY'RE FROM A BAKERY or the food court at the mall, gooey, softball-sized cinnamon buns are worth every last calorie. This mammoth breed of cinnamon bun is distinguished from its leaner, punier cousins by its size, yes, but also by the richness of the soft, buttery yeasted dough, the abundance of cinnamon-sugar filling, and the thickness of the sticky cream cheese glaze. I wanted to re-create the best of its kind at home.

My research turned up recipes based on various types of dough. After trying several iterations of each, my tasters rejected recipes based on sweet bread dough (too lean), Danish dough (too buttery, flaky, and labor intensive), and challah (not rich or soft enough). Buttery, tender brioche proved the best base for rich cinnamon buns.

Most recipes use 2 or 3 cups of all-purpose flour to make eight buns. To bump them up to "ultimate" status, I started my recipe with 4½ cups of flour. To this I added sugar and salt, then slowly stirred in the wet ingredients:

ULTIMATE CINNAMON BUNS

3 beaten eggs, ¾ cup whole milk, and yeast. I tested various amounts of butter and my tasters liked the richness brought by 12 tablespoons. The dough is kneaded and left to rise until doubled in size. It's then rolled out, sprinkled with filling, rolled up, cut into buns, and baked. These buns tasted fabulous, but they were a little tough.

I hoped I could tenderize the buns by replacing the all-purpose flour with lower-protein cake flour. But in this case the cake flour worked too well, producing buns that baked up so soft that they never rose properly. In the test kitchen, we sometimes approximate cake flour by cutting all-purpose flour with a little cornstarch (the ratio is ⅞ cup flour to 2 tablespoons cornstarch). I found that if I manipulated that formula (I ended up at 4¼ cups of all-purpose flour and ½ cup cornstarch), I got the benefit of good structure and height from the flour, and tenderness from the cornstarch.

My tasters found granulated sugar too bland for the filling and dark brown sugar too bold. Light brown sugar worked best, and I doubled the amount of sugar most recipes use to 1½ cups. For big cinnamon pop, I blended 1½ tablespoons of cinnamon with the sugar. To keep this thick filling from spilling out as the dough was rolled up, I needed more than a simple brushing of butter, and instead slathered 4 tablespoons of softened butter all over the dough. Baked together, the butter and cinnamon sugar turned into a truly rich, gooey filling.

Many recipes cover the buns with a frosting made of butter, cream cheese, and confectioners' sugar—which pushed these already rich buns over the edge. I wondered if a thick glaze made with just cream cheese, confectioners' sugar, and milk would do. I spread this mixture over the warm buns. Everything seemed fine—until I came back 30 minutes later to find that the glaze had soaked into the buns. For the next batch, I reserved a little of the glaze to apply again after the buns cooled. Now my "ultimate buns" truly looked the part.

—ERIKA BRUCE, *Cook's Country*

Ultimate Cinnamon Buns

MAKES 8 BUNS

In step 2, if after mixing for 10 minutes the dough is still wet and sticky, add up to ¼ cup flour (1 tablespoon at a time) until the dough releases from the bowl. For smaller cinnamon buns, cut the dough into 12 pieces in step 3.

DOUGH
- ¾ cup whole milk, heated to 110 degrees
- 1 envelope (2¼ teaspoons) rapid-rise or instant yeast
- 3 large eggs, at room temperature
- 4¼ cups (21¼ ounces) unbleached all-purpose flour
- ½ cup (2 ounces) cornstarch
- ½ cup (3½ ounces) granulated sugar
- 1½ teaspoons salt
- 12 tablespoons (1½ sticks) unsalted butter, cut into 12 pieces and softened

FILLING
- 1½ cups packed (10½ ounces) light brown sugar
- 1½ tablespoons ground cinnamon
- ¼ teaspoon salt
- 4 tablespoons (½ stick) unsalted butter, softened

GLAZE
- 4 ounces cream cheese, softened
- 1 tablespoon whole milk
- 1 teaspoon vanilla extract
- 1½ cups (6 ounces) confectioners' sugar

NOTES FROM THE TEST KITCHEN

ASSEMBLING CINNAMON BUNS

1. Roll the dough into an 18-inch square on a lightly floured counter.

2. Leaving a ½-inch border around the edges, spread the softened butter over the dough, sprinkle with the sugar mixture, and lightly press the butter-sugar mixture into the dough.

3. Use a knife (or metal dough scraper) to cut the rolled log in half and then into 8 equal pieces.

1. FOR THE DOUGH: Adjust an oven rack to the middle position and heat the oven to 200 degrees. When the oven reaches 200 degrees, shut it off. Following the photos on page 93, line a 13 by 9-inch baking pan with foil, allowing the excess foil to hang over the pan edges. Grease the foil and a medium bowl.

2. Whisk the milk and yeast in a liquid measuring cup until the yeast dissolves, then whisk in the eggs. In the bowl of a standing mixer fitted with the dough hook, mix the flour, cornstarch, granulated sugar, and salt until combined. With the mixer on low, add the warm milk mixture in a steady stream and mix until the dough comes together, about 1 minute. Increase the speed to medium and add the butter, one piece at a time, until incorporated. Continue to mix until the dough is smooth and comes away from the sides of the bowl, about 10 minutes. Turn the dough out onto a clean surface and knead to form a smooth, round ball. Transfer the dough to the prepared bowl, cover with plastic wrap, and place in the warm oven. Let rise until doubled in size, about 2 hours.

3. FOR THE FILLING: Combine the brown sugar, cinnamon, and salt in a small bowl. Turn the dough out onto a lightly floured counter. Following the photos on page 90, roll the dough into an 18-inch square, spread with the butter, and sprinkle evenly with the brown-sugar mixture. Starting with the edge nearest you, roll the dough into a tight cylinder, pinch lightly to seal the seam, and cut into 8 pieces. Transfer the pieces, cut-side up, to the prepared pan. Cover with plastic wrap and let rise in a warm spot until doubled in size, about 1 hour. (After transferring the pieces to the prepared pan, the buns, covered with plastic wrap, can be refrigerated for up to 24 hours. When ready to bake, let sit at room temperature for 1 hour. Remove the plastic wrap and continue with step 4 as directed.)

4. FOR THE GLAZE AND TO BAKE: Heat the oven to 350 degrees. Whisk the cream cheese, milk, vanilla, and confectioners' sugar in a medium bowl until smooth. Discard the plastic wrap and bake the buns until deep golden brown and the filling is melted, 35 to 40 minutes. Transfer to a wire rack and top the buns with ½ cup of the glaze; let cool for 30 minutes. Using the foil overhang, lift the buns from the pan and top with the remaining glaze. Serve.

ST. LOUIS GOOEY BUTTER CAKE

AS ANY ST. LOUIS NATIVE WILL TELL YOU, there are actually two distinct styles of gooey butter cake—and everyone I talked to during a two-day visit to the city had a favorite. Many bakeries and coffee shops sell squares of gooey butter cake that are more like a chewy (and messy) bar cookie than a cake. The base is cake dough and the topping is similar to cheesecake. The second style is more like an old-fashioned coffee cake, with a rich yeast dough and custardy topping. The secret to this style is the one I hoped to uncover: The combination of tender yeast cake and silky custard literally melts in your mouth.

My initial recipe tests were pretty far from the mark. The bases were dry and tough (more like pizza dough than coffee cake) and the toppings were runny and soupy. The cake portion of the best of these early recipes combined 1½ cups of flour, 1 egg, and 4 tablespoons of butter, which were then mixed with yeast, water, sugar, and salt; once the dough was kneaded it was left to rise before being pressed into a pan. The topping was made by creaming butter and sugar, then mixing in corn syrup, an egg, vanilla, and flour. Once assembled, the cake was baked in a 350-degree oven.

I knew I needed to enrich, tenderize, and sweeten the cake base. Taking inspiration from rich yeasted doughs like brioche and Danish, I doubled the number of eggs. Doubling the butter to a full stick made the dough a little greasy; 6 tablespoons was the right compromise. Switching from water to milk gave the cake even more substance. Doubling the sugar (from 2 tablespoons to 4) lent more than the obvious sweetness; it also helped tenderize the cake. With a richer, more tender foundation in place, I moved on to the topping.

Bakers in St. Louis told me that by the time the cake base is cooked through, the topping should still jiggle slightly. As the gooey butter cake cools, the topping will set up into a velvety, custard-like consistency. Unfortunately, my experience with the topping was quite different. It was much too runny and puddled like melted ice cream when the cake was sliced.

My first thought was to add more flour, but the filling became pasty. I had better luck when I beat some cream cheese in with the butter and sugar. The cream cheese partially firmed up the filling without making it pasty, but using any more than 2 ounces made the topping too tangy and cheesecake-like. Cornstarch gave the filling an

ST. LOUIS GOOEY BUTTER CAKE

unpleasant slippery texture, but spurred the idea of trying instant pudding (which contains cornstarch as a thickener). Sure enough, a few tablespoons of vanilla pudding mix added flavor and provided the creamy, gooey-yet-sliceable texture I'd been looking for. With a dusting of confectioners' sugar, I had finally created a recipe that can compete with the best St. Louis bakeries.

—CALI RICH, *Cook's Country*

St. Louis Gooey Butter Cake

SERVES 9

Remove the cake from the oven when the perimeter is golden brown and the center is still slightly loose; the topping will continue to set as the cake cools.

DOUGH

- ¼ cup whole milk, heated to 110 degrees
- 1½ teaspoons rapid-rise or instant yeast
- ¼ cup (1¾ ounces) granulated sugar
- 2 large eggs, room temperature
- ½ teaspoon vanilla extract
- ½ teaspoon salt
- 1½ cups (7½ ounces) unbleached all-purpose flour
- 6 tablespoons (¾ stick) unsalted butter, cut into 6 pieces and softened

TOPPING

- ½ cup (3½ ounces) granulated sugar
- 4 tablespoons (½ stick) unsalted butter, softened
- 2 ounces cream cheese, softened
- 2 tablespoons light corn syrup
- 1 large egg, room temperature
- 1 teaspoon vanilla extract
- ⅓ cup (1⅝ ounces) unbleached all-purpose flour
- 3 tablespoons instant vanilla pudding mix
- 2 tablespoons confectioners' sugar

1. FOR THE DOUGH: Adjust an oven rack to the lower-middle position and heat the oven to 200 degrees. When the oven reaches 200 degrees, shut the oven off. Following the photos, line an 8-inch square baking pan with a foil sling. Grease the foil and a medium bowl.

2. In the bowl of a standing mixer fitted with the paddle attachment, mix the milk and yeast on low speed until the yeast dissolves. Add the sugar, eggs, vanilla, salt, and flour and mix until combined, about 30 seconds. Increase the speed to medium-low and add the butter, one piece at a time, until incorporated, then continue mixing for 5 minutes. Transfer the dough to the prepared bowl, cover with plastic wrap, and place in the warm oven. Let rise until doubled in size, about 30 minutes. Spread the dough into the prepared pan. Heat the oven to 350 degrees.

3. FOR THE TOPPING: In the bowl of a standing mixer fitted with the paddle attachment, beat the granulated sugar, butter, and cream cheese on medium speed until light and fluffy, about 2 minutes. Reduce the speed to low and add the corn syrup, egg, and vanilla until combined. Add the flour and pudding mix and mix until just incorporated. Portion dollops of the topping evenly over the dough, then spread into an even layer.

4. Once the oven is fully heated, bake until the exterior is golden and the center of the topping is just beginning to color (the center should jiggle slightly when the pan is shaken), about 25 minutes. Cool in the pan at least 3 hours. Use the foil overhang to lift the cake from the pan. Dust the cake with the confectioners' sugar and serve. (The cake can be refrigerated in an airtight container for up to 2 days.)

VARIATIONS

Butterscotch Gooey Butter Cake

Follow the recipe for St. Louis Gooey Butter Cake, substituting ¼ cup packed (1¾ ounces) light brown sugar for the granulated sugar in the dough in step 2. Substitute

---

NOTES FROM THE TEST KITCHEN

MAKING A FOIL SLING

1. Fold two long sheets of aluminum foil so that they are as wide as the baking pan. Lay the sheets of foil in the pan, perpendicular to one another, with the extra foil hanging over the edges of the pan.

2. Push the foil into the corners and up the sides of the pan. Grease the sides and bottom before adding the dough. Once the cake has cooled, you can use the foil overhang to remove it from the pan easily.

3 tablespoons instant butterscotch pudding mix for the vanilla pudding mix in the topping in step 3.

Chocolate Gooey Butter Cake

Follow the recipe for St. Louis Gooey Butter Cake, replacing 3 tablespoons of the flour with an equal amount of Dutch-processed cocoa in the dough in step 2. Substitute 3 tablespoons instant chocolate pudding mix for the vanilla pudding mix in the topping in step 3.

CORNMEAL BISCUITS

AS BISCUITS GO, CORNMEAL RANKS AS ONE OF MY favorites. Ideally, they have a tender crumb, a cheerful yellow hue, and the sweetness and subtle crunch of cornmeal. But how much cornmeal is right? The amount in recipes ranges from as little as 2 tablespoons (an afterthought) to as much as 1½ cups for a dozen biscuits (overkill)—enough to befuddle even the experienced biscuit maker.

Not surprisingly, such recipes delivered vastly different results. Biscuits with just a sprinkling of cornmeal had a tender, fluffy crumb but scant corn flavor. Those made with a lot of cornmeal offered lots of flavor, but were dry and leaden. I was looking for a biscuit that combined the advantages of both—tall and tender yet with distinct cornmeal flavor.

Since none of these recipes was very promising, I decided to start with the test kitchen's stamped buttermilk biscuit recipe and figure out how to add the cornmeal from there. This recipe calls for pulsing cubes of chilled butter with the dry ingredients (flour, baking powder and soda, and salt) in a food processor until only pea-sized pieces remain. The baker stirs in buttermilk, pats out the dough, stamps out the rounds, and bakes. For my first test, I substituted cornmeal for half the flour.

The biscuits looked promising coming out of the oven, but my hopes were soon deflated—they tasted dry and were overwhelmingly gritty. Working with the same recipe, I ran through a gamut of tests comparing different ratios. In the end, my work yielded mixed results. Tasters agreed that twice as much flour as cornmeal supplied the right cornmeal flavor, but they remained dissatisfied with the texture. Give us a little cornmeal crunch, they said, but show some restraint.

To soften the cornmeal grit, I first tried increasing the buttermilk. This dough was too wet to handle.

Some recipes for cornbread suggest softening cornmeal in hot water; I wondered if that approach might lead to success here. Since my liquid ingredient was buttermilk, I microwaved that with the cornmeal. Alas, this worked too well, yielding a heavy biscuit with zero crunch. Next, I tried soaking the cornmeal in the buttermilk without applying any heat. A mere 10-minute soak produced the just-soft crumb tasters were after.

As I watched a group of fans drizzling honey onto their biscuits, it occurred to me to add honey directly to the dough. Sure enough, just a tablespoon provided a subtle sweetness that drew out even more of the cornmeal's sweet corn flavor.

—CALI RICH, *Cook's Country*

Cornmeal Biscuits

MAKES 12 BISCUITS

If you don't have buttermilk, whisk 1 tablespoon lemon juice into 1¼ cups of milk and let it stand until slightly thickened, about 10 minutes. Avoid coarsely ground cornmeal, which makes gritty biscuits.

- 1 **cup (5 ounces) cornmeal (see note)**
- 1¼ **cups buttermilk (see note)**
- 1 **tablespoon honey**
- 2 **cups (10 ounces) unbleached all-purpose flour**
- 1 **tablespoon baking powder**
- ½ **teaspoon baking soda**
- 1 **teaspoon salt**
- 12 **tablespoons (1½ sticks) unsalted butter, cut into ½-inch pieces and chilled**

1. Adjust an oven rack to the middle position and heat the oven to 450 degrees. Line a baking sheet with parchment paper. Whisk the cornmeal, buttermilk, and honey in a large bowl; let sit for 10 minutes.

2. Pulse the flour, baking powder, baking soda, salt, and butter in a food processor until the mixture resembles coarse meal, about 10 pulses. Add to the bowl with the buttermilk mixture and stir until the dough forms.

3. Turn the dough out onto a lightly floured counter and knead until smooth, 8 to 10 times. Pat the dough into a 9-inch circle, about ¾ inch thick. Using a 2½-inch biscuit cutter dipped in flour, cut out rounds (dipping the cutter in flour after each cut) and transfer to the prepared baking sheet. Gather the remaining dough and pat into a ¾-inch-thick circle. Cut more rounds from

CORNMEAL BISCUITS

the dough and transfer to the baking sheet (you should have 12 rounds total).

4. Bake until the biscuits begin to rise, about 5 minutes, then reduce the oven temperature to 400 degrees and bake until golden brown, 8 to 12 minutes more. Let cool for 5 minutes on the sheet, then transfer to a wire rack. Serve warm or let cool to room temperature. (The biscuits can be stored in an airtight container at room temperature for up to 2 days.)

NOTES FROM THE TEST KITCHEN

THE NEED TO KNEAD
It's an adage as old as biscuit making: Light hands make tender biscuits. So why do we instruct you to knead our cornmeal biscuit dough? When biscuit recipes warn you not to overhandle the dough, they are cautioning against the development of gluten. It's desirable for chewy doughs (say, for bagels), but gluten is typically the enemy of tender, flaky biscuits. We replace some of the flour with 1 cup cornmeal, which has no gluten, so gluten development poses less of a risk. Also, the buttermilk in the dough is an acidic ingredient that helps break down gluten. Kneading the dough briefly ensures evenly textured biscuits that rise high instead of spreading.

MAKING CORNMEAL BISCUITS

1. Soak the cornmeal in buttermilk.

2. Transfer the dough to a lightly floured counter and knead it briefly before patting it into a 9-inch circle.

3. Use a biscuit cutter to cut the dough into rounds, dipping the cutter into flour between cuts.

POPOVERS

NOTHING EXEMPLIFIES THE MAGIC OF BAKING more than the popover. The classic recipe is quite simple: A pancake-like batter of milk, eggs, flour, melted butter, and salt is poured into the deep cups of a popover pan and baked in a very hot oven. Even without leaveners or whipped egg whites for lift, the batter somehow climbs the pan until it pops over the top into a sky-high balloon. Crack into the hot popover and you'll be met with a shattering crust and a hollow, custardy interior ready for butter or jam.

I've chased the perfect popover for years, but cookbook recipes led me only to squat, tough, or sunken versions. I wanted to develop a recipe that guaranteed a high rise every time. I had no idea that it would take over 100 batches—yes, I made more than 600 popovers—and some debunking of popover mythology to get the job done.

The most common formula for popover batter is 1 cup each of flour and whole milk, 2 eggs, and 1 tablespoon of melted butter; since these amounts made for skimpy popovers, my first move was to double the recipe to fill the same 6-cup popover pan. Tasters wanted more butter flavor, so I increased the amount to 4 tablespoons. As for the flour, I tested my working recipe using cake flour (a favorite of modern recipes), all-purpose flour, and bread flour. The bread flour has the highest protein content of the three, so it built the strongest structure—the highest rise and crispest crust—in the popovers. The bread flour proved so sturdy that it sometimes set up too quickly, impeding the initial rise. Resting the batter for an hour before baking gave the proteins in the flour time to relax and prevented the popovers from setting up too quickly, promoting a consistently better rise. But I wanted the popovers to rise even higher.

The 2 cups of whole milk, 4 eggs, and 4 tablespoons of melted butter I was using were making for flavorful popovers, but at a cost: The fat in these ingredients was weighing down the batter and inhibiting the popovers' rise. Reducing the amount of milk made them dry; switching to low-fat milk made for a higher-rising, moist finished product. Heating the milk allowed the batter to come together with less mixing, which was key to avoiding an overworked batter (which makes for tough popovers). I found I could cut the eggs from four to three, and the butter from 4 to 3 tablespoons to help the popovers maximize their rising potential; further reductions made the popovers taste too lean. A pinch of salt and sugar enhanced the flavor further.

Popovers baked at 450 degrees were too crusty on the outside by the time they were fully cooked, but reducing the starting temperature meant the popovers didn't rise as high. I had the best results baking the popovers for 20 minutes at 450 degrees to initiate the rise and then turning the oven down to 300 degrees so the interior would be done at the same time as the crust.

These popovers were showstoppers in the oven, but they collapsed like leaking tires as they cooled. The problem was steam trapped inside the popover; this moisture slowly dissolved the lofty, crusty structure I'd worked so hard to build. I solved the problem by poking a hole in the top of the popovers when they were almost done cooking, and then again as they cooled. This allowed the steam to escape and kept the crisp structure intact. After more than 100 tests, I finally had the perfect popover.

—DIANE UNGER, *Cook's Country*

Popovers

MAKES 6 POPOVERS

Greasing the pans with shortening ensures the best release, but vegetable oil spray may be substituted; do not use butter. To gauge the popovers' progress without opening the oven door, use the oven light during baking. Bread flour makes for the highest and sturdiest popovers, but 2 cups (10 ounces) unbleached all-purpose flour may be substituted.

Vegetable shortening (see note)

2 cups (11 ounces) bread flour (see note), plus extra for dusting the pan

3 large eggs

2 cups low-fat milk, heated to 110 degrees

3 tablespoons unsalted butter, melted and cooled slightly

1 teaspoon salt

1 teaspoon sugar

1. Adjust an oven rack to the lower-middle position and heat the oven to 450 degrees. Grease the interior of a 6-cup popover pan with the shortening, then dust lightly with flour. Whisk the eggs in a medium bowl until light and foamy. Slowly whisk in the milk and butter until incorporated.

2. Combine the flour, salt, and sugar in a large bowl. Whisk three-quarters of the milk mixture into the flour mixture until no lumps remain, then whisk in the remaining milk mixture. Transfer the batter to a large measuring cup, cover with plastic wrap, and let rest at room temperature for 1 hour. (Alternatively, the batter can be refrigerated for up to 1 day. Bring to room temperature before proceeding with the recipe.)

3. Whisk the batter to recombine, then pour into the prepared popover pan (the batter will not quite reach the top of the cups). Bake until just beginning to brown, about 20 minutes. Without opening the oven door, decrease the oven temperature to 300 degrees and continue to bake until the popovers are golden brown all over, 35 to 40 minutes longer. Poke a small hole in the top of each popover with a skewer and continue to bake until deep golden brown, about 10 minutes longer. Transfer the popover pan to a wire rack. Poke again with a skewer and let cool for 2 minutes. Turn out the popovers and serve. (Once the popovers have cooled completely, they can be stored at room temperature in a zipper-lock bag for up to 2 days. To serve, set the popovers on a rimmed baking sheet and bake on the middle rack at 400 degrees until crisp and heated through, 5 to 8 minutes.)

NOTES FROM THE TEST KITCHEN

A RELIABLE POPOVER PAN

Popover pans are composed of six tall, heavyweight steel cups affixed to one another with thick steel wire. The open design maximizes heat transfer, which is crucial to high-rising popovers. Very few companies manufacture popover pans these days; in fact, most cookware stores carry only one brand—the **Chicago Metallic Professional Nonstick Popover Pan**, $20. Made of nonstick, heavyweight steel, it is designed for maximum heat transfer, and it browns popovers well and releases them easily.

MAKING POPOVERS IN A MUFFIN TIN

If you don't have a popover pan, you can bake the popovers in a nonstick 12-cup muffin tin—with a sacrifice in stature. To ensure even cooking, fill only the 10 outer cups to ¼ inch from the top (you may have some batter left over). Reduce the initial baking time in step 3 to 15 minutes, and reduce the secondary baking time to 20 to 25 minutes after the oven temperature has been lowered. Poke the popovers as directed and continue to bake them for another 10 minutes.

RUSTIC DINNER ROLLS

RUSTIC DINNER ROLLS

I HAVE ALWAYS HAD A WEAKNESS for European-style dinner rolls. These lean, rustic rolls boast an airy crumb and yeasty, savory flavor worlds away from their richer American cousins. But the best part is their crust—so crisp it practically shatters when you bite into it, yet chewy enough to offer satisfying resistance.

This magnificent crust is what keeps these rolls the provenance of professionals, who typically rely on a steam-injected oven to expose the developing crust to moisture. I didn't have a steam-injected oven, but I did have a library of cookbooks and a kitchen full of experienced test cooks to consult. With these reinforcements and a little ingenuity, I was sure I could create a reliable recipe for rustic dinner rolls that looked—and tasted—like they came from an artisanal bakery.

After testing various recipes, I found the best rolls had two things in common: no butter or oil, and bread flour instead of all-purpose. This made sense, as fat inhibits gluten formation while the higher protein content of bread flour encourages it. (Gluten is the network of proteins that gives bread its chew.) For a working recipe, I settled on 3 cups bread flour, 10 ounces water, 1¼ teaspoons instant yeast, and salt. Following bread-making protocol, I mixed and kneaded the dough in a standing mixer, then transferred it to a bowl to rise. A couple hours later, I shaped the dough into balls, let them rise briefly, and baked them in a 425-degree oven.

My first batch emerged looking the part, with appealingly burnished exteriors. When I broke open a roll, however, I discovered a dense, bland crumb beneath a thin, leathery crust. The flavor was easy enough to improve; replacing 3 tablespoons of bread flour with whole wheat flour contributed subtle earthiness, while 2 teaspoons honey added some sweetness yet left the rolls' savory profile intact.

To create an airy crumb, I tried increasing the yeast. But I was able to add only a scant ¼ teaspoon before the rolls took on a sour, fermented flavor. This modest addition provided some lift, but not enough. That's when two fellow test cooks suggested making the dough wetter. Their logic was simple: During baking, the water within the dough turns to steam, creating hollow pockets as moisture rushes to escape. In addition, extra water creates looser dough, which allows the steam bubbles to expand more easily. The higher the hydration level, the theory goes, the airier the crumb.

Determining the hydration of my dough to be nearly 60 percent (in other words, there are, by weight, 6 ounces of water for every 10 ounces of flour), I assembled several batches of dough with varying amounts of water. Sure enough, increasing the hydration opened the crumb considerably. Working my way up, I found about 72 percent hydration to be optimal before the dough started getting too wet to shape into rolls.

From past experience, I knew that giving the dough a couple turns (gently folding it over on itself when partially risen) would encourage the yeast to produce more carbon dioxide, creating even more bubbles in the dough and thus an airier crumb. This technique was indeed effective, yielding the airiest and chewiest texture yet.

Using more water improved the finished rolls, but it also made the dough extremely sticky, oozy, and hard to shape. In fact, the very process of forming rolls sometimes caused the delicate dough to deflate, making its texture too dense. Wondering if I could forgo shaping altogether, I tried using a bench scraper to divide the dough into rough (but even) pieces. Bingo! With less handling, these rolls retained far more of the open texture I had taken such pains to achieve. Still, a problem remained: how to keep the soft dough from spreading and baking into a squat shape.

To prevent the dough from spreading, I tried crowding the dough in a cake pan. I coated these pieces lightly with flour to keep them from fusing together during baking and to make them easier to pull apart afterward. This batch looked good, but the spots where the rolls had rested against each other stayed soft. The solution: I removed the rolls from the oven halfway through baking, pulled them apart, and returned them to the oven spaced out on a baking sheet. With this two-stage baking method, they finished uniformly golden and crisp.

My rolls were now airy, with excellent flavor and an appealing shape. But I still wasn't satisfied with their crust. Playing around with oven temperature, I tried an old baking technique (popularized by Fannie Farmer in the late 19th century) of starting the rolls at a high temperature, then reducing the heat to finish them. I baked the rolls at 500 degrees for 10 minutes, separated them on a baking sheet, and lowered the heat to 400 degrees. This initial blast of heat made all the difference between a so-so crust and one with real crackling crispness. It had another advantage—boosting the oven spring (the rise that yeasted dough experiences when it first hits the heat of the oven), so the crumb was even airier than before. Misting the rolls with water before baking made the crust even crisper. Finally, I had rustic dinner rolls from my home oven. Light, chewy, and shatteringly crisp, with a perfectly airy crumb, they could give any artisanal bakery rolls a run for the money.

—CHARLES KELSEY, *Cook's Illustrated*

Rustic Dinner Rolls

MAKES 16 ROLLS

Because this dough is sticky, keep your hands well floured when handling it. Use a spray bottle to mist the rolls with water.

1½ **cups plus 1 tablespoon (12½ ounces) water, at room temperature**

1½ **teaspoons rapid-rise or instant yeast**

2 **teaspoons honey**

3 **cups plus 1 tablespoon (16½ ounces) bread flour, plus extra for forming the rolls**

3 **tablespoons (about 1 ounce) whole wheat flour**

1½ **teaspoons salt**

1. Whisk the water, yeast, and honey in the bowl of a standing mixer until well combined, making sure no honey sticks to the bottom of the bowl. Add the flours and mix on low speed with a dough hook until a cohesive dough is formed, about 3 minutes. Cover the bowl with plastic wrap and let sit at room temperature for 30 minutes.

2. Remove the plastic wrap and evenly sprinkle the salt over the dough. Knead on low speed for 5 minutes. (If the dough creeps up the attachment, stop the mixer and scrape it down using well-floured hands or a greased spatula.) Increase the speed to medium and continue to knead until the dough is smooth and slightly tacky, about 1 minute. If the dough is very sticky, add 1 to 2 tablespoons flour and continue mixing for 1 minute. Lightly spray a 2-quart bowl with vegetable oil spray; transfer the dough to the bowl and cover with plastic wrap. Let the dough rise in a warm, draft-free place until doubled in size, about 1 hour.

3. Fold the dough over itself; rotate the bowl a quarter turn and fold again. Rotate the bowl again and fold once more. Cover with plastic wrap and let rise for 30 minutes. Repeat the folding, replace the plastic wrap, and let the dough rise until doubled in volume, about 30 minutes. Spray two 9-inch round cake pans with vegetable oil spray and set aside.

4. Transfer the dough to a floured counter and sprinkle the top with more flour. Using a bench scraper, cut the dough in half and gently stretch each half into a 16-inch cylinder. Divide each cylinder into quarters, then each quarter into 2 pieces (you should have 16 pieces total), and dust the top of each piece with more flour. With floured hands, gently pick up each piece and roll in your palms to coat with flour, shaking off any excess, and place it in the prepared cake pan. Arrange 8 dough pieces in each cake pan, placing one piece in the middle and the others around it, with the long side of each piece running from the center of the pan to the edge and making sure the cut side faces up. Loosely cover the cake pans with plastic wrap and let the rolls rise until doubled in size, about 30 minutes (the dough is ready when it springs back slowly when pressed lightly with a finger). Thirty minutes before baking, adjust an oven rack to the middle position and heat the oven to 500 degrees.

5. Remove the plastic wrap from the cake pans, spray the rolls lightly with water, and place in the oven. Bake for 10 minutes until the tops of the rolls are brown; remove from the oven. Reduce the oven temperature to 400 degrees; using kitchen towels or oven mitts, invert the rolls from both cake pans onto a rimmed baking sheet. When the rolls are cool enough to handle, turn them right-side up, pull them apart, and space them evenly on the baking sheet. Continue to bake until the rolls develop a deep golden brown crust and sound hollow when tapped on the bottom, 10 to 15 minutes, rotating the baking sheet halfway through the baking time. Transfer the rolls to a wire rack and cool to room temperature, about 1 hour. Serve. (The rolls can be stored in a zipper-lock bag at room temperature for up to 2 days. To recrisp the crust, place the rolls in a 450-degree oven for 6 to 8 minutes. They can also be frozen for several months wrapped in foil and placed in a large zipper-lock bag. Thaw the rolls at room temperature and recrisp using the instructions above.)

THE REASON FOR HIGH HEAT

Cranking up the heat when the rolls go into the oven maximizes what professional bakers call "oven spring," the rapid rise in volume that all yeasted dough experiences when it first hits a hot oven. The higher this initial lift, the higher the finished bread.

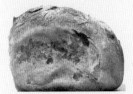

HIGHER HEAT= HIGHER RISE

LOWER HEAT= LESS LIFT

THE KEY TO PERFECTLY BROWNED ROLLS

1. Partially baking the rolls in a cake pan helps set their shape but leaves soft spots where they touch.

2. Separating the rolls and returning them to the oven on a baking sheet ensures finished rolls that are golden and crisp all around.

ONE GOOD TURN

Some bread recipes call for punching the dough down after its initial rise, while others call for merely "turning" it (gently folding the sides over into the center). To see what worked best, we tried both methods, along with an untouched batch of dough as a control. The untouched dough produced bland rolls that lacked chewiness, while the simple turn yielded the highest rise and the most open texture. Why? As the dough gets jostled around, the yeast cells are introduced to new food sources that allow them to continue multiplying, improving flavor and creating gas to help it rise. While turning does this in a very gentle way that helps the dough retain its air pockets, punching actually deflates the dough—great for dense, fine-crumbed bread like a sandwich loaf, but not for airy, open-crumbed rustic rolls.

PIZZA BIANCA

DURING A TRIP TO ROME a few years ago, I couldn't help but notice the lines of people waiting outside local bakeries for a regional specialty: pizza bianca. Intrigued, I waited my turn. With no cheese or sauce—just a gloss of olive oil and flakes of salt—it looked more like focaccia than pizza. But one bite into its crisp exterior and chewy, bubbly middle and I immediately forgot all about nomenclature—even toppings. I headed right back to the end of the line for more.

When I got home I collected a few pizza bianca recipes and even spent a day working with an American practitioner of the craft, cookbook author Daniel Leader, owner of Bread Alone, a bakery in Boiceville, New York. I discovered it's made from the same basic ingredients as our familiar pizza crusts: flour, water, yeast, and salt (plus a little sugar). And the general method is no more difficult: Mix the ingredients, knead them until dough forms, allow the dough to rise for a couple of hours, and you're good to go. So what's the difference?

As it turns out, there's a big one: Italians use significantly more water, creating a dough so wet it's impossible to roll out. While most pizza doughs don't exceed 60 percent hydration—meaning that, by weight, there are 6 ounces of water for every 10 ounces of flour—pizza bianca dough ranges from 70 to over 100 percent. The pizza makers then deposit and stretch the gloppy dough across the inside of the oven (to do this they use a long-handled wooden peel, or paddle).

There was no way I was going to try stretching dough out in my own oven, no matter how good the resulting crust. But if I could simply press this very wet dough into a baking sheet—and add a few toppings to turn a snack into dinner—I might never go back to making any other kind of pizza again.

I combined flour, water, yeast, and salt in a mixing bowl, opting for a hydration level around 90 percent. More water might make the dough gooey and difficult to handle; any less and I wouldn't get the super chewy, bubbly interior I was hoping for. Though I knew wet batter would require a lengthy kneading time, I wasn't prepared for the 30 minutes it took for dough to form. At high speed (a must for wet dough), I had to babysit the mixer to keep it from wobbling off the countertop. Unless I could cut down the kneading process, this dough would be more hassle than it was worth.

I took a step back and thought about the mechanics of bread-making. The goal in making any dough is to create gluten, the strong elastic network of cross-linked proteins that give bread its crumb structure. Kneading aids gluten formation by bringing the protein molecules in flour into alignment so they can bind. But we've also learned that a long rest has the same exact effect. I didn't want to wait around all day just to make pizza, but what if I allowed the flour and water to sit for a modest interval—say, less than an hour? After experimenting, I found that 20 minutes of resting was enough to reduce the kneading time to less than 10 minutes.

After letting the dough rise and triple in volume, it was wet and sticky but remarkably easy to shape. As I pressed it out over an 18 by 13-inch baking sheet, it showed little of the "spring back" that can make firmer dough annoying to work with.

Now the dough was ready to bake, and I tried our typical protocol for pizza recipes: Let the dough rest 5 to 10 minutes, then place it on a heated pizza stone positioned on a lower rack of a 500-degree oven. But when I tried to remove the baked pizza from the pan, it stuck resolutely, leaving behind swaths of crust—a clear sign that not enough moisture had cooked off. I reduced the oven temperature to 450 degrees and baked the dough on the middle rack, which allowed me to leave it in the oven longer. The pizza I pulled from the oven was as golden and crisp on the outside, and as chewy and flavorful on the inside, as the pizza bianca I had sampled in Italy.

Up to now, I had been loyal to authentic versions, adorning my pizzas with nothing more than salt, a handful of rosemary, and a thin coat of olive oil brushed on at the end. As good as this was, I wanted a pizza I could serve as a meal. I settled on tomato sauce and mozzarella for a variation I knew would please even the pickiest eaters in my household, and sausage for another. Adding these toppings halfway through baking was the key—spreading them over the raw dough at the beginning led to a gummy crust. Using a light hand was also essential, as too much of any one ingredient overpowers the flavor of the crust and detracts from its texture.

With the technique for dealing with wet dough perfected, and toppings successfully added, I had discovered how to adapt a classic Italian recipe for my kitchen at home. This easy, all-purpose pizza crust is one I'll return to again and again.

—DAVID PAZMIÑO, *Cook's Illustrated*

Pizza Bianca

SERVES 6 TO 8

Serve the pizza by itself as a snack or with soup or salad for a light meal. When kneading the dough on high speed, the mixer tends to wobble and move on the counter; watch it at all times during mixing. Handle the dough with slightly oiled hands. Resist flouring your fingers or the dough might stick. This recipe was developed using an 18 by 13-inch baking sheet. Smaller baking sheets can be used, but because the pizza will be thicker, the baking times will be longer. If not using a pizza stone, increase the oven temperature to 500 degrees and set the rack to the lowest position; the cooking time might increase by 3 to 5 minutes and the exterior won't be as crisp.

    3 cups (15 ounces) unbleached all-purpose flour
    1⅔ cups (13½ ounces) water, room temperature
    1¼ teaspoons table salt
    1½ teaspoons rapid-rise or instant yeast
    1¼ teaspoons sugar
    5 tablespoons extra-virgin olive oil
    1 teaspoon kosher salt
    2 tablespoons whole fresh rosemary leaves

1. Place a towel or shelf liner beneath a standing mixer to prevent wobbling. Mix the flour, water, and table salt in the bowl of the mixer fitted with the dough hook on low speed until no patches of dry flour remain, 3 to 4 minutes, occasionally scraping the sides and bottom of the bowl. Turn off the mixer and let the dough rest for 20 minutes.

2. Sprinkle the yeast and sugar over the dough. Knead on low speed until fully combined, 1 to 2 minutes, occasionally scraping the sides and bottom of the bowl. Increase the mixer speed to high and knead until the dough is glossy, smooth, and pulls away from the sides of the bowl, 6 to 10 minutes. (The dough will pull away from the sides only while the mixer is on. When the mixer is off, the dough will fall back to the sides.)

3. Using your fingers, coat a large bowl with 1 tablespoon of the oil, rubbing the excess oil from your fingers onto the blade of a rubber spatula. Using the oiled spatula, transfer the dough to the bowl and pour 1 tablespoon oil over the top. Flip the dough over once so it is well coated with oil; cover tightly with plastic wrap. Let the dough rise at room temperature until nearly tripled in volume and large bubbles have formed, 2 to 2½ hours. (Once the dough has been placed in the oiled bowl, it

PIZZA BIANCA

can be refrigerated for up to 24 hours. Bring the dough to room temperature, 2 to 2½ hours, before proceeding with step 4.)

4. One hour before baking the pizza, adjust an oven rack to the middle position, place a pizza stone on the rack, and heat the oven to 450 degrees.

5. Coat a rimmed baking sheet with 2 tablespoons more oil. Following the photos, use a rubber spatula to turn the dough out onto the baking sheet along with any oil in the bowl. Using your fingertips, press the dough out toward the edges of the pan, taking care not to tear it. (The dough will not fit snugly into the corners. If the dough resists stretching, let it relax for 5 to 10 minutes before trying to stretch it again.) Let the dough rest in the pan until slightly bubbly, 5 to 10 minutes. Using a dinner fork, poke the surface of the dough 30 to 40 times and sprinkle with the kosher salt.

6. Bake until golden brown, 20 to 30 minutes, sprinkling the rosemary over the top and rotating the baking sheet halfway through the baking time. Using a metal spatula, transfer the pizza to a cutting board. Brush the dough lightly with the remaining 1 tablespoon oil. Slice and serve.

VARIATIONS

Pizza Bianca with Tomatoes and Mozzarella

Pour one 28-ounce can of crushed tomatoes into a fine-mesh strainer set over a bowl. Let sit for 30 minutes, stirring 3 times to enable the juices to drain. Combine ¾ cup of the tomato solids, 1 tablespoon olive oil, and ⅛ teaspoon table salt. (Save the remaining solids and juice for another use.) Follow the recipe for Pizza Bianca, omitting the kosher salt and rosemary. In step 6, bake the pizza until spotty brown, 15 to 17 minutes. Remove the pizza from the oven, spread the tomato mixture evenly over the surface, and sprinkle with 6 ounces (1½ cups) shredded mozzarella (do not brush the pizza with oil). Return the pizza to the oven and continue to bake until the cheese begins to brown in spots, 5 to 10 minutes longer.

Pizza Bianca with Tomatoes, Sausage, and Fontina

Remove ¾ pound sweet Italian sausage from its casings. Cook the sausage in a large nonstick skillet over medium heat, breaking it into small pieces with a wooden spoon, until no longer pink, about 8 minutes. Use a slotted spoon to transfer sausage to a paper towel–lined plate. Follow the recipe for Pizza Bianca with Tomatoes and

Mozzarella, substituting 8 ounces (2 cups) shredded fontina cheese for the mozzarella and sprinkling the sausage over the pizza with the cheese.

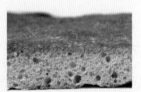

NOTES FROM THE TEST KITCHEN

WHY MORE WATER IS BETTER

To achieve its chewy, bubbly texture, our recipe calls for an almost 30 percent higher level of hydration than in most other pizza dough. Water aids the development of gluten, the network of cross-linked proteins that give bread its internal structure and chew. Up to a point, the more water in the dough, the stronger and more elastic the gluten strands and the chewier the bread. These strands, in turn, help to support the air bubbles formed as the dough bakes, preventing them from bursting and creating an open, airy crust.

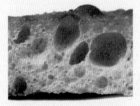

90 PERCENT HYDRATION
More water, bubblier crust

60 PERCENT HYDRATION
Less water, denser crust

MAKING PIZZA BIANCA

1. Turn the dough out onto a well-oiled baking sheet.

2. Press the dough from its middle toward the edges of the pan.

3. Bake the crust on a pizza stone on the middle rack of a 450-degree oven.

SKILLET PIZZA

A CRISP, THIN-YET-STURDY CRUST simply topped with fresh tomato sauce and melted cheese is pizza at its finest. But making good thin-crust pizza at home requires a pizza stone (which, in turn, requires plenty of time to get good and hot in the oven), not to mention the agility required to maneuver the dough onto the stone and the piping hot pizza off it without burning fingers or arms. I wanted to ditch the stone and come up with an easier, quicker way to make pizza in a home oven.

I thought a skillet might help fill the role of a pizza stone. My idea was to build the pizza in the skillet and give it a jump start with heat from the stovetop before transferring it to the oven.

First, I'd have to perfect the crust. We already had a handful of great pizza dough recipes in our library, but would any of these translate to the thin skillet-based crust I was after? For my first attempt, I heated some oil in a skillet over medium-high heat, gently laid the pizza dough inside, and cooked it on the stovetop before adding the toppings and baking it. The pizza looked perfect as it emerged from the oven, but once I cut into it I could see that the crust was thick and gummy, not thin and crispy. Plus, dropping an 11-inch round of dough into a skillet full of hot oil was a bit challenging to say the least.

I would need to test a slew of methods to get the dough right. First, I realized that a pound of pizza dough was a bit much for one 11-inch thin-crust pizza; I decided to cut the dough in half and make two pizzas, setting half aside and building and baking one pizza at a time. Also, I used bread flour instead of all-purpose flour to increase the chewiness in the finished crust. As for the cooking technique, I tried the simplest possible method—putting the dough into a cold skillet. Testing heat levels, I cooked pizzas over high, medium-high, and medium. The medium-heat pizza crust took six minutes to set and turn brown, and it was gummy when it was done. The pizza crust cooked over medium-high heat took four minutes to cook and was also a little gummy. The high-heat crust took three minutes, and it was crisp with a chewy center. A cold skillet and high heat was the right combination. As for oven temperature, I knew that, with pizza, the hotter the better, so I cranked the oven up to 500 degrees.

The crust was ready for toppings, but I wasn't sure when to add them. Should they go on just before the pizza went into the oven or before the dough was cooked on the stovetop? I tested both methods, and found no difference between the two pizzas. For simplicity's sake, I decided to top the pizza before placing it on the stovetop.

Next, I tested cooked and no-cook pizza sauce. The no-cook pizza sauce—a simple mix of canned whole tomatoes, olive oil, garlic, and salt that I pureed in the food processor—was favored by tasters. For the cheese, I used traditional shredded mozzarella, with a sprinkling of fresh grated Parmesan for a nice saltiness.

For those nights when I want something more festive than cheese pizza, I came up with a few variations. In my first one, I replaced the mozzarella with fontina cheese, then topped the fully cooked pizzas with arugula and prosciutto, which add nice textural variations. For a flavorful vegetarian option, I made a pizza with goat cheese, olives, and spicy garlic oil. Saving the best for last, I created a pizza with ricotta, bacon, and scallions—tasters couldn't get enough of this addictive combination.

—MEGAN WYCOFF, *America's Test Kitchen Books*

Skillet Cheese Pizza

MAKES TWO 11-INCH PIZZAS, SERVES 4

Our pizza dough and sauce are easy to make, but you can substitute premade pizza dough or sauce (or both) from the supermarket. All-purpose flour can be substituted for the bread flour, but the resulting crust will be a little less chewy. For whole wheat pizza dough, substitute 1 cup of whole wheat flour for 1 cup of the bread flour. The dough shrinks some after you roll it out, but may come up the sides of the pan a bit.

DOUGH

- 2 **cups (11 ounces) bread flour, plus extra as needed (see note)**
- 1⅛ **teaspoons (about ½ envelope) rapid-rise or instant yeast**
- ¾ **teaspoon salt**
- 5 **tablespoons olive oil, plus extra for the bowl**
- ¾ **cup warm water (110 degrees)**

SAUCE AND TOPPINGS

- 1 **(14.5-ounce) can whole peeled tomatoes, drained, with juice reserved**
- 1 **tablespoon extra-virgin olive oil**
- 1 **garlic clove, minced**
- ¼ **teaspoon salt**
- 6 **ounces mozzarella cheese, shredded (about 1½ cups)**
- ¼ **cup grated Parmesan cheese**

SKILLET PIZZA WITH RICOTTA, BACON, AND SCALLIONS

1. FOR THE DOUGH: Pulse the flour, yeast, and salt together in a food processor (fitted with a dough blade, if possible) to combine, about 5 pulses. With the processor running, slowly pour 1 tablespoon of the oil, then water through the feed tube and process until the dough forms a sticky ball that clears the sides of the workbowl, 1½ to 2 minutes. (If, after 1 minute, the dough is sticky and clings to the blade, add extra flour, 1 tablespoon at a time, as needed until it clears the side of the workbowl.)

2. Turn the dough out onto a lightly floured counter and form it into a smooth, round ball. Place the dough in a lightly oiled large bowl and cover tightly with greased plastic wrap. Let rise in a warm place until doubled in size, 1 to 1½ hours. (If desired, you can slow the dough's rising time by letting it rise in the refrigerator for 8 to 16 hours; let the refrigerated dough soften at room temperature for 30 minutes before using. Once risen, the dough can be sealed in a zipper-lock bag and frozen for up to 1 month; let thaw on the counter for 2 to 3 hours, or overnight in the refrigerator, before using.)

3. FOR THE SAUCE AND TOPPINGS: Meanwhile, pulse the drained tomatoes, oil, garlic, and salt together in a food processor until coarsely ground and no large pieces remain, about 12 pulses. Transfer the mixture to a liquid measuring cup and add the reserved canned tomato juice until the sauce measures 1 cup. Set aside.

4. Adjust an oven rack to the upper-middle position and heat the oven to 500 degrees. Grease a 12-inch oven-safe skillet with 2 tablespoons more oil.

5. Turn the dough out onto a lightly floured counter, divide it into 2 equal pieces, and cover one piece with greased plastic wrap. Press and roll the other dough piece into an 11-inch round. Transfer the dough to the prepared skillet.

6. Spread ½ cup of the pizza sauce over the dough, leaving a ½-inch border around the edge. Sprinkle ¾ cup of the mozzarella and 2 tablespoons of the Parmesan over the top. Set the skillet over high heat and cook until the outside edge of the dough is set, the pizza is lightly puffed, and the bottom crust is spotty brown when gently lifted with a spatula, about 3 minutes.

7. Transfer the pizza to the oven and bake until the edges are brown and the cheese is golden in spots, 7 to 10 minutes. Using pot holders (the skillet handle will be hot), transfer the pizza to a carving board, slice into wedges, and serve.

8. Let the skillet cool slightly, then wipe it clean and repeat with the remaining 2 tablespoons oil, remaining dough, remaining ½ cup pizza sauce, remaining ¾ cup mozzarella, and remaining 2 tablespoons Parmesan to make a second pizza.

VARIATIONS

Skillet Pizza with Fontina, Arugula, and Prosciutto

Follow the recipe for Skillet Cheese Pizza, omitting the Parmesan and substituting 6 ounces fontina cheese, shredded (1½ cups), for the mozzarella. Immediately after baking, sprinkle 2 ounces thinly sliced prosciutto, cut into 1-inch strips, and 1 cup fresh arugula over the top of each pizza before serving (you will need 4 ounces prosciutto and 2 cups arugula for both pizzas).

Skillet Pizza with Goat Cheese, Olives, and Spicy Garlic Oil

If your olives are particularly salty, be sure to rinse them.

Follow the recipe for Skillet Cheese Pizza, omitting the Parmesan. Mix 2 tablespoons olive oil, 1 minced garlic clove, and ¼ teaspoon red pepper flakes together in a small bowl. Brush half of the garlic-oil mixture over the top of each pizza before adding the sauce in step 6. Sprinkle 5 ounces goat cheese, crumbled (⅓ cup), and ¼ cup pitted kalamata olives, halved, on top of the mozzarella on each pizza before baking (you will need 10 ounces goat cheese and ½ cup olives for both pizzas).

Skillet Pizza with Ricotta, Bacon, and Scallions

Cook 4 slices bacon, cut into ¼-inch pieces, in a small skillet over medium heat until browned and most of the fat has rendered, about 10 minutes; use a slotted spoon to transfer bacon to a paper towel–lined plate. Mix 7 ounces whole milk ricotta cheese (⅔ cup), 2 thinly sliced scallions, ¼ teaspoon salt, and a pinch of pepper together. Follow the recipe for Skillet Cheese Pizza, omitting the Parmesan. Dollop half of the ricotta mixture, 1 tablespoon at a time, on top of the mozzarella on each pizza, then sprinkle with half of the bacon. Sprinkle each pizza with 1 more sliced scallion before serving.

CHAPTER 5

PASTA

Quick Tomato Sauce   111

Skillet Penne alla Vodka   112

Baked Ziti   115

Skillet Pasta with Peas and Prosciutto   117

Garlicky Shrimp Pasta   118

Make-Ahead Creamy Macaroni and Cheese   120

Skillet Ramen with Beef, Shiitakes, and Spinach   123

Slow-Cooker Meatballs in Marinara Sauce   124

QUICK TOMATO SAUCE

QUICK TOMATO SAUCE

IN A PERFECT WORLD, when you set out to make a quick tomato sauce, you'd simply reach for a few fresh, garden-ripe tomatoes to get started. But that isn't a realistic option for most of the year. Canned tomatoes far surpass the bland, rock-hard offerings in the produce aisle, but they have their own disadvantages. First, great tomato flavor is as much about taste as it is about smell, and the canning process cooks off many of the key aromatic compounds (16 in all) that food scientists have identified as prime contributors to full, fruity tomato taste. Second, researchers know that people perceive tomatoes to have the best flavor when sweetness and acidity are in balance (for optimal flavor, both should be high). The addition of citric acid as a preservative throws off that delicate but crucial equation.

I wanted to create a complex, brightly flavored sauce, one that tasted first and foremost of tomatoes, in the time it takes to boil pasta. I could never hope to restore the exact flavor of fresh tomatoes—but, with the right ingredients, maybe I could come close.

Starting with the right can of tomatoes should greatly improve the odds of success. Of the four major types of canned tomato products (whole, diced, crushed, and pureed), whole and diced tend to be the least cooked and have the freshest flavor. But I wanted a quick recipe, and crushed tomatoes would save me the step of pureeing them myself. Fortunately, crushed tomato brands such as Tuttorosso or Muir Glen (winners of our taste tests) are also minimally processed. I had another reason to choose one of these high-quality producers. While all brands heat their tomatoes to kill off any harmful microorganisms, these two producers use a lower temperature (between 160 and 185 degrees) to preserve an enzyme called lipoxygenase. Lipoxygenase oxidizes two of the pigments found in ripe tomatoes (lycopene and beta-carotene), creating new aromatic compounds that can make a canned tomato literally taste fresh.

Adding just ¼ teaspoon of sugar and a couple cloves of garlic instantly boosted flavor, as did a small amount of dried oregano. But my tasters wanted more depth. I tried a range of other ingredients commonly added to tomato sauce, with little success. Tasters quickly outlawed tomato paste for tasting overcooked. Red wine

brought too much of its own distinct profile. Ditto with carrots (too earthy) and lemon zest (too citrusy).

Conversations with several tomato industry specialists provided a clue as to why none of these "enhancers" was in fact enhancing the sauce: A good canned tomato will retain at least some of the fresh fruit's volatile components, but contact with other foods can alter their makeup, turning them into compounds that lack the aromas tasters recognize as tomato-like. If I wanted a sauce to taste primarily of tomatoes, I'd have to single out ingredients that didn't take me too far from their flavor.

One ingredient I hadn't tried was onion, for no other reason than cooking it down to the melting sweetness required by a good sauce takes time, and I wanted a streamlined recipe. Onions contain long chains of fructose molecules linked together in compounds known as inulin. Breaking down inulin releases the fructose, causing onions to become sweet, a reaction I could intensify if I caramelized them. I shredded a small amount of onion on a box grater, which would make it cook faster and release fructose more efficiently.

I started to sauté the onion in olive oil, but then thought better of it. Why not use butter, which also caramelizes in the presence of heat, creating its own new flavor compounds that would hopefully enhance, rather

than detract from, my sauce? After about five minutes, when the onions were lightly browned, I added two cloves of minced garlic, the sugar, and the crushed tomatoes, then allowed the sauce to simmer 10 minutes. (I found cooking times under 15 minutes produced fresher, brighter flavor.)

This was definitely the best sauce I had made yet. But I had one last tweak. To make up for the lost fragrance of fresh tomatoes, I added two highly aromatic ingredients: chopped fresh basil and extra-virgin olive oil. Swirled in just before serving, these ingredients perfumed the sauce with bright, grassy notes.

This sauce, to which I'd done so little, was a huge hit with my tasters, who praised it over and over for a bright, well-balanced flavor that tasted like it had come straight from the garden, not the pantry.

—KEITH DRESSER, *Cook's Illustrated*

Quick Tomato Sauce

MAKES ABOUT 3 CUPS, ENOUGH FOR 1 POUND OF PASTA

High-quality canned tomatoes will make a big difference in this sauce. Our preferred brands of crushed tomatoes are Tuttorosso and Muir Glen. Grate the onion on the large holes of a box grater.

- 2 tablespoons unsalted butter
- ¼ cup grated onion (see note)
- ¼ teaspoon dried oregano
  Salt
- 2 garlic cloves, minced
- 1 (28-ounce) can crushed tomatoes (see note)
- ¼ teaspoon sugar
- 2 tablespoons coarsely chopped fresh basil
- 1 tablespoon extra-virgin olive oil
  Pepper

Melt the butter in a medium saucepan over medium heat. Add the onion, oregano, and ½ teaspoon salt; cook, stirring occasionally, until the liquid has evaporated and the onion is golden brown, about 5 minutes. Add the garlic and cook until fragrant, about 30 seconds. Stir in the tomatoes and sugar; increase the heat to high and bring to a simmer. Lower the heat to medium-low and simmer until thickened slightly, about 10 minutes. Off the heat, stir in the basil and oil; season with salt and pepper to taste and serve.

SKILLET PENNE ALLA VODKA

PENNE ALLA VODKA QUICKLY BECAME A FEATURED item at trendy restaurants when it won first place in a 1970s recipe contest promoting vodka. This dish relies on a few simple ingredients—cream, red pepper flakes, and vodka—to emphasize the pure flavor of tomatoes. My goal was to fine-tune its elements and strike just the right balance of sweet, tangy, spicy, and creamy. While I was at it, I also hoped to streamline this modern classic by assembling it all in one pan—a skillet.

Most recipes for penne alla vodka begin with a basic tomato sauce (canned tomatoes, garlic, and red pepper flakes), but the textures run the gamut from thick-and-chunky to ultra-smooth. Tasters preferred a middle-of-the-road texture, so I pulsed whole peeled tomatoes in the food processor, which provided the desired consistency and helped the sauce cling to the pasta. In 10 minutes, my simmering sauce was just right; but before I could finesse the flavors, I needed to figure out how to cook the sauce and pasta together in one skillet.

Fortunately, this task was easier than I expected. It turns out that small amounts of pasta (about 12 ounces—perfect for a recipe that serves four) cook very well in a nonstick skillet with a brothy, creamy, or diluted sauce. Cooked at a vigorous simmer, the pasta absorbs the cooking liquid and becomes tender in a reasonable amount of time. And because the pasta was cooking right in our tomato sauce, it absorbed maximum flavor. Adding 2 cups of water to the sauce provided just the right amount of liquid to allow the pasta to cook through; I also found that covering the skillet while simmering the pasta prevented the tomato sauce from reducing too much.

With the specifics of the skillet technique in place, I focused on rounding out the flavors of my sauce. First, I sautéed some minced onion in the skillet, before simmering the tomatoes, to underscore the tomatoes' sweetness. I found that this sweetness, which was essential to the balanced flavor profile I sought, faded when I added the cream and vodka later on. I stirred in a tablespoon of tomato paste, which both reinforced the sweetness and provided depth to the overall flavor of the sauce. Also, I noticed that when I added the vodka near the end of the recipe, as many recipes specify, its flavor dominated the finished dish. I looked more closely at the role alcohol was playing in my penne alla vodka.

Besides cutting through the richness of the cream, vodka contributes another nuance to the sauce, which tasters identified as "zinginess." Raw alcohol is an irritant, creating a stinging sensation on the tongue and in the throat. When cooked, alcohol doesn't entirely evaporate, and a mild burning sensation (aka zinginess) is left behind. It was this sensation I wanted in my dish, not an overly boozy flavor. I realized I'd have to add the vodka to the skillet earlier in the process (with the pasta and water), so that the alcohol mostly—but not completely—cooked off. I stirred a small amount of vodka into the sauce when I added the water and pasta. It took just 15 minutes at a vigorous simmer for the pasta to become tender and absorb the flavor of the sauce.

It was time for the finishing touches: I swirled in ½ cup of heavy cream for a rich but not over-the-top consistency, then I garnished the pasta with chopped basil and grated Parmesan. Finally, I had a quick and delicious penne alla vodka that struck the flavor balance I'd been looking for.

—SUZANNAH MCFERRAN, *America's Test Kitchen Books*

NOTES FROM THE TEST KITCHEN

MEASURING PASTA

In skillet pasta recipes, the ratio of pasta to cooking liquid is critical to success. If you do not own a scale, you can use these equivalent cup measurements for various shapes.

PASTA TYPE	8 OUNCES	12 OUNCES
Penne	2½ cups	3¾ cups
Ziti	2½ cups	3¾ cups
Orecchiette	2⅓ cups	3½ cups
Campanelle	3 cups	4½ cups
Farfalle (Bow Ties)	3 cups	4½ cups
Medium Shells	3 cups	4½ cups
Small Shells	2 cups	3 cups
Elbow Macaroni	2 cups	3 cups

THE BEST TOMATO PASTE

Tomato paste is great for adding a slightly deeper, rounder flavor and color to soups, stews, and sauces. Our favorite—which comes in a tube, not a can—is **Amore Tomato Paste.** Because it's packaged in a tube, Amore lacks the tinny aftertaste that plagues many canned tomato pastes. One note: The label marks this as a "double concentrated" tomato paste, but we found no differences between this and other tomato pastes; just use the amount called for in a recipe.

Skillet Penne alla Vodka
SERVES 4

You can substitute ziti, medium shells, farfalle, campanelle, or orecchiette for the penne; however, the cup measurements will vary. See the chart for more information on measuring pasta. If possible, use premium vodka; inexpensive brands will taste harsh in this sauce. Pepper vodka imparts a pleasant flavor and can be substituted for plain. Be sure to simmer the tomatoes gently in step 2 or the sauce will become too thick.

- 3 (14.5-ounce) cans whole peeled tomatoes
- 2 tablespoons extra-virgin olive oil
- ¼ cup minced onion
- 1 tablespoon tomato paste
  Salt
- 2 garlic cloves, minced
- ¼–½ teaspoon red pepper flakes
- 2 cups water
- ⅓ cup vodka (see note)
- 12 ounces (about 3¾ cups) penne (see note)
- ½ cup heavy cream
- 2 tablespoons chopped fresh basil
  Pepper
  Freshly grated Parmesan cheese, for serving

1. Pulse the tomatoes with their juice in a food processor until coarsely ground and no large pieces remain, about 12 pulses.

2. Heat the oil in a 12-inch nonstick skillet over medium heat until shimmering. Add the onion, tomato paste, and ½ teaspoon salt and cook, stirring often, until softened, 5 to 7 minutes. Stir in the garlic and red pepper flakes and cook until fragrant, about 30 seconds. Stir in the processed tomatoes. Reduce the heat to medium-low and simmer gently, stirring occasionally, until the tomatoes no longer taste raw, about 10 minutes.

3. Stir in the water and vodka, then add the pasta. Cover, increase the heat to medium-high, and cook, stirring often and adjusting the heat to maintain a vigorous simmer, until the pasta is tender, 15 to 18 minutes.

4. Stir in the cream and cook until hot, about 1 minute. Stir in the basil and season with salt and pepper to taste. Serve, passing the Parmesan separately.

BAKED ZITI

BAKED ZITI

BAKED ZITI IS SUPPOSED TO BE SIMPLE: just pasta and a robust tomato sauce baked under a cover of bubbling, gooey cheese. But over time the dish has devolved from simple to merely lazy. Most versions seem like they went directly from the pantry into the oven, calling for little more than cooked pasta, jarred tomato sauce, a container of ricotta, and some preshredded cheese. The results—overcooked ziti in a dull, grainy sauce topped with a rubbery mass of mozzarella—more than earn the dish its reputation as mediocre church-supper fare. Without turning baked ziti into a weekend project, I wanted to get the same rewarding outcome from ziti that I've come to expect from any other baked pasta.

The first problem to tackle was the sauce. I wanted a sauce that was big on flavor and light on prep. (I'd deal with the dairy question later; for now, I'd finish my sauce by mixing in ricotta cheese.) Whole canned tomatoes and crushed tomatoes both had good flavor but took a long time to cook down. To speed things up, what if I used a tomato product that was already concentrated? Canned sauce provided the viscous texture I wanted but lacked bright tomato flavor. Adding a can of diced tomatoes struck the ideal balance of texture and flavor, and some basil and oregano contributed rich, aromatic savor.

Just when my tomato sauce seemed perfect, I added the ricotta, and a familiar problem reared its head: Rather than baking up creamy and rich, the ricotta was grainy and dulled the sauce. Maybe a different dairy product was in order? Straight-up heavy cream added lushness but dulled the flavor just as much as ricotta. I needed something creamy yet bright.

A colleague suggested I try her mother's baked ziti recipe, which called for two unorthodox ingredients: cottage cheese and jarred Alfredo sauce. I was skeptical, but I tried the cottage cheese. To my surprise, it was a smashing success. Its pillowy curds have a texture similar to ricotta, but it possesses a much creamier consistency and a more distinct, tangy flavor. And since its curds are bigger, cottage cheese bakes up with none of ricotta's graininess.

Alfredo sauce sounded intriguing—what could be wrong with a rich sauce made of reduced cream and Parmesan cheese? But why go with jarred? A quick scan of the jar's label revealed that commercial Alfredo sauce also contains eggs and thickener. Plain heavy cream didn't work in my previous tests, but maybe thickening it and enriching it with eggs would help. For my next batch, I combined cottage cheese with eggs, Parmesan, and heavy cream thickened with a bit of cornstarch. Combining this milky, tangy mixture with the bright tomato sauce won instant converts. I now had a sauce that was bright, rich, and creamy—all at the same time.

The pasta presented its own challenges. Most recipes cook the ziti in boiling water until al dente before tossing it with the sauce and baking. But pasta continues to absorb sauce as it bakes, with two unfortunate consequences: overcooked pasta and sauce that has been robbed of moisture. Covering the casserole with aluminum foil as it baked helped to retain moisture and keep the top from drying out, but I needed more drastic measures. I ran a series of tests, finding that cooking the pasta for roughly five minutes—about half the cooking time that most recipes call for—and using more than 8 cups of sauce—nearly twice the amount of sauce usually specified—yielded perfectly al dente pasta in the baked dish with plenty of sauce left to keep the whole thing moist.

The only remaining question was how to deal with the cheese. Grated cheese congeals into a mass that makes the dish not only unappetizing but difficult to portion, as some pieces get more than their share of cheese while others get none. Instead of shredding the mozzarella, I tried cutting it into small cubes—reasoning that they would melt into distinct but delectable little pockets of cheese—but they ended up flowing into each other and, like the shredded cheese, forming a heavy crust on top. What if I mixed half of the cheese with the sauce just before adding it to the pasta, and then sprinkled the rest over the top? This strategy yielded a hot, bubbly success. The cubes on top remained perfectly distributed, and the casserole below was dotted with gooey bits of cheese.

While second-rate red-sauce restaurants continue to make "lazy-man's" baked ziti, my family will have this dish the way it's meant to be—with perfectly al dente pasta, a rich and flavorful sauce, and melted cheese in every bite.

—DAVID PAZMIÑO, *Cook's Illustrated*

Baked Ziti

SERVES 8 TO 10

The test kitchen prefers baked ziti made with heavy cream, but whole milk can be substituted by increasing the amount of cornstarch to 2 teaspoons and increasing the cooking time in step 3 by 1 to 2 minutes. Either whole milk or part-skim mozzarella can be used, but avoid preshredded cheese, as it does not melt well. Do not use nonfat cottage cheese; it will break when the dish is baked.

- 1 **pound whole milk or 1 percent cottage cheese (see note)**
- 2 **large eggs, lightly beaten**
- 3 **ounces Parmesan cheese, grated (about 1½ cups)**
  Salt
- 1 **pound ziti or other short, tubular pasta**
- 2 **tablespoons extra-virgin olive oil**
- 5 **garlic cloves, minced**
- 1 **(28-ounce) can tomato sauce**
- 1 **(14.5-ounce) can diced tomatoes**
- 1 **teaspoon dried oregano**
- ½ **cup plus 2 tablespoons chopped fresh basil**
- 1 **teaspoon sugar**
  Pepper
- ¾ **teaspoon cornstarch**
- 1 **cup heavy cream (see note)**
- 8 **ounces low-moisture mozzarella cheese, cut into ¼-inch pieces (about 1½ cups) (see note)**

1. Adjust an oven rack to the middle position and heat the oven to 350 degrees. Whisk the cottage cheese, eggs, and 1 cup of the Parmesan together in a medium bowl; set aside. Bring 4 quarts water to a boil in a large Dutch oven over high heat. Stir in 1 tablespoon salt and the pasta; cook, stirring often, until the pasta is just shy of al dente, 5 to 7 minutes. Drain the pasta and leave it in the colander (do not wash the Dutch oven).

2. Meanwhile, heat the oil and garlic in a 12-inch skillet over medium heat until the garlic is fragrant but not brown, about 2 minutes. Stir in the tomato sauce, diced tomatoes, and oregano and simmer until thickened, about 10 minutes. Off the heat, stir in ½ cup of the basil and sugar, then season with salt and pepper to taste.

3. Stir the cornstarch into the cream in a small bowl; transfer the mixture to the now-empty Dutch oven set over medium heat. Bring to a simmer and cook until thickened, 3 to 4 minutes. Remove the pot from the heat and add the cottage cheese mixture, 1 cup of the tomato sauce, and ¾ cup of the mozzarella, then stir to combine. Add the pasta and stir to coat thoroughly with sauce.

4. Transfer the pasta mixture to a 13 by 9-inch baking dish and spread the remaining tomato sauce evenly over the pasta. Sprinkle the remaining ¾ cup mozzarella and the remaining ½ cup Parmesan over the top. Cover the baking dish tightly with foil and bake for 30 minutes.

5. Remove the foil and continue to cook until the cheese is bubbling and beginning to brown, about 30 minutes longer. Let cool for 20 minutes. Sprinkle with the remaining 2 tablespoons basil and serve.

NOTES FROM THE TEST KITCHEN

BUILDING A BETTER BAKED ZITI

DICED CHEESE
Diced mozzarella (rather than shredded), stirred into the sauce and sprinkled on top of the dish, leads to melted cheese in every bite.

COTTAGE CHEESE
Our recipe swaps ricotta with cottage cheese, which maintains its creamy texture even when hot.

TWO SAUCES
We combine traditional tomato sauce with nontraditional Alfredo sauce to achieve a perfect balance of brightness and richness.

OUR FAVORITE COTTAGE CHEESE

Americans have enjoyed cottage cheese since Colonial times. Today, most refrigerators have a container. Textures range from wet to dry, although you would never know it from the marketing lingo. "California style" refers to a drier cottage cheese, while "country style" refers to a creamier, wetter mixture. Which tastes best? We tasted three national brands of small-curd cottage cheese with 4 percent fat, plain and in baked ziti. Our favorite was **Hood Country Style Cottage Cheese.** Tasters praised its creamy flavor and texture.

SKILLET PASTA WITH PEAS AND PROSCIUTTO

THE COMBINATION OF PASTA, PROSCIUTTO, AND PEAS is a favorite here in the test kitchen. They taste great together, but the textural contrast of the prosciutto and peas is what really steals the show; the subtle pop of the pea's shell and its starchy flesh are juxtaposed with the crisp yet chewy strands of sautéed prosciutto. Add to that the pasta and a rich sauce, and you have something to talk about. I set out to incorporate them into a flavorful skillet pasta dinner that was quick and easy.

I started at the very beginning, by deciding what my base would be—a red sauce or a creamy white sauce? Tasters unanimously favored the idea of a creamy white sauce—they felt a red sauce would compete with the peas and prosciutto, while a creamy sauce would add a subtle richness. After sautéing onion and garlic for flavor, I added 2 cups of cream along with some water, stirred in the pasta, and simmered it over high heat until the pasta was tender. I already knew that when cooking pasta in a cream-based sauce, leaving it uncovered is important; it allows most of the liquid to be absorbed by the pasta, reducing the remainder down to a nice, silky sauce. At least that's how it usually works. But here the resulting sauce was bland and too thick. I replaced some water with vegetable broth to add flavor, and reduced the cream to 1 cup. The texture of the sauce was much improved, but tasters wanted something to bring out the meaty flavor of the prosciutto in the finished dish. Finally, I came up with the winning combination of chicken broth, water, and cream. I found that 5 cups of liquid (2 cups each of chicken broth and water, and 1 cup cream) is the right amount for 12 ounces of pasta. The pasta—we chose medium shells, although many similar-sized shapes would also work well to capture the sauce—absorbed most of the liquid as it cooked, and the remainder of the liquid reduced to a nice saucy consistency.

Next I moved on to the peas. While we normally avoid frozen vegetables, peas are an exception. Peas are so delicate that their flavor is compromised as soon as they are picked; like corn, their sugars instantly begin converting to starch after harvesting. Fortunately, frozen peas are processed within hours of being picked, when their flavor is at its peak. I knew they would need just a minute of cooking—after the pasta was done—to warm through and still maintain their fresh, vibrant flavor.

I turned my attention to the prosciutto and how best to incorporate it into the sauce. Prosciutto is an uncooked, unsmoked ham that is salted and cured for eight months to two years, depending on the processor. One of the secrets of traditional prosciutto-making is that the pigs are fed on the leftover whey from the production of Parmesan cheese, which imparts its characteristic nuttiness to the meat. While prosciutto can be eaten raw, and generally is, I sautéed it briefly in olive oil to crisp it up, then set it aside until the end, when I

NOTES FROM THE TEST KITCHEN

REGULAR VERSUS PETITE PEAS
We've always been big fans of frozen peas. Individually frozen right after being shucked from the pod, they are often sweeter and fresher-tasting than the shuck-'em-yourself "fresh" peas that may have spent days in storage, slowly losing sweetness and gaining starchiness. We've seen two varieties in the freezer aisle: regular frozen peas, and bags labeled "petite peas." To see if there is a difference, we tasted each type with butter. Tasters unanimously favored the smaller peas for their sweeter flavor and creamier texture. Regular peas were by no means unacceptable but had tougher skins and mealier interiors. Since both varieties are available for the same price, we're going with the petite peas from now on.

THE BEST NONSTICK SKILLET
We've always recommended buying inexpensive nonstick skillets, because with regular use the nonstick coating inevitably scratches, chips off, or becomes ineffective. Why spend big bucks on a pan that will last only a year or two? We rounded up eight models priced under $60 and pitted them against our gold standard, the $135 nonstick skillet from All-Clad, to see how they measured up.

We sautéed onions and carrots, cooked thin fillets of sole, made omelets, and fried eggs (with no added fat) in each pan. We found that they all did an acceptable job cooking and releasing these foods. There were noticeable differences in sauté speed, but most home cooks know if their cookware runs a bit fast or slow and adjust accordingly. To gauge durability, we cooked 12-egg frittatas while doing several things that manufacturers specifically forbid in each pan: broiling, cutting with a sharp knife, removing the slices with a metal pie server, and washing with an abrasive metal scrubber. And the results? Although the $135 All-Clad is still the best pan out there, our favorite among the group of less-expensive pans was the **Calphalon Simply Calphalon Nonstick 12-Inch Omelette Pan,** $54.95, which not only performed well, but also was preferred for its light weight and comfortable handle.

sprinkled it over the pasta. Tasters favored this approach because it provided a textural contrast with the peas.

My dish was good, but tasters wanted a bit more creaminess. Looking back over my research, I remembered that fresh ricotta had been used in some recipes. Ricotta, with its hint of sweetness, pairs particularly well with peas, but its grainy texture can be distracting when stirred into a hot sauce. To combat this, I placed heaping tablespoons of ricotta over the pasta just as it finished cooking, covered the dish, and let it stand off the heat so the ricotta would melt slightly. The sauce was at once silky and creamy. I added Parmesan and a touch of lemon zest to the ricotta, which perked things up and complemented the prosciutto. For an even fresher flavor reminiscent of spring, I finished my dish with a handful of fresh mint.

—SUZANNAH MCFERRAN, *America's Test Kitchen Books*

Skillet Pasta with Peas and Prosciutto

SERVES 4

Use either whole milk or part-skim ricotta; do not use fat-free ricotta, which has a very dry texture and bland flavor. You can substitute ziti, farfalle, campanelle, or orecchiette for the shells; however, the cup measurements will vary. See page 113 for more information on measuring pasta.

- 1 cup ricotta cheese (see note)
- 1 ounce Parmesan cheese, grated (about ½ cup)
- 1 teaspoon grated lemon zest plus 1 tablespoon fresh lemon juice
  Salt and pepper
- 1 tablespoon extra-virgin olive oil
- 4 ounces thinly sliced prosciutto, cut into ¼-inch pieces
- 1 onion, minced (about 1 cup)
- 2 garlic cloves, minced
- 2 cups low-sodium chicken broth
- 2 cups water
- 1 cup heavy cream
- 12 ounces (about 4½ cups) medium pasta shells (see note)
- 2 cups frozen peas
- 2 tablespoons unsalted butter, cut into 8 pieces
- 2 tablespoons chopped fresh mint

1. Combine the ricotta, Parmesan, lemon zest, ¼ teaspoon salt, and ¼ teaspoon pepper in a medium bowl and set aside.

2. Heat the oil in a 12-inch nonstick skillet over medium-high heat until shimmering. Add the prosciutto and cook until well browned and crisp, 2 to 3 minutes. Transfer the prosciutto to a paper towel–lined plate, leaving the oil in the skillet.

3. Add the onion and ½ teaspoon salt to the oil left in the skillet and cook over medium heat, stirring often, until softened, 5 to 7 minutes. Stir in the garlic and cook until fragrant, about 30 seconds.

4. Stir in the broth, water, and cream, then add the pasta. Increase the heat to high and cook at a vigorous simmer, stirring often, until the pasta is tender and the liquid has thickened, 15 to 18 minutes.

5. Stir in the peas, butter, and lemon juice and cook until the peas are hot, about 1 minute. Season with salt and pepper to taste. Dot heaping tablespoons of the ricotta mixture over the pasta. Cover and let stand off the heat until the cheese warms and softens, 2 to 4 minutes. Sprinkle with the prosciutto and mint and serve.

GARLICKY SHRIMP PASTA

IN THEORY, garlic shrimp pasta has all the makings of an ideal weeknight meal. Toss a few quick-cooking ingredients—shrimp, garlic, oil, and wine—with boiled dried pasta, and only the salad's left holding up dinner.

As with most theories, of course, reality has a way of rearing its ugly head. Delicate shrimp cooks fast, which translates to overcooked in a matter of seconds. Meanwhile, volatile garlic is all over the map: Like a high-maintenance friend, it can become overbearing or bitter (or simply disappear), depending on how it's treated. Add to that the challenge of getting a brothy sauce to coat the pasta, and this simple recipe turns into a precarious balancing act. But I still wanted it all: al dente pasta and moist shrimp bound by a supple sauce infused with a deep garlic flavor.

Before facing the garlic problem, I tackled the shrimp. Because most shrimp are frozen once caught—and the flavor and texture degrade quickly once thawed—the test kitchen prefers buying IQF (individually quick-frozen) shrimp and thawing it ourselves (which takes only minutes in a colander under cold running water).

We've also found that freezing prepeeled, deveined shrimp sabotages flavor, so it's worth saving those tasks for home, too. I ruled out medium-sized shrimp because they cook too fast, as well as expensive extra-large and jumbo, landing on mid-priced-but-meaty large shrimp.

In most shrimp pasta recipes, the shrimp are cooked separately, then tossed with the sauce and pasta at the end. But how to cook them? Searing quickly over high heat was too risky, yielding an overcooked texture. Poaching in a court-bouillon (water enhanced with wine and aromatics) kept the shrimp moist but didn't contribute much flavor. I tentatively settled on sautéing them gently in garlic and oil while building the sauce.

Starting with a basic working recipe, I sautéed the shrimp with three cloves of minced garlic in a modest amount of olive oil. Removing the shrimp, I added a pinch of red pepper flakes and a cup of white wine, reduced the sauce, then tossed it with the shrimp and boiled linguine. The results were just OK: weak garlic, moist but lackluster shrimp, and a thinnish sauce that dripped off the pasta.

Upping the garlic by increments until I reached six cloves gave me indisputably garlicky pasta. But now I had a new problem: All that garlic cooked unevenly. Sautéed too little, and the pasta suffered that raw flavor that takes your breath away; too long, and random burnt granules imparted a bitter taste. Turning the heat to the lowest setting and simmering the garlic longer yielded a sweet, nutty taste, but we missed the brasher notes.

I decided to split the difference. First, I slowly simmered the oil with smashed garlic cloves (more effective in this task than minced) over low heat, discarded the toasted cloves, and built the sauce using the infused oil. Just before adding the wine, I quickly sautéed a smaller amount of minced garlic. With sweet low notes from the infused oil and brasher high notes from the minced, I finally had the balanced, deeply layered garlic flavor I wanted. When tasters noted that the shrimp itself was still short on flavor, I marinated it for 20 minutes with additional minced garlic.

Next, I tinkered with the sauce. To deglaze the pan, I tried replacing the wine with sherry, Marsala, and Madeira, but tasters preferred the cleaner taste of dry vermouth or white wine. Bottled clam broth added after the vermouth contributed seaworthy complexity, bolstering the shrimp flavor. To get the sauce to cling to the pasta, I stirred a little flour into the oil as a

thickener just before adding the liquid and added some cold butter to finish.

Presumably at the finish line, I served up my deep-flavored, luxurious-textured pasta. But tasters remarked that the shrimp stayed hidden in a tangle of linguine, and there simply weren't enough bites. Swapping out traditional linguine for a chunky tubular pasta (we liked mezze rigatoni) made it easy to find the shrimp, and cutting each shrimp into thirds before cooking ensured that nearly every bite boasted a tasty morsel.

—FRANCISCO J. ROBERT, *Cook's Illustrated*

Garlicky Shrimp Pasta

SERVES 4

Marinate the shrimp while you prepare the remaining ingredients.

5	garlic cloves, minced (about 5 teaspoons), plus 4 cloves, smashed
1	pound large shrimp (21 to 25 per pound), peeled and deveined, each shrimp cut into 3 pieces
3	tablespoons olive oil
	Salt
1	pound short tubular pasta such as mezze rigatoni, fusilli, or campanelle
¼–½	teaspoon red pepper flakes
2	teaspoons unbleached all-purpose flour
½	cup dry vermouth or white wine
¾	cup clam juice
½	cup chopped fresh parsley
3	tablespoons unsalted butter
1	teaspoon fresh lemon juice plus 1 lemon, cut into wedges for serving
	Pepper

1. Toss 2 teaspoons of the minced garlic, shrimp, 1 tablespoon of the oil, and ¼ teaspoon salt in a medium bowl. Let the shrimp marinate at room temperature for 20 minutes.

2. Heat the smashed garlic cloves and remaining 2 tablespoons oil in a 12-inch skillet over medium-low heat, stirring occasionally, until the garlic is light golden brown, 4 to 7 minutes. Remove the skillet from the heat and use a slotted spoon to remove the garlic from the skillet; discard the garlic. Set the skillet aside.

3. Bring 4 quarts water to a boil in a large Dutch oven over high heat. Add 1 tablespoon salt and the pasta. Cook, stirring often, until just al dente. Drain the pasta, reserving ¼ cup of the cooking water, and transfer the pasta back to the Dutch oven.

4. Meanwhile, return the skillet with the oil to medium heat; add the shrimp with the marinade to the skillet in a single layer. Cook the shrimp, undisturbed, until the oil starts to bubble gently, 1 to 2 minutes. Stir the shrimp and continue to cook until almost cooked through, about 1 minute longer. Using a slotted spoon, transfer the shrimp to a medium bowl. Add the remaining 3 teaspoons minced garlic and the red pepper flakes to the skillet and cook until fragrant, about 1 minute. Add the flour and cook, stirring constantly, for 1 minute; stir in the vermouth and cook for 1 minute. Add the clam juice and parsley; cook until the mixture starts to thicken, 1 to 2 minutes. Off the heat, whisk in the butter and lemon juice. Add the shrimp and sauce to the pasta, adjusting the consistency with up to ¼ cup reserved pasta cooking water. Season with pepper to taste. Serve, passing the lemon wedges separately.

NOTES FROM THE TEST KITCHEN

THE BEST CLAM JUICE
We sampled three brands of bottled clam juice and found that the fresh, bright taste of **Bar Harbor** boosted our pasta's seafood flavor best, keeping the shrimp from getting stranded in a sea of garlic.

STORING DEFROSTED SHRIMP
Since almost all shrimp you buy from a fish counter have been frozen (and usually thawed by the retailer), we recommend buying individually quick-frozen (IQF) shrimp rather than thawed shrimp. This puts you in control of how long the shrimp are stored once they are defrosted. To find out how long defrosted shrimp can be stored, we defrosted 1 pound of frozen shrimp every day for a week, refrigerating each defrosted batch. At the end of the week we peeled and deveined the shrimp and steamed each batch separately to evaluate differences in flavor and texture. Shrimp stored in the refrigerator for five days had a mushy texture, a slight off-flavor, and a distinctly fishy and ammoniated odor. (Shrimp stored longer were inedible.) As raw shrimp age, enzymes begin breaking down the proteins in the flesh, creating a mealy texture. So the best approach is to defrost them the same day you plan to cook them. If you want to buy defrosted shrimp at the fish counter, insist on smelling them first to assess freshness. If they're firm and have no ammonia-like odor, go ahead and buy the defrosted shrimp, but make sure to cook them within a day.

MAKE-AHEAD CREAMY MACARONI AND CHEESE

HOMEMADE MACARONI AND CHEESE is an easy dish with unbeatable payoff in creamy goodness. But just try freezing it. Or rather, don't. I did, and it was a disaster: The noodles bloated, the sauce curdled, and the entire dish dried out. I wanted to be able to pull macaroni and cheese from the freezer on busy weeknights for an easy supper. But it's not convenient if it's not edible.

To make mac and cheese from scratch, you boil macaroni until al dente; make a white sauce by whisking flour into melted butter and stirring in milk and shredded cheese; combine the two; dot with seasoned, buttered bread crumbs; and bake. One from-the-freezer recipe I found used a higher ratio of sauce to macaroni than typical—about 5½ cups sauce to 1 pound pasta. I figured the extra sauce was intended to keep the pasta from drying out. Since it wasn't quite accomplishing that, I increased the volume of milk. An additional ¼ cup did little, so I tried an extra ½ cup. I stirred in the cheese (a blend of mild colby, which melts nicely, and extra-sharp cheddar, for bold flavor), mixed the sauce and noodles together, and poured it all into a 13 by 9-inch baking dish. The loose mix looked like soup but, amazingly, when I baked it after freezing, it was thick and moist.

It was still curdling, though. I knew from test kitchen experience that heavy cream might be my answer. Cream has more fat and therefore less protein (casein) than milk, and it's the protein that's prone to curdling. When I tried the sauce with heavy cream, the problem disappeared, as predicted. But it was far too rich. Cutting the cream with chicken broth lightened it. For added insurance, I cooled the boiled noodles on a baking sheet instead of rinsing them in a colander. I knew the starch that clings to cooked noodles would do its bit to keep the sauce nice and thick.

The flavor was getting there, but the noodles remained mushy. They seemed to be drinking up the cream sauce. A colleague suggested I try undercooking them. Instead of boiling them until al dente, I pulled them out of the boiling water after just 3 minutes. I made, froze, and baked a casserole with the undercooked noodles. Problem solved. But the final product took an eternity to bake, and I began to doubt that the frozen lump in its center would ever thaw. The solution? I divided the mixture between two 8-inch square baking dishes. I took one out of the freezer and microwaved it for about 10 minutes to speed

MAKE-AHEAD CREAMY MACARONI AND CHEESE

ASSEMBLING MAKE-AHEAD MAC AND CHEESE

The freezer wreaks havoc with foods, robbing them of moisture and causing other problems. We had to figure out how to safeguard our make-ahead macaroni and cheese.

1. Undercook the pasta, boiling it for just 3 minutes; it will finish cooking in the oven.

2. Spread the pasta on a baking sheet instead of rinsing to cool it quickly but retain its starches (which help stabilize the sauce).

3. Make a soupy sauce to keep the dish creamy.

THE BEST ELBOW MACARONI

This pasta has become a staple in such distinctly American recipes as macaroni salad and macaroni and cheese. But with so many brands of elbow macaroni on the market, which one should you buy? To find out, we rounded up eight contenders and tasted them simply dressed with vegetable oil and in macaroni and cheese. **Barilla**, an Italian brand that makes pasta for the American market at the company's plant in Ames, Iowa, won our tasting by a large margin. Our tasters praised this pasta for its "wheaty," "buttery" flavor and "firm texture," and they especially liked that these elbows have small ridges and a slight twist that "holds sauce well." (See page 295 for more information about our testing results.)

EASIER GRATING

When grating large quantities of cheese, spray the grater or shredding disk lightly with cooking spray before grating; this reduces clumping as well as cleanup time.

the thawing process. Portioning let me reduce the oven time from an hour and 15 minutes to just 40 minutes.

One small problem remained. My mixture was soupy before I froze it, and I was stirring it periodically in the microwave to help it thaw evenly. As a result, I had to figure out when to spread the crumb topping over the casseroles. I froze the crumbs separately, sprinkling them over the macaroni and cheese after it had baked for 20 minutes and had a chance to firm up a bit. In the remaining 20 minutes, the topping crisped and browned, and the inviting smell called everyone to dinner.

—MEGHAN ERWIN, *Cook's Country*

Make-Ahead Creamy Macaroni and Cheese

SERVES 8 TO 10

You will need 2 microwave-safe 8-inch square baking dishes for this recipe.

- 4 slices high-quality white sandwich bread, torn into pieces
- ¼ cup grated Parmesan cheese
- 1 garlic clove, minced
- 8 tablespoons (1 stick) unsalted butter, melted
  Salt
- 1 pound elbow macaroni
- 6 tablespoons unbleached all-purpose flour
- 1 teaspoon dry mustard
- ⅛ teaspoon cayenne pepper
- 4½ cups low-sodium chicken broth
- 1½ cups heavy cream
- 1 pound colby cheese, shredded (about 4 cups)
- 8 ounces extra-sharp cheddar cheese, shredded (about 2 cups)
- ½ teaspoon pepper

1. Pulse the bread, Parmesan, garlic, and 2 tablespoons of the butter in a food processor until coarsely ground. Divide the crumb mixture between 2 zipper-lock bags and freeze for up to 2 months.

2. Bring 4 quarts water to a boil in a large Dutch oven over high heat. Add 1 tablespoon salt and the macaroni and cook, stirring often, until barely softened, about 3 minutes. Drain the pasta, then spread it out on a rimmed baking sheet and let cool.

3. Heat the remaining 6 tablespoons butter, flour, mustard, and cayenne in the now-empty pot over medium-high heat, stirring constantly, until golden and fragrant, 1 to 2 minutes. Slowly whisk in the broth and cream and bring to a boil. Reduce the heat to medium and simmer until slightly thickened, about 15 minutes. Off the heat, whisk in the colby, cheddar, 1 teaspoon salt, and the pepper until smooth.

4. Stir the cooled pasta into the sauce, breaking up any clumps, until well combined. Divide the pasta mixture between two 8-inch square baking dishes. Cool to room temperature, about 2 hours. Cover the dishes tightly with plastic wrap, cover with foil, and freeze for up to 2 months.

5. Adjust an oven rack to the middle position and heat the oven to 375 degrees. Remove the foil from the casserole and reserve. Microwave the casserole until the mixture is thawed and beginning to bubble around the edges, 7 to 12 minutes, stirring and replacing the plastic halfway through the cooking time. (If preparing both dishes, microwave them one at a time.) Discard the plastic and cover the pan with the reserved foil. Bake for 20 minutes, then remove the foil and sprinkle with 1 bag of the frozen bread crumbs. (If preparing both dishes, sprinkle the second bag of crumbs over the second dish.) Continue to bake until the crumbs are golden brown and crisp, about 20 minutes longer. Let cool for 10 minutes and serve.

SKILLET RAMEN WITH BEEF, SHIITAKES, AND SPINACH

RAMEN NOODLES HAVE THE REPUTATION OF BEING a mainstay on college campuses across the country. They are cheap and cook quickly, making them a convenient dinner for the thrifty, time-crunched cook. However, in Japan, ramen (or ramen soup) is a much more serious endeavor, with ramen shops on almost every street corner and noodles served in a variety of richly flavored broths. I wanted to see if I could give these noodles a fresh, new flavor by incorporating them into a simple one-skillet dish.

I started by pitching the seasoning packets that come in packages of ramen—they're loaded with a day's worth of sodium, not to mention stale, dehydrated ingredients that I can't even pronounce. To create my own broth in which to simmer the noodles, I sautéed fresh garlic and ginger; to that I added chicken broth and a splash of soy sauce, which provided a nice base for the broth.

It took me a few tries to get the correct ratio of broth to noodles. If I used too much broth, the flavors were diluted and the noodles turned mushy. In the end I settled on 3½ cups of broth and 12 ounces of noodles.

To turn my ramen dish into a substantial meal, I decided to add some beef. Tasters approved of thinly sliced flank steak, to which I added shiitake mushrooms and spinach for a classic Asian combination. Before cooking the beef, I sliced it thin and tossed it with a little soy sauce for flavor and to promote browning. I sautéed it briefly over high heat until it was just cooked through and then set it aside, to be returned to the skillet when the noodles were done simmering in the broth.

Finally, I focused on the noodles. I was a little hesitant to use the dried ramen noodles that flood grocery store shelves. For comparison, I sought out dried ramen from an Asian market (although they seemed indistinguishable from their supermarket counterpart), along with high-end chuka soba noodles (noodles made from all wheat flour or a combination of wheat and buckwheat flours) and fresh Chinese egg noodles. Chuka soba noodles were much thinner and, frankly, didn't have as much flavor as the more common dried ramen noodles. That might be because dried ramen noodles are actually fried as part of the drying process. This frying instills a richer flavor, which in my tests gave

HOW TO SLICE FLANK STEAK
To make cutting the steak easier, place the whole flank in the freezer for 20 minutes to firm up.

1. Cut the flank steak in half lengthwise.

2. Working with one half at a time, slice the steak on the bias into ¼-inch-thick pieces.

them an advantage over fresh noodles. Plus, the ramen noodles instantly soaked up the rich broth when they hit the skillet.

Quick-cooking and easy to prepare, this simple skillet supper makes a unique and satisfying weeknight meal.

—SUZANNAH MCFERRAN, *America's Test Kitchen Books*

Skillet Ramen with Beef, Shiitakes, and Spinach

SERVES 4

Do not substitute other types of noodles for the ramen noodles here. The sauce will seem a bit brothy when finished, but the liquid will be absorbed quickly by the noodles.

- 1 pound flank steak, trimmed and sliced thin across the grain on the bias (see page 123)
- 8 teaspoons soy sauce
- 2 tablespoons vegetable oil
- 8 ounces shiitake mushrooms, stemmed and sliced thin
- 3 garlic cloves, minced
- 1 tablespoon grated or minced fresh ginger
- 3½ cups low-sodium chicken broth
- 4 (3-ounce) packages ramen noodles, seasoning packets discarded (see note)
- 3 tablespoons dry sherry
- 2 teaspoons sugar
- 1 (6-ounce) bag baby spinach

1. Pat the beef dry with paper towels and toss with 2 teaspoons of the soy sauce. Heat 1 tablespoon of the oil in a 12-inch nonstick skillet over high heat until just smoking. Add the beef, break up any clumps, and cook without stirring until beginning to brown, about 1 minute. Stir the beef and continue to cook until it is nearly cooked though, 1 minute longer. Transfer the beef to a bowl, cover to keep warm, and set aside.

2. Wipe out the skillet with paper towels. Add the remaining 1 tablespoon oil to the skillet and return to medium-high heat until shimmering. Add the mushrooms and cook until browned, about 4 minutes. Stir in the garlic and ginger and cook until fragrant, about 30 seconds.

3. Stir in the broth. Break the bricks of ramen into small chunks and add to the skillet. Bring to a simmer and cook, tossing the ramen constantly with tongs to separate, until the ramen is just tender but there is still liquid in the pan, about 2 minutes.

4. Stir in the remaining 2 tablespoons soy sauce, the sherry, and sugar. Stir in the spinach, one handful at a time, until it is wilted and the sauce is thickened. Return the beef, along with any accumulated juices, to the skillet and cook until warmed through, about 30 seconds. Serve.

SLOW-COOKER MEATBALLS IN MARINARA SAUCE

MAKING BIG, LITTLE ITALY–SIZED MEATBALLS IS EASY. Making them tender and moist, with enough structure to hold their shape in the slow cooker, is not so simple. Most recipes rely on two tricks: mixing the usual ground beef with ground pork (for flavor and texture) and adding a panade, a paste made from bread and milk. The panade adds both moisture and tenderness to the meatballs. But as soon as I made my first batch I could see that I was in trouble. The moment the meatballs went into the slow cooker, they collapsed under their own weight.

Stepping back, I took a good look at meatball basics: the meat, the binders, and the flavorings. Cutting back on the milk was an obvious way to make the meatballs sturdier, but I quickly learned that cutting the milk out completely wasn't an option—without it, the meatballs turned rubbery and tough. Adding back the milk a tablespoon at a time, I landed on a good balance of tenderness and sturdiness by using just ⅓ cup.

Using a higher ratio of beef to pork also helped the meatballs hold together better during the long cooking time. A beef-to-pork ratio of 5 to 1 was just right. Without the extra pork, however, the flavor of the meatballs was a bit bland. Then a colleague suggested substituting raw Italian sausage for the ground pork. This turned out to be a great idea—not only was I able to boost the flavor of the meatballs a bit, but buying small amounts of sausage is often easier and more convenient than buying small amounts of ground pork. To boost the flavor of the meatballs further, I found it important to add some sautéed onion, garlic, red pepper flakes, and dried oregano. Finished with some fresh parsley and a handful of Parmesan cheese, these meatballs now had some serious flavor.

Most meatball recipes fry the meatballs first to help firm them up and rid them of excess grease, and the browned bits left in the pan after frying are used to flavor the sauce. Yet frying these huge meatballs, even in our largest pan, needed to be done in two batches, and the resulting crust on the exterior of the meatballs was tough. I thought of baking the meatballs in the oven to release some of their fat without creating a crust, but waiting for the oven to heat up didn't make this recipe any more convenient. Frustrated, I did something unexpected and turned to the microwave. My reasoning was this—I needed to cook the meatballs just enough to allow them to exude most of their fat and firm up the meat without making the exterior tough, while still keeping things simple. As it turned out, this worked beautifully; it took only about five minutes on high power.

I finally turned my attention to the sauce. To compensate for the missing fried-meatball flavor, I sautéed my aromatics with tomato paste, then deglazed the pan with red wine before pouring the mixture into the slow cooker along with tomatoes, the foundation of the sauce, and soy sauce for added depth. As it turned out, the sauce required exactly the same sautéed aromatics as the meatballs, so to simplify things I sautéed a single large batch, using half for the meatballs and half for the sauce.

I experimented with various tomato products for my sauce—diced, pureed, and crushed. Diced tomatoes didn't blend into the sauce as much as I would have liked, and everyone agreed that tomato puree was too sweet and too thick. Crushed tomatoes gave me both the fresh flavor and the smooth, light texture that I was seeking. The resulting sauce had a deep crimson color and a deep, rich flavor. Once my sauce was in the slow cooker and ready to go, I added my microwaved meatballs and let the cooking go from there.

With the pairing of a satisfying sauce and perfected meatballs, I had a dish that tasted like it was delivered straight from Little Italy—maybe even better.

—BRYAN ROOF, *America's Test Kitchen Books*

Slow-Cooker Meatballs in Marinara Sauce

SERVES 6, ENOUGH FOR 1½ POUNDS OF PASTA

The quality of crushed tomatoes varies quite a bit from brand to brand; we prefer Tuttorosso and Muir Glen. Be sure to reserve half of the mixture for the meatballs before adding the wine to the skillet.

- 2 tablespoons vegetable oil
- 2 onions, minced (about 2 cups)
- ¼ cup tomato paste
- 8 garlic cloves, minced
- 1½ teaspoons dried oregano
- ¼ teaspoon red pepper flakes
- Salt
- ½ cup dry red wine
- 2 (28-ounce) cans crushed tomatoes (see note)
- ½ cup water
- 2 tablespoons soy sauce
- 2 slices high-quality white sandwich bread, torn into large pieces
- ⅓ cup milk
- 1½ ounces Parmesan cheese, grated (about ¾ cup)
- ¼ cup chopped fresh parsley
- 2 large eggs, lightly beaten
- 1¼ pounds 90 percent lean ground beef
- ¼ pound sweet Italian sausage, casings removed
- 2 tablespoons chopped fresh basil
- 1-2 teaspoons sugar

1. Heat the oil in a 12-inch nonstick skillet over medium-high heat until shimmering. Add the onions, tomato paste, 6 cloves of the garlic, oregano, red pepper flakes, and ¼ teaspoon salt and cook, stirring often, until the onions are softened and lightly browned, 8 to 10 minutes.

2. Transfer half the onion mixture to a large bowl and set aside. Stir the wine into the skillet with the remaining onion mixture, scraping up any browned bits. Transfer the onion–red wine mixture to the slow cooker and stir in the tomatoes, water, and soy sauce until evenly combined.

3. Add the bread and milk to the bowl of reserved onion mixture and mash together until smooth. Stir in ½ cup of the Parmesan, parsley, eggs, remaining 2 garlic cloves, and ¾ teaspoon salt. Add the ground beef and sausage and knead with your hands until thoroughly combined. Form the mixture into twelve 2-inch meatballs. Place the meatballs on a large microwave-safe plate and microwave on full power until most of the fat is rendered, about 5 minutes.

4. Nestle the meatballs in the slow cooker, discarding the rendered fat. Cover and cook on low until the meatballs are tender and the sauce is slightly thickened, 4 to 5 hours.

5. Let the cooking liquid settle for 5 minutes, then gently tilt the slow cooker and remove as much fat as possible from the surface using a large spoon. Gently stir the remaining ¼ cup Parmesan and basil into the sauce and season with salt and sugar to taste before serving.

CHAPTER 6

MEAT

Green Chile Cheeseburgers   128

Steak Tacos with Sweet
and Spicy Pickled Onions   130

Reuben Sandwiches   134

Braised Beef Short Ribs   135

Braised Beef Short Ribs
with Guinness and Prunes

Pan-Seared Strip Steak
with Crispy Potatoes and
Salsa Verde   137

Chicken-Fried Steak   139

Swedish Meatballs
with Pickled Cucumbers   142

Grilled Beef Teriyaki   144

Shredded Barbecued Beef   148

Slow-Cooker Barbecued
Beef Brisket   149

Texas Barbecued Beef Ribs   152

Baltimore Pit Beef   155

Roast Beef Tenderloin   157

Beef en Cocotte with
Caramelized Onions   159

Classic Roast Beef
and Gravy   160

Glazed Meat Loaf   163

Pan-Fried Pork Chops   164

Barbecued Pan-Fried
Pork Chops

Herbed Pan-Fried
Pork Chops

Spiced Pork Tenderloin
with Potato Rösti   167

Atomic Ribs   168

Grill-Roasted Ham   170

Holiday Stuffed Roast Pork   172

Holiday Roast Pork
with Cherry Stuffing

Grilled Rack of Lamb   174

Grilled Rack of Lamb
with Sweet Mustard Glaze

GREEN CHILE CHEESEBURGERS

GREEN CHILES SHOW UP ON MENUS everywhere in New Mexico. Farmers harvest the chiles in late summer, when they are bought by the bushel to be roasted and frozen for year-round use. It's no wonder the chiles make their way into so many dishes, including muffins, apple pie, and even chocolate ice cream. One especially beloved tradition is the green chile burger. At roadside restaurants all over New Mexico, ground beef patties are grilled to a crusty brown and topped with fire-roasted, chopped chiles and a slice of cheese.

Wanting to duplicate these burgers without hopping on a plane, I mail-ordered a batch of fire-roasted, hot green chiles from Hatch, New Mexico, the self-proclaimed green chile capital of the country. Almost as soon as they arrived, I headed out to grill some burgers. As advertised, the chiles had intense heat and a captivating sweet and smoky flavor. Nonetheless, waiting for chiles in the mail so I could make a burger was out of the question. To bring this regional favorite out of the Southwest, I'd need to use ordinary supermarket ingredients.

Most recipes suggest canned chiles as a substitute. We found them tinny and so mild that you could eat them by the spoonful. Casting about at the supermarket for an alternative, I spied Anaheim chiles, which do, in fact, grow in New Mexico. Experts say that the state's hot, arid climate produces hotter Anaheims than those grown in California or Florida, the states that supply most supermarkets around the country. I roasted my supermarket Anaheims and found them far milder than the Hatch ones I'd mail-ordered. To fix that, I tried combining them with poblano peppers, which have a spicy, smoky edge. The mix tasted unpleasantly vegetal, and the heat barely registered. Moving up the heat scale, I combined the Anaheims with jalapeños. Much better! These came close to the mail-order chiles. To round out the flavor, I added sautéed onions and garlic to the chiles. Rather than dirtying a pan, I simply grilled the onions with the chiles, then chopped them with fresh garlic in the food processor.

Now that the topping was in order, I turned to the burger. Tasters preferred the flavor of 85 percent lean ground beef. To shape the burgers, I used a proven test kitchen technique—making a small indentation in each patty to keep them from buckling and dislodging the topping. I grilled the burgers to medium doneness over high heat. They were juicy and meaty, but tasters complained the chiles were being upstaged. The obvious solution was extra topping, but if I heaped on any more, it'd just fall into the grill. What if I put chiles into the burgers? This time, I set aside some of my chile mixture for the topping and pureed the rest into a smooth sauce, which I then mixed into the ground raw meat. These burgers packed a pleasurable, hot punch through and through.

I flipped a final batch of burgers over and topped them with spoonfuls of chile mixture and a slice of cheese (tasters preferred American to cheddar or Monterey Jack for its melting ability); the cheese melted as the burgers finished cooking, which helped the topping stay put. The burgers, by contrast, were ready to travel—from New Mexico straight into your kitchen.

—LYNN CLARK, *Cook's Country*

Green Chile Cheeseburgers

SERVES 4

For more heat, include the jalapeño ribs and seeds. In step 3, you may need to add a teaspoon or two of water to the food processor to help the chile mixture puree. Pressing a shallow divot in the center of each burger patty keeps the burgers flat during grilling.

- 3 **Anaheim chiles, stemmed, seeded, and halved lengthwise**
- 3 **jalapeño chiles, stemmed, seeded, and halved lengthwise (see note)**
- 1 **onion, sliced into ½-inch-thick rounds**
- 1 **garlic clove, minced**
  Salt and pepper
- 1½ **pounds 85 percent lean ground beef**
- 4 **slices deli American cheese**

1A. FOR A CHARCOAL GRILL: Open the bottom grill vents completely. Light a large chimney starter filled with charcoal briquettes (100 briquettes; 6 quarts). When the coals are hot, pour them in an even layer over the grill. Set the cooking grate in place, cover, and open the grill vents completely. Heat the grill until hot, about 5 minutes.

1B. FOR A GAS GRILL: Turn all the burners to high, cover, and heat the grill until hot, about 15 minutes. (Adjust the burners as needed to maintain a hot fire; see page 130).

GREEN CHILE CHEESEBURGERS

2. Clean and oil the cooking grate. Lay the chiles and onion on the grill and cook until the vegetables are lightly charred and tender, 2 to 4 minutes per side. Transfer the vegetables to a bowl, cover, and let sit for 5 minutes. Remove the skins from the chiles and discard; separate the onion rounds into rings.

3. Transfer the chiles, onion, and garlic to a food processor and pulse until coarsely chopped, about 10 pulses. Transfer all but ¼ cup of the chopped chile mixture to the empty bowl and season with salt and pepper to taste; set aside. Process the remaining mixture until smooth.

4. Combine the beef, pureed chile mixture, ½ teaspoon salt, and ¼ teaspoon pepper in a large bowl and knead gently until well incorporated. Shape into four ¾-inch-thick patties and press a shallow divot in the center of each (see note).

5. Grill the burgers, covered, until well browned on the first side, 3 to 5 minutes. Flip the burgers, top each with the chopped chile mixture and 1 slice of cheese, and continue to grill, covered, until the cheese is melted and the burgers are cooked to desired doneness, 3 to 5 minutes longer. Serve.

NOTES FROM THE TEST KITCHEN

USE TWO TYPES OF CHILES
For complex green chile flavor outside of New Mexico, we found that a 1:1 ratio of Anaheims and jalapeños has a nice peppery balance. Anaheim chiles add a mildly sweet, grassy flavor, while jalapeño chiles have just enough heat to stand up to the beefiness of the burger.

ANAHEIM CHILE   **JALAPEÑO CHILES**

HOW HOT IS YOUR FIRE?
To determine the heat level of the cooking grate itself, heat up the grill and hold your hand 5 inches above the cooking grate, counting how long you can comfortably keep it there. This works with both charcoal and gas grills.

Hot fire	2 seconds
Medium-hot fire	3 to 4 seconds
Medium fire	5 to 6 seconds
Medium-low fire	7 seconds

STEAK TACOS

BEEF TACOS MADE INDOORS are typically the pedestrian ground-beef kind, stuffed into a crisp corn tortilla and loaded with cheese and shredded lettuce. More upscale steak tacos, modeled after authentic Mexican carne asada, are generally reserved for the grill. Here a thin cut of beef, typically skirt or flank steak, is marinated, then grilled, cut into pieces, and served in a soft corn tortilla with simple garnishes. Done properly, the meat has rich, grilled flavor and the tacos themselves are simple to throw together.

Given the choice, I'd almost always prefer the beefier (and let's face it—better) flavors of a steak taco over a ground beef one, but what about those times when cooking outdoors isn't possible? I wanted to develop a method for bringing steak tacos indoors that would yield meat as tender, juicy, and rich-tasting as the grilled kind.

My first task was to choose the right cut of meat. Traditional Mexican recipes typically call for skirt or flank steak for taco meat, both of which come from the belly of the cow. Tasters liked the well-marbled skirt steak, but I found that availability of this cut was spotty. Flank steak is more widely available, has a nice beefy flavor, and, when sliced thinly against the grain, is very tender.

Unadorned, the flank steak was good, but I wondered if I could render the meat even juicier. I found that, similar to brining, sprinkling the meat with a liberal dose of salt and allowing it to sit for an hour markedly boosted juiciness. I was able to reduce that time to just 30 minutes by poking holes into the steak with a fork, which allowed the salt to sink more quickly into the meat's interior.

Given that the grill was the inspiration for this recipe, I wanted to try to mimic the browned exterior and crisp, brittle edges of grilled meat as much as possible. I figured that the intense heat of the oven's broiler would most closely resemble that of a grill and decided to start there. But after several tests, I knew the oven would never work with a thin cut like flank steak. While the broiler was able to brown the exterior of the meat, this didn't occur until the steak was way overcooked.

Pan-searing proved to be a much more promising method that allowed me to achieve some decent browning. But I wanted more. I tried increasing the surface area by butterflying the steak, but this was a tedious process that didn't yield significantly better results. Next I experimented with cutting the steak lengthwise with the grain into four long strips about 2½ inches wide and 1 inch thick. The results were great. Because the strips were relatively thick, I now had double the number of exposed edges—four sides instead of two—to make crisp and super-flavorful. I had two more tricks up my sleeve to promote caramelization and boost flavor even further: I sprinkled the steak pieces with a little sugar before browning and increased the oil I was cooking them in from 2 teaspoons to 2 tablespoons.

With a successful cooking method squared away, I now looked at adding some other flavor dimensions to the steak. My first thought was to incorporate a dry spice rub when I salted the meat. But after a couple of tests I found that the spice rub just tasted dusty and raw. A wet rub or paste, provided it was removed before cooking so it wouldn't impede browning, seemed a better option. After looking into traditional marinades, I settled on a combination of cilantro, scallions, garlic, and jalapeño. Processed into a pestolike paste with some oil, this marinade added fresh flavors to the steak. And when coupled with the salt, the oil-based marinade was pulled into the steak, flavoring it throughout. I reserved some of the marinade to toss with the steak after it was sliced. This brightened the flavor and presentation considerably.

For garnishes, I chose raw onion, cilantro leaves, and lime wedges—all of which echoed the flavors in my marinade. Tasters also liked thinly sliced radishes and cucumber for the contrast in texture they provided to the steak. Lastly, I experimented with making some quick pickled vegetables, which I loosely based on *curtido* (a relish commonly served in Latin America). Tasters loved onions I "pickled" in a mixture of sugar and red wine vinegar enlivened by a couple of jalapeños. I now had a great-tasting alternative to the ubiquitous ground beef taco—one that could even be made in the middle of winter and in no time at all.

—KEITH DRESSER, *Cook's Illustrated*

OUR FAVORITE SPATULAS

We evaluated 10 heatproof rubber (also called silicone) spatulas, all dishwasher-safe, running each through nine tests, including lifting omelets, scraping the bowl of a food processor, making a pan sauce, and stirring risotto. We also simmered the spatulas in a pot of tomato-curry sauce and then ran them through the dishwasher to see if they would come through clean and odor-free. Our favorites are the **Rubbermaid Professional 13½-Inch Heat Resistant Scraper,** $23.50 (top), and the **Tovolo Silicone Spatula** (bottom), which at $8.99 is our best buy. The Rubbermaid is a practical, no-nonsense spatula that aced every cooking test, with a great balance of flexibility and firmness in both the head and the handle. The Tovolo passed every performance test, scraping, stirring, folding, and sautéing like a champ. It also withstood our attempts to stain and melt it. The Tovolo's good looks and nice price make it hard to resist, but, in the end, the larger overall size and sturdiness of the Rubbermaid won our highest accolades. (See page 304 for more information about our testing results.)

SHOPPING FOR CORN TORTILLAS

The rule of thumb when buying tortillas is to buy a brand made with nothing more than ground corn treated with lime (an alkali that removes the germ and hull) and water. Look for brands sold in the refrigerator case of the supermarket, as these have few, if any, preservatives and tend to be more moist and flavorful.

HOW TO WARM TORTILLAS

Warming tortillas over the open flame of a gas burner or in a skillet gives them a toasted flavor; however, an oven or microwave will also work. If your tortillas are dry, pat them with a little water first.

If using a gas stove, toast the tortillas, one at a time, directly on the cooking grate over a medium flame until slightly charred around the edges, about 30 seconds per side. If using a skillet, toast the tortillas, one at a time, over medium-high heat until softened and speckled with brown, 20 to 30 seconds per side. Wrap the warmed tortillas in foil or a kitchen towel to them keep warm and soft until serving time.

If using an oven, stack the tortillas in a foil packet and heat at 350 degrees until warm and soft, about 5 minutes. Keep them in the foil until serving time. To use a microwave, stack the tortillas on a plate, cover with microwave-safe plastic wrap, and heat on high until warm and soft, 1 to 2 minutes. Remove the plastic wrap and cover the tortillas with a kitchen towel or foil to keep them warm and soft.

Steak Tacos with Sweet and Spicy Pickled Onions

SERVES 4 TO 6

For more heat, include the jalapeño ribs and seeds. We prefer this steak cooked to medium-rare, but if you prefer it more or less done see "Testing Meat for Doneness" on page 139. In addition to the toppings suggested below, try serving the tacos with thinly sliced radishes or cucumber, or salsa.

PICKLED ONIONS

- 1 red onion, halved and sliced thin
- 1 cup red wine vinegar
- ⅓ cup sugar
- 2 jalapeño chiles, seeds and ribs removed, cut into thin rings (see note)
- ¼ teaspoon salt

HERB PASTE

- ½ cup packed fresh cilantro leaves
- 3 garlic cloves, roughly chopped
- 3 scallions, roughly chopped (about ⅓ cup)
- 1 jalapeño chile, seeds and ribs removed, roughly chopped (see note)
- ½ teaspoon ground cumin
- ¼ cup vegetable oil
- 1 tablespoon fresh lime juice

STEAK

- 1 (1½ to 1¾-pound) flank steak, trimmed and cut lengthwise (with the grain) into 4 equal pieces
- 1 tablespoon kosher salt or 1½ teaspoons table salt, plus extra to taste
- ½ teaspoon sugar
- ½ teaspoon pepper
- 2 tablespoons vegetable oil

TORTILLAS AND GARNISHES

- 12 (6-inch) corn tortillas, warmed (see page 131)
  Fresh cilantro leaves
  Minced white onion
  Lime wedges

1. FOR THE PICKLED ONIONS: Place the onion in a medium heat-resistant bowl. Bring the vinegar, sugar, jalapeños, and salt to a simmer in a small saucepan over medium-high heat, stirring occasionally, until the sugar dissolves. Pour the vinegar mixture over the onions, cover loosely, and let cool to room temperature, about 30 minutes. Once cool, drain and discard the liquid. (The pickled onions can be refrigerated in an airtight container for up to 1 week.)

2. FOR THE HERB PASTE: Pulse the cilantro, garlic, scallions, jalapeño, and cumin in a food processor until finely chopped, about 12 pulses, scraping down the sides of the bowl as necessary. Add the oil and process until the mixture is smooth and resembles pesto, about 15 seconds, scraping down the sides of bowl as necessary. Transfer 2 tablespoons of the herb paste to a medium bowl; whisk in the lime juice and set aside.

3. FOR THE STEAK: Using a dinner fork, poke each piece of steak 10 to 12 times on each side. Place in a large baking dish; rub all sides of the steak pieces evenly with the salt and then coat with the remaining herb paste. Cover with plastic wrap and refrigerate for at least 30 minutes or up to 1 hour.

4. Scrape the herb paste off the steak and sprinkle all sides of the pieces evenly with the sugar and pepper. Heat the oil in a 12-inch nonstick skillet over medium-high heat until just smoking. Place the steak in the skillet and cook until well browned, about 3 minutes. Flip the steak and sear until the second side is well browned, 2 to 3 minutes. Using tongs, stand each piece on a cut side and cook, turning as necessary, until all the cut sides are well browned and the center of the steak registers 120 to 125 degrees on an instant-read thermometer (for medium-rare), 2 to 7 minutes. Transfer the steak to a cutting board and let rest for 5 minutes.

5. Using a sharp chef's knife or carving knife, slice the steak pieces across the grain into ⅛-inch-thick pieces. Transfer the sliced steak to a bowl with the herb paste–lime juice mixture and toss to coat. Season with salt to taste. Spoon a small amount of sliced steak into the center of each warm tortilla and serve immediately, passing the pickled onions and garnishes separately.

STEAK TACOS WITH SWEET AND SPICY PICKLED ONIONS

REUBEN SANDWICHES

THE GRILLED REUBEN—sliced corned beef, tangy sauerkraut, creamy Russian or Thousand Island dressing, and melted Swiss cheese on rye—is the epitome of a New York deli sandwich. But even the *New York Times* reports that the Reuben was created in the 1920s at the Blackstone Hotel in Omaha, Nebraska, when a local grocer, Reuben Kulakofsky, concocted it for his poker buddies, then convinced the hotel owner to put it on the menu. A waitress there won a national contest with the sandwich in the 1950s, and it soon swept the country. Today, Reubens are everywhere, but most recipes I tried produced sandwiches with chilly centers, unmelted cheese, soggy rye, watery sauerkraut, and sugary supermarket dressing.

Bottled Russian and Thousand Island dressings are nearly identical: Both are made from mayonnaise, ketchup, pickle relish, vinegar, and sugar, and both were unacceptably sweet here. A homemade dressing using the same ingredients—minus the sugar—was much better, but my tasters wanted more punch. Hot peppers tasted out of place, but horseradish provided welcome heat. To streamline ingredients, I tried replacing the ketchup and horseradish with prepared cocktail sauce, and my tasters couldn't tell the difference. While most recipes use pickle relish, tasters preferred the fresher flavor and crunch of hand-chopped pickles. Finally, replacing the vinegar with pickle juice balanced tang with sweetness.

I spread the dressing on rye bread, and to combat soggy sandwich syndrome, I drained the sauerkraut and also layered it in the middle of the sandwich, with meat and cheese on either side. But the sauerkraut still exuded enough moisture to saturate the bread. Even worse, since the meat and cheese had come straight from the refrigerator, the contents of the sandwich were cold (and the cheese unmelted) by the time the bread was sufficiently browned. I tried cooking the sauerkraut in a skillet before assembling the sandwiches. This allowed the excess moisture to evaporate, plus the hot sauerkraut helped warm the meat. Cooking the sauerkraut also presented an opportunity to add flavor, and I found that adding 2 tablespoons of cider vinegar and a little brown sugar improved the sauerkraut considerably.

The interior of my Reubens was warmer, but the cheese still wasn't melting fully. The test kitchen uses shredded cheese to make grilled cheese sandwiches, and switching to shredded Swiss helped a little. A colleague suggested covering the skillet, which is how her mother taught her to make grilled cheese. I always thought covering made for soggy sandwiches, but condensation never developed in the short cooking time, and the higher temperature under the lid melted the cheese perfectly.

—LYNN CLARK, *Cook's Country*

Reuben Sandwiches

SERVES 4

Corned beef is typically made from either the brisket or the round. We prefer the corned beef brisket. We like pouched sauerkraut, sold near the pickles in most supermarkets, to jarred or canned varieties.

¼ **cup mayonnaise**

¼ **cup finely chopped sweet pickles plus 1 teaspoon sweet pickle juice**

2 **tablespoons cocktail sauce**

1 **cup sauerkraut, drained and rinsed (see note)**

2 **tablespoons cider vinegar**

1 **teaspoon brown sugar**

8 **slices rye bread**

4 **ounces Swiss cheese, shredded (about 1 cup)**

12 **ounces thinly sliced deli corned beef (see note)**

4 **tablespoons (½ stick) unsalted butter**

1. Whisk the mayonnaise, pickles, pickle juice, and cocktail sauce together in a small bowl; set aside. Cook the sauerkraut, vinegar, and sugar in a large skillet over medium-high heat, stirring occasionally, until the liquid evaporates, about 3 minutes. Transfer the sauerkraut to a bowl and wipe out the skillet.

2. Spread the dressing evenly on 1 side of each slice of bread. Layer half of the cheese on 4 slices of the bread, then top with half of the corned beef. Divide the sauerkraut evenly over the meat, then top with the remaining corned beef and remaining cheese. Arrange the remaining bread, dressing-side down, over the cheese.

3. Melt 2 tablespoons of the butter in the now-empty skillet over medium heat. Place 2 sandwiches in the pan and cook until golden brown on the first side, 2 to 3 minutes. Flip the sandwiches and cook, covered, over medium-low heat until the second side is golden brown and the cheese is melted, about 2 minutes longer. Transfer to a wire rack and repeat with the remaining butter and sandwiches. Serve.

COOK THE SAUERKRAUT

Soggy bread and a cold interior are common problems for Reuben sandwiches.

Quickly cooking the sauerkraut evaporates the excess moisture that can cause a soggy sandwich; it also helps to warm the meat and melt the cheese when placed in the middle of the sandwich.

SELECTING SAUERKRAUT

Briny, salty sauerkraut is an essential component of Reuben sandwiches. To see which brand of sauerkraut is best, we tasted eight national contenders—in jars, cans, and vacuum-sealed bags—both plain and in a Reuben. Right off the bat, tasters panned the heavily processed (and long-cooked) canned brands as limp, flavorless, and flat. Jarred and bagged brands are cooked less; these generally had more crunch and flavor. Our winning sauerkraut, **Boar's Head,** is a bagged variety that was praised for its "chewy-crisp" texture and "fresh, vinegary kick."

BRAISED BEEF SHORT RIBS

THERE MAY BE NO CUT OF MEAT BETTER suited for braising than the rich, beefy short rib. Thanks to copious amounts of fat and sinews of connective tissue, these "short" portions cut from a cow's ribs start out tough and chewy but are transformed into tender, succulent morsels through hours of braising.

Browning the ribs, then placing them in the oven with plenty of liquid until tender, is about as hands-off as it gets. But since so much fat is rendered during the ribs' three- or four-hour stint in the oven, most recipes call for resting the ribs in the braising liquid overnight, so that the fat solidifies into an easy-to-remove layer. Recognizing that most people don't plan their dinners days in advance, those same recipes usually offer home cooks the option of just skimming the fat with a spoon. That method may work fine for leaner cuts. But short ribs simply give off too much fat, and the meat and

sauce come out greasy, no matter how diligent one's spoon-wielding. There had to be a better way.

My first task was to choose the right rib. Cutting the ribs between the bones and into lengths between 2 and 6 inches yields what butchers call "English" style, a cut typically found in European braises. Cutting the meat across the bone yields the "flanken" cut, more typically found in Asian cuisines. Since English-style short ribs are more widely available, I focused my attention there, and 4-inch-long ribs were just the right size.

In an attempt to get rid of some of the excess fat, I trimmed the hard, waxy surface fat from each rib, leaving only a thin layer. But short ribs also contain a layer of fat and connective tissue between the meat and the bone. Once fully cooked, this layer shrinks into a tough, chewy strip called "strap meat." To get rid of that strip would mean cutting the meat off the bone and serving the ribs boneless.

Come to think of it, every time I'd ordered braised short ribs in a restaurant, the meat was served off the bone. Calling around to a few local chefs, I found out that most restaurant kitchens cook the meat on the bone, but since they cool the braising liquid overnight, they don't have to worry about removing all the fat on the meat. When it's time to serve the ribs, they remove the bones and excess connective tissue before reheating the meat in the defatted and reduced braising liquid.

What if I followed suit but in reverse, removing the bones before cooking? For my next batch, I simply lopped the meat from the bone in one easy cut and then trimmed the fat on both sides of the meat. As an added benefit, I now had more surface area for browning.

I was shocked by the difference in the amount of fat I ended up with. The bone-in batch rendered nearly 1½ cups of hardened fat. The boneless? A mere ¼ cup. Talk about lean and mean! The results were so shocking that I repeated the test. The outcome was the same. Removing the bones (and the fat between the bones and meat) nearly solved the greasy sauce problem. To further streamline the recipe, why not just buy boneless short ribs? Boneless short ribs generally cost about $1 more per pound than bone-in ribs, but are actually cheaper in the end. The 3 pounds of meat I wanted required 7 pounds of bone-in ribs. With boneless, I needed to buy just 3½ pounds of meat.

Using boneless ribs cut time, money, and fat, but conventional wisdom holds that bones equal flavor. I wondered if this was really the case. So I saved some bones after removing and trimming the meat and placed them into the pot along with the braising liquid. At the same time, I made a batch with only the boneless ribs. They tasted almost the same. But the dish with cooked bones did come out differently in other ways: It had significantly more body, which came from the connective tissue attached to the bone that had broken down into gelatin over time. Sprinkling a small amount (just half a teaspoon) of powdered gelatin into the sauce a few minutes before serving was easy and provided a similar supple texture.

Now I wanted to ramp up the richness of the sauce a bit. After the meat is seared in a pan over relatively high heat, most recipes call for cooking aromatics such as onions, shallots, celery, and carrots in the pan drippings before returning the meat to the pot with several cups of stock and some wine. After a few hours, meat cooked this way was certainly tender, but the liquid was thin and not very bold. Reducing the liquid improved matters somewhat, but the sauce tasted acidic and lacked balance.

I poured 2 cups of wine right over the browned aromatics and reduced it in the pan. This added just the right intensity, but I didn't end up with enough liquid to keep the meat half-submerged (the right level for braises). I needed another cup of liquid. More wine yielded too much wine flavor; tested against water and chicken broth, beef broth won out for its intensity.

But what about the ¼ cup of excess fat—much more manageable than the 2 cups I'd ended up with using bone-in ribs, but excess all the same? I found that straining and defatting the liquid in a fat separator was all I needed to produce a silky, grease-free sauce. Reducing the degreased cooking liquid to 1 cup concentrated the flavors, making a rich, luxurious sauce—the perfect complement to the fork-tender short-rib meat. And all in a few hours' work.

—DAVID PAZMIÑO, *Cook's Illustrated*

USE GELATIN

The bones in short ribs contain marrow, which contributes flavor and body to a braise. But they also contain lots of fat and have connective tissue attached to them that looks unsightly when the meat is cooked. We eliminated these problems by using boneless short ribs in our braise. Surprisingly, we didn't miss much flavor from the bones, and adding half a teaspoon of gelatin to the sauce restored any missing suppleness.

THE DIFFERENCE BETWEEN BONE-IN AND BONELESS SHORT RIBS

Although we expected that bone-in short ribs would exude more fat than their boneless counterparts, we were shocked by the dramatic difference—1½ cups versus ¼ cup (six times as much)! No wonder most short rib recipes call for letting the fat solidify overnight in the fridge.

BONE-IN = LOTS OF FAT

BONELESS = MANAGEABLE FAT

BONING AND TRIMMING SHORT RIBS

1. With a chef's knife, carefully remove the meat as close as possible to the bone.

2. Trim the excess hard fat and silver skin from both sides of the meat.

Braised Beef Short Ribs

SERVES 6

Make sure that the ribs are at least 4 inches long and 1 inch thick. If boneless ribs are unavailable, substitute 7 pounds of bone-in beef short ribs at least 4 inches long with 1 inch of meat above the bone. To remove the meat from the bone, see page 136. We recommend a bold red wine such as Cabernet Sauvignon or Côtes du Rhône. Serve with egg noodles, mashed potatoes, or roasted potatoes.

3½ pounds boneless short ribs, trimmed (see page 136) (see note)

    Kosher salt and pepper

2 tablespoons vegetable oil

2 large onions, halved and sliced thin (about 4 cups)

1 tablespoon tomato paste

6 garlic cloves, peeled

2 cups red wine (see note)

1 cup low-sodium beef broth

4 large carrots, peeled and cut crosswise into 2-inch pieces

4 sprigs fresh thyme

1 bay leaf

¼ cup cold water

½ teaspoon powdered gelatin

1. Adjust an oven rack to the lower-middle position and heat the oven to 300 degrees. Pat the beef dry with paper towels and season with 2 teaspoons salt and 1 teaspoon pepper. Heat 1 tablespoon of the oil in a large Dutch oven over medium-high heat until just smoking. Add half of the beef and cook, without moving, until well browned, 4 to 6 minutes. Turn the beef and continue to cook on the second side until well browned, 4 to 6 minutes longer, reducing the heat if the fat begins to smoke. Transfer the beef to a medium bowl. Repeat with the remaining 1 tablespoon oil and remaining meat.

2. Reduce the heat to medium, add the onions, and cook, stirring occasionally, until softened and beginning to brown, 12 to 15 minutes. (If the onions begin to darken too quickly, add 1 to 2 tablespoons water to the pan.) Add the tomato paste and cook, stirring constantly, until it browns on the sides and bottom of the pan, about 2 minutes. Add the garlic and cook until fragrant, about 30 seconds. Increase the heat to medium-high, add the wine and simmer, scraping the bottom of the pan with a wooden spoon to loosen any browned bits,

until reduced by half, 8 to 10 minutes. Add the broth, carrots, thyme, and bay leaf. Add the beef and any accumulated juices to the pot; cover and bring to a simmer. Transfer the pot to the oven and cook, using tongs to turn the meat twice during cooking, until a fork slips easily in and out of the meat, 2 to 2½ hours.

3. Place the water in a small bowl and sprinkle the gelatin on top; let stand for at least 5 minutes. Using tongs, transfer the meat and carrots to a serving platter and tent with foil. Strain the cooking liquid through a fine-mesh strainer into a fat separator or bowl, pressing on the solids to extract as much liquid as possible; discard the solids. Allow the liquid to settle about 5 minutes and strain off the fat. Return the cooking liquid to the Dutch oven and cook over medium heat until reduced to 1 cup, 5 to 10 minutes. Remove from the heat and stir in the gelatin mixture; season with salt and pepper to taste. Pour the sauce over the meat and serve.

VARIATION

Braised Beef Short Ribs with Guinness and Prunes
Follow the recipe for Braised Beef Short Ribs, substituting 1 cup Guinness (or other full-flavored porter or stout) for the red wine and omitting the 8 to 10-minute reduction time in step 2. Add ⅓ cup pitted prunes to the pot along with the broth.

PAN-SEARED STEAK WITH FRIES

WHILE STEAK AND FRIES MIGHT SEEM MUNDANE, in American chophouses this pairing has been elevated to an art form. The steak is always perfectly cooked, nicely seared and juicy-tender, and the potato wedges are fluffy on the inside with perfectly crisped exteriors. But when the home cook attempts to re-create this dish, all too often the steak is bland and flavorless, and the fries almost instantly turn soggy sitting among the steak's juices on the plate. I set out to create chophouse-caliber pan-seared steak with steak fries in my own kitchen—and all in one skillet.

I started with the steak. For a perfectly seared steak, a large, heavy skillet is key for even heat distribution, as is the right level of heat. I quickly discovered that to achieve the perfect crust, it was important to make sure of two things: the skillet should be just smoking before adding the steaks, and don't overcrowd the skillet. If the skillet is not hot enough, or if the steaks are jammed too tightly together (which will cause the pan to cool down), the steaks will end up stewing rather than searing. And because moving the steaks releases their liquid, once they were in the pan I made sure to let them be. Getting a deep brown crust on the first side took about five minutes, then I flipped them, reduced the heat to medium, and continued cooking until they were medium-rare (120 to 125 degrees), another five to ten minutes. I found it best to always undercook the steaks a bit to allow for carryover cooking as the steaks rest.

Next I tackled the potatoes. Not only did sautéing them allow me to forgo the messy business of deep-frying, but the results were far less greasy. From past test kitchen experience, I knew that high-starch russet potatoes make the best steak fries, but simply dumping a handful of raw potato wedges into a hot skillet with a modicum of oil left tasters chewing on charred fries with raw centers. Upping the amount of oil to 4 tablespoons helped me achieve more evenly golden fries, but it did little to solve the undercooked middles. That's when I decided I should parcook the potatoes in the microwave before adding them to the skillet. This meant I could get the potatoes started while the steaks seared, and then sauté the potatoes just long enough to finish cooking their interiors and crisp up their exteriors. The microwave also helped make the interior of the fries light and fluffy, as if they had been deep-fried.

As a crowning touch, we decided to top our steak with salsa verde, a rustic, pureed parsley and olive oil sauce flavored with capers and lemon juice.

—BRYAN ROOF, *America's Test Kitchen Books*

Pan-Seared Strip Steak with Crispy Potatoes and Salsa Verde
SERVES 4

We prefer this steak cooked to medium-rare, but if you prefer it more or less done see "Testing Meat for Doneness" on page 139.

SALSA VERDE
- 1 slice high-quality white sandwich bread
- ½ cup extra-virgin olive oil
- 2 tablespoons fresh lemon juice
- 2 cups lightly packed fresh parsley leaves
- 2 medium anchovy fillets
- 2 tablespoons drained capers
- 1 small garlic clove, minced
- ⅛ teaspoon salt

STEAK AND POTATOES
- 1¾ pounds russet potatoes (3 to 4), scrubbed and each cut lengthwise into 6 wedges
- 6 tablespoons vegetable oil
- Salt and pepper
- 2 (1-pound) boneless strip steaks, about 1½ inches thick, each steak cut in half crosswise

1. FOR THE SALSA VERDE: Toast the bread in a toaster at the lowest setting until the surface is dry but not browned, about 15 seconds. Remove and discard the crust and cut the bread into rough ½-inch pieces (you should have about ½ cup). Process the bread pieces, oil, and lemon juice together in a food processor until smooth, about 10 seconds. Add the parsley, anchovies, capers, garlic, and salt. Pulse until the mixture is finely chopped (the mixture should not be smooth), about 5 pulses, scraping down the sides of the bowl as necessary. Transfer the sauce to a serving bowl and set aside.

2. FOR THE STEAK AND POTATOES: Toss the potatoes with 1 tablespoon of the oil, ¼ teaspoon salt, and ⅛ teaspoon pepper in a microwave-safe bowl. Cover the bowl with plastic wrap and microwave on high power until the potatoes begin to soften, 7 to 10 minutes, stirring the potatoes halfway through cooking.

3. While the potatoes microwave, pat the steaks dry with paper towels and season with salt and pepper. Heat 1 tablespoon more oil in a 12-inch nonstick skillet over medium-high heat until just smoking. Carefully lay the steaks in the skillet and cook without moving until well browned on the first side, 3 to 5 minutes.

4. Flip the steaks over, reduce the heat to medium, and continue to cook without moving until the center of the steak registers 120 to 125 degrees on an instant-read thermometer (for medium-rare), 5 to 10 minutes longer. Transfer the steaks to a plate, tent loosely with foil, and let rest while finishing the potatoes.

5. Drain the microwaved potatoes well. Add the remaining 4 tablespoons oil to the skillet and return to medium-high heat until shimmering. Add the potatoes and cook, without stirring, until golden brown on one side, about 6 minutes. Flip the potatoes and continue to cook, without stirring, until golden brown on the second side, about 6 minutes longer. (If the potatoes are browning unevenly, use tongs and gently move them around as necessary.)

6. Transfer the potatoes to a platter and serve with the steak and salsa verde.

NOTES FROM THE TEST KITCHEN

TESTING MEAT FOR DONENESS

An instant-read thermometer is the most reliable method for checking the doneness of chicken, beef, and pork. To use an instant-read thermometer, simply insert it through the side of a chicken breast, steak, or pork chop. The chart below lists temperatures at which the meat should be removed from the heat (the temperature of the meat will continue to climb between 5 and 10 degrees as it rests before serving).

WHEN IS IT DONE?

MEAT	COOK UNTIL IT REGISTERS	SERVING TEMPERATURE
Chicken and Turkey Breasts	160 to 165 degrees	160 to 165 degrees
Chicken Thighs	175 degrees	175 degrees
Duck Breasts		
Medium-rare	120 to 125 degrees	130 degrees
Medium	130 to 135 degrees	140 degrees
Medium-well	140 to 145 degrees	150 degrees
Well-done	150 to 155 degrees	160 degrees
Pork	140 to 145 degrees	150 degrees
Beef and Lamb		
Rare	115 to 120 degrees	125 degrees
Medium-rare	120 to 125 degrees	130 degrees
Medium	130 to 135 degrees	140 degrees
Medium-well	140 to 145 degrees	150 degrees
Well-done	150 to 155 degrees	160 degrees

CHICKEN-FRIED STEAK

LIKE NEW YORKERS AND THEIR BAGELS, Texans are passionate and partisan (some might say a little nuts) about chicken-fried steak—cheap steak pounded to tenderness, coated, fried, and served (always!) with a peppery cream gravy and mashed potatoes. Most culinary historians trace its origins to Wiener schnitzel, brought by German immigrants to Texas in the mid-19th century. According to this theory, the coating and the cooking method were adapted for local beef. (No tender veal on the range.)

CFS (its nickname in many diners) has moved beyond the borders of Texas, and today you can find versions all over the South and Midwest. Some demand adherence to the "original" concept: Only a simple flour dredge and a skillet will do. Others coat the steaks in batter and cook them in a bubbling deep-fat fryer. As someone who was only casually familiar with chicken-fried steak, I was uncommitted. As long as the steaks lived up to the advance billing—crunchy on the outside, tender within, and hot, salty, and big enough to hang over the edge of a dinner plate—I was willing to throw my lot in with either camp.

All the recipes in my initial testing used cube steak—steaks cut from the round and put through a tenderizing machine that makes small, cubelike indentations. Breaded and fried, it makes serviceable steak. Unfortunately, overzealous supermarket butchers often mangle the job, turning out cube steak the texture of coarse hamburger.

I turned to other cheap beef options. Blade steaks had an obstructive line of gristle, so I ruled them out, but tasters loved the flavor of sirloin tips. Even pounded, coated, and fried, however, the tips were a little tough. I borrowed an idea from the cubing process and tried scoring the meat at ¼-inch intervals on both sides, then bashed the tips with a meat mallet until they were thin and would fry up nice and tender.

Some recipes called for the steaks to be dredged in flour. The result was too bare. Other recipes used a tempura-like batter, which gave me puffy, pasty coatings. Since the very name CFS suggests fried chicken, I wondered how a test kitchen recipe for fried chicken would fare with steak tips. I pulled out the recipe, then dredged the steaks in seasoned flour (plus baking powder to lighten and cornstarch for extra crispness), dipped them in egg, and then coated them in a pebbly mixture of more seasoned flour, to which I'd added a little milk. These steaks were light and crisp right out of the oil but within moments, the crust became soggy and peeled off the meat.

CHICKEN-FRIED STEAK

I looked through my recipes and found unexpected guidance from the *Household Searchlight Recipe Book,* Topeka, Kansas (1949), which included the oldest published recipe for chicken-fried steak I'd been able to find. It gave instructions to pound the flour into the steak. I'd been lightly coating the steaks in flour, not pounding it in. What would that do? So, after scoring the sirloin tips on both sides, I pounded in flour until it disappeared, dipped the steaks in egg, and again applied my fried chicken coating. Now the crust held on, the flour essentially "gluing" the coating to the meat. Alas, the crust was as soggy as ever.

I discussed the challenge with our science editor. Pound more, he suggested. Pounding damages the cell structure of meat, releasing moisture to the surface. Second, ditch the deep-fry method I'd been using in favor of a shallower fry. Submerging the coated meat in deep fat traps the moisture and prevents it from evaporating. I returned to the kitchen, where I pounded the steaks to ⅛ inch thick and added just enough oil to the skillet, about 1½ cups, for my steaks to float. The difference was dramatic. Visible steam wisped upward, and as I flipped the steaks, the juices sputtered away. Sure enough, a tuck-in with a fork and knife rewarded me with heat, salt, beefy flavor, and serious crunch.

The traditional recipe for cream gravy starts by cooking flour in the pan drippings, then whisking in milk, salt, and pepper. I took the opportunity to buck tradition and amp up the flavors with the addition of chicken broth and garlic powder. This was tasty, but the real problem with the gravy was that by the time it was ready, my steaks were almost cold. I decided a preemptive strike was in order and made the gravy before frying the steaks, using butter in place of any pan drippings. By the time the steaks were golden brown and crispy, the cream gravy was good to go.

—DIANE UNGER, *Cook's Country*

Chicken-Fried Steak

SERVES 4

Avoid using low-fat or skim milk in the gravy. For this recipe, buy a whole 1-pound steak and cut it yourself. Serve with mashed potatoes.

GRAVY

- 3 tablespoons unsalted butter
- 3 tablespoons unbleached all-purpose flour
- ½ teaspoon garlic powder
- 1½ cups low-sodium chicken broth
- 1½ cups whole milk (see note)
- ¾ teaspoon salt
- ½ teaspoon pepper

STEAK

- 3½ cups unbleached all-purpose flour
- ½ cup cornstarch
- 1 tablespoon garlic powder
- 1 tablespoon onion powder
- ½ teaspoon cayenne pepper
- 2 teaspoons baking powder
  Salt and pepper
- 4 large eggs
- ¼ cup whole milk
- 1 pound sirloin steak tips (flap meat), trimmed and cut into four 4-ounce pieces (see note)
- 1½ cups peanut or vegetable oil

1. FOR THE GRAVY: Melt the butter in a large skillet over medium heat. Stir in the flour and garlic powder and cook until golden, about 2 minutes. Slowly whisk in the broth, milk, salt, and pepper and simmer until thickened, about 5 minutes. Cover and keep warm while preparing the steak. (The gravy can be refrigerated in an airtight container for up to 2 days.)

2. FOR THE STEAK: Whisk the flour, cornstarch, garlic powder, onion powder, cayenne, baking powder, 1 teaspoon salt, and 2 teaspoons pepper in a large bowl. Transfer 1 cup of the seasoned flour mixture to a shallow dish. Beat the eggs in a second shallow dish. Add the milk to the bowl with the remaining flour mixture and rub with your fingers until the mixture resembles coarse meal.

3. Pat the steaks dry with paper towels and season with salt and pepper. Following the photos on page 142, score the meat lightly and then dredge the meat in the seasoned flour. Using a meat pounder, pound the steaks to between ⅛ and ¼ inch thick. One at a time, coat the steaks lightly with the seasoned flour again, dip them in the egg, and then transfer to the bowl with the milk and flour mixture, pressing to adhere. Arrange the steaks on a wire rack set inside a rimmed baking sheet and refrigerate for 15 minutes or up to 4 hours; do not discard the milk and flour mixture.

4. Adjust an oven rack to the middle position and heat the oven to 200 degrees. Heat the oil in a large Dutch oven over medium-high heat until just smoking. Return 2 of the steaks to the bowl with the milk and flour mixture and turn to coat. Fry the steaks until deep golden brown and crisp, 2 to 3 minutes per side. Transfer to a clean wire rack set inside a rimmed baking sheet and keep warm in the oven. Repeat with the remaining steaks. Serve with the gravy.

NOTES FROM THE TEST KITCHEN

PREPARING CHICKEN-FRIED STEAK

1. Score the meat at ¼-inch intervals in a crosshatch pattern. Repeat on the other side.

2. Dredge each steak in seasoned flour, then use a meat pounder to flatten.

3. After the final dredge, fry two steaks at a time in a heavy-bottomed Dutch oven.

AVOID CUBE STEAK

The classic choice for chicken-fried steak is cube steak (also known as minute steak), a tough, relatively bland cut from the hind quarters of the steer. After a run through the meat tenderizer, where it is twice cut (or cubed), the meat takes on its characteristic dimpled look—or, in sloppy hands, becomes ragged. Our tasters preferred the beefy flavor and tender texture of flap meat (a.k.a. sirloin or steak tips) that we pounded ourselves.

CUBE STEAK
Tough, ragged, and bland

SWEDISH MEATBALLS

MOST OF US KNOW SWEDISH MEATBALLS as lumps of flavorless ground beef or pork covered in heavy gravy that congeals as it all sits. After countless years enduring the sinkers that a relative inflicts on my family at reunions, I made a resolution: Meatballs had to be Sweden's national dish for a reason, and I was going to find out why.

The answer came when I visited Aquavit, Swedish chef Marcus Samuelsson's high-end New York restaurant, where I found meatballs that tasted as they were meant to taste. Unlike Italian meatballs, which are melt-in-your-mouth tender, these main-course meatballs were substantial yet delicate. Biting into them, I noticed the springiness and satisfying snap you get from a good sausage or hot dog. Even better, the heavy brown gravy had been replaced by a light cream sauce.

The most successful recipes I tried back in the test kitchen used two Italian meatball tricks: a combination of meats (usually beef and pork) and a panade (a paste of bread and liquid that is mixed into the meat). Although these tricks yielded a moist finished product, the meatballs were too tender—they practically fell apart. While this trait is desirable in Italian meatballs, I wanted springy, Swedish-style meatballs to rival those at Aquavit.

My working recipe started with two slices of bread soaked in ½ cup of cream and then mixed by hand with ¾ pound ground beef, ¼ pound ground pork, an egg, and a few basic flavorings: onions, nutmeg, and allspice. The balls were cooked to a golden brown color before being simmered in the gravy. Thinking that less panade might make my meatballs more cohesive, I tried reducing the amount of bread. The meatballs gained substance, but they also became progressively drier and tougher.

When meat is ground and mixed, the proteins in it get tangled up, producing a weblike matrix that gives meatballs a cohesive structure. Without anything to break up this web, however, the proteins wrap together tightly and squeeze out moisture, making the meatballs dry and tough. A panade works in two ways: Its liquid adds moisture, and the bread starch gets in the way of the proteins, preventing them from interconnecting too strongly. But it can also take things too far, resulting in meatballs that barely hold together. I needed to find just the right balance.

Thinking of other ingredients used to lighten food, I turned to baking powder. Combining a single teaspoon of baking powder and a slice of bread mixed with cream provided the ideal balance of moistness, substance, and lightness.

The next step in perfecting my meatballs was adding a bit of sausagelike springiness. I scanned our library for books on sausage-making, which turned up an interesting technique: using a standing mixer to combine the meat, fat, and flavorings. This approach finely distributes the fat into the lean meat, guaranteeing a juicy finished product. It also causes the meat proteins to stretch out and link up end to end. This creates tension in the sausage that breaks when you bite into it—hence the snap.

This approach was a disaster. These meatballs were more like mini hot-dog nuggets than Swedish meatballs. Since everything I read about sausage-making indicated that this technique worked best with pork, which has a higher fat content and less robust muscle structure than beef, what if I were to separate the meats? Starting with equal parts beef and pork, I whipped the pork with the salt, baking powder, and seasonings until an emulsified paste formed, added the panade, and then gently folded in the ground beef. The results were exactly what I wanted: The panade and baking powder kept the meatballs delicate and juicy, the whipped pork provided just enough spring, and the barely mixed beef offered heartiness.

Now that I'd mastered texture, all the meatballs needed was a little flavor adjustment. A teaspoon of brown sugar added complexity without being cloying. Tasters liked pinches of nutmeg and allspice, and grated onions dispersed easily and evenly in the meat mixture.

As for the cooking technique, baking turned out meatballs that overcooked before they had browned properly, while sautéing in oil resulted in spotty browning. My solution: shallow frying, which browned the meatballs evenly and cooked them through.

The final step was perfecting the gravy. Most recipes call for a flour-thickened blend of stock and cream in roughly equal proportions, but this was too rich for my taste. Using mostly stock and just a touch of cream was a big improvement. I had already added sugar to the meatballs, but adding more to the sauce helped balance flavors. A splash of lemon juice contributed brightness.

I finally had my ideal Swedish meatball recipe, which I accompanied with some easy pickled cucumbers. I couldn't avoid the occasional lead ball at family reunions, but in my own home I would serve Swedish meatballs as they're meant to be—light and juicy, bursting with sweetness and meaty flavor.

—J. KENJI ALT, *Cook's Illustrated*

Swedish Meatballs with Pickled Cucumbers
SERVES 4 TO 6

The traditional accompaniments for the meatballs are Swedish pickled cucumbers and lingonberry preserves. Kirby cucumbers are also called pickling cucumbers. If these small cucumbers are unavailable, substitute 1 large American cucumber. For a slightly less sweet dish, omit the brown sugar in the meatballs and reduce the brown sugar in the sauce to 2 teaspoons. A 12-inch slope-sided skillet can be used in place of the sauté pan—use 1½ cups of oil to fry instead of 1¼ cups. Serve the meatballs with mashed potatoes, boiled red potatoes, or egg noodles.

PICKLED CUCUMBERS
- 1 pound Kirby cucumbers (3 small), sliced into ⅛ to ¼-inch-thick rounds (see note)
- 1½ cups white vinegar
- 1½ cups granulated sugar
- 1 teaspoon salt
- 12 whole allspice berries

MEATBALLS
- 1 large egg
- ¼ cup heavy cream
- 1 slice high-quality white sandwich bread, crusts removed, torn into 1-inch pieces
- 8 ounces ground pork
- ¼ cup grated onion
- ⅛ teaspoon freshly grated nutmeg
- ⅛ teaspoon ground allspice
- ⅛ teaspoon pepper
- 1 teaspoon brown sugar (see note)
- 1½ teaspoons salt
- 1 teaspoon baking powder
- 8 ounces 85 percent lean ground beef
- 1¼ cups vegetable oil

SAUCE
- 1 tablespoon unsalted butter
- 1 tablespoon unbleached all-purpose flour
- 1½ cups low-sodium chicken broth
- 1 tablespoon brown sugar (see note)
- ½ cup heavy cream
- 2 teaspoons fresh lemon juice
- Salt and pepper

1. FOR THE PICKLED CUCUMBERS: Place the cucumber slices in a medium heatproof bowl. Bring the vinegar, granulated sugar, salt, and allspice to a simmer in a small saucepan over high heat, stirring occasionally to dissolve the sugar. Pour the vinegar mixture over the cucumbers and stir to separate the slices. Cover the bowl with plastic wrap and let sit for 15 minutes. Uncover and cool to room temperature, about 15 minutes. (The pickles can be refrigerated in their liquid in an airtight container for up to 2 weeks.)

2. FOR THE MEATBALLS: Whisk the egg and cream together in a medium bowl. Stir in the bread and set aside. In a standing mixer fitted with the paddle attachment, beat the pork, onion, nutmeg, allspice, pepper, brown sugar, salt, and baking powder on high speed until smooth and pale, about 2 minutes, scraping down the bowl as necessary. Using a fork, mash the bread mixture until no large dry bread chunks remain; add the mixture to the mixer bowl and beat on high speed until smooth and homogeneous, about 1 minute, scraping down the bowl as necessary. Add the beef and mix on medium-low speed until just incorporated, about 30 seconds, scraping down the bowl as necessary. Using moistened hands, form a generous 1 tablespoon of the meat mixture into a 1-inch round meatball; repeat with the remaining mixture to form 25 to 30 meatballs.

3. Heat the oil in a 10-inch straight-sided sauté pan over medium-high heat until the edge of a meatball dipped in the oil sizzles (the oil should register 350 degrees on an instant-read thermometer), 3 to 5 minutes. Add the meatballs in a single layer and fry, flipping once halfway through cooking, until lightly browned all over and cooked through, 7 to 10 minutes. (Adjust the heat as needed to keep the oil sizzling but not smoking.) Using a slotted spoon, transfer the browned meatballs to a paper towel–lined plate. (The fried meatballs can be frozen for up to 2 weeks. Thaw the meatballs in the refrigerator overnight before proceeding with step 4, using a clean pan.)

4. FOR THE SAUCE: Pour off and discard the oil in the pan, leaving any fond (browned bits) behind. Melt the butter over medium-high heat. Add the flour and cook, whisking constantly, until the flour is light brown, about 30 seconds. Slowly whisk in the broth, scraping the pan bottom to loosen any browned bits. Add the brown sugar and bring to a simmer. Reduce the heat to medium and cook until the sauce is reduced to about 1 cup, about 5 minutes. Stir in the cream and return to a simmer.

5. Add the meatballs to the sauce and simmer, turning occasionally, until heated through, about 5 minutes. Stir in the lemon juice, season with salt and pepper to taste, and serve with the pickled cucumbers.

GRILLED BEEF TERIYAKI

TRUE JAPANESE TERIYAKI is as simple as it is restrained: Take a glossy, salty-sweet glaze made with soy sauce, sake, and mirin (a sweet Japanese rice wine) and paint it over char-grilled fish to accent its delicately smoky flavor. After Japanese immigrants introduced this dish to Hawaii in the 19th century, beef and chicken all but replaced the fish, and additions such as sugar and garlic became standard in the sauce. Over time, these perfectly reasonable adaptations morphed into the tired renditions of teriyaki now found at many Japanese-American restaurants: chewy, flavorless slivers of meat daubed with a thick, overly sweet sauce.

I wanted to see this translated dish fulfill its potential, with a juicy, charred steak embellished by a well-balanced, sweet and savory glaze that would be robust enough to stand up to the beef.

To begin, I created a traditional glaze combining equal parts sake, mirin, and soy sauce and simmering the mixture on the stovetop for an hour until it reduced to a syrupy glaze. My next decision concerned the beef.

NOTES FROM THE TEST KITCHEN

MEATBALL TIPS

1. Keep a bowl of water nearby and dip your fingers after every two or three meatballs to prevent the meat from sticking as you form the balls.

2. Starting near the skillet handle, arrange the meatballs in a clockwise spiral to keep track of when each one needs to be flipped.

GRILLED BEEF TERIYAKI

I tried moderately priced options such as top blade, top sirloin, skirt steak, flank steak, and sirloin tips (also known as flap meat). Tasters quickly ruled out the top blade (gristly) and the top sirloin (bland), but the three remaining cuts all boasted good beefy flavor—sirloin tips in particular. This cut's marbling melted into the coarse muscle fibers of the beef as it cooked, adding flavor and making it seem more tender than other cheap steaks.

As for the meat's preparation, thin pieces on skewers were uniformly dry and leathery. Cooking a whole steak, glazing it with sauce, and slicing before serving also had its issues: The juiciness of the steak caused the glaze to wash off as soon as I sliced the meat, no matter how long I let it rest.

What if I sliced the steak before it went onto the grill? Slicing the meat into thin cutlets across the grain worked great; this shortened the muscle fibers so that the texture was tender and yielding, and the ½-inch-thick cutlets provided plenty of surface area for charring on the grill. Applied to the browned, caramelized exterior of each slice, the glaze adhered firmly.

I was making progress, but the meat was still a little dry and tasters thought the sugarless sauce was too understated for beef. I experimented with adding various proportions of sugar until I was adding as much sugar as the other ingredients. Tasters liked this new balance of flavors, but overall the dish was a little one-dimensional. To boost the flavor of the meat, I tried marinating it, soaking the strips of meat for 30 minutes in a combination of soy sauce, sugar, and mirin. This worked beautifully. Not only did the soy promote browning on the grill, but the beef was also juicier. Reducing the amount of soy sauce in the glaze prevented the dish from being too salty.

Teriyaki is often served with a garnish of sliced scallions and ginger. I decided to add them directly to the marinade (along with a few cloves of garlic) for an aromatic boost, while a small amount of orange zest contributed freshness that tasters appreciated.

I was nearly there but thought that the beef could be smokier and more charred. My single-level fire—a full chimney of charcoal spread over the entire surface of the grill—was not concentrating the heat enough, so I banked all the coals to one side of the grill for a modified two-level fire. Positioned over this higher mound of coals, the steak came out well charred and juicy.

I had perfectly cooked steak with robust flavors and just the right complement of a spare, salty-sweet sauce.

The only problem? The sauce took an hour of simmering to reach the perfect consistency. I decided to try the obvious shortcut: cornstarch. A teaspoon was all it took to achieve a nice syrupy consistency, and a mere 15 minutes on the stovetop softened the raw alcohol edge. I now had a sauce that was perfect for both glazing the meat in its final minutes on the grill and passing at the table. This beef teriyaki wasn't true to any tradition, hybrid or otherwise, but it was very, very good.

—KEITH DRESSER, *Cook's Illustrated*

Grilled Beef Teriyaki

SERVES 4

If you can't find flap meat, flank steak is a good alternative. We prefer sake in the sauce, but vermouth may be substituted in a pinch. Mirin, a sweet Japanese rice wine, is a key component of teriyaki; it can be found in Asian markets and the international section of most supermarkets. Alternatively, substitute ¼ cup vermouth or sake and 2 teaspoons sugar for every ¼ cup mirin. Serve the beef with steamed rice, preferably short-grain.

STEAK

- 2 pounds sirloin steak tips (flap meat), trimmed (see note)
- ⅓ cup soy sauce
- ¼ cup mirin (see note)
- 2 tablespoons vegetable oil
- 3 garlic cloves, minced
- 1 tablespoon grated or minced fresh ginger
- 1 tablespoon sugar
- 1 teaspoon grated orange zest
- 2 scallions, white parts minced and green parts sliced thin on the bias, separated

SAUCE

- ½ cup sugar
- ½ cup sake (see note)
- ½ cup mirin (see note)
- ⅓ cup soy sauce
- 1 teaspoon grated or minced fresh ginger
- 1 teaspoon cornstarch

1. FOR THE STEAK: Following the photos on page 147, cut the steak with the grain into 2 to 3 even pieces. (If the total length of the steak is 12 inches or less, cut it into 2 pieces. If over 12 inches, cut it into 3 pieces.)

Holding the knife at a 45-degree angle, slice each piece against the grain into 4 to 5 slices about ½ inch thick. Combine the remaining ingredients, except the scallion greens, in a gallon-sized zipper-lock bag and toss to combine. Place the meat in the bag, press out as much air as possible, and seal. Refrigerate for 30 minutes or up to 1 hour, flipping the bag every 15 minutes to ensure that the meat marinates evenly.

2A. FOR A CHARCOAL GRILL: Open the bottom grill vents completely. Light a large chimney starter filled with charcoal briquettes (100 briquettes; 6 quarts). When the coals are hot, pour them in an even layer over half the grill, leaving the other half empty. Set the cooking grate in place, cover, and heat the grill until hot, about 5 minutes.

2B. FOR A GAS GRILL: Turn all the burners to high, cover, and heat the grill until hot, about 15 minutes. Leave the primary burner on high and turn the other burner(s) to low. (Adjust the burners as needed to maintain a hot fire and a low fire on separate sides of the grill; see page 130.)

3. FOR THE SAUCE: While the grill is heating, whisk the sauce ingredients together in a small saucepan until combined. Bring the sauce to a boil over medium-high heat, stirring occasionally. Reduce the heat to medium-low and simmer, stirring occasionally, until the sauce is syrupy and reduced to 1 cup, 12 to 15 minutes. Transfer ¾ cup of the sauce to a small bowl and set aside to serve with the cooked meat.

4. Clean and oil the cooking grate. Remove the meat from the marinade and pat dry with paper towels. Place the steaks on the hotter part of the grill and cook, uncovered, until well seared and dark brown on the first side, 3 to 4 minutes. Using tongs, flip the steak and grill until the second side is well seared and dark brown, 3 to 4 minutes. Brush the top of the meat with 2 tablespoons of the sauce; flip and cook 30 seconds. Brush the meat with the remaining 2 tablespoons sauce; flip and cook 30 seconds longer.

5. Transfer the meat to a serving platter and let rest for 5 minutes. Sprinkle with the scallion greens and serve, passing the reserved sauce separately.

NOTES FROM THE TEST KITCHEN

CUTTING SIRLOIN STEAK TIPS FOR GRILLING

1. Cut the steak with the grain into 2 or 3 even pieces.

2. Hold the knife at a 45-degree angle and cut ½-inch-thick slices.

3. Each piece of steak should yield 4 to 5 slices.

BUYING FLAP MEAT

Beef labeled "steak tips" can be cut from various muscles of the cow into cubes, strips, or steaks. Our favorite kind is cut into a steak that boasts a coarse, longitudinal grain. Butchers call this form of steak tips "flap meat" or "sirloin tips." Look for pieces that range from 1 to 1½ inches thick.

SKIP THE STRIPS   **GO FOR WHOLE**

THE BEST MIRIN

Prized in Asian marinades and glazes, this Japanese rice wine has a subtle, salty-sweet flavor. We tasted four brands—three from the supermarket and one high-priced mail-order bottle. Mail-ordering mirin was not worth the trouble—when it's cooked into teriyaki sauce, its finer flavors were hard to detect. Our favorite is **Eden Mirin Rice Cooking Wine.**

SHREDDED BARBECUED BEEF

BARBECUED BEEF BRISKET IS GREAT FOR SLICING, but when you want shredded barbecued beef, most experts rely on a fatty, flavorful chuck roast. Long, slow cooking is supposed to melt the fat and connective tissue in this large shoulder roast and yield moist, tender meat.

I rounded up several recipes for shredded beef barbecue and fired up the grills. The savory smoke that filled the air outside the test kitchen had my tasters eager with anticipation. Their enthusiasm turned to disappointment as they chewed their way through beef that was dry and stringy on the outside and lacked smoke flavor. Given the work involved, these recipes were true failures.

For my next test, I decided to try cooking a chuck roast the same way the test kitchen cooks a pork shoulder for pulled pork: I rubbed the outside with salt, pepper, and cayenne (a classic Texas-style rub for beef) and set the roast to smoke on the cooler side of the grill. After two hours, the meat was sufficiently crusty, so I transferred it to a baking pan, wrapped the pan in foil, and placed the roast in the oven to finish cooking to fall-apart tenderness. (This grill-to-oven method is much quicker than cooking the meat entirely on the grill.)

It took four hours in the oven to tenderize the tough chuck, but by that time the meat was dried out—except for where the bottom of the roast had been sitting in the exuded juices. I cooked the next roast in a disposable aluminum pan from the outset (starting with its time on the grill) to catch those juices, which helped keep more—but not all—of the meat moist. Cutting the roast into four pieces solved the problem, as the smaller pieces of meat sat lower in the pan and thus deeper in the juices. Flipping the pieces before transferring them to the oven ensured that more of meat was "basted" and moist (by the end of cooking, the juices were coming about halfway up the sides of the pieces). What's more, the smaller pieces of beef absorbed more smoke flavor, and they cooked faster than a single large roast.

Meat this good demanded a homemade sauce. Many recipes start by sautéing onions in oil, but for richer flavor I used some beef fat from the pan instead. Chili powder and black pepper added bite, while ketchup, vinegar, coffee, Worcestershire sauce, brown sugar, and some of the rendered beef juices rounded out the flavors. This beef was tender, juicy, smoky, and ready to be piled on a sandwich.

—MEREDITH BUTCHER, *Cook's Country*

Shredded Barbecued Beef
SERVES 8 TO 10

If you prefer a smooth barbecue sauce, strain the sauce before tossing it with the beef in step 5. We like to serve this beef on white bread with plenty of pickle chips.

SPICE RUB AND BEEF
- 1 tablespoon salt
- 1 tablespoon pepper
- 1 teaspoon cayenne pepper
- 1 (5 to 6-pound) boneless beef chuck-eye roast
- 1 (13 by 9-inch) disposable aluminum roasting pan
- 3 cups wood chips, soaked in water for 15 minutes and drained

BARBECUE SAUCE
- 1 onion, minced (about 1 cup)
- 4 garlic cloves, minced
- ½ teaspoon chili powder
- 1¼ cups ketchup
- ¾ cup brewed coffee
- ½ cup cider vinegar
- ½ cup packed brown sugar
- 3 tablespoons Worcestershire sauce
- ½ teaspoon pepper

1. FOR THE SPICE RUB AND BEEF: Combine the salt, pepper, and cayenne in a small bowl. Following the photos on page 149, quarter the roast and remove any excess fat and gristle. Rub the meat all over with the salt mixture and transfer to the disposable aluminum roasting pan. (The salt-rubbed meat can be covered tightly with plastic wrap and refrigerated for up to 24 hours.) Seal the soaked wood chips in a foil packet and cut vent holes in the top (see page 149).

2A. FOR A CHARCOAL GRILL: Open the bottom grill vents halfway. Light a large chimney starter half full with charcoal briquettes (50 briquettes; 3 quarts). When the coals are hot, pour them into a steeply banked pile against one side of the grill. Place the wood chip packet on top of the coals. Set the cooking grate in place, cover, and open the lid vents halfway. Heat the grill until hot and the wood chips begin to smoke heavily, about 5 minutes.

2B. FOR A GAS GRILL: Place the wood chip packet directly on the primary burner. Turn all the burners to high, cover, and heat the grill until hot and the wood chips begin to smoke heavily, about 15 minutes. Leave the primary burner on medium and turn off the other burner(s). (Adjust the burners as needed to maintain the grill temperature around 275 degrees.)

3. Clean and oil the cooking grate. Place the roasting pan with the beef on the cooler part of the grill and cook, covered, until the meat is deep red and smoky, about 2 hours. During the final 20 minutes of grilling, adjust an oven rack to the lower-middle position and heat the oven to 300 degrees.

4. Flip the meat over in the roasting pan, cover the pan tightly with foil, and roast the beef in the oven until

a fork inserted into the center meets no resistance, 2 to 3 hours. Transfer the meat to a large bowl, tent loosely with foil, and let rest for 30 minutes. While the meat rests, skim the fat from the accumulated juices in the pan; reserve 2 tablespoons of the fat. Strain the defatted juices; reserve ½ cup juice.

5. FOR THE BARBECUE SAUCE AND TO FINISH: Combine the onion and reserved fat in a saucepan and cook over medium heat until the onion has softened, about 10 minutes. Add the garlic and chili powder and cook until fragrant, about 30 seconds. Stir in the remaining ingredients and reserved meat juices and simmer until thickened, about 15 minutes. Using 2 forks, pull the meat into shreds, discarding any excess fat or gristle. Toss the meat with ½ cup barbecue sauce. Serve, passing the remaining sauce at the table.

NOTES FROM THE TEST KITCHEN

PREPARING BARBECUED BEEF

1. Cut the chuck roast into quarters, removing and discarding excess fat and gristle.

2. Place the disposable roasting pan with the spice-rubbed meat on the grill opposite the coals and packet of soaked wood chips.

3. Before wrapping the pan with foil and transferring it to the oven to finish cooking, flip the pieces of meat to maximize contact with the pan juices.

MAKING A FOIL PACKET

After soaking the wood chips in water for 15 minutes, drain and spread them in the center of a 15 by 12-inch piece of heavy-duty foil. Fold to seal the edges, then cut three or four slits to allow smoke to escape.

SLOW-COOKER BARBECUED BEEF BRISKET

BARBECUED BRISKET SHOULD BE TENDER and moist, with a deep brown crust and robust spice and smoke flavor. That's hard enough to pull off on a backyard grill, but try translating it to the slow cooker and the problems seem insurmountable. Most recipes throw a slab of brisket in the slow cooker, cover it with bottled barbecue sauce, and hope for the best. The result is meat with a boiled, stringy exterior and an interior so dry that no amount of sauce can salvage it. Was I expecting too much from a slow cooker?

First up was a simple spice rub, often the hallmark of great barbecue. I combined salt, pepper, brown sugar, cumin, and paprika. To bump up the flavor and start building the smoky component, I added chipotle chiles. I scored the fat to allow the flavor to permeate and rubbed the mixture all over the brisket. I put the brisket in the slow cooker with a little barbecue sauce and waited. The test kitchen smelled great—but that was as good as it got. The brisket was bobbing in more than two cups of liquid that had been forced out of the meat as it cooked; this made it taste more like pot roast than barbecue.

Elevating the meat off the bottom of the slow cooker so that it wasn't sitting in any accumulated juices seemed worth a try. So for my next test, I balled up some aluminum foil and set the brisket on top. Seven hours later, the results were promising: Half of the meat was out

SLOW-COOKER BARBECUED BEEF BRISKET

of the pool. The other half was listing precariously. I needed something sturdier to support the brisket's weight. Scanning the test kitchen's supply room, I spied a loaf pan. I inverted it in the slow cooker like a pedestal and placed the brisket on top. So far, so good.

I couldn't check the meat because opening the lid allows too much heat to escape. And condensation blocked my view through the lid, so when I took the lid off seven hours later, I did a double take. The brisket looked great: dark brown with a caramelized exterior. What really threw me, though, was that instead of the usual couple of inches of juice in the slow cooker, there was barely any. Where had it gone? I lifted up the loaf pan and got my answer: Out came a flood of thin but concentrated beef juice, which had been drawn into the pan by a vacuum effect. What a brilliant accident! Containing the liquid under the loaf pan made the cooking environment even drier, which is closer to how real barbecue is cooked. To bump up the flavor of the juice, I sautéed onion, garlic, tomato paste, and more of the chipotle that I'd put in the rub and added that to the slow cooker, under the loaf pan, to cook along with the brisket. Adding a little water to the pan provided protection against scorching.

After the brisket rested for 30 minutes, I sliced it thinly against the grain and poured half of the flavorful, thin sauce over the meat. I turned the remaining juices into a thicker serving sauce by adding ketchup, vinegar, and a few drops of liquid smoke to drive home the outdoor flavor. One bite of this brisket and I knew I'd hit the mark. The meat was moist and tender; the sauce was spicy, a bit smoky, and packed with concentrated flavor. I expected more from my slow cooker and I got it!

—DIANE UNGER, *Cook's Country*

Slow-Cooker Barbecued Beef Brisket

SERVES 8 TO 10

Scoring the fat on the brisket at ½-inch intervals will allow the rub to penetrate the meat. Two disposable aluminum loaf pans stacked inside one another can be substituted for the metal loaf pan.

SPICE RUB AND BRISKET

½ cup packed dark brown sugar

2 tablespoons minced canned chipotle chiles in adobo sauce

1 tablespoon ground cumin

1 tablespoon paprika

1 teaspoon salt

2 teaspoons pepper

1 (4 to 5-pound) beef brisket, preferably flat cut, fat trimmed to ¼-inch thickness and scored lightly (see note)

SAUCE

3 tablespoons vegetable oil

1 onion, minced (about 1 cup)

2 tablespoons tomato paste

1 tablespoon chili powder

1 tablespoon minced canned chipotle chiles in adobo sauce

2 garlic cloves, minced

½ cup water

¼ cup ketchup

1 tablespoon cider vinegar

¼ teaspoon liquid smoke

Salt and pepper

1. FOR THE SPICE RUB AND BRISKET: Combine the sugar, chipotles, cumin, paprika, salt, and pepper in a bowl. Rub the sugar mixture all over the brisket. Cover with plastic wrap and let sit at room temperature for 1 hour or refrigerate for up to 24 hours.

2. FOR THE SAUCE: Heat the oil in a large skillet over medium-high heat until shimmering. Add the onion and cook until softened, 5 to 7 minutes. Add the tomato paste and cook until beginning to brown, about 1 minute. Stir in the chili powder, chipotles, and garlic and cook until fragrant, about 30 seconds. Following the photos on page 152, mound the onion mixture in the center of the slow cooker, arrange an inverted metal loaf pan over the onion mixture, and place the brisket, fat-side up, on top of the loaf pan. Add the water to the slow cooker, cover, and cook on high until a fork inserted into the brisket meets no resistance, 7 to 8 hours (or cook on low for 10 to 12 hours).

3. Transfer the brisket to a 13 by 9-inch baking dish, cover with foil, and let rest for 30 minutes. Carefully remove the loaf pan from the slow cooker. Pour the onion mixture and accumulated juices into a large bowl and skim the fat. (You should have about 2 cups defatted juices; if you have less, supplement with water.) (The brisket can be wrapped tightly in foil and refrigerated for up to 3 days. Refrigerate the juices separately in an airtight container. To serve, transfer the foil-wrapped brisket to a baking dish and place in a 350-degree oven until

MINIMIZING MOISTURE

To minimize the moisture absorbed by the brisket, we place the meat on top of a loaf pan. The juices exuded by the meat are drawn under the pan by a vacuum effect, creating less moisture directly below the meat.

1. Pile the onion mixture in the bottom of the slow cooker and top with an inverted loaf pan.

2. Place the brisket on top of the loaf pan.

3. Remove the loaf pan to release the juices.

TWO CUTS OF BRISKET

Cut from the cow's breast section, a whole brisket is a boneless, coarse-grained cut comprised of two smaller roasts: the flat (or first) cut and the point (or second) cut. The knobby point cut (A) overlaps the rectangular flat cut (B). The point cut has more marbling and fat, and the flat cut's meat is lean and topped with a thick fat cap. Our recipe calls for the widely available flat cut (B). Make sure that the fat cap isn't overtrimmed and is about ¼ inch thick.

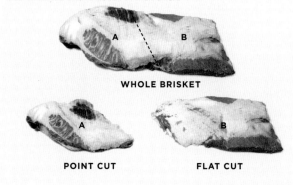

WHOLE BRISKET

POINT CUT　　　　**FLAT CUT**

the brisket is heated through, about 1 hour. Reheat the juices in a microwave or saucepan set over medium heat. Continue with the recipe as directed.)

4. Transfer the brisket to a cutting board, slice thinly across the grain, and return to the baking dish. Pour 1 cup of the reserved defatted juices over the sliced brisket. Whisk the ketchup, vinegar, and liquid smoke into the remaining juices. Season with salt and pepper to taste. Serve, passing the sauce at the table.

TEXAS BARBECUED BEEF RIBS

PORK RIBS MAY REIGN SUPREME across most of this country, but Texans do things their own way. In Texas, you have to have beef ribs, and they differ from barbecued pork ribs in nearly every way, from the Flinstonian size to an unapologetically meaty flavor. You don't have to wear pointy boots to eat them, but your expectations may need some corralling. While pork ribs often cook until the meat slips off the bone, beef ribs retain some chew. Bite into a good beef rib and it'll fight back—just a little. Don't expect a sticky coat of sauce on beef ribs, either. While a sauce is sometimes served on the side, beef ribs need no distractions.

The challenge to replicating these ribs at home is twofold: lack of equipment and lack of patience. I've seen industrial smoke pits 20 feet long, the interior grates lined with beef ribs. A smoke box at one end is fed around the clock on a steady diet of seasoned hickory, post oak, or mesquite logs. As the wood burns, the low heat and smoke waft through the meat, melting away the fat, building smoldering flavor, and creating unforgettable crust—known to barbecue fans as bark. The process can take 10 hours, plus a lot of dedication. Could I streamline it to work on my kettle grill without shortchanging the ribs?

I tried smoking the ribs indirectly (all the coals banked to one side of the grill, and the ribs placed over the empty side) and used wood chips to try to duplicate the smoke of a pit. The ribs required seven long hours. The beef itself is the toughest problem—literally. Beef ribs contain a lot of connective tissue sometimes referred to as collagen. Collagen needs a slow, steady supply of low heat to break down and tenderize. I'd found plenty of recipes that parboiled the ribs before placing them on a smoker. It makes sense, as boiling, braising, and steaming are all efficient ways to break down collagen. But in the test

TEXAS BARBECUED BEEF RIBS

kitchen we've found that any tenderness gained by boiling meat is canceled out by its washed-out flavor. Might one of those other techniques help render the fattier bits and speed things along?

Next I smoked the ribs over indirect heat for just an hour and a half. I then brought them inside, placed them on a baking rack set over a pan of water, wrapped both ribs and pan tightly with foil, and cooked them in a 300-degree oven until tender. Two hours later, the smoky flavor was strong and the ribs were tender with just a tug of resistance. The low, moist heat had done the trick. Unfortunately, the bark turned soggy in the oven.

I thought a hotter oven might speed the cooking time (making for a drier exterior), but this succeeded only in making the meat overcook and shred. I next eliminated the water from the pan, and instead clustered the ribs in a heavy sheet of foil, figuring their natural juices would finish steaming them. The bark was as soggy as before, and the ribs were far from tender. Finally, it dawned on me that I should try reversing the order of cooking: Steam the ribs first, then finish by smoking them on the grill. I tried my reverse two-step cooking process: The meat was tender with just the right amount of chew and was surrounded by a crusty layer of spice and smoke. I balanced the heat from the rub by adding 3 tablespoons of sugar and went out to the grill one last time. I now had the flavors of Texas in my own backyard.

—KRIS WIDICAN, *Cook's Country*

Texas Barbecued Beef Ribs

SERVES 4

Make sure the ribs you buy have a substantial amount of meat on the bones; otherwise, the rewards of making this recipe are few. Beef ribs are sold in slabs with up to 7 bones, but we prefer slabs with 3 to 4 bones, which are easier to manage on the grill.

SAUCE

- 2 tablespoons unsalted butter
- ¼ cup minced onion
- 2 garlic cloves, minced
- 1½ teaspoons chili powder
- 1½ teaspoons pepper
- ½ teaspoon dry mustard
- 2 cups tomato juice
- 6 tablespoons white vinegar
- 2 tablespoons Worcestershire sauce
- 2 tablespoons brown sugar
- 2 tablespoons molasses
- Salt

RIBS

- 3 tablespoons brown sugar
- 4 teaspoons chili powder
- ½ teaspoon cayenne pepper
- 1 tablespoon salt
- 2 teaspoons pepper
- 3-4 (3 to 4-rib) beef rib slabs (about 5 pounds) (see note)
- 1 cup wood chips, soaked in water for 15 minutes and drained

1. FOR THE SAUCE: Melt the butter in a saucepan over medium heat. Cook the onion until softened, about 5 minutes. Stir in the garlic, chili powder, pepper, and mustard and cook until fragrant, about 30 seconds. Stir in the tomato juice, vinegar, Worcestershire, sugar, and molasses and simmer until the sauce is reduced to 2 cups, about 20 minutes. Season with salt to taste. (The sauce can be refrigerated in an airtight container for up to 1 week.)

2. FOR THE RIBS: Adjust an oven rack to the middle position and heat the oven to 300 degrees. Combine the sugar, chili powder, cayenne, salt, and pepper in a bowl. Pat the ribs dry with paper towels and rub the sugar mixture all over the ribs. (The ribs can be covered in plastic wrap and refrigerated for up 24 hours.)

3. Arrange the ribs on a wire rack set inside a rimmed baking sheet. Add just enough water to cover the pan bottom, then cover the pan tightly with aluminum foil and bake until the fat has rendered and the meat begins to pull away from the bones, about 2 hours. Seal the soaked wood chips in a foil packet and cut vent holes in the top (see page 149).

4A. FOR A CHARCOAL GRILL: Open the bottom grill vents halfway. Light a large chimney starter filled with charcoal briquettes (100 briquettes; 6 quarts). When the coals are hot, pour them into a steeply banked pile against one side of the grill. Place the wood chip packet on top of the coals. Set the cooking grate in place, cover, and open the lid vents halfway. Heat the grill until hot and the wood chips begin to smoke heavily, about 5 minutes.

4B. FOR A GAS GRILL: Place the wood chip packet directly on the primary burner. Turn all the burners to high, cover, and heat the grill until hot and the wood chips begin to smoke heavily, about 15 minutes. Leave the primary burner on high and turn off the other burner(s). (Adjust the burners as needed to maintain the grill temperature around 350 degrees.)

5. Clean and oil the cooking grate. Place the ribs on the cooler side of the grill and cook, covered, flipping and rotating the slabs once, until the ribs are lightly charred and smoky, about 1½ hours. Transfer to a cutting board, tent with foil, and let rest for 10 minutes. Serve, passing the sauce separately.

NOTES FROM THE TEST KITCHEN

SHOPPING FOR BEEF RIBS

Texas-style barbecued beef ribs are all about the meat. Because beef ribs are located on the cow next to expensive cuts such as rib-eye and prime rib, butchers often overtrim the ribs so they can maximize the meat on the pricier cuts. Be sure to buy slabs with a thick layer of meat that covers the bones. Also, steer clear of the seven-rib slabs, which won't fit on the kettle grill. A three or four-rib slab works best.

TOO SKIMPY
Bony ribs are better suited for the stockpot than the smoke pit.

TOO BIG
Mammoth ribs are hard to squeeze onto a kettle grill.

JUST RIGHT
It's easy to place and move smaller three to four-rib slabs.

THE BEST CHIMNEY STARTER

We wouldn't dream of starting a charcoal fire without a chimney starter. These cylindrical canisters quickly ignite quarts of briquettes without lighter fluid. You put briquettes in the large top chamber, place a crumpled sheet of newspaper in the smaller chamber under the coals, and light it. In about 20 minutes, the coals are red-hot, covered with a fine, gray ash, and ready to pour into your grill. Our favorite is the **Weber RapidFire Chimney Starter,** $14.95, for its sturdy construction, generous capacity, heat-resistant handle, and second handle for better leverage. It also has plenty of ventilation holes in its canister, maximizing airflow and allowing coals to ignite quickly.

BALTIMORE PIT BEEF

ASK JUST ABOUT ANYONE what food Baltimore is famous for and the answer is likely to be blue crabs. That said, the city's one-of-a-kind style of barbecue deserves its due, too. Known as Baltimore pit beef, this regional specialty calls for a large roast to be grilled (but not smoked) over intensely hot coals while being flipped constantly to avoid burning. The meat comes off the grill well charred, almost black on the exterior but not burned, and rosy pink in the center, bordering on rare. The meat is sliced thin, piled on Kaiser rolls, and topped with sliced onions and a horseradish-mayonnaise mixture some locals refer to as "tiger sauce." The final result is tender, smoky, and spicy. I wanted to re-create this relatively unknown player, tiger sauce and all.

Round cuts, the traditional choice of Baltimore pit masters, are a varied lot, consisting of bottom, top, and eye round roasts. I wanted a piece of meat that was tender, flavorful, and manageable on the grill and would cook evenly. Eye round fit the bill.

Although most pit beef is seasoned with salt and pepper only, a few pit masters swear by using no seasoning at all, while others favor a spice rub. I tried all these approaches, and tasters liked the spice-rubbed meat best. Allowing the rub to sit on the meat for at least one hour, or up to 24 hours (the longer the better), yielded the best flavor.

Throughout my early tests, I adhered religiously to the test kitchen's approach to attaining medium-rare meat, pulling the meat off the grill once it reached between 120 and 125 degrees and allowing it to rest. After resting, however, my roasts were repeatedly cooked beyond medium-rare. After some research, I discovered that the amount of carryover cooking a piece of meat experiences is directly proportional to the intensity of the cooking heat. Usually we take meat off the grill when it reaches 5 to 10 degrees below the final target. But I was cooking over unusually red-hot coals for upward of half an hour, so to achieve a perfect medium-rare I needed to cook the roast only to between 95 and 100 degrees in order to reach medium-rare after a 30-minute rest.

With my cooking technique perfected, I turned my attention to the sauce. I learned from several pit masters in Baltimore that most sauces just stick to the basics: mayonnaise and horseradish with little or no embellishment. I followed suit, adding a touch of garlic, cayenne, and a splash of lemon juice for a little extra oomph.

—BRYAN ROOF, *America's Test Kitchen Books*

Baltimore Pit Beef

SERVES 8

In Baltimore, a deli slicer is often used to shave the meat thinly for sandwiches. We found it easiest to cut the roast in half lengthwise before slicing it as thinly as possible. We prefer this beef cooked medium-rare, but if you prefer it more or less done see "Testing Meat for Doneness" on page 139; plan on the temperature of the meat rising 20 to 30 degrees while resting in step 5.

SAUCE

- ⅓ cup prepared horseradish
- ⅓ cup mayonnaise
- 1 teaspoon fresh lemon juice
- 1 garlic clove, minced
  Pinch cayenne pepper
  Salt and pepper

BEEF

- 2 teaspoons salt
- 2 teaspoons paprika
- 1 teaspoon pepper
- ½ teaspoon garlic powder
- ½ teaspoon dried oregano
- ¼ teaspoon cayenne pepper
- 1 (3-pound) boneless eye round roast, trimmed
- 2 teaspoons vegetable oil
- 8 Kaiser rolls, warmed
- 1 onion, halved and sliced thin

1. FOR THE SAUCE: Whisk the horseradish, mayonnaise, lemon juice, garlic, and cayenne together in a bowl and season with salt and pepper to taste. (The sauce can be refrigerated in an airtight container for up to 2 days.)

2. FOR THE BEEF: Combine the salt, paprika, pepper, garlic powder, oregano, and cayenne in a bowl. Pat the meat dry with paper towels and rub it evenly with the spice mixture. Cover the meat with plastic wrap and let sit at room temperature for at least 1 hour, or refrigerate for up to 24 hours. (If refrigerated, let sit at room temperature for 1 hour before grilling.) Before cooking, unwrap the meat and rub it evenly with the oil.

3A. FOR A CHARCOAL GRILL: Open the bottom grill vents completely. Light a large chimney starter filled with charcoal briquettes (100 briquettes; 6 quarts). When the coals are hot, pour them in an even layer over half the grill, leaving the other half empty. Set the cooking grate in place, cover, and heat the grill until hot, about 5 minutes.

3B. FOR A GAS GRILL: Turn all the burners to high, cover, and heat the grill until hot, about 15 minutes. (Adjust the burners as needed to maintain a hot fire; see page 130).

4. Clean and oil the cooking grate. Place the meat on the hotter part of the grill. Cook (covered, if using gas), turning often, until evenly blackened on all sides and the center of the meat registers 95 to 100 degrees on an instant-read thermometer (for medium-rare), about 30 minutes.

5. Transfer the meat to a carving board, tent loosely with foil, and let rest for 30 minutes. Cut the roast in half lengthwise, then slice it, against the grain, as thinly as possible. Divide the sliced meat equally among the rolls, top with the sliced onion and sauce, and serve.

NOTES FROM THE TEST KITCHEN

OUR FAVORITE SLICING KNIFE

A slicing knife is indispensable year-round for cutting everything from brisket on the Fourth of July to roasts during the holidays. Specially designed to cut neatly through meat's muscle fibers and connective tissues, no other knife can cut with such precision in a single stroke. We already knew the key attributes to look for: an extra-long, sturdy, tapered blade with a round tip, which allows for easy, trouble-free strokes; a granton edge, which means the knife has oval scallops carved into both sides of the blade, making a thinner edge on the blade possible without sacrificing the heft or rigidity carried by the top of the blade—perfect for producing thinner slices with little effort; and, finally, a comfortable handle. After testing eight knives that fit this criteria, the **Forschner Fibrox 12-inch Granton Edge Slicing Knife Model 47645**, $44.95, came out in front, scoring top points in slicing, sharpness, and comfort. (See page 305 for more information about our testing results.)

ROAST BEEF TENDERLOIN

THOUGH IT IS MILD IN FLAVOR, nothing beats the extravagantly buttery texture of beef tenderloin. The challenge is in expertly cooking the meat—typically the roast either emerges from the oven without the dark, caramelized crust that gives meat a deep roasted flavor, or is marred by a thick, gray band of overdone meat near the edge. And considering its steep price, overcooking this special-occasion roast is not an option.

With only two tenderloin roast options, whole and center-cut, we faced a straightforward choice. Whole tenderloin is huge—the typical roast is 5 or 6 pounds, serving up to 16 people. It often comes covered in a thick layer of fat and sinew that is time-consuming to trim and peel, plus its long, tapered shape is a challenge to cook evenly. We prefer the smaller center-cut roast, known as the Châteaubriand. Some butchers charge significantly more for center-cut versus whole tenderloin, but it comes already trimmed (so there's no waste) and its cylindrical shape practically guarantees that both ends cook to the same degree of doneness. What you're getting is the best of the best—the centerpiece of the most exquisitely tender part of the cow.

To achieve a good crust on the meat, I could either sear it first in a skillet or simply crank up the oven as high as it would go, at the beginning or end of cooking. A few tests ruled out oven-searing. No matter what I tried—starting out high (at 500 degrees) and dropping down much lower (400 degrees), or the reverse—the meat would not brown adequately. My best results came from simply cooking the tenderloin at 425 degrees for half an hour and turning it after 15 minutes, but the pesky band of gray, overcooked meat at the edge remained.

Pan-searing it would have to be. I heated a few tablespoons of vegetable oil in a large skillet and then added my roast, browning it on all sides before transferring it to the oven. I placed it on a wire rack set inside a rimmed baking sheet to promote air circulation and more even cooking. I prepared several roasts this way and experimented with different oven temperatures, from 500 degrees on down to 350. Naturally, each of these roasts had a good-looking crust, but each also had an overdone "ring around the collar." The best of the bunch was the tenderloin roasted at 350, but there was still room for improvement. Tinkering around, I decided to try reversing the cooking order, roasting first, then searing, a technique we've used successfully in other meat recipes. The switch worked wonders here as well. Searing the roast when it was warm and dry meant that it could reach the necessary browning temperature of 310 degrees a lot faster than searing it raw, cold, and wet. Less searing time, in turn, minimized the overcooked layer of gray.

Could I get rid of the gray band altogether by taking the oven temperature down further? In the past, the test kitchen has roasted meat at even lower temperatures with great success, transforming tough, inexpensive cuts into meltingly tender meat. I hadn't initially thought to try slow roasting because tenderloin is so soft to begin with. Now I reconsidered. After tying several more roasts, I put them in the oven and began dialing back the temperature from 350 degrees. As it turned out, I didn't have that far to go: 300 degrees proved the magic temperature for yielding consistent ruby coloring from edge to edge.

Despite decent progress, I still hadn't coaxed deep beefy flavor from my mild-mannered tenderloin. The issue was the meat itself: With so little fat, it was lacking ideal flavor, even after searing to create a crust and carefully calibrating the cooking. I was curious to explore some of the offbeat techniques I'd come across in my research. The most appealing involved roasting the meat wrapped in a couple slices of bacon, which then get discarded when the meat is seared. But bacon caused the meat to steam and didn't really add or detract flavor. Shrouding the tenderloin in butter-soaked cheesecloth produced similarly uninspiring results. And soaking the meat in a soy-Worcestershire mix—ingredients often used to accentuate beef flavor—was just plain overpowering.

In the end, a tried-and-true method proved best—sprinkling the meat with salt, covering it with plastic wrap, and letting it sit at room temperature. After sitting for an hour, the roast cooked up with significantly more flavor. Here's why: The salt draws juices out of the meat, then the reverse happens and the salt and moisture flow back in, drawing flavor deep into the meat.

I got the best results of all when, after salting the meat, I rubbed it with a couple of tablespoons of softened butter before cooking, which added surprisingly satisfying richness. In fact, this technique was so effective that I decided against a rich, complex sauce and instead created an easy compound butter, combining shallot, garlic, and parsley. The wafting aroma of the flavored butter melting into the crevices of the meat proved irresistible to tasters. I had spent $1,200 on more than 25 tenderloins, but that satisfaction made it worth every penny.

—CHARLES KELSEY, *Cook's Illustrated*

THE TROUBLE WITH TENDERLOIN

There are two common problems with beef tenderloin: Either it has a good flavorful crust but a band of gray, overcooked meat near the edge, or it is rosy from edge to edge but lacks a good crust and meaty flavor. Our recipe solves both problems.

CRUSTY BUT OVERCOOKED   **EVENLY COOKED BUT NO CRUST**

PREPARING BEEF TENDERLOIN

1. After salting the meat and letting it stand for 1 hour, rub the roast with a small amount of softened butter.

2. Roast the tenderloin in a 300-degree oven.

3. Sear the tenderloin on the stovetop after roasting.

4. Top with the herb butter before the meat rests.

Roast Beef Tenderloin

SERVES 4 TO 6

Ask your butcher to prepare a trimmed, center-cut Châteaubriand from the whole tenderloin, as this cut is not usually available without special ordering. If you are cooking for a crowd, this recipe can be doubled to make two roasts. Sear the roasts one after the other, wiping out the pan and adding new oil after searing the first roast. Both pieces of meat can be roasted on the same rack. We prefer this roast cooked to medium-rare, but if you prefer it more or less done see "Testing Meat for Doneness" on page 139.

SHALLOT-PARSLEY BUTTER

- 4 tablespoons (½ stick) unsalted butter, softened
- 1 small shallot, minced (about 2 tablespoons)
- 1 garlic clove, minced
- 1 tablespoon chopped fresh parsley
- ¼ teaspoon salt
- ¼ teaspoon pepper

BEEF

- 1 (2-pound) beef tenderloin center-cut Châteaubriand, trimmed of fat and silver skin (see note)
- 2 teaspoons kosher salt or 1 teaspoon table salt
- 1 teaspoon coarsely ground pepper
- 2 tablespoons unsalted butter, softened
- 1 tablespoon vegetable oil

1. FOR THE SHALLOT-PARSLEY BUTTER: Combine all the ingredients in a medium bowl and set aside.

2. FOR THE BEEF: Using 12-inch lengths of twine, tie the roast crosswise at 1½-inch intervals. Sprinkle the roast evenly with the salt, cover loosely with plastic wrap, and let stand at room temperature for 1 hour. Meanwhile, adjust an oven rack to the middle position and heat the oven to 300 degrees.

3. Pat the roast dry with paper towels. Sprinkle the roast evenly with the pepper and spread the unsalted butter evenly over the surface. Transfer the roast to a wire rack set in a rimmed baking sheet. Roast until the center of the roast registers 120 to 125 degrees on an instant-read thermometer (for medium-rare), 40 to 55 minutes, flipping the roast halfway through cooking.

4. Heat the oil in a 12-inch skillet over medium-high heat until just smoking. Place the roast in the skillet and sear until well browned on all four sides, 1 to 2 minutes per side (for a total of 4 to 8 minutes). Transfer the roast to a carving board and spread 2 tablespoons of the flavored butter evenly over the top of the roast; let rest for 15 minutes. Remove the twine and cut the meat crosswise into ½-inch-thick slices. Serve, passing the remaining flavored butter separately.

BEEF EN COCOTTE

COOKING EN COCOTTE, or casserole-roasting, is a common cooking method in France. The approach is simple: Place a piece of meat in a pot, scatter in a small handful of chopped vegetables, cover, and bake. Cooking beef en cocotte, I hoped, would combine the best aspects of both braising and roasting. It would allow me to take an inexpensive cut of beef and make it tender in much the same way that braising does—the low, slow heat allows the fibers time to break down, rendering a tough piece of meat tender. But unlike braising, no liquid is added to the pot; instead, juices are drawn from the meat and into the pot, and the meat cooks in its own juices. These juices create a moist-heat environment, so that the meat cooks gently and its flavors are concentrated. As with roasting, the technique would allow me to cook the meat to the desired doneness (such as medium-rare) without having to spend a lot of money on an already-tender, prime piece of meat.

Three inexpensive roasts immediately came to mind as possibilities for this method: eye round roast (a lean cut from the leg that usually becomes tender when cooked slowly), chuck roast (the popular choice for stews and pot roast, it contains a higher than usual amount of sinew and collagen), and top sirloin roast (lean with bold, beefy flavor and ideal for grill-roasting and roasting to medium-rare).

To determine which roast we liked best, I seared each in a Dutch oven, then placed the covered pot in the oven at 250 degrees. I was surprised to discover how quickly these roasts cooked—they all took about 25 minutes to reach medium-rare. This was not enough time for the chuck roast to become tender; instead, it was unbearably chewy, with strands of sinew throughout. The eye round roast was a bit more promising but was still tough despite its rosy interior. Top sirloin was far and away the best option as it was noticeably more tender, with

concentrated beef flavor. Sticking with top sirloin, I settled on a 3 to 4-pound roast, which I trimmed of excess fat and then tied prior to searing to help ensure even cooking. With my cut of meat and the cooking time settled, all I needed to do was work on building some other flavors to complement the beef.

Onions are a classic accompaniment to beef, and I thought the sweetness of caramelized onions would provide a nice balance of flavors. I had the best results caramelizing the onions in the pot after the beef was seared. To boost the flavor of the onions I added some garlic and then deglazed the pot with a little sherry, scraping up the fond as the liquid reduced. (Since I didn't want liquid in the pot when it went into the oven, I made sure to let the sherry reduce before adding the seared beef back in.) I placed the beef on top of the onions and covered the pot, then into the oven it went. Once the meat was cooked to medium-rare, I let it rest while I completed my sauce. I added chicken broth to the onions and reduced the mixture slightly to concentrate the flavors, then finished the sauce with a little butter for richness. I was pleased with the results—cooking beef en cocotte allowed me to take an inexpensive cut of meat and turn it into a tender, perfectly cooked roast.

—BRYAN ROOF, *America's Test Kitchen Books*

Beef en Cocotte with Caramelized Onions
SERVES 6 TO 8

Be sure to trim the meat well or you'll wind up with a greasy sauce; feel free to ask your butcher to trim and tie the roast for you. We prefer this roast cooked to medium-rare, but if you prefer it more or less done see "Testing Meat for Doneness" on page 139.

1 (3 to 4-pound) top sirloin roast, trimmed and tied once around the middle (see page 160) (see note)
  Salt and pepper
3 tablespoons vegetable oil
3 onions, halved and sliced thin
3 garlic cloves, peeled and crushed
¼ cup dry sherry
2 cups low-sodium chicken broth
1 tablespoon unsalted butter

1. Adjust an oven rack to the lowest position and heat the oven to 250 degrees. Pat the beef dry with paper towels and season with salt and pepper.

2. Heat 2 tablespoons of the oil in a large Dutch oven over medium-high heat until just smoking. Brown the beef well on all sides, 7 to 10 minutes, reducing the heat if the pot begins to scorch. Transfer the beef to a large plate.

3. Add the remaining 1 tablespoon oil to the pot and heat over medium heat until shimmering. Add the onions and garlic, cover, and cook until softened and wet, about 5 minutes. Remove the lid and continue to cook the onions, stirring often, until dry and well browned, 10 to 12 minutes. Stir in the sherry, scraping up any browned bits, and cook until almost all of the liquid has evaporated, about 1 minute.

4. Off the heat, nestle the beef, along with any accumulated juices, into the pot. Place a large sheet of foil over the pot and press tightly to seal, then cover with the lid. Transfer the pot to the oven and cook until the center of the roast registers 120 to 125 degrees on an instant-read thermometer (for medium-rare), 20 to 30 minutes.

5. Remove the pot from the oven. Transfer the beef to a cutting board, tent loosely with foil, and let rest for 20 minutes. Stir the chicken broth into the onions and simmer over medium-high heat until slightly thickened, about 2 minutes. Off the heat, whisk in the butter, season with salt and pepper to taste, and cover to keep warm.

6. Remove the twine, slice the meat against the grain into ¼-inch-thick slices, and transfer to a platter. Spoon the sauce over the meat and serve.

NOTES FROM THE TEST KITCHEN

TYING TOP SIRLOIN

To correct for an unevenly cut or oddly shaped top sirloin roast, and to ensure even cooking, tie a piece of kitchen twine around the center of the roast.

CLASSIC ROAST BEEF AND GRAVY

THE BEST ROAST BEEF IS COOKED GENTLY to keep all its juices inside. But without enough pan drippings, how do you make rich, beefy gravy? The worst roasts produce the best gravy. That's because when roast beef is cooked at too high a temperature, the fibers in the meat contract, forcing out the flavorful juices. These juices are the foundation of great gravy, but if you find a lot in the roasting pan, it means the meat will be dry and tough. For beef roasts that cook evenly and retain their flavorful juices, we've learned that a low-to-moderate oven is best. But how do you make rich, meaty gravy from a roast that doesn't throw off much liquid?

I began with top sirloin roast, the test kitchen's choice for a beef roast that balances flavor, tenderness, and economy. To determine the ideal roasting temperature, I seasoned five top sirloin roasts with salt and pepper (letting the salted roast sit for an hour or more promoted well-seasoned, even juicier meat) and browned each roast on the stovetop to develop a flavorful crust. I roasted each one at a different oven temperature until the meat registered about 125 degrees (for medium-rare). The roast cooked at 375 degrees threw off a plethora of juice, leaving the meat dry and with an overcooked gray ring around the exterior. The roast improved with each step down in roasting temperature. The best temperature was 275, which produced juicy meat (having expelled very little liquid), a uniformly rosy interior (no gray ring from too much heat) in under two hours—and precious little liquid in the roasting pan.

Gravy is usually made by pouring these liquid contents into a fat separator. The fat is heated in a pan (sometimes the empty roasting pan), and flour is stirred in to make a roux. Then the flavorful juices are whisked in and reduced into rich, viscous gravy. I didn't have any meat juices to work with, but I did have some rendered fat (and fond, the flavorful browned bits that form on the pan bottom) in my Dutch oven from searing the roast. I started my gravy by sautéing onion, carrot, and celery in the rendered fat. Once the vegetables were soft, I stirred in the flour, then store-bought beef broth, scraping up the flavor-rich fond. I reduced and strained the gravy, but without the meat juices it was missing richness. For the next batch, I added garlic to the vegetables and

CLASSIC ROAST BEEF AND GRAVY

red wine to the broth. Both additions helped, but the gravy still lacked complexity and roasted flavor.

We often use sautéed mushrooms and tomato paste to add depth of flavor reminiscent of roasted meats. These two ingredients greatly improved the "meaty" flavor of the gravy (with the tomato paste also contributing body), but something was still missing. That something turned out to be Worcestershire sauce, whose salty, sweet, and acidic essence made the gravy taste truly rich and meaty. After dozens of tests, I'd finally made a gravy—without pan drippings—that was worthy of my perfectly cooked roast beef.

—KELLEY BAKER, *Cook's Country*

Classic Roast Beef and Gravy

SERVES 6 TO 8

For the best flavor and texture, refrigerate the roast overnight after salting. If you don't have a V-rack, cook the roast on a wire rack set inside a rimmed baking sheet. We prefer this roast cooked to medium-rare, but if you prefer it more or less done see "Testing Meat for Doneness" on page 139.

1	**(4-pound) top sirloin roast, fat trimmed to ¼-inch thickness (see note)**
	Salt and pepper
1	tablespoon vegetable oil
8	ounces white mushrooms, chopped
2	onions, minced (about 2 cups)
1	carrot, peeled and chopped
1	celery rib, chopped
1	tablespoon tomato paste
4	garlic cloves, minced
¼	cup unbleached all-purpose flour
1	cup red wine
4	cups low-sodium beef broth
1	teaspoon Worcestershire sauce

1. Pat the roast dry with paper towels. Rub 2 teaspoons salt evenly over the surface of the meat. Cover with plastic wrap and refrigerate for at least 1 hour or up to 24 hours.

2. Adjust an oven rack to the lower-middle position and heat the oven to 275 degrees. Pat the roast dry with paper towels and rub with 1 teaspoon pepper. Heat the oil in a large Dutch oven over medium-high heat until just smoking. Brown the roast on all sides, 8 to 12 minutes, then transfer to a V-rack set inside a roasting pan (do not wipe out the Dutch oven). Transfer to the oven and cook until the center of the meat registers 120 to 125 degrees on an instant-read thermometer (for medium-rare), 1½ to 2 hours.

3. Meanwhile, add the mushrooms to the fat in the Dutch oven and cook over medium heat until golden, about 5 minutes. Stir in the onions, carrot, and celery and cook until browned, 8 to 10 minutes. Stir in the tomato paste, garlic, and flour and cook until fragrant, about 2 minutes. Stir in the wine and broth, scraping up any browned bits with a wooden spoon. Bring to a boil, then reduce the heat to medium and simmer until thickened, about 10 minutes. Strain the gravy, then stir in the Worcestershire and season with salt and pepper to taste; cover and keep warm.

4. Transfer the roast to a cutting board, tent with foil, and let rest for 20 minutes. Slice the roast crosswise against the grain into ½-inch-thick slices. Serve with the gravy.

NOTES FROM THE TEST KITCHEN

THE BEST PLASTIC WRAP

Plastic wrap is essential for storing, freezing, and keeping food fresh, but problems with plastic wrap abound: the plastic clings to itself more than the dish or won't stick at all, and more important, it doesn't keep food from spoiling quickly. Has any brand overcome these failings? As it turns out, plastic wrap today can be made from two distinctly different substances: a food-safe version of PVC (polyvinyl chloride) or LDPE (low-density polyethylene). The main difference? PVC clings but is not impermeable; LDPE is impermeable but has far less cling. The bottom line? Clingy PVC wraps such as Reynolds, Stretch-Tite, and FreezeTite are preferable if you are transporting food or are worried about spills and leaks, but to keep foods fresh longer, select plastic wraps made from LDPE and reach for a box of our all-around winner, **Glad Cling Wrap**, $1.20 per 100 square feet. (See page 307 for more information about our testing results.)

GLAZED MEAT LOAF

SAY MEAT LOAF AND MOST AMERICANS THINK 1950S comfort food and Mom, but this humble recipe has surprisingly elegant roots in a now-forgotten dish called "cannelon." A typical cannelon recipe from the *Fannie Farmer Original 1896 Boston Cooking-School Cook Book* calls for chopping and seasoning beef, shaping it into a log, and basting with melted butter as it bakes. The wide availability of meat grinders and the advent of reliable refrigeration made ground beef a household staple in the early 20th century, and meat loaf recipes gained wide circulation. But popularity rarely translates into perfection. My goal was to make meat loaf special again.

Over the years, meat loaves have been dressed up and down every which way. I tested recipes that used a range of ingredients and cooking methods. Some were OK, but none had everything my tasters and I wanted: moist meat, hearty beef flavor, classic seasonings, and a well-browned crust enhanced with a simple ketchup-based glaze. The one thing these early trials reaffirmed is the test kitchen's technique of cooking the meat loaf free-form; one and all, meat loaves baked in pans emerged with greasy, mushy undersides.

Many recipes rely on meat loaf mix, a blend of ground chuck, pork, and veal available in most supermarkets. Loaves made from this blend can be good, but because the mix varies from store to store it yields inconsistent results. I wanted something more reliable, so I first tried an all-beef meat loaf made from ground sirloin. This loaf had good meaty flavor—so good that it now tasted too much like a burger. Cutting the ground beef with an equal portion of sweet ground pork (ground veal isn't as readily available) balanced the beefy flavor. The traditional seasonings of salt, pepper, Dijon mustard, Worcestershire sauce, and parsley emerged as clear favorites—especially when mixed with sautéed onion and garlic.

The meat loaf now had great flavor, but it was dry and crumbly. Eggs were the obvious binder; two eggs, plus an extra yolk for richness, proved perfect. We sometimes use a panade (a paste of milk and bread or crackers) to add moisture to meat loaves and meatballs, so I tested different versions. My tasters preferred the mild saltiness of the panade made with milk and saltines to those that contained bread. Combining the panade in a food processor and then pulsing it with the meat gave the loaf the most cohesive, tender texture.

I had been following test kitchen protocol, letting the meat loaf bake to near doneness before turning on the broiler and brushing on an easy glaze of brown sugar and ketchup. But the top and sides of the loaf beaded with moisture in the oven, preventing a flavorful crust from forming. And without a dry, textured crust, the glaze slid off before it could caramelize and thicken. After I tried several fruitless tests that involved fiddling with baking and broiling specifics, a colleague suggested I broil the meat loaf before glazing and baking, to evaporate the surface moisture that was inhibiting the formation of a crust. This worked beautifully, and the browned crust gave the glaze—applied twice for extra effect—something to hang onto. This technique, combined with the tender, flavorful meat, made for one heck of a meat loaf.

—KRIS WIDICAN, *Cook's Country*

Glazed Meat Loaf

SERVES 6 TO 8

Both ground sirloin and ground chuck work well here, but avoid ground round—it is gristly and bland.

GLAZE
- 1 cup ketchup
- ¼ cup packed brown sugar
- 2½ tablespoons cider vinegar
- ½ teaspoon hot sauce

MEAT LOAF
- 2 teaspoons vegetable oil
- 1 onion, minced (about 1 cup)
- 2 garlic cloves, minced
- ⅔ cup crushed saltine crackers (about 17 crackers)
- ⅓ cup whole milk
- 1 pound 90 percent lean ground beef (see note)
- 1 pound ground pork
- 2 large eggs plus 1 large yolk
- 2 teaspoons Dijon mustard
- 2 teaspoons Worcestershire sauce
- ½ teaspoon dried thyme
- ⅓ cup chopped fresh parsley
- 1 teaspoon salt
- ¾ teaspoon pepper

1. FOR THE GLAZE: Whisk all the ingredients together in a saucepan until the sugar dissolves. Reserve ¼ cup of the glaze mixture, then simmer the remaining glaze over medium heat until slightly thickened, about 5 minutes. Cover and keep warm.

2. FOR THE MEAT LOAF: Line a rimmed baking sheet with foil and coat lightly with vegetable oil spray. Heat the oil in a nonstick skillet over medium heat until shimmering. Cook the onion until golden, about 8 minutes. Add the garlic and cook until fragrant, about 30 seconds. Transfer to a large bowl and set aside.

3. Process the saltines and milk in a food processor until smooth, about 10 seconds. Add the beef and pork and pulse until well combined, about 10 pulses. Transfer the meat mixture to the bowl with the cooled onion mixture. Add the eggs and yolk, mustard, Worcestershire, thyme, parsley, salt, and pepper to the bowl and mix with your hands until combined.

4. Adjust the oven racks to the upper (about 4 inches away from the broiler element) and middle positions and heat the broiler. Transfer the meat mixture to the prepared baking sheet and shape into a 9 by 5-inch loaf. Broil on the upper rack until well browned, about 5 minutes. Brush 2 tablespoons of the uncooked glaze over the top and sides of the loaf and return to the oven and broil until the glaze begins to brown, about 2 minutes.

5. Transfer the meat loaf to the middle rack and brush with the remaining uncooked glaze. Reduce the oven temperature to 350 degrees and bake until the center of the meat loaf registers 160 degrees on an instant-read thermometer, 40 to 45 minutes. Transfer to a cutting board, tent with foil, and let rest for 20 minutes. Slice and serve, passing the cooked glaze at the table.

NOTES FROM THE TEST KITCHEN

PREPARING MEAT LOAF

1. Sauté the onions.

2. Process the saltines, milk, and meat until smooth.

3. Bake the loaf on a rimmed baking sheet.

4. Broil the meat loaf, then glaze it.

PAN-FRIED PORK CHOPS

ORDER A PAN-FRIED PORK CHOP at a family-style restaurant in the South and what you're served is a thing of beauty. Bone-in pork chops are dredged in highly seasoned flour and given a quick fry in lots of sizzling fat, traditionally bacon fat. At their best, the chops have a juicy, meaty interior set off by a thick, highly seasoned crust. For some reason, this no-fuss method has fallen out of favor with home cooks.

Is it because recipes can be maddeningly vague ("Season pork chop, cook in frying oil until done")? Other recipes I found called for gobs of bacon fat, harkening back to a time when cooks kept coffee cans of the stuff by their stoves. Dredging a chop, then sliding it into a pan of hot fat (more fat than with searing, less than with deep-frying) seems straightforward. But in fact, when I tried it, a few real challenges emerged. For one, that crispy crust kept chipping off. Also, the seasonings in many recipes proved musty, salty, or unbalanced. Finally, without the can of fat, the flavor of the chops left a lot to be desired.

Simply dredging the pork chops in flour, as most recipes instruct, produced a spotty, insubstantial crust that

PAN-FRIED PORK CHOPS

wouldn't stay put. I tried dipping them in buttermilk first, but the tang was a distraction, so I went back to the simple flour dredge. After several unsuccessful test batches, I noticed that the coatings on the dredged chops that sat around for a few minutes were getting a little wet and gummy. The test kitchen has had success letting floured chicken rest (just 10 minutes is enough) before redredging and frying. The second dredge makes for a sturdier, more substantial crust. Sure enough, my double-dipped chops emerged from the pan with a hefty, crisp, golden brown crust.

But the crust didn't taste like much. I added seasoned salt to the flour (too dusty and lacking punch), then supermarket spice mixes (musty and stale tasting). I tried making my own spice mix but went a little overboard concocting an elaborate 10-spice blend. Tasters eventually helped me pare it down to the essentials: garlic powder, paprika, salt, pepper, and cayenne. Applying the spices directly to the meat, rather than adding them to the flour, let me season the chops more thoroughly.

I'd been frying the pork chops in ½ cup vegetable oil—just enough to come about halfway up the sides of the chops. In a nod to older recipes, a colleague suggested I render some bacon and use the fat to flavor the oil. Augmenting the oil with the fat from three slices of bacon gave the cooked chops a depth of smoky flavor that, combined with the garlicky, golden crust, had tasters licking their chops.

—MEGHAN ERWIN, *Cook's Country*

NOTES FROM THE TEST KITCHEN

PREVENTING CURLY CHOPS
Pork chops have a tendency to curl as they cook. When exposed to the high heat of the pan, the ring of fat and connective tissue that surrounds the exterior tightens, causing the meat to buckle and curl. To prevent this, we cut two slits about 2 inches apart through the fat and connective tissue on each chop.

| **BUCKLED CHOP** | **FLAT CHOP** |
| No Slits | Slits Cut |

Pan-Fried Pork Chops
SERVES 4

Chops between ¾ and 1 inch thick are best for this recipe.

- 1 **teaspoon garlic powder**
- ½ **teaspoon paprika**
- ½ **teaspoon salt**
- ½ **teaspoon pepper**
- ¼ **teaspoon cayenne pepper**
- 1 **cup unbleached all-purpose flour**
- 4 **bone-in rib or center-cut pork chops, about ¾ inch thick (see note)**
- 3 **slices bacon, chopped**
- ½ **cup vegetable oil**

1. Combine the garlic powder, paprika, salt, pepper, and cayenne in a bowl. Place the flour in a shallow dish. Pat the chops dry with paper towels. Cut 2 slits about 2 inches apart through the fat on the edges of each chop (see photo). Season both sides of the chops with the spice mixture, then dredge the chops lightly in the flour (do not discard the flour). Transfer to a plate and let rest for 10 minutes.

2. Meanwhile, cook the bacon in a large nonstick skillet over medium heat until the fat renders and the bacon is crisp, about 8 minutes. Using a slotted spoon, transfer the bacon to a paper towel–lined plate and reserve for another use. Do not wipe out the pan.

3. Add the oil to the fat in the pan and heat over medium-high heat until just smoking. Return the chops to the flour dish and turn to coat. Cook the chops until well browned, 3 to 4 minutes per side. Serve.

VARIATIONS

Barbecued Pan-Fried Pork Chops
Follow the recipe for Pan-Fried Pork Chops, replacing the first five ingredients with 3 tablespoons light brown sugar, 1 teaspoon chili powder, 1 teaspoon paprika, ½ teaspoon salt, ½ teaspoon dry mustard, ¼ teaspoon ground cumin, and ¼ teaspoon cayenne pepper.

Herbed Pan-Fried Pork Chops
Follow the recipe for Pan-Fried Pork Chops, replacing the first five ingredients with ½ teaspoon dried marjoram, ½ teaspoon dried thyme, ¼ teaspoon dried basil, ¼ teaspoon dried rosemary (crumbled), ¼ teaspoon dried sage, pinch ground fennel, and ½ teaspoon salt.

SPICED PORK TENDERLOIN WITH POTATO RÖSTI

FOR A WEEKNIGHT SUPPER, nothing is simpler or tastier than a juicy pork tenderloin dressed up with a flavorful spice rub and roasted to perfection. That is, unless you want to take it to the next level and pair it with a wedge of crispy potato rösti. The national potato dish of Switzerland, rösti is made of strands of grated potato cooked until crisp with salt, pepper, and a healthy dose of butter and pressed into a single skillet-sized pancake. When it is served with a pork tenderloin seasoned with warm, bold spices, the pair evolves from uninspired pork and potatoes to a perfect flavor and texture combination.

I knew I wanted to brown the tenderloin in the skillet to flavor not only the meat but also the potatoes, which I would cook in the skillet once I moved the tenderloin to the oven to finish up. I browned the pork all over, then transferred it to the oven to finish cooking. After numerous tests, I found that about 15 minutes in a 425-degree oven produced the most evenly cooked, moist tenderloins.

The meat was perfectly cooked, but because pork tenderloin is so lean it has a very mild flavor—making it a perfect candidate for a spice rub. I cobbled together a warm spice mixture of caraway seeds, coriander, allspice, and nutmeg, rubbed it over the tenderloin, then browned it (switching from oil to butter for a rich, nutty flavor). Now I could turn my attention to the rösti.

I started by choosing the potato. I tested both Yukon Gold and russet potatoes, the two most popular choices used in my researched recipes, and tasters slightly favored the buttery flavor of the Yukon Golds. (In a pinch russets would work just fine.)

I really didn't anticipate the work involved in achieving a perfect rösti. My initial test involved simply shredding the potatoes, seasoning them with salt and pepper, then adding them to a hot skillet with some butter. This left me with a crispy, burnt exterior and raw, starchy strands of potato on the inside. Browning the outside wasn't going to be the challenge, it was cooking the inside while somehow removing the starchy gumminess.

As it turns out, excess moisture and starch are your worst enemies when making rösti. Too much moisture prevents proper browning of the exterior, and too much starch leaves the potatoes gummy. Soaking the shredded potatoes in a bowl of water, in effect rinsing them, removed enough of the starch to banish gumminess, and drying them lessened the moisture. Drying progressed from laying the potato strands on paper towels to ultimately squeezing them in a clean kitchen towel, which yielded the driest strands and, in turn, produced the lightest, fluffiest rösti yet.

The only problem with my method was that some starch was necessary to hold the rösti together, and now I had removed so much that my rösti was falling apart. My solution was to add a teaspoon of cornstarch. This was enough to hold it all together without making things gummy again.

One final trick led me to rösti perfection: covering the rösti as it cooked. My instincts told me that this would trap moisture and make the cake dense and gummy, yet just the opposite occurred. The gumminess had been due in part to undercooked potatoes, and the cover addressed that problem. The batches of rösti that were cooked covered for a period were surprisingly light, with the moist heat cooking the potatoes through more fully than dry heat alone. Further testing allowed me to zero in on a covered cooking time of six minutes, followed by two minutes uncovered to crisp and brown the bottom. Flipping the rösti, I continued cooking just long enough to brown the second side.

Served with a dollop of sour cream and applesauce, my spiced pork tenderloin and crispy potato rösti were a match made in heaven. Easy enough for a weeknight dinner but elegant enough for company, this skillet supper delivers big on flavor and small on labor.

—BRYAN ROOF, *America's Test Kitchen Books*

NOTES FROM THE TEST KITCHEN

REMOVING THE SILVER SKIN FROM PORK TENDERLOIN

The silver skin is a tough, thin, translucent membrane that covers parts of the tenderloin. Slip a knife under the silver skin, angle it slightly upward, and use a gentle back and forth motion to remove it.

Spiced Pork Tenderloin with Potato Rösti

SERVES 4

We prefer to shred the potatoes using the large shredding disk of a food processor. You can use a box grater, but the potatoes should be shredded lengthwise, so you are left with long shreds. It is important to squeeze the potatoes as dry as possible in step 1 to ensure a crisp exterior. Serve with applesauce and sour cream.

- 1½ pounds Yukon Gold or russet potatoes (3 to 4), peeled and shredded (see note)
- 1 teaspoon cornstarch
  Salt and pepper
- 1 teaspoon caraway seeds
- ½ teaspoon ground allspice
- ½ teaspoon ground coriander
- ¼ teaspoon ground nutmeg
- 2 (1 to 1¼-pound) pork tenderloins, trimmed (see page 167)
- 6 tablespoons (¾ stick) unsalted butter

1. Adjust an oven rack to the middle position and heat the oven to 425 degrees. Place the potatoes in a large bowl, fill with cold water, and swirl to remove excess starch. Drain the potatoes into a strainer. Working in two batches, wrap the potatoes in a clean kitchen towel, squeeze out the excess liquid, and transfer the potatoes to a dry bowl. Sprinkle the cornstarch, ½ teaspoon salt, and ¼ teaspoon pepper over the potatoes and gently toss until thoroughly incorporated; set aside.

2. Mix the caraway, allspice, coriander, nutmeg, 1 teaspoon salt, and ½ teaspoon pepper together in a small bowl. Pat the tenderloins dry with paper towels and rub them with the spice mixture.

3. Melt 2 tablespoons of the butter in a 12-inch nonstick skillet over medium-high heat. Brown the tenderloins on all sides, reducing the heat if the pan begins to scorch, 6 to 8 minutes. Transfer the tenderloins to a 13 by 9-inch baking dish and roast in the oven until the thickest part of the tenderloins registers 140 to 145 degrees on an instant-read thermometer, 15 to 18 minutes. Transfer the tenderloins to a cutting board, tent loosely with foil, and let rest until the center registers 150 degrees.

4. While the pork cooks in the oven, melt 2 tablespoons more butter in the skillet over medium heat. Add the potato mixture and spread it into an even layer. Cover and cook for 6 minutes.

5. Uncover and use a spatula to gently press the potatoes down to form a compact, round cake. Continue to cook, uncovered, occasionally pressing on the potatoes to shape into a uniform round cake, until the bottom is deep golden brown, about 2 minutes longer. Shake the skillet to loosen the rösti, then slide it onto a large plate.

6. Melt the remaining 2 tablespoons butter in the skillet. Cover the rösti with a second plate, then invert the rösti and slide it back into the skillet, browned side facing up. Continue to cook, uncovered and occasionally pressing down on the cake, until the bottom is well browned, 5 to 7 minutes.

7. Remove the pan from the heat and allow the rösti to cool in the pan for 5 minutes. Slice the pork into ½-inch-thick slices. Slide the rösti onto a cutting board, cut into 4 wedges, and serve with the pork.

ATOMIC RIBS

SOME RIB FANS PUT THE EMPHASIS ON THE MEAT, and others focus on the sauce, whether it's thick and sweet or a vinegary mop. Then there are those who pick up a rib looking for nothing but pure fire—not a touch of spice but real four-alarm heat. I rounded up several recipes for "atomic" ribs—pork ribs that make you feel the burn—some of which made us sweat after just one bite. Armed with multiple racks of ribs, the entire contents of our spice cabinet, and every condiment I could find, I set out to develop a recipe for really great (and seriously hot) atomic ribs.

The actual cooking technique required little testing, as the test kitchen already has a grill-to-oven method for cooking pork ribs that is straightforward and virtually guarantees tender meat. The ribs develop a deep smoky flavor on the grill for the first two hours over indirect heat. They are then wrapped in foil to seal in moisture and placed on a baking sheet in a low oven to finish cooking. The ribs emerge from the oven tender and juicy—and best of all, there is no need to rebuild the fire with freshly lit coals halfway through cooking.

The recipes I tested for the spicy sauce agreed on the presence of chiles, but there was little consensus on the other ingredients. After testing numerous condiments in the fridge, I settled on an unlikely combination. Yellow mustard contributed bright flavor and color, a welcome pungency, and a thick consistency that helped the sauce cling nicely to the barbecued ribs. As for the heat, tasters liked habanero chiles for their unapologetic burn, but they wanted more complexity. I added pickled banana peppers (plus some of their pickling juice) for a nice tang, and dry mustard for its sinus-clearing heat. A few minced garlic cloves and a handful of sliced scallions rounded out the flavors of the sauce.

I knew from experience that applying the sauce toward the end of cooking was the best way to avoid burning and charring. I slathered the ribs (I opted for spareribs over baby back simply because they are meatier and stand up better to the heat) with my sauce just as they came off the grill, then wrapped them in foil and placed them in the oven to finish cooking through. But once the ribs were removed from the oven, disappointment loomed—my bright, fresh sauce was now a muddy hue and its heat was dulled. Brushing the ribs just before serving was a better approach—the sauce retained its bright yellow color and flavor.

My ribs were packing a punch, but the spice fanatics in our kitchen were still demanding more heat and bold flavor, so I tried cranking up the heat of my spice rub. After trying numerous combinations, I settled on a hefty dose of paprika, chili powder, pepper, and cayenne. Salt and brown sugar were musts, adding flavor and a touch of sweetness to balance the spice.

Finally, I had ribs with a smoky, spicy crust that penetrated deep into the meat. Finished with the fresh fiery mustard sauce, these ribs were finally worthy of their name.

—SUZANNAH MCFERRAN, *America's Test Kitchen Books*

Atomic Ribs

SERVES 4 TO 6

Buy St. Louis–style ribs, which are more manageable than untrimmed pork spareribs. If you can't find them, baby back ribs will work fine; just reduce the cooking time in the oven in step 5 to 1 to 2 hours. This sauce is very spicy. For the maximum amount of heat, include the ribs and seeds, which are the hottest parts of the pepper, when mincing the habanero. For less heat, use only one habanero and remove the ribs and/or seeds.

SAUCE

- ¼ cup sliced pickled banana peppers, chopped fine, and 2 tablespoons pickling liquid
- ¼ cup fresh lemon juice from 2 lemons
- ¼ cup vegetable oil
- ¼ cup yellow mustard
- 4 scallions, sliced thin
- 3 tablespoons dry mustard
- 2 tablespoons chili sauce
- 2 tablespoons brown sugar
- 3 garlic cloves, minced
- 1-2 habanero chiles, minced (see note)
- Salt and pepper

RIBS

- 3 tablespoons paprika
- 2 tablespoons chili powder
- 2 tablespoons brown sugar
- 2 tablespoons pepper
- 1 tablespoon salt
- 1 tablespoon cayenne pepper
- 2 (2½ to 3-pound) full racks pork spareribs, preferably St. Louis cut (see note), trimmed of any large pieces of fat and membrane removed (see photos)
- 2 cups wood chips, soaked in water for 15 minutes and drained

ST. LOUIS-STYLE SPARERIBS

Spareribs are flavorful ribs from near the pig's fatty belly, but they require a fair amount of home trimming. St. Louis-style spareribs on the other hand, have been trimmed of skirt meat and excess cartilage, creating minimal fuss.

REMOVING THE RIB MEMBRANE

1. At one end of the rack, loosen the edge of the membrane with the tip of a paring knife or your fingernail.

2. Grab the membrane with a paper towel and pull slowly—it should come off in one piece. The membrane itself is very thin, so removing it should not expose the rib bones.

1. FOR THE SAUCE: Whisk the banana peppers, pickling liquid, lemon juice, oil, mustard, scallions, dry mustard, chili sauce, brown sugar, garlic, and habaneros together in a bowl. Season with salt and pepper to taste. (The sauce can be refrigerated in an airtight container for up to 4 days.)

2. FOR THE RIBS: Combine the paprika, chili powder, sugar, pepper, salt, and cayenne in a bowl. Pat the ribs dry with paper towels and rub them evenly with the spice mixture. Cover the meat with plastic wrap and let sit at room temperature for at least 1 hour, or refrigerate for up to 24 hours. (If refrigerated, let sit at room temperature for 1 hour before grilling.) Seal the soaked wood chips in a foil packet and cut vent holes in the top (see page 149).

3A. FOR A CHARCOAL GRILL: Open the bottom grill vents halfway. Light a large chimney starter three-quarters full with charcoal briquettes (75 briquettes; 4½ quarts). When the coals are hot, pour them into a steeply banked pile against one side of the grill. Place the wood chip packet on top of the coals. Set the cooking grate in place, cover, and open the lid vents halfway. Heat the grill until hot and the wood chips begin to smoke heavily, about 5 minutes.

3B. FOR A GAS GRILL: Place the wood chip packet directly on the primary burner. Turn all the burners to high, cover, and heat the grill until hot and the wood chips begin to smoke heavily, about 15 minutes. Turn the primary burner to medium-high and turn off the other burner(s). (Adjust the primary burner as needed to maintain the grill temperature around 325 degrees.)

4. Clean and oil the cooking grate. Place the ribs, meat side down, on the cooler part of the grill; the ribs may overlap slightly. Cover (positioning the lid vents over the meat if using charcoal) and cook until the ribs are deep red and smoky, about 2 hours, flipping and rotating the racks halfway through. During the final 20 minutes of grilling, adjust an oven rack to the middle position and heat the oven to 250 degrees.

5. Remove the ribs from the grill and wrap tightly with foil. Arrange the foil-wrapped ribs on a rimmed baking sheet and continue to cook in the oven until tender and a fork inserted into the ribs meets no resistance, 1½ to 2½ hours.

6. Remove the ribs from the oven and let rest, still wrapped, for 30 minutes. Unwrap the ribs and brush with half of the sauce. Slice the ribs between the bones and serve with the remaining sauce.

GRILL-ROASTED HAM

OVER THE YEARS IN THE TEST KITCHEN, we've baked wet-cured hams in oven bags and in foil, brushed them with glazes, and rubbed them with sugar and spice. We thought we'd cooked ham every which way, so when a colleague talked about grilling ham for Easter, I was intrigued. Apparently, with unexpected guests on the way and a turkey hogging the oven, she'd thought fast and stuck a spiral-sliced ham on the grill. A couple hours later, guests sat down to an intensely smoky ham with a crisp, charred crust unmatched by any oven-roasted ham. She admitted it was far from perfect. The meat had dried out and there were random charred bits, but these were problems I was confident I could solve.

I tested recipes that called for an array of techniques, but the results were disappointing. Hams cooked over direct heat developed a crusty exterior but either burned or dried out. Those cooked in disposable pans or over indirect heat were moist, but developed no crust and simply tasted baked. The most promising recipe combined the two methods. It called for grilling the ham in a disposable pan over indirect heat to warm it through, then removing it from the pan and placing it over direct heat to obtain a tasty char.

The first thing I realized was that a spiral-sliced ham was never going to work on the grill. Moisture evaporated from the interior, drying out the meat and creating a tough, unappetizing crust. By contrast, an uncut ham, with a protective layer of fat on the outside and scant exposed meat, stayed relatively moist.

I was cooking uncut ham over indirect heat and finishing it over direct heat when a new problem emerged: The fat kept dripping onto the grill, setting fire to grill and meat. Setting the ham in a roasting V-rack kept it a safe distance from the flames. I made the switch to direct heat when the ham reached 100 degrees, and the exterior fat transformed into a crisp, pleasingly charred, flavorful crust. Unfortunately, only the side of the ham facing the fire developed that crust.

For a well-rounded crust, I'd obviously have to turn the ham. But with a hot, open flame, how the heck could I rotate a bulky 10-pound ham safely? I was stymied—until it occurred to me to use metal skewers to simulate a rotisserie. I skewered the meat on either side of the bone, creating handles. Once the ham had cooked through, I began to turn it every five or so minutes on my makeshift rotisserie. The fat rendered off, creating a tantalizing, smoky charred exterior all around.

GRILL-ROASTED HAM

The ham now had unrivaled grilled flavor, but to me it didn't qualify as holiday ham without a glaze. I tried basting it with a glaze near the end of cooking, but even with protection from the V-rack, the sugary glaze burned. Next, I coated the ham with a traditional dry barbecue rub of dark brown sugar, paprika, black pepper, and cayenne before grilling. The rub had sugar too, but far less, and because it was dry it stayed put, caramelizing nicely on the ham into a tasty, crunchy coating. The indirect cooking ensured moist, tender meat. The direct grill contact accentuated the ham's smoky flavor. Combining the two techniques made this grilled ham a thing of beauty.

—LYNN CLARK, *Cook's Country*

Grill-Roasted Ham

SERVES 16 TO 20

Do not use a spiral sliced ham; it will dry out on the grill. You will need two 12-inch metal skewers.

- 1 (7 to 10-pound) cured bone-in ham, preferably shank end, skin removed and fat trimmed to ¼-inch thickness (see note)
- ¼ cup packed dark brown sugar
- 2 tablespoons paprika
- 1 teaspoon pepper
- ¼ teaspoon cayenne pepper

1. Score the ham at 1-inch intervals in a crosshatch pattern. Combine the sugar, paprika, pepper, and cayenne in a small bowl. Rub the spice mixture all over the ham. Transfer to a V-rack and let stand at room temperature for 1½ hours. Thread the ham with metal skewers on both sides of the bone.

NOTES FROM THE TEST KITCHEN

SKEWERING THE HAM

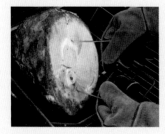

To develop the smoky char of the grill on all sides, we needed a way to manipulate an unwieldy ham as it sits in a V-shaped roasting rack. Metal skewers make a great makeshift rotisserie, allowing us to turn the ham with ease.

2A. FOR A CHARCOAL GRILL: Open the bottom grill vents halfway. Light a large chimney starter filled with charcoal briquettes (100 briquettes; 6 quarts). When the coals are hot, pour them in an even layer over half of the grill, leaving the other half empty. Set the cooking grate in place, cover, and open the lid vents halfway. Heat the grill until hot, about 5 minutes.

2B. FOR A GAS GRILL: Turn all the burners to high, cover, and heat the grill until hot, about 15 minutes. Leave the primary burner on high and turn off the other burner(s). (Adjust the burners as needed to maintain the grill temperature around 350 degrees.)

3. Clean the cooking grate. Place the V-rack on the cooler side of the grill. Cook the ham, covered, rotating it once halfway through cooking, until the meat registers 100 degrees, about 1½ hours.

4. For a charcoal grill, light about 25 coals. When the coals are hot, remove the grill grate and scatter over the top of the spent coals. Replace the grill grate and position the V-rack directly over the coals. (For a gas grill, turn all the burners to low.) Grill the ham until lightly charred on all sides, about 30 minutes, turning the ham every 5 minutes. Transfer to a cutting board, tent with foil, and let rest for 15 minutes. Carve and serve.

STUFFED ROAST PORK

I'M A LONGTIME FAN of the test kitchen recipe for pork roast, which slowly cooks a well-marbled, tough Boston butt to meltingly tender effect. The recipe is always such a hit that I wondered if I could dress up the same cut for the holidays. To elevate this roast to holiday status, I decided to try stuffing it.

I cut a pocket in the roast, crammed in the test kitchen's recipe for poultry bread stuffing, and tied and roasted it. Unfortunately, not much stuffing fit into my roast, and what did was too bland to stand up to the pork. Clearly, I'd need a more potent stuffing, one that would deliver big flavor in every bite.

I'd come across a promising pork roast recipe from northern Minnesota called porketta (or porchetta), introduced by Italian immigrant miners to the state's Iron Range region. It calls for opening up a pork butt like a book, lavishing it with gutsy seasonings, and then rolling and roasting. I decided to borrow the seasoning mix but aim for a more substantial filling.

In a side-by-side tasting of six variations, a stuffing made with garlic, fennel seeds, red pepper flakes, plenty of onion, and ground pork stood out. (Old recipes call for minced lard, prosciutto, or pancetta, so ground pork wasn't much of a stretch.)

Although the flavor was just where I wanted it to be, my job was far from done: The stuffing was baking up dry. I'd been using cooked ground pork; now I tried adding it raw. Bingo. It made for moister stuffing, especially when bound with fresh bread crumbs and egg.

Tasters liked the stuffing so much that they wanted more. To increase the surface area of the pork so that I could pile it high with stuffing, I butterflied it as before and then pounded it to an even ¾-inch thickness. This increased the stuffing-to-meat ratio as I'd intended, but my rolled and tied meat was too long for most roasting pans. Cutting the large butterflied meat into two smaller roasts neatly solved this problem. As a bonus, the smaller roasts cooked in less than half the time.

I'd been covering the pork with foil as it roasted to ensure that it stayed moist, but this method prevented flavorful browning. Searing the meat in a skillet before roasting fixed that, but the technique was cumbersome. What if I simply rubbed the raw roast with salt, pepper, and brown sugar (the last to promote browning)? For the final half hour of cooking, I uncovered the roast and upped the heat. Success! My stuffed roast, with its crisp crust, juicy meat and assertive stuffing, could fittingly grace any holiday table.

—MEGHAN ERWIN, *Cook's Country*

Holiday Stuffed Roast Pork

SERVES 8

Boneless pork shoulder, often labeled Boston butt, is usually wrapped in netting. If all you can find is a bone-in roast, have the butcher remove the bone.

STUFFING

    2 slices high-quality white sandwich bread
    2 tablespoons vegetable oil
    1 onion, minced (about 1 cup)
   10 garlic cloves, minced
    8 ounces ground pork
    3 tablespoons chopped fresh parsley
    1 teaspoon fennel seeds
    ½ teaspoon red pepper flakes
    1 teaspoon salt
    1 large egg, lightly beaten

PORK

    2 tablespoons brown sugar
    1 tablespoon salt
    1 tablespoon pepper
    1 (4 to 5-pound) boneless pork shoulder roast
       (see note)

1. FOR THE STUFFING: Pulse the bread in a food processor until coarsely ground, about 10 pulses (you should have about 1 cup crumbs). Heat the oil in a large nonstick skillet over medium heat until shimmering. Add the onion and cook until golden, about 8 minutes. Stir in the garlic and cook until fragrant, about 30 seconds; transfer to a large bowl and let cool. Add the bread crumbs, ground pork, parsley, fennel seeds, red pepper flakes, salt, and egg to the bowl with the onion mixture and knead with your hands until well combined.

NOTES FROM THE TEST KITCHEN

BUTTERFLYING A BOSTON BUTT

1. Insert a chef's knife into the opening where the bone has been removed. Cut horizontally, stopping at least 1 inch before the edge, and open the meat like a book.

2. Make another cut diagonally into the thicker portion of the roast. Open this flap, smoothing out the butterflied rectangle of meat.

3. Cover the pork with plastic wrap and, using a meat pounder, pound the meat to an even ¾-inch thickness. The pork is now ready to be cut in half, stuffed, rolled, and tied.

2. FOR THE PORK: Adjust an oven rack to the middle position and heat the oven to 300 degrees. Combine the sugar, salt, and pepper in a small bowl. Following the photos on page 173, butterfly the pork and pound to a ¾-inch thickness; you should have a rectangle measuring about 15 by 8 inches. With the long side facing you, cut the pounded pork in half crosswise. Spread the stuffing in an even layer over each half of the pork, leaving a 1-inch border around the edges. Roll and tie each half securely with kitchen twine at 1-inch intervals. Rub the roasts evenly with the sugar mixture and transfer to a rimmed baking sheet. Cover the baking sheet tightly with foil and roast until the center of the meat registers 170 degrees on an instant-read thermometer, about 2 hours.

3. Remove the foil and increase the oven temperature to 400 degrees. Cook until the roasts are well browned and the meat registers 190 degrees, about 30 minutes. Transfer the roasts to a cutting board, tent with foil, and let rest for 20 minutes. Remove the kitchen twine. Slice and serve.

VARIATION

Holiday Roast Pork with Cherry Stuffing

Follow the recipe for Holiday Stuffed Roast Pork, substituting 1 cup crumbled cornbread for the bread crumbs, 2 tablespoons minced fresh thyme for the parsley, and 1 teaspoon black pepper for the red pepper flakes. Omit the fennel seeds and add 1 cup chopped dried cherries to the stuffing in step 1.

GRILLED RACK OF LAMB

RACK OF LAMB IS LIKE PRIME RIB: You don't cook an expensive cut like this very often, and when you do, you want it to be spectacular. The meat should be pink and juicy, surrounded by a well-browned crust that provides a contrast in texture to the lush, ultra-tender interior. While it's possible to achieve these results in the oven, lamb and the grill have unbeatable chemistry. The intense heat of the coals produces a great crust and melts away the meat's abundance of fat, distributing flavor throughout. Plus grilling imparts a smokiness that's the perfect complement to lamb's rich, gamey flavor. The only hitch: I'd have to figure out how to keep all the rendering fat from creating the meat-scorching flare-ups and sooty flavors that are the surest way to ruin this pricey cut.

Before I looked into the best way to grill the racks, I needed to figure out which type to buy. The racks sold by supermarkets are typically domestic or imported from Australia or New Zealand. My tasters in the test kitchen preferred the milder domestic lamb to the imported meat, which is bred for gamier flavors. Domestic lamb also has the advantage of coming in bigger sizes. While I knew that the larger racks would be a challenge to cook evenly, I also figured a heftier size would translate to a longer stay on the grill, thus better grilled flavor. The key to lamb's unique flavor and tenderness is its high proportion of fat, most of which covers one side of the rack like a cap. The fat also leads to aggressive flare-ups, but removing all of the cap leaves the racks dry with very little of the distinctive lamb flavor that makes this meat superb. As a compromise, I left a thin layer of fat over the loin and removed most of the fat between the bones.

But lamb still has enough interior fat that it would only be a matter of minutes before the flare-ups started. When grilling fattier meat, we often build a two-level fire by pushing all the coals to one side of the grill to create hot and cool areas. Starting the lamb over the cooler side (indirect heat) allowed the fat to render first. Once that fat was sufficiently rendered, I could move the racks to the hotter side (direct heat) to brown the exterior. The only drawback to this approach was the need to crowd the large racks on one side of the grill, leaving them catty-cornered to the fire and causing them to cook unevenly. This method also left small pockets of unrendered fat that made the meat taste greasy.

To solve this problem, I turned to a solution we devised for other large cuts: Instead of a traditional two-level fire with all the coals on one side, I heaped two smaller mounds on either side of the grill and placed an aluminum pan between them to act as a divider. (The pan would also serve as a drip tray to catch rendering fat.) I then positioned the lamb racks over the cooler center of the grill. Situated this way, all parts of the meat were exposed to the same amount of heat, allowing the racks to cook more evenly. And because the heat was more diffuse, the fat also rendered more thoroughly. When the racks were lightly browned and the fat sufficiently rendered, I could then slide them over to the hot sides for just a short while to brown the exterior without fear of flare-ups. (Concerned that this setup might be hard to replicate on a gas grill, I did some quick tests. I found that the larger surface area of the gas grill allowed me

GRILLED RACK OF LAMB

to abandon the split-fire method and simply leave one burner on high and turn the others off.)

My biggest challenge met, I set out to flavor the lamb. Because lamb tastes so good on its own, I wanted to enhance the meat's flavor without overwhelming it. Many recipes call for marinating the lamb before grilling, but the several I tried succeeded only in making the lamb mushy. With my particular cooking method, a dry rub, applied to the racks before they went on the grill, did add some flavor, but much of it trickled away with the rendering fat, ending up in the drip pan. The best option turned out to be a wet rub consisting of garlic and a couple of robust herbs (rosemary and thyme) mixed with a little oil (just enough to adhere the flavorings to the lamb without causing flare-ups). Brushed on the racks as they browned over the direct heat, the wet rub added just the right note to the perfectly cooked meat.

—KEITH DRESSER, *Cook's Illustrated*

Grilled Rack of Lamb
SERVES 4

We prefer the milder taste and bigger size of domestic lamb, but you may substitute imported lamb from New Zealand and Australia. Since imported racks are generally smaller, follow the shorter cooking times given in the recipe. While most lamb is sold frenched (meaning part of each rib bone is exposed), chances are there will still be some extra fat between the bones. Remove the majority of this fat, leaving an inch at the top of the small eye of meat. Also, make sure that the chine bone (along the bottom of the rack) has been removed to ensure easy cutting between the ribs after cooking. Ask the butcher to do this; it's very hard to cut off at home. We prefer the lamb cooked to medium-rare, but if you prefer it more or less done, see "Testing Meat for Doneness" on page 139. You do not need the roasting pan if using a gas grill.

- 1 (12 by 8-inch) disposable aluminum roasting pan (see note)
- 4 teaspoons olive oil
- 4 teaspoons minced fresh rosemary
- 2 teaspoons minced fresh thyme
- 2 garlic cloves, minced
- 2 (1½ to 1¾-pound) racks of lamb, rib bones frenched and meat trimmed of all excess fat (see page 177) (see note)
  Salt and pepper

1A. FOR A CHARCOAL GRILL: Open the bottom grill vents completely and place the roasting pan in the center of the grill. Light a large chimney starter filled with charcoal briquettes (100 briquettes; 6 quarts). When the coals are hot, pour them into even piles on each side of the pan. Set the cooking grate in place, cover, and open the lid vents completely. Heat the grill until hot, about 5 minutes.

1B. FOR A GAS GRILL: Turn all the burners to high, cover, and heat the grill until hot, about 15 minutes. Leave the primary burner on high and turn off the other burner(s). (Adjust the burner as needed to maintain the grill temperature around 350 degrees.)

2. Combine 3 teaspoons of the oil, rosemary, thyme, and garlic in a small bowl; set aside. Rub the lamb with the remaining 1 teaspoon oil and season generously with salt and pepper.

3. Clean and oil the cooking grate. Following the photos on page 177, place the racks bone-side up on the cooler part of grill (over the aluminum pan on a charcoal grill) with the meaty side of the racks very close to, but not quite over, the hot coals. Cover and grill until the meat is lightly browned, faint grill marks appear, and the fat has begun to render, 8 to 10 minutes.

4. Flip the racks over, bone-side down, and move to the hotter parts of the grill. Grill, without moving, until well-browned, 3 to 4 minutes. Brush the racks with the herb-garlic mixture. Flip the racks bone-side up and continue to grill over the hotter parts of grill until well browned, 3 to 4 minutes. Stand the racks up and lean them against each other; continue to grill over one hotter side of the grill until the bottom is well-browned and an instant-read thermometer inserted from the side of the rack into the center, but away from any bone, registers 120 degrees (for medium-rare), 3 to 8 minutes longer

5. Transfer the lamb to a cutting board, tent with foil, and let rest for 15 minutes (the racks will continue to cook while resting). Cut between the ribs to separate the chops, and serve immediately.

VARIATION
Grilled Rack of Lamb with Sweet Mustard Glaze
Follow the recipe for Grilled Rack of Lamb, omitting the rosemary and adding 3 tablespoons Dijon mustard, 2 tablespoons honey, and ½ teaspoon grated lemon zest to the oil, thyme, and garlic in step 2. Brush the racks with the mustard glaze as directed in step 4, reserving 2 tablespoons. Brush the racks with the reserved glaze once removed from the grill in step 5.

TRIMMING FAT FROM THE RACK

1. Peel back the thick outer layer of fat from the rack. Cut any tissue connecting the fat cap to the rack.

2. Trim the remaining thin layer of fat that covers the loin, leaving the thin strip of fat between the loin and the bone.

3. Make a straight cut along the top side of the bones, an inch up from the small eye of meat.

4. Remove any fat above this line and scrape any remaining meat or fat from the exposed bones.

CLEANING THE GRATE

After cleaning the grate with a grill brush, it is important to oil it to prevent food from sticking. Dip a large wad of paper towels in vegetable oil, using tongs, and wipe the cooking grate thoroughly several times.

GRILLING RACKS OF LAMB

1. Place an aluminum pan between two mounds of coals to create a cooler center area flanked by 2 hotter areas. Place the racks bone-side up on the cooler center of the grill and grill until lightly browned.

2. Grill the racks, bone-side down, over the hotter sides of the grill for 3 to 4 minutes, and then brush them with the herb paste.

3. Flip each rack bone-side up and brown the meat, then stand the racks together and brown their bottoms.

BUYING LAMB

Domestic lamb is distinguished by its larger size and milder flavor, while lamb imported from Australia and New Zealand features a far gamier taste. The reason for this difference in taste boils down to diet—and the chemistry of lamb fat. Imported lamb is pasture-fed on mixed grasses, while lamb raised in the United States begins on a diet of grass but finishes with grain. The switch to grain has a direct impact on the composition of the animal's fat, reducing the concentration of the medium-length branched fatty-acid chains that give any lamb its characteristic "lamb-y" flavor—and ultimately leading to sweeter-tasting meat.

DOMESTIC   **DOWN UNDER**

CHAPTER 7

POULTRY

Barbecued Chicken Wings   180

Sautéed Chicken Cutlets with Porcini Sauce   181

Enchiladas Verdes   184

Skillet Phyllo Pie with Chicken   187

Spiedies   189

Cornell Chicken   193

Roast Lemon Chicken   194

Glazed Roast Chicken   197

Huli Huli Chicken   199

Old-Fashioned Roast Turkey and Gravy   202

BARBECUED CHICKEN WINGS

WHEN PEOPLE THINK OF WINGS, the spicy, deep-fried Buffalo version inevitably comes to mind. But wings are also a great food for the grill. Grilling is naturally more healthful than frying, and you can cook more wings at once on the grill, not to mention avoid the laborious project of deep-frying at home. But grill wings incorrectly and you end up with greasy meat surrounded by charred, rubbery skin. I set out to develop a hassle-free recipe for grilled wings with crisp, thin, caramelized skin; tender and moist meat; and smoky barbecue flavor.

Wings are made up of three parts: the meaty, drumsticklike piece that is closest to the breast section of the bird, the two-boned center portion that is surrounded by a band of meat and skin, and the small, almost meatless wingtip. After several tests, I concluded that wingtips, which offer almost no meat and tend to char, are just not worth it. So I had two options: already cut pieces (affectionately referred to as "drumettes") or whole wings. Whole wings (with wingtips removed) were somewhat difficult to maneuver on the grill and awkward to eat, but the precut wings were often poorly cut and unevenly sized. I chose to buy whole wings and butcher them myself. With a sharp chef's knife (kitchen shears would also work), I halved the wings at the main joint and lopped off and discarded the wingtips.

Tackling cooking technique next, I learned early on that grilling the wings over medium and medium-low heat produced the most acceptable results. The skin was crisp and thin, but these wings lacked a nicely caramelized crust. Giving the wings a high-heat finish quickly solved the problem.

Last, I focused on the seasonings and sauce. I tossed the wings in a mixture of salt, pepper, and cayenne to flavor them and add a dash of heat. Knowing the sauce would burn if I brushed it on too soon, I found that it was best to start basting the wings with sauce (I made a simple barbecue sauce from basic pantry ingredients) once I moved them to the hot side of the grill. Flipping the wings as they cooked gave the sauce a chance to caramelize and prevented it from charring. These wings came off the grill juicy and tender, with crispy, flavorful skin. No dipping sauce required for this Super Bowl favorite.

—RACHEL TOOMEY, *America's Test Kitchen Books*

Barbecued Chicken Wings
MAKES ABOUT 2 DOZEN WINGS

Although we think our quick and easy homemade barbecue sauce tastes best, feel free to substitute your favorite store-bought sauce. You do not need the disposable aluminum roasting pan if using a gas grill.

SAUCE
- 1½ cups ketchup
- ½ cup molasses
- 2 tablespoons cider vinegar
- 1½ teaspoons hot sauce
- ½ teaspoon liquid smoke
- Salt and pepper

CHICKEN
- 1 teaspoon salt
- 1 teaspoon pepper
- ⅛ teaspoon cayenne pepper
- 2½ pounds whole chicken wings, wingtips discarded and wings split (see photo)
- 1 (13 by 9-inch) disposable aluminum roasting pan (see note)

1. FOR THE SAUCE: Whisk the ketchup, molasses, vinegar, hot sauce, and liquid smoke together in a bowl and season with salt and pepper to taste. (The sauce can be refrigerated in an airtight container for up to 4 days.)

2. FOR THE CHICKEN: Combine the salt, pepper, and cayenne in a bowl. Pat the chicken wings dry with paper towels, and rub them evenly with the spice mixture.

3A. FOR A CHARCOAL GRILL: Open the bottom grill vents completely and place the roasting pan in the center

NOTES FROM THE TEST KITCHEN

CUTTING UP CHICKEN WINGS

Using kitchen shears or a sharp chef's knife, cut through the wing at the two joints and discard the wingtip.

of the grill. Light a large chimney starter filled with charcoal briquettes (100 briquettes; 6 quarts). When the coals are hot, pour them into two even piles on either side of the roasting pan. Set the cooking grate in place, cover, and open the lid vents completely. Heat the grill until hot, about 5 minutes.

3B. FOR A GAS GRILL: Turn all the burners to high, cover, and heat the grill until hot, about 15 minutes. Turn all the burners to medium-low. (Adjust the burners as needed to maintain the grill temperature around 350 degrees.)

4. Clean and oil the cooking grate. Place the wings on the grill (in the center of the grill if using charcoal). Cover and cook until the skin is crisp and golden, 15 to 20 minutes, flipping the wings halfway through.

5. Slide the chicken to the hotter part of the grill if using charcoal, or turn all the burners to high (adjusting the burners as needed to maintain a hot fire; see page 130) if using gas. Continue to cook the chicken wings, flipping and brushing with some of the barbecue sauce, until glazed and deep brown, about 5 minutes longer.

6. Transfer the chicken wings to a platter, brush with the remaining sauce, and serve.

SAUTÉED CHICKEN CUTLETS WITH PORCINI SAUCE

ON THE SURFACE, *pollo ai funghi porcini* isn't the likeliest candidate for a quick weeknight dinner. This classic Northern Italian dish simmers fresh porcini, white wine, tomato, and a whole chicken until the chicken is fall-off-the-bone tender and the broth rich and satisfying. But with deeply flavored porcini mushrooms on my side, maybe I could distill the essence of this braise into a complex-tasting pan sauce served over simple sautéed chicken cutlets. My goal was dinner on the table in no more than 30 minutes, start to finish.

I started the countdown by sautéing eight thinly pounded cutlets in two speedy batches (each batch only required 2½ minutes). I transferred the chicken to a plate and added fresh porcini and a minced shallot to the pan, sautéing them briefly. Then I deglazed the pan with white wine, tomato paste, and chicken broth, finishing with butter. Even with the earthy savor of

porcini in the mix, the sauce tasted weak; plus, its consistency was thin, barely clinging to the chicken. Clearly I needed to bump up flavor. But first, I had to get the sauce to coat the chicken. Adding flour as I sautéed the mushrooms and the shallot made the sauce thicker, but it still slid off the cutlets. The solution was to also dredge the cutlets in flour before sautéing, which not only improved browning but also added a rough surface to capture the sauce.

Now, what to do about flavor? When a wine-based liquid simmers for a long time, flavor compounds in the wine break down and recombine to form new compounds known as esters, which bring fruity depth to the mix. A pan sauce reduced for five minutes doesn't cook long enough for this reaction to happen. But what if I were to swap wine for vermouth—which has many of the qualities of a good dry white wine but more concentrated flavor? While vermouth helped, tasters still missed the subtle sweetness contributed by long-simmered wine. The answer proved as simple as adding half a teaspoon of sugar.

It was time to take a step back and consider my choice of fresh porcini. Their rich, woodsy flavor is superior to the dried kind, but as they're so hard to find, I knew I had to at least try substituting dried. A half-ounce of dried porcini soaked in chicken broth, then strained and chopped, was all my tasters could handle before protesting about too many soggy mushroom bits in the sauce. Yet this wasn't enough to deliver the same degree of flavor as 4 ounces of fresh. Trying to add flavor by browning the reconstituted porcini was fruitless—they were too wet to caramelize properly. Then I remembered a test kitchen trick to increase savory flavor: adding a dash of soy sauce. The natural glutamates found in soy sauce (the compound that gives food umami, or savory flavor) are the same compounds that make mushrooms taste meaty. I was afraid tasters might complain about an Asian condiment in an Italian-inspired dish, but all they noticed was deeper porcini flavor—exactly what I wanted.

To perfect the sauce, all I needed was fresh thyme and a shot of lemon juice stirred in before serving. Ready in just 30 minutes, this new chicken dish was so full of flavor, it tasted like it had been slow-cooked in a traditional Italian kitchen.

—J. KENJI ALT, *Cook's Illustrated*

SAUTÉED CHICKEN CUTLETS WITH PORCINI SAUCE

Sautéed Chicken Cutlets with Porcini Sauce

SERVES 4

For even more intense mushroom flavor, grind an additional half-ounce of dried porcini mushrooms in a spice grinder until it is reduced to fine dust. Sift the dust through a fine-mesh strainer and then stir it into the flour before dredging the chicken. The chicken breasts will be easier to slice in half if you freeze them for 15 minutes first.

½ **ounce (about ¾ cup) dried porcini mushrooms (see note)**

1 **cup low-sodium chicken broth**

¼ **cup plus 1 teaspoon unbleached all-purpose flour**
  Salt and pepper

4 **(6 to 8-ounce) boneless, skinless chicken breasts, trimmed, halved horizontally, and pounded ¼ inch thick (see photos) (see note)**

2 **tablespoons plus 1 teaspoon vegetable oil**

1 **small shallot, minced (about 2 tablespoons)**

¼ **cup dry vermouth**

1 **teaspoon tomato paste**

1 **teaspoon soy sauce**

½ **teaspoon sugar**

2 **tablespoons unsalted butter, chilled**

½ **teaspoon minced fresh thyme**

½ **teaspoon fresh lemon juice**

1. Rinse the porcini in a large bowl of cold water, agitating them with your hands to release any dirt and sand. Allow the dirt and sand to settle to the bottom of the bowl, then lift the porcini from the water and transfer them to a microwave-safe 2-cup measuring cup. Add the chicken broth, submerging the porcini beneath the surface of the liquid. Microwave on high power 1 minute, until the broth is steaming. Let stand for 10 minutes. Using tongs, gently lift the porcini out of the broth and transfer to a cutting board, reserving the broth. Chop the porcini into ¾-inch pieces and transfer to a medium bowl. Strain the broth through a fine-mesh strainer lined with a large coffee filter into the bowl with the chopped porcini.

2. Combine ¼ cup of the flour, 1 teaspoon salt, and ½ teaspoon pepper in a pie plate. Pat the chicken dry with paper towels. Working with one piece at a time, dredge the chicken in the flour mixture, shaking gently to remove any excess. Set aside on a plate.

3. Heat 1 tablespoon of the oil in a 12-inch skillet over medium-high heat until just smoking. Place 4 of the cutlets in the skillet and cook without moving until browned, about 2 minutes. Flip the cutlets and continue to cook until the second sides are opaque, 15 to 20 seconds. Transfer to a large plate. Add 1 tablespoon more oil to the skillet and repeat with the remaining cutlets. Tent the plate loosely with foil.

4. Add the remaining 1 teaspoon oil to the skillet and return the pan to medium heat. Add the shallot and cook, stirring often, until softened, about 2 minutes. Add the remaining 1 teaspoon flour and cook, whisking constantly,

---

NOTES FROM THE TEST KITCHEN

SLICING BREASTS INTO CUTLETS

1. Lay the chicken breast smooth-side up on a cutting board. Place one hand on top to steady the chicken, and carefully slice the breast in half horizontally to yield two pieces.

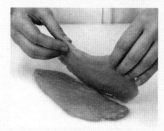

2. The two pieces should be about ¼ inch thick. If necessary, pound the cutlets to an even ¼-inch thickness.

PICKING PROPER PORCINI
Like fresh fruits and vegetables, the quality of dried porcini mushrooms can vary dramatically from package to package and brand to brand. Always inspect the mushrooms before you buy. Small holes indicate that the mushroom was maybe home to pinworms, so look for large, smooth porcini, free of worm holes, dust, and grit.

PREVIOUSLY OCCUPIED　　　**CLEAN & CLEAR**

about 30 seconds. Increase the heat to medium-high and whisk in the vermouth, soaked porcini and their liquid, tomato paste, soy sauce, and sugar. Simmer until reduced to 1 cup, 3 to 5 minutes.

5. Transfer the cutlets and any accumulated juices to the skillet. Cover and simmer until the cutlets are heated through, about 1 minute. Remove the skillet from the heat and transfer the cutlets to a serving platter. Whisk the butter, thyme, and lemon juice into the sauce and season with salt and pepper to taste. Spoon the sauce over the chicken and serve.

ENCHILADAS VERDES

IN MEXICO, ENCHILADAS COME IN MYRIAD FORMS. In this country, these stuffed and baked corn tortillas are defined almost exclusively by whether they're covered in a red sauce or a green one. Red sauces boast the deep, earthy flavor of dried red chiles, while green sauces feature the brighter taste of fresh green chiles and tomatillos, the tangy little tomatolike fruit that is common in authentic Mexican cooking. For me, enchiladas topped by green sauce—enchiladas verdes—are as perfect a comfort food as any I know, especially when they include moist, tender pieces of chicken. I love the way the fresh, citrusy flavors and coarse texture of the sauce contrast with the richness of chicken wrapped in soft corn tortillas and topped with melted cheese.

For the home cook, enchiladas verdes offer a distinct advantage over red-sauce versions: To preserve its vibrant flavors, the sauce is relatively quick-cooking. But while I've had memorable enchiladas verdes with chicken in restaurants, I've never had much success re-creating them at home. The sauce is often too watery and thin, the tortillas mushy, and the filling marred by bland, dried-out chicken overpowered by cheese. Armed with a stack of recipes, I headed into the test kitchen to figure out how to get this Mexican restaurant classic right.

My first step was to nail down the sauce. I began my tests using broad, dark green poblano chiles. Poblanos have mild to moderate heat and a deep herbal flavor that is far more complex than the straightforward grassy taste of chiles such as jalapeños or serranos. As for the tomatillos, I decided from the outset to use fresh instead of canned to ensure that as much of their tangy flavor as possible made it into the dish. (Luckily, the fruit is increasingly available fresh year-round in supermarkets across the country.)

Traditional recipes dry-roast whole tomatillos and chiles on the stovetop until soft and charred. This method, which employs a flat cast-iron vessel known as a *comal,* imparts smokiness and concentrates flavor, all the while wicking away excess moisture that makes for a watery sauce. The blackened skins on the tomatillos have good flavor, but the chile skins taste bitter and need to be removed. These ingredients are then ground up in a mortar and pestle to form a sauce. More modern recipes skip the comal for similarly fast, intense cooking techniques such as sautéing, high-heat oven-roasting, or broiling and use a blender or food processor to create the sauce.

I quickly eliminated sautéing and oven-roasting from consideration; neither method added enough char to create the smokiness I was looking for. Broiling, however, tempered the tartness of the tomatillos and brought a near-sweet richness to the poblanos. The tomatillos did fine left whole on a baking sheet under the broiler, but I found that slicing the poblanos in half and placing them skin-side up helped blacken them more evenly.

Whirring the tomatillos and chiles in the blender made the sauce too smooth; a few pulses in the food processor better approximated the coarse, rustic texture produced by a mortar and pestle. But it was now a little too thick and pulpy. I tried thinning it with a number of ingredients; dairy in any form deadened the bright flavors, but just ¼ cup of chicken broth lent a subtle richness and thinned the sauce while maintaining its body.

In my preliminary test, tasters preferred white meat over dark in the filling. But what was the best method for cooking the chicken? With an eye on keeping the recipe streamlined, I settled on the fastest, simplest approach: poaching. Spiking some chicken broth with sautéed onion, garlic, and cumin before adding the chicken infused the meat with a deeper, richer flavor. In addition, I now had a great-tasting broth I could use to thin the sauce; I reserved ¼ cup before discarding the rest.

I planned to leave cheese out of the filling entirely as it can weigh down the dish, but tasters complained that the enchiladas lacked richness, even with the traditional sprinkling of cheese on top. What if I added a moderate amount of cheese to the filling? I tried a few obvious types: pepper Jack, cheddar, and queso fresco, a salty, crumbly fresh cheese from Mexico resembling feta. Though queso fresco might have bested the others south of the border, it is not a melting cheese, and my tasters wanted gooeyness in their filling. Cheddar lost out to 1½ cups of shredded pepper Jack, a milder cheese that nonetheless added a spicy kick. To keep the richness of the cheese in check, I added a handful of chopped cilantro.

Traditionally, corn tortillas are dipped in hot oil to make them pliable and to keep them from breaking apart when rolled. I opted for the quicker, less messy method we've developed in the test kitchen: spraying the tortillas with vegetable oil and gently baking them for a few minutes. Once they were soft and warm, I took them out of the oven and proceeded to assemble the enchiladas: distributing filling in each, rolling them up, and placing them in a baking dish before topping them with sauce and Jack cheese. Quickly baked until heated through, then served with thinly sliced scallion, radish slices, and a dollop of sour cream, my enchiladas verdes were as good as any I'd enjoyed in my favorite Mexican restaurants.

—CHARLES KELSEY, *Cook's Illustrated*

Enchiladas Verdes

SERVES 4 TO 6

You can substitute three 11-ounce cans of tomatillos, drained and rinsed, for the fresh ones in this recipe. Halve large tomatillos (more than 2 inches in diameter) and place them skin-side up for broiling in step 2 to ensure even cooking and charring. If you can't find poblanos, substitute 4 large jalapeño chiles (with seeds and ribs removed). To increase the spiciness of the sauce, reserve some of the chiles' ribs and seeds and add them to the food processor in step 3.

4	teaspoons vegetable oil
1	onion, chopped medium (about 1 cup)
3	garlic cloves, minced (about 3 teaspoons)
½	teaspoon ground cumin
1½	cups low-sodium chicken broth
1	pound boneless, skinless chicken breasts (2 to 3 breasts), trimmed
1½	pounds tomatillos (16 to 20), husks and stems removed, rinsed well and dried (see note)
3	poblano chiles, halved lengthwise, stemmed, and seeded (see note)
1–2½	teaspoons sugar
	Salt and pepper
½	cup chopped fresh cilantro
8	ounces pepper Jack or Monterey Jack cheese, shredded (about 2 cups)
12	(6-inch) corn tortillas
	Vegetable oil spray

GARNISH

2	scallions, sliced thin
	Thinly sliced radishes
	Sour cream

1. Adjust the oven racks to the middle and highest positions and heat the broiler. Heat 2 teaspoons of the oil in a medium saucepan over medium heat until shimmering; add the onion and cook, stirring frequently, until golden, 8 to 10 minutes. Add 2 teaspoons of the garlic and cumin; cook, stirring frequently, until fragrant, about 30 seconds. Decrease the heat to low and stir in the broth. Add the chicken, cover, and simmer until the thickest part of the breasts registers 160 to 165 degrees on an instant-read thermometer, 15 to 20 minutes, flipping the chicken halfway through cooking. Transfer the chicken to a large bowl and place in the refrigerator to cool, about 20 minutes. Reserve ¼ cup of the liquid from the saucepan; discard any remaining liquid.

2. Meanwhile, toss the tomatillos and poblanos with the remaining 2 teaspoons oil; arrange on a rimmed baking sheet lined with foil, with the poblanos skin-side up. Broil until the vegetables blacken and start to soften, 5 to 10 minutes, rotating the pan halfway through cooking. Cool for 10 minutes, then remove the skin from the poblanos (leave the tomatillo skins intact). Transfer the tomatillos and chiles to a food processor. Decrease the oven temperature to 350 degrees. Discard the foil from the baking sheet and set the baking sheet aside for warming the tortillas.

3. Add 1 teaspoon of the sugar, 1 teaspoon salt, remaining 1 teaspoon garlic, and reserved cooking liquid to the food processor; pulse until the sauce is somewhat chunky, about 8 pulses. Season with salt and pepper to taste and adjust the tartness by stirring in the remaining sugar, ½ teaspoon at a time. Set the sauce aside (you should have about 3 cups).

4. When the chicken is cool, pull it into shreds using your hands or 2 forks, then chop into small bite-sized pieces. Combine the chicken with the cilantro and 1½ cups of the cheese; season with salt to taste.

5. Smear the bottom of a 13 by 9-inch baking dish with ¾ cup of the tomatillo sauce. Place the tortillas on 2 baking sheets. Spray both sides of the tortillas lightly

ENCHILADAS VERDES

with vegetable oil spray. Bake until the tortillas are soft and pliable, 2 to 4 minutes. Increase the oven temperature to 450 degrees. Place the warm tortillas on the counter and spread ⅓ cup filling down the center of each tortilla. Roll each tortilla tightly and place in the baking dish, seam-side down. Pour the remaining tomatillo sauce over the top of the enchiladas. Use the back of a spoon to spread the sauce so that it coats the top of each tortilla. Sprinkle with the remaining ½ cup cheese and cover the baking dish with foil.

6. Bake the enchiladas on the middle rack until heated through and the cheese is melted, 15 to 20 minutes. Uncover, sprinkle with the scallions, and serve, passing the radishes and sour cream separately.

NOTES FROM THE TEST KITCHEN

SHOPPING FOR TOMATILLOS

Called *tomates verdes* (green tomatoes) in much of Mexico, small green tomatillos have a tangier, more citrusy flavor than true green tomatoes. When choosing tomatillos, look for pale-green orbs with firm flesh that fills and splits open the fruit's outer papery husk, which must be removed before cooking. Avoid tomatillos that are too yellow and soft, as these specimens are past their prime and will taste sour and muted. Canned tomatillos are a reasonable substitute for fresh, though they won't contribute the same depth of flavor.

GREEN AND JUST RIGHT   **TOO YELLOW**

FINE STAND-IN FOR FRESH

THE IMPORTANCE OF BROILING

Quickly charring the tomatillos and chiles under the broiler intensifies their flavor and adds smokiness.

SKILLET PHYLLO PIE WITH CHICKEN

MOST TAVERNS IN GREECE, and certainly every Greek-American restaurant, offer some version of phyllo pie on the menu. The most common is spanakopita, which is filled with spinach and cheese. A less widely known alternative, called *kotopita,* replaces the spinach with chicken. This version layers sheets of phyllo dough with a filling of chicken and tangy feta cheese, spiked with garlic and herbs. The pies are then baked, resulting in the perfect marriage of crisp, flaky pastry and savory, satisfying filling.

But phyllo pie can be a tough dish to get right at home. The chicken can be dense and dry, characteristics that are only amplified by thin, dried-out pastry. And random chunks of feta cheese don't do much to improve the dish. Add to that the difficulty of working with store-bought phyllo dough, and you might as well dine out. I knew I could improve upon this classic dish; I wanted a simpler version, with a moist chicken filling, bright flavors, and evenly spaced bites of feta that didn't dull after baking. I also wanted to build and bake the whole pie in one skillet and, to keep things simple, use the phyllo as the topping instead of layering it throughout the dish.

I focused first on perfecting the chicken and feta filling, which would form the base of my pie. Ground chicken was my first choice for the meat—it cooks quickly and is easy to use for a weeknight meal. After a couple of tests, I determined that ground dark meat surpassed ground white meat for both its flavor and its ability to remain moist in the baked phyllo pie. It was crucial to break the chicken meat into small pieces as it cooked. If the meat remained in large clumps, it didn't create a uniform filling. I added some garlic for flavor and chicken broth to keep the meat moist. To avoid big chunks of feta in the filling and ensure that it was evenly distributed, I first crumbled it up, then mixed it with eggs. The eggs bound the filling ingredients together, adding richness and flavor, and lightened the layer of chicken that would otherwise be dense when baked in the oven.

Scallions and mint are traditional ingredients in phyllo pies, but they are usually added in such paltry amounts that the flavors disappear. I increased the quantities of each and mixed them in with the feta and eggs. Lemon juice and cayenne pepper are less commonly included, but tasters unanimously approved of both. In search of more punch, I added chopped kalamata olives, which gave a bold flavor to my ground chicken filling. With the flavors now bright and clean, I mixed the feta filling into the cooked ground chicken. It was time to move on to the phyllo.

The single most important thing to know when working with phyllo dough is that it needs to be at room temperature. Most problems arise when packages are hastily thawed; sheets that are still cold will crack along the folds or stick together at the corners.

Phyllo is famous for its crisp, flaky layers, but it was this quality that gave me the most trouble once the pie hit the hot oven. In every test, the papery layers curled and separated from each other as they baked. Cutting into the baked dish sent shattered pieces of phyllo everywhere. Looking for a solution, I tried brushing each layer with olive oil, which helped the pastry layers stick together. One teaspoon of oil per sheet is adequate if spread carefully, but I preferred the added flavor and crispness of a slightly more generous amount of fat, about half a tablespoon per sheet. To fit my skillet, I placed the layers over each other in a pinwheel pattern, then folded the edges over the top to make a circle. I found it helpful to prepare the phyllo first and have it ready to go when my filling was done, so in subsequent tests I assembled my stack of phyllo sheets first, then stored them in the freezer to keep them firm for the short amount of time it took to make the filling.

Lastly, I wondered about the lengthy baking times specified by most recipes—usually an hour in the oven at 350 degrees, until the phyllo is golden and crisp. But when the hour was up, my bright flavors were washed out and flat, and the phyllo topping was dried out and more prone to shattering. Increasing the temperature to 450 degrees and reducing the cooking time to about 15 minutes resulted in a filling and crust that were both done to perfection.

—MEGAN WYCOFF, *America's Test Kitchen Books*

NOTES FROM THE TEST KITCHEN

MAKING A PHYLLO CRUST

1. Lay the first sheet of phyllo on a large piece of parchment paper and brush the pastry lightly, but thoroughly, with oil.

2. Lay the remaining sheets on top of the first, in a pinwheel fashion, to make a circle, brushing each sheet with more oil.

3. Fold the edges of phyllo over the top so the circle measures 11 inches across, then slide the parchment and phyllo onto a baking sheet and freeze until firm before using.

Skillet Phyllo Pie with Chicken
SERVES 4

Thaw the phyllo completely before using, either in the refrigerator overnight or on the counter for several hours; don't thaw the phyllo in the microwave. Do not substitute white chicken meat here, or the filling will taste very dry and bland.

PHYLLO CRUST

½ **pound (14 by 9-inch) phyllo, thawed (see note)**
⅓ **cup olive oil**

FILLING

8 **ounces feta cheese, crumbled fine (about 2 cups)**
3 **large eggs, lightly beaten**
1 **bunch scallions, sliced thin**
½ **cup pitted kalamata olives, chopped coarse**
⅓ **cup chopped fresh mint**
3 **tablespoons fresh lemon juice**
½ **teaspoon salt**
¼ **teaspoon pepper**
¼ **teaspoon cayenne pepper**
1 **tablespoon olive oil**
2 **pounds ground dark meat chicken (see note)**
3 **garlic cloves, minced**
½ **cup low-sodium chicken broth**

1. **FOR THE PHYLLO CRUST:** Adjust an oven rack to the middle position and heat the oven to 450 degrees. Following the photos on page 188, lay 1 phyllo sheet on a large sheet of parchment paper and brush the pastry lightly with oil. Repeat with 9 more phyllo sheets, placing them in a pinwheel pattern and brushing each sheet with oil. Fold the edges of the phyllo over so that the circle measures 11 inches. Slide the parchment and phyllo circle onto a baking sheet and freeze while making the filling.

2. **FOR THE FILLING:** Mix the feta, eggs, scallions, olives, mint, lemon juice, salt, pepper, and cayenne together in a large bowl. Set aside.

3. Heat the oil in a 12-inch ovensafe skillet over medium heat until shimmering. Add the chicken and cook, breaking up the meat with a wooden spoon, until no longer pink, about 5 minutes. Stir in the garlic and cook until fragrant, about 30 seconds. Stir in the chicken broth, scraping up any browned bits. Off the heat, stir in the feta mixture until well combined.

4. Smooth the filling into an even layer in the skillet. Lay the frozen phyllo circle on top of the filling and press lightly to adhere. Bake the pie until the phyllo is golden and crisp, about 15 minutes. Let the pie cool for 10 minutes before serving.

SPIEDIES

SPIEDIES—grilled, marinated chicken sandwiches—are upstate New York's best-kept secret. The sandwich (pronounced "speedy") gets its name not from haste but from *spiedo*, which is Italian for spit. Cubed meat—anything from chicken to venison—sits in an acidic, highly seasoned marinade for up to a week before it is skewered and grilled. For easy eating, the meat cubes are slid off the skewers and cradled in a slice of Italian bread or a hoagie bun. The sandwich is so popular in the Greater Binghamton region of New York that every summer 100,000 people attend Spiedie Fest, a summer weekend festival devoted to it.

Spiedies were originally made with lamb, which may account for the historically long marinade time and the strong seasoning, kitchen tricks that would mitigate gaminess and break down tough cuts of meat. Although tender chicken is now the most popular

choice for spiedies, the tradition of the long marinade continues. Not one recipe I found called for a marinade time shorter than 24 hours, so I wasn't surprised that my first batch of spiedies tasted pickled. Worse, the chicken was grainy and chalky, as if it had been overcooked. My goals for this sandwich were simple: I wanted to keep the chicken moist during cooking, develop a flavorful but not overwhelming seasoning combination, and reduce the time it took to get the chicken from my prep counter to the table.

I began with a variation of the marinade recipe tasters preferred from my first round of testing—lemon juice, red wine vinegar, olive oil, garlic, dried oregano, red pepper flakes, and fresh basil. I was pretty sure that simply reducing the marinade time from 24 hours to a few would vastly improve the texture of the chicken, but exactly how long did it need to sit in the marinade to achieve optimum texture—as well as flavor? Chicken marinated longer than four hours had the same texture problem as recipes that required an overnight marinade, but even when I reduced the marinade time to just two hours, tasters still complained that it was dry. A consultation with our science editor confirmed my suspicion that the acid in the marinade was to blame: It chemically "cooked" the chicken before it even hit the grill.

The logical next step was to remove the acid from the marinade. This chicken was moister and well seasoned, but the tangy, bright flavor—the essence of a spiedie—was missing. A colleague reminded me that, to offset dryness and add flavor, the test kitchen often brushes or rolls grilled meat in a fresh batch of marinade after it comes off the grill. I split the oil-based marinade into two bowls, adding the chicken to one and the vinegar and lemon juice to the other, making a "dressing" to drizzle on the cooked meat. The oil, salt, spices, and garlic in the marinade flavored the meat and improved its texture by acting as a brine, while the dressing "refreshed" the marinade flavors and the acidic components reintroduced the bright notes that had been missing. Adding lemon zest to the marinade boosted flavor, and, although unconventional, whisking 3 tablespoons of mayonnaise into the dressing gave it body and helped it cling to the chicken.

I was almost done, but I still wanted to further reduce the time the chicken spent in the marinade. I had been using 2-inch cubes of chicken, but I found that when

SPIEDIES

I cut the chicken into 1¼-inch cubes, the marinade flavored the meat more rapidly. Borrowing another test kitchen technique, I pricked the raw chicken all over with a fork before marinating it to see if that would help the marinade penetrate. In just half an hour, the chicken cubes were flavorful and ready to grill. This was a speedy sandwich, indeed.

—KRIS WIDICAN, *Cook's Country*

Spiedies

SERVES 6

You will need six 12-inch metal skewers for this recipe.

- ½ cup olive oil
- 2 garlic cloves, minced
- 2 tablespoons chopped fresh basil
- ½ teaspoon dried oregano
- 2 teaspoons grated lemon zest plus 1 tablespoon fresh lemon juice
- 1 teaspoon salt
- ½ teaspoon pepper
- ¼ teaspoon red pepper flakes
- 3 tablespoons mayonnaise
- 1 tablespoon red wine vinegar
- 1½ pounds boneless, skinless chicken breasts (about 4 breasts), trimmed
- 6 (6-inch) submarine rolls, slit partially open lengthwise, or 6 large slices Italian bread

1. Combine the oil, garlic, basil, oregano, lemon zest, salt, pepper, and pepper flakes in a large bowl. Transfer 2 tablespoons of the oil mixture to a separate bowl and whisk in the mayonnaise, vinegar, and lemon juice; refrigerate until ready to serve. (The sauces can be refrigerated, covered, for up 2 days.)

2. Following the photos, prick the chicken breasts all over with a fork, cut them into 1¼-inch chunks, and transfer to the bowl with the remaining oil mixture. Refrigerate, covered, for 30 minutes or up to 3 hours.

3. Remove the chicken from the marinade and thread the chunks onto six 12-inch metal skewers.

4A. FOR A CHARCOAL GRILL: Open the bottom grill vents completely. Light a large chimney starter filled with charcoal briquettes (100 briquettes; 6 quarts). When the coals are hot, spread them evenly over the grill. Set the cooking grate in place, cover, and heat the grill until hot, about 5 minutes.

4B. FOR A GAS GRILL: Turn all the burners to high, cover, and heat the grill until hot, about 15 minutes. (Adjust the burners as needed to maintain a hot fire; see page 130).

5. Clean and oil the cooking grate. Place the skewers on the grill and cook (covered if using gas), turning frequently, until lightly charred and cooked through, 10 to 15 minutes.

6. Transfer the chicken to the rolls, remove the skewers, and drizzle with the mayonnaise mixture. Serve.

NOTES FROM THE TEST KITCHEN

SPEEDY SPIEDIE PREP

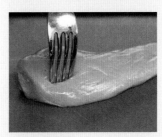

1. To help the marinade penetrate the meat, prick the chicken breasts all over with a fork.

2. To expose more surface area to the marinade, cut the chicken into 1¼-inch cubes.

3. Marinate the chicken in a highly seasoned mixture that will transfer flavor in just 30 minutes.

CORNELL CHICKEN

CORNELL CHICKEN

CORNELL CHICKEN WAS INVENTED IN THE 1940S by the late Robert Baker, a Cornell University professor, and it has been a star attraction at the New York State Fair ever since (it is also referred to as "State Fair Chicken"). Baker's recipe and method remain unchanged at the Baker's Chicken Coop stand at the fair today: Half-chickens are basted with a tangy sauce (vinegar, oil, poultry seasoning, and an egg) while they cook over a custom-made grill that elevates the birds exactly 26 inches above the coals. The combination of low heat and continual basting produces tangy, crisp-skinned chicken.

Unfortunately, recipes that try to adapt Baker's chicken to the backyard grill, where the fire is much closer to the cooking grate, are problematic. The oily basting sauce inevitably drips off the chicken and into the fire, where it causes flare-ups that blacken the outside of the chicken before the inside has cooked through. I wanted to create a backyard Cornell chicken that featured crisp (but not charred) skin and meat that was deeply seasoned.

I started with the grilling method. Since Dr. Baker used low heat, I first tried grilling chicken halves over indirect heat; this method worked OK, but it meant I'd have to finish the chicken over high heat to get the crispy skin I desired. It was much easier (on either a gas or a charcoal grill) to grill two split chickens over gentle direct heat for the entire cooking time. To crisp the skin without burning it, I started the chicken skin-side up to slowly render the fat, then flipped the chicken skin-side down to brown it to a crisp.

The sauce for Cornell chicken is pretty standard: 2 parts vinegar to 1 part vegetable oil, along with poultry seasoning, salt, and a beaten egg. I discovered quickly that basting adds flavor only if the baste stays on the chicken—and in my tests, it ran off the chicken as fast as I could brush it on, causing flare-ups that led to charred chicken (this is not a problem at the Baker's Chicken Coop stand, where the distance between the coals and the chicken makes the issue of flare-ups moot). The egg was supposed to thicken the sauce; since the sauce wasn't thick enough to stay on the meat, I tried increasing the number of eggs, all the way up to four. This baste adhered to the chicken, all right, creating a scrambled-egg crust that sent my tasters running for the door.

Since the eggs weren't adding desirable flavor, and I had to use too many of them to achieve any thickening power, I decided to eliminate egg from the sauce altogether (some claim that Baker included the egg in his recipe solely to aid local egg sales). I needed to find another ingredient to thicken the basting sauce so that it would adhere to the chicken. Since the sauce is essentially a vinaigrette, I tried adding mustard (which we often use to help emulsify vinaigrettes), and it worked perfectly, contributing flavor and thickening the sauce. The sauce was now thick enough that I had to lift the grill lid and apply it only three times during cooking to match the amount of flavor achieved by continual basting with a thinner sauce; less basting also meant crisper skin.

The baste was working well, but it was flavoring only the outside of the chicken. Soaking the raw chicken in a saltwater brine helped to season the meat, and adding vinegar to the brine brought the tangy pucker all the way down to the bone. For even more flavor, I rubbed poultry seasoning (along with salt and pepper) into the skin of the meat before grilling and replaced the poultry seasoning in the sauce (where, uncooked, it tasted a little dusty) with fresh rosemary and sage. Backyard Cornell Chicken has finally gotten an education of its own.

—DIANE UNGER, *Cook's Country*

Cornell Chicken

SERVES 4 TO 6

It's easy to halve chickens yourself, but you can also buy split chicken halves at the supermarket. Do not brine the chicken longer than 2 hours or the vinegar will make the meat mushy. Baste the chicken carefully in step 5, as any excess will drip onto the fire and flare up.

CHICKEN

¼ cup table salt

3½ cups cider vinegar

2 (3½ to 4-pound) whole chickens, giblets discarded and halved (see page 194; see note)

SEASONING AND SAUCE

1 tablespoon poultry seasoning

Salt and pepper

½ cup cider vinegar

3 tablespoons Dijon mustard

1 tablespoon chopped fresh sage

1 tablespoon minced fresh rosemary

½ cup olive oil

1. FOR THE CHICKEN: Dissolve the salt in the vinegar and 2 quarts cold water in a large container. Submerge the chicken in the brine, cover, and refrigerate for 1 to 2 hours.

2. FOR THE SEASONING AND SAUCE: Combine the poultry seasoning, 2 teaspoons salt, and 2 teaspoons pepper in a small bowl; set aside. Process the vinegar, mustard, sage, rosemary, ½ teaspoon salt, and ½ teaspoon pepper in a blender until smooth, about 1 minute. With the blender running, slowly add the oil until incorporated. Transfer the vinegar sauce to a small bowl and reserve. (Both the spice rub and the sauce can be made up to 3 days ahead. Store the spice rub in an airtight container on the counter and the sauce in an airtight container in the refrigerator.)

3A. FOR A CHARCOAL GRILL: Open the bottom grill vents halfway. Light a large chimney starter three-quarters full with charcoal briquettes (75 briquettes; 4½ quarts). When the coals are hot, pour them evenly over the grill. Set the cooking grate in place, cover, and open the lid vents halfway. Heat the grill until hot, about 5 minutes.

3B. FOR A GAS GRILL: Turn all the burners to high, cover, and heat the grill until hot, about 15 minutes. Turn all the burners to medium-low. (Adjust the burners as need to maintain the grill temperature around 350 degrees).

NOTES FROM THE TEST KITCHEN

HALVING CHICKENS

1. Using kitchen shears, cut along both sides of the backbone to remove it. (You can freeze the backbone for making stock.) Trim any excess fat or skin at the neck.

2. Flip the chicken over and, using a chef's knife, cut through the breastbone to separate the chicken into halves.

---

4. Clean and oil the cooking grate. Remove the chicken from the brine, rinse well, and pat dry with paper towels. Rub the chicken all over with the poultry seasoning mixture. (The chicken can be brined, patted dry, and rubbed with the seasoning mixture up to 8 hours ahead.)

5. Arrange the chicken skin-side up on the grill and baste with the reserved vinegar sauce. Grill, covered, until the chicken is well browned on the bottom and the thickest part of the thighs registers 120 degrees on an instant-read thermometer, 25 to 30 minutes, basting with the sauce halfway through cooking. Flip the chicken skin-side down and baste with the sauce. Continue to grill, covered, until the skin is golden brown and crisp, the thickest part of the breasts registers 160 to 165 degrees, and the thickest part of the thighs registers 175 degrees, 20 to 25 minutes longer. Transfer the chicken to a platter (do not cover) and let rest for 5 minutes. Serve.

ROAST LEMON CHICKEN

FLAVORING A ROAST CHICKEN with lemon seems simple and ought to be out-and-out delicious. But after trying several recipes, I realized it wasn't so straightforward. The flavors can be bitter or bland. Add sauce and the problems multiply. Some sauces taste lemon-less, others pucker-up harsh. I wanted a recipe quick enough for a weeknight meal, one that wouldn't require me to squeeze a bushel of lemons yet would infuse the meat with lemon flavor that actually appealed.

Putting lemon halves in the cavity of a chicken is a common technique, but it did little to flavor the meat. Next, I brined a chicken in a lemon-saltwater solution. It made for a moist chicken, but with diluted lemon flavor. After that, I slid lemon butter under the skin of a bird; the flavor melted away. I roasted a fourth chicken, this time tucking strips of peel under its skin. The pigment from the lemon strips turned the chicken meat Big Bird yellow, but the lemon flavor seemed worth pursuing—maybe in a more user-friendly form? I started my next round of testing there.

Instead of strips of peel, I tried grating lemon zest and mixing it with a little sugar. I figured grating the

ROAST LEMON CHICKEN

zest would strengthen the lemon flavor and the sugar would tame its tang. Grated zest was also easier to distribute under the skin of the chicken and eliminated the unwieldy strips of sour peel. I roasted the chicken breast-side down at 375 degrees for about 35 minutes, increased the heat (to 450 degrees), and flipped the chicken breast-side up to crisp the skin. The lemon flavor was stronger, but tasters still felt the lemon flavor wasn't permeating the chicken.

One of the first recipes I'd tried called for carving the bird after roasting, then arranging the pieces in a lemony sauce and broiling the chicken to crisp the skin. Tedious, yes, but the meat that came in contact with the sauce as the chicken broiled tasted fantastic.

What if I split the chicken open and roasted it, start to finish, right in a lemony sauce? I removed the backbone with a pair of kitchen shears, rubbed my lemon-sugar mixture under the skin (easier now that the bird was butterflied), and set the chicken in a roasting pan.

I added ⅓ cup fresh lemon juice mixed with water and chicken broth (to tame the acidity and guard against burning) so that the meat of the chicken was resting in the flavorful liquid, with the skin safely above the juice to let it get crisp. After roasting one chicken, I realized that a higher temperature of 475 degrees for the entire time made it crisper. This chicken had golden, incredibly crisp skin with a salty-sweet hit, plus meat with bright, balanced lemon flavor in every bite.

The juices were almost perfect straight from the roasting pan. But with just a little work, I could take them over the top. While the chicken was resting, I skimmed the fat, reduced the liquid to concentrate its flavor, and thickened it slightly with butter and cornstarch.

—DIANE UNGER, *Cook's Country*

NOTES FROM THE TEST KITCHEN

MORE LEMON FLAVOR IN LESS TIME

1. Butterflying the chicken makes it easier to flavor with lemon—and speeds roasting, too. Use kitchen shears to cut out the backbone. Flip the bird over and press to flatten the breastbone.

2. Carefully loosen the skin, then rub the zest mixture into the breast, thigh, and leg meat.

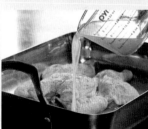

3. Roast the flattened chicken in the lemony sauce so that its flavor can permeate the meat.

Roast Lemon Chicken

SERVES 3 TO 4

Avoid using nonstick or aluminum roasting pans in this recipe. The former can cause the chicken to brown too quickly, while the latter may react with the lemon juice, producing off-flavors.

    Table salt
½   cup plus 1 teaspoon sugar
1   (3½ to 4-pound) whole chicken, giblets discarded, backbone removed, and butterflied (see photo)
3   tablespoons grated lemon zest plus
    ⅓ cup fresh lemon juice from 3 lemons
    Pepper
2   cups low-sodium chicken broth
1   cup plus 1 tablespoon water
1   teaspoon cornstarch
3   tablespoons unsalted butter
1   tablespoon chopped fresh parsley

1. Dissolve ½ cup salt and ½ cup of the sugar in 2 quarts cold water in a large container. Submerge the chicken in the brine, cover, and refrigerate for 1 hour.

2. Adjust an oven rack to the middle position and heat the oven to 475 degrees. Remove the chicken from the brine, rinse well, and pat dry with paper towels. Combine the lemon zest and remaining 1 teaspoon sugar in a small bowl. Rub 2 tablespoons of the zest mixture under the skin of the chicken (see photo 2). Season the chicken with pepper and transfer to the roasting pan. (The seasoned chicken can be refrigerated for up to 2 hours.)

3. Whisk the broth, 1 cup of the water, lemon juice, and remaining zest mixture in a 4-cup liquid measuring cup, then pour into the roasting pan. (The liquid should just reach the skin of the thighs. If the liquid does not reach this level, add enough water so that it does.) Roast until the skin is golden brown and the thickest part of the breast registers 160 to 165 degrees and the thickest part of the thighs registers 175 degrees on an instant-read thermometer, 40 to 45 minutes. Transfer to a cutting board and let rest for 20 minutes.

4. Pour the liquid from the pan, along with any accumulated chicken juices, into a saucepan (you should have about 1½ cups). Skim the fat, then cook over medium-high heat until reduced to 1 cup, about 5 minutes. Whisk the cornstarch with the remaining 1 tablespoon water in a small bowl until no lumps remain, then whisk into the saucepan. Simmer until the sauce is slightly thickened, about 2 minutes. Off the heat, whisk in the butter and parsley and season with salt and pepper to taste. Carve the chicken and serve, passing the sauce at the table.

GLAZED ROAST CHICKEN

MOST GLAZED ROAST CHICKEN RECIPES offer some variation on these instructions: Roast a chicken as you would normally, painting on a sweet glaze 15 to 30 minutes before the bird is done. It sounds simple, but following these recipes actually turns up a host of troubles, as the problems inherent in roasting chicken (dry breast meat, flabby skin, big deposits of fat under the skin) are compounded by the problems of a glaze (won't stick to the meat, burns in patches, introduces moisture to already flabby skin).

Yet I know that great glazed chicken is possible. Barbecued rotisserie chicken turns slowly as it cooks, making it a cinch to apply sauce to every nook and cranny while also ensuring even cooking. Likewise, Chinese chefs glaze whole ducks that roast while suspended from hooks, turning out perfectly lacquered, crisp-skinned birds. With these techniques as my inspiration, I set out to develop a method for evenly glazed roast chicken with crisp skin and moist, tender meat.

I chose a large roaster chicken (6 to 7 pounds), enough to feed four to six people, and started with an approach we've used before in the test kitchen. I separated the skin from the meat and pricked holes in the fat deposits (to allow rendering fat to escape, resulting in crisper skin), then rubbed it with salt and baking soda (to dehydrate the skin and help it to crisp) and let the chicken rest. I then roasted the chicken breast-side down on a V-rack at 450 degrees for 30 minutes, flipped it over, and roasted it another 30 minutes. Then, with the chicken nearly done, I brushed it with a simple glaze of maple syrup, marmalade, vinegar, and Dijon mustard, and finished it with a blast of 500-degree heat.

While the meat was moist and evenly cooked, the glaze was disappointing. The top of the bird was a lacquered mahogany, while the bottom was merely golden brown—not the deep, even tone I expected with a glaze. And although the precautions I'd taken helped the fat render from beneath the skin, 15 minutes of steaming under a moist glaze left the skin woefully soggy.

With one side of the chicken facing down during the entire glazing process, I could never hope to glaze the whole bird evenly. Short of installing meat hooks or a rotisserie in my oven, what could I do? A vertical roaster, which cooks chicken standing up, was a possibility, but then I remembered a simpler alternative, found right in my fridge: a beer can. We've had great success placing a beer can in the chicken cavity and standing it upright on the grill, which allows heat to circulate freely so that the bird cooks evenly from all sides. Why not bring this popular technique indoors?

I prepared the chicken and applied a rub as before. After allowing the chicken to rest for an hour, I grabbed a 16-ounce can of beer (the large bird didn't fit on anything smaller), took a few sips to prevent spills, and straddled the chicken on top. I then placed it in a roasting pan and slid it into the oven. The technique seemed like a winner—no awkward flipping, glazing every nook and cranny was easy, and fat dripped freely out of the bird. But cutting into the chicken revealed that the breast, now exposed to the high oven heat for the entire cooking time, was dry and tough. Scaling back the oven temperature to a gentler 325 degrees resolved this issue, but even without steaming under a glaze, the skin was far from crisp.

To develop a crisp skin, the chicken needs to finish roasting at a very high heat (around 500 degrees) for

VERTICAL ROASTERS

When it comes to cost, it's hard to beat a beer can as a tool for vertical roasting. But is the real deal worth having on hand? Like a beer can, vertical roasters can support poultry to crisp the skin all over. We tested five models priced from $11.99 to $110. Some seemed so flimsy, we worried the chicken might tip over; we also didn't like designs that allowed the chicken to sit in its own rendered fat. Our top performer, the **Norpro Vertical Roaster with Infuser,** $27.95, had the longest cone and excelled in even roasting and sturdiness. That said, a beer can—though it requires a bit more maneuvering of the chicken—works nearly as well.

PRIMING CHICKEN FOR CRISPER SKIN

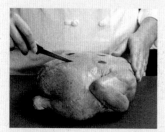

1. Cut channels in the skin along the chicken's back.

2. Loosen the skin from the thighs and breast.

3. Poke holes in the skin of the breast and thighs.

4. Apply a rub of salt, pepper, and baking powder, then air-dry the chicken in the refrigerator before roasting.

about 30 minutes. But in the time it takes the oven to heat from 325 to 500 degrees, the delicate breast meat overcooks. With regular roast chicken, we've solved this problem by letting it rest at room temperature while the oven heats up for its final blast. Would that work with a vertically roasted chicken? Though the rested-before-blasted chicken came out much crisper than before, and the breast meat was perfectly cooked, the glaze was still robbing my chicken of optimum skin quality.

This was the problem: Most recipes call for a watery glaze that slowly reduces and thickens as the bird cooks—a hindrance when you're trying to crisp the skin. What if I reduced the glaze on the stovetop before I applied it? That way, I could wait to brush on the glaze until the very end, when it wouldn't ruin the texture of the skin. I made another glaze, this time thickening it with cornstarch. I reduced it to a syrupy consistency and applied it before the final five minutes of roasting. This chicken emerged from the oven with a burnished sheen of deep brown, and its rendered skin crackled as I cut into it, revealing moist, tender meat. For good measure, I brushed more glaze on the chicken and made extra to pass tableside. Now when I hanker for perfect glazed chicken, I'll forget about the rotisserie—all I need is a beer can to get the job done right.

—DAVID PAZMIÑO, *Cook's Illustrated*

Glazed Roast Chicken

SERVES 4 TO 6

For best results, use a 16-ounce can of beer. A larger can will work, but avoid using a 12-ounce can, as it will not support the weight of the chicken. A vertical roaster can be used in place of the beer can, but we recommend using only a model that can be placed in a roasting pan. Taste your marmalade before using it; if it is overly sweet, reduce the amount of maple syrup in the glaze by 2 tablespoons.

CHICKEN

- 1 (6 to 7-pound) whole chicken, giblets discarded
- 5 teaspoons kosher salt or 2½ teaspoons table salt
- 1 teaspoon baking powder
- 1 teaspoon pepper
- 1 (16-ounce) can beer (see note)

GLAZE

- 1 **teaspoon cornstarch**
- 1 **tablespoon water**
- ½ **cup maple syrup**
- ½ **cup orange marmalade (see note)**
- ¼ **cup cider vinegar**
- 2 **tablespoons unsalted butter**
- 2 **tablespoons Dijon mustard**
- 1 **teaspoon pepper**

1. FOR THE CHICKEN: Place the chicken breast-side down on the countertop. Following the photos on page 198, use the tip of a sharp knife to make 1-inch incisions below each thigh and breast along the back of the chicken (four incisions total). Using your fingers or the handle of a wooden spoon, carefully separate the skin from the thighs and breast. Using a metal skewer, poke 15 to 20 holes in the fat deposits on top of the breast and thighs. Tuck the wings behind the back.

2. Combine the salt, baking powder, and pepper in a small bowl. Pat the chicken dry with paper towels and sprinkle evenly all over with the salt mixture. Rub in the mixture with your hands, coating the entire surface evenly. Set the chicken, breast-side up, on a rimmed baking sheet and refrigerate, uncovered, for 30 to 60 minutes. Meanwhile, adjust an oven rack to the lowest position and heat the oven to 325 degrees.

3. Open a beer can and pour out (or drink) about half of the liquid. Spray the can lightly with vegetable oil spray and place in the middle of a roasting pan. Slide the chicken over the can so the drumsticks reach down to the bottom of the can, the chicken stands upright, and the breast is perpendicular to the bottom of the pan. Roast until the skin starts to turn golden and the thickest part of the breast registers 140 degrees on an instant-read thermometer, 75 to 90 minutes. Carefully remove the chicken and pan from the oven and increase the oven temperature to 500 degrees.

4. FOR THE GLAZE: While the chicken cooks, stir the cornstarch and water together in a small bowl until no lumps remain; set aside. Bring the remaining glaze ingredients to a simmer in a medium saucepan over medium-high heat. Cook, stirring occasionally, until reduced to ¾ cup, 6 to 8 minutes. Slowly whisk the cornstarch mixture into the glaze. Return to a simmer and cook for 1 minute. Remove the pan from the heat.

5. When the oven is heated to 500 degrees, pour 1½ cups water into the bottom of the roasting pan and return to the oven. Roast until the entire chicken skin is browned and crisp and the thickest part of the breast registers 160 to 165 degrees and the thickest part of thighs registers 175 degrees, 25 to 30 minutes. Check the chicken halfway through roasting; if the top is becoming too dark, place a 7-inch square piece of foil over the neck and wingtips of the chicken and continue to roast (if the pan begins to smoke and sizzle, add an additional ½ cup water to the roasting pan).

6. Brush the chicken with ¼ cup of the glaze and continue to roast until browned and sticky, about 5 minutes. (If the glaze has become stiff, return to low heat to soften.) Carefully remove the chicken from the oven, transfer the chicken, still on the can, to a cutting board, and brush with ¼ cup more glaze. Let rest for 20 minutes.

7. While the chicken rests, strain the juices from the pan through a fine-mesh strainer into a fat separator; allow the liquid to settle for 5 minutes. Whisk ½ cup of the juices into the remaining ¼ cup glaze in the saucepan and set over low heat. Using a kitchen towel, carefully lift the chicken off the can and onto a platter or cutting board. Carve the chicken, adding any accumulated juices to the sauce. Serve, passing the sauce separately.

HULI HULI CHICKEN

"HULI! HULI!" workers shout to one another as they man the 10-foot portable grills that dot the roads and parking lots of Hawaii, each grill cooking more than 30 split chickens at a time. The birds are continually basted with a sticky-sweet sauce and "huli"-ed (turned, in Hawaiian) to keep from burning. True huli huli chicken is something most people buy instead of make at home, as the grill apparatus and incessant flipping discourage even the most adventurous grillers. Could I find a way to adapt the technique for the home cook?

I started by rummaging around cookbooks and the Internet, where I found adaptations of the teriyaki-like sauce to which sweet ingredients are added. I made, remade, adapted, developed, and tweaked. Ultimately, tasters picked a version with soy sauce, rice vinegar, and

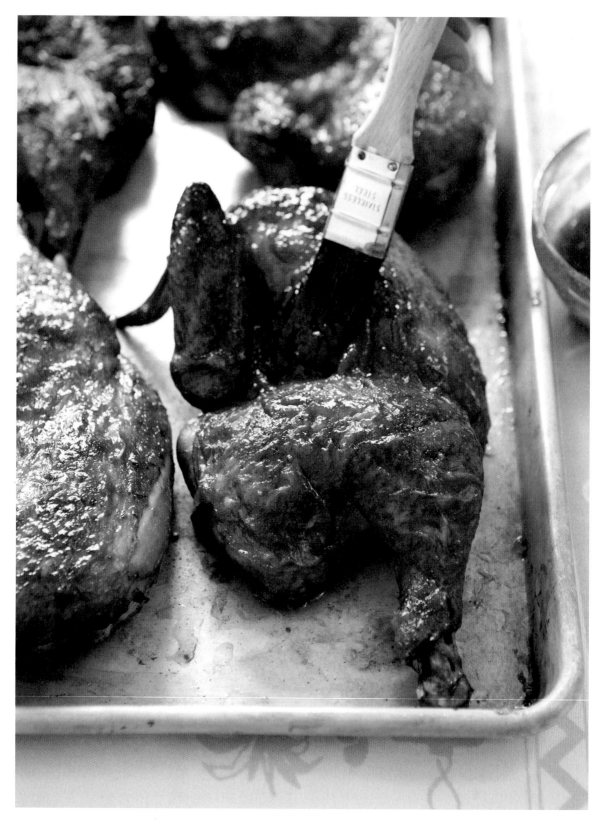

HULI HULI CHICKEN

ginger with garlic, chili sauce, ketchup, brown sugar, and lots and lots of pineapple juice. I boiled the sauce down until it was thick, glossy, and sweet. Then I marinated the chicken in the sauce, as most recipes instruct. But on the grill, by the time the chicken was cooked through, its skin had incinerated. Also, the meat was dry, and though you'd think soaking it in sticky sauce would let it soak up flavor, that wasn't the case.

First order of business: I'd tackle the grill setup. On a Hawaiian rotisserie, the chicken halves are strapped to parallel poles, suspended way above the coals and continually turned. For me, high, direct heat proved a direct path to scorched chicken. Indirect heat (banking the coals to one side and grilling the chicken on the other side) resulted in flabby chicken skin. My best bet was a moderate number of coals (about 75) spread in a single layer over the entire grill. The direct heat rendered the fat and crisped the skin, but the chicken was far enough from the coals to eliminate burning—or so I hoped.

The test kitchen often brines chicken to keep it moist and flavorful. For my next test, instead of soaking the chicken in sauce, I brined it in lots of salt and water, planning to paint on the sauce while the chicken was grilling. This chicken was moist, but as soon as I started to baste, it burned yet again. Despite my careful grill setup, with so much sugar in the sauce the chicken didn't stand a chance. Also, the flavor was only skin-deep; those great sauce flavors just weren't getting into the meat. What if I used some of my sauce ingredients as a brine? Instead of salt, I mixed together soy sauce, water, garlic, and ginger (I sautéed the last two to bring out their flavors) to make a brine. In another bid for flavor, I added soaked mesquite chips to my grill. (Kiawe, the Hawaiian wood typically used, is a species of mesquite.) This chicken had a deep, seasoned-to-the-bone flavor.

If only I could fix that smoldering problem. Since the glaze was to blame, why not save it until the chicken came off the grill? After all, the chicken was already highly seasoned from the brine and well smoked from the wood. I grilled the chicken skin-side up to render the fat, and then huli-ed it skin-side down to finish cooking and crisp the skin (just one turn sufficed). As soon as the chicken came off the grill, I painted

on the glaze. This chicken was bronzed and beautiful, smoky, moist, sweet, and flavorful throughout.

—DIANE UNGER, *Cook's Country*

Huli Huli Chicken

SERVES 4 TO 6

It's easy to halve chickens yourself, but you can also buy split chicken halves at the supermarket.

CHICKEN

- 2 **cups soy sauce**
- 1 **tablespoon vegetable oil**
- 6 **garlic cloves, minced**
- 1 **tablespoon grated or minced fresh ginger**
- 2 **(3½ to 4-pound) whole chickens, giblets discarded and halved (see page 194; see note)**

GLAZE

- 3 **(6-ounce) cans pineapple juice**
- ¼ **cup packed light brown sugar**
- ¼ **cup soy sauce**
- ¼ **cup ketchup**
- ¼ **cup rice vinegar**
- 4 **garlic cloves, minced**
- 2 **tablespoons grated or minced fresh ginger**
- 2 **teaspoons Asian chili-garlic sauce**
- 2 **cups wood chips, soaked in water for 15 minutes and drained**

1. FOR THE CHICKEN: Combine the soy sauce and 2 quarts cold water in a large bowl. Heat the oil in a large saucepan over medium-high heat until shimmering. Add the garlic and ginger and cook until fragrant, about 30 seconds. Stir into the soy sauce mixture. Add the chicken and refrigerate, covered, for 1 hour or up to 8 hours.

2. FOR THE GLAZE: Combine the pineapple juice, sugar, soy sauce, ketchup, vinegar, garlic, ginger, and chili-garlic sauce in an empty saucepan and bring to a boil. Reduce the heat to medium and simmer until thick and syrupy (you should have about 1 cup), 20 to 25 minutes. (The glaze can be refrigerated in an airtight container for up to 3 days.) Seal the soaked wood chips in a foil packet and cut vent holes in the top (see page 149).

3A. FOR A CHARCOAL GRILL: Open the bottom vents halfway. Light a large chimney starter three-quarters full with charcoal briquettes (75 briquettes; 4½ quarts). When the coals are hot, spread them evenly over the grill. Place the wood chip packet on top of the coals. Set the cooking grate in place, cover, and open the lid vents halfway. Heat the grill until hot and the wood chips begin to smoke heavily, about 5 minutes.

3B. FOR A GAS GRILL: Place the wood chip packet directly on the primary burner. Turn all the burners to high, cover, and heat the grill until hot and the wood chips begin to smoke heavily, about 15 minutes. Turn all the burners to medium-low. (Adjust the burners as needed to maintain the grill temperature around 350 degrees.)

4. Clean and oil the cooking grate. Remove the chicken from the brine and pat dry with paper towels. Arrange the chicken skin-side up on the grill (do not place the chicken directly above the foil packet). Grill, covered, until the chicken is well browned on the bottom and the thickest part of the thighs registers 120 degrees on an instant-read thermometer, 25 to 30 minutes. Flip the chicken skin-side down and continue to grill, covered, until the skin is well browned and crisp, the thickest part of the breasts registers 160 to 165 degrees, and the thickest part of the thighs registers 175 degrees, 20 to 25 minutes longer. Transfer the chicken to a platter, brush with half of the glaze, and let rest for 5 minutes. Serve, passing the remaining glaze at the table.

NOTES FROM THE TEST KITCHEN

FOR AUTHENTIC FLAVOR, USE MESQUITE
Authentic huli huli chicken is grilled over kiawe wood, a hardwood tree that is a species of mesquite. The test kitchen finds mesquite wood chips too assertive for long-cooked barbecue dishes, such as brisket. After a couple of hours, the smoke turns bitter. But we liked them in this comparatively quick recipe. Our recipe will work with any variety of wood chips, but if you care about authenticity, mesquite is the chip of choice.

OLD-FASHIONED ROAST TURKEY AND GRAVY

THE PROSPECT OF ROASTING A HOLIDAY TURKEY can make me pull the covers up over my head on Thanksgiving morning. It's a lot of work and a huge time commitment, and the results are all too often dry and disappointing. The only thing to be thankful for is a giant ladle of gravy that can make it all palatable.

The problem is that the white and dark meat need to be cooked to different temperatures. While the white meat starts to dry out if cooked past 165 degrees, the dark meat isn't tender and fully cooked until it reaches 175 degrees. There are ways to solve this issue, but none are particularly effortless. Brining a turkey ensures that even overcooked breast meat will be juicy, but this step takes many hours and a lot of refrigerator space. Or you can start the bird breast-side down to expose the dark meat to more heat and then flip the turkey so the breast skin can crisp. To my mind, wrestling with a hot, heavy bird when the house is filled with guests isn't all that appealing. I wanted to find an easier way to perfectly cooked turkey.

I remembered seeing my grandmother cook a holiday turkey by covering the breast meat with cheesecloth soaked in chicken broth, the idea being that the broth would slowly drip, keeping the meat moist and helping to prevent overcooking. While the test kitchen has learned that traditional basting doesn't work (repeatedly opening the oven leads to too much heat loss, and the liquid runs off the bird as fast as you apply it), the cheesecloth technique seemed promising. It took me a few tests to discover that the soaked cheesecloth did help to slow down the cooking of the breast meat, but if you didn't baste the cheesecloth (and keep it moist), it blackened and fused to the turkey.

For my next test, I covered the breast meat with cheesecloth soaked in chicken broth and then covered the cheesecloth with a double layer of aluminum foil to insulate it from drying out. I stuck a temperature probe into the thickest portion of the breast and another into the thickest portion of the thigh. I connected the probes to a computer program that could chart the temperature throughout the cooking time.

OLD-FASHIONED ROAST TURKEY AND GRAVY

FAT EQUALS FLAVOR

Covering the breast and tops of the legs of the turkey with salt pork helps to season the meat and insulate it from overcooking. Don't confuse salt pork with bacon. Although both come from the belly of the pig and are salt-cured, bacon is heavily smoked and is typically leaner and meatier. Salt pork is unsmoked and used primarily as a flavoring agent. Buy blocks of salt pork that have at least a few streaks of meat throughout. Salt pork can be refrigerated for up to one month.

PREPARING OLD-FASHIONED ROAST TURKEY

1. Use a fork to pierce the skin of the turkey breast and legs all over.

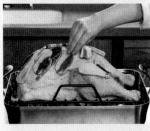

2. Cover the entirety of the breast and the tops of the legs with strips of salt pork.

3. Soak cheesecloth in cold water, then drape it over the salt pork on the breast and legs.

4. Cover the cheesecloth completely with foil.

As I had hoped, this method caused the breast meat to lag a perfect 10 degrees behind the thighs—with very little effort. When the breast meat reached 140 degrees, I took the cheesecloth and foil off and turned the oven up (from 350 to 425 degrees), and continued to roast the turkey until the breast meat was done and the skin was nicely browned.

My insulation was working, but I wanted to add more flavor to the bird. I tried adding herbs and peppercorns to the broth I used for soaking the cheesecloth, but the added flavor was superficial at best. Butter wasn't much better—it quickly dripped off the turkey and into the bottom of the pan. Looking for a potent ingredient that would slowly release its flavor during cooking, I thought of a technique that has been used for poultry for ages: larding, a process of inserting strips of lard (or other animal fat) into the turkey meat so it could slowly release its flavor and moisture throughout roasting. While I didn't want to cut holes in my turkey—or infuse it with lard—I decided to try covering the breast with bacon before layering on my broth-soaked cheesecloth and foil. Once the breast meat hit 140 degrees, I took off the covering and bacon slices and finished cooking the turkey as before. The meat was definitely better seasoned, but tasters objected to the smoky flavor that the bacon had imparted to the meat and drippings.

I tried replacing the bacon with ¼-inch slices of salt pork, which further insulated the breast and slowly melted in the oven, basting the turkey with flavorful pork fat. Since the tops of the turkey legs were drying out during cooking, I also gave them the salt pork, soaked cheesecloth, and foil treatment. The breast meat was moist and flavorful, the dark meat tender, and the skin beautifully browned and crisp. The salt pork added so much richness that I didn't need to soak the cheesecloth in broth—plain water worked just fine. Now that I had the perfect turkey, it was time to make the perfect gravy.

I started by simmering a stock made from the turkey giblets and neck, onion, and herbs while the turkey was in the oven. I strained the stock and was ready to start building the gravy once the turkey came out of the oven. I made a roux from turkey fat (for flavor) and flour, then added my stock and defatted pan drippings and simmered my gravy until it was nicely thickened. The gravy was richly seasoned from my homemade stock, the turkey drippings, and the salt pork. I finally had a perfectly cooked, moist turkey with great gravy— and a minimum of fuss.

—DIANE UNGER, *Cook's Country*

Old-Fashioned Roast Turkey and Gravy

SERVES 10 TO 12

You will need one 2-yard package of cheesecloth for this recipe. Because we layer the bird with salt pork, we prefer to use a natural turkey here; self-basting turkeys may become too salty. If using a self-basting turkey, use all water in the gravy rather than a combination of water and broth. Make sure to start the gravy as soon as the turkey goes into the oven.

TURKEY

- 1 **package cheesecloth (see note)**
- 4 **cups cold water**
- 1 **(12 to 14-pound) turkey, neck and giblets reserved (see note)**
- 1 **pound salt pork, cut into ¼-inch-thick slices**

GRAVY

- 1 **tablespoon vegetable oil**
  Reserved turkey neck and giblets
- 1 **onion, chopped medium (about 1 cup)**
- 5 **cups water**
- 2 **cups low-sodium chicken broth (see note)**
- 4 **sprigs fresh thyme**
- 1 **bay leaf**
- 6 **tablespoons unbleached all-purpose flour**
  Salt and pepper

1. FOR THE TURKEY: Adjust an oven rack to the lowest position and heat the oven to 350 degrees. Remove the cheesecloth from the package and fold into an 18-inch square. Place the cheesecloth in a large bowl and cover with the water. Tuck the wings behind the back and arrange the turkey, breast-side up, on a V-rack set inside a roasting pan. Following the photos on page 204, prick the skin of the breast and legs of the turkey all over with a fork, cover the breast and legs of the turkey with the salt pork, top with the soaked cheesecloth (pouring any remaining water into the roasting pan), and cover the cheesecloth completely with heavy-duty aluminum foil.

2. Roast the turkey until the thickest part of the breast registers 140 degrees on an instant-read thermometer, 2½ to 3 hours. Remove the foil, cheesecloth, and salt pork and discard. Increase the oven temperature to 425 degrees. Continue to roast until the thickest part of the breast registers 160 to 165 degrees and the thickest part of thighs registers 175 degrees, 40 to 60 minutes longer. Transfer the turkey to a cutting board and let rest for 30 minutes.

3. FOR THE GRAVY: While the turkey is roasting, heat the oil in a large saucepan over medium-high heat until shimmering. Cook the turkey neck and giblets until browned, about 5 minutes. Add the onion and cook until softened, 5 to 7 minutes. Stir in the water, broth, thyme, and bay leaf and bring to a boil. Reduce the heat to low and simmer until reduced by half, about 3 hours. Strain the stock into a large measuring cup (you should have about 3½ cups), reserving the giblets if desired.

4. Carefully strain the contents of the roasting pan into a fat separator. Let the liquid settle so that the fat separates, then skim, reserving ¼ cup of the fat. Pour the defatted pan juices into the measuring cup with the giblet stock to yield 4 cups stock.

5. Heat the reserved fat in an empty saucepan over medium heat until shimmering. Stir in the flour and cook until honey-colored and fragrant, about 4 minutes. Slowly whisk in the giblet stock and bring to a boil. Reduce the heat to medium-low and simmer until slightly thickened, about 5 minutes. Chop the giblets and add to the gravy, if desired, and season with salt and pepper to taste. Carve the turkey and serve with the gravy.

CHAPTER 8

SEAFOOD

Grilled Salmon Fillets with Almond Vinaigrette   208

Salmon en Cocotte   210

　　Salmon en Cocotte with Leeks and White Wine

　　Salmon en Cocotte with Celery and Orange

Skillet Salmon and Leek Pot Pie   213

Skillet Shrimp and Grits   215

New Orleans Barbecue Shrimp   217

Southern Shrimp Burgers   218

Shrimp Tempura with Ginger-Soy Dipping Sauce   220

GRILLED SALMON FILLETS

COOKING DELICATE SALMON CAN BE TRICKY. Even when I'm using a nonstick skillet, I still end up breaking the occasional fillet, which requires a patch job on the plate. Introduce the same fillet to a grill, and you've got a real challenge: When it's time to flip the fish, the skin invariably gets stuck and the flesh gets mangled. And if you've got a grate that's encrusted with gunk, things get even messier. So how is it that any halfway decent chophouse or pub manages to serve char-grilled salmon with a tender interior and crisp skin, the fillet perfectly intact? There had to be a secret behind the swinging doors.

In truth, part of the solution was already behind the test kitchen's back door, in a protocol we developed to clean the grill thoroughly before grilling fish: Place an overturned disposable aluminum pan over the grate as the grill warms up, trapping hot air and super-heating the grate to temperatures that exceed 800 degrees. Just like in a self-cleaning oven, the high heat causes grease and debris to disintegrate. By swapping the disposable pan for aluminum foil pressed against the grate (with spaces left on each side for ventilation), I was able to bump this temperature up to nearly 900 degrees, making the technique even more effective.

With a clean grill at the ready, I reviewed dozens of recipes that claimed to solve the sticking quandary. Many advise using a foil boat to keep the fish from ever touching the grill. This trick works, but it creates a new problem: The fish never picks up true char-grilled flavor. Elevating the salmon on fennel fronds, citrus slices, and other foods created steam that made the fish taste more poached than grilled—definitely not the result I wanted. Other recipes suggest boosting the flame. Thanks to the preheating-with-foil technique, however, my grill was already nearly 900 degrees, yet the salmon still stuck to the grate.

Stumped, I did a bit of research and discovered the cause of my problem. Unlike the superficial stickiness caused by, say, barbecue sauce or a sweet glaze, the bond between proteins and grill is a molecule-to-molecule fusion. Since this reaction happens almost the instant the fish hits the grill, trying to separate them is an exercise in futility. To prevent sticking, I had two options: altering the proteins on the surface of the fish so they wouldn't bond with the metal grate, or creating a barrier between fish and grill.

The most obvious way to alter proteins is to cook them. Since even a grill as hot as 900 degrees wasn't cooking the salmon fast enough to prevent bonding, I theorized that perhaps the moisture on and just underneath the surface of the fish was slowing things down. Drying the fish's exterior by wrapping it in kitchen towels and putting it in the refrigerator before grilling helped, but not enough. What if I parcooked the fish just until its exterior was set and then placed it on the grill? I quickly learned there was no efficient way to parcook it. Poaching took too long, microwaving proved uneven, and sautéing seemed silly—if I started it in a pan, after all, I might as well finish it there.

Since altering the proteins didn't seem to be the solution, I was left wondering how I might create a barrier between fish and grill. Scores of recipes advise oiling both the cooking grate and the fish. I found this method only moderately effective at reducing sticking, but it did make me realize that when oil is applied to a hot cooking grate, it vaporizes almost instantly, leaving a black, weblike residue. Here's what happens: As oil heats up, its fatty-acid chains form polymers (that is, they stick together), creating that crisscross pattern over the surface of the metal.

I had observed this reaction while seasoning a cast-iron pan. A single layer of these polymers won't prevent sticking, but applying and heating oil repeatedly will build up a thick layer of them. Eventually, this will mean that proteins can no longer come into direct contact with the metal and therefore cannot bond with it. It was suddenly clear to me why restaurant cooks rarely have the same sticking problems as home grillers: With a grill in use throughout the day, there must be a hefty buildup of polymers. Could I speed the process and "season" my cooking grate in one session?

Instead of brushing the cooking grate with a single coat of oil, I decided to try brushing it over and over again, until it had developed a dark, shiny coating, and then lay the fillets on the grate. With the help of two spatulas—one in each hand—I easily flipped each fillet without even the tiniest bit of sticking.

Finally, I could focus on the grilling. From experience, I expected that preheating the grill to high and then turning it down to medium once I added the fish would achieve optimum charring without overcooking, and my salmon was no exception. As for flavor, tasters liked a tangy almond vinaigrette. It perfectly complemented the char-grilled taste I'd worked so hard to achieve.

—J. KENJI ALT, *Cook's Illustrated*

Grilled Salmon Fillets with Almond Vinaigrette

SERVES 4

To ensure uniform pieces of fish that cook at the same rate, we prefer to buy a whole center-cut fillet and cut it into evenly sized individual fillets ourselves. If buying individual fillets, make sure they are the same size and thickness. This recipe works best with salmon fillets but can also be used with any thick, firm-fleshed white fish, including red snapper, grouper, halibut, and sea bass (cook white fish to 140 degrees, up to 2 minutes longer per side). If you are using skinless fillets, treat the skinned side of each as if it were the skin side. If your fillets are thicker than 1 inch, increase the cooking time on the second side in step 6 until the center of the fillet registers 125 degrees (or 140 degrees for white fish).

VINAIGRETTE

- ⅓ cup almonds, toasted
- 2 teaspoons honey
- 1 teaspoon Dijon mustard
- 4 teaspoons white wine vinegar
- 1 small shallot, minced (about 2 tablespoons)
- ⅓ cup extra-virgin olive oil
- 1 tablespoon cold water
- 1 tablespoon chopped fresh tarragon
- Salt and pepper

SALMON

- 1 (1¾ to 2-pound) skin-on salmon fillet, ¾ to 1 inch thick at thickest part (see note)
- Vegetable oil
- Kosher salt and pepper

1. FOR THE VINAIGRETTE: Place the almonds in a zipper-lock bag and, using a rolling pin, pound until no pieces larger than ½ inch remain. Combine the pounded almonds, honey, mustard, vinegar, and shallot in a medium bowl. Whisking constantly, drizzle in the olive oil until an emulsion forms. Add the water and tarragon and whisk to combine, then season with salt and pepper to taste and set aside.

2. FOR THE SALMON: Trim any whitish fat from the belly of the fillet, then cut the fish into 4 equal pieces. Place the fillets skin-side up on a rimmed baking sheet or large plate lined with a clean kitchen towel. Place a second clean kitchen towel on top of the fillets and press down to blot liquid. Refrigerate the fish, wrapped in the towels, while preparing the grill, at least 20 minutes.

3A. FOR A CHARCOAL GRILL: Open the bottom grill vents completely. Cover the cooking grate with a large piece of heavy-duty aluminum foil (see photo 2). Light a large chimney starter filled two-thirds with charcoal (65 briquettes; 4 quarts). When the coals are hot, pour them in an even layer over half the grill. Set the cooking

---

NOTES FROM THE TEST KITCHEN

THE SECRETS TO NONSTICK GRILLING

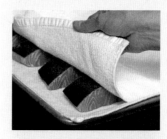

1. Drying the fillets prevents moisture on their surface from cooling the cooking grate, which can lead to sticking.

2. Super-heating the grill by covering it with aluminum foil ensures that all stuck-on debris disintegrates.

3. Seasoning the cooking grate with multiple layers of oil builds a nonstick surface.

4. Positioning the fish diagonally on the cooking grate creates attractive grill marks and makes flipping easier.

5. Doubling up on spatulas supports the fish from two sides while it's being flipped.

grate in place, cover, and open the lid vents completely. Heat the grill until hot, about 5 minutes.

3B. FOR A GAS GRILL: Cover the cooking grate with a large piece of heavy-duty aluminum foil (see page 209). Turn all the burners to high, cover, and heat the grill until hot, about 15 minutes.

4. Remove the foil with tongs and discard. Use a grill brush to scrape the cooking grate clean. Lightly dip a wad of paper towels in oil; holding the wad with tongs, wipe the grate. Continue to wipe the grate with the oiled paper towels, redipping the towels in oil between applications, until the grate is black and glossy, 5 to 10 times. (Turn all the burners to medium if using gas.)

5. Brush both sides of the fish with a thin coat of oil and season with kosher salt and pepper. Place the fish skin-side down on the grill diagonal to the grate (over the coals if using charcoal), cover the grill, and cook without moving until the skin side is brown, well marked, and crisp, 3 to 5 minutes. (Try lifting the fish gently with a spatula after 3 minutes; if it doesn't cleanly lift off the grill, continue to cook, checking at 30-second intervals until it releases.)

6. Using 2 spatulas, flip the fish over and cook, covered, until the centers of the fillets are opaque and register 125 degrees on an instant-read thermometer, 2 to 6 minutes longer. Serve with the vinaigrette.

SALMON EN COCOTTE

COOKING EN COCOTTE is a common cooking method in France that is typically used for chicken, lamb, and even eggs. The technique is surprisingly simple; you essentially just place the meat and some chopped vegetables in a pot, cover, and bake. The result is tender meat and ultra-concentrated flavor.

We've used this technique successfully with beef (see page 159), and have learned a few essentials in the process: A heavy, large Dutch oven is important for even heating, and a tight-fitting lid is also key, as it prevents steam from escaping (we seal the pot with aluminum foil before adding the lid to ensure a tight seal). Also, a surprisingly low oven temperature—250 degrees—is best, yielding incredibly tender meat, thanks to delicate heat and a relatively long cooking time. I couldn't help but wonder if cooking en cocotte might also work for fish. There was only one problem: Fish tends to cook quickly.

Since the whole premise of cooking en cocotte is to slow down cooking to concentrate flavor, I was a little skeptical that this technique would successfully translate to fish. Nevertheless, I decided to head into the kitchen to find out just how far I could push the limits of cooking en cocotte.

Salmon is the fish most often found on home dinner tables, so it became my fish of choice. I knew it would be important to have uniform pieces of fish that would cook evenly, so I settled on using a whole center-cut fillet that I could cut myself into four individual servings. I also found it best to remove the skin from the salmon so that the actual flesh of the fish would pick up the flavors of the aromatics. Removing the skin also made my final sauce less greasy. As we have done with chicken and beef, I started by searing the fish to develop a crust and deepen its flavor. The results were good, but I wondered what would happen if I streamlined my technique. For my next test I skipped the searing and was happy to discover that this extra step was not necessary with fish.

Leeks, with their delicate, onion-like sweetness, are a nice complement to salmon so I decided to use them as my aromatic. I added the leeks (along with some thyme and garlic) to the pot, then placed the fish on top of the leeks and placed the covered pot in the oven. Just to be sure that 250 degrees was the right temperature for my salmon, I tested oven temperatures ranging from 250 degrees to 400 degrees. I determined that, as with meat, lower was indeed better. Sure, it takes a little longer for the salmon to cook through (about 30 minutes, which is a relatively long time for fish), but it was all walk-away time and tasters raved about the salmon's rich, concentrated flavor.

Due to the low oven temperature, the leeks did not have a chance to fully soften and develop their flavor. The solution was to sauté the leeks on the stovetop first before adding the salmon. After removing the salmon from the pot, I added a healthy dose of white wine to the leeks and simmered the mixture until it had reduced slightly, then whisked in some butter for richness before spooning it over the salmon.

I now had just what I wanted: perfectly cooked, moist salmon that flaked apart into large, buttery chunks topped with a flavorful sauce. Tasters raved about the combination of flavors and textures. Elegant enough for a dinner party, yet simple enough for a weeknight, this flavorful dish will undoubtedly become an instant classic.

—BRYAN ROOF, *America's Test Kitchen Books*

SALMON EN COCOTTE WITH LEEKS AND WHITE WINE

Salmon en Cocotte with Leeks and White Wine

SERVES 4

To ensure uniform pieces of fish that cook at the same rate, we prefer to buy a whole center-cut fillet and cut it into evenly sized individual fillets ourselves. If buying individual fillets, make sure they are the same size and thickness. If the fillets are thicker or thinner than 1½ inches, you may need to adjust the cooking time slightly. If you can only find skin-on fillets, be sure to remove the skin before cooking or the sauce will be greasy; have the fishmonger do this for you, or see the photos to do it yourself. You can substitute arctic char or cod fillets for the salmon.

1 (1¾ to 2-pound) skinless salmon fillet, about 1½ inches thick at thickest part (see note)
   Salt and pepper
2 tablespoons extra-virgin olive oil
2 leeks, white and light green parts only, halved lengthwise, sliced thin, and rinsed thoroughly (see page 213)
2 sprigs fresh thyme
2 garlic cloves, minced
½ cup dry white wine
2 tablespoons unsalted butter, cut into 2 pieces

1. Adjust an oven rack to the lowest position and heat the oven to 250 degrees. Trim any whitish fat from the fillet, then cut the fish into 4 equal pieces. Pat the salmon dry with paper towels and season with salt and pepper.

2. Heat the oil in a large Dutch oven over medium-low heat until shimmering. Add the leeks, thyme, and a pinch of salt, cover, and cook until softened, 8 to 10 minutes. Stir in the garlic and cook until fragrant, about 30 seconds. Remove the pot from the heat.

3. Lay the salmon, skinned-side down, on top of the leeks. Place a large sheet of foil over the pot and press to seal, then cover tightly with the lid. Transfer the pot to the oven and bake until the centers of the fillets are opaque and register 125 degrees on an instant-read thermometer, 25 to 30 minutes.

4. Transfer the fish to a platter and tent loosely with foil. Stir the wine into the leeks and simmer over medium-high heat until slightly thickened, about 2 minutes. Off the heat, whisk in the butter and season with salt and pepper to taste. Spoon the sauce over the salmon and serve.

VARIATION

Salmon en Cocotte with Celery and Orange

Follow the recipe for Salmon en Cocotte with Leeks and White Wine, adding 2 celery ribs, sliced thin, and 1 teaspoon minced fresh orange zest along with the garlic in step 2. Substitute ½ cup orange juice for the wine, and add 1 orange, segmented, when thickening the sauce in step 4.

NOTES FROM THE TEST KITCHEN

THE BEST EXTRA-VIRGIN OLIVE OIL

For most cooked dishes we're perfectly happy reaching for an inexpensive olive oil, but sometimes only a good-quality extra-virgin olive oil will do. Typically produced in Italy, Greece, and Spain, extra-virgin oils range wildly in price, color, and packaging, so it's hard to know what you're really purchasing. Many things can impact the quality and flavor of olive oil, but the type of olive, the harvest (earlier means greener, more bitter, and pungent; later, milder and more buttery), and processing are the most important factors. The best-quality oil comes from olives picked at their peak and processed as soon as possible, without heat (which can coax more oil from the olives but at the expense of flavor). Our favorite oils were produced from a blend of olives and, thus, were well rounded—no one element came on too strong. Out of those tasted, we most liked **Columela Extra Virgin Olive Oil** from Spain for its fruity flavor and excellent balance. (See page 290 for more information about our testing results.)

HOW TO SKIN SALMON FILLETS

1. Insert a sharp boning knife just above the skin about 1 inch from the end of the fillet. Cut through the nearest end, keeping the blade just above the skin.

2. Rotate the fish and grab the loose piece of skin. Run the knife between the flesh and the skin, keeping the knife just above the skin.

SKILLET SALMON AND LEEK POT PIE

POT PIES COME IN ALL STRIPES—some classic, some not so classic. Fish pies fall into the former category, and we found recipes dating back hundreds of years. Unfortunately, for a dish with such a lengthy history, modern fish pie often tends to be no better than a use for leftover fish. But with the right ingredients and technique, I knew I could elevate this dish to a showstopping elegant entrée. And I hoped to do it all in one skillet, making my pot pie perfect for a weeknight supper.

The most common fish pies use either flaky white fish, such as cod, or firm-fleshed salmon. Since salmon is wildly popular and reasonably priced, I decided it would be just the thing for my first tests. I collected a variety of salmon pie recipes and prepared those that seemed the most promising. The best were reasonably light and simple, highlighting the fish's distinct flavor. Tasters' favorites bound the fish and a complementary vegetable or two in a fairly light, milk-based sauce. As for toppings, flaky pastry and mashed-potato crusts were common, as was puff pastry—an option I favored because the pastry's elegance and light texture suited the rich salmon, and because it's so easy to use.

There was one big problem with all the recipes I tried: The salmon was overcooked in every single one. The recipes required precooking the fish before mixing it into the sauce; this method resulted in a chalky texture and flavorless fish. It was pretty obvious to me that the fish could be cut into pieces and added raw to the hot filling; it would have plenty of time to cook through by the time the pastry browned.

I wanted to use vegetables that complemented the salmon but held their own ground in the sauce. I chose a simple combination of leeks and peas—both classic accompaniments to salmon because of their mild, sweet flavor. I included a good amount of leeks, cooking them in butter until they were soft and supple. As for the peas, I knew that frozen peas require little cooking—like the salmon, they would cook through in the oven.

Next, I tackled the sauce. It would need to be light so the flavors of the salmon and leeks could shine through, yet flavorful in its own right. I made a sauce right in the skillet by stirring milk, bottled clam juice, and vermouth in with the sautéed leeks, garlic, and flour. The brininess of the clam juice paired well with the salmon's sweet flesh.

Balanced but rather bland, my sauce needed some seasoning. A tablespoon each of Dijon mustard and lemon juice helped to cut through the richness. For herbs, I looked no further than dill—its light, almost tangy flavor is without parallel as a complement to salmon.

It was time to turn my attention to the puff-pastry topping. Readily available in most supermarkets, frozen puff pastry is a cinch to prepare: just defrost, roll out, and bake. In my first attempt, I rolled out sheets

NOTES FROM THE TEST KITCHEN

TOPPING A SKILLET POT PIE WITH PUFF PASTRY

Carefully place nine of the baked rectangles around the edge of the skillet and fit three of the baked rectangles in the center of the skillet.

PREPARING LEEKS

1. Trim and discard the roots and dark green leaves.

2. Slice the trimmed leek in half lengthwise, then slice thin.

3. Rinse the cut leeks thoroughly to remove dirt and sand.

of the defrosted dough and trimmed them to fit snugly over the top of the skillet, sealing the filling beneath. Unfortunately, the tight seal of the pastry yielded an overcooked filling. I suspected that the topping trapped escaping steam, thereby prompting the filling to boil. In addition, the puff pastry itself was more soggy than crisp. Clearly, a solid sheet would not do.

I shifted gears and experimented with cutting the pastry into smaller pieces, prebaking them before laying them on the filling. Parbaking helped crisp up the pastry before placing it over the wet filling, and using smaller pieces of pastry had the added benefit of allowing excess steam from the filling to evaporate in the oven. To make prepping the pastry easy, I simply cut it into rectangles with a sharp knife. Because this pot pie was covered by pastry pieces, not a whole layer of pastry, it needed just 10 minutes to cool off.

Prepared all in one skillet, my salmon and leek pot pie couldn't be easier to make, yet the rich, flavorful filling and delicate puff-pastry topping make it an elegant meal any night of the week.

—MEGAN WYCOFF, *America's Test Kitchen Books*

Skillet Salmon and Leek Pot Pie

SERVES 4

If desired, cut the pastry into 12 large circles using a 3-inch round cookie cutter instead of cutting it into rectangles in step 1; don't twist the cutter when stamping out the pastry rounds, or the pastry will rise crookedly during baking. If you can only find skin-on fillets, have the fishmonger remove the skin for you, or see the photos on page 212 to do it yourself. Be sure to check the salmon for pinbones before cutting it into pieces. Do not substitute dried dill for the fresh dill here.

TOPPING

Unbleached all-purpose flour, for dusting the counter

1 (9½ by 9-inch) sheet frozen commercial puff pastry, thawed at room temperature for 30 minutes

1 large egg, lightly beaten

FILLING

1½ pounds skinless salmon fillet, cut into ½-inch pieces (see note)

Salt and pepper

2 tablespoons unsalted butter

2 leeks, white and light green parts only, halved lengthwise, sliced thin, and rinsed thoroughly (see page 213)

1 garlic clove, minced

¼ cup unbleached all-purpose flour

1 tablespoon Dijon mustard

⅓ cup dry vermouth or dry white wine

1½ cups whole milk

1 (8-ounce) bottle clam juice

1 cup frozen peas

¼ cup chopped fresh dill (see note)

1 tablespoon fresh lemon juice

Lemon wedges, for serving

1. FOR THE TOPPING: Adjust an oven rack to the middle position and heat the oven to 425 degrees. Line a baking sheet with parchment paper. Dust the counter lightly with flour and unfold the sheet of puff pastry. Use a pizza cutter or sharp paring knife to cut the dough into 3 pieces along the seams, then crosswise in fourths to make 12 rectangles (see note).

2. Brush each square with the beaten egg and transfer to the baking sheet. Chill the dough on the baking sheet in the freezer for 10 minutes. Remove the pan from the freezer and place it directly in the oven. Bake until the rectangles are puffed and lightly browned, about 10 minutes. Let the pastry cool on the baking sheet and set aside until needed.

3. FOR THE FILLING: Reduce the oven temperature to 400 degrees. Season the salmon with salt and pepper and set aside.

4. Melt the butter in a 12-inch ovensafe skillet over medium-low heat. Add the leeks and ½ teaspoon salt and cook, stirring occasionally, until softened, 8 to 10 minutes. Stir in the garlic and cook until fragrant, about 30 seconds. Stir in the flour and mustard and cook, stirring constantly, until incorporated, about 1 minute.

5. Slowly stir in the vermouth and cook until evaporated, about 30 seconds. Slowly stir in the milk and clam juice and bring to a simmer.

6. Off the heat, season with salt and pepper to taste, then stir in the salmon, peas, dill, and lemon juice.

7. Place the baked puff-pastry rectangles on top of the filling (see page 213). Bake the pot pie until the pastry is a deep golden brown and the filling is bubbling, 13 to 15 minutes. Using a potholder (the skillet handle will be hot), remove the skillet from the oven. Let the pot pie cool for 10 minutes and serve, passing the lemon wedges separately.

SKILLET SHRIMP AND GRITS

IN SOUTH CAROLINA, shrimp and grits has long been a basic breakfast for coastal fishermen and families during the shrimp season. The dish consists of a pot of grits with shrimp that have been cooked in a little bacon fat. Over the years, this humble dish has taken on a whole new life as an anytime casserole, chock-full of shrimp, cheese, and grits. I wanted to develop a recipe for shrimp and grits casserole, with cheesy grits (not overcooked and pasty, which tend to be the trend) and tender, succulent shrimp. And I wanted to do it all in one skillet, as opposed to the usual skillet and the extra casserole dish used for baking.

I started by looking at the grits available in our local grocery store. There were two kinds: instant, which cook in five minutes; and old-fashioned, which cook in 15 minutes. In a side-by-side taste test, most tasters thought the instant grits were too creamy and tasted overprocessed. The old-fashioned grits were creamy yet retained a slightly coarse texture that tasters liked—these grits deserve their name.

After doing some research, I uncovered recipes that were simple yet devoid of any kick of flavor. I began to look at the options that might add pizzazz to this dish. Tasters approved of some sautéed minced onion and garlic, but they wanted a stronger flavor to complement the other elements of the dish. Minced chipotle chile in adobo sauce provided a touch of smokiness and spice to the dish—just what I was looking for. Sliced scallions, stirred in just before baking, also perked up the casserole with their color and mild onion flavor. Now for the grits.

To add richness without relying solely on butter, as many recipes do, I decided to try cooking the grits in milk rather than water. The flavor of the grits disappeared behind the lactose-heavy milk flavor. I then tried cooking them in a small amount of heavy cream and water mixed together. Everyone liked this batch—the grits were rich, but without an overwhelming dairy flavor. Cooked cream does not develop the same strong "cooked" flavor as milk because the extra fat in cream keeps the milk proteins from breaking down when heated. After a few more batches of varying proportions, I found that using just ½ cup of cream to 3½ cups of water for 1 cup of grits offered the best balance of richness and flavor.

Next I looked at cheese options. Monterey Jack made the grits taste bland, so it was out. Regular cheddar was also bland, but the flavor was getting there. Extra-sharp cheddar proved to be the winner. The flavor was assertive and complemented the subtle corn flavor.

My grits were good, but the texture wasn't quite what I wanted. I wanted a denser, heartier dish, one closer to baked polenta than custardy spoon bread. I decided to add a couple eggs to bind the grits and give the dish the dense texture tasters desired. Two eggs didn't change the texture of my grits much, and four eggs made them too heavy and imparted an eggy flavor. Three eggs, on the other hand, provided just enough structure without making the grits taste eggy.

It was time for the star of the show—the shrimp. I knew that I would have to be careful not to overcook them, as most of the recipes I had tested did just that. I thought the best option would be to simply nestle them into the fully cooked grits before transferring the skillet to the oven. When the grits were cooked, I stirred in half of the shredded cheddar cheese and the eggs, nestled in the shrimp, sprinkled the remaining cheese over the top, and baked the whole dish right in the skillet. The shrimp were perfectly cooked, and the combination of flavors was in balance. This was the best shrimp and grits casserole any of us had ever eaten.

—BRYAN ROOF, *America's Test Kitchen Books*

NOTES FROM THE TEST KITCHEN

OUR FAVORITE TRADITIONAL SKILLET

The variation in price of traditional skillets is dizzying—pans can cost anywhere from $30 to $150 or more. Preliminary tests of traditional skillets confirmed our suspicions that cheap was not the way to go, but how much do you really need to spend? We zeroed in on a group of eight pans from well-known manufacturers. All of the pans tested had flared sides, and most had uncoated stainless steel cooking surfaces, which we prize for promoting a fond. We concluded that medium-weight pans are ideal—they brown food beautifully, and most testers handled them comfortably. These pans have enough heft for heat retention and structural integrity, but not so much that they are difficult to manipulate. For its combination of excellent performance, optimum weight and balance, and overall ease of use, the **All-Clad Stainless Steel Fry Pan,** which comes in 8-inch ($85), 10-inch ($100), and 12-inch ($135) sizes, was the hands-down winner. (See page 303 for more information about our testing results.)

SKILLET SHRIMP AND GRITS

Skillet Shrimp and Grits

SERVES 4

Do not substitute instant grits here. Be sure to remove the shrimp shells completely (including the tails) before nestling them into the grits in step 4. Feel free to substitute smoked cheddar or smoked Gouda for the extra-sharp cheddar.

- 2 tablespoons unsalted butter
- 1 onion, minced (about 1 cup)
- 1 teaspoon salt
- 2 garlic cloves, minced
- 1 teaspoon minced canned chipotle chile in adobo sauce
- 3½ cups water
- ½ cup heavy cream
- 1 cup old-fashioned grits (see note)
- 6 ounces extra-sharp cheddar cheese, shredded (about 1½ cups) (see note)
- 3 large eggs, lightly beaten
- 4 scallions, thinly sliced
- ¼ teaspoon pepper
- 1½ pounds extra-large shrimp (21 to 25 per pound), peeled and deveined (see page 219) (see note)

1. Adjust an oven rack to the middle position and heat the oven to 450 degrees.

2. Melt the butter in a 12-inch ovensafe skillet over medium heat. Add the onion and salt and cook until softened, 5 to 7 minutes. Stir in the garlic and chipotle and cook until fragrant, about 30 seconds.

3. Stir in the water and cream and bring to a boil. Slowly whisk in the grits. Reduce the heat to low and cook, stirring frequently, until the grits are thick and creamy, about 15 minutes.

4. Off the heat, whisk in the cheddar, eggs, scallions, and pepper. Lay the shrimp on their sides in a pinwheel formation over the grits, then press on them lightly to submerge about halfway. Bake the casserole until the top is browned, the grits are hot, and the shrimp are cooked through, about 15 minutes. Using a potholder (the skillet handle will be hot), remove the skillet from the oven. Let the casserole cool for 10 minutes before serving.

NEW ORLEANS BARBECUE SHRIMP

BARBECUE SHRIMP IS A DELICIOUS MISNOMER. It is not grilled or barbecued, nor is it smoky, and you won't see this particular recipe on the barbecue circuit anytime soon. It is, instead, a uniquely New Orleans skillet dish that sauces peel-on shrimp in a velvety mixture of butter and seafood stock fortified with cayenne, herbs, garlic, and Worcestershire. This dish is named for its "barbecue" kick and color, and like barbecued ribs, the messy peel-and-eat shrimp are best served with a stack of napkins—plus a hunk of soft French bread to sop up the sauce.

I turned to recipes from regional cookbooks as a starting point. Most begin by cooking shrimp in melted butter (up to two entire sticks!) seasoned with Worcestershire, red pepper flakes, cayenne, thyme, rosemary, oregano, and garlic. The liquids—some combination of fish or shrimp stock, beer, and white wine—are reduced in the shrimp-filled skillet, and the sauce is finished with even more butter to thicken. It sounds tasty and easy, but the shrimp were overcooked and rubbery, and the wallop of butter dulled the other flavors and made the sauce greasy.

Working on the cooking method first, I tested fully cooking the shrimp in plain butter and removing them from the pan. Then I sautéed the garlic, herbs, and Worcestershire in the empty skillet, poured in the liquid (a bottle of beer for now), and returned the shrimp to the sauce to warm through. This gave me more control over the texture of the shrimp, but their flavor suffered from spending so little time in the sauce. For my next test, I just seared the shrimp—removing them from the pan before they were fully cooked—before sautéing the aromatics, adding the liquid, and then finally returning the shrimp to gently finish cooking in the rich sauce. These shrimp were tender and just cooked through, and much more flavorful than before.

Now I could work on perfecting the sauce, starting with the liquid base. The test kitchen has had good results replacing seafood stocks with bottled clam juice, and sure enough, it worked well here, too. To round out the liquid, my tasters preferred mellow beer to acidic wine, hands down. I added tomato paste to the sautéing aromatics to enrich the sauce—it also reinforced the "barbecue" color. Cutting the amount of butter from two sticks to less than one helped the other flavors shine through and reduced the greasiness, but it also created a new problem. The sauce was now so thin, it ran right off the shrimp. I turned to a classic New Orleans technique for thickening: starting the sauce with a roux. Adding 2 teaspoons of flour to the sautéing aromatics created a sauce that was thick enough to coat the shrimp. Armed with a bowlful of the shrimp and a mug of cold beer, I could have been in the Crescent City.

—CALI RICH, *Cook's Country*

New Orleans Barbecue Shrimp

SERVES 4

Although authentic barbecue shrimp is always made with shell-on shrimp, peeled and deveined shrimp may be used. Light or medium-bodied beers work best here. Serve with hot sauce and French bread, if desired.

2	pounds extra-large shrimp (21 to 25 per pound) (see note)
½	teaspoon salt
½	teaspoon cayenne pepper
2	tablespoons vegetable oil
6	tablespoons (¾ stick) unsalted butter, cut into 6 pieces
2	teaspoons unbleached all-purpose flour
1	teaspoon tomato paste
1	teaspoon minced fresh rosemary
1	teaspoon minced fresh thyme
½	teaspoon dried oregano
3	garlic cloves, minced
¾	cup bottled clam juice
½	cup beer (see note)
1	tablespoon Worcestershire sauce

1. Pat the shrimp dry with paper towels and sprinkle with the salt and cayenne. Heat 1 tablespoon of the oil in a large skillet over medium-high heat until just smoking. Cook half of the shrimp, without moving, until spotty brown on one side, about 1 minute; transfer to a large plate. Repeat with the remaining 1 tablespoon oil and shrimp.

2. Melt 1 tablespoon of the butter in the now-empty skillet over medium heat. Add the flour, tomato paste, rosemary, thyme, oregano, and garlic and cook until

fragrant, about 30 seconds. Stir in the clam juice, beer, and Worcestershire, scraping up any browned bits, and bring to a boil. Return the shrimp and any accumulated juices to the skillet. Reduce the heat to medium-low and simmer, covered, until the shrimp are cooked through, about 2 minutes. Off the heat, stir in the remaining 5 tablespoons butter until incorporated. Serve.

SOUTHERN SHRIMP BURGERS

ALTHOUGH NOT AS WELL KNOWN as other Southern favorites such as fried chicken or collard greens, shrimp burgers are a long-standing specialty in coastal towns in South Carolina and Georgia, where seafood is abundant. Although the particulars may vary, a good shrimp burger should be first and foremost about the shrimp. Unfortunately, some of the shrimp burgers I've had were reminiscent of fish-flavored rubber patties; others were more bread ball than shrimp burger. With these pitfalls in mind, I set out to develop a recipe for my ideal shrimp burger: moist, chunky yet still cohesive, and with seasoning that complements the sweet shrimp flavor but doesn't overpower it. Pan-frying is the most common way to cook these burgers, but I thought they would be even better on the grill, where they could develop a nice crust.

The first issue was how to prepare the shrimp. After early testing I decided I needed a combination of textures—finely chopped shrimp to help bind the burgers, as well as some larger, bite-sized chunks. I peeled and thoroughly dried 1½ pounds of shrimp, tossed half in the food processor until finely minced, then chopped the other half by hand. This worked well, but I realized I could eliminate a step and pulse it all in the food processor, which resulted in an inconsistent texture anyway—annoying for some applications but exactly what I was looking for in this recipe.

As for a binder, I wanted as little as possible. Most of the recipes I found used some combination of mayonnaise, egg, and bread crumbs, but these recipes yielded burgers with shrimp swathed in a soggy, unappealing mush. The mayonnaise was adding much-needed fat and moisture (unlike beef, shrimp have little fat of their own), but the egg seemed less helpful—it only made the burgers wet, requiring more bread crumbs. I made a batch of burgers without the egg and decreased the bread crumbs to a single slice of bread. Since packing the patties makes them rubbery, I handled them as little as possible, instead allowing them to firm up in the refrigerator. Despite the small amount of binder, I was surprised at how well these burgers held together. Even better, they stayed together on the grill, and tasters loved their moist texture and sweet shrimp flavor, with no hint of soggy filling.

NOTES FROM THE TEST KITCHEN

DEVEINING SHRIMP

1. After removing the shell, use a paring knife to make a shallow cut along the back of the shrimp so that the vein is exposed.

2. Use the tip of the knife to lift the vein out of the shrimp. Discard the vein by wiping the blade against a paper towel.

THE BEST BLACK PEPPERCORNS

Beyond its heat and sharp bite, black pepper enhances our ability to taste food, stimulating our salivary glands so we experience flavors more fully. This effect comes only from freshly ground pepper. Once the hard, black shell of the peppercorn is cracked open, its aroma immediately starts to fade, and most of its flavor and scent disappear within half an hour. Can choosing a better variety of peppercorn improve it even more? To find out, we tasted eight brands of freshly ground whole black peppercorns plain and in white rice. Our favorites were the mail-order **Kalustyan's Indian Tellicherry Black Peppercorns** (left), for its fruity, pungent, complex flavor, and super-market winner **Morton & Bassett Organic Whole Black Peppercorns** (right), which tasters found to be spicy but not hot, with a bold flavor. (See page 291 for more information about our testing results.)

For seasonings, tasters preferred simplicity—some minced scallion and parsley, as well as lemon zest, which accentuated the sweetness of the shrimp, and a touch of cayenne. By themselves or on a bun with lettuce and tartar sauce, these burgers are sure to disappear as fast as they come off the grill.

—ADELAIDE PARKER, *America's Test Kitchen Books*

Southern Shrimp Burgers

MAKES 4 BURGERS

Be sure to use raw, not cooked, shrimp here. Dry the shrimp thoroughly before processing, or the burgers will be mushy. Handle the burgers gently when shaping and grilling; if overhandled while being shaped, the burgers will be dense and rubbery, and if handled roughly during cooking, they will break apart.

TARTAR SAUCE

- ¾ cup mayonnaise
- 1½ tablespoons minced cornichons (about 3 large), plus 1 teaspoon cornichon juice
- 1 tablespoon minced scallion
- 1 tablespoon minced red onion
- 1 tablespoon drained capers, rinsed and minced

SHRIMP BURGERS

- 1 slice high-quality white sandwich bread, torn into large pieces
- 1½ pounds extra-large shrimp (21 to 25 per pound), peeled, deveined, and patted dry (see photos) (see note)
- ¼ cup mayonnaise
- 2 scallions, minced
- 2 tablespoons chopped fresh parsley
- 2 teaspoons grated fresh lemon zest
  Pinch cayenne pepper
- ¼ teaspoon salt
- ⅛ teaspoon pepper
  Vegetable oil

1. FOR THE TARTAR SAUCE: Whisk all of the ingredients together in a bowl. Cover and refrigerate until the flavors meld, at least 30 minutes. (The sauce can be refrigerated in an airtight container for up to 4 days.)

2. FOR THE SHRIMP BURGERS: Pulse the bread in a food processor to coarse crumbs, about 8 pulses. Transfer to a bowl. Pulse the shrimp in the food processor until some pieces are finely minced and others are coarsely chopped, about 7 pulses. Transfer the shrimp to a large bowl.

3. Combine the mayonnaise, scallions, parsley, lemon zest, cayenne, salt, and pepper in a large bowl until uniform, then gently fold into the processed shrimp until just combined. Sprinkle the bread crumbs over the mixture and gently fold until incorporated.

4. Scrape the shrimp mixture onto a small baking sheet, divide it into 4 equal portions, and loosely pack each into a 1-inch-thick patty. Cover and refrigerate the patties for at least 30 minutes, or up to 3 hours.

5A. FOR A CHARCOAL GRILL: Open the bottom grill vents completely. Light a large chimney starter three-quarters full with charcoal briquettes (75 briquettes; 4½ quarts). When the coals are hot, pour them in an even layer over the grill. Set the cooking grate in place, cover, and heat the grill until hot, about 5 minutes.

5B. FOR A GAS GRILL: Turn all the burners to high, cover, and heat the grill until hot, about 15 minutes. Turn all the burners to medium-high. (Adjust the burners as needed to maintain a medium-hot fire; see page 130.)

6. Clean and oil the cooking grate. Lightly brush the tops of the burgers with oil, lay them on the grill, oiled-side down, and lightly brush the other side with oil. Cook the burgers, without pressing on them, until lightly browned and cooked through, 10 to 14 minutes, flipping them halfway through. Transfer the burgers to a platter, tent loosely with foil, and let rest for 5 minutes before serving with the tartar sauce.

SHRIMP TEMPURA

A PERFECTLY COOKED PIECE OF SHRIMP TEMPURA is a beautiful thing—a fried food so light, crisp, and fresh-tasting that it barely seems fried. When shrimp tempura is done properly, the essence of sweet, tender shrimp defines its taste. Portuguese missionaries introduced quick-fried seafood to Japan in the 16th century, but over the course of the next few centuries Japanese cooks made this technique their own.

The approach sounds simple enough: Stir together a batter of flour, egg, and water; dip in shrimp (or other ingredients); drop into hot oil; and fry just until crisp and light golden. But success hinges almost entirely on

the batter—which is maddeningly hard to get right. Undermix by just a hair and the batter remains thin, barely providing a barrier against the hot oil and allowing the shrimp to overcook. Overmix by a similarly small degree and you wind up with a coating so thick and doughy that it seems more at home on a corn dog than on shrimp.

I started with the batter formula found in most traditional recipes: one egg and equal parts ice water and flour. To make dinner for four, I'd need 1½ pounds of shrimp. Since it's all too easy to overcook small shrimp, I chose the largest available (8 to 12 per pound).

I heated 3 quarts of oil to 400 degrees—a little hotter than most recipes called for, but a higher temperature would help the shrimp cook quickly, limiting the absorption of oil. I first tried cooking the batter-soaked shrimp in one batch, but this caused the oil temperature to plunge to 300 degrees, and the shrimp needed to stay the pot so long that their coating was practically dripping with grease. But cooking in two batches immediately brought the problems of batter consistency to the fore: Even when my first batch achieved just the right crisp and delicate texture, the second batch still turned out thick and doughy. Why?

When water and flour are mixed, the proteins in the flour form gluten, giving structure to the coating. Protein from the egg buttresses this structure and adds flavor and color. As it hits the hot oil, the water in the batter rapidly expands into steam, creating small bubbles. At the same time, the egg and gluten coagulate and stiffen, strengthening the bubbles. This chain of reactions is what gives tempura its intricate, lacy-crisp texture—and also what makes the batter so persnickety. In addition, gluten develops even without stirring; as my batter sat untouched on the counter between batches, it was thickening with every second that passed.

Many chefs claim to make the batter failsafe with "secret" ingredients or novel techniques. It couldn't hurt to try a few. One idea—adding whipped egg white to the batter—led to shrimp encased in a coating so voluminous it resembled a balloon. Baking soda created a coating so crumbly that it fell right off the shrimp. As a last shot, I replaced the flour with cornstarch, which develops no gluten at all. The coating looked delicate and crisp, but turned out to be as tough as Styrofoam.

Replacing all the flour with cornstarch hadn't worked, but what if I just reduced the amount of gluten instead of eliminating it? Starting with 2 cups of flour

SHRIMP TEMPURA WITH GINGER-SOY DIPPING SAUCE

and 1 tablespoon of cornstarch, I gradually increased the ratio until I arrived at a mixture of 1½ cups of flour and ½ cup of cornstarch. This significantly improved the structure and lightness in the first batch, but did nothing to address consistency.

Moving on to the egg, I tried adjusting the number of yolks and whites; a single egg produced the best results in every test. Then I considered the final ingredient: water. I was using ice water, which slows down gluten development—until the water warms up. Searching for an alternative, I recalled a recipe that used seltzer water. I swapped out the ice water for 2 cups of effervescent seltzer water, hoping that its multitude of bubbles would make my batter even more delicate and lacy. Seltzer produced the desired effect—and then some. It turns out that seltzer is slightly more acidic than regular tap water, enough to slow down gluten development. My batter now fried up into a wonderfully airy coating—but it was still too easy to overmix, and it turned thicker yet as it sat.

Then it hit me: A couple of years ago, a fellow test cook faced the same conundrum trying to master pie crust. To ensure a perfectly tender crust, he had to minimize gluten development in the dough. His solution? Eighty-proof vodka, which consists of about 60 percent water and 40 percent alcohol. While water contributes to gluten, alcohol doesn't. I fried two batches of shrimp made with 1 cup of seltzer water and 1 cup of vodka, and the shrimp I pulled out of the hot oil were not only consistent from the first batch to the second, but also the lightest and crispest I'd made yet.

With a foolproof batter at last, I could now fine-tune the details. Even though the batter was perfectly light and lacy, it still clumped on the inside curl of the shrimp. To set that straight, I made two shallow cuts on the underside of its flesh. The traditional sauce uses dashi, a Japanese stock made from dried kelp and bonito (tuna) flakes. I streamlined it and came up with a sweet ginger-soy dip.

My recipe was quite a departure from tradition, but you would never know it from the featherweight coating and supremely tender shrimp on my plate.

—FRANCISCO J. ROBERT, *Cook's Illustrated*

Shrimp Tempura with Ginger-Soy Dipping Sauce
SERVES 4

If you are unable to find colossal shrimp (8 to 12 per pound), jumbo (16 to 20) or extra-large (21 to 25) may be substituted. Do not omit the vodka; it is critical for a crisp coating. For safety, use a Dutch oven with a capacity of at least 7 quarts. Be sure to begin mixing the batter when the oil reaches 385 degrees (the final temperature should reach 400 degrees). It is important to maintain a high oil temperature throughout cooking. Fry smaller shrimp in three batches, reducing the cooking time to 1½ to 2 minutes per batch.

SAUCE
- ¼ cup soy sauce
- 3 tablespoons mirin
- 1 teaspoon sugar
- 1 teaspoon toasted sesame oil
- 1 garlic clove, minced
- 2 teaspoons grated or minced fresh ginger
- 1 scallion, minced

SHRIMP
- 3 quarts vegetable oil
- 1½ pounds colossal shrimp (8 to 12 per pound), peeled and deveined, tails left on (see page 219) (see note)
- 1½ cups unbleached all-purpose flour
- ½ cup cornstarch
- 1 large egg
- 1 cup vodka (see note)
- 1 cup seltzer water
- Kosher salt

1. FOR THE SAUCE: Whisk all the ingredients together in a bowl and set aside.

2. FOR THE SHRIMP: Adjust an oven rack to the upper-middle position and heat the oven to 200 degrees. Heat the oil in a large Dutch oven to 385 degrees, 18 to 22 minutes. (Use an instant-read thermometer that registers high temperatures, or clip a candy/deep-fat thermometer onto the side of the pan.)

3. While the oil heats, make 2 shallow cuts about ¼ inch deep and 1 inch apart on the underside of each shrimp. Whisk the flour and cornstarch together in a large bowl. Whisk the egg and vodka together in a second large bowl. Whisk the seltzer water into the egg mixture.

4. When the oil reaches 385 degrees, pour the liquid mixture into the bowl with the flour mixture and whisk gently until just combined (it is OK if some small lumps remain). Submerge half of the shrimp in the batter. Using tongs, remove the shrimp from the batter 1 at a time, allowing the excess batter to drip off, and carefully place in the oil (the temperature should now be at 400 degrees). Fry, stirring with a chopstick or wooden skewer to prevent sticking, until light brown, 2 to 3 minutes. Using a slotted spoon, transfer the shrimp to a paper towel–lined plate and sprinkle with salt. Once the paper towels absorb the excess oil, place the shrimp on a wire rack set in a rimmed baking sheet and place in the oven.

5. Return the oil to 400 degrees, about 4 minutes, and repeat with the remaining shrimp. Serve with the dipping sauce.

NOTES FROM THE TEST KITCHEN

BOOZE FOR BETTER BATTER?

In the past, we've guaranteed tender, flaky pie crust by replacing some of the water in the dough with vodka. To see if this would work with tempura, we fried shrimp in two different batters. The first batter contained egg, flour, cornstarch, and seltzer water. In the second, we replaced some of the seltzer water with vodka.

The vodka-batter shrimp was identical from the first batch to the second, turning out light and crisp each time. The shrimp dipped in the batter without vodka came out heavier and greasier in the second batch. When water (in this case seltzer) and flour are mixed, the proteins in the flour form gluten, which provides structure—but it takes only a few too many stirs (or too many minutes of sitting) to develop too much gluten and an overly heavy batter. Because vodka is about 60 percent water and 40 percent alcohol (which does not combine with protein to form gluten), it makes the batter fluid and keeps gluten formation in check.

THE BEST INEXPENSIVE DUTCH OVEN

So what should you consider when selecting a Dutch oven? Look for one that is roughly twice as wide as it is tall, with a minimum capacity of 6 quarts, though 7 is even better. The bottom should be thick to prevent food from scorching, and the lid should fit tightly to prevent excessive moisture loss. Looking for a less expensive alternative to our favorites made by All-Clad and Le Creuset, we tested Dutch ovens in the under-$100 range. The **Tramontina 6.5-Quart Cast Iron Dutch Oven** is comparable in size to the All-Clad and Le Creuset ovens and performs nearly as well. Better yet, at $45, it costs a fraction of the price of either.

ACHIEVING THE RIGHT BATTER CONSISTENCY

TOO THICK
Overmixed batter fries into a thick, breadlike coating.

TOO PUFFY
Whisking whipped egg white into the batter creates a balloonlike coating.

TOO THIN
Undermixed batter remains thin, contributing to overcooked shrimp.

JUST RIGHT
A surprise ingredient—vodka—and the right technique keep our coating crisp and airy.

CHAPTER 9

DESSERTS

Perfect Chocolate Chip Cookies   226

Chewy Chocolate Cookies   228

Hermits   231

Dream Bars   233

Easy Chocolate Ice Cream   235

Chocolate Bread Pudding   238

Skillet Cherry Cobbler   239

   Skillet Cherry-Almond Cobbler

   Skillet Cherry, Red Wine, and Cinnamon Cobbler

Skillet Apple Pie   242

Blueberry Pie   245

Foolproof Double-Crust Pie Dough   247

Foolproof Single-Crust Pie Dough   249

Jefferson Davis Pie   249

French Silk Chocolate Pie   251

Pumpkin Pie   253

Emergency Chocolate Cake   257

Bold and Spicy Gingerbread Cake   258

Easy Caramel Cake   260

7Up Pound Cake   263

Skillet Lemon Soufflé   265

   Skillet Chocolate-Orange Soufflé

Triple-Chocolate Mousse Cake   269

PERFECT CHOCOLATE CHIP COOKIES

SINCE NESTLÉ FIRST BEGAN PRINTING the recipe for Toll House cookies on the back of chocolate chip bags in 1939, generations of cooks have packed them into lunches, taken them to bake sales, and kept them on hand for snacking. The Toll House cookie's cakey texture and buttery flavor certainly have their appeal. But is it really the best that a chocolate chip cookie can be? In my opinion, a truly great cookie offers real complexity, not just a one-note sweet taste and uniform texture. My ideal has always been this: a chocolate chip cookie that's moist and chewy on the inside and crisp at the edges, with deep notes of toffee and butterscotch to balance its sweetness. What would it take to achieve the perfect specimen?

I'm not the first to think the Toll House cookie could stand improvement. Chefs everywhere have employed unusual techniques for creating a better chocolate chip cookie—from resting the dough for up to three days (to create a drier dough that caramelizes more quickly in the oven and achieves richer flavor) to portioning and freezing dough before baking (to prevent the dough from spreading, thereby keeping the center moist and chewy). These are fine ideas for professional kitchens—but who at home wants to wait two days to bake or try jamming multiple cookie sheets into the freezer?

Other chefs endorse "pet" ingredients to get better results; I tried milk powder (for depth of flavor) but it just made the cookies taste milky. I also experimented with a slew of even less likely additives, including tapioca powder, brown rice flour, and xanthan gum—all suggestions for ensuring chewier texture. In each case, tasters were unanimous: No, thanks.

I wasn't having luck on the flavor or chewiness fronts, but an approach for increasing crispness from the Toll House creator herself, Ruth Wakefield, seemed worth trying: In a variation on her chocolate chip cookie recipe published in *Toll House Tried and True Recipes* (1940), Wakefield swaps all-purpose flour for cake flour. But the swap yielded a cookie so crumbly that it practically disintegrated after one bite. Cake flour has less protein (6 to 8 percent) than all-purpose flour (10 to 12 percent). Protein is one of the building blocks of gluten, which gives baked goods their structure.

It was time to come up with my own ideas. I decided to start by tackling texture, first zeroing in on the impact of the fat. Butter was definitely my fat of choice—there was no way vegetable shortening or oil could ever compete with its rich flavor. The Toll House recipe calls for creaming the butter with the sugar to create tiny air bubbles that bring a cakey lift to cookies. But I already knew that melting the butter before combining it with the other ingredients leads to a chewier texture. Here's why: Butter contains up to 18 percent water. When butter melts, the water separates from the fat and can then interact with the proteins in flour to create more structure-enhancing gluten—and a noticeably chewier cookie.

Since I was melting the butter, I saw an opportunity to brown it, a technique we often use in the test kitchen to add nutty flavors to food. Sure enough, it worked here as well. But since browning burns off some of the butter's moisture, I decided to brown only a portion of it.

Next ingredient under the microscope: sugar. Besides adding sweetness, sugar affects texture. White sugar granules lend crispness, while brown sugar, which is hygroscopic (meaning it attracts and retains water, mainly from the air), enhances chewiness. The Toll House recipe calls for an equal amount of white and brown sugar; I got the best results when I simply upped the brown sugar (tasters preferred dark for its deeper flavor) to 60 percent and knocked the granulated down to 40 percent.

Next came flour. I had already seen how cake flour, with its low protein content, yields a crunchy, crumbly cookie. What if I took the opposite tack and tried bread flour, with its higher protein content of 12 to 14 percent? Again, this was going too far: The cookies were so dense and chewy that they were breadlike. In the end, just cutting back on the all-purpose flour by ½ cup increased moistness in the cookies and allowed the chewiness contributed by the brown sugar to come to the fore. The only problem: With less flour, the cookies were a little greasy. To resolve the issue, I decreased the butter by 2 tablespoons.

Finally, I was ready to evaluate the role of eggs in my batter. I knew from experience that egg whites, which contain much of the protein in the egg, tend to create cakey texture in baked goods—not what I wanted in my cookies. Eliminating one egg white was the right way to go, resulting in cookies that were supremely moist and chewy.

I had achieved chewiness, but what about my other goals? The crisp edges and deep toffee flavor were still missing, and, short of melting candy into the dough, I was stumped on how to create these effects. That's when batch number 43 came along.

In the middle of stirring together the butter, sugar, and eggs, I stopped to take a phone call. Ten minutes later, I found the sugars had dissolved and the mixture had turned thick and shiny, like frosting. I didn't think much of it until I pulled the finished cookies from the oven. Instead of the smooth, matte surface of the previous batches, these cookies emerged with a slightly glossy sheen and an alluring surface of cracks and crags. One bite revealed a rush of deep, toffeelike flavor. Mysteriously, these cookies finally had just the texture I was aiming for: crisp on the outside and chewy within.

I knew it wasn't just luck, so I pulled our science editor onto the case. He theorized that allowing the sugar to rest in the liquids enabled more of it to dissolve in the small amount of moisture before baking. The dissolved sugar caramelizes more easily, creating a spectrum of toffee flavors and influencing texture. When sugar dissolved in water is heated, the moisture burns off and its molecules break apart, creating a brittle, amorphous structure that translates to crisper texture. But that effect occurs mainly at the cookie's outer edges, with the remaining moisture becoming concentrated in the center.

Now all that was left was finessing the baking time and oven temperature. With caramelization in mind, I kept the temperature hot, 375 degrees—the same as for Toll House cookies. Watching carefully, I left the cookies in the oven until they were golden brown, just set at the edges, and soft in the center, between 10 and 14 minutes.

I sat down with a tall glass of milk and a sample from my weeks of labor and more than 700 cookies baked. My cookie was crisp and chewy, gooey with chocolate, and with a complex medley of sweet, buttery, caramel, and toffee flavors. Perfection is a subjective judgment at best, so I held one more blind tasting, pitting my cookie against the Toll House classic. The verdict? My cookies weren't just better—they were perfect.

—CHARLES KELSEY, *Cook's Illustrated*

Perfect Chocolate Chip Cookies
MAKES 16 COOKIES

Avoid using a nonstick skillet to brown the butter; the dark color of the nonstick coating makes it difficult to gauge when the butter is browned. Use fresh, moist brown sugar instead of hardened brown sugar, which will make the cookies dry. This recipe works with light brown sugar, but the cookies will be less full-flavored.

- 1¾ cups (8¾ ounces) unbleached all-purpose flour
- ½ teaspoon baking soda
- 14 tablespoons (1¾ sticks) unsalted butter
- ½ cup (3½ ounces) granulated sugar
- ¾ cup packed (5¼ ounces) dark brown sugar (see note)
- 1 teaspoon salt
- 2 teaspoons vanilla extract
- 1 large egg plus 1 large yolk
- 1¼ cups semisweet chocolate chips or chunks
- ¾ cup chopped pecans or walnuts, toasted (see page 16; optional)

1. Adjust an oven rack to the middle position and heat the oven to 375 degrees. Line 2 large baking sheets with parchment paper. Whisk the flour and baking soda together in a medium bowl and set aside.

2. Melt 10 tablespoons of the butter in a 10-inch skillet over medium-high heat, about 2 minutes. Continue cooking, swirling the pan constantly, until the butter is dark golden brown and has a nutty aroma, 1 to 3 minutes. Remove the skillet from the heat and, using a heatproof spatula, transfer the browned butter to a large heatproof bowl. Stir the remaining 4 tablespoons butter into the hot butter until completely melted.

3. Add both of the sugars, salt, and vanilla to the bowl with the butter and whisk until fully incorporated. Add the egg and yolk and whisk until the mixture is smooth with no sugar lumps remaining, about 30 seconds. Let the mixture stand for 3 minutes, then whisk for 30 seconds. Repeat the process of resting and whisking 2 more times until the mixture is thick, smooth, and shiny. Using a rubber spatula or wooden spoon, stir in the flour mixture until just combined, about 1 minute. Stir in the chocolate chips and nuts (if using), giving the dough a final stir to ensure no flour pockets remain.

4. Divide the dough into 16 portions, each about 3 tablespoons, and roll the dough into balls. Place the cookies on the prepared baking sheets, spacing them about 2 inches apart, 8 dough balls per sheet.

(Smaller baking sheets can be used, but will require 3 batches.) (The dough can be portioned and shaped into balls and then frozen on a tray or large plate; when they are frozen solid, transfer them to a large zipper-lock bag. To bake, arrange the frozen cookies on the baking sheets—do not thaw—and bake as directed, increasing the baking time to 19 to 24 minutes.)

5. Bake the cookies 1 tray at a time until the cookies are golden brown and still puffy, and the edges have begun to set but the centers are still soft, 10 to 14 minutes, rotating the sheet halfway through the baking time. Transfer the baking sheet to a wire rack and cool the cookies completely on the sheet before serving. (The cookies can be stored in an airtight container at room temperature for up to 3 days.)

NOTES FROM THE TEST KITCHEN

OUR FAVORITE CHOCOLATE CHIPS
Chocolate has just three basic ingredients—cocoa butter, cocoa solids, and sugar. So does it matter which brand of chocolate chips you buy? After sampling eight brands, we found that it does. The higher the cacao percentage (the total amount of cocoa butter and cocoa solids), the darker and more intense the chocolate flavor. Our favorite, **Ghirardelli 60% Cacao Bittersweet Chocolate Chips,** had the highest percentage of cacao in our lineup—comparable to bar chocolate—and by far the most cocoa butter; in addition, its low sugar content allowed the chocolate flavor to shine. A wider, flatter shape and high percentage of fat helped the chips melt into thin layers for a pleasing balance of cookie and chocolate in every bite. (See page 294 for more information about our testing results.)

THE BEST INNOVATIVE MIXING BOWL
Made of classic stainless steel or heat-resistant glass, our mixing bowls are kitchen workhorses. Yet they have their shortcomings: They wobble as you mix, the rim can make pouring a mess, and metal bowls can't go in the microwave. Would innovative new designs do better? We tested nine models in glass, plastic, metal, and silicone, with features such as silicone- or rubber-lined bottoms to prevent skidding and handles and spouts to make pouring easier. Only one was a true improvement over the old classics: the **Pyrex Grip-Rite 5-Quart Teardrop Mixing Bowl,** $16.99. Silicone strips around the base grip the counter firmly, and the teardrop shape, spout, and handle allow for neat pouring, making this bowl a real winner.

CHEWY CHOCOLATE COOKIES

WHENEVER A COOKIE RECIPE TRUMPETS its extreme chocolate flavor, I'm always a bit suspicious. It's not the flavor I doubt, it's the texture. Cookies with names like "Death by Chocolate" and "Super-Duper Chocolate" provide plenty of intensity. But these over-the-top confections also tend to be delicate and crumbly, more like cakey brownies than cookies. I wanted an exceptionally rich chocolate cookie I could really sink my teeth into—without having it fall apart in my hand.

Surveying the options, I soon discovered that no recipe offered it all. Chocolate butter cookies were rich and crisp, but not particularly chocolaty. Chocolate sugar cookies were soft and moist, but without the chewiness I wanted. Chocolate "crinkle" cookies looked the part—the sturdy exterior mottled with sugary cracks offering hints of the molten center within—but they were so delicate they collapsed on impact.

Baking is all about how ingredients interact, with even the smallest changes transforming flavor and texture. So before I began my quest for rich chocolate flavor and chewiness, I needed to review my main ingredients. Most chocolate cookie recipes call for flour, butter, eggs, sugar, chocolate or cocoa powder (or both), leavener, salt, and vanilla. Flour builds structure; when mixed with liquid, it forms gluten, the protein that gives baked goods their chew. Butter adds flavor and tender texture, while eggs contribute richness and lift. Sugar not only offers sweetness but, when melted, also brings more chewiness to the final product—think caramel. Chocolate can challenge even the most experienced baker. The cocoa butter it contains coats the proteins in flour, preventing it from forming gluten and thereby tenderizing dough, making it very difficult to develop solid structure.

Using one of the extreme-chocolate cookie recipes as a starting point, I creamed 12 tablespoons of butter with a cup of sugar in a standing mixer, whipped in two eggs, then blended in a whopping half pound of melted semisweet chocolate, followed by a dry mixture of 1¾ cups flour, ½ cup cocoa powder, and some baking soda and salt. These cookies baked up rich and fudgy, but they were overly tender and much too cakey.

The melted chocolate was an obvious culprit for my tenderness trouble: All its fat was softening up my dough. But before I made cutbacks there, I decided to

CHEWY CHOCOLATE COOKIES

try decreasing the butter. When I knocked off a few tablespoons, I found the cookies didn't spread as well. Though I was loath to do it, I looked to the melted chocolate, scaling back by increments over the course of several batches. Sure enough, the less chocolate I used, the progressively less cakey and tender (and thus more like a cookie) the texture became. When I eliminated melted chocolate entirely, they were finally sturdy but—no surprise!—not very chocolaty despite some cocoa powder in the mix.

To restore the lost chocolate flavor without adding too much in the way of fat, I replaced some of the flour with more cocoa powder—in particular, Dutch-processed cocoa (which the test kitchen has found delivers fuller chocolate flavor than the "natural" variety). Increasing the cocoa by ¼ cup and reducing the flour by the same amount yielded both decent chocolate flavor and reasonably sturdy texture.

But how to get the texture sturdier still? Eggs were another prime suspect for fat, and I zeroed in on them, decreasing from two to just one. The reduction improved matters—could I take it further? In my next test, I eliminated the yolk. With just an egg white, the cookies finally had the stalwart structure I was looking for.

At this point, I had cookies with fine chocolate flavor and good structure—but they simply weren't chewy enough. Replacing some of the white sugar with dark brown sugar resulted in distinctly moister cookies with a better flavor and slightly more chew, but still not enough. I tried to remember where I'd experienced the ultimate chewy cookie. Of course: It was the molasses cookie—the chewiest cookie in the modern world! Could molasses hold the key to the chocolate cookie of my dreams?

For texture, it was absolutely perfect. But the assertive molasses flavor was clearly the wrong companion for chocolate. Swapping out the molasses for dark corn syrup yielded an incredibly moist and chewy cookie. What's more, it offered an agreeable hint of caramel flavor that enhanced the chocolate taste without overwhelming it.

Still, some tasters wanted more chocolate flavor, but I hated to risk ruining all my hard work getting the dough just so. Then it occurred to me: What if I simply added some chocolate at the end of mixing, à la chocolate chip cookies? The structure of the dough would be unaffected. I folded in 4 ounces of chopped dark chocolate.

The half-inch chunks stayed intact, adding intense flavor—and gooey bites of pure chocolate satisfaction.

Another pleasing textural improvement came from rolling the dough into balls and dipping them in granulated sugar, giving the finished cookies a slightly sweet crunch and an attractive crackled appearance. An oven temperature of 375 degrees baked the cookies quickly without drying them, so that their exteriors were firm and crisp while their interiors remained delectably moist and chewy.

—YVONNE RUPERTI, *Cook's Illustrated*

NOTES FROM THE TEST KITCHEN

THE RIGHT-SIZED CHUNK
Tiny chocolate pieces will melt and disappear into the cookie dough when baked. Half-inch chunks contribute chocolate flavor while staying intact.

TOO SMALL

JUST RIGHT

KNOWING WHEN COOKIES ARE DONE

When the cookies have cracked but still look wet between the fissures, take them out of the oven. This ensures a moist, chewy texture.

THE BEST CHOCOLATE CHIPPER
We hate clogging our kitchen drawers with unnecessary equipment, but chipping chocolate into the right-sized pieces with a chef's knife is so tiresome that we wondered: Could a tool designed for the task make things easier? We found two models, both shaped like mini pitchforks with tiny tines. The top chipper, **Lehman's Porcelain-Handled Chocolate Chipper**, $6.95, was comfortable to hold, didn't damage our cutting board, and broke uniform pieces of chocolate without excess force. Given its modest price tag, we're happy to add this handy tool to our drawer.

Chewy Chocolate Cookies

MAKES 16 COOKIES

Light brown sugar can be substituted for the dark, as can light corn syrup for the dark, but with some sacrifice in flavor.

⅓ cup (2⅓ ounces) granulated sugar, plus ½ cup for coating

1½ cups (7½ ounces) unbleached all-purpose flour

¾ cup Dutch-processed cocoa powder

½ teaspoon baking soda

¼ teaspoon plus ⅛ teaspoon salt

½ cup dark corn syrup (see note)

1 large egg white

1 teaspoon vanilla extract

12 tablespoons (1½ sticks) unsalted butter, softened

⅓ cup packed (2⅓ ounces) dark brown sugar (see note)

4 ounces bittersweet chocolate, chopped into ½-inch pieces (see page 230)

1. Adjust the oven racks to the upper-middle and lower-middle positions and heat the oven to 375 degrees. Line 2 large baking sheets with parchment paper. Place ½ cup of the granulated sugar in a shallow baking dish or pie plate. Whisk the flour, cocoa powder, baking soda, and salt together in a medium bowl. Whisk the corn syrup, egg white, and vanilla together in a small bowl.

2. In a large bowl, beat the butter, brown sugar, and remaining ⅓ cup granulated sugar with an electric mixer at medium speed until light and fluffy, 3 to 6 minutes. Beat in the corn syrup mixture until fully incorporated, about 20 seconds, scraping down the bowl and beaters as needed. Reduce the mixer speed to low and add the flour mixture and chopped chocolate; mix until just incorporated, about 30 seconds, scraping down the bowl and beaters as needed. Give the dough a final stir with a rubber spatula to ensure that no pockets of flour remain at the bottom. Chill the dough for 30 minutes to firm slightly (do not chill longer than 30 minutes).

3. Divide the dough into 16 portions, each about 2 tablespoons, and roll the dough into balls. Working in batches, drop 8 dough balls into the baking dish with the sugar and toss to coat. Place the cookies on the prepared baking sheets, spacing them about 2 inches apart, 8 dough balls per sheet. (The dough can be portioned and shaped into balls and then frozen on a tray or large plate; when they are frozen solid, transfer them to a large zipper-lock bag. To bake, arrange the frozen cookies on

the baking sheets—do not thaw—and bake as directed, increasing the baking time to 16 to 21 minutes.)

4. Bake until the cookies are puffed and cracked and the edges have begun to set but the centers are still soft (the cookies will look raw between the cracks and seem underdone), 10 to 11 minutes, switching and rotating the sheets halfway through the baking time. Do not overbake.

5. Cool the cookies on the baking sheets for 5 minutes, then use a wide metal spatula to transfer the cookies to a wire rack; cool the cookies to room temperature before serving. (The cookies can be stored in an airtight container at room temperature for up to 3 days.)

HERMITS

I PRIDE MYSELF ON BEING the in-house cookie expert, so I was surprised when a colleague reminisced about a favorite childhood cookie I'd never heard of: hermits. A chewy raisin spice cookie with a sweet glaze, this New England specialty (unknown where I grew up in North Carolina) sounded appealing.

Some initial reading revealed many generations of fond memories, as hermits date back to the late 1800s. But after making a handful of recipes, I wondered if nostalgia had clouded my colleague's recollections. Most baked up more hard tack than soft batch and were peppered with bland, tough raisins. As for flavor, all but one tasted like a spice rack clearinghouse. My colleague insisted that hermits could be better, so I set out on a monthlong baking odyssey.

Hermits typically involve creaming softened butter and brown sugar, adding eggs and molasses, and then mixing in the dry ingredients (flour, spices, baking soda, and salt). But all of the recipes I made using this method produced dry, almost biscuit-y cookies. Melted butter generally makes cookies moister and chewier, and melting the butter had the desired effect in this recipe. Taking this a step further, I cooked the butter in a saucepan until it turned light brown and fragrant, which added a nutty flavor to the cookies.

It seems like no two hermit recipes use the same combination of warm spices. Most recipes I tested used too many spices, giving the cookies an unappealing dusty quality. After testing various combinations of cinnamon, cloves, nutmeg, allspice, ginger, black pepper, cardamom, and mace, my tasters settled on the simple—yet potent—combination of cinnamon, allspice, and ginger. Adding the spices to the browned butter bloomed their natural flavor and allowed me to use less, thus avoiding the dusty texture of hermits made with too much ground spice.

My tasters were starting to warm to these cookies, but the bland, tough raisins were still a problem. Steeping the raisins in melted butter softened them and greatly improved their flavor. Pureeing the raisins into a rough paste helped distribute chewy, raisin-y goodness into every bite. Spying a bag of crystallized (or candied) ginger, I wondered if I could puree the ginger with the raisins for more flavor. Sure enough, the pureed ginger lent pungent sweetness—and even

more chew—to the baked cookies, and allowed me to omit the dried ginger.

Recipes are divided as to how hermits should be shaped. One camp calls for dropping balls of dough to form round cookies; the other calls for the dough to be shaped into logs, baked, and then cut into individual cookies. A side-by-side test revealed that the hermits baked in logs and then cut were much chewier and moister, as the larger mass of dough better held its moisture through baking. As a crowning touch, I made a simple glaze of orange juice and confectioners' sugar to drizzle over the just-baked cookies. These old-fashioned cookies might not look like much, but they've earned a regular spot in my cookie jar.

—CALI RICH, *Cook's Country*

NOTES FROM THE TEST KITCHEN

MAKING HERMITS

1. Roll each quarter of dough into a 10-inch log, transfer to a baking sheet, then use a ruler to neatly square off the sides before baking.

2. Once the baked hermits have completely cooled, drizzle with the glaze before slicing into individual bars.

MOLASSES PRIMER

Thick, sticky-sweet molasses is a by-product of the sugar-refining process—it is the liquid that is drawn off after the cane juice has been boiled and has undergone crystallization. Once the sugar crystals are removed, the remaining liquid is packaged and sold as mild (or light) molasses, or it is boiled again and marketed as robust or full-flavored molasses. If the molasses is reduced a third time, it is labeled blackstrap. With each boil, the molasses becomes darker, more concentrated in flavor, and more bitter. Though we prefer mild molasses in our cookies—its subtle flavor allows the spice flavor to shine through—robust molasses is an acceptable substitute. Avoid the assertive, overpowering bitterness of blackstrap molasses.

Hermits

MAKES ABOUT 1½ DOZEN COOKIES

Crystallized (or candied) ginger is available in the spice aisle of most supermarkets. For this recipe, we prefer using mild (or light) molasses; robust molasses is an acceptable substitute, but avoid blackstrap.

- 1 **cup raisins**
- 2 **tablespoons finely chopped crystallized ginger (see note)**
- 8 **tablespoons (1 stick) unsalted butter**
- ¼ **teaspoon ground cinnamon**
- ¼ **teaspoon ground allspice**
- 2 **cups (10 ounces) unbleached all-purpose flour**
- ½ **teaspoon baking soda**
- ½ **teaspoon salt**
- ¾ **cup packed (5¼ ounces) dark brown sugar**
- ½ **cup molasses (see note)**
- 2 **large eggs**
- 1½ **tablespoons orange juice**
- ¾ **cup (3 ounces) confectioners' sugar**

1. Adjust the oven racks to the upper-middle and lower-middle positions and heat the oven to 350 degrees. Line two large baking sheets with parchment paper. Process the raisins and ginger in a food processor until the mixture sticks together and only small pieces remain, about 10 seconds. Transfer to a large bowl.

2. Melt the butter in a small saucepan over medium-low heat, swirling the pan occasionally, until nutty brown in color, about 10 minutes. Stir in the cinnamon and allspice and cook until fragrant, about 15 seconds. Stir the butter mixture into the raisin mixture until well combined and cool to room temperature.

3. Whisk the flour, baking soda, and salt together in a bowl. Stir the brown sugar, molasses, and eggs into the cooled butter mixture until incorporated. Fold in the flour mixture (the dough will be very sticky) and refrigerate, covered, until firm, at least 1½ hours or up to 24 hours.

4. Divide the dough into quarters. Following the photos on page 232, transfer one piece of the dough to a lightly floured counter, roll into a 10-inch log, and transfer to the prepared baking sheet. Repeat with the remaining dough (you will have two logs per sheet). Bake until only shallow indentations remains on the edges when touched (the center will appear slightly soft), 15 to 20 minutes, switching and rotating the sheets halfway through the baking time. Let cool on the sheet for 5 minutes, then transfer the parchment with the logs to a wire rack and cool completely.

5. Whisk the orange juice and confectioners' sugar together in a small bowl until smooth. Drizzle the glaze onto the cooled logs and let sit until the glaze hardens, about 15 minutes. Cut the logs into 2-inch bars. Serve. (The cookies can be stored in an airtight container at room temperature for up to 5 days.)

DREAM BARS

IN THE DEPTHS OF THE DEPRESSION, Americans badly needed sweet dreams. And that's exactly when recipes for dream bars—rich, nutty coconut bars—first made the rounds in newspapers. Within 20 years, dream bars were so popular that manufacturers had taken to using them to promote a wide range of ingredients. A Domino sugar advertisement went so far as to promise that the housewife who used its brown sugar to make her dream bars would become known as "a cook with a touch of genius."

Early recipes called for a simple brown-sugar pat-in-the-pan shortbread crust topped by a sticky, uncluttered filling (eggs, more brown sugar, shredded "cocoanut," and "nut meats"). By the 1940s and '50s, dream bars might include chocolate chips, cornflakes, graham cracker crumbs, dried apricots, or even rolled oats. A number of these fully loaded versions originated as back-of-the-box

recipes (most famously for bars that incorporate sweetened condensed milk). As the ingredient list swelled, the recipes were rechristened several times over. But Hello Dolly bars, seven-layer bars, and magic bars all are a far cry from the pared-down, toffee-flavored original that I was determined to re-create.

Even the simplest versions I tested were too sweet for modern tastes, and the coconut and pecans all but disappeared because the sugar was so forward. To bring out their flavor, I tried toasting them. Now the pecans tasted crunchy and rich. The shredded coconut, alas, dried out. Perhaps a structural change was in order: If I separated the filling into two layers, I figured the coconut had a fighting chance to hold its own. Wrong.

I was stumped—until a colleague came up with an interesting idea. She suggested I intensify the flavor of the shredded coconut by soaking it in coconut milk. Nobody liked the white, cottony topping that resulted, but the test wasn't a total failure: It led me to cream of coconut, which has almost 10 times as much sugar as coconut milk. That sugar helped the coconut topping caramelize.

Unfortunately, my initial problem resurfaced with a vengeance—the bars were cloyingly sweet. Up to now, I'd been using a standard shortbread crust. Reducing the amount of brown sugar in the crust was a good first step. Making the crust thicker and adding pecans to it created a nutty density that helped counterbalance the sweet topping.

To create an even crust, I scattered the crust mixture into the prepared baking pan and then used the bottom of a metal measuring cup to firmly compact it into a uniform layer before baking. These chewy, butterscotch-y Dream Bars were their own advertisement.

—MARÍA DEL MAR SACASA, *Cook's Country*

DREAM BARS

Dream Bars

MAKES 24 BARS

Spread the coconut mixture as evenly as possible over the pecan layer, but don't worry if it looks patchy. Cream of coconut is available in the baking aisle alongside other coconut products.

CRUST

- **2 cups (10 ounces) unbleached all-purpose flour**
- **¾ cup packed (5¼ ounces) dark brown sugar**
- **½ cup pecans**
- **¼ teaspoon salt**
- **10 tablespoons (1¼ sticks) unsalted butter, cut into ½-inch pieces and chilled**

TOPPING

- **1½ cups sweetened shredded coconut**
- **1 cup cream of coconut (see note)**
- **2 large eggs**
- **¾ cup packed (5¼ ounces) dark brown sugar**
- **2 tablespoons unbleached all-purpose flour**
- **1½ teaspoons baking powder**
- **1 teaspoon vanilla extract**
- **½ teaspoon salt**
- **1 cup pecans, toasted and chopped rough (see page 16)**

1. FOR THE CRUST: Adjust an oven rack to the middle position and heat the oven to 350 degrees. Line a 13 by 9-inch baking pan with foil, allowing the excess foil to hang over the pan edges. Coat the foil lightly with vegetable oil spray.

2. Process the flour, sugar, pecans, and salt in a food processor until the pecans are coarsely ground, about 10 seconds. Add the butter and pulse until the mixture resembles coarse meal, about 10 pulses. Using the bottom of a metal measuring cup, press the mixture firmly into the prepared baking pan. Bake until golden brown, about 20 minutes. Cool on a wire rack for 20 minutes.

3. FOR THE TOPPING: Combine the coconut and cream of coconut in a bowl. In another bowl, whisk the eggs, sugar, flour, baking powder, vanilla, and salt until smooth. Stir in the pecans, then spread the filling over the cooled crust. Dollop heaping tablespoons of the coconut mixture over the filling, then spread into an even layer.

4. Bake until the topping is a deep golden brown, 35 to 40 minutes. Cool on a wire rack, about 2 hours. Using the foil overhang, lift the bars from the pan and cut into 24 pieces. Serve. (The bars can be refrigerated in an airtight container for up to 5 days.)

EASY CHOCOLATE ICE CREAM

AN ICE CREAM MAKER TURNS UP in just about every wedding registry. The young couples envision themselves churning out batches of creamy homemade ice cream, but once the honeymoon is over, most machines wind up in the back of a closet. It's easy to see why. Few people can remember to freeze the insert ahead of time. If your freezer doesn't get cold enough, neither will the insert, and the ice cream machine won't work. Many recipes use a fussy French egg custard that must be cooked, strained, cooled, and chilled before churning. Could we make really good ice cream—with intense chocolate flavor and lush texture—without the machine or the hassle?

Ice cream makers work by incorporating air, which reduces ice crystals and helps ensure a smooth, creamy texture. Recipes I tried that called for simply freezing a mixture of melted chocolate, cream, and sugar were more like frozen truffles than ice cream. Other recipes incorporated air by freezing the mixture and then stirring it every 30 minutes for hours; this was tedious, to say the least. I found one recipe based on semifreddo (an Italian dessert) that called for folding whipped egg whites or whipped cream into an egg yolk base, but it tasted too light and icy. I also considered the old summer camp method in which a small coffee can is filled with cream, sugar, and chocolate syrup and set inside a larger coffee can filled with rock salt and ice; the entire contraption is then shaken vigorously for 30 minutes. Unless you happen to have the cans, rock salt, and a crew of campers willing to shake, rattle, and roll, this approach hardly makes sense.

Things began looking up when I found a recipe that used sweetened condensed milk in place of cream. I added chopped semisweet chocolate to the condensed milk, melted the mixture in the microwave, and then froze it. In the freezer, the condensed milk maintained its velvety texture. Unfortunately, its cloying sweetness overpowered the chocolate. Thinking about the semifreddo, I tried folding in whipped cream to lighten the mixture. After several hours, I pulled my container from the freezer and found dense, creamy chocolate ice cream with a luscious texture that rivaled any I'd ever made in a machine. But while the texture hit the mark, the flavor was sickly sweet and barely tasted of chocolate.

I tried replacing semisweet chocolate with unsweetened. That cut the sweetness but—alas—spoiled the texture. Because unsweetened chocolate (and cocoa powder, which I also tried) have more cocoa solids than semisweet chocolate, they made the ice cream chalky. Next, I tried using equal parts of unsweetened and white chocolate (which has no cocoa solids). Although this did lighten the ice cream, the white chocolate masked the dark chocolate flavor. Bittersweet

chocolate, which has slightly less sugar than semisweet, worked best in maintaining the texture, but tasters continued to find the ice cream too sweet and the chocolate flavor lacking.

In the test kitchen, we often add instant coffee granules to heighten chocolate flavor. The note of bitterness intensifies the chocolate without making it taste like a cup of coffee. Not only did the coffee enhance the chocolate, the ice cream—balanced by the coffee—tasted less sweet. A pinch of salt and a little vanilla extract rounded out the flavor of this mousselike, ultra-rich, full-on chocolate dessert. As a final test, we tasted our ice cream against some premium commercial brands: Ours won hands down.

—LYNN CLARK, *Cook's Country*

NOTES FROM THE TEST KITCHEN

CHOCOLATE ICE CREAM MADE SIMPLE

1. Microwave the chocolate, coffee, and condensed milk until the chocolate is melted.

2. Gently fold in whipped cream.

3. Pour the mixture into a container and freeze for at least six hours.

Easy Chocolate Ice Cream

MAKES 1 QUART

If you plan to store the ice cream for more than a few days, place plastic wrap directly on its surface before freezing.

- 1 teaspoon instant coffee or espresso powder
- 1 tablespoon hot water
- 4 ounces bittersweet chocolate, chopped fine
- ½ cup sweetened condensed milk
- ½ teaspoon vanilla extract
  Pinch salt
- 1¼ cups heavy cream, chilled

1. Combine the coffee powder and hot water in a small bowl. Let stand until the coffee dissolves, about 5 minutes. Microwave the chocolate, sweetened condensed milk, and coffee mixture in a bowl on high power, stirring every 10 seconds, until the chocolate is melted, about 1 minute. Stir in the vanilla and salt and let cool.

2. In a large bowl, whip the cream with an electric mixer on medium-low speed until light and frothy, about 1 minute. Increase the mixer speed to high and continue to whip until the cream forms soft peaks, 1 to 3 minutes. Whisk one-third of the whipped cream into the chocolate mixture. Fold the remaining whipped cream into the chocolate mixture until incorporated. Freeze in an airtight container until firm, at least 6 hours or up to 2 weeks. Serve.

EASY CHOCOLATE ICE CREAM

CHOCOLATE BREAD PUDDING

CREAMY, CUSTARDY BREAD PUDDING has humble origins as a way to use up stale bread, and its rustic nature—and ease of preparation—make it all the more appealing. The simplest versions call for soaking stale or toasted bread in a mixture of eggs, sugar, and dairy (cream or milk) and then baking. Adding chocolate to the mix sounds like a winning proposition, but the reality isn't so rosy.

I tested eight published recipes from reputable sources and had a hard time convincing my colleagues that adding chocolate to bread pudding was even a good idea. Recipes that simply stirred cocoa powder into the custard base were pale and lacked chocolate punch. Recipes that added melted chocolate tasted better, but the dense chocolate thickened the base so it never fully permeated the bread, making for bland, dry bread cubes suspended in chocolate custard.

I started over with a test kitchen bread pudding recipe that soaks cubed, toasted white sandwich bread in a custard base of egg yolks, heavy cream, milk, and sugar. For round chocolate flavor, I knew a combination of cocoa powder and melted chocolate would be key. Dutch-processed cocoa gave the mixture a good foundation of chocolate flavor, and my tasters much preferred the richness of melted semisweet chocolate to milk chocolate (too sweet and bland) or unsweetened (sour and grainy). Just a tablespoon of instant espresso powder enhanced the chocolate flavor without being identifiable on its own. Since the sandwich bread was a little light for my chocolaty custard, I made a batch using toasted challah, a richer bread that suited the chocolate base better.

The base tasted chocolaty, but it was so thick that it still wasn't fully soaking into the bread. To thin it, I made a batch that omitted the melted chocolate (which I would add back later) and was happy to find that it soaked through the toasted challah more efficiently. To further loosen the liquid, I removed the egg yolks (again, I'd add them back later) from the soaking mixture, which was now just cream, milk, cocoa, espresso powder, and sugar. Without the yolks, I could heat the mixture to better dissolve the cocoa and sugar and to promote a deeper soak.

Now that the bread cubes were fully saturated with my "hot cocoa" mixture, I could combine the egg yolks and melted chocolate with more cream and sugar to make a rich chocolate custard for the bread pudding. I poured this thick mixture over the soaked bread and baked the pudding in a gentle 325-degree oven for 45 minutes. When it came out of the oven, the tantalizing smell lured a horde of hungry test cooks to my work station. To tempt them further, I drizzled a little reserved chocolate sauce (just melted chocolate and cream) over the warm bread pudding. Judging from the way my colleagues enthusiastically crowded around for seconds, I knew that this chocolate bread pudding recipe was finally a winner.

—KELLEY BAKER, *Cook's Country*

Chocolate Bread Pudding

SERVES 12

Challah can be found in most bakeries and many supermarkets. It is important to use Dutch-processed cocoa in this recipe. Natural cocoa powder will make the bread pudding too bitter.

- 1 **(12-inch) loaf challah, cut into ½-inch cubes (about 12 cups) (see note)**
- 4 **cups heavy cream**
- 2 **cups whole milk**
- ½ **cup Dutch-processed cocoa powder (see note)**
- 1 **tablespoon instant espresso powder**
- 1 **cup (7 ounces) sugar**
- 8 **ounces semisweet chocolate, chopped**
- 10 **large egg yolks**

1. Adjust an oven rack to the middle position and heat the oven to 300 degrees. Toast the bread on a rimmed baking sheet, stirring occasionally, until golden and crisp, about 30 minutes. Transfer to a large bowl.

2. Increase the oven temperature to 325 degrees. Grease a 13 by 9-inch baking pan. Heat 1½ cups of the cream, milk, cocoa, espresso, and ½ cup of the sugar in a saucepan over medium-high heat, stirring occasionally, until steaming and the sugar dissolves. Pour the warm cream mixture over the toasted bread and let stand, tossing occasionally, until the liquid has been absorbed, about 10 minutes.

3. Meanwhile, bring 1 cup more cream to a simmer in a saucepan over medium-high heat. Remove from the heat and stir in the chocolate until smooth. Transfer 1 cup of the chocolate mixture to a medium bowl and let cool for 5 minutes (cover the pan and reserve the remaining chocolate mixture for serving). Add the egg yolks, remaining 1½ cups cream, and remaining ½ cup sugar to the bowl with the chocolate mixture and whisk to combine.

4. Transfer the soaked bread mixture to the prepared pan and pour the chocolate custard mixture evenly over the bread. Bake until the pudding is just set and the surface is slightly crisp, about 45 minutes. Let cool for 30 minutes. Warm the reserved chocolate mixture over low heat, then pour over the bread pudding. Serve. (Leftover bread pudding should be refrigerated; reheat individual portions in the microwave. The unbaked bread pudding can also be made in advance. Once the soaked bread mixture has been transferred to the prepared pan and the chocolate custard poured over the bread, the pan can be covered with plastic wrap and refrigerated overnight. When ready to bake, remove the plastic and proceed with the recipe as directed, increasing the baking time to 55 to 60 minutes. Let the reserved chocolate serving sauce cool, then cover with plastic wrap and refrigerate. Heat the sauce in the microwave when needed.)

NOTES FROM THE TEST KITCHEN

SECRET TO A PROPER SOAK

Melted semisweet chocolate adds big flavor to our chocolate bread pudding, but it's so thick that it doesn't soak into the bread. Soaking toasted bread in a warm mixture of heavy cream, milk, cocoa powder, and sugar helps infuse each piece with chocolate flavor before adding the rich custard made with melted chocolate.

SOAKED IN DAIRY, COCOA, AND SUGAR
Bread is fully saturated.

SOAKED IN CUSTARD MADE WITH MELTED CHOCOLATE
Bread remains dry in spots.

SKILLET CHERRY COBBLER

A FLEET OF TENDER BISCUITS on a sea of sweet, saucy cherries, a good cherry cobbler can hold its own against other fruit desserts, especially because this down-to-earth dessert comes together in just a couple of quick steps and can be dished up right away, ready to be devoured with a scoop of vanilla ice cream. The filling is traditionally cooked on the stovetop, so I figured this simple dish would be easy to make—and bake—in a skillet.

First I had to decide on the ideal cherries for this cobbler. Sour cherries were the obvious choice, as they have sufficient acidity to cook up well and become truly flavorful with a touch of sugar and some heat. Since fresh sour cherries have such a short season, I knew that using jarred or canned sour cherries would be easier—they're always available and already pitted, plus they're usually packed in a juice that can be used to flavor the sauce.

I tested several canned and jarred varieties, and found jarred Morello cherries to be the best; they were plump, meaty, and tart, right out of the jar. To make the sauce, I drained two 24-ounce jars of Morello cherries, reserved the juice, and set the cherries aside for the time being. I had 2 cups of juice, which I would thicken to form the base of my rich, saucy cobbler. For sweetness, I found that ¾ to 1 cup of sugar was the right amount, depending on the brand and sweetness level of the cherries. To heighten the cherry flavor, I also added some vanilla extract, then cooked the mixture (along with 3 tablespoons of cornstarch) until it had thickened. Off the heat, I stirred in the cherries. Since jarred (and canned) cherries have been processed, they are already cooked, so the less heat they're exposed to thereafter the better. By fully cooking the sauce on the stove prior to adding the cherries, I could also lessen the baking time—the sauce wouldn't have to cook in the oven—ensuring that the topping wouldn't burn.

Moving on to the cobbles, I omitted the eggs, which I've learned can give biscuits a dense texture, and added buttermilk for the opposite effect, creating biscuits that were light and tender. I tested several biscuit variations and settled on a fairly standard mix of all-purpose flour, butter, baking powder and soda, sugar, salt, and buttermilk.

My biggest question was how to cook the biscuit dough evenly without burning it. I started out by dropping heaping spoonfuls of dough over the cooked

SKILLET CHERRY COBBLER

cherry filling, instead of the more time-consuming method of rolling out the dough and cutting out biscuits. Although this technique was promising and gave our cobbler a rustic look, I found that the large drops of dough took too long to bake through, and the undersides remained raw and gummy. For the next test, I traded in the large spoon for a teaspoon and dropped small scoops of biscuit dough evenly over the fruit for a truly cobbled effect. These mini-cobbles worked perfectly and cooked through in just half an hour without issue—no soggy bottoms here. To give the topping a bit more oomph, I sprinkled turbinado sugar over the tops before baking. This gave our biscuits a crispy texture that contrasted nicely against the softened cherries and sweet sauce.

With my topping perfected and juicy cherry filling hot and bubbling, I let the finished cobbler sit for a short time before digging in. The biscuits were brown and crisp, and the cherry filling was just right, somewhere between sweet and tart. My cherry cobbler was ready in minutes, and, since I used jarred cherries, it could satisfy my down-home dessert cravings any time of the year.

—MEGAN WYCOFF, *America's Test Kitchen Books*

NOTES FROM THE TEST KITCHEN

THE BEST VANILLA EXTRACTS

Vanilla extract is sold in pure and imitation varieties. So which should you buy? If you're buying only one bottle of vanilla for cooking, baking, and making cold and creamy desserts, our top choice is a real extract—real vanilla has around 250 flavor and aroma compounds compared to imitation vanilla's one, giving it a complexity tasters appreciated in certain applications. Our favorite pure vanilla is **McCormick Pure Vanilla Extract.** But if you use vanilla only for baking, we have to admit there's still not much difference between a well-made synthetic vanilla and the real thing (the flavor and aroma compounds in pure vanilla begin to bake off at higher temperatures, so the subtleties are lost). Tasters liked the "well-balanced and full" vanilla flavor and budget-friendly price of our top-rated imitation vanilla, **Gold Medal.** (See page 292 for more information about our testing results.)

Skillet Cherry Cobbler
SERVES 6

The amount of sugar you use will depend on the sweetness of your cherries; if they are very sweet, use the smaller amount of sugar given. We prefer the crunchy texture of turbinado sugar sprinkled over the biscuits before baking, but regular granulated sugar can be substituted.

BISCUIT TOPPING

1½ cups (7½ ounces) unbleached all-purpose flour

5 tablespoons granulated sugar

1½ teaspoons baking powder

¼ teaspoon baking soda

¼ teaspoon salt

¾ cup buttermilk

4 tablespoons (½ stick) unsalted butter, melted and cooled

FILLING

¾–1 cup (5¼ to 7 ounces) granulated sugar (see note)

3 tablespoons cornstarch

Pinch salt

2 (24-ounce) jars Morello cherries, drained (about 4 cups cherries), with 2 cups juice reserved

½ teaspoon vanilla extract

2 tablespoons turbinado sugar (see note)

1. FOR THE BISCUIT TOPPING: Adjust an oven rack to the middle position and heat the oven to 400 degrees. Whisk the flour, granulated sugar, baking powder, baking soda, and salt together in a medium bowl. Stir in the buttermilk and melted butter until a dough forms. Cover and set aside.

2. FOR THE FILLING: Whisk the granulated sugar, cornstarch, and salt together in a 12-inch ovensafe skillet. Whisk in the reserved cherry juice and vanilla. Set the skillet over medium-high heat and cook, whisking frequently, until the mixture simmers and is slightly thickened, about 5 minutes. Off the heat, stir in the cherries.

3. Using a spoon, scoop and drop 1-inch pieces of the dough, spaced about ½ inch apart, over the cherry filling in the skillet, then sprinkle with the turbinado sugar. Transfer the skillet to the oven and bake the cobbler until the biscuits are golden brown and the filling is thick and glossy, 25 to 30 minutes.

4. Using a potholder (the skillet handle will be hot), remove the skillet from the oven. Let the cobbler cool in the skillet for at least 15 minutes before serving.

VARIATIONS

Skillet Cherry-Almond Cobbler

Follow the recipe for Skillet Cherry Cobbler, substituting ½ teaspoon almond extract for the vanilla. Sprinkle ¼ cup sliced almonds, toasted, over the top before serving.

Skillet Cherry, Red Wine, and Cinnamon Cobbler

Follow the recipe for Skillet Cherry Cobbler, substituting 1 cup dry red wine for 1 cup of the reserved jarred cherry juice. Add 1 cinnamon stick to the skillet with the cherry juice in step 2; remove and discard the cinnamon stick when stirring in the cherries.

SKILLET APPLE PIE

AS GREAT AS APPLE PIE IS, LET'S FACE IT: It can be a time-consuming affair. So when I came across a recipe for apple pandowdy, I was immediately intrigued. A colonial New England original, pandowdy is essentially an apple pie filling baked with a top crust. During or after baking, the cook breaks the pastry and pushes it into the filling, a technique known as "dowdying" (and a reference, perhaps, to the dessert's resulting "dowdy" appearance). Rustic looks aside, I loved the idea of this no-frills approach. With no fussy crimping, no filling that must be finessed to make it sliceable, and no bottom crust that could get soggy, this kind of pie sounded manageable enough to make all the time.

I wondered if I could make apple pandowdy by simply putting an apple pie filling in a baking dish and topping it with dough. I decided to try this with a basic filling of sweet and tart apples, sugar, and lemon juice. As for the topping, a traditional pandowdy may be topped with a cakelike batter, biscuit dough, or pie pastry. Because I was drawn to the idea of a simple apple pie, I decided to stick with a pie pastry topping.

When the dessert came out of the oven, I gave dowdying a try, using the back of a spoon to push the crust into the filling. The crust quickly became soggy and bloated—not what I wanted at all. In colonial times, dowdying was likely practiced in order to soften a tough dough with the juice from the apples.

My tender modern dough was much more delicate than its sturdy ancestors, and dowdying just didn't make sense. I decided to skip the dowdying and pursue a dessert modeled on a one-crust pie.

Even after abandoning the dowdying step, I knew that I needed to make some adjustments. First and foremost, the apple filling was dry and lacked flavor. I wanted a juicy, rich filling that really tasted of apples. Unlike a pie, which needs to be thick and sliceable, my pandowdy could afford to be somewhat saucy—and then I could concentrate on building superior flavor without having to worry about sliceability.

Perhaps I could produce a juicier filling by drawing out some of the liquid in the apples? I tried macerating the apples in sugar to coax out moisture, but this was unsuccessful: Apples aren't as juicy as berries or stone fruits. I would have to add some extra liquid to the apples. An additional ½ cup of apple juice made the filling moist but diluted its taste. Simmering a cup of apple juice until it was reduced by half intensified the flavor, but using apple cider was easier—it provided resonant apple flavor straight from the jug. I thickened the cider with two teaspoons of cornstarch, yielding a juicy filling with just the right amount of body.

Pandowdies were originally sweetened with molasses, maple syrup, or brown sugar. Compared with these old-fashioned choices, the granulated sugar that I had been using tasted plain and boring. But molasses and brown sugar were both overpowering. One-third of a cup of maple syrup struck the perfect balance, complementing the natural sweetness of the apples without being cloying. After testing—and dismissing—a few different spices, I concluded that a classic pinch of cinnamon was a nice optional addition.

At this point I had a juicy apple filling and could focus on improving the crust. I wanted it to be extra-crisp to stand up to the moist, saucy fruit. After some trial and error, I found that the best approach was to use a standard pie crust that had been brushed with egg white and sprinkled with sugar (for a crackly finish), and then to bake the pandowdy in a 500-degree oven. But there was a problem: Although the crust was browned and crisp with a beautiful golden color, the apples were sadly undercooked. Lowering the oven temperature eventually cooked the apples through, but left the crust pale.

As I struggled to solve this dilemma, I turned to my historical sources again and rediscovered a chief point

SKILLET APPLE PIE

about early pandowdies: They were cooked in a heavy skillet or pot that was placed directly over the heat source. Could I mimic this old-fashioned technique by starting my pandowdy in a skillet on the stovetop? I could give the apples a head start by sautéing them first, then add the crust and quickly brown it in a hot oven.

My new method worked beautifully, yielding caramelized apples that were richly flavored and perfectly cooked. In just about 20 minutes, the apples baked evenly, the sauce was nicely thickened and sticky around the edges, and the crust developed a lovely deep brown hue.

As a final touch, I cut the dough into six pieces before the pandowdy went into the oven. This extra step enabled each piece of pastry to bake up with multiple crisp, flaky edges, and the cider-enriched filling bubbled up and caramelized nicely around the edges of the tender pastry. With results so good and so simple to come by, I might never go back to conventional apple pie again.

—YVONNE RUPERTI, *Cook's Illustrated*

Skillet Apple Pie

SERVES 6 TO 8

If you do not have apple cider, reduced apple juice may be used as a substitute—simmer 1 cup apple juice in a small saucepan over medium heat until reduced to ½ cup (about 10 minutes). Use a combination of sweet, crisp apples such as Golden Delicious and firm, tart apples such as Cortland or Empire. Serve the pie warm or at room temperature with vanilla ice cream or whipped cream.

CRUST
- 1 cup (5 ounces) unbleached all-purpose flour, plus extra for the counter
- 1 tablespoon sugar
- ½ teaspoon salt
- 2 tablespoons vegetable shortening, chilled
- 6 tablespoons (¾ stick) unsalted butter, cut into ¼-inch pieces and chilled
- 3–4 tablespoons ice water

FILLING
- ½ cup apple cider (see note)
- ⅓ cup maple syrup
- 2 tablespoons fresh lemon juice
- 2 teaspoons cornstarch
- ⅛ teaspoon ground cinnamon (optional)
- 2 tablespoons unsalted butter
- 2½ pounds sweet and tart apples (about 5 medium), peeled, cored, halved, and cut into ½-inch-thick wedges (see note)
- 1 egg white, lightly beaten
- 2 teaspoons sugar

1. FOR THE CRUST: Pulse the flour, sugar, and salt in a food processor until combined. Add the shortening and process until the mixture has the texture of coarse sand, about 10 seconds. Scatter the butter pieces over the flour mixture and process until the mixture is pale yellow and resembles coarse crumbs, with butter bits no larger than small peas, about 10 seconds. Transfer the mixture to a medium bowl.

2. Sprinkle 3 tablespoons of the ice water over the mixture. With a rubber spatula, use a folding motion to mix. Press down on the dough with the broad side of the spatula until the dough sticks together, adding up to 1 tablespoon more ice water if the dough does not come together. Turn the dough out onto the counter and flatten into a 4-inch disk. Wrap in plastic wrap and refrigerate for 1 hour or up to 2 days. Let the dough stand at room temperature for 15 minutes before rolling.

3. FOR THE FILLING: Adjust an oven rack to the upper-middle position (between 7 and 9 inches from the heating element) and heat the oven to 500 degrees. Whisk the cider, syrup, lemon juice, cornstarch, and cinnamon (if using) together in a medium bowl until smooth. Melt the butter in a 12-inch ovensafe skillet over medium-high heat. Add the apples and cook, stirring 2 or 3 times, until the apples begin to caramelize, about 5 minutes. (Do not fully cook the apples.) Remove the pan from the heat, add the cider mixture, and gently stir until the apples are well coated. Set aside to cool slightly.

4. TO ASSEMBLE AND BAKE: Roll the dough on a lightly floured counter to an 11-inch circle. Roll the dough loosely around the rolling pin and unroll it over the apple filling. Brush the dough with the egg white and sprinkle with the sugar. With a sharp knife, gently cut the dough into 6 pieces by making 1 vertical cut followed by 2 evenly spaced horizontal cuts (perpendicular to the first cut). Bake until the apples are tender and the crust is a deep golden brown, about 20 minutes. Using a potholder (the skillet handle will be hot), remove the skillet from the oven. Let cool for 15 minutes and serve.

BUYING AND STORING APPLES

Apples that aren't going to be sold within a few weeks of harvest are placed in refrigerated "controlled atmosphere" (CA) storage with regulated levels of oxygen and carbon dioxide. Because apples continue to ripen after harvest, these conditions are designed to halt the ripening process. But once they are removed from CA storage and put on display at the grocery store, they begin an accelerated ripening process. The apple's structure will then quickly break down upon cooking. The longer apples are kept in CA storage, the faster they ripen once removed, and the more likely they are to turn mushy during baking. Because it is impossible to know how long or under what conditions supermarket apples have been stored, your best bet is to use fresh, local apples whenever possible. If you purchase fresh apples, refrigerate and use them as soon as you can.

KEYS TO A FLAKY, FLAVORFUL SKILLET APPLE PIE

1. Precook the apples in butter to deepen their flavor.

2. Coat the apples with ½ cup apple cider to create a juicy, flavorful filling.

3. Cut the dough before baking to allow juices to bubble up and caramelize around the edges.

4. Place the skillet in the oven. Precooked apples need less time in the oven than traditional apple pie.

BLUEBERRY PIE

THERE'S NOTHING LIKE BLUEBERRY PIE to shake the confidence of even the most experienced baker. Unlike apple pie, which requires little (if any) starch to thicken the fruit, the filling in blueberry pie needs special attention because the berries are so juicy. The very first slice reveals success or failure. Triumph brings a firm, glistening filling full of fresh, bright flavor and still-plump berries. Defeat can range from a wedge that collapses into a soupy puddle topped by a sodden crust, to filling so dense and gelatinous that just cutting into it is a challenge.

I started my search for a juicy yet sliceable pie by filling a basic pie dough with a fairly standard mixture of 6 cups fresh blueberries, ¾ cup sugar, and our usual thickener for berry pies, tapioca. The 6 tablespoons recommended on the back of the tapioca box produced a stiff, congealed mass, so I slowly cut back the amount. At 4 tablespoons, the filling was still too congealed for my tasters' liking, but this amount proved to be the tipping point; any less and the pie needed to be served with a spoon.

The problem, of course, was the juiciness of the berries. Could I reduce some of their liquid by cooking them before they were baked in the pie shell? I put all 6 cups in a pan. As the berries simmered, I mashed them with a potato masher to release their juices. Excess liquid did indeed boil away—but so did a lot of fresh berry flavor.

After some experimentation, I found that cooking just half of the berries was enough to adequately reduce the liquid. I then folded the remaining raw berries into the mixture, creating a satisfying combination of intensely flavored cooked fruit and bright-tasting fresh fruit that allowed me to cut the tapioca down to 3 tablespoons. Encouraged by this success, I wondered if I could decrease the tapioca even further.

As I watched the blueberries for my pie bubble away in the pot, I thought about blueberry jam. Well-made jam boasts a soft, even consistency that is neither gelatinous nor slippery. The secret to this great texture is pectin, a carbohydrate found in fruit. Blueberries are low in natural pectin, so commercial pectin in the form of a liquid or powder is usually added when making blueberry jam. The only downside to commercial pectin is that it needs the presence of a certain proportion of sugar and acid in order to work. I added an ounce of pectin, along with some extra sugar, but this made the filling sickeningly sweet. A test with "no sugar needed" pectin set up properly, but this additive contains lots of natural acid, which compensates for the lack of extra sugar—and its sourness made my tasters wince. I was ready to give up when a colleague offered a suggestion: Since apples contain a lot of natural pectin, could an apple be added to the blueberries to help set the filling?

I folded one peeled and grated Granny Smith apple into a new batch of fresh and cooked berries I had mixed with 2 tablespoons of tapioca. When I sliced into this pie, I knew I'd hit on a great solution. Combined with a modest 2 tablespoons of tapioca, the apple provided enough thickening power to set the pie beautifully, plus it enhanced the flavor of the berries without anyone guessing my secret ingredient. Just as important, it left no evidence of its own texture.

Tweaking the crust was the last step. I found that baking the pie on a heated baking sheet on the bottom rack of the oven produced a crisp, golden bottom crust that didn't get soggy. As for the top crust, berry pies are often made with a decorative lattice topping that allows the steam from the berries to gently escape. But after making more than 50 lattice tops, I was determined to find a faster, easier approach. I had seen in my research a crust that had vents in the form of simple round cutouts, and I decided to try this method. After rolling out the dough, I used a small biscuit cutter to cut out circles, and then I transferred the dough onto the pie. This method saved time and made an attractive, unusual-looking top crust that properly vented the steam from the berry filling as it baked. At long last, my blueberry blues had turned to blueberry bliss.

—YVONNE RUPERTI, *Cook's Illustrated*

NOTES FROM THE TEST KITCHEN

THE IMPORTANCE OF A THICKENER

PRETTY BUT PASTY
Too much tapioca (or the wrong thickener, such as flour or cornstarch) results in a filling that holds its shape but tastes gluey and dull.

FRESH BUT SOUPY
With no thickener at all, there is plenty of fresh berry flavor, but the filling is loose and runny.

A NO-FUSS TOP CRUST

We found that simply cutting holes in the top crust is a much faster (and easier) alternative to making a lattice top. We use a 1¼-inch biscuit cutter to cut the holes in the dough, but a spice-jar lid will also do the trick.

Blueberry Pie

MAKES ONE 9-INCH PIE

This recipe was developed using fresh blueberries, but unthawed frozen blueberries will work as well. In step 3, cook half the frozen berries over medium-high heat, without mashing, until reduced to 1¼ cups, 12 to 15 minutes. Grind the tapioca to a powder in a spice grinder or mini food processor. If using pearl tapioca, reduce the amount to 5 teaspoons.

- 1 recipe Foolproof Double-Crust Pie Dough (page 247)
- 6 cups (about 30 ounces) fresh blueberries (see note)
- 1 Granny Smith apple, peeled and grated on the large holes of a box grater
- 2 teaspoons grated lemon zest plus 2 teaspoons fresh lemon juice
- ¾ cup (5¼ ounces) sugar
- 2 tablespoons instant tapioca, ground (see note)
  Pinch salt
- 2 tablespoons unsalted butter, cut into ¼-inch pieces
- 1 large egg, lightly beaten with 1 teaspoon water

1. Remove 1 disk of the dough from the refrigerator and let stand at room temperature for 15 minutes. Roll the dough out on a generously floured (up to ¼ cup) counter to a 12-inch circle, about ⅛ inch thick. Roll the dough loosely around the rolling pin and unroll into a 9-inch pie plate, leaving at least a 1-inch overhang. Ease the dough into the plate by gently lifting the edge of the dough with one hand while pressing into the plate bottom with the other hand. Leave any dough that overhangs the plate in place; cover with plastic wrap and refrigerate until the dough is firm, about 30 minutes.

2. Meanwhile, remove the second disk of dough from the refrigerator and let stand at room temperature for 15 minutes. Roll the dough out on a generously floured (up to ¼ cup) counter to an 11-inch circle, about ⅛ inch thick. Transfer the dough to a parchment-lined baking sheet; using a 1¼-inch round biscuit cutter, cut a round from the center of the dough. Cut another 6 rounds from the dough, 1½ inches from the edge of the center hole and equally spaced around the center hole (see page 246). Cover with plastic wrap and refrigerate until firm, about 30 minutes.

3. Adjust an oven rack to the lowest position, place a foil-lined rimmed baking sheet on the oven rack, and heat the oven to 400 degrees. Place 3 cups of the berries in a medium saucepan and set over medium heat. Using a potato masher, mash the berries several times to release their juice. Continue to cook, stirring frequently and mashing occasionally, until about half of the berries have broken down and the mixture is thickened and reduced to 1½ cups, about 8 minutes. Let cool slightly.

4. Place the grated apple in a clean kitchen towel and wring dry. Transfer the apple to a large bowl. Add the cooked berries, remaining 3 cups uncooked berries, lemon zest, juice, sugar, tapioca, and salt; toss to combine. Transfer the mixture to the dough-lined pie plate and scatter the butter pieces over the filling.

5. Flip the remaining dough round onto the filling. Pinch the edges of the top and bottom dough rounds firmly together. Using kitchen shears, trim the bottom layer of overhanging dough, leaving a ½-inch overhang. Fold the dough under itself so that the edge of the fold is flush with the outer rim of the pie plate. Flute the edges using your thumb and forefinger or press with the tines of a fork to seal. Brush the top and edges of the pie with the egg mixture. If the dough is very soft, chill in the freezer for 10 minutes.

6. Place the pie on the heated baking sheet and bake for 30 minutes. Reduce the oven temperature to 350 degrees and continue to bake until the juices bubble and the crust is deep golden brown, 30 to 40 minutes longer. Transfer the pie to a wire rack and cool to room temperature, at least 4 hours. Cut into wedges and serve.

Foolproof Double-Crust Pie Dough

MAKES ENOUGH FOR ONE 9-INCH DOUBLE-CRUST PIE

Vodka is essential to the texture of the crust and imparts no flavor. This dough will be moister and more supple than most standard pie doughs and will require more flour to roll out (up to ¼ cup).

2½ cups (12½ ounces) unbleached all-purpose flour
1 teaspoon salt
2 tablespoons sugar
12 tablespoons (1½ sticks) unsalted butter,
    cut into ¼-inch pieces and chilled
½ cup vegetable shortening, cut into 4 pieces and chilled
¼ cup cold vodka (see note)
¼ cup cold water

1. Pulse 1½ cups of the flour, salt, and sugar in a food processor until combined, about 2 pulses. Add the butter and shortening and process until a homogeneous dough just starts to collect in uneven clumps, about 15 seconds

---

NOTES FROM THE TEST KITCHEN

KEY STEPS TO FOOLPROOF PIE DOUGH

1. Completely blending part of the flour with all of the butter and shortening ensures a consistent amount of fat-coated flour in the final dough.

2. Pulsing the remaining flour ensures a consistent amount of uncoated flour in the finished dough.

3. Sprinkling the dough with water and vodka ensures even distribution. No need to skimp—unlike water, vodka won't make the dough tough.

BLUEBERRY PIE

(the dough will resemble cottage cheese curds and there should be no uncoated flour). Scrape down the bowl with a rubber spatula and redistribute the dough evenly around the processor blade. Add the remaining 1 cup flour and pulse until the mixture is evenly distributed around the bowl and the mass of dough has been broken up, 4 to 6 quick pulses. Empty the mixture into a medium bowl.

2. Sprinkle the vodka and water over the mixture. With a rubber spatula, use a folding motion to mix, pressing down on the dough until the dough is slightly tacky and sticks together. Divide the dough into 2 even balls and flatten each into a 4-inch disk. Wrap each disk in plastic wrap and refrigerate at least 1 hour or up to 2 days.

Foolproof Single-Crust Pie Dough

MAKES ENOUGH FOR ONE 9-INCH SINGLE-CRUST PIE

Vodka is essential to the texture of the crust and imparts no flavor. This dough will be moister and more supple than most standard pie doughs and will require more flour to roll out (up to ¼ cup).

- 1¼ **cups (6¼ ounces) unbleached all-purpose flour**
- ½ **teaspoon salt**
- 1 **tablespoon sugar**
- 6 **tablespoons (¾ stick) unsalted butter, cut into ¼-inch pieces and chilled**
- ¼ **cup vegetable shortening, cut into 2 pieces and chilled**
- 2 **tablespoons cold vodka**
- 2 **tablespoons cold water**

1. Pulse ¾ cup of the flour, salt, and sugar together in a food processor until combined, about 2 pulses. Add the butter and shortening and process until a homogeneous dough just starts to collect in uneven clumps, about 10 seconds (the dough will resemble cottage cheese curds with some very small pieces of butter remaining, but there should be no uncoated flour). Scrape down the sides of the bowl with a rubber spatula and redistribute the dough evenly around the processor blade. Add the remaining ½ cup flour and pulse until the mixture is evenly distributed around the bowl and the mass of dough has been broken up, 4 to 6 quick pulses. Empty the mixture into a medium bowl.

2. Sprinkle the vodka and water over the mixture. With a rubber spatula, use a folding motion to mix, pressing down on the dough until the dough is slightly tacky and

sticks together. Flatten the dough into a 4-inch disk. Wrap the disk in plastic wrap and refrigerate at least 1 hour or up to 2 days.

JEFFERSON DAVIS PIE

THE SOUTH REMAINS SWEET on its Civil War leaders: A lemon curd–filled cake is named after Robert E. Lee, while Confederate President Jefferson Davis ("Jeff" to some recipe writers) has a pie named after him. Despite my Southern upbringing, I wasn't acquainted with Jefferson Davis pie, a simple brown-sugar chess pie studded with dried fruit and nuts. Most recipes make a no-cook filling by combining brown sugar, egg yolks, butter, milk, warm spices, dried fruit, pecans, and a few tablespoons of flour; the mixture is poured into a raw pie shell and the pie is baked until the custard sets. This sounded like a pie worth getting to know!

But when I baked off a handful of recipes, I wasn't sure Mr. Davis and I were going to be friends. Most of my test pies baked up with saccharine, loose fillings and soggy crusts. And while my tasters appreciated the flavor of the fruit and nuts, they didn't like the distraction of having them suspended in the otherwise smooth custard.

My first goal was sliceable custard with a good balance of sweetness and spice. Most recipes started out with 2 (or more) cups of brown sugar, but I found that 1 cup was just fine, as less sugar let the flavors of the cinnamon and allspice (favored over common but imposing additions like cloves, nutmeg, and mace) shine through. Using heavy cream instead of milk gave the pie a silkier, thicker texture and much richer flavor.

Most custard pies are made with whole eggs, which set faster than just the yolks used in Jefferson Davis pie, so custard pies bake faster (in a half hour or less) and require a parbaked pie shell to ensure even cooking. Jeff Davis pie usually bakes in a raw pie shell for about 45 minutes. The pies are typically started at a high temperature (about 425 degrees) to firm up the crust and finished at a moderate 350 degrees. But without fail, this method resulted in custards that dried out around the edges before they were fully set in the center. After several tests, I found that a slightly longer bake (about an hour) in a gentle 325-degree oven allowed the crust to brown in the same time it took for the custard to set to the requisite firmness.

Some recipes saddle this pie with 2 cups of raisins and dates and more than a cup of pecans. I started by halving those amounts and finely grinding them in the food processor for a more homogeneous filling. But my tasters still balked at the bits of fruit and nuts in the custard. So instead of folding them in, I tried pressing them into the bottom of the raw crust and gently pouring the custard over. This pie baked up with a thin, distinct layer of fruit and nuts on the bottom and a creamy, smooth custard layer on top. A dollop of bourbon-fortified whipped cream was all I needed to make this pie worthy of a national introduction.

—CALI RICH, *Cook's Country*

Jefferson Davis Pie

SERVES 8

We prefer the mild flavor of golden raisins in this recipe, but regular raisins will work.

PIE

1	recipe Foolproof Single-Crust Pie Dough (page 249)
½	cup raisins (see note)
½	cup chopped dates
½	cup pecans, toasted and chopped (see page 16)
3	tablespoons unbleached all-purpose flour
1	teaspoon ground cinnamon
¼	teaspoon ground allspice
½	teaspoon salt
1	cup packed (7 ounces) light brown sugar
8	tablespoons (1 stick) unsalted butter, softened
5	large egg yolks
1¼	cups heavy cream

BOURBON WHIPPED CREAM

1	cup heavy cream
2	tablespoons bourbon
1½	tablespoons light brown sugar
½	teaspoon vanilla extract

1. FOR THE PIE: Remove the dough from the refrigerator and let stand at room temperature for 15 minutes. Roll the dough out on a lightly floured counter to a 12-inch circle, about ⅛ inch thick. Roll the dough loosely around the rolling pin and unroll into a 9-inch pie plate, leaving at least a 1-inch overhang. Ease the dough into the plate by gently lifting the edge of the dough with one hand while pressing into the plate bottom with the other hand. Leave any dough that overhangs the plate in place.

2. Trim the overhang to ½ inch beyond the lip of the pie plate. Fold the overhang under itself; the folded edge should be flush with the edge of the pie plate. Using your thumb and forefinger, flute the edge of the dough. Cover with plastic wrap and refrigerate until firm, about 30 minutes.

3. Adjust an oven rack to the lowest position and heat the oven to 325 degrees. Pulse the raisins, dates, and pecans in a food processor until finely ground, about 10 pulses. Transfer the mixture to the chilled pie shell and gently press into an even layer.

4. Combine the flour, cinnamon, allspice, and salt in a small bowl. In a large bowl, beat the sugar and butter with an electric mixer on medium-low speed until just combined, about 1 minute. Mix in the yolks, one at a time, until incorporated. Add the flour mixture and cream and mix, scraping down the bowl and beaters as needed, until just combined.

5. Pour the filling over the fruit and nuts in the prepared crust and bake until the surface is deep brown and the center jiggles slightly when the pie is shaken, 55 to 65 minutes. Cool completely on a wire rack, about 4 hours. (The pie can be refrigerated, covered in plastic wrap, for up to 2 days.)

6. FOR THE BOURBON WHIPPED CREAM: In a large bowl, beat the cream, bourbon, sugar, and vanilla on medium-low speed until frothy, about 1 minute. Increase the mixer speed to high and continue to whip until the cream forms soft peaks, 1 to 3 minutes. (The whipped cream can be refrigerated for up to 4 hours.) Serve with the pie.

NOTES FROM THE TEST KITCHEN

THE BEST PIE PLATE

A pie plate's rim should be wide enough to support a fluted edge. We found that pie plates with rims narrower than ½ inch were not up to the task. Of all the pie plates we have tested, the classic **Pyrex Bakeware 9-Inch Pie Plate**, $2.99, is our favorite, delivering a solid performance across the board: good crisping and browning; a see-through bottom to monitor the crust; a half-inch rim; shallow, angled sides; and a low price. (See page 306 for more information about our testing results.)

FRENCH SILK
CHOCOLATE PIE

DON'T LET THE NAME FOOL YOU: French silk pie was "born" in America. Betty Cooper, who lived in Maryland, won a $1,000 prize for the recipe in 1951 in the third annual Pillsbury Bake-Off. Betty's recipe is an old-fashioned icebox pie—the name reflects the international curiosity of postwar America.

To make the filling for her icebox pie, Betty whipped together butter, sugar, melted-and-cooled unsweetened chocolate, and raw eggs until the mixture was light and fluffy. She poured the filling into a homemade pre-baked pie crust and chilled it until it was firm; no baking required. Served with dollops of whipped cream, French silk chocolate pie was an instant hit.

Although you can find commercial versions of French silk pie in the freezer section of the supermarket, not many home cooks tackle it these days, possibly because the recipe calls for raw eggs. When I made Betty's original prize-winning recipe, I uncovered another reason: The pie barely tasted like chocolate. It may have pleased eaters nearly 60 years ago, but Americans today have become accustomed to ramped-up chocolate flavor.

In the interest of food safety, the recipe on the Pillsbury website calls for egg substitutes in place of the original raw eggs. I tested a few pies with various brands, but the fillings had an artificial, off-flavor. I decided to stick with real eggs and cook the eggs and sugar on the stovetop, almost like making a custard. Once the egg and sugar mixture was light and thick (and cooked to a safe 160 degrees), I removed it from the heat and continued whipping it until it was fully cooled.

The original recipe called for 3 ounces of unsweetened chocolate. Wanting a more chocolaty pie, I tried doubling the amount, but the unsweetened chocolate was acidic and harsh at that volume (and adding more sugar ruined the texture). Next, I made pies with semisweet and bittersweet chocolate, in combination and alone. Across the board, tasters preferred the bold-but-balanced flavor of pies made with bittersweet chocolate. I tried different amounts and settled on 8 ounces, which I folded into the cooled egg and sugar mixture.

The filling tasted terrific, but it was much too dense when I beat in the two sticks of softened butter called for in the original recipe. Cutting the amount of butter in half got me closer to the satiny texture I wanted. But the filling still wasn't quite silky or light enough.

Most recipes suggest serving the pie with whipped cream. I wondered if I could lighten the pie by incorporating whipped cream into the filling. I whipped 1 cup of cream, folded it into the chocolate mixture, and spooned the filling into the pie shell. I waited patiently for the pie to set (it took about three hours), sliced the pie, and dug in. The filling was light, but rich, thick, and chocolaty all at once. It was, finally, as smooth as French silk.

—DIANE UNGER, *Cook's Country*

French Silk Chocolate Pie
SERVES 8 TO 10

We prefer ceramic or metal pie weights for prebaking the pie shell. If you don't own any weights, rice or dried beans can stand in, but since they're lighter than pie weights, be sure to fill up the foil-lined pie shell completely. Serve with lightly sweetened whipped cream.

- 1 recipe Foolproof Single-Crust Pie Dough (page 249)
- 1 cup heavy cream, chilled
- 3 large eggs
- ¾ cup sugar
- 2 tablespoons water
- 8 ounces bittersweet chocolate, melted and cooled
- 1 tablespoon vanilla extract
- 8 tablespoons (1 stick) unsalted butter, cut into ½-inch pieces and softened

1. Adjust an oven rack to lowest position, place a foil-lined rimmed baking sheet on the rack, and heat the oven to 400 degrees. Remove the dough from the refrigerator and let stand at room temperature for 15 minutes. Roll the dough out on a generously floured (up to ¼ cup) counter to a 12-inch circle, about ⅛ inch thick. Roll the dough loosely around the rolling pin and unroll into a 9-inch pie plate, leaving at least a 1-inch overhang. Ease the dough into the plate by gently lifting the edge of the dough with one hand while pressing into the plate bottom with the other hand. Leave any dough that overhangs the plate in place.

2. Trim the overhang to ½ inch beyond the lip of the pie plate. Fold the overhang under itself; the folded edge should be flush with the edge of the pie plate. Using your thumb and forefinger, flute the edge of the dough. Cover with plastic wrap and refrigerate until firm, about 30 minutes.

FRENCH SILK CHOCOLATE PIE

3. Remove the pie plate from the refrigerator, line the crust with heavy-duty foil, folding the excess foil over the edges of the pan, and fill with pie weights (see note). Bake on the rimmed baking sheet for 15 minutes. Carefully remove the foil and weights, rotate the baking sheet, and bake until the crust is golden brown and crisp, 5 to 10 additional minutes. Remove the pie plate and baking sheet from the oven.

4. In a large bowl, whip the cream with an electric mixer on medium low-speed until frothy, about 1 minute. Increase the mixer speed to medium-high and continue to whip until the cream forms stiff peaks, 2 to 4 minutes. Transfer the whipped cream to a small bowl and refrigerate.

5. Combine the eggs, sugar, and water in a large heatproof bowl set over a medium saucepan filled with ½ inch of barely simmering water (don't let the bowl touch the water). With an electric mixer on medium speed, beat until the egg mixture is thickened and registers 160 degrees on an instant-read thermometer, 7 to 10 minutes. Remove the bowl from the heat and continue to beat the egg mixture until fluffy and cooled to room temperature, about 8 minutes.

6. Add the chocolate and vanilla to the cooled egg mixture and beat until incorporated. Beat in the butter, a few pieces at a time, until well combined. Using a spatula, fold in the whipped cream until no streaks of white remain. Scrape the filling into the pie shell and refrigerate until set, at least 3 hours or up to 24 hours. Serve.

PUMPKIN PIE

SERVING PUMPKIN PIE AT THANKSGIVING is an exercise in futility. After a rich, filling repast, the last part of the ritual appears, problematic as ever: grainy, canned-pumpkin custard encased in a soggy crust. If pumpkin pie is so important that it wouldn't be Thanksgiving without it, why not make it a first-class finish to the meal? Could we turn this holiday dessert into more than an obligatory endnote for already-sated guests?

All too often, pumpkin pie does a poor job of showcasing the flavor of its star ingredient. But I knew better than to think the answer was to use fresh pumpkin. In numerous tests, we've found that very few tasters can distinguish between fresh and canned pumpkin once it's baked in a pie—and cooking fresh pumpkin is a whole lot of work. The real problem is that pumpkin, fresh or canned, contains a lot of moisture, which ultimately dilutes the pie's flavor. This point was driven home when I wrapped the contents of a can of pumpkin puree in cheesecloth and left it overnight in a colander to drain. By the next morning, the pumpkin had released copious amounts of liquid. Out of curiosity, I tasted a spoonful of the liquid and was surprised to find it had an intense flavor.

To maximize flavor, it made sense to concentrate the pumpkin's liquid rather than just remove it. I emptied a can of puree into a saucepan along with some sugar and spices, then cranked up the heat. I whisked in some dairy and eggs and poured the filling into a prebaked shell. Not only did cooking the pumpkin improve its

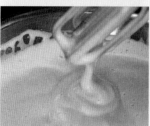

flavor, but the hot filling also allowed the custard to firm up quickly in the oven, preventing it from soaking into the crust and turning it soggy.

Now that I had great flavor, did I even need spices? My tasters unanimously agreed that a small amount complemented the pumpkin, singling out nutmeg, cinnamon, and ginger as their favorites. Substituting a couple of teaspoons of freshly grated ginger for the dry equivalent was a hit, imparting a bright, almost fruity flavor to the pie. Cooking the ginger and spices along with the pumpkin puree intensified their taste—the direct heat bloomed their flavors. I also experimented with a number of different sweeteners, including honey, maple syrup, and brown sugar. On their own, maple syrup and honey were overpowering; brown sugar resulted in a grainy texture and a too-distinct flavor. In the end, tasters favored a combination of granulated sugar and a small amount of maple syrup, which added a layer of complexity. But not enough complexity—tasters still craved a more flavorful pie.

NOTES FROM THE TEST KITCHEN

KEEPING THE CUSTARD FROM CURDLING
The right oven temperature is essential to the success of our pumpkin pie. A pie cooked at 425 degrees curdles and becomes watery and grainy. Starting the pie at 400 degrees and finishing it at 300 degrees allow it to bake without curdling.

OVERCOOKED   **SILKY SMOOTH**

COOKING THE FILLING

Simmering the filling drives off moisture and concentrates the flavor of the pumpkin and sweet potatoes. It also helps the filling firm up quickly in the oven, rather than soaking into the pastry and causing the crust to become soggy.

On a whim, I borrowed a few roasted sweet potatoes that a colleague was testing for a side dish and mashed them into my pumpkin mixture without telling anyone. Tasters immediately recognized a new and deeper flavor in the pie. I had hit on a secret ingredient! But I didn't really want to take the time to roast the sweet potatoes for this effect. Would canned sweet potatoes work? I drained the sugar syrup from a can of sweet potatoes (commonly labeled as yams) and cooked them with the canned pumpkin. Once again, my tasters loved the pie and never guessed the true source of the flavor.

With richly flavored filling at hand, it was time to tackle the texture. My goal was to eliminate the graininess that plagues most custard for a creamy, sliceable, not-too-dense pie. To achieve this, I first played with the type of dairy and quantity of eggs. Whole milk yielded a looser pie than one made with cream, but tasters found the latter too rich. Using equal amounts of whole milk and cream provided balance. But this filling was barely sliceable, and using extra whole eggs to firm it up just made the pie taste too eggy. Since the white contains most of the water in an egg, I replaced a few of the whole eggs with yolks to firm up the custard, settling on a ratio of three whole eggs to two yolks. I then whisked the milk, cream, and eggs with some vanilla into the cooked pumpkin–sweet potato mixture and passed the filling through a fine-mesh strainer to remove any stringy bits, ensuring a smooth texture.

Most pumpkin pie recipes call for a high oven temperature (425 degrees) to expedite cooking time. But once the temperature of custard rises above 175 degrees it curdles, turning the filling coarse and grainy. Lowering the temperature to 350 degrees wasn't the solution: I now had a pie that curdled and overcooked at the outer edges but was still underdone in the center. I tried the opposite extreme—baking the pie at 300 degrees, a temperature that would give me a wide margin of safety—but it took two hours. What if I combined both approaches: a high initial oven temperature to give the already-warm filling a blast of heat, followed by a gentle 300 degrees for the remainder of the baking time? Not only did the dual temperatures reduce the total baking time to less than an hour, but they produced a creamy pie fully and evenly cooked from edge to center.

PUMPKIN PIE

Months of testing and hundreds of pies later, I had finally created a pumpkin pie destined to be a new classic: velvety smooth, packed with pumpkin flavor, and redolent of just enough fragrant spices. This year I'll see if anyone can turn down a slice—even after the heavy meal.

—FRANCISCO J. ROBERT, *Cook's Illustrated*

Pumpkin Pie

MAKES ONE 9-INCH PIE

We prefer ceramic or metal pie weights for prebaking the pie shell. If you don't own any weights, rice or dried beans can stand in, but since they're lighter than pie weights, be sure to fill up the foil-lined pie shell completely. If candied yams are unavailable, regular canned yams can be substituted. The pie finishes cooking with residual heat; to ensure that the filling sets, cool it at room temperature and not in the refrigerator. To ensure accurate cooking times and a crisp crust, the filling should be added to the prebaked crust when both the crust and filling are warm. Serve at room temperature with whipped cream.

1 recipe Foolproof Single-Crust Pie Dough (page 249)
1 cup heavy cream
1 cup whole milk
3 large eggs plus 2 large yolks
1 teaspoon vanilla extract
1 (15-ounce) can pumpkin puree
1 cup drained candied yams from 15-ounce can (see note)
¾ cup sugar
¼ cup maple syrup
2 teaspoons grated fresh ginger
½ teaspoon ground cinnamon
¼ teaspoon ground nutmeg
1 teaspoon salt

1. Adjust an oven rack to lowest position, place a foil-lined rimmed baking sheet on the rack, and heat the oven to 400 degrees. Remove the dough from the refrigerator and let stand at room temperature for 15 minutes. Roll the dough out on a generously floured (up to ¼ cup) counter to a 12-inch circle, about ⅛ inch thick. Roll the dough loosely around the rolling pin and unroll into a 9-inch pie plate, leaving at least a 1-inch overhang. Ease the dough into the plate by gently lifting the edge of the dough with one hand while pressing into the plate bottom with the other hand. Leave any dough that overhangs the plate in place.

2. Trim the overhang to ½ inch beyond the lip of the pie plate. Fold the overhang under itself; the folded edge should be flush with the edge of the pie plate. Using your thumb and forefinger, flute the edge of the dough. Cover with plastic wrap and refrigerate until firm, about 30 minutes.

3. Remove the pie plate from the refrigerator, line the crust with heavy-duty foil, folding the excess foil over the edges of the pan, and fill with pie weights (see note). Bake on the rimmed baking sheet for 15 minutes. Carefully remove the foil and weights, rotate the baking sheet, and bake until the crust is golden brown and crisp, 5 to 10 additional minutes. Remove the pie plate and baking sheet from the oven.

4. While the pie shell is baking, whisk the cream, milk, eggs, yolks, and vanilla together in a medium bowl. Set aside. Combine the pumpkin puree, yams, sugar, syrup, ginger, cinnamon, nutmeg, and salt in a large heavy-bottomed saucepan; bring to a sputtering simmer over medium heat, 5 to 7 minutes. Continue to simmer the pumpkin mixture, stirring constantly and mashing the yams against the sides of the pot, until thick and shiny, 10 to 15 minutes.

5. Remove the pan from the heat and whisk in the cream mixture until fully incorporated. Strain the mixture through a fine-mesh strainer set over a medium bowl, using the back of a ladle or spatula to press the solids through the strainer. Rewhisk the mixture and transfer to the warm pie shell. Return the pie plate with the baking sheet to the oven and bake the pie for 10 minutes. Reduce the heat to 300 degrees and continue baking until the edges of the pie are set and the center registers 175 degrees on an instant-read thermometer, 20 to 35 minutes longer (the center should look firm but jiggle slightly). Transfer the pie to a wire rack and cool to room temperature, 2 to 3 hours. Cut into wedges and serve.

EMERGENCY CHOCOLATE CAKE

WHEN INGREDIENTS LIKE BUTTER and fresh eggs were scarce during World War II, cooks came up with cakes that worked without them. Homemakers found these wartime recipes so convenient (the cakes could be whipped up with ingredients on hand), they continued to bake them long after rationing was over. I recently came across a classic from this era in a collection of family recipes: my grandmother's Emergency Chocolate Cake. Of course I had to try it. The recipe called for water and ingredients straight from the pantry: flour, sugar, cocoa powder, baking soda, vanilla, and the real kicker—mayonnaise, a stand-in for butter and eggs.

I followed her instructions, mixing the water with the mayonnaise, combining this liquid with the dry ingredients, pouring the batter into an 8-inch square pan, and then baking the whole thing at 350 degrees. The dark, shiny cake I took out of the oven a half hour later was remarkably moist and tender, with no trace of a mayonnaise taste. But a dessert this easy had to have at least one hitch, and it did: The chocolate flavor, while decent, was far from decadent. I didn't want to turn this snack cake into a pan of brownies, but if I did a little tinkering, could I ramp up the chocolate flavor enough to take the cake from good to great?

Increasing the cocoa powder was an obvious first step, and I quickly discovered that my grandmother knew what she was doing when she arrived at ½ cup. Cocoa powder is composed mainly of cocoa solids; any more than that turned the cake dry and chalky. Good-quality bar chocolate has deeper flavor than cocoa powder, but swapping one for the other wasn't a solution, either. Solid chocolate contains lots of cocoa butter. To get the intense flavor I wanted, I needed to use so much that the cake became greasy and soft. I got the best results supplementing the cocoa powder with 2 ounces of melted bittersweet chocolate. But before I was done with the chocolate, I had a trick I wanted to try: In other recipes calling for cocoa powder, we've intensified its flavor by "blooming" it in hot water first. Cocoa powder contains solid particles of fat and protein with tiny flavor molecules trapped inside. The hot water causes these flavor molecules, which would otherwise remain imprisoned, to burst forth, amplifying overall flavor.

These measures helped, but could I take things further? We've also had success getting deeper chocolate flavor by combining chocolate with coffee. Instead of blooming the cocoa in hot water, I used a hot cup of coffee to great effect: The chocolate flavor became richer with coffee as a silent partner. I also found that if the dark chocolate was chopped fine enough, I could add it to the cocoa to melt while the cocoa was blooming—no need to melt it separately.

Now it was time to think about the oddball ingredient in the mix: mayonnaise. I wondered if I could make my cake richer by replacing the mayo with eggs and butter or even eggs and oil. I made two more cakes: one with melted butter and an egg and one with vegetable oil and an egg. While perfectly fine specimens, these cakes weren't quite as moist and velvety as the mayonnaise version. How could this be? Research revealed that oil, butter, and mayo each interact a little differently with flour. While all three coat the protein particles and reduce gluten development, creating a tender crumb, commercially prepared mayonnaise contains lecithin, an emulsifier that helps keep the oil in mayonnaise suspended in microdroplets. These small droplets greatly aid the oil's ability to coat the flour's protein particles, leading to a supremely tender cake.

While butter and oil were out, the egg was a keeper, contributing a richer flavor and springier texture. With only a little more work, I now had a super-easy cake with such velvety texture and deep chocolate flavor that it was good enough for special occasions as well as emergencies.

—KEITH DRESSER, *Cook's Illustrated*

Emergency Chocolate Cake

MAKES ONE 8-INCH SQUARE CAKE

Instead of confectioners' sugar, the cake can also be served with sweetened whipped cream.

- 1½ cups (7½ ounces) unbleached all-purpose flour
- 1 cup (7 ounces) sugar
- ½ teaspoon baking soda
- ¼ teaspoon salt
- ½ cup Dutch-processed cocoa powder
- 2 ounces bittersweet chocolate, chopped fine
- 1 cup hot coffee
- ⅔ cup mayonnaise
- 1 large egg
- 2 teaspoons vanilla extract
  Confectioners' sugar, for serving (optional) (see note)

1. Adjust an oven rack to the middle position and heat the oven to 350 degrees. Lightly spray an 8-inch square baking dish with vegetable oil spray.

2. Whisk the flour, sugar, baking soda, and salt together in a large bowl. In a separate bowl, combine the cocoa and chocolate; pour the hot coffee over the cocoa mixture and whisk until smooth; let cool slightly. Whisk in the mayonnaise, egg, and vanilla. Stir the mayonnaise mixture into the flour mixture until combined.

3. Scrape the batter into the prepared pan and smooth the top. Bake until a wooden skewer inserted into the center of the cake comes out with few crumbs attached, 30 to 35 minutes.

4. Let the cake cool in the pan on a wire rack, 1 to 2 hours. Dust with confectioners' sugar (if using), cut into squares, and serve straight from the pan; or turn the cake out onto a platter and dust with confectioners' sugar (if using).

NOTES FROM THE TEST KITCHEN

DOES VANILLA EXTRACT GO BAD?
Some people bake enough cookies and cakes to blow through a whole bottle of vanilla extract in just a month, while less enthusiastic bakers may keep the same bottle for years. Does vanilla extract ever go bad or lose potency? We located 3-year-old and 10-year-old bottles of vanilla extract and compared them with a fresh bottle of the same brand in cupcakes, vanilla frosting, and chocolate chip cookies. Although the older bottles took a bit of effort to open, once the extract was incorporated into recipes, tasters could detect no difference between the old and the new. Vanilla extract has a minimum alcohol content of 35 percent, which, according to Matt Nielsen of vanilla manufacturer Nielsen-Massey, makes it the most shelf-stable form of vanilla. It will last indefinitely if stored in a sealed container away from heat and light.

OUR FAVORITE DARK CHOCOLATES
We've tasted, and baked with, lots of chocolate that falls into the "gourmet" category, and although many brands have distinctive flavors that tasters liked in particular desserts, two chocolates consistently produce great results in a variety of baked goods— **Callebaut Intense Dark Chocolate L-60-40NV** and **Ghirardelli Bittersweet Chocolate Baking Bar.** We liked them better than more expensive dark chocolates, and both are widely available.

BOLD AND SPICY GINGERBREAD CAKE

TRADITIONAL GINGERBREAD CAKE IS EASY TO MAKE. Most recipes combine butter, sugar, eggs, flour, leavener, warm spices, molasses, and water; pour the batter into a square pan and bake. But the recipes I tried produced cakes that were dry and far too sweet, with unbalanced spicing dominated by the dusty burn of powdered ginger. Without unduly complicating the recipe, I wanted to turn this neglected cake into a moist, boldly flavored yet balanced cake.

The first thing to go was the square baking pan; for more substantial slices, I decided to bake my gingerbread in a Bundt pan. I found that 2½ cups flour, 16 tablespoons butter, and 4 eggs filled the pan nicely. Creaming the butter and sugar in a mixer made the cake a little too light and fluffy. Searching for a denser, moister texture, I tried a dump-and-stir mixing method that replaced the butter with an equal volume of vegetable oil, but that made for a greasy cake that lacked richness. I tried the same method using melted butter, which proved the best path to a moist, dense, rich cake.

The standard liquid combination of mild molasses and water seemed lackluster, so I switched to robust molasses. In place of water, I tried milk and buttermilk; both were fine but didn't add much. I tested unexpected liquids like coffee (too bitter) and orange juice (too sour) before I remembered a recipe I'd seen that used stout. I stirred the beer in and was shocked that it gave the cake a deep malty tang that my tasters loved.

Powdered ginger gave the cake some bite, and a little cinnamon and allspice supported the ginger flavor nicely. A surprising ingredient, black pepper, helped draw out even more of the ginger's pleasing burn.

Ground spices used in large quantities gave the cake a dusty texture. Rather than increasing amounts to promote flavor, I tried cooking the spices in melted butter, a technique we use in the test kitchen for savory spiced dishes like curry and chili. The flavors bloomed (and any dusty feel was gone), but tasters still wanted more ginger. Maybe old-fashioned recipes were stuck with just powdered ginger; I went to the real McCoy and found that grated fresh ginger added an unmistakable element that the dried spices couldn't muster.

With a glaze of confectioners' sugar and ginger ale, I'd finally managed to put the ginger back in gingerbread.

—ERIKA BRUCE, *Cook's Country*

BOLD AND SPICY GINGERBREAD CAKE

Bold and Spicy Gingerbread Cake

SERVES 12

Guinness is the test kitchen's favorite brand of stout. An equal amount of orange or lemon juice can be substituted for the ginger ale in the glaze. Be sure to use finely ground black pepper here.

CAKE

- 2½ cups (12½ ounces) unbleached all-purpose flour
- 2 teaspoons baking powder
- ¾ teaspoon baking soda
- ¾ teaspoon salt
- 16 tablespoons (2 sticks) unsalted butter
- 2 tablespoons ground ginger
- 2 teaspoons ground cinnamon
- 1 teaspoon ground allspice
- ¼ teaspoon pepper (see note)
- 4 large eggs, at room temperature
- 1½ cups (10½ ounces) sugar
- 4 teaspoons grated or minced fresh ginger
- ¾ cup robust or dark molasses
- ¾ cup stout beer (see note)

GLAZE

- 1¾ cups (7 ounces) confectioners' sugar
- 3 tablespoons ginger ale (see note)
- 1 teaspoon ground ginger

1. FOR THE CAKE: Adjust an oven rack to the middle position and heat the oven to 375 degrees. Grease and flour a 12-cup nonstick Bundt pan. Whisk the flour, baking powder, baking soda, and salt in a large bowl. Melt the butter in a saucepan over medium heat until bubbling. Stir in the ground ginger, cinnamon, allspice, and pepper and cook until fragrant, about 30 seconds. Remove from the heat and let cool slightly.

2. Whisk the eggs, sugar, and fresh ginger in a large bowl until light and frothy. Stir in the melted butter mixture, molasses, and beer until incorporated. Whisk the flour mixture into the egg mixture until no lumps remain.

3. Pour the batter into the prepared pan and gently tap the pan on the countertop to release any trapped air bubbles. Bake until a toothpick inserted into the center comes out clean, about 45 minutes. Cool the cake in the pan for 20 minutes, then turn it out onto a wire rack set inside a rimmed baking sheet; let cool completely.

4. FOR THE GLAZE: Whisk the ingredients in a bowl until smooth. Pour the glaze over the cooled cake. Let the glaze set for 15 minutes. Serve. (The cake can be stored at room temperature, covered in plastic wrap, for up to 2 days.)

NOTES FROM THE TEST KITCHEN

GINGERBREAD WITH A KICK
Once spicy and bold, gingerbread has become sweet and bland over time. Here's how we breathed new life into a tired recipe.

Ground and fresh ginger in the cake and ginger ale in the glaze ensure a strong ginger presence.

Robust molasses and stout add richness and a bitter edge that balance the spicy ginger.

EASY CARAMEL CAKE

I LOVE THE RICH, TOFFEE-FLAVORED FROSTING on a caramel cake. Spread over yellow cake layers, this unique frosting starts out creamy but quickly firms up to a fudgelike consistency. The exterior of the frosting develops a thin, crystalline crust while the frosting closest to the cake remains silky and smooth.

While the appeal of this Southern specialty is clear, it's easy to understand why few bakers make it, even in the South. Caramel frosting is notoriously tricky. Traditional recipes call for cooking granulated sugar (sometimes with water) in a saucepan until dark amber, carefully adding cream while it violently sputters, then beating in butter and confectioners' sugar. Some recipes shortcut the process by starting with brown sugar, but you generally still need a candy thermometer to recognize when the caramel has reached the "soft ball" stage. If these challenges aren't enough, the frosting can harden at lightning speed. My goal was an easier, foolproof caramel icing that would stay creamy

EASY CARAMEL CAKE

long enough to frost a two-layer cake—without racing the clock.

I first needed a sturdy cake with enough flavor to stand up to the sweet frosting. I started with the test kitchen's recipe for classic yellow cake, which relies on the "reverse creaming" mixing method. Standard creaming beats butter and sugar until fluffy, then alternately adds the wet and dry ingredients. The result is a tender, fluffy cake. Reverse creaming beats the butter (followed by dairy) into the dry ingredients. Less air is beaten into the batter, and the crumb is finer and less fluffy.

Tests confirmed that reverse creaming produced a somewhat sturdier cake better suited to caramel frosting. Switching from cake flour to higher-protein all-purpose flour gave the cake yet more structure to handle the heavy frosting. To temper the cake's sweetness, I tried cutting back on the 1½ cups of sugar, but even a slight reduction made the cake dry. I had better luck replacing the milk with tangy buttermilk.

I researched "easy" caramel frostings made with brown sugar. The most promising recipe cooked 2 cups brown sugar, 12 tablespoons butter, and ½ cup heavy cream over medium heat; when bubbles formed around the perimeter of the saucepan, the mixture was transferred to a mixer to beat in confectioners' sugar. This method was easy, but because the brown sugar was cooking in so much liquid, it never developed enough caramelized flavor. For my next test I simmered just the sugar and butter before adding the cream; now the flavor of caramel was unmistakable.

But the icing still stiffened before I finished frosting the cake. Upping the amount of butter kept the mixture soft for longer, but it also made the frosting greasy. Thinking of how creamy buttercream frostings

NOTES FROM THE TEST KITCHEN

CARAMEL MADE EASY

Our foolproof caramel uses brown sugar and a simple visual cue—a ring of bubbles around the perimeter of the pan—to signal when it's time to add the cream and, later, to remove the mixture from the heat.

whip softened butter with confectioners' sugar, I tried beating a little softened butter into the finished frosting. This frosting was rich and silky, and the fat from the butter kept the frosting soft and spreadable for a few precious extra minutes. The best part? The signature of a Southern caramel cake, the crystalline crust, formed in about 30 minutes.

—CALI RICH, *Cook's Country*

Easy Caramel Cake
SERVES 8

In step 5, the cooled frosting stays soft and spreadable longer than other recipes, but it will harden over time. If the frosting does begin to stiffen, you can microwave it for about 10 seconds (or until it returns to a spreadable consistency).

CAKE
- ½ cup buttermilk, at room temperature
- 4 large eggs, at room temperature
- 2 teaspoons vanilla extract
- 2¼ cups (11¼ ounces) unbleached all-purpose flour
- 1½ cups (10½ ounces) granulated sugar
- 1½ teaspoons baking powder
- ½ teaspoon baking soda
- ¾ teaspoon salt
- 16 tablespoons (2 sticks) unsalted butter, cut into 16 pieces and softened

FROSTING
- 12 tablespoons (1½ sticks) unsalted butter, cut into 12 pieces and softened
- 2 cups packed (14 ounces) dark brown sugar
- ½ teaspoon salt
- ½ cup heavy cream
- 1 teaspoon vanilla extract
- 2½ cups (10 ounces) confectioners' sugar, sifted

1. FOR THE CAKE: Adjust an oven rack to the middle position and heat the oven to 350 degrees. Grease and flour two 9-inch round cake pans. Whisk the buttermilk, eggs, and vanilla in a large measuring cup. In a large bowl, mix the flour, granulated sugar, baking powder, baking soda, and salt with an electric mixer on low speed until combined. Beat in the butter, 1 piece at a time, until only pea-sized pieces remain. Pour in half of the buttermilk mixture and beat at medium-high speed until light and fluffy, about 1 minute. Slowly add the remaining buttermilk mixture to the bowl and beat until incorporated, about 15 seconds.

2. Scrape equal amounts of batter into the prepared pans and bake until golden and a toothpick inserted in the center comes out clean, 20 to 25 minutes. Cool the cakes in the pans for 10 minutes, then turn out onto wire racks. Let cool completely, at least 1 hour.

3. FOR THE FROSTING: Heat 8 tablespoons of the butter, brown sugar, and salt in a large saucepan over medium heat until small bubbles appear around the perimeter of the pan (see page 262), 4 to 8 minutes. Whisk in the cream and cook until a ring of bubbles reappears, about 1 minute. Off the heat, whisk in the vanilla.

4. Transfer the hot frosting mixture to a bowl and, with an electric mixer on low speed, gradually mix in the confectioners' sugar until incorporated. Increase the speed to medium and beat until the frosting is pale brown and just warm, about 5 minutes. Add the remaining 4 tablespoons butter, 1 piece at a time, and beat until light and fluffy, about 2 minutes.

5. TO ASSEMBLE: Place 1 cake round on a platter. Spread ¾ cup of the frosting over the cake, then top with the second cake round. Spread the remaining frosting evenly over the top and sides of the cake. Serve.

7UP POUND CAKE

IN THE EARLY 1950S, soda companies began marketing their products as more than mere drink, urging consumers to think of soda as a pantry staple. For one such effort, an advertising campaign to "get some extra 7UP for cooking," the company distributed free promotional recipe booklets that touted dishes like 7UP salad (blend lime Jell-O, applesauce, and soda) and 7UP parfait pie (add the soda to both ice cream filling and crust). Over the years, most of these recipes have (mercifully) been forgotten. But 7UP pound cake remains a treasured favorite. The effervescent, slightly acidic soda gives this cake its flavor, lift, and uniquely tender texture.

Except for the 7UP, the recipes I found for 7UP pound cake mirror traditional pound cake in both method and ingredients: Sugar and softened butter (or shortening) are beaten together until light and fluffy. Eggs are added, followed by 7UP and lemon extract or zest. The flour is mixed in until just combined, and the batter is poured into a tube pan and baked at a moderate temperature (to prevent overbrowning) for a little over an hour. While traditional pound cakes can be dense, the 7UP version emerged with a tight yet light crumb, thanks to the soda's citric acid (which tenderizes) and carbonated water (which lifts).

Unfortunately, the flavor didn't wow me as much as the texture. The cake made with extract tasted like I'd dusted it with furniture polish, while the sugar (a generous 3 cups) overwhelmed the citrus flavor of those made with zest. Also, every last recipe omitted lime altogether—surprising, given 7UP's hallmark lemon-lime combination.

Working from a recipe that fortified the 7UP cake with zest, I began scaling back the sugar to bring out some citrus zing. Eventually, I achieved balanced sweetness by cutting out ½ cup of sugar. But the flavor of the cake remained flat. Unlike juice, finely grated zest can be added without affecting texture, so I added increasing amounts of both lemon and lime zest until I'd topped off at 1 tablespoon of each. The zest lent a fragrant quality, but the cake still lacked conviction. Realizing I'd need to add fresh (highly acidic) lemon and lime juice despite the troubles they might cause, I gradually added each until I'd settled on ¼ cup between the two in place of an equal amount of 7UP. Now the cake tasted great, but, as I'd feared, the texture had taken a turn for the worse. A perfect pound cake hinges on a fragile emulsion of butter and eggs. The extra acid (from the juice) was causing the batter to curdle, resulting in a tough, gummy cake.

The test kitchen has had success using melted butter in acidic cake batters. While softened butter provides an uneven coating that exposes the batter to the structure-wrecking acid, melted butter readily coats and therefore protects the gluten. To put this to the test, I simply melted the butter and, using a technique the test kitchen has liked in the past, pulled out the food processor. (The brawn of the machine ensures the emulsification.) Once the sugar and wet ingredients were combined, I slowly poured the melted butter down the feed tube. I stirred in the flour, baked and cooled the cake, then helped myself to a slice. This big, buttery cake had a fine, even crumb plus a forceful lemon-lime flavor that warranted the 7UP name.

—CALI RICH, *Cook's Country*

7UP POUND CAKE

7UP Pound Cake

SERVES 12

Fresh, not flat, 7UP is essential for the best texture and rise. You can also bake the cake in a 12-cup nonstick Bundt pan.

CAKE

- 2½ cups (17½ ounces) granulated sugar
- 5 large eggs, at room temperature
- ½ cup 7UP, at room temperature (see note)
- 1 tablespoon grated lemon zest plus 2 tablespoons fresh lemon juice
- 1 tablespoon grated lime zest plus 2 tablespoons fresh lime juice
- ½ teaspoon salt
- 20 tablespoons (2½ sticks) unsalted butter, melted and cooled slightly
- 3¼ cups (13 ounces) cake flour

GLAZE

- 1 cup (4 ounces) confectioners' sugar
- 1 tablespoon fresh lemon juice
- 1 tablespoon fresh lime juice

1. FOR THE CAKE: Adjust an oven rack to the lower-middle position and heat the oven to 300 degrees. Grease and flour a 12-cup nonstick tube pan. Process the granulated sugar, eggs, 7UP, lemon zest and juice, lime zest and juice, and salt in a food processor until smooth, about 10 seconds. With the machine running, slowly pour in the butter and process until incorporated. Transfer to a large bowl. Add the flour in three additions, whisking until combined.

2. Spread the batter in the prepared pan. Gently tap the pan on the counter to release any trapped air bubbles. Bake until a toothpick inserted in the center comes out clean, 75 to 90 minutes. Cool the cake in the pan for 10 minutes, then turn it out onto a wire rack set inside a rimmed baking sheet to cool completely, about 2 hours.

3. FOR THE GLAZE: Whisk the ingredients together in a bowl until smooth. Pour the glaze over the cooled cake. Let the glaze set for 10 minutes. Serve. (The cake can be covered in plastic wrap and stored at room temperature for up to 3 days.)

NOTES FROM THE TEST KITCHEN

DOES IT HAVE TO BE 7UP?
Curious if other clear sodas could stand in for 7UP, we compared cakes made with Sprite, Fresca, Mountain Dew, and ginger ale with one using 7UP. The 7UP cake was indistinguishable from all but one—the Fresca cake, which was pale and tough. Blame it on the artificial sweeteners, and be sure to avoid Diet 7UP for the same reason.

THE ORIGINAL, BUT NOT THE ONLY SODA FOR THE JOB

SKILLET LEMON SOUFFLÉ

WHILE SOUFFLÉS CAN BE FINICKY AND FUSSY, they are not nearly as daunting as people think. And, for the chef, it is a rewarding exercise; serving a soufflé for dessert guarantees complete admiration from fellow diners, since the soufflé's airy, foamy texture is in a realm all its own. I wondered if I could simplify soufflé by making it in a skillet. I hypothesized that the skillet would help make a soufflé foolproof, because I could utilize heat from the stovetop to activate the batter and ensure a tall, sturdy rise from the egg whites, instead of baking the batter for almost half an hour, as many recipes do.

In classical French cooking, soufflés are made with either a béchamel base (a classic French sauce made from butter, flour, and milk) or a bouillie base (a paste made from flour and milk) mixed in to help stabilize the whipped egg whites. But I thought I could eliminate the fussy step of making a béchamel or bouillie, and instead make a simpler base and utilize a skillet and the direct heat of the stovetop to cook and stabilize the egg whites in the batter. I pitted three skillet soufflés—one with béchamel, one with bouillie, and one with raw whipped egg yolks as the base—against one another to see if I was right. Lemon, a common dessert soufflé variation, was the flavor I wanted because the bright, citrus notes burst through the eggy base especially well.

Giving all three soufflés a head start on the stovetop, I found that my theory worked out just as I had hoped. Sure, the béchamel- and bouillie-based soufflés tasted fine, but the soufflé with a whipped egg yolk base was far easier to make—I didn't have to cook anything in advance—and boasted a cleaner, fresher lemon flavor. My theory confirmed, I began to tweak the ratio of soufflé batter ingredients in search of the ultimate skillet soufflé texture.

I started with the eggs, which give the soufflé its delicate and lofty texture, using a simple ingredient list—egg whites, egg yolks, and sugar. To determine the proper ratio of egg whites to egg yolks, I tried four variations, whipping whites and yolks separately, then folding the egg whites into the whipped yolk base. I found that too many egg whites resulted in a foamy but stiff soufflé. Eventually I hit on using an equal amount of yolks and whites—five of each—for a supremely rich and creamy soufflé.

The technique used to beat the egg whites is crucial to a successful soufflé—its structure comes solely from the aerated eggs. The objective is to create a strong, stable foam that rises well and doesn't collapse during either folding or baking. I knew that adding sugar to the whites during beating would result in stable whites that would be more resilient when it came time to fold them into the yolks, and the soufflé would be less apt to fall quickly after baking. I made sure my mixing bowl was clean—a bowl with even the tiniest speck of oil or dirt can prevent the whites from rising well—and began whipping my whites, adding sugar at various intervals. Most of the sugar, it turned out, should be added not at the outset of whipping but after the whites break up and become foamy. I also learned that the sugar must be added gradually; dumping in the sugar all at once produced a soufflé with an uneven, shorter rise and an overly sweet taste. Adding an acid (I used cream of tartar) to the whites as they were whipped also helped them build to a sturdy texture and retain their shape.

At this point, my soufflé was slightly foamier than I wanted. Having tinkered with the egg whites already, I looked to make a few adjustments to my whipped yolk base. I followed the lead of many classic soufflé recipes and added some flour. Two tablespoons turned our foamy soufflé creamy—exactly the texture I was looking for.

A good lemon soufflé should burst with bright, citrus flavors and not taste overly eggy. I wanted a clean, natural lemon flavor, so I added a mixture of fresh lemon juice and lemon zest. Starting out with a mere 2 tablespoons of juice and 1 teaspoon zest whipped in with the yolks, I felt that the lemon flavor was hardly present. More zest wasn't the answer, as increased amounts simply added an unwelcome bitter flavor. I upped the lemon juice to ⅓ cup; now I was happy with the lemony flavor and zing.

With the whites sturdily whipped and the egg yolk base brightly flavored, I folded the whites gently into the yolks. I poured the entire batter into a buttered skillet and let it cook for a couple minutes over medium-low heat until just set around the edges and on the bottom, setting up the base for the soufflé to rise in the oven. As a bonus, the direct heat on the bottom of the skillet gave the finished soufflé a great crust that tasters loved.

Almost there, I moved the soufflé into the oven to finish cooking. Although I had been using a 350-degree oven with decent success up to this point, I wondered if either a higher or a lower temperature would work even better. Lower oven temperatures produced heavy, dense soufflés, but a slightly higher temperature of 375 degrees produced a more dramatic rise and sharper contrast between the cooked exterior and the creamy interior.

I expected the soufflé to be done quickly and started checking on it after seven minutes—just one extra minute in the oven makes all the difference between a perfectly cooked soufflé and one that's overdone. Looking through the oven window, I saw that the top was lightly golden—just right. I dipped into the soufflé with a spoon and found it was perfectly lemony, creamy and moist in the middle, and firm around the outside—a skillet soufflé success.

—MEGAN WYCOFF, *America's Test Kitchen Books*

SKILLET LEMON SOUFFLÉ

Skillet Lemon Soufflé

SERVES 6

Don't open the oven door during the first 7 minutes of baking, but do check the soufflé regularly for doneness during the final few minutes in the oven. Be ready to serve the soufflé immediately after removing it from the oven. Using a 10-inch traditional (not nonstick) skillet is essential to getting the right texture and height for the soufflé.

5	large eggs, separated
¼	teaspoon cream of tartar
⅔	cup (4⅔ ounces) granulated sugar
⅛	teaspoon salt
1	teaspoon grated lemon zest plus ⅓ cup fresh lemon juice from 2 lemons
2	tablespoons unbleached all-purpose flour
1	tablespoon unsalted butter
	Confectioners' sugar, for dusting

1. Adjust an oven rack to the middle position and heat the oven to 375 degrees. In a large bowl, whip the egg whites and cream of tartar together with an electric mixer on medium-low speed until foamy, about 1 minute. Slowly add ⅓ cup of the granulated sugar and the salt, then increase the mixer speed to medium-high and continue to whip until stiff peaks form, 3 to 5 minutes. Gently transfer the whites to a clean bowl and set aside.

2. In the same bowl (no need to wash the bowl), whip the yolks and the remaining ⅓ cup sugar together on medium-high speed until pale and thick, about 1 minute. Whip in the lemon zest, juice, and flour until incorporated, about 30 seconds.

3. Fold one-quarter of the whipped egg whites into the yolk mixture until almost no white streaks remain. Gently fold in the remaining egg whites until just incorporated.

4. Melt the butter in a 10-inch ovensafe skillet over medium-low heat. Swirl the pan to coat it evenly with the melted butter, then gently scrape the soufflé batter into the skillet and cook until the edges begin to set and bubble slightly, about 2 minutes.

5. Transfer the skillet to the oven and bake the soufflé until puffed, the center jiggles slightly when shaken, and the surface is golden, 7 to 11 minutes. Using a potholder (the skillet handle will be hot), remove the skillet from the oven. Dust the soufflé with the confectioners' sugar and serve immediately.

VARIATION

Skillet Chocolate-Orange Soufflé

Grating the chocolate fine is key here; we find it easiest to use either a rasp grater or the fine holes of a box grater.

Follow the recipe for Skillet Lemon Soufflé, substituting 1 tablespoon grated zest from 1 orange for the lemon zest, and ⅓ cup orange juice for the lemon juice. Gently fold 1 ounce finely grated bittersweet chocolate (about ½ cup) into the soufflé batter after incorporating all of the whites in step 3.

NOTES FROM THE TEST KITCHEN

THE BEST RASP GRATER
To grate raw vegetables or big hunks of cheese, we rely on our sturdy, stand-up box grater. But for zesting a lemon or grating chocolate, we turn to the compact rasp grater. To find out which rasp grater performs best, we tested four models currently on the market. The one that came out on top was the **Microplane 8.5-Inch Grater/Zester,** $12.95. Shaped like a ruler, but with lots and lots of tiny, sharp teeth, the Microplane can grate cheese, zest, chocolate, and whole nutmegs smoothly and almost effortlessly. The black plastic handle, which we found more comfortable than any of the others, also earned high praise.

TRIPLE-CHOCOLATE MOUSSE CAKE

TRIPLE-CHOCOLATE MOUSSE CAKE is a cocoa-charged tower of dark, milk, and white chocolate that looks three times more decadent than a mere bowl of mousse ever could. But time and again I've sliced into this triumvirate only to be let down. Here's the problem: The triple layers don't add up to anything more interesting than the sum of their parts. Most times the texture is exactly the same from one layer to the next and so overpoweringly rich that I can barely finish more than a few forkfuls. To be worth the effort, this showy confection would need to be more than just a color study in chocolate. By finessing one layer at a time, I aimed to build a triple-decker that was incrementally lighter in texture—and richness—with each new tier.

"Mousse"—a French word meaning froth or foam—is a simple concoction, often combining nothing more than fruit puree or melted chocolate with sugar, whipped cream, and/or egg whites (though many also enrich the mixture with egg yolks and even butter). Once incorporated, tiny air bubbles from the whipped cream or beaten egg whites (or both) help develop its signature billowy texture, while chilling crystallizes the cocoa butter in the chocolate and the fat in the cream, enabling it to remain solid even at room temperature.

I would need a bottom layer that wasn't just solid but that also had the heft to support the upper two tiers. My plan was to start with a typical recipe and adjust from there: I gently cooked four yolks and a few tablespoons sugar until thick and custardy; whisked the mixture into 7 ounces of melted bittersweet chocolate; then folded in 2 cups of whipped heavy cream. As I might have predicted, even after hours of chilling, the resulting mousse was a little too soft and airy. Adding extra chocolate turned the dessert into a slab of truffle—way too rich, even for the bottom.

Rather than tinkering endlessly, I decided to reconsider the foundation and try an actual cake for my base. Both chocolate sponge cake and devil's food cake turned gummy and chewy in the fridge (where any base layer would necessarily sit for at least a few hours as the two mousse layers chilled—for simplicity's sake I wanted to build all three components, tier by tier, in the same pan). For a dense yet velvety texture, why not try flourless chocolate cake, which shares the same ingredients as mousse (butter, chocolate, eggs, and sugar) but gets cooked in the oven instead of on the stove? Just out of the oven, the cake fit the bill. But once again chilling interfered, turning this layer overly heavy and sludgy. Somehow the batter needed to be airier from the start.

Then it hit me: Why not just separate the eggs, whip the whites to soft peaks, then gently fold them into the batter—essentially transforming my flourless cake into a baked version of chocolate mousse? Fifteen minutes in the oven yielded a decadent (but not fudge-like) base. Espresso powder added complexity to the chocolate without announcing its presence, as did swapping out the white sugar for light brown sugar's hint of smoky molasses.

Moving on to the middle layer, I started with a basic dark chocolate mousse recipe—bittersweet chocolate, cocoa powder, and a splash of water. Texture-wise, this recipe was perfect, but its deep chocolate flavor was almost indistinguishable from the bottom layer. I tried substituting milk chocolate for the bittersweet chocolate. Bad call; the latter has fewer cocoa solids, which made the mousse too soft to slice. Next I tried reducing the chocolate, starting with the bittersweet bar. Halving the amount was too drastic, destroying texture and deadening flavor, but a minimal cutback—from 8 ounces to just 7—moderated richness without sacrificing structure. The eggs—a fat source—would have to go, too, but at the expense of the texture; now the mousse was too dense. To compensate, I upped the whipped cream from 1 cup to 1½ cups. Voila! My second tier was now light, chocolaty, and creamy—noticeably different than the über-rich base.

Finally, I made it to the top—and met another challenge. Ideally, this crowning mousse layer would be ethereally silky with a delicate chocolate sweetness, but lightening each consecutive layer while maintaining its structural integrity was getting harder. Plus, this layer would be white chocolate: sweet, milky, buttery, and a striking color contrast, but completely cocoa solid-free. After melting 6 ounces of white chocolate, I folded in whipped cream and layered it on top of the dark chocolate mousse. The texture was light and creamy, but it had a tendency to ooze during slicing. I tried increasing the chilling time, to no avail. Instead I turned to gelatin. One teaspoon stiffened the topping to a fault, but ¾ teaspoon was just right. The only accessorizing this crown needed was a few wispy curls of chocolate. My tasting panel agreed: This triple-decker rated a 10.

—YVONNE RUPERTI, *Cook's Illustrated*

Triple-Chocolate Mousse Cake

MAKES ONE 9½-INCH CAKE, SERVING 12 TO 16

This recipe requires a springform pan at least 3 inches high to fit all three layers. It is imperative that each layer be made in sequential order. Cool the base completely before topping with the middle layer. We recommend Ghirardelli Bittersweet Chocolate Baking Bar for the base and middle layers; our other recommended brand of chocolate, Callebaut Intense Dark L-60-40NV, may be used but will produce drier, slightly less sweet results. For best results, chill the mixer bowl before whipping the heavy cream. For neater slices, use a cheese wire (see page 271) or dip your knife into hot water before cutting each slice.

BASE LAYER

- 6 tablespoons (¾ stick) unsalted butter, cut into 6 pieces
- 7 ounces bittersweet chocolate, chopped fine (see note)
- ¾ teaspoon instant espresso powder
- 1½ teaspoons vanilla extract
- 4 large eggs, separated
  Pinch salt
- ⅓ cup packed (2½ ounces) light brown sugar

MIDDLE LAYER

- 2 tablespoons cocoa powder, preferably Dutch-processed
- 5 tablespoons hot water
- 7 ounces bittersweet chocolate, chopped fine (see note)
- 1½ cups cold heavy cream
- 1 tablespoon sugar
- ⅛ teaspoon salt

TOP LAYER

- ¾ teaspoon powdered gelatin
- 1 tablespoon water
- 6 ounces white chocolate, chopped fine
- 1½ cups cold heavy cream

  Shaved chocolate or cocoa powder for serving (optional) (see note)

1. FOR THE BASE LAYER: Adjust an oven rack to the middle position and heat the oven to 325 degrees. Grease the bottom and sides of 9½-inch springform pan. Melt the butter, chocolate, and espresso powder in a large heatproof bowl set over a saucepan filled with 1 inch of barely simmering water, stirring occasionally until smooth. Remove from the heat and cool the mixture slightly, about 5 minutes. Whisk in the vanilla and egg yolks; set aside.

2. In the clean bowl of a standing mixer fitted with the whisk attachment, beat the egg whites and salt at medium speed until frothy, about 30 seconds. Add half of the brown sugar and beat until combined, about 15 seconds. Add the remaining brown sugar and beat at high speed until soft peaks form when the whisk is lifted, about 1 minute longer, scraping down the sides halfway through. Using a whisk, fold one-third of the beaten egg whites into the chocolate mixture to lighten. Using a rubber spatula, fold in the remaining egg whites until no white streaks remain. Carefully transfer the batter to the prepared springform pan, gently smoothing the top with a spatula.

3. Bake until the cake has risen and is firm around the edges, and the center has just set but is still soft (the center of the cake will spring back after pressing gently with your finger), 13 to 18 minutes. Transfer the cake to a wire rack to cool completely, about 1 hour. (The cake will collapse as it cools.) Do not remove the cake from the pan.

4. FOR THE MIDDLE LAYER: Combine the cocoa powder and hot water in a small bowl; set aside. Melt the chocolate in a large heatproof bowl set over a saucepan filled with 1 inch of barely simmering water, stirring occasionally until smooth. Remove from the heat and cool slightly, 2 to 5 minutes.

5. In the clean bowl of a standing mixer fitted with the whisk attachment, whip the cream, sugar, and salt at medium speed until it begins to thicken, about 30 seconds. Increase the speed to high and whip until soft peaks form when the whisk is lifted, 15 to 60 seconds. Whisk the cocoa powder mixture into the melted chocolate until smooth. Using a whisk, fold one-third of the whipped cream into the chocolate mixture to lighten. Using a rubber spatula, fold in the remaining whipped cream until no white streaks remain. Spoon the mousse into the springform pan over the cooled cake and gently tap the pan on the counter 3 times to remove any large air bubbles; gently smooth the top with an offset spatula. Wipe the inside edge of the pan with a damp cloth to remove any drips. Refrigerate the cake at least 15 minutes while preparing the white chocolate mousse.

6. FOR THE TOP LAYER: In a small bowl, sprinkle the gelatin over the water; let stand at least 5 minutes. Place the white chocolate in a medium bowl. Bring ½ cup of the cream to a simmer in a small saucepan over medium-high heat. Remove from the heat; add the gelatin mixture and stir until fully dissolved. Pour the cream mixture over the chocolate and whisk until the chocolate is melted and the mixture is smooth, about 30 seconds. Cool to room temperature, stirring occasionally, 5 to 8 minutes (the mixture will thicken slightly).

7. In the clean bowl of a standing mixer fitted with the whisk attachment, whip the remaining 1 cup cream at medium speed until it begins to thicken, about 30 seconds. Increase the speed to high and whip until soft peaks form when the whisk is lifted, 15 to 60 seconds. Using a whisk, fold one-third of the whipped cream into the white chocolate mixture to lighten. Using a rubber spatula, fold the remaining whipped cream into the white chocolate mixture until no white streaks remain. Spoon the white chocolate mousse into the pan over the bittersweet chocolate mousse layer. Smooth the top with an offset spatula. Return the cake to the refrigerator and chill until set, at least 2½ hours. (The cake can be refrigerated up to 1 day; let it sit at room temperature for 45 minutes before releasing from the cake pan and serving.)

8. TO SERVE THE CAKE: Garnish the top of the cake with chocolate curls or dust with cocoa (if using). Run a thin knife between the cake and side of the springform pan; remove the side of the pan. Clean the knife and run it along the outside of the cake to smooth the sides. Cut into slices and serve.

NOTES FROM THE TEST KITCHEN

TRIPLE DECKER CONSTRUCTION

BOTTOM: BAKED MOUSSE
A baked mousse made with eggs, butter, dark chocolate, and sugar provided a sturdy— but not dense—base. The cake collapses as it cools.

MIDDLE: BITTERSWEET CHOCOLATE MOUSSE
This layer's silky yet sliceable consistency is the closest to regular mousse in texture, with chocolate flavor from dark bar chocolate and cocoa powder.

TOP: WHITE CHOCOLATE MOUSSE
Made with whipped cream and white chocolate, this layer is the lightest in flavor and texture. The addition of a little gelatin helps to make the topping sliceable.

OUR FAVORITE WHITE CHOCOLATE CHIPS

White chocolate isn't really chocolate at all. While it contains the cocoa butter of true chocolate, it lacks cocoa solids, the element responsible for milk and dark chocolate's characteristic brown color and nutty roasted flavor. Other pale confections labeled simply "white" chips or bars (these boast less than the 20 percent cocoa butter required to earn the designation "white chocolate") are just as common in the baking aisle of the supermarket. **Guittard Choc-Au-Lait White Chips** lack a high enough concentration of cocoa butter to qualify as true white chocolate, but impressed tasters with smooth texture, strong vanilla flavor, and mild sweetness, beating out four real white chocolates. Turns out a lesser amount of cocoa butter has its advantages: Fake whites boast a longer shelf life and were less finicky in cooking than the real white chocolate brands.

MAKING THE CUT

The thin yet sturdy wire of a cheese cutter does not drag against the delicate interior of our triple mousse cake, and it worked far better than a cake knife in creating precise slices.

TEST KITCHEN RESOURCES

Best Kitchen Quick Tips   274

Techniques Illustrated

Basic Vegetable Prep 101   278

Chef's Knife 101   280

Keeping Produce
Fresh 101   282

Mushrooms 101   284

Keeping Kitchen
Staples Fresh 101   286

Marinating 101   288

Tastings & Testings

Supermarket
Extra-Virgin Olive Oil   290

Black Peppercorns   291

Vanilla Extract   292

Maple and
Pancake Syrups   293

Chocolate Chips   294

Elbow Macaroni   295

Premium
Applewood Bacon   296

Microwave Popcorn   297

Boxed Brownie Mixes   298

Tastings & Testings (Cont.)

Hot Cocoa Mixes   299

Low-Fat
Strawberry Yogurt   300

Baked Beans   301

Automatic Drip
Coffee Makers   302

Traditional Skillets   303

Silicone Spatulas   304

Slicing Knives   305

Pie Plates   306

Plastic Wrap   307

Blenders   308

Cookware Sets   309

Safety Can Openers   310

Nonscratch Scrubbers   311

Paper Plates   312

Inexpensive
Four-Slice Toasters   313

Conversions & Equivalencies   314

BEST KITCHEN QUICK TIPS

HOMEMADE CLIP-ON THERMOMETER

Geoff Craig of Northport, N.Y., wanted to deep-fry a batch of donuts and couldn't find the clip for his thermometer to attach it to the side of the pot. Here's how he improvised.

1. Crumple a 12-inch sheet of aluminum foil into a rope. Wrap one end of the foil rope around the probe, directly under the face of the thermometer.

2. Add oil to the pan. Before heating it, secure the other end of the foil to the pot's handle so that the probe is stable and submerged at the desired level in the oil. (Make sure that the tip of the probe does not touch the bottom of the pot.)

MEAT MASH

While cooking ground beef and sausage for meat sauce, Jodi Comiskey of Chehalis, Wash., discovered that a whisk works better than a wooden spoon to break up the meat, especially leaner sausage, into evenly sized bits.

NEW USE FOR COOKIE CUTTERS

Finding herself without a roasting rack, Susan Chi of Lawrence, Kan., improvised by placing several open-style metal cookie cutters in the bottom of a roasting pan. She then placed the item to be roasted on the cutters, successfully suspending it above the bottom of the pan.

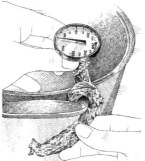

PREVENTING MICROWAVE SPLATTERS

Food often splatters when it is being heated in the microwave. Jane Weis of Elk Rapids, Mich., found that a basket-style coffee filter is ideal for covering food and keeping the walls of the microwave clean.

PLASTIC BAG STORAGE

Claudia Carrier of Sagle, Idaho, saves the cardboard tubes from paper towel rolls and stores plastic grocery bags inside them. She's amazed by how many she can squeeze into each tube, and the tube fits in a drawer so it is tucked away out of sight.

STRING STORAGE

To keep her kitchen twine clean, Deborah Tanaka of Richwood, Ohio, keeps the ball in a sealed, plastic pint-sized container—deli containers or clean cottage cheese tubs are perfect. She cuts a small "X" in the lid and threads the twine through, pulling out however much twine she needs for the job at hand. The container is easily wiped down and neatly stored.

TURKEY LEFTOVERS

Microwaving or reheating leftover turkey in the oven often dries it out. Elaine Parker of Edmonton, Alberta, Canada, found an ingenious way to keep the meat moist. Place slices of leftover turkey in a steamer basket set in a pot of simmering water, then cover the pot with a lid and check it every few minutes. The turkey heats up quickly and stays juicy.

HANDY TEMPERATURE GUIDE

Tired of fumbling through recipe books every time she cooked fish, meat, or poultry, Alice Pruce of Edmonds, Wash., created an index card with a list of final internal cooking temperatures. Enclosing the card in a zipper-lock bag keeps it clean, and storing the card with her digital thermometer allows her to reference it quickly.

NO MORE STACKING

Elaine Darrah of Merced, Calif., used to stack her baking dishes and skillets, but got tired of lifting them all out of the cupboard to get to the one she needed, which was inevitably on the bottom of the stack. Now she uses several metal bookends to hold the dishes and skillets upright, on their sides, in the cupboard. She can slide out the one she wants without having to move everything around.

CRISP STUFFING TOPS

Norma Wrenn of Abilene, Texas, has a family that prizes the crisp topping of baked stuffing. To please everyone at the table, she bakes individual portions of stuffing in muffin tins so that there is plenty of crispness to go around: The sides and top of each "muffin" become browned and crunchy. (A bonus: the baking time for the stuffing is also reduced.)

EXTRA-LARGE TRIVET

When roasts, casseroles, and cookies are parading out of her oven during the holidays, Adele Wilde of Las Vegas, Nev., always runs out of places to put hot pans. In a pinch, she uses an inverted, rimmed baking sheet as a makeshift trivet. Not only does it give her an extra landing zone for hot pans, it works especially well for large roasting pans or Dutch ovens.

KEEPING CHIVES IN CHECK

When prepping a bunch of chives, the slender herbs can roll all over the cutting board, making them difficult to chop. Angela Helman of Somerville, Mass., secures the chives with a rubber band to keep the leaves together.

MAKESHIFT PASTRY CUTTER

Arlene Stolley of Dallas, Texas, found herself in a bind when she was in the middle of preparing a pie dough recipe and realized it called for a pastry cutter, a tool she didn't own. With some creative thinking, she came up with the idea of using a stiff wire whisk as a substitute tool. By tilting the bowl and holding the whisk at an angle, she was able to cut the butter into the flour.

EGGSHELL MAGIC

Trying to remove small bits of stray yolk or eggshell from freshly cracked eggs can test the patience of any cook. Jennifer Mulder of Saratoga Springs, N.Y., solves the problem with the egg itself.

A. Dip an eggshell half into egg whites to scoop out bits of yolk. The eggshell acts as a magnet, attracting the wayward yolk.

B. An eggshell half can also be used to attract smaller pieces of eggshell that have fallen into cracked eggs.

KITCHEN RULES

Danielle Beauchesne of Southborough, Mass., purchased a plastic ruler just for the kitchen and keeps it in her utensil jar. It's handy for everyday kitchen tasks like measuring pie dough diameter, making sure you have the right size pan or cookie cutter, or preparing to cut ingredients to a certain size. It cleans up easily—she has even thrown it in her dishwasher!

RESCUING OVERWHIPPED CREAM

When whipping cream, it's always wise to pay careful attention so that the cream doesn't become too stiff. But if it's been whipped just a bit too much, Dartagnan Brown of Everett, Mass., has a trick to ensure all is not lost.

1. Add unwhipped cream into the overwhipped mixture 1 tablespoon at a time.

2. Gently fold the mixture, adding more unwhipped cream until the desired consistency is reached.

NO-SLIP MIXING

When using a handheld mixer to make cookies or cake, Livie Zuccaro of Westlake, Ohio, likes to keep one hand free for adding ingredients to the mixing bowl. She keeps the bowl from sliding around by placing it on a rubber shelf liner or silicone baking sheet liner. The mixing bowl sticks to the liner and keeps it stable.

BEST KITCHEN QUICK TIPS

STABILIZING A MIXING BOWL

When scooping cake frosting or cookie dough out of a bowl, Carly Anderson of New York, N.Y., finds that if the bowl is angled, it is much easier to dig into. To do this, she places the mixing bowl in a pot lined with a dish towel. The now-secure bowl can be tilted in any direction.

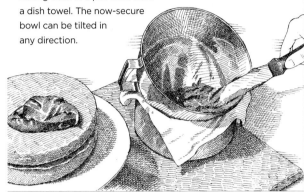

NOT JUST FOR MELON

Arthur Augustus of Fort Monmouth, N.J., hates kitchen tools that only have one use, so he's always looking for new ways to use different gadgets. A melon baller pulls double-duty by serving as a spoon for jarred olives and capers. Its small size allows him to reach into the narrow neck of the jars, and the hole in the bottom allows the juice to drain out with no effort.

GRATE GINGER TIP

To keep fresh ginger on hand, Marcia Entzel of George, Wash., purchases several large pieces at a time. She grates them ahead and measures teaspoon-sized mounds onto a baking sheet. She freezes the whole sheet until the ginger is firm and tosses all the premeasured mounds into a freezer zipper-lock bag. Keep the bag in the freezer and use the pre-grated ginger as needed.

NO MORE FRUIT FLIES

Many fruits, such as tomatoes and bananas, are best stored at room temperature. During the warmer months, however, fruit flies find ripening produce irresistible. Kendra Grady of Newburgh, N.Y., entices the pests with this trick. She places ¼ cup of orange juice in a small drinking glass and then tops it with a funnel. Placed next to a fruit bowl, the juice lures the tiny flies into the funnel, where they are unable to escape.

STEADIER ROLLING

When Meg Gallagher of Santa Monica, Calif., rolls out biscuit or pie dough between two sheets of parchment or wax paper, the bottom has a tendency to slide around. To prevent this, she wets the bottom sheet with a little bit of water—it sticks to the counter and keeps everything in place.

NO MORE STICKY HANDS

Washing your hands after working with sticky dough can be a difficult task. Aya Alt of Ithaca, N.Y., has a solution. She keeps a small bowl of cornmeal next to her work station. When she's ready to clean up, she rubs her hands in the cornmeal to help scrape off much of the dough before she goes to the sink.

VEGETABLE REVIVAL

To keep bagged salad greens or carrots from getting slimy, Kristen Sansoni of Pittsburgh, Pa., places a folded paper towel in the bag immediately after opening it. The paper towel absorbs the excess water and keeps the greens fresh and long lasting.

EXTRA DISH-DRYING SPACE

Yolanda Coroy of Houston, Texas, keeps her dish-drying rack underneath a cabinet. For those times when the rack is overflowing with dishes and utensils, she uses hooks attached to the underside of the cabinet. Extra wet items can be suspended from the hooks to drip dry.

SAUSAGE CASING SOLUTION

When eating hard sausage or salami, Janet Gilbert of Eugene, Ore., finds it a nuisance to peel off the sticky white casing from each individual slice. If the casing won't peel off the whole sausage easily before slicing, she uses a vegetable peeler to quickly remove the casing in advance.

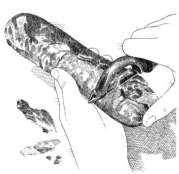

NEATER LEMON WEDGES

The thick strand of white pith along the center ridge of a lemon wedge can cause the juice to squirt out in all directions during squeezing.

1. For juice that lands in her teacup (and not in her eye), Lois Jacobson of Memphis, Tenn., uses a paring knife to remove the tough pith from wedges.

2. The resulting wedges will squeeze neatly into food and drinks.

EASIER ZESTING

Licia Jaccard of Culver City, Calif., found that when she zested fruit over her Microplane grater onto a cutting board, she couldn't see how much zest was accumulating. She decided to hold the fruit with her hand and run the zester over the fruit instead. This method allows the zest to collect in the grater's chute, neatly and in full view.

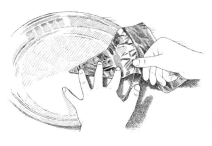

A PRETTIER PIECE OF PIE

Prying out the first piece of pie usually results in a broken, messy slice. Koji Nakanishi of New York, N.Y., offers a trick to make the first piece as pretty as the rest.

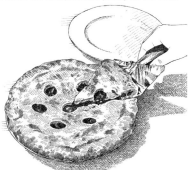

1. Fold a 12- by 12-inch sheet of foil in half, then in half again to make a 6-inch square. Fold this square diagonally to form a triangle. Press one point of the triangle into the center of the pie plate and let the other two points hang over the edge.

2. After baking and cooling, slice a piece of pie following the lines of the triangle. Pull up on the overhang and use a spatula to lift out the slice.

KEEPING SPONGES STRAIGHT

To avoid using the same sponge for washing dishes as for cleaning grimy countertops and kitchen surfaces, Dan Cully-Rapata of San Francisco, Calif., used to assign a different color sponge to each task. But packages of sponges always contain multiple colors, making it difficult to keep track. Now he has a better system: He snips off a corner from sponges that he intends to use for cleaning counters and stovetops, reserving uncut sponges for washing dishes.

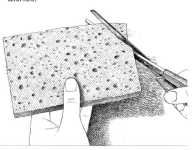

CORN FOR A CROWD

When James Montgomery of Chicago, Ill., needs to butter corn on the cob for a crowd, he melts butter in the empty pot that he used for boiling the corn. Then he returns the corn to the pot and tosses the ears with melted butter. The residual heat of the pot also keeps the corn warm while he finishes cooking the rest of the meal.

REMINDER TO TURN OFF THE GRILL

MaryAnn Grecco of El Paso, Texas, often found herself in a hot spot whenever she forgot to turn off the gas tank after grilling. She now jogs her memory by slipping a rubber band around the knob of the gas tank. When she turns the tank on, she places the rubber band around her wrist, only removing it when she turns the tank off. As long as she's wearing the rubber band, she knows that the tank is on.

BASIC VEGETABLE PREP 101

ONIONS

DICING AND MINCING

1. Using a chef's knife, halve the onion pole to pole. Lop off the tops of each half, leaving the root end intact, and peel the onion.

2. Make horizontal cuts, starting with the heel of the blade and carefully pulling the knife toward you, without cutting through the root end.

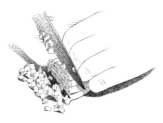

3. Using the tip of the knife, make several vertical cuts, dragging the knife toward you and making sure to keep the tip against the board.

4. Slice across the lengthwise cuts, using your knuckles as a guide for the knife while holding the onion with your fingertips.

STORING

DO store onions at cool room temperature and away from light.

DON'T store onions in the refrigerator, where their odors can permeate other foods.

WHAT'S THE YIELD?

MINCED GARLIC	
Small clove	½ tsp.
Medium clove	1 tsp.
Large clove	2 tsp.

CHOPPED ONION	
Small (2-inch diameter)	½ cup
Medium (2½- to 3-inch diameter)	1 cup
Large (4-inch diameter)	2 cups

MINCED SHALLOT	
Medium	3 Tbs.

CHOPPED LEEK	
Medium	1½ cups

CHOPPED CARROT/CELERY	
Medium	½ cup

GARLIC

BUYING

DO buy loose garlic; cellophane-wrapped boxes don't allow for close inspection.

DON'T buy heads that feel spongy or have skins where cloves used to reside. Also avoid garlic that smells fermented or unusually fragrant or has spots of mold—all signs of spoilage.

STORING

DO keep unpeeled garlic heads and cloves in a cool, dry, pantry space away from direct sunlight.

DON'T store garlic in the refrigerator. This causes it to soften and deteriorate far more quickly.

NEVER store raw garlic cloves in oil; this can result in botulism.

THE ONLY WAY TO SKIN A CLOVE

Forget trying to painstakingly peel skin off garlic. Crush the clove with the side of a chef's knife. The skin will loosen for easy removal.

PREPPING

DO remove any green sprout from the center of the clove. It contains strong-tasting compounds that can add bitterness to food.

DO use a garlic press to mince cloves. A good press can break down the cloves more finely and evenly (and far faster) than the average cook wielding a knife, which means better distribution of garlic flavor.

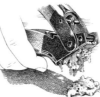

MAKE (GARLIC) PASTE

Here's an easy way to turn minced garlic into a smooth puree for applications such as aioli or pesto, where you want the garlic texture to be as unobtrusive as possible.

Sprinkle minced garlic with a coarse salt such as kosher. Repeatedly drag the side of a chef's knife over the mixture until all the garlic turns into a smooth paste.

KNOW YOUR CUTS

Minced	⅛-inch pieces or smaller
Chopped fine	⅛- to ¼-inch pieces
Chopped medium	¼- to ½-inch pieces
Chopped coarse	½- to ¾-inch pieces
Cut into chunks	¾-inch pieces or larger
Sliced	Cut into flat, thin pieces
Diced	Cut into uniform cubes
Cut on the bias	Cut at an angle

CARROTS

BUYING

DO look for sturdy, hard carrots—a sign of freshness.

DON'T buy extra-large carrots, which are often woody and bitter.

STORING

Store them in the crisper, wrapped in their original plastic bag or in a partially open plastic bag.

DICING

1. Remove a thin slice from one side of the carrot to form a flat edge.

2. Place the carrot on that edge and slice it lengthwise into strips.

3. Turn the strips 90 degrees and cut horizontally to complete the dice.

LEEKS

BUYING

DO buy leeks with sprightly, unblemished leaves and long white stems, as the white and light green parts are the only edible portions. The size of the leek has no impact on taste or texture.

DON'T buy leeks pretrimmed down to the lighter base—the purpose of this procedure is to trim away aging leaves and make old leeks look fresher.

STORING

Store leeks in a partially open plastic bag in your refrigerator's crisper.

WHEN TO USE

Turn to leeks in place of onions when you want a milder, sweeter flavor and a texture that turns tender and silky when cooked.

CLEANING

1. Trim and discard the roots and dark green leaves. Slice the trimmed leek in half lengthwise, then cut it into ¼-inch pieces.

2. Rinse the cut leeks thoroughly in a bowl of water to remove the dirt and sand.

TEST KITCHEN FAVORITES

Fast, precise slicing, chopping, and mincing begins with the right tools. Here are our test kitchen winners:

Chef's Knife: Victorinox Fibrox 8-Inch Chef's Knife ($24.95)

Paring Knife: Victorinox 4-Inch Paring Knife ($12.95)

Peeler: Messermeister Pro-Touch Swivel Peeler ($5.95)

Cutting Board: Totally Bamboo Congo Board ($49.99)

SHALLOTS

WHEN TO USE

Shallots have a more mild and delicate flavor than onions—a difference accentuated by cooking. A finely minced shallot will also melt away during cooking until its texture is all but indiscernible.

MINCING

1. Place the peeled shallot flat-side down and make closely spaced vertical cuts, leaving the root end intact.

2. Make 2 or 3 horizontal cuts.

3. Thinly slice the shallot crosswise, creating a fine mince.

CELERY

BUYING

DO look for tightly packed stalks.

DON'T buy bunches with brown spots or stalks that have begun to shrivel.

STORING

Store in the crisper in its original wrapping or a partially open plastic bag.

DICING

Slice a rib in half crosswise. Then, cut each half lengthwise into strips of equal width. Cut across the strips to form even dice.

CHEF'S KNIFE 101

ANATOMY OF A CHEF'S KNIFE

HANDLE

The knife handle helps balance the blade's weight. The handle should be comfortable and resist slipping, even when your hand is wet or greasy.

BLADE CURVE

A good chef's knife blade should have a long, gently sloping curve suited to the rocking motion of mincing and chopping.

BLADE MATERIAL

We prefer knives made with high-carbon stainless steel that, once sharpened, stay that way.

BLADE LENGTH

An 8-inch blade provides plenty of power without being unwieldy.

FORGED VS. STAMPED BLADES

Forged blades—made by hammering or forming a steel blade between dies—are weightier than stamped blades, which are punched out of steel. Both perform equally well. The blade above is stamped.

Test Kitchen Favorites

The inexpensive, lightweight **Victorinox Forschner Fibrox 8-Inch Chef's Knife** ($24.95; above, left) is a test kitchen favorite. We also like the **Glestain Indented-Blade 8.2-Inch Gyutou Chef's Knife** ($157.50) for its razor-sharp blade and double row of granton-style oval hollows to minimize resistance between blade and food.

BLADE MAINTENANCE

A KNIFE'S LIFE CYCLE

A sharp blade tapers down to a thin edge (below, left). However, even a few minutes of cutting can make that edge roll over (below, center) and cause the blade to feel slightly dull. A quick steeling will remove the folded edge and restore sharpness.

After the sharp angles become rounded and very dull (below, right), the knife needs a new edge, achievable only through true sharpening, not steeling.

VERY SHARP

SLIGHTLY DULL

VERY DULL

IS IT SHARP?

Hold a folded, but not creased, sheet of newspaper by one end. Lay the blade against the top edge at an angle and slice outward. If the knife fails to slice clearly, try steeling it. If it still fails, it needs sharpening.

WHEN TO USE A SHARPENING STEEL

A so-called sharpening steel, the metal rod sold with most knife sets, doesn't sharpen at all: It's a tune-up device. As you cut with a sharp knife, the edge of the blade can actually get knocked out of alignment. The knife may seem dull, but its edge is simply misaligned. Running the knife blade over the steel repositions that edge. But it can't reshape a blade that's rounded and worn down—that's when you need a sharpener.

MAKE IT SHARP

To reshape the edge of a dull knife, you have three choices: You can send it out, you can use a whetstone (tricky for anyone but a professional), or you can use an electric or manual sharpener.

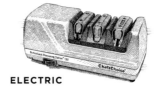 

ELECTRIC

MANUAL

DULL AND DANGEROUS

The duller the blade of a knife, the more force it takes to do the job—and the easier it is for the blade to slip and miss the mark, quickly sending the knife toward your hand. With a sharp knife, the blade does the work—and the razorlike edge is far less likely to slip. To protect your knife from dulling, avoid hard cutting surfaces such as glass or acrylic (stick with bamboo and plastic cutting boards) and keep it out of the dishwasher, where getting knocked around might damage its edge.

Test Kitchen Favorites

Our favorite electric model is the **Chef's Choice 130 Professional Sharpening Station** ($149.95) and our preferred manual tool is the **AccuSharp Knife and Tool Sharpener** ($10.99), a simple plastic hand-held device.

MAKING THE CUT

Different cuts make use of different parts of the blade. Here's how to utilize all parts of the blade safely and efficiently.

WHOLE BLADE

To make fast work of mincing fresh herbs, garlic, and the like, place one hand on the handle and rest the fingers of the other hand lightly on the knife tip. This lighter two-handed grip facilitates the up-and-down rocking motion needed for quick mincing. To make sure the food is evenly minced, pivot the knife as you chop.

TIP

We rarely use a cutting motion that brings the blade toward the body. However, when using the tip, drawing the knife inward is unavoidable.

1. Place the knife into the food with the tip facing slightly down. Pivot the blade so the tip slices through the ingredient and rests on the board.

2. Drag the knife toward you, making sure to keep the tip against the board as you pull.

MIDDLE

While using the blade's curve to guide the knife through a series of smooth cutting strokes, push the blade forward and down. If the food is small enough (e.g., celery or scallions), the tip of the blade should touch the cutting board at all times (below, left). However, for large ingredients such as eggplant or sweet potatoes, the tip of the blade should come off the board while making smooth cutting strokes through the ingredient (below, right).

HEEL

The heel is the sturdiest part of the blade, offering a flat cutting edge for hacking up chicken bones, or splitting winter squash. To apply a lot of force using the heel, hold the handle and place the flat palm of your other hand over the top of the blade (use a towel to cushion your hand) and cut straight down on the item. Use utmost caution and make sure your knife, hands, and cutting surface are completely dry (to avoid slippage).

SAFETY BASICS

STABILIZED FOR SAFETY

Knife work and wobbly ingredients don't mix. Halve round foods like onions to create a flat, stable side and place each half cut-side down before slicing or dicing. For narrow ingredients such as carrots, remove a thin sliver from one side to create a stable edge.

POSITIONED FOR PROTECTION

Prevent slippage, control cut size, and protect your fingers by curling the ingredient-holding hand.

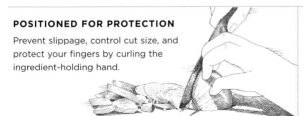

Tuck your fingertips away from the knife in a "bear claw" to hold the food in place, while the knuckles rest against the side of the blade, providing guidance while minimizing danger. During the upward motion of slicing, reposition your guiding hand for the next cut.

GET A GRIP

Most people tend to hold a chef's knife by keeping their fingers entirely on the handle (top). For added control, choke up on the knife, with the thumb and index finger actually gripping the heel of the blade (bottom).

LESS CONTROL

MORE CONTROL

KEEPING PRODUCE FRESH 101

Most people tend to treat all fruits and vegetables the same, fitting them wherever there's room in the fridge. The reality is, different types of produce have different storage requirements. Some need to be placed in the coldest part of the refrigerator, some need humidity, and some don't need to be chilled at all. Storing your produce under the appropriate conditions is the key to prolonging its shelf life.

REFRIGERATOR MICROCLIMATES

We often think of our refrigerator as having a single temperature: around 34 degrees Fahrenheit, the average temperature recommended for a home refrigerator. In fact, every refrigerator has its own microclimates, with warmer, cooler, and more humid zones. When we hooked up a special device to one of our refrigerators in the test kitchen to monitor temperatures in various locations, we found that temperature ranged from as low as 33 degrees to as high as 43.

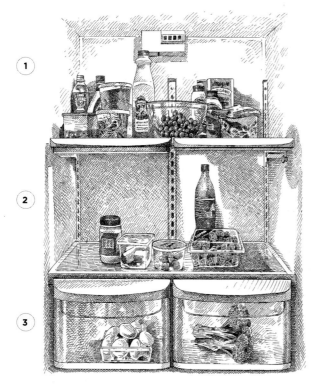

1. COLD ZONE: Back, Top to Middle
The top and middle shelves at the back of the fridge are normally the coldest, with temperatures that can dip below 34 degrees. Fruits and vegetables that are not prone to chill-injury should be stored here.

2. MODERATE ZONE: Front, Middle to Bottom
The areas at the front of our refrigerator, from the middle to the bottom shelves, were the most moderate, with temperatures above 37 degrees. Put fruits and vegetables that need refrigeration but are sensitive to chill-injury here.

3. HUMID ZONE: Crisper Drawer
Crispers provide a humid environment that helps keep produce with a high water content from shriveling and rotting. However, if the humidity is too high, water can build up on fruits and vegetables and hasten spoilage. You can regulate humidity by adjusting the vents.

WHERE TO STORE PRODUCE

KEEP IN THE FRONT OF THE FRIDGE
These items are sensitive to chill-injury and should be placed in the front of the fridge, where the temperatures tend to be higher.

Berries	Melons
Citrus	Peas
Corn on the cob	

BEST IN THE CRISPER
These items do best in the humid environment of the crisper.

Artichokes	Chiles	Mushrooms
Asparagus	Cucumbers	Peppers
Beets	Eggplant	Radishes
Broccoli	Fresh herbs	Scallions
Cabbage	Green beans	Summer squash
Carrots	Leafy greens	
Cauliflower	Leeks	Turnips
Celery	Lettuce	Zucchini

CHILL ANYWHERE
These items are not prone to chill-injury and can be stored anywhere in the fridge (including its coldest zones), provided the temperature doesn't freeze them.

Apples	Cherries	Grapes

ON THE COUNTER
Some produce is sensitive to chill-injury and is subject to dehydration, internal browning, and/or internal and external pitting if stored in the refrigerator.

Apricots	Mangos	Pears
Avocados*	Nectarines	Pineapple
Bananas	Papayas	Plums
Kiwis*	Peaches	Tomatoes

*Once they've reached their peak ripeness, these fruits can be stored in the refrigerator to prevent overripening, but some discoloration may occur.

IN THE PANTRY
The following produce should be kept at cool room temperature and away from light to prevent sprouting (in the case of potatoes) and to prolong shelf life.

Garlic	Shallots	Winter squash
Onions	Sweet potatoes	
Potatoes		

STORAGE TECHNIQUES

HERB KEEPER

The **Herb Keeper** ($12.99) is an acrylic canister that holds long-stemmed herbs upright in water. It has a rubber lid and a removable bottom piece that can be unscrewed to refill with fresh water every three to four days. Compared to storing herbs wrapped in a damp paper towel placed in a plastic bag, we found that the Herb Keeper added three to four days to an herb's life.

KEEPING CORN SWEET

The general rule with corn is to eat it the same day you buy it, as its sugars start converting to starches as soon as it is harvested, causing the corn to lose sweetness. Never refrigerate corn without wrapping it—and letting it sit on the counter is worse still.

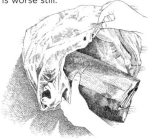

Wrap the unshucked corn in a wet paper bag to slow down the conversion from sugar to starch. Place the wet paper bag in a plastic bag and refrigerate.

STORAGE BASICS

ETHYLENE: ENEMY OF FRESHNESS

As produce ripens, it emits small amounts of the ripening hormone ethylene. If ethylene is allowed to build up, the gas will activate enzymes that break down and soften the cell walls of produce, speeding moisture loss and spoilage. Most storage techniques are designed to slow the production of ethylene or mitigate its impact.

When to Wash

With few exceptions, it's best to wash produce just before you use it. Moisture promotes the growth of mold, which in turn causes spoilage. If you do wash ahead of time, make sure to dry the produce thoroughly before storing.

It's a Wrap

In general, store produce in the packaging in which it was sold. Sometimes ready-made packaging has a function beyond simple convenience. For example, though they appear solid, the bags in which greens are now sold are made of a polymer that allows ripening gases to pass through freely, staving off spoilage. Other types of packaging often feature small perforations or other openings to allow gases to escape while also protecting the produce from the drying effects of air.

KEEPING LETTUCE CRISP

When lettuce comes in bags, store it in its original packaging. Store lettuce without packaging as follows.

1. SHORT-TERM STORAGE: Wash and dry lettuce, then line the empty salad spinner with paper towels. Layer in the lettuce, covering each layer with additional paper towels.

2. LONGER-TERM STORAGE: Loosely roll the washed and dried lettuce in paper towels and then place inside a large zipper-lock bag; leave the bag open to allow gases to escape. Lettuce will keep for up to one week.

WATER YOUR SPEARS

To keep asparagus spears tender and flavorful, trim the ends and store them upright in cool water. Limp broccoli and celery benefit from the same treatment.

BETTER BERRY TREATMENT

While damp berries turn mushy faster than dry berries, we've discovered that cleaning with a mild vinegar solution and carefully drying destroys bacteria and mold spores, extending a berry's life.

1. Wash the berries in a bowl with 3 cups water and 1 cup white vinegar. Drain in a colander and rinse under running water.

2. Place the berries in a salad spinner lined with paper towels. Spin until the berries are completely dry. Store in a loosely covered paper towel–lined container.

MUSHROOMS 101

BUYING

We recommend buying loose rather than prepackaged mushrooms so you can inspect their condition and quality. Look for mushrooms with whole, intact caps; avoid those with discoloration or dry, shriveled patches. The mushrooms should feel faintly damp, but not moist or slimy. Their texture should be springy and light, never spongy. Aroma is another important indicator of quality and intensity—the stronger the sweet, earthy scent, the more potent and flavorful the mushrooms. Sour or fishy-smelling mushrooms should always be avoided. Pick mushrooms with large caps and minimal stems since the latter are often discarded.

STORING

Due to their high moisture content, mushrooms are very perishable. Over the years we've tested numerous storage methods to find the best approach.

DO store loose mushrooms in a partially open zipper-lock bag, which maximizes air circulation without drying out the mushrooms. Leaving the bag slightly open allows for the release of the ethylene gas emitted from the mushrooms.

DON'T wrap mushrooms in a paper bag—as directed by many sources—as it turns the fungi spongy and wrinkly.

DO store packaged mushrooms in their original containers. These containers are designed to "breathe," maximizing the life of the mushrooms by balancing the retention of moisture and release of ethylene gas. If you open a sealed package of mushrooms but don't use all the contents, simply rewrap the remaining mushrooms in the box with plastic wrap.

DON'T cover mushrooms with a damp paper towel, as it only speeds up their deterioration.

CLEANING

Many sources advise against washing mushrooms to avoid their soaking up any additional moisture and suggest brushing them instead. But after we learned that mushrooms are over 80 percent water, we began to question their ability to absorb more liquid. To find out, we rinsed mushrooms in cold water, weighing them before and after their wash. We found that six ounces of mushrooms gained only about a quarter ounce of water, and most of this was beaded on the surface. Cut mushrooms are another story. The exposed flesh will absorb water like a sponge, so rinse mushrooms before slicing them. And be careful not to wash mushrooms until you are ready to cook them or they will turn slimy.

BRUSHING

Brushing off mushrooms with a dry toothbrush makes sense when you plan to serve them raw, as rinsing can cause discoloration.

WASHING

Place mushrooms in a salad spinner basket and spray with water until dirt is removed. Put the basket into the salad spinner and spin the mushrooms dry. Use a paper towel to blot up any remaining moisture.

HOW TO USE DRIED MUSHROOMS

To boost mushroom flavor in soups, stews, stuffings, and risottos, we often turn to dried porcini, also known as cèpes.

BUYING

Look for packages with large, thick, tan or brown (not black) pieces. Avoid packages with lots of dust and crumbled bits and keep an eye out for small pinholes, telltale signs that worms got into the mushrooms.

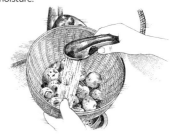

REHYDRATING

Place the dried porcini in a small strainer and rinse. Transfer them to a microwave-safe bowl, add water to cover, and seal the bowl with plastic wrap. Cut steam vents in the plastic wrap and microwave on high power for 30 seconds. Remove the bowl from the microwave and let stand, covered, until the mushrooms soften, about 5 minutes.

GETTING RID OF GRIT

1. Use a fork to lift the rehydrated mushrooms from the soaking liquid without stirring up the sand. If the mushrooms still feel gritty, rinse them briefly under cool running water.

2. To remove grit from the soaking liquid, pour it through a strainer lined with a coffee filter or a paper towel set over a measuring cup. Save this flavorful liquid for other uses.

MUSHROOM VARIETIES

PORTOBELLO

Ranging in diameter from 4 to 6 inches, portobellos are the giants of the Agaricus clan. Their dense flesh is steaklike, with a robust flavor.

BUYING: Choose portobellos with fully intact caps and dry gills; avoid those with wet, damaged gills.

PREPPING: To avoid a muddy-looking sauce, gently scrape out the portobello's black gills with a spoon before cooking.

BEST WAYS TO COOK: Grill, sauté, roast

SHIITAKE

This variety is tan to dark brown. The caps have a chewy texture and nutty flavor, but the stems are tough, woody, and inedible and should be trimmed and discarded.

BUYING: Look for smaller shiitakes that have domed, thick caps, with edges that curl under the cap (a sign of freshness). They should be dry—but not desiccated or wrinkly—with a nutty, earthy aroma.

BEST WAY TO COOK: Sauté

WHITE BUTTON

The mild flavor of this most common cultivated variety becomes rich and meaty when cooked.

BEST WAYS TO COOK: Grill, sauté, roast

CREMINI

Basically miniature portobellos harvested before reaching maturity, cremini are browner and firmer than white buttons and have a more intense flavor.

BEST WAYS TO COOK: Grill, sauté, roast

OYSTER

These large, fan-shaped mushrooms are commonly beige, cream, or gray. Delicate and best cooked only briefly, they have a springy texture and subtle briny flavor.

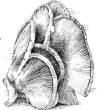

BEST WAY TO COOK: Sauté

BLACK TRUMPET/HORN OF PLENTY

Related to chanterelles, black trumpets are hollow and drier. They have a chewy texture and an almost smoky flavor.

BUYING: Avoid dried-out, leathery mushrooms and those that are solid black (a sign of old age).

CLEANING: These particularly dirty mushrooms need to be rinsed in several changes of water. Halve them first to loosen any grit hiding inside their hollow center.

BEST WAY TO COOK: Sauté

MOREL

Ranging from blond to black, morels are hollow and porous with a mild, nutty flavor that's less potent than other wild mushrooms.

BUYING: When buying wild morels, pick mushrooms with minimal grit and be sure to check inside the hollow center for insects.

CLEANING: While the cultivated kind is very clean, wild morels need to be thoroughly washed. After trimming off and discarding the bottoms of the stems, halve the mushrooms and rinse them in several changes of water.

BEST WAY TO COOK: Sauté

MAITAKE/HEN-OF-THE-WOODS

Maitake is the Japanese name for these densely clustered fungi; "hen" comes from their feathery caps. Their complex red-wine flavor contains garlic subtleties.

BEST WAY TO COOK: Sauté

CHANTERELLE

Pale yellow to deep orange, chanterelles are trumpet-shaped and dense. They have an assertively nutty, almost fruity flavor. Wild versions are intensely flavored.

BEST WAY TO COOK: Sauté

KEEPING KITCHEN STAPLES FRESH 101

Few things last forever—including some of the pantry staples you might think are fine to squirrel away for years. And even if you do observe expiration and sell-by dates, we've found they can't always be trusted. Here's how to preserve the freshness of pantry items—and how to know when it's time to restock.

SPICES & DRIED HERBS

SHELF LIFE:
Whole Spices: 2 years
Ground Spices and Dried Herbs: 1 year

DO buy spices whole, versus ground, whenever possible and grind them just before using. Grinding releases the volatile compounds that give a spice its flavor and aroma. The longer the spice sits around (or is stored), the more compounds disappear.

DON'T store spices and herbs on the counter close to the stove. Heat, light, and moisture shorten their shelf life.

CHECKING FOR FRESHNESS

Crumble a small amount of the dried herb between your fingers and take a whiff. If it releases a lively aroma, it's still good to go. If the aroma and color of a spice have faded, it's time to restock.

VINEGARS

SHELF LIFE: Long-lasting

DON'T toss old vinegar. Most vinegars contain about 5 percent acetic acid, which (along with pasteurization) prevents the growth of harmful bacteria, and will last indefinitely.

DO ignore any sediment in your vinegar. The sediment is a harmless cellulose that our testing has shown doesn't affect taste; it can be easily strained out.

BEYOND THE PANTRY

While not pantry staples per se, eggs and butter are essential to everyday cooking.

BUTTER

Butter can pick up off-flavors and turn rancid if kept in the refrigerator for longer than a month. If you don't use a lot, store butter in the freezer for up to 4 months in a zipper-lock bag and thaw sticks as needed.

EGGS

NEVER put eggs in the egg tray on the refrigerator door, which is too warm. Keep them in the carton, which holds in moisture and protects against odor absorption.

Checking for Freshness

Legally, eggs may already be up to two months old by the end of the "sell by" date, so it's best to check for freshness yourself. If an egg has an unpleasant odor, discard it. Store eggs in the refrigerator for 3 to 5 weeks.

OLIVE OIL

SHELF LIFE:
Unopened: 1 year
Open: 3 months

DO check the harvest date printed on the label of high-end oils to ensure the freshest bottle possible. (Some labels cite an expiration date, which producers typically calculate as 18 months from harvesting. We think unopened olive oil can go rancid 1 year after the harvest date.)

DO Keep olive oil in a dark pantry or cupboard. Strong sunlight will oxidize the chlorophyll in the oil, producing stale, harsh flavors.

DON'T buy olive oil in bulk. Once opened, it has a very short shelf life.

CHECKING FOR FRESHNESS

Heat a little olive oil in a skillet. If it smells rancid, throw out the bottle. (This test works for all vegetable oils.)

OTHER OILS

Here's a quick guide to storing open bottles of oil in your kitchen. For optimal flavor, replace these oils 6 months after opening.

STORE IN PANTRY
Canola
Corn
Peanut
Vegetable

STORE IN FRIDGE
Sesame
Walnut

SWEETENERS

SHELF LIFE:
Granulated Sugar, Honey, and Molasses: Long-lasting

Maple Syrup: 2 years unopened, 1 year open

DO store granulated sugar in an airtight container to protect it from heat, moisture, and critters.

DO keep molasses and honey in the pantry (in the fridge, molasses temporarily turns into a thick, unpourable sludge, and honey crystallizes).

DO store unopened maple syrup in the pantry, but move the opened syrup to the refrigerator. Because of its high moisture level and lack of preservatives, maple syrup is susceptible to the growth of yeast, mold, and bacteria.

LEAVENERS

SHELF LIFE:
Baking Powder and Baking Soda: 6 months

Instant or Active Dry Yeast: 4 months (in freezer)

DO replace baking powder and soda regularly (see below).

DON'T keep yeast in the pantry—put it in the freezer to slow deterioration. And because yeast is a living organism, the expiration date on the package should be observed.

WHEN BAKING POWDER LOSES PUNCH

Over time, baking powder loses its ability to produce carbon dioxide and give baked goods their lift. We compared biscuits made with a newly opened can of baking powder to biscuits made with cans opened and stored for 1 month all the way up to a year. The rise of the biscuits began to decrease with the 6-month-old powder and continued to decline to half the height of fresh at the 10-month-old mark. For best results, replace your baking powder (and soda) every 6 months.

CHOCOLATE

SHELF LIFE:
Unsweetened and Dark Chocolate: 2 years

Milk and White Chocolate: 6 months

DON'T store chocolate in the refrigerator or freezer, as cocoa butter easily absorbs off-flavors from other foods and changes its crystal structure.

DO keep in mind that the milk solids in milk and white chocolate give them a shorter shelf life than unsweetened and dark chocolate.

DO wrap open bars in plastic and store in a cool pantry. If chocolate is exposed to rapid changes in humidity or temperature, sugar or fat may soften and migrate, discoloring the surface. This cosmetic condition, called bloom, doesn't affect flavor.

VANILLA

SHELF LIFE: Long-lasting

DO keep vanilla in a tightly sealed container away from light and heat.

DON'T get rid of old vanilla. Vanilla's high alcohol content makes it extremely shelf-stable. In tests, we've found that even 10-year-old vanilla is indistinguishable from fresh.

CHILL OUT

These items stay fresher in the freezer than the pantry:

Bay leaves   Yeast   Nuts and seeds

Flours with heavy germ content (such as whole wheat) and cornmeal

FLOUR

SHELF LIFE:
All-Purpose Flour: 1 year

Whole Wheat Flour and Cornmeal: 1 year (in freezer)

DO transfer all-purpose flour out of its paper bag and into an airtight container to protect it from humidity.

DON'T leave whole wheat flour or cornmeal in the pantry; they contain natural oils that will go rancid in as little as 3 months.

DO enclose whole wheat flour and cornmeal in zipper-lock bags and store them in the freezer.

DRY STORAGE CONTAINERS

Airtight containers keep moisture at bay. Our preferred storage choice for flour and sugar is a container that easily accommodates an entire 5-pound bag, with an opening wide enough to dip in a measuring cup and level off the excess right back into the container.

Test Kitchen Favorite

The **Rubbermaid 4-Quart Carb-X Commercial Food Storage** container ($14.99), has measurement marks, sturdy handles, and clear plastic for visibility.

MARINATING 101

Marinating is often regarded as a cure-all for bland, chewy meat. Years of testing have taught us that while it can bump up flavor, it will never turn a tough cut tender. But with the right ingredients in the mix, marinating can enhance juiciness and add complexity to steak, chicken, and pork.

BUSTING THE MYTHS

MYTH: THE LONGER THE SOAK, THE BETTER
FACT: A LONG SOAK IS POINTLESS

Because marinades don't penetrate deeply, a lengthy soak is pointless. Furthermore, too long a soak in an acidic (or enzymatic) marinade can weaken the protein bonds near the surface so that they turn mushy—or worse, can no longer hold moisture and dry out.

MYTH: BOTTLED DRESSING IS A GREAT TIME-SAVER
FACT: BOTTLED DRESSING MAKES MEDIOCRE MARINADE

Due to high levels of acidity, salad dressings don't add complex flavor and only make meat mushy. Plus, they are laden with sweeteners, stabilizers, and gums, which add a gelatinous consistency and unnatural flavor.

BAN THE BOTTLE

MYTH: ACIDS TENDERIZE MEAT
FACT: ACIDS TURN MEAT MUSHY

To tenderize meat, you have to break down muscle fiber and collagen, the connective tissue that makes meat tough, thus increasing the meat's ability to retain moisture. While acidic ingredients like citrus juice, vinegar, yogurt, buttermilk, and wine do weaken collagen, their impact is confined to the meat's surface. We find that if left too long, acids turn the outermost layer of meat mushy, not tender. To minimize mushiness, we use acidic components sparingly (or cut them out entirely) and only for short marinating times.

USE WITH DISCRETION

MYTH: MARINADES PENETRATE MEAT DEEPLY
FACT: MOST IMPACT IS SUPERFICIAL

Contrary to popular belief, marinades do most of their work on the surface of meat or just below. Some ingredients in a marinade do penetrate the meat—but only by a few millimeters (and oil-soluble herbs and spices in the mix merely add flavor to the exterior). To prove the point, we soaked beef short ribs in red wine for intervals from one hour to 18, then measured the band of purple created by the wine. Our finding? Even after 18 hours of soaking, the wine penetrated less than 1 millimeter. Additional testing with marinated boneless chicken breasts confirmed that the flavors of other kinds of soaking liquids do not penetrate to the center of the meat.

MYTH: ENZYMES TENDERIZE MEAT
FACT: ENZYMES MAKE MEAT MUSHY

The enzymes in many plants—such as papain in papaya and bromelain in pineapple, to name two—can break down collagen in meat. But as with acids, their impact is limited to the meat's surface, where we find they likewise turn the texture mushy, not tender.

MYTH: MARINADES ADD FLAVOR TO ANY MEAT
FACT: MARINADES ARE BEST FOR THIN CUTS

With their influence limited mostly to the surface of meat, we reserve marinades for relatively thin cuts like chicken breasts, pork chops, steaks, cutlets, and meat cut into chunks or slices for kebabs and stir-fries.

THICK: PROBLEMATIC

THIN: OPTIMAL

A BETTER WAY TO MARINATE: BRINERATE

Successful marinating is all about getting as much of the soaking liquid flavors into (and on) the meat as possible. Brining in a saltwater solution is a way to create more juiciness. To pump up flavor as well as juiciness, our marinades combine both approaches, with soaking liquids that not only contain lots of seasonings and flavorings but so much salt, you might even call them "brinerades." As in a brine, salt in a marinade affects meat in two ways. Through osmotic pressure, it pulls moisture from a place of higher water concentration (the marinade) into a place with a lower one (the meat). In addition, it restructures the protein molecules in the meat, creating gaps that fill with water to further increase juiciness. It also seasons the meat, enhancing its inherent flavors.

TIPS FOR SUCCESS

USE LOTS OF FLAVORINGS AND SEASONINGS

In tests, we've found that a high concentration of salt in a marinade (and we use plenty) can inhibit meat from absorbing the flavors of other ingredients, unless they're included in copious quantities (i.e., 3 or 4 cloves of garlic and at least a tablespoon of chopped herbs, if using).

SCORE MEAT BEFORE MARINATING

To help the marinade penetrate as deeply as possible (especially thicker cuts like flank steak), prick the surface of the meat with a fork or score it with a knife.

FLIP OR STIR

Place meat in a zipper-lock bag with the air squeezed out or use a large baking dish covered with plastic wrap. Flip the bag or stir the meat halfway through the soaking time to ensure that the meat is thoroughly coated.

REFRIGERATE WHILE MARINATING

To eliminate the risk of microorganisms spreading in raw meat, don't leave meat on the counter—refrigerate it. This keeps it out of the temperature danger zone of 40 to 140 degrees, within which bacteria spread rapidly.

REMOVE MARINADE BEFORE COOKING

To prevent flare-ups on the grill and ensure properly browned meat when sautéing or stir-frying, wipe off most of the excess marinade before cooking. Keep just a little marinade on the meat surface to maximize flavor.

DON'T RECYCLE USED MARINADE

Used marinade is contaminated with raw meat juice and is therefore unsafe. If you want sauce to serve with the cooked meat, just make a little extra marinade and set it aside before adding the bulk of the marinade to the raw meat.

MARINADE MUST-HAVES

Both salt and oil are critical to a successful marinade; soy, sugar, and honey are great flavor boosters.

SALT: Not Just Seasoning

To increase the meat's juiciness, our marinades usually include a high concentration of salt (typically about 1½ teaspoons per 3 tablespoons of liquid), and thus serve as "brinerades" that combine the benefits of both marinating and brining.

OIL: Flavor Facilitator

Most of the herbs and spices we add to marinades are oil-soluble, which means they only release their full flavor when mixed in oil. So, to get the most out of a marinade, always include oil. But note: These flavors will merely coat, not penetrate, the meat. Meat proteins are saturated with water, so they won't absorb the oil or its flavors.

SOY: Flavor Enhancer

For more complex flavor, use soy sauce instead of salt—besides being salty, it contains glutamic acid, which boosts meaty flavor.

SUGAR/HONEY: Browning Boosters

Sweeteners like sugar and honey not only add complexity, they also help foods brown during cooking, further developing flavor.

THE SHORT JOURNEY OF A MARINADE

To determine how far flavors in different marinades might penetrate into meat, we placed boneless, skinless chicken breasts in four different soaking liquids (variously made with soy sauce, yogurt, wine, and lemon juice and garlic). We soaked all four batches a full 18 hours, then cooked them in a 300-degree oven until the internal temperature registered 160 degrees. We then cut off 3 millimeters from the exterior of each breast (a good 2 millimeters beyond where it was clear the soy and wine marinades had penetrated). Finally, we tasted the trimmed chicken side by side with breasts we baked at 300 degrees without marinating. Tasters could find no distinguishable flavor differences among any of the batches. Our conclusion: Marinade flavors do not penetrate meat beyond the first few millimeters, no matter what is in the mix.

SUPERMARKET EXTRA-VIRGIN OLIVE OIL

When you set out to buy superior extra-virgin olive oil at the supermarket, good luck. Rows of bottles fill the shelves, with even the most ordinary of grocery stores offering more than a dozen choices. We chose 10 of the top-selling brands and conducted a blind tasting—first plain, and then warmed and tossed with pasta. We also compared them with our favorite high-end brand. While a few supermarket oils passed muster, most ranged from plain Jane to distinctly unpleasant. Many things can impact the quality and flavor of extra-virgin olive oil, but the type of olive, the timing of the harvest, and processing are the most important factors. The best-quality oil comes from olives picked at their peak and processed as soon as possible, without heat. Our favorite oil was Columela, which is made with a blend of olives grown in Spain. Available at specialty stores (and a few supermarkets), Columela is actually cheaper than Lucini, our top supermarket brand. This raises the question: Is the supermarket the best place to buy your extra-virgin olive oil? Unfortunately, we'd have to say no. Olive oils are listed in order of preference.

HIGHLY RECOMMENDED

COLUMELA Extra Virgin Olive Oil
PRICE: $17.95 for 17 oz ($35.90 per liter)
ORIGIN: Spain
COMMENTS: Columela is composed of a blend of intense Picual, mild Hojiblanca, Ocal, and Arbequina olives. This oil took top honors for its fruity flavor and excellent balance. Tasters praised it as having "big olive aroma, big olive taste" with a "buttery" flavor that is "sweet" and "full," with a "peppery finish."

RECOMMENDED

LUCINI ITALIA Premium Select Extra Virgin Olive Oil
PRICE: $19.99 for 500 ml ($39.98 per liter)
ORIGIN: Italy
COMMENTS: Tasters noted this oil's flavor was "much deeper than the other samples," describing it as "fruity, with a slight peppery finish," "buttery undertones," and a "clean, green taste" that was "aromatic, with a good balance."

COLAVITA Extra Virgin Olive Oil
PRICE: $17.99 for 750 ml ($23.98 per liter)
ORIGIN: Italy
COMMENTS: Virtually tied for second place, this oil was deemed "round and buttery," with a "light body" and flavor that was "briny and fruity," "very fine and smooth," and "almost herbal," with "great balance."

RECOMMENDED WITH RESERVATIONS

BERTOLLI Extra Virgin Olive Oil
PRICE: $12.49 for 750 ml ($16.65 per liter)
ORIGIN: Italy, Greece, Spain, and Tunisia
COMMENTS: A clear step down from the top oils, tasters noted "overall mild" flavor and "very little aroma," with only a "hint of green olive" and a "hint of spiciness at the end."

FILIPPO BERIO Extra Virgin Olive Oil
PRICE: $10.99 for 750 ml ($14.65 per liter)
ORIGIN: Italy, Spain, Greece, and Tunisia
COMMENTS: While some tasters found this oil "sweet" and "buttery" with "medium body" and "slight spice at the end," others complained that it had "zero olive flavor" and noted a "bitter" aftertaste. In pasta, it was "extremely mild" to the point of being "boring."

RECOMMENDED WITH RESERVATIONS (continued)

GOYA Extra Virgin Olive Oil
PRICE: $13.99 for 1 liter
ORIGIN: Spain
COMMENTS: The best comments tasters could muster were "mild" and "neutral." Some liked it on pasta, but complaints were myriad: "metallic," "soapy," "briny," "hints of dirt."

POMPEIAN Extra Virgin Olive Oil
PRICE: $9.99 for 473 ml ($21.12 per liter)
ORIGIN: Spain
COMMENTS: While some tasters called this oil "mild" and "smooth," others found it "thin, greasy" and "not very interesting." "I bet the cooking water had more olive flavor," speculated one taster.

BOTTICELLI Extra Virgin Olive Oil
PRICE: $10.99 for 1 liter
ORIGIN: Italy
COMMENTS: While a few tasters liked this "potent" oil, others deemed it "overpowering" and "musky," with a "rank, off-flavor."

NOT RECOMMENDED

CARAPELLI Extra Virgin Olive Oil
PRICE: $10.99 for 750 ml ($14.65 per liter)
ORIGIN: Italy, Greece, Spain, Tunisia, Turkey, Cypress, Morocco, and Syria
COMMENTS: "Nothing remarkable here—just greasy, no flavor," summarized one taster. "Where did the olive go?" said another. This oil was judged to have a "kind of rancid" aftertaste that was reminiscent of "soil," "tree resin," and "ammonia and grass."

DAVINCI Extra Virgin Olive Oil
PRICE: $17.99 for 1 liter
ORIGIN: Italy, Greece, Spain, Tunisia, and Turkey
COMMENTS: Although this oil won top place in a previous tasting, because olive oil is an agricultural product, it can differ from year to year. This time, tasters found it "washed out and muted."

STAR Extra Virgin Olive Oil
PRICE: $11.99 for 750 ml ($15.99 per liter)
ORIGIN: Spain, Italy, Greece, and Tunisia
COMMENTS: "Boring" and "not very complex," this oil came across as "plastic-y and industrial; some hint of olives, but it fades quickly." Tasters identified "unpleasant and dirty" off-flavors.

BLACK PEPPERCORNS

Beyond its heat and sharp bite, black pepper also enhances our ability to taste food, stimulating our salivary glands so we experience flavors more fully. This effect comes only from freshly ground pepper. Once the hard, black shell of the peppercorn is cracked open, its aroma immediately starts to fade, and most of its flavor and scent disappear within a half hour. After tasting freshly ground supermarket and mail-order black peppers, we knew immediately that there were significant differences among brands. Some were searingly hot, others mild; some were one-dimensional, others complex. While all peppercorns are defined by the heat-bearing compound piperine, the flavor of a peppercorn depends on exactly where it is cultivated, when the berries are picked, and how they are processed. We gave top marks to highly aromatic peppercorns with complex flavor and preferred moderate rather than strong heat, which tended to overpower any other taste. Cooking did have some leveling effect on the pepper's complexity, with tasters struggling to detect differences between the top and bottom-ranked brands when just a pinch was used. The verdict? In applications that call for a small dose, just about any pepper will be fine as long as it is freshly ground. But if you're cooking a peppery specialty, or if you like to grind fresh pepper over your food before eating, choosing a superior peppercorn can make a difference. Black peppercorns are listed in order of preference.

RECOMMENDED

KALUSTYAN'S Indian Tellicherry Black Peppercorns

PRICE: $6.99 for 2.5-ounce jar ($2.80 per ounce)
COMMENTS: With high marks for "enticing" aroma and complex flavor, tasters praised these peppercorns for a "beautiful scent," "like licorice, sweet and spicy; rich, a little smoky," "winey," "floral," with a "hint of sweetness," and a "fruity" taste with "mild heat that gradually builds."

MORTON & BASSETT Organic Whole Black Peppercorns **BEST BUY**

PRICE: $5.39 for 2-ounce jar ($2.70 per ounce)
COMMENTS: "Spicy but not hot," this organic Lampong pepper from Indonesia (sold by a San Francisco-based spice company) won our initial supermarket-brand tasting, and was the only non-tellicherry pepper to make it to our final lineup. It won praise for being "very fragrant and floral and piney, very spicy," with notes of "cinnamon" and "citrus," with "some good berry notes." In sum: "What I expect pepper to taste like."

ZINGERMAN'S Tellicherry Peppercorns

PRICE: $8 for 2.53-ounce jar ($3.16 per ounce)
COMMENTS: "This smells like green peppercorns, ripe, pungent, sharp and hot," noted one taster of this pepper from a Michigan-based gourmet catalog and retailer, while others described its "creeping heat and lovely floral undertones," including "herb, lavender, and rosemary," and called it "bright," "lively," and "grassy, with balanced heat and spice, nice and aromatic."

RECOMMENDED WITH RESERVATIONS

VANNS SPICES Tellicherry Peppercorns

PRICE: $3.77 for 2.25-ounce jar ($1.68 per ounce)
COMMENTS: With a "bright, fresh scent" and a "mellow bite," this pepper from a Baltimore spice purveyor was described as "floral" and "fruity" while others less flatteringly mentioned "slightly pungent barnyard flavors" and "no depth of flavor."

RECOMMENDED WITH RESERVATIONS (continued)

McCORMICK Gourmet Collection Tellicherry Black Peppercorns

PRICE: $4.99 for 1.87-ounce jar ($2.67 per ounce)
COMMENTS: While several tasters noted this supermarket pepper's "very nice" "floral" aroma, they also noted that, compared to other samples, it was "bland" and "flat" and offered "not as complicated or layered flavors."

PENZEYS India Tellicherry Peppercorns

PRICE: $3.49 for 2.2-ounce jar ($1.59 per ounce)
COMMENTS: Tasters enjoyed this gourmet spice purveyor's offering for its "piney, rosemary scent" with "citrus" and "lavender" notes, but many complained of "a lot of burning heat" that was "not very pleasant." "I taste mostly heat, not flavor," said one unhappy taster. "It finishes very hot but without much depth."

THE SPICE HOUSE Tellicherry Black Peppercorns

PRICE: $2.98 for 2.5-ounce jar ($1.19 per ounce)
COMMENTS: With a "super strong aroma" that was "very appealing—piney, citrus, fresh Christmas tree," these peppercorns from the Chicago spice purveyor founded by a branch of the Penzey family also came across with a peppery intensity that "is really assertive— a smack-you-in-the-face kind of heat." But reactions were mixed: Several found it "slightly bitter" and "stale."

DEAN & DELUCA Tellicherry Peppercorns

PRICE: $5.75 for 2-ounce tin ($2.88 per ounce)
COMMENTS: Tasters noted this pepper's "mild aroma and flavor"—described as "soft," "faint," and even "dull"—and "barely detectable heat." What little flavor and aroma tasters did perceive they mostly liked: "almost like cloves or allspice," "a cinnamony aroma" that was "a little chocolatey on the finish." Overall: "Not great; smells better than it tastes."

VANILLA EXTRACT

Vanilla enhances our ability to taste other foods, including chocolate, coffee, fruit, and nuts, and boosts our perception of sweetness. While this is true for both pure and imitation vanilla, the two choices are far from identical. Scientists have identified around 250 flavor and aroma compounds in real vanilla, while the artificial version has just one: vanillin, the predominant flavor in natural vanilla. In our quest for great vanilla, we sampled 12 of the country's top-selling supermarket brands of vanilla extract, both fake and pure, stirring them into milk and pudding before trying a few choices in cake and cookies. So what's our conclusion? If you're buying only one bottle of vanilla for cooking, baking, and making cold and creamy desserts, our top choice is a real extract. If you use vanilla just for baking, we have to admit there's not much difference between a well-made synthetic vanilla and the real thing. Vanillas are listed in order of preference.

RECOMMENDED

McCORMICK Pure Vanilla Extract
PRICE: $7.99 for 2 ounces ($4 per ounce)
COMMENTS: This vanilla won top praise for being "strong," "rich," and "spicy," with a "sweet undertone." It had "clear vanilla flavor with nice balance" and notes of "dried fruit," "caramel," and "chocolate," "like Kahlúa or Bailey's."

RODELLE Pure Vanilla Extract
PRICE: $7.99 for 4 ounces ($2 per ounce)
COMMENTS: "Smoky" and "earthy," with "caramel," "prune," and "chocolate" notes, it was praised for offering "deep, rich flavor." Prepared in pudding, it was "subtle" and "well-balanced."

NIELSEN-MASSEY Madagascar Bourbon Pure Vanilla Extract
PRICE: $9.99 for 4 ounces ($2.50 per ounce)
COMMENTS: "Sweeter and more pleasant" than other vanillas, it lacked the "boozy burn" of some of the pure extracts and offered a "sweet floral flavor," with "honey" and "maple" notes. In pudding, it had a "nutty" finish.

GOLD MEDAL Imitation Vanilla Extract
BEST BUY
PRICE: $2.25 for 8 ounces (28 cents per ounce)
COMMENTS: Tasters felt that this imitation vanilla ranked with the pure extracts. "Lovely, seemed like pure vanilla," said one; another described it as "mild and gentle; maybe it's not real, but it tastes good." Others said it was "perfumy," with notes of "toasted rice."

SAUER'S Pure Vanilla Extract
PRICE: $5.25 for 2 ounces ($2.62 per ounce)
COMMENTS: "Sweet," with "a nice depth" was a common reaction to this extract. Some noted that it had "elements of tea," "chocolate," and "a little caramel" with "assertive vanilla" flavor. But the alcohol struck many as "overpowering."

SPICE ISLANDS Pure Vanilla Extract
PRICE: $7.43 for 2 ounces ($3.72 per ounce)
COMMENTS: "Sweet," but with a "harsh, boozy finish" and a "peaty, almost smoky flavor," it "smells great, but tastes blah." In pudding, it was "smoky and heavy."

RECOMMENDED (continued)

DURKEE Pure Vanilla Extract
PRICE: $27.87 for 16 ounces ($1.74 per ounce)
COMMENTS: The ingredient list shows "vanilla bean extractives" in last place, after corn syrup. "Good aroma, but flavor is straightforward and somewhat lacking," said one taster; others called it "mild," with a "malted flavor." In pudding, it was "subtle." In sum: "decent but unremarkable."

RECOMMENDED WITH RESERVATIONS

MORTON & BASSETT Pure Vanilla Extract
PRICE: $9.09 for 4 ounces ($2.27 per ounce)
COMMENTS: Has a "sharp scent, followed by a sharp flavor"; "heavy on the alcohol," it was "slightly herbaceous, a mix of floral and earthy." In pudding, tastes "like melted Breyers vanilla ice cream," but with a "harsh" aftertaste.

McCORMICK Premium Imitation Vanilla Extract
PRICE: $3.69 for 2 ounces ($1.85 per ounce)
COMMENTS: Includes cocoa and tea extractives "and other artificial flavorings" to mimic the complexity of pure vanilla. Tasters detected "some vanilla, but that dissipates, and tastes almost fruity," with "cherry cola" and "coffee" notes. In pudding, it was "bright," like a "girly cocktail."

McCORMICK Gourmet Collection Organic Pure Madagascar Vanilla Extract
PRICE: $10.55 for 2 ounces ($5.28 per ounce)
COMMENTS: With a "barely there aroma and flavor," this gourmet line from McCormick is not worth its high price. In pudding, tasters said there was "not much vanilla coming through."

ADAMS Pure Vanilla Extract
PRICE: $7.88 for 4 ounces ($1.97 per ounce)
COMMENTS: "Mild," "thin," "sharp," and "weak," this came across as "all nose, no flavor," with an aftertaste of "bitterness at the back of the throat like Robitussin." In pudding, it was "bland."

DURKEE Imitation Vanilla Flavor
PRICE: $2.84 for 16 ounces (18 cents per ounce)
COMMENTS: Tasters liked its "sweet" aroma, but complained that this imitation had "virtually no vanilla taste," and what there was seemed "way too mild." In pudding, tasters described it as "soft-serve vanilla" and "commercial-tasting."

MAPLE AND PANCAKE SYRUPS

Sold side by side in the supermarket, genuine maple syrup and so-called pancake syrup can range from more than $1 per ounce for the real deal to a mere 14 cents per ounce for an imitation. To find out which tastes best, we pitted four top-selling national brands (and one mail-order brand) of maple syrup against five popular pancake syrups. Maple syrup costs much more than pancake syrup for some very good reasons: Its production is labor-intensive (tree sap is boiled to reduce its water content and concentrate its sugar), with a short season and limited supply. Pancake syrup, on the other hand, is a manufactured mix of high-fructose corn syrup and other ingredients engineered to taste like maple. Whether tasted on waffles or baked in a pie, the pancake syrups universally got the thumbs-down. As for the maple syrups, we preferred dark syrups with intense maple flavor to the delicate flavor of pricey Grade A light amber syrup. Syrups are listed in order of preference.

RECOMMENDED

MAPLE GROVE FARMS Pure Maple Syrup
Grade A Dark Amber
(Product of U.S. and Canada)
PRICE: $5.29 for 8.5 ounces (62 cents per ounce)
SUGAR CONTENT: 62.9g/100g
COMMENTS: "A good balance of maple and sweetness," "potent," "clean," and "intense." A "perfect consistency, not too thick or thin." In pie, it was "very mild, but tasted real and satisfying."

HIGHLAND SUGARWORKS
Grade B Cooking Maple (Product of Vermont)
PRICE: $16.95 per pint ($1.06 per ounce) by mail order plus shipping
SUGAR CONTENT: 63.3g/100g
COMMENTS: While tasters agreed on our favorite mail-order syrup's "intense, complex maple flavor," a few found it "a bit much" when tasted plain. But this dark syrup shone in pie, earning praise for "very rich, deep" maple flavor.

CAMP Maple Syrup
Grade A Dark Amber (Product of Canada)
PRICE: $12.49 for 12.5 ounces ($1 per ounce)
SUGAR CONTENT: 61.8g/100g
COMMENTS: Tasters found this syrup "clean" with "light maple flavor" that was "pleasantly thin and sweet." In pie, it was "mild" and "barely there."

RECOMMENDED WITH RESERVATIONS

SPRING TREE Pure Maple Syrup
Grade A Dark Amber (Product of Canada)
PRICE: $9.49 for 12.5 ounces (76 cents per ounce)
SUGAR CONTENT: 65.4g/100g
COMMENTS: This syrup had a "light body and a slight burned taste," though it was also deemed "sweet, natural," and "clearly maple." A few tasters detected a "slightly acidic" off-note.

MAPLE GOLD Syrup
Grade A Dark Amber (Product of Canada)
PRICE: $5.29 for 8.5 ounces (62 cents per ounce)
SUGAR CONTENT: 64.9g/100g
COMMENTS: Tasters enjoyed the "solid maple flavor" of this contender, but also noted that it was "thin, achingly sweet, and astringent."

NOT RECOMMENDED

KELLOGG'S EGGO Original Syrup
PRICE: $3.49 for 23 ounces (15 cents per ounce)
COMMENTS: "Very sugary. Slightly plastic. Maple aftertaste, but weak." In pie, while a minority of tasters liked its "nice, toasted sweetness," many complained: "Where's the maple?"

AUNT JEMIMA Original Syrup
PRICE: $3.59 for 24 ounces (15 cents per ounce)
COMMENTS: A few tasters liked this syrup's "honey and vanilla" notes, but most comments were less forgiving: "Fake, viscous corn syrup," with a "fake maple smell" and "fake butter flavor."

MRS. BUTTERWORTH'S Original Syrup
PRICE: $3.49 for 24 ounces (15 cents per ounce)
COMMENTS: Tasters likened this syrup to "melted candy," "cheap butterscotch," and "what a maple-flavored Life Saver would taste like." In pie, it was "saccharine sweet," with "no off-flavors, but not very mapley either."

LOG CABIN Pancake Syrup
PRICE: $3.59 for 24 ounces (15 cents per ounce)
COMMENTS: The sweetness of this syrup was inoffensive, but tasters found its "salty, strong artificial butter flavor—like movie-theater popcorn" thoroughly off-putting. In pie, it fared better, but most agreed it was "cloyingly sweet."

HUNGRY JACK Original Syrup
PRICE: $3.99 for 27.6 ounces (14 cents per ounce)
COMMENTS: Tasters described this syrup as "super sweet and sloppy, with a vanilla flavor." They also said it was "thick and buttery, but tastes like corn syrup." Its texture was decried as "so thick you could stand a spoon in it."

CHOCOLATE CHIPS

Given that chocolate chips have just three basic ingredients—cocoa butter, cocoa solids, and sugar—does it matter which brand you buy? We rounded up eight high-end and middle-market brands, all of which are widely available at supermarkets. We then sampled them plain and in nearly 300 cookies. The "cacao percentage" you hear so much about in bar chocolate refers to the total amount of cocoa butter and cocoa solids contributed by ground-up cacao beans. As a general rule, the higher the cacao percentage, the darker and more intense the chocolate. Our favorite chips—Ghirardelli 60% Cacao Bittersweet Chocolate Chips—contained the highest cacao percentage of all the chips in the lineup, as well as the most cocoa butter by far. Sugar was another consideration—and for the most part, more wasn't better. Our favorite chip had the least amount of sugar in the lineup. Chocolate chips are listed in order of preference. (Note numbers are approximations.)

HIGHLY RECOMMENDED

GHIRARDELLI 60% Cacao Bittersweet Chocolate Chips
PRICE: $3.50 for an 11.5-ounce bag
SUGAR: 40%
CACAO: 60%
FAT: 44% (included in cacao percentage)
COMMENTS: Distinct "wine" and "fruit," flavors made this "adult chocolate" a winner. Low sugar content allowed the chocolate flavor to shine. In cookies, a wider, flatter shape and high percentage of fat helped the chips melt into thin layers for a pleasing balance of cookie and chocolate in every bite.

RECOMMENDED

HERSHEY'S Special Dark Mildly Sweet Chocolate Chips
PRICE: $2.39 for a 12-ounce bag
SUGAR: 53%
CACAO: 45%
FAT: 38% (included in cacao percentage)
COMMENTS: Tasters liked the "strong cocoa flavor," which stood up to the sweetness of cookies. This chip was the only one that contained Dutch-processed cocoa powder, resulting in a "bold" chocolate flavor. A higher fat percentage gave it a creamier texture in cookies.

GUITTARD Real Semisweet Chocolate Chips
PRICE: $3.29 for a 12-ounce bag
SUGAR: 53%
CACAO: 43%
FAT: 29% (included in cacao percentage)
COMMENTS: A "complex" chip with cinnamon and caramel undertones. Some tasters felt it needed a bolder chocolate presence to stand up to other flavors when baked in cookies.

HERSHEY'S Semi-Sweet Chocolate Chips
PRICE: $2.29 for a 12-ounce bag
SUGAR: 53%
CACAO: 42%
FAT: 30% (included in cacao percentage)
COMMENTS: Though praised for "good cocoa" flavor in cookies, this chip didn't have enough chocolate flavor to balance out the high sugar content. Tasters found its flavor more similar to milk chocolate than semisweet chocolate.

RECOMMENDED *(continued)*

GHIRARDELLI Semi-Sweet Chips
PRICE: $3.50 for a 12-ounce bag
SUGAR: 53%
CACAO: 46%
FAT: 34% (included in cacao percentage)
COMMENTS: The unique "tangy, fruity" flavor of this chip rated well when baked in cookies. But tasters commented that it was "a bit too sweet" and lacking the "strong chocolate flavor" of its 60 percent cacao sister chip.

RECOMMENDED WITH RESERVATIONS

BAKER'S Real Semi-Sweet Chocolate Chunks
PRICE: $2.69 for a 12-ounce bag
SUGAR: 53%
CACAO: 47%
FAT: 35% (included in cacao percentage)
COMMENTS: Tasters detected "pleasant coffee and cinnamon tones" in this chip but also an "off, coconut-like" flavor. Overall, tasters noticed "more sweetness than chocolate flavor."

NOT RECOMMENDED

NESTLÉ Toll House Real Semi-Sweet Chocolate Morsels
PRICE: $2.50 for a 12-ounce bag
SUGAR: 57%
CACAO: 47%
FAT: 30% (included in cacao percentage)
COMMENTS: With the highest sugar content in the lineup, tasters agreed this best-selling chip was "unpleasantly sweet" and compared its "fleeting" chocolate flavor to "cheap Halloween candy."

NESTLÉ Toll House Real Semi-Sweet Chocolate Chunk Morsels
PRICE: $2.50 for an 11.5-ounce bag
SUGAR: 50%
CACAO: 45%
FAT: 27% (included in cacao percentage)
COMMENTS: Tasters panned this chip's "odd" flavor, variously described as "grassy," "like dirt," and "oily." The chunks, which are heavier than the classic morsels, didn't melt enough.

ELBOW MACARONI

Elbow macaroni has become a staple in such distinctly American recipes as macaroni salad and macaroni and cheese. But with so many brands of elbow macaroni on the market, which one should you buy? To find out, we rounded up eight contenders and tasted them simply dressed with vegetable oil and in our recipe for classic macaroni and cheese. Barilla, an Italian brand that makes pasta for the American market at its plant in Ames, Iowa, won our tasting by a large margin. Our tasters praised this pasta for its "wheaty," "buttery" flavor and "firm texture," and they especially liked that these elbows have small ridges and a slight twist that "holds sauce well." After Barilla, our tasters didn't notice much difference among other major brands, all of which were deemed acceptable. Elbow macaronis are listed in order of preference.

HIGHLY RECOMMENDED

BARILLA Elbows
PRICE: $1.33 for 16 ounces
COMMENTS: Tasters were nearly unanimous in praising this pasta's "hearty texture" and "rich," "wheaty" flavor. The ridged surface and slight twist in shape were big hits, especially in the macaroni and cheese portion of the tasting, where this pasta held the sauce particularly well.

RECOMMENDED

MUELLER'S Elbow Macaroni
PRICE: $1.19 for 16 ounces
COMMENTS: The "mild wheaty" flavor and "buttery aftertaste" of this pasta brought several tasters back to their childhood: "Just like Ma's" was one happy observation. The "firm and toothsome" texture held up well in the heavy cheese sauce. A few tasters complained about the "thick walls" and "chewy, dense" texture of these elbows.

RONZONI Smart Taste Elbows
PRICE: $2 for 14.5 ounces
COMMENTS: "Simple and straightforward," "neutral," and "bland but decent" were common sentiments concerning this product, which is enriched with fiber and calcium. Several tasters commented on the noodles being "blown out" and "mushy."

RONZONI Elbows
PRICE: $1.35 for 16 ounces
COMMENTS: This product scored especially well in the macaroni and cheese tasting, with tasters lauding its "creamy," "substantive" texture. A few tasters perceived a "slightly stale," "grassy" flavor that led to slightly lower scores in plain tasting.

RECOMMENDED *(continued)*

DECECCO No. 81 Elbows
PRICE: $2.29 for 16 ounces
COMMENTS: This Italian import received mixed comments, with some tasters calling it "classic" while others deemed it "generic." The "tender" texture was stressed under the weight of the cheese sauce, making the elbows "squishy" and "mushy."

DAVINCI Elbows Macaroni
PRICE: $1.30 for 16 ounces
COMMENTS: This "simple but pleasant" brand (also from Italy) was commended for its "good springy texture," but a few tasters were put off by its "dinky," "thin," and "wimpy" size. It had average scores for flavor and texture across the board.

PRINCE Elbow Macaroni
PRICE: $1.29 for 16 ounces
COMMENTS: "Just average," "nothing special," "unremarkable," and "a bit bland but okay" were common refrains for these elbows. While some tasters found these elbows "mushy," others liked the "soft" texture.

NOT RECOMMENDED

BARILLA Plus Elbows
PRICE: $2.29 for 14.5 ounces
COMMENTS: This "dusty," "cardboard-y" brand was found by one panelist to "taste like it was fortified with sawdust." If the other samples prove that average noodles are just fine, this one makes the emphatic point that you shouldn't mess too much with a proven entity. "Scary looking," "gross," and "weird."

PREMIUM APPLEWOOD BACON

While there's probably no such thing as terrible bacon, we know that there is definitely better bacon, with mass-market supermarket strips varying a lot from producer to producer. In recent years we've been hearing about small, artisanal producers crafting premium bacon using old-fashioned curing methods and hand labor. (Mass-produced bacon is made in a matter of hours and by machine.) But at double or even triple the price of ordinary bacon, is this premium pork worth it? We bought six artisanal bacons by mail order in a single style—applewood smoked—and pitted these premium strips against applewood-smoked bacon from the supermarket. Great bacon is all about a balance of sweet, smoky, salty, and meaty—and striking that flavor balance turned out to be the biggest factor for success with our tasters. While our top picks were artisanal bacons, two supermarket brands weren't far behind. Bacons are listed in order of preference.

HIGHLY RECOMMENDED

VANDE ROSE FARMS Artisan Dry Cured Bacon, Applewood Smoked
PRICE: $13.95 for 12 ounces, plus shipping
DESCRIPTION: Dry-cured with brown sugar, salt, and pepper; hand-rubbed; applewood-smoked
SIZE OF SLICE: 33g
COMMENTS: Tasters raved that this bacon had it all: "Nice balance of sweetness to salt, complex ham flavor and very meaty." "A nice, thick cut, hearty and substantial."

NODINE'S SMOKEHOUSE Apple Smoke Flavored Bacon
PRICE: $8 for 16 ounces, plus shipping
DESCRIPTION: Wet-cured with brown sugar, salt, and spices; smoked over dried apple pomace and hickory or maple hardwood
SIZE OF SLICE: 37g
COMMENTS: "Wow, this is some huge piece of amazing bacon. Nice meatiness." "Apple flavor is subtle and it isn't too smoky." While it had "good pork flavor," several tasters felt it "needs more salt."

APPLEGATE FARMS Uncured Sunday Bacon BEST BUY
PRICE: $5.39 for 8 ounces
DESCRIPTION: Wet-cured with water, sea salt, celery juice, evaporated cane juice, and lactic acid starter culture; smoked over applewood
SIZE OF SLICE: 7g
COMMENTS: One taster praised this nitrite-free brand for a "subtle smokiness, sweetness of pork, but not sugary." Two identified it as supermarket bacon, "with its heavy salt and mild smoke."

RECOMMENDED WITH RESERVATIONS

FARMLAND/CARANDO Apple Cider Cured Bacon, Applewood Smoked BEST BUY
PRICE: $5.99 for 16 ounces
DESCRIPTION: Wet-cured with water, sugar, salt, sodium phosphate, natural apple flavoring, sodium erythorbate, and sodium nitrite; smoked over applewood
SIZE OF SLICE: 7.5g
COMMENTS: Some found this supermarket bacon far too sweet. Others enjoyed its "applelike flavor" and "caramelized" notes.

RECOMMENDED WITH RESERVATIONS *(continued)*

OSCAR'S SMOKE HOUSE Applewood Smoked Bacon
PRICE: $9.95 for 16 ounces, plus shipping
DESCRIPTION: Wet-cured with brown sugar and honey; applewood-smoked
SIZE OF SLICE: 4g
COMMENTS: A few tasters noted an "Asian" flavor to this bacon, describing it as like "teriyaki bacon, sweet and tangy." Several noted a "chewy" (a few said "tough") texture and "relatively meaty" consistency. Others found it "too sweet," and "one-dimensional."

NORTH COUNTRY SMOKEHOUSE Applewood Smoked Bacon
PRICE: $18.50 for 2 pounds, plus shipping
DESCRIPTION: Wet-cured in maple syrup and spices; smoked and cooked for eight hours
SIZE OF SLICE: 12g
COMMENTS: Smoke flavor dominated, and those who liked smokiness liked this bacon. But the majority disagreed: "Wow, a lot of smoke, like barbecued bacon. Too much for me."

NOT RECOMMENDED

NIMAN RANCH Applewood Smoked Dry-Cured Bacon
PRICE: $7.98 for 12 ounces, plus shipping
DESCRIPTION: Dry cured, smoked over applewood chips
SIZE OF SLICE: 15g
COMMENTS: "A fairly average piece of bacon," "thin," and "not sweet or deeply flavorful." One taster noted it "tastes like smoke, but not much else; very fatty."

NUESKE'S Applewood Smoked Bacon
PRICE: $19.95 for 2 pounds, plus shipping
DESCRIPTION: Wet-cured with salt, sugar, sodium phosphate, sodium erythorbate, and sodium nitrite for 24 hours; hung to dry for 24 hours, then applewood-smoked for 24 hours
SIZE OF SLICE: 9g
COMMENTS: Despite the company's claims of using particularly lean hogs, our tasters found this bacon "very fatty" with "hardly any meat," and many complained of its "overwhelming smoke flavor."

MICROWAVE POPCORN

Americans spend over $1 billion annually on unpopped popcorn kernels, and corn producers develop as many as 30,000 hybrids (which have varying flavor, textural, and volume characteristics) a year in search of better products. To find out which supermarket microwave popcorn we liked best, we popped up seven national brands in their basic butter flavor. As a baseline, we also tasted plain popcorn kernels popped in a microwave popper and dressed with a modest amount of melted butter and salt. The homemade popcorn won by a landslide. Out of the seven store-bought brands, only two received acceptable grades—the almost underseasoned Orville Redenbacher's Natural and the highly seasoned Pop Secret. The biggest problem with the prepackaged popcorns was "artificial tasting" flavors from the "natural and/or artificial butter flavor" and preservatives. It wasn't surprising that popcorns with "artificial butter flavor" would taste artificial. We were, however, very surprised that brands with "natural butter flavor" weren't better. Since butter is perishable, it needs heavy processing and/or added preservatives to be shelf-stabilized for these packages—and both of those roads lead to unnatural or weak butter flavor. Microwave popcorns are listed in order of preference.

HIGHLY RECOMMENDED

Freshly popped kernels with butter and salt
PRICE: About $.54 for 3.3 ounces, or $1.62 for the equivalent of one box
COMMENTS: Tasters sang the praises of this popcorn's "clean butter flavor" and "pleasant balance of corn and butter." It stood out for having "no artificial aftertaste."

RECOMMENDED WITH RESERVATIONS

ORVILLE REDENBACHER'S Gourmet Popping Corn Natural Butter Flavor
PRICE: $2.79 for three 3.3-ounce bags
COMMENTS: Tasters viewed this popcorn's "muted," "neutral" flavor as a positive, as it had "only a touch of butter" and a "mellow corn after-taste." While this popcorn didn't knock tasters' socks off, it was our overall favorite.

POP-SECRET Premium Popcorn Butter Flavor
PRICE: $2.29 for three 3.5-ounce bags
COMMENTS: "Oh my, a butter bomb!" said one happy taster. While many tasters commented on this popcorn's "fake butter flavor" that a few compared to "butter buds," others liked the "sweet aftertaste" and its resemblance to "movie theater popcorn."

NOT RECOMMENDED

ACT II Butter Microwave Popcorn
PRICE: $2.49 for three 3.3-ounce bags
COMMENTS: Tasters noted the "less overt fake (butter) flavor" and "natural tasting" flavor. A few dissenters likened this brand's "squishy," "soft" texture to "Styrofoam."

JOLLY TIME Better Butter Butter Flavor
PRICE: $2.59 for three 3.35-ounce bags
COMMENTS: "Buttery in that awesome artificial way," said one taster. "Bland but okay" and "chewy" were common themes. Some tasters thought this popcorn was too salty.

NEWMAN'S OWN Organics Pop's Corn Butter Organic Microwave Popcorn
PRICE: $3.29 for three 3.5-ounce bags
COMMENTS: This sample scored very high for its "natural, toasty" corn fla-vor, but its butter flavor was deemed "bland and boring" and "flat."

ORVILLE REDENBACHER'S Gourmet Popping Corn Butter
PRICE: $2.79 for three 3.3-ounce bags
COMMENTS: One taster felt this brand resembled popcorn with "golden top-ping." Tasters didn't mince words, call-ing this sample "awful," "gross," and "truly inedible."

NEWMAN'S OWN Oldstyle Picture Show Microwave Popcorn Butter Flavor
PRICE: $2.59 for three 3.5-ounce bags
COMMENTS: This brand had the lowest sodium, fat, and scores of our lineup. A few tasters likened its "fishy," "chem-ical" flavors to "buttered popcorn jelly beans."

BOXED BROWNIE MIXES

There are times, such as a last-minute bake sale or Cub Scout troop meeting, when the convenience of a boxed brownie mix is appealing. To find out just how good these mixes are, we rounded up seven national brands of boxed brownie mixes and baked them according to package instructions. The majority of the brownies were awful, featuring "chemical" flavors, cloying sweetness, and a distinct lack of chocolate flavor. There were, however, two bright spots. The brownies from chocolate manufacturer Ghirardelli and gourmet brand Barefoot Contessa were actually pretty good—not as good as homemade, but surprisingly close. They were the only mixes to include additional sources of chocolate (other than chips). The Ghirardelli mix comes with a packet of chocolate syrup; the Barefoot Contessa mix has both semisweet chocolate chunks and mini chocolate chips. Tasters praised the "rich," "balanced" chocolate flavor of these mixes, which comes in part from their inclusion of both natural and Dutch-processed cocoa powder. Most mixes, including the winning Ghirardelli, call for vegetable oil; the Barefoot Contessa mix calls for butter, which contributes richness and flavor and gave this brand a significant leg up in our tasting. Brownie mixes are listed in order of preference.

RECOMMENDED

GHIRARDELLI Chocolate Syrup Brownie Mix
PRICE: $3.69 for 18.75 ounces
REQUIRES: ⅓ cup vegetable oil, 1 egg, and ¼ cup water for 8- by 8-inch pan of brownies (can also bake in 9- by 9-inch pan)
COMMENTS: "Balanced chocolate (flavor) and sweetness" was tasters' assessment of these "moist, chewy" brownies, which were also praised for their "perfect texture." One taster gushed, "Just like Mom used to make."

BAREFOOT CONTESSA Outrageous Brownie Mix
PRICE: $8.99 for 20.8 ounces
REQUIRES: 8 tablespoons (1 stick) unsalted butter, 2 eggs, and ¾ cup chopped walnuts (optional; we did not use them) for 8- by 8-inch pan of brownies
COMMENTS: Most tasters lauded the "very rich," "real," and "natural" chocolate flavor of this upscale brand from television personality and cookbook author Ina Garten. The "dense and chewy," "moist and fudgy" texture was also a hit. A few naysayers complained about "burnt" or "acrid" notes.

RECOMMENDED WITH RESERVATIONS

PILLSBURY Brownie Classics Traditional Fudge Premium Brownie Mix
PRICE: $2.59 for 19.5 ounces
REQUIRES: ½ cup oil, 2 eggs, and ¼ cup water for 13- by 9-inch pan of brownies
COMMENTS: "Sweeter than most and not as chocolaty" and "pretty sweet but good" sum up tasters' opinions of this brand's middle-of-the-road flavor. Comments on texture were not as kind: "spongy," "extremely oily," and "weird chewy clumps."

RECOMMENDED WITH RESERVATIONS *(continued)*

BETTY CROCKER Hershey's Ultimate Fudge Supreme Brownie Mix
PRICE: $2.99 for 21 ounces
REQUIRES: ½ cup vegetable oil, 2 eggs, and 2 tablespoons water for 8- by 8-inch pan of brownies (can also bake in 9- by 9-inch or 13- by 9-inch pan)
COMMENTS: With the longest ingredient list in our lineup, it wasn't surprising that tasters found these "very chewy" brownies to have a "fake" chocolate flavor and an "off aftertaste."

NOT RECOMMENDED

DUNCAN HINES Family-Style Chewy Fudge Brownies
PRICE: $1.69 for 21 ounces
REQUIRES: ½ cup vegetable oil, 2 eggs, and ¼ cup water for 8- by 8-inch pan of brownies (can also bake in 9- by 9-inch or 13- by 9-inch pan)
COMMENTS: Cries of "too sweet" and "lacks flavor" dominated the comment sheets. "Looks awesome," but "tastes like microwave brownies" were other complaints.

KING ARTHUR FLOUR All-American Fudge Brownie Mix
PRICE: $3.83 for 18 ounces
REQUIRES: ⅓ cup vegetable oil, 2 eggs, and 3 tablespoons water for 8- by 8-inch pan of brownies
COMMENTS: Our tasters clamored over strange flavors: "offensive molasses," "rank artificial chocolate," "strange cinnamon aftertaste," and "prune-y" were among the telling remarks.

CHERRYBROOK KITCHEN Fudge Brownie Mix with Chocolate Chips
PRICE: $5.29 for 16 ounces
REQUIRES: ⅓ cup melted margarine, 2 teaspoons vegetable oil, and ¾ cup water for 9- by 9-inch pan of brownies
COMMENTS: The "stale and sour" flavors didn't come from the margarine—these eggless brownies were still last across the board when made with butter. The non-dairy chocolate chips in the mix didn't seem to boost chocolate flavor.

HOT COCOA MIXES

It's not difficult to make homemade hot cocoa—stir together cocoa, sugar, hot milk, and maybe a splash of vanilla and a pinch of salt—but we admit that instant mixes are unbeatably convenient. To find out which are best, we rounded up leading supermarket brands as well as mixes from a few upscale chocolatiers. Following the instructions on the package, we used either water or milk to reconstitute the cocoa mixes. Across the board, tasters valued creaminess, which can come from either the added milk or from dry milk in the mix (all mixes that can be reconstituted with water contain some form of dried milk). In the end, however, what separated winners from losers was big chocolate flavor. The cocoa mix from Godiva won in a landslide. The mix includes both Dutch-processed cocoa powder and bittersweet chocolate. The mixes reconstituted with hot water tasted, well, watery, while another was overbearingly sweet. Cocoas are listed in order of preference.

HIGHLY RECOMMENDED

GODIVA CHOCOLATIER Dark Chocolate Hot Cocoa

PRICE: $10 for 14.5 ounces (about $0.91 per serving) at Godiva.com
COMMENTS: The "deep, rich chocolate flavor" and "nice depth" of this cocoa made it a hit: "I love everything about this one!" Tasters described it as "balanced and complex," with "intense" flavor and "a nice bitter edge" that made it "actually taste like chocolate."

RECOMMENDED

GHIRARDELLI Chocolate Premium Double Chocolate Hot Cocoa

PRICE: $5.19 for 16 ounces (about $0.47 per serving)
COMMENTS: The second most-chocolaty cocoa in our lineup (according to tasters), it won high marks for a "good balance of chocolate and sugar" and "good bitter chocolate taste." A few tasters complained, however, that the texture was "chalky."

NESTLÉ Rich Chocolate Flavor Hot Cocoa Mix

PRICE: $2.09 for 7.12 ounces (about $0.21 per serving)
COMMENTS: This "creamy and sweet" hot chocolate transported several tasters back to the skating rinks and sledding hills of their childhoods. They described it as "frothy," "more milky than chocolaty," "bland but not unpleasant," and "just like Mom used to make."

BAREFOOT CONTESSA Sinful Hot Chocolate Mix

PRICE: $11.98 for 16 ounces (about $1.09 per serving) at Cooking.com
COMMENTS: With both coffee and cinnamon supplementing the cocoa powder, this brand may not please children. But tasters found this "very dark and chocolaty" mix "rich, complex, a bit exotic." It's "not classic hot chocolate," one said, but many tasters liked it.

NOT RECOMMENDED

HERSHEY'S Goodnight Kisses Milk Chocolate Hot Cocoa Mix

PRICE: $2.19 for 5 ounces (about $0.55 per serving)
COMMENTS: "Tastes cheap," tasters said of this "thin, watery" mix. The ingredient list includes partially hydrogenated soybean and coconut oils as well as artificial flavors, so it's not surprising tasters detected a "weird, artificial taste."

STARBUCKS Gourmet Hot Cocoa

PRICE: $18.99 for 30 ounces (about $0.79 per serving)
COMMENTS: This hot cocoa mix had "strong," "dark" chocolate flavor but was also "thin," "dull," and "watery," perhaps because the package calls for it to be stirred into hot water, not milk. Although this mix does contain nonfat dry milk, it was rated the least creamy of the lineup.

LAND O'LAKES Cocoa Classics Hot Cocoa Mix

PRICE: $6.46 for 15 ounces (about $0.54 per serving)
COMMENTS: With its ingredient list full of polysyllabic items, we weren't surprised that tasters called this cocoa mix "plasticky." Tasters detected little chocolate flavor, but did note a vanilla or "white chocolate" presence. "Like a hot Yoo-hoo: thin and watery."

SWISS MISS Milk Chocolate Hot Cocoa Mix

PRICE: $1.99 for 10 ounces (about $0.20 per serving)
COMMENTS: Its first two ingredients are sugar and corn syrup; tasters found this cocoa "really sweet," with "more sugar than chocolate." They rated it the sweetest of all with the second-weakest chocolate profile; one called it "super-mild and artificial."

LOW-FAT STRAWBERRY YOGURT

Low-fat yogurt far outsells full-fat and nonfat versions in American supermarkets. In the past year, more strawberry yogurts have been introduced to the market than any other flavor. To see which low-fat strawberry yogurt was best, we rounded up eight national brands. Our tasters' preferences tracked closely to berry flavor (ahead of tang or texture), with Dannon leading the pack. Along with our two other recommended yogurts, Dannon puts strawberries second (after milk) on its ingredient list; by law, ingredients are listed on labels in order of amounts. By comparison, the yogurts that list sugar second (ahead of berries) had lackluster berry flavor. And our lowest-rated brand contains no strawberries at all—just artificial strawberry flavor. Every brand we tested, save one, contained at least two stabilizers. While the type of stabilizers used didn't fully correlate with our textural preferences, none of our three recommended brands contains kosher gelatin. When shopping for strawberry yogurt, look for brands that list strawberries ahead of sugar—the more strawberries, the more strawberry flavor. If you like its strong tang and thick texture, Greek-style Fage 2% is an excellent choice; otherwise we recommend the yogurts from Dannon and Wallaby. Yogurts are listed in order of preference.

RECOMMENDED

DANNON Fruit on the Bottom Strawberry Yogurt
PRICE: $.75 for 6 ounces
MILK FAT CONTENT: 1%
COMMENTS: This brand scored either first or second in all three criteria we rated: tang, texture, and strawberry flavor. Tasters liked that it "wasn't too sweet," and had "good strawberry flavor" and a "creamy" texture. "Actually tastes like it has strawberries in it," one pleased taster said.

WALLABY ORGANIC Creamy Australian Style Lowfat Strawberry Yogurt
PRICE: $1.19 for 6 ounces
MILK FAT CONTENT: 1½%
COMMENTS: This "sweet and milky" yogurt has a "strong, fresh dairy flavor." Tasters liked the flavor more than the texture, however, noting, "a bit thin, but tastes nice and bright." "Good-sized strawberry bits" contributed to its "bright berry flavor."

FAGE 2% All Natural Greek Strained Yogurt with Strawberry
PRICE: $1.99 for 5.3 ounces
MILK FAT CONTENT: 2%
COMMENTS: Tasters compared this polarizing sample to "sour cream," "brie," and "crème fraîche." The pros: "What yogurt should taste like"; "creamy and super thick." The cons: "chalky," "too thick," and "funky." Everybody agreed that this was "not your average yogurt."

RECOMMENDED WITH RESERVATIONS

YOPLAIT Original Strawberry Lowfat Yogurt
PRICE: $.75 for 6 ounces
MILK FAT CONTENT: 1%
COMMENTS: Several panelists faulted Yoplait's "very sweet," "generic berry flavor" as "fake-tasting." One compared it (unfavorably, of course) to Pop Rocks candy.

RECOMMENDED WITH RESERVATIONS *(continued)*

BREYERS Fruit on the Bottom Smart Strawberry Lowfat Yogurt
PRICE: $.79 for 6 ounces
MILK FAT CONTENT: 1%
COMMENTS: Tasters found this "very sweet" yogurt "artificial," "plasticky," and "not memorable." "Not really any yogurt or strawberry flavor," an unimpressed taster said.

BROWN COW Strawberry Low Fat Yogurt
PRICE: $.99 for 6 ounces
MILK FAT CONTENT: 1%
COMMENTS: The "thick, smooth" texture was fine; the flavor was not. "Strange perfume taste," one taster said. "Very strong floral-fruity flavor," another seconded. "Why," asked a third, "does this taste like banana?"

STONYFIELD FARM Organic Lowfat Strawberry Yogurt
PRICE: $.99 for 6 ounces
MILK FAT CONTENT: 1%
COMMENTS: Tasters disliked Stonyfield's "loose," "watery" texture. "Why is it separated?" asked one. The yogurt won points for its "milky," "natural-tasting" tang, but lost them for "bland," "too mild" strawberry flavor.

NOT RECOMMENDED

COLOMBO Lowfat Strawberry Flavored Yogurt
PRICE: $1.69 for 32 ounces
MILK FAT CONTENT: ½%
COMMENTS: This "overly sweet," "fake-tasting" yogurt (which does not contain strawberries) ranked last in every category—tang, strawberry flavor, and texture. Tasters compared it to "Jell-O mixed with cornstarch," "strawberry Quik," and "strawberry shampoo."

BAKED BEANS

Baked beans are a staple of backyard gatherings, but few of us bother to make them from scratch. Canned baked beans deliver convenience, especially in the heat of summer. But are they any good? We gathered several brands of beans, all of which were heated in saucepans and sampled plain. Tasters universally liked sweet, slightly firm beans. Surprisingly, a meatless product, B&M Vegetarian Baked Beans, came out on top, just ahead of Bush's and Van Camp's. Tasters rated these three brands the sweetest, and a check of the ingredient list confirmed that they did indeed contain the most sugars. The top brands were also judged to have the best texture, which makes sense when you consider that sugar slows the softening process (our tasters liked beans with a little bite). More important, the type of sweetener had a big impact on flavor. Our top brands all contain molasses, a classic baked bean seasoning that adds complexity and depth. By contrast, our least-favorite brands rely instead on high fructose corn syrup, evaporated cane juice and maple syrup, or sorghum. The lowest-ranked brands also contain tomato puree, which made the beans taste inappropriately "ketchup-y." Baked beans are listed in order of preference.

RECOMMENDED

B&M Vegetarian Baked Beans
PRICE: $2 for 28 ounces
SUGARS: 12g per serving
COMMENTS: Tasters loved the "very molasses-y" flavor of the these beans, calling them "slightly sweet, complex, with a slow-cooked feeling." "Richer than the others" was a common refrain. Their "firm" and "pleasant" texture was another big plus.

BUSH'S BEST Original Baked Beans
PRICE: $2 for 28 ounces
SUGARS: 12g per serving
COMMENTS: Bush's came in a close second over-all, and were given the highest scores for their texture, which was described as "creamy" but "firm." Tasters deemed these beans the sweetest of the lot, and praised their "smoky, rich flavor," which had a "nice balance of salty and sweet."

VAN CAMP'S Original Baked Beans
PRICE: $1.89 for 28 ounces
SUGARS: 11g per serving
COMMENTS: These "very smoky" (they contain natural smoke flavor) beans received solid scores across the board. "Nicely complex, with a texture that is soft but not mushy," said one taster. But there was no mistaking this brand for home-made beans, with a few tasters picking up a range of (not unpleasant) flavors from "cola" to "salad dressing."

RECOMMENDED WITH RESERVATIONS

B&M Original Baked Beans
PRICE: $2 for 28 ounces
SUGARS: 10g per serving
COMMENTS: These beans have less total sugars than their vegetarian cousins. Tasters liked the "nice molasses" flavor, but were none too keen on the "refried-bean-like" (and lowest-scoring) texture, which was "thick and sludgy" and "sticky."

NOT RECOMMENDED

CAMPBELL'S Pork & Beans
PRICE: $1.69 for 15.75 ounces
TOTAL SUGARS: 8g per serving
COMMENTS: To be fair, these are labeled "Pork and Beans" and not baked beans. Tasters found them "bland," "runny," and "entirely unremark-able." "I feel no compulsion to keep eating them."

AMY'S Organic Vegetarian Baked Beans
PRICE: $2.69 for 15 ounces
SUGARS: 9g per serving
COMMENTS: Ironically, tasters likened this relatively wholesome brand's flavor to highly processed foods like "SpaghettiOs" and "Chef Boyardee." "Tastes like grade school," said one. Another thought these "ketchup-y" beans tasted of "tinny tomato, chemicals, and shoe polish." Enough said.

EDEN Organic Baked Beans
PRICE: $1.99 for 15 ounces
SUGARS: 6g per serving
COMMENTS: With just half as much sugars as our winners, tasters found these beans to be "mushy" (as sugar retards softening, less sugar usually means softer beans) and "bitter." Tasters disliked the "clove-y," "burnt," and "metallic," flavors. "I couldn't even swallow these" sums things up.

AUTOMATIC DRIP COFFEE MAKERS

Have manufacturers finally developed an automatic drip coffee maker that can produce a terrific brew? We found seven brands with thermal carafes and at least a 10-cup capacity at prices from $47 to nearly $300. Unfortunately, most made the same kind of mediocre coffee we've come to expect: bitter, weak, or one-dimensional. What was the problem? Aside from fresh, high-quality coffee beans and good-tasting cold water, the two most important factors in making good coffee are the water temperature as it passes through the grounds and the length of time the grounds are exposed to the water. In the end, only one coffee maker stood out: The Technivorm Moccamaster consistently brewed smooth, full-flavored coffee that our tasters ranked highest. It turns out that the most expensive part of the coffee maker is the heating element, something most manufacturers skimp on by using inexpensive aluminum. In contrast, the Technivorm's heating element is made of far more expensive copper. Its price tag is high, but its consistently full-flavored, smooth brew will pay for itself when you start skipping a few trips to Starbucks. Coffee makers are listed in order of preference.

RECOMMENDED	PERFORMANCE	TESTERS' COMMENTS
TECHNIVORM Moccamaster Coffeemaker, Model KBT741 PRICE: $239.95	BREWING: ★★★ FLAVOR: ★★★ USER-FRIENDLINESS: ★★★	Fast, very simple to operate. Tasters described coffee as "clean, flavorful and expressive," "very good; robust but smooth." Achieved perfect temperatures for brewing and serving and was the closest of all the coffee makers to reaching the ideal brewing time. Pieces disassemble easily for cleaning. Though not programmable, this machine was so fast and easy to use, we didn't mind.

RECOMMENDED WITH RESERVATIONS	PERFORMANCE	TESTERS' COMMENTS
KRUPS 10-Cup Programmable Thermal Coffee Machine, Model FMF5 PRICE: $95.93	BREWING: ★ FLAVOR: ★★ USER-FRIENDLINESS: ★★★	Compact and attractive, this programmable machine is simple to use, but it lost points for too-slow and slightly too-hot brewing. Thin water line down front of machine magnifies as water is added, making it easy to read levels. Optional beeper indicates when brewing is complete. Tasters deemed its coffee "slightly too bitter."
CUISINART Grind & Brew Thermal 12-Cup Automatic Coffeemaker, Model DGB-900BC PRICE: $199	BREWING: ★ FLAVOR: ★★ USER-FRIENDLINESS: ★★	The attached burr grinder is so loud it will wake anyone who isn't already up in the morning. Controls and carafe were well designed, but brewing water spent most of the cycle well below optimal temperature. While a few tasters called the coffee "mellow," others deemed it "bitter," and "thin."
BLACK & DECKER 10-Cup Thermal Stainless Steel Coffeemaker, Model TCM830 PRICE: $59.99	BREWING: ★ FLAVOR: ★★ USER-FRIENDLINESS: ★★	Innovative lift-out water reservoir you can take to the sink and fill, but controls could use improvement: one button turned the machine on and off and set programs with different numbers of pushes. Coffee was "strong," but "nothing exceptional." Brewing water remained too cool for most of the cycle, then spiked up too high near the end.

NOT RECOMMENDED	PERFORMANCE	TESTERS' COMMENTS
HAMILTON BEACH Stay or Go Deluxe 10-Cup Thermal Coffeemaker, Model 45238 PRICE: $89.99	BREWING: ★ FLAVOR: ★ USER-FRIENDLINESS: ★★★	This programmable machine is easy to use and fill, with simple controls, and we liked the two commuter cups you can brew into directly. But it's by far the slowest coffee make in the lineup, taking 18 minutes to produce a pot. Brewing water was too cool and took 16 minutes of the brew cycle to reach the proper temperature. Tasters found the coffee "strong" but too "bitter."
MR. COFFEE 10-Cup Thermal Programmable Coffee Maker, Model FTTX95 PRICE: $47.24	BREWING: ★ FLAVOR: ★ USER-FRIENDLINESS: ★★	Attractive machine, but water filter is fussy. Tasters found the coffee the most bitter of the lineup, and rated it near the bottom for complexity of flavor. Brewing temperature fluctuated too much.
CAPRESSO CoffeeTEAM Therm, Model 455 PRICE: $299	BREWING: ★ FLAVOR: ★ USER-FRIENDLINESS: ★	For the price, the coffee should taste better, and it takes up too much counter space. Coffee was brewed at too high a temperature, making it "too hot to drink," "weak and watery," and "bitter." Tiny parts for brew basket were easily lost and had to be in exactly the right place for proper function.

TRADITIONAL SKILLETS

You can cook almost anything in a 12-inch skillet, whether you want to sauté, shallow-fry, pan-roast, or even stir-fry. Its shape encourages evaporation, which is why skillets excel at searing, browning, and sauce reduction. In particular, a skillet with a traditional, rather than nonstick, surface allows food to adhere slightly, which helps create fond, the foundation for great flavor. We chose six skillets from leading manufacturers; five were fully clad with layers of aluminum and stainless steel covering the entire pan, while one had an aluminum-steel disk bottom. The best skillets transmitted heat steadily and evenly; had even, moderate sauté speed; and came up to temperature at a moderate pace. They also had a generous cooking surface, lower sides, and a good balance of weight between handle and pan. Skillets are listed in order of preference.

HIGHLY RECOMMENDED

ALL-CLAD Stainless 12-Inch Fry Pan Model 5112
PRICE: $135
WEIGHT: 2.75 lbs
BOTTOM THICKNESS: 3.18mm
COOKING SURFACE DIAMETER: 9¾ inches
HEIGHT OF SIDES: 1⅞ inches

PERFORMANCE
PERFORMANCE: ★★★
SAUTÉ SPEED: ★★★
USER-FRIENDLINESS: ★★★
DURABILITY: ★★★

TESTERS' COMMENTS
Testers praised this pan for having "everything you need in a skillet" with enough surface for sautéing eight chicken pieces; steady heat for excellent browning; and low sides. The weight balance was outstanding; it was easy to manipulate and lift.

RECOMMENDED

CALPHALON Contemporary Stainless 12-Inch Omelette Pan MODEL LR 1392
PRICE: $119.95
WEIGHT: 2.9 lbs
BOTTOM THICKNESS: 2.44mm
COOKING SURFACE DIAMETER: 9¾ inches
HEIGHT OF SIDES: 2¼ inches

PERFORMANCE
PERFORMANCE: ★★★
SAUTÉ SPEED: ★★
USER-FRIENDLINESS: ★★★
DURABILITY: ★★

TESTERS' COMMENTS
This handle-heavy skillet struck testers as "lightweight, almost flimsy." This pan is the thinnest of the lineup, which made it hard to control: We had to keep reducing the flame, but once we did, the results were excellent.

WEIL by Spring, The Healthy Kitchen 12-Inch Fry Pan Model 1812
PRICE: $120
WEIGHT: 3.95 lbs
BOTTOM THICKNESS: 3.5mm
COOKING SURFACE DIAMETER: 9 inches
HEIGHT OF SIDES: 1⅞ inches

PERFORMANCE
PERFORMANCE: ★★
SAUTÉ SPEED: ★★★
USER-FRIENDLINESS: ★★
DURABILITY: ★★

TESTERS' COMMENTS
This "five-ply" pan with extra layers of aluminum alloy around an aluminum core had slow and steady heat. Its smaller cooking surface left steaks slightly crowded and chicken unevenly browned. It is heavier than we prefer, but handled well despite its weight.

ALL-CLAD 13-Inch Stainless French Skillet Model 5113
PRICE: $99.95
WEIGHT: 3.6 lbs
BOTTOM THICKNESS: 3.42mm
COOKING SURFACE DIAMETER: 11 inches
HEIGHT OF SIDES: 2⅛ inches

PERFORMANCE
PERFORMANCE: ★★
SAUTÉ SPEED: ★★
USER-FRIENDLINESS: ★★
DURABILITY: ★★

TESTERS' COMMENTS
Testers loved the generous span of this pan's cooking surface, but it was heavy and awkward to manipulate, with a fast sauté speed that required vigilance. It dented and the handle loosened in our abuse test.

NOT RECOMMENDED

CUISINART Chef's Classic Stainless 12-Inch Skillet Model 722-30H
PRICE: $49.95
WEIGHT: 3.05 lbs
BOTTOM THICKNESS: 4.0mm
COOKING SURFACE DIAMETER: 10½ inches
HEIGHT OF SIDES: 2 inches

PERFORMANCE
PERFORMANCE: ★
SAUTÉ SPEED: ★
USER-FRIENDLINESS: ★★
DURABILITY: ★

TESTERS' COMMENTS
Heat built up in the thick aluminum disk and transmitted abundantly through the cooking surface, making the temperature climb precipitously. Onions scorched, even when we lowered the heat. In the durability test, the disk bottom fell off.

SILICONE SPATULAS

Old-fashioned rubber spatulas melt in high heat. Some are so stiff they can't fold egg whites. Others are so flexible they bend when confronted with thick cookie dough. In our quest to find one spatula that could do it all, we singled out 8 contenders—all dishwasher-safe and priced between $7 and $19. The ideal material for the head is silicone, which is heat-resistant, inert (it doesn't release chemicals into the air or your food), and endlessly customizable. Testers liked silicone heads that were not only soft and flexible enough to sweep all traces of batter out of a mixing bowl but stiff enough to remove sticky brown bits, or fond, from a skillet. They also wanted the top edge of the head to be flat, fairly rigid, and squared off; the edges thin enough to maneuver into hard-to-reach corners; and a flat face that would scrape clean in one stroke against the rim of a pot or bowl. Spatulas are listed in order of preference.

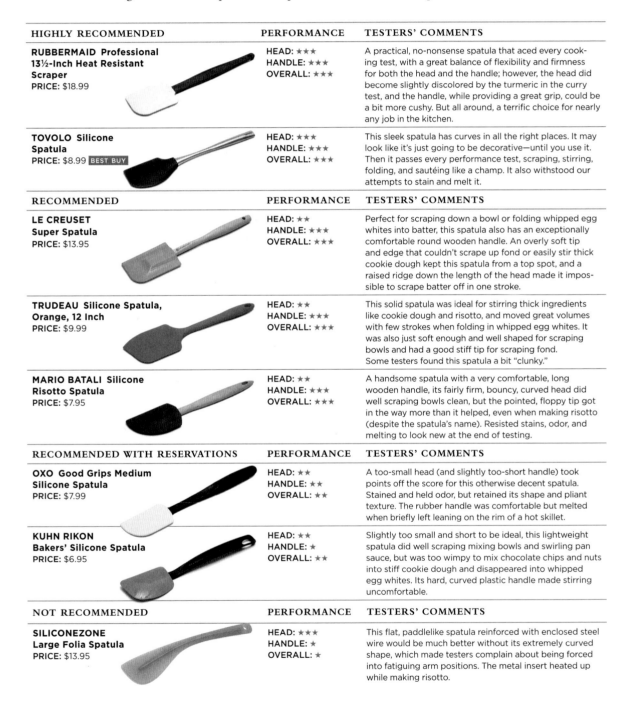

HIGHLY RECOMMENDED	PERFORMANCE	TESTERS' COMMENTS
RUBBERMAID Professional 13½-Inch Heat Resistant Scraper PRICE: $18.99	HEAD: ★★★ HANDLE: ★★★ OVERALL: ★★★	A practical, no-nonsense spatula that aced every cooking test, with a great balance of flexibility and firmness for both the head and the handle; however, the head did become slightly discolored by the turmeric in the curry test, and the handle, while providing a great grip, could be a bit more cushy. But all around, a terrific choice for nearly any job in the kitchen.
TOVOLO Silicone Spatula PRICE: $8.99 BEST BUY	HEAD: ★★★ HANDLE: ★★★ OVERALL: ★★★	This sleek spatula has curves in all the right places. It may look like it's just going to be decorative—until you use it. Then it passes every performance test, scraping, stirring, folding, and sautéing like a champ. It also withstood our attempts to stain and melt it.

RECOMMENDED	PERFORMANCE	TESTERS' COMMENTS
LE CREUSET Super Spatula PRICE: $13.95	HEAD: ★★ HANDLE: ★★★ OVERALL: ★★★	Perfect for scraping down a bowl or folding whipped egg whites into batter, this spatula also has an exceptionally comfortable round wooden handle. An overly soft tip and edge that couldn't scrape up fond or easily stir thick cookie dough kept this spatula from a top spot, and a raised ridge down the length of the head made it impossible to scrape batter off in one stroke.
TRUDEAU Silicone Spatula, Orange, 12 Inch PRICE: $9.99	HEAD: ★★ HANDLE: ★★★ OVERALL: ★★★	This solid spatula was ideal for stirring thick ingredients like cookie dough and risotto, and moved great volumes with few strokes when folding in whipped egg whites. It was also just soft enough and well shaped for scraping bowls and had a good stiff tip for scraping fond. Some testers found this spatula a bit "clunky."
MARIO BATALI Silicone Risotto Spatula PRICE: $7.95	HEAD: ★★ HANDLE: ★★★ OVERALL: ★★★	A handsome spatula with a very comfortable, long wooden handle, its fairly firm, bouncy, curved head did well scraping bowls clean, but the pointed, floppy tip got in the way more than it helped, even when making risotto (despite the spatula's name). Resisted stains, odor, and melting to look new at the end of testing.

RECOMMENDED WITH RESERVATIONS	PERFORMANCE	TESTERS' COMMENTS
OXO Good Grips Medium Silicone Spatula PRICE: $7.99	HEAD: ★★ HANDLE: ★★ OVERALL: ★★	A too-small head (and slightly too-short handle) took points off the score for this otherwise decent spatula. Stained and held odor, but retained its shape and pliant texture. The rubber handle was comfortable but melted when briefly left leaning on the rim of a hot skillet.
KUHN RIKON Bakers' Silicone Spatula PRICE: $6.95	HEAD: ★★ HANDLE: ★ OVERALL: ★★	Slightly too small and short to be ideal, this lightweight spatula did well scraping mixing bowls and swirling pan sauce, but was too wimpy to mix chocolate chips and nuts into stiff cookie dough and disappeared into whipped egg whites. Its hard, curved plastic handle made stirring uncomfortable.

NOT RECOMMENDED	PERFORMANCE	TESTERS' COMMENTS
SILICONEZONE Large Folia Spatula PRICE: $13.95	HEAD: ★★★ HANDLE: ★ OVERALL: ★	This flat, paddlelike spatula reinforced with enclosed steel wire would be much better without its extremely curved shape, which made testers complain about being forced into fatiguing arm positions. The metal insert heated up while making risotto.

SLICING KNIVES

A good slicing knife cuts cleanly through muscle fiber and connective tissue and produces thin, uniform slices. We chose eight models with the following criteria: an extra-long blade that could slice through large cuts of meat, enough sturdiness to ensure a straight cutting path, and a round tip that wouldn't get caught. We also knew to single out knives with a hollow or granton edge and eliminate carving knives, because their pointed tip and narrow blade make them too agile to maintain a straight cutting path. After slicing more than 180 pounds of roast beef, ham, turkey, and smoked salmon, we learned a few more things: a 12-inch blade was ideal and it should be neither overly stiff nor too flexible. Heavier knives were more stable and knives with a significantly tapered blade performed best. Knives are listed in order of preference.

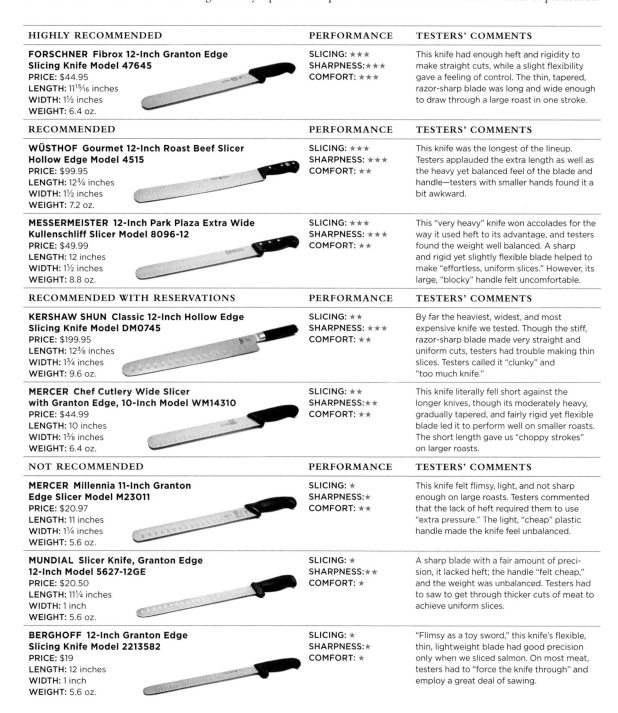

HIGHLY RECOMMENDED	PERFORMANCE	TESTERS' COMMENTS
FORSCHNER Fibrox 12-Inch Granton Edge Slicing Knife Model 47645 PRICE: $44.95 LENGTH: 11¹⁵⁄₁₆ inches WIDTH: 1½ inches WEIGHT: 6.4 oz.	SLICING: ★★★ SHARPNESS: ★★★ COMFORT: ★★★	This knife had enough heft and rigidity to make straight cuts, while a slight flexibility gave a feeling of control. The thin, tapered, razor-sharp blade was long and wide enough to draw through a large roast in one stroke.

RECOMMENDED	PERFORMANCE	TESTERS' COMMENTS
WÜSTHOF Gourmet 12-Inch Roast Beef Slicer Hollow Edge Model 4515 PRICE: $99.95 LENGTH: 12¾ inches WIDTH: 1½ inches WEIGHT: 7.2 oz.	SLICING: ★★★ SHARPNESS: ★★★ COMFORT: ★★	This knife was the longest of the lineup. Testers applauded the extra length as well as the heavy yet balanced feel of the blade and handle—testers with smaller hands found it a bit awkward.
MESSERMEISTER 12-Inch Park Plaza Extra Wide Kullenschliff Slicer Model 8096-12 PRICE: $49.99 LENGTH: 12 inches WIDTH: 1½ inches WEIGHT: 8.8 oz.	SLICING: ★★★ SHARPNESS: ★★★ COMFORT: ★★	This "very heavy" knife won accolades for the way it used heft to its advantage, and testers found the weight well balanced. A sharp and rigid yet slightly flexible blade helped to make "effortless, uniform slices." However, its large, "blocky" handle felt uncomfortable.

RECOMMENDED WITH RESERVATIONS	PERFORMANCE	TESTERS' COMMENTS
KERSHAW SHUN Classic 12-Inch Hollow Edge Slicing Knife Model DM0745 PRICE: $199.95 LENGTH: 12⅜ inches WIDTH: 1¾ inches WEIGHT: 9.6 oz.	SLICING: ★★ SHARPNESS: ★★★ COMFORT: ★★	By far the heaviest, widest, and most expensive knife we tested. Though the stiff, razor-sharp blade made very straight and uniform cuts, testers had trouble making thin slices. Testers called it "clunky" and "too much knife."
MERCER Chef Cutlery Wide Slicer with Granton Edge, 10-Inch Model WM14310 PRICE: $44.99 LENGTH: 10 inches WIDTH: 1⅜ inches WEIGHT: 6.4 oz.	SLICING: ★★ SHARPNESS: ★★ COMFORT: ★★	This knife literally fell short against the longer knives, though its moderately heavy, gradually tapered, and fairly rigid yet flexible blade led it to perform well on smaller roasts. The short length gave us "choppy strokes" on larger roasts.

NOT RECOMMENDED	PERFORMANCE	TESTERS' COMMENTS
MERCER Millennia 11-Inch Granton Edge Slicer Model M23011 PRICE: $20.97 LENGTH: 11 inches WIDTH: 1¼ inches WEIGHT: 5.6 oz.	SLICING: ★ SHARPNESS: ★ COMFORT: ★★	This knife felt flimsy, light, and not sharp enough on large roasts. Testers commented that the lack of heft required them to use "extra pressure." The light, "cheap" plastic handle made the knife feel unbalanced.
MUNDIAL Slicer Knife, Granton Edge 12-Inch Model 5627-12GE PRICE: $20.50 LENGTH: 11¼ inches WIDTH: 1 inch WEIGHT: 5.6 oz.	SLICING: ★ SHARPNESS: ★★ COMFORT: ★	A sharp blade with a fair amount of precision, it lacked heft; the handle "felt cheap," and the weight was unbalanced. Testers had to saw to get through thicker cuts of meat to achieve uniform slices.
BERGHOFF 12-Inch Granton Edge Slicing Knife Model 2213582 PRICE: $19 LENGTH: 12 inches WIDTH: 1 inch WEIGHT: 5.6 oz.	SLICING: ★ SHARPNESS: ★ COMFORT: ★	"Flimsy as a toy sword," this knife's flexible, thin, lightweight blade had good precision only when we sliced salmon. On most meat, testers had to "force the knife through" and employ a great deal of sawing.

PIE PLATES

In search of a versatile, all-around pie plate, we tested eight models by baking an unfilled pie shell, a quiche, an apple pie, and a pat-in-the-pan graham cracker crust. The best pans produced blind-baked shells that were golden brown on both sides and bottoms, apple pies with evenly cooked fillings, and graham cracker crusts that didn't slump, crack, or crumble. But the real litmus test turned out to be quiche. Our winning pie plates conducted enough heat to set the egg custard to a creamy texture without overbaking the crust. The best plates were made of glass or ceramic; both conduct heat slowly, so heat gradually builds and spreads throughout the plate. Our favorite all-purpose pie plate is the glass Pyrex plate, which provides slow, steady, insulating heat for even baking. Its shallow, angled sides prevent crusts from slumping and its basic, functional design, flawless performance, and low price made it the clear winner. Pie plates are listed in order of preference.

HIGHLY RECOMMENDED		PERFORMANCE	TESTERS' COMMENTS
PYREX Bakeware **9-Inch Pie Plate Model 6001003** PRICE: $2.99 MATERIAL: Ovenproof tempered glass		BLIND-BAKED SHELL: ★★★ QUICHE: ★★★ APPLE PIE: ★★★ DESIGN: ★★★	Good crisping and browning; a see-through bottom to monitor the bottom crust; a half-inch rim; shallow, angled sides; and a low price made this our winner—again.

RECOMMENDED		PERFORMANCE	TESTERS' COMMENTS
ROSE'S Perfect Pie Plate by Rose Levy Beranbaum Model RL3 PRICE: $19.99 MATERIAL: Glazed ceramic		BLIND-BAKED SHELL: ★★★ QUICHE: ★★★ APPLE PIE: ★★★ DESIGN: ★★	Rose Levy Beranbaum, author of *The Pie and Pastry Bible*, designed this scalloped-edge ceramic plate to help create attractive pies. It made perfect filling, but browned edges a bit too quickly.

RECOMMENDED WITH RESERVATIONS		PERFORMANCE	TESTERS' COMMENTS
PYREX 9½-Inch Advantage Pie Plate Model 1073356 PRICE: $5.99 MATERIAL: Ovenproof tempered glass		BLIND-BAKED SHELL: ★★★ QUICHE: ★★★ APPLE PIE: ★★★ DESIGN: ★	Good browning and crisping, evenly cooked fillings, and large handles made this plate appealing. But scallop-shaped depressions around the edges for press-in fluting actually made pies look messy.
CORNINGWARE SimplyLite 9-Inch Pie Plate Model 1080843 PRICE: $9.99 MATERIAL: Glass laminate		BLIND-BAKED SHELL: ★★ QUICHE: ★★★ APPLE PIE: ★★★ DESIGN: ★	This plate made impressively crisp bottom crusts, but was too deep for ready-made pie dough and produced a graham cracker crust that slumped.
DOUGHMAKERS Pie Pan with Crust Protector Model 10595825 PRICE: $19.99 MATERIAL: Aluminum		BLIND-BAKED SHELL: ★★ QUICHE: ★★ APPLE PIE: ★★ DESIGN: ★	Pies baked in this plate required 25 percent more oven time than recipes called for—and still had pockets of unevenly cooked filling. The so-called crust "protector" crushed the fluted pastry as it baked.

NOT RECOMMENDED		PERFORMANCE	TESTERS' COMMENTS
NORPRO Nonstick Pie Crust Pan with Shield Model 3913 PRICE: $9.99 MATERIAL: Steel with nonstick coating		BLIND-BAKED SHELL: ★ QUICHE: ★ APPLE PIE: ★★ DESIGN: ★	The perforated shield/pie weight conducted heat too well and overbrowned the blind-baked crust. The nonstick coating scratched deeply at the first cut.
CHICAGO Metallic Perforated Pie Pans Model 10517934 PRICE: $8.99 for 2 MATERIAL: Aluminum alloy		BLIND-BAKED SHELL: ★ QUICHE: ★ APPLE PIE: ★ DESIGN: ★	A perforated bottom let moisture escape and evaporate from the bottom of the pie plate, which made the crust soggy.
CRISPY CRUST Pie Pan MODEL 1543-79271-1334 PRICE: $14.99 MATERIAL: Aluminum with stainless steel mesh bottom		BLIND-BAKED SHELL: ★ QUICHE: ★ APPLE PIE: ★ DESIGN: ★	The mesh bottom let steam and heat escape, so the bottom crust never baked through. Fillings leaked through the mesh. The crust fused to the leaking fillings and created a sticky mess.

PLASTIC WRAP

Plastic wrap is essential for keeping food fresh as well as for storing and freezing, but using it can drive you crazy: The roll rips and wraps around itself; the plastic clings to itself more than the dish or won't stick at all; and most important, it doesn't keep food from spoiling quickly. We measured strength by pulling pieces of wrap until they tore or lost their shape. We then tested the ability of the wraps to cling by placing grapes in plastic, metal, and glass bowls, covering each with wrap, and shaking the inverted bowls. Finally, we tested the ability of the wraps to keep foods fresh. For this we put 1 tablespoon of Drierite (an absorbent used in packaging) in small glass bowls covered tightly with a sheet of each wrap. If the Drierite turned bright pink, it indicated that the wrap had allowed moisture in, which means food would spoil faster. As it turns out, plastic wrap can be made from two distinctly different substances: a food-safe version of PVC or low-density polyethylene (LDPE). PVC clings but is not impermeable; LDPE is impermeable but has far less cling. Our advice? Clingy PVC wraps are preferable if you are transporting food or are worried about spills and leaks, but to keep foods fresh longer, select plastic wraps made from LDPE. Plastic wraps are listed in order of preference.

RECOMMENDED	PERFORMANCE	TESTERS' COMMENTS
GLAD Cling Wrap Clear Plastic PRICE: $1.20 per 100 square feet MATERIAL: Low-Density Polyethylene (LDPE)	IMPERMEABILITY: ★★★ STRENGTH AND CLING: ★★ PACKAGING: ★★	This wrap aced the impermeability test. Its box featured well-placed, sharp teeth, and an adhesive pad to hold the cut end of the wrap. It clung slightly less well than PVC-based wraps, but it got the job done and offered good value.

RECOMMENDED WITH RESERVATIONS	PERFORMANCE	TESTERS' COMMENTS
STRETCH-TITE Plastic Food Wrap PRICE: $1.72 per 100 square feet MATERIAL: Polyvinyl Chloride (PVC)	IMPERMEABILITY: ★ STRENGTH AND CLING: ★★★ PACKAGING: ★★	This wrap had the most cling and was by far the toughest of the lineup. Unfortunately, it was one of the first wraps to turn pink in the Drierite test, meaning it allowed moisture to penetrate.
SARAN Premium Wrap PRICE: $2.99 per 100 square feet MATERIAL: Low-Density Polyethylene (LDPE)	IMPERMEABILITY: ★★★ STRENGTH AND CLING: ★ PACKAGING: ★★	Its easy "tear and restart" strip earned this wrap points, as did its ability to keep moisture out. However, it bombed the cling test. Plus, it wouldn't stick to plastic bowls.
GLAD Press'n Seal Plastic Wrap PRICE: $4.56 per 100 square feet MATERIAL: Low-Density Polyethylene (LDPE) with Griptex	IMPERMEABILITY: ★★★ STRENGTH AND CLING: ★★ PACKAGING: ★	This wrap will stick to anything, and it performed well in our moisture test, but its price and inability to restick once the initial seal is broken pushed its rating down. Also, the frosted film makes it impossible to see into the bowl.
SARAN Cling Plus Wrap PRICE: $1 per 100 square feet MATERIAL: Low-Density Polyethylene (LDPE)	IMPERMEABILITY: ★★★ STRENGTH AND CLING: ★ PACKAGING: ★	It passed the moisture-proof test and offered the best value of the lineup. But the sharp teeth along the bottom sent testers running for Band-Aids. The wrap clung tightly to glass, but the seal broke after six shakes of a metal bowl and just three in a plastic one.

NOT RECOMMENDED	PERFORMANCE	TESTERS' COMMENTS
FREEZE-TITE Freezer Wrap PRICE: $4.01 per 100 square feet MATERIAL: Polyvinyl Chloride (PVC)	IMPERMEABILITY: ★ STRENGTH AND CLING: ★★★ PACKAGING: ★	This brand offered the widest sheets of the wraps we tested, but it failed our moisture-proof test. In the kitchen, that would mean freezer burn. Also, this wrap often tore as it was dispensed, and its price was among the highest.
REYNOLDS Seal-Tight Plastic Wrap PRICE: $2 per 100 square feet MATERIAL: Polyvinyl Chloride (PVC)	IMPERMEABILITY: ★ STRENGTH AND CLING: ★★ PACKAGING: ★	A "quick release" tab tore off, causing the wrap to stick to itself before testing even began. While its sticking performance was fine, it allowed moisture to penetrate within two days (compared to three weeks for other wraps).

BLENDERS

When you come right down to it, a blender has one basic job—to blend food into a uniform consistency, whether it's crushing ice or producing lump-free purees. And just two things matter for success at this basic job: the configuration of the blender blades and a V-shaped jar that keeps food close to the blade edges. We gathered 9 models of blenders, including basic machines as well as those that boasted fancy new features. Our top performer impressed us with both its brute strength and efficiency. Each of its four blades was positioned at a different angle, maximizing its ability to pulverize food. Blenders are listed in order of preference.

HIGHLY RECOMMENDED	PERFORMANCE	TESTERS' COMMENTS
KITCHENAID 5-Speed Blender MODEL: KSB580 PRICE: $149.99 JAR MATERIAL AND CAPACITY: Polycarbonate, 56 ounces	ICE CRUSHING: ★★★ SMOOTHIE: ★★★ HUMMUS: ★★★ SPEED: ★★★ SOUND LEVEL: ★★★	A large, powerful machine. Ice was quickly pulverized, smoothies were lump-free, and hummus was perfectly consistent. Although the blades could not be removed, the entire jar is dishwasher-safe.

RECOMMENDED	PERFORMANCE	TESTERS' COMMENTS
KALORIK BL Blender MODEL: 16909 PRICE: $49.99 BEST BUY JAR MATERIAL AND CAPACITY: Glass, 50 ounces	ICE CRUSHING: ★★★ SMOOTHIE: ★★ HUMMUS: ★★★ SPEED: ★★ SOUND LEVEL: ★★★	Excelled at ice crushing and hummus mixing but left pulp in the smoothie. This ultra-quiet blender had six blades—two serrated—and a steeply tapered glass jar that helped keep the contents moving.

RECOMMENDED WITH RESERVATIONS	PERFORMANCE	TESTERS' COMMENTS
L'EQUIP RPM Blender MODEL: 228 PRICE: $165.99 JAR MATERIAL AND CAPACITY: Plastic, 56 ounces	ICE CRUSHING: ★ SMOOTHIE: ★★★ HUMMUS: ★★★ SPEED: ★★★ SOUND LEVEL: ★	Our past winner fell seriously short when it came to crushing ice, leaving lots of solid chunks stuck to the walls beyond reach of the blades. This model also lost points for noise.
HAMILTON BEACH Dual Wave Blender MODEL: 52147H PRICE: $69.99 JAR MATERIAL AND CAPACITY: Plastic, 80 ounces	ICE CRUSHING: ★★★ SMOOTHIE: ★★★ HUMMUS: ★ SPEED: ★★ SOUND LEVEL: ★	A huge jar and side-by-side "dual-action" blades. With ice and smoothies, the two blades tag-teamed to pulverize ingredients, but they turned hummus into a frothy drink instead of a puree. Not a good all-purpose blender.
WARING Professional Bar Blender MODEL: MBB518 PRICE: $129.95 JAR MATERIAL AND CAPACITY: Glass, 40 ounces	ICE CRUSHING: ★ SMOOTHIE: ★★ HUMMUS: ★★ SPEED: ★★ SOUND LEVEL: ★★★	Struggled to crush ice efficiently; only a middling performer with smoothies and hummus. The cloverleaf-shaped jar was extremely narrow.
CUISINART SmartPower Premiere 600-Watt Blender MODEL: CBT-500 PRICE: $99.95 JAR MATERIAL AND CAPACITY: Glass, 50 ounces	ICE CRUSHING: ★★★ SMOOTHIE: ★★ HUMMUS: ★ SPEED: ★★ SOUND LEVEL: ★★	Crushed ice with ease, but its bulky jar didn't push food to the center. To remove the jar you must lift without twisting, or the contents pour out the bottom.
VIKING Professional Blender MODEL: VBLG01 PRICE: $149.95 JAR MATERIAL AND CAPACITY: Glass, 40 ounces	ICE CRUSHING: ★ SMOOTHIE: ★★ HUMMUS: ★★ SPEED: ★★ SOUND LEVEL: ★★	Not powerful enough to crush ice, and it left small chunks in the smoothies. The base stands so tall that the model felt unsteady during blending.

NOT RECOMMENDED	PERFORMANCE	TESTERS' COMMENTS
OSTER Counterforms 2-in-1 Appliance MODEL: BVLB07-L PRICE: $89.99 JAR MATERIAL AND CAPACITY: Glass, 48 ounces	ICE CRUSHING: ★ SMOOTHIE: ★ HUMMUS: ★★ SPEED: ★ SOUND LEVEL: ★★	Ineffective at ice-crushing, and testers had to run the cycle twice to get fruit to break down into smoothies.
BLACK & DECKER Cyclone 12-Speed Blender MODEL: BLC12650HB PRICE: $29.88 JAR MATERIAL AND CAPACITY: Glass, 48 ounces	ICE CRUSHING: ★ SMOOTHIE: ★ HUMMUS: ★★ SPEED: ★ SOUND LEVEL: ★★	Ice jammed the blades, leaving large chunks on top; fruit fibers and seeds clogged the smoothie, and the hummus was grainy.

COOKWARE SETS

Most cookware sets bundle together a lot of pans we don't need and not enough of the ones we do. That said, buying pieces one by one gets expensive—particularly with high-end brands. Our ideal set would have a 12-inch traditional skillet, 10-inch nonstick skillet, 12-inch cast iron skillet, 2- and 4-quart saucepans, an enameled cast-iron Dutch oven, and a large stockpot. After testing all the pieces in five cookware sets to assess construction, cooking speed, and design, we found that, while none had everything we wanted in a cookware set, there were a few we could recommend—including one that is an astonishingly good buy. Cookware sets are listed in order of preference.

RECOMMENDED	PERFORMANCE	TESTERS' COMMENTS
ALL-CLAD Stainless Steel Cookware Set, 10-piece PRICE: $699.95 MATERIAL: Fully clad, stainless steel with aluminum core; stainless steel lids PIECES: 10- and 12-inch stainless fry pans, 2-qt. and 4-qt. saucepans with lids, 4-qt. sauté pan with lid, 8-qt. stockpot with lid 	COOKING: ★★★ DESIGN: ★★★ PAN SIZES: ★★★	This set came closest to our ideal and includes winning pans from previous testings in sizes we've identified as the most useful. The fry pans have low, flaring sides and broad cooking surfaces; the saucepans are sturdy and hefty for slow, steady cooking; the stockpot is roomy enough for most big cooking jobs.
TRAMONTINA 18/10 Stainless Steel TriPly-Clad Cookware Set, 8-piece PRICE: $144.97 **BEST BUY** MATERIAL: Fully clad, stainless steel with aluminum core; stainless steel lids PIECES: 8- and 10-inch fry pans, 1-qt. and 2-qt. saucepans with lids, 5-qt. Dutch oven with lid 	COOKING: ★★★ DESIGN: ★★★ PAN SIZES: ★	This fully clad cookware set is an amazing bargain, with performance, design, and construction comparable to All-Clad cookware (though cooking surfaces are slightly smaller). Sturdy and moderately heavy, with riveted handles and slow, steady heating.
CALPHALON Tri-Ply Stainless Steel Cookware Set, 8-piece, Model LS 8 PRICE: $299.99 MATERIAL: Fully clad, stainless steel with aluminum core; tempered glass lids safe to 450 degrees PIECES: 8- and 10-inch fry pans, 1.5-qt. and 2.5-qt. saucepans with lids, 6-qt. stockpot with lid 	COOKING: ★★★ DESIGN: ★★ PAN SIZES: ★★	Wide, low saucepans made it easy to see the food inside; fry pans with low, angled sides encouraged evaporation during simmering. We only wish that instead of glass, the lids were stainless steel, which is more durable and heatproof at any temperature.

RECOMMENDED WITH RESERVATIONS	PERFORMANCE	TESTERS' COMMENTS
KITCHENAID Gourmet Reserved Brushed Stainless Cookware Set, 10-piece Model 71984 PRICE: $179.99 MATERIAL: Stainless steel with aluminum disk bottom; break-resistant glass lids PIECES: 8- and 10-inch fry pans, 1-qt. and 2-qt. saucepans with lids, 3-qt. sauté pan with lid, 8-qt. stockpot with lid	COOKING: ★★ DESIGN: ★★ PAN SIZES: ★★	Pans are less solidly constructed than we prefer and were the lightest of all the sets we tested. The stockpot shifted as we stirred our chili, and its handles didn't protrude as far as we like for a good grip. The disk bottoms tended to heat up a little too quickly so that chili boiled instead of simmered.
KENMORE Stainless Steel Cookware Set, 10-piece Model 71787-T PRICE: $159.99 MATERIAL: Stainless steel sides with aluminum disk bottom; stainless steel lids; silicone handle grips PIECES: 8- and 10-inch fry pans, 1-qt. saucepan with lid, 2-qt. saucepan with lid and steamer insert, 3-qt. sauté pan (shares lid with stockpot), 6-qt. stockpot with lid 	COOKING: ★★ DESIGN: ★★ PAN SIZES: ★	We liked the low, open shape of the saucepans, but the silicone handles, while comfortable, got very hot. Pans were all on the lightweight side, and flames tended to darken meatballs, onions, and pan sauces along the perimeter where the heat bypassed the disk bottom. The fry pan heated oil too fast, forcing us to throw out a batch we were using for a frittata, and its sides were a little too high.

SAFETY CAN OPENERS

Traditional can openers cut through can lids from the top, leaving sharp edges on the lids (which sit atop the contents and must be fished out). Safety can openers, on the other hand, cut from the side and remove the entire top part of the can (lid and all), leaving dull "safe" edges behind. We rounded up six safety openers as well as two traditional openers boasting "safer" operation—all priced under $20. Safety can openers come in two basic designs: top mounting and side mounting. Side-mounting can openers proved to be much less intuitive for first-time users; top-mounting can openers were easier to attach. The two traditional can openers had locking mechanisms with push-button releases. Our surprise winner, the traditional-style OXO Good Grips, did leave sharp edges on the lid, but its lid-catching magnet made disposing of the lid easy and safe. Openers are listed in order of preference.

RECOMMENDED	PERFORMANCE	TESTERS' COMMENTS
OXO Good Grips i-Series Can Opener TYPE: Traditional opener with magnet for lid removal PRICE: $19.95	PERFORMANCE: ★★★ COMFORT: ★★★ SAFETY: ★★	Intuitive to use and easy to attach and detach from cans. It was "comfortable," and very efficient in operation. Because it is a traditional opener, this model leaves a lid with sharp edges, but minimizes potential danger with a magnet that allows "neat and safe" lid disposal.
KUHN RIKON Slim Safety LidLifter TYPE: Top-mounting safety opener with pincers for lid removal PRICE: $11.95	PERFORMANCE: ★★ COMFORT: ★★★ SAFETY: ★★★	Testers praised the handy "change in feeling" once the can was completely open. There were no changes in performance or appearance after several wash cycles. A few testers had mild complaints about the "awkward position" of the oversized turning knob.
PROGRESSIVE International Safety I-Can Opener TYPE: Top-mounting safety opener with pincers for lid removal PRICE: $12.79	PERFORMANCE: ★★ COMFORT: ★★★ SAFETY: ★★★	The unique ratchet cutting wheel mechanism was "easy to operate" but was "hard to know when finished." Pincers disposed of the cut lid safely. For some testers, the instructions for this opener were "not obvious."
GOOD COOK 4-1WHT Safe Can Opener TYPE: Side-mounting safety opener PRICE: $9.99	PERFORMANCE: ★★★ COMFORT: ★★ SAFETY: ★★	"Clearly written instructions" and "smooth gears" made this opener easy and efficient. Testers appreciated the "perceptible change in feeling" when the can opener had rounded the entire can. Lost a few points for not having a lid-gripper.
RECOMMENDED WITH RESERVATIONS	PERFORMANCE	TESTERS' COMMENTS
ZYLISS Safe Edge Can Opener TYPE: Top-mounting safety opener PRICE: $14.95	PERFORMANCE: ★★ COMFORT: ★★★ SAFETY: ★★	Although the handle was "very comfortable," its angle made opening short cans of tuna awkward and messy. Testers could not operate the lid lifter and had to dispose of the cut lid by hand.
MIU CanDo Safety Can Opener TYPE: Side-mounting safety opener PRICE: $9.99	PERFORMANCE: ★★ COMFORT: ★★ SAFETY: ★★	Downgraded for its lack of instructions, this opener operated smoothly once testers figured out how to use it. This model claimed to be dishwasher-safe, but the cutting wheel rusted after several washes.
NOT RECOMMENDED	PERFORMANCE	TESTERS' COMMENTS
CHEF'N EZ Squeeze 1-Handed Can Opener TYPE: Traditional opener with magnet for lid removal PRICE: $14.99	PERFORMANCE: ★★ COMFORT: ★★ SAFETY: ★	Testers found the instructions unclear. The gripper handle was "easy to squeeze," but was angled such that opening short cans of tuna was "messy and awkward." The release button struggled to disengage the opener from the can and the magnet failed to pick the lids out of most cans.
CIA Masters Collections Side Can Opener TYPE: Side-mounting safety opener PRICE: $14.95	PERFORMANCE: ★ COMFORT: ★ SAFETY: ★★	Most testers found the instructions to be "a little vague." The opener was tricky to attach to the can, and the handle was remarkably difficult to turn, once attached.

NONSCRATCH SCRUBBERS

What kind of scrubber is most effective on delicate nonstick surfaces? To find out, we rounded up eight nonscratch scrubbers, rolled up our sleeves, and got scrubbing. Our two most important criteria were effectiveness in cleaning and whether they truly lived up to the "nonscratch" name. Of secondary importance were durability and comfort. Our top three scrubbers were rectangular and employed a scrubbing surface of raised, ribbonlike nylon strands that gently but efficiently removed residue. We recommend avoiding scrubbers with curved edges (which can't reach into tough corners) and those with thick, abrasive scouring surfaces, which aren't comfortable or as effective. Scrubbers are listed in order of preference.

HIGHLY RECOMMENDED	PERFORMANCE	TESTERS' COMMENTS
CHORE BOY Scratch-Free LongLast Scrubber PRICE: $1.19 each	PERFORMANCE: ★★★ NO-SCRATCH TEST: ★★★	The raised, ribbonlike nylon strands made for an effective yet gentle scrubber. The bonus: This winning scrubber has a smooth sponge side, making it a great all-purpose sponge. The thin, pliable design made it easy to maneuver into tight corners. A few threads came loose after repeated use, but the scrubber continued to perform well.
CHORE BOY Soap-Filled Scrubber PRICE: $1.69 for 2	PERFORMANCE: ★★★ NO-SCRATCH TEST: ★★★	This scrubber employs the same raised, ribbonlike nylon strand technology as the Chore Boy Scratch-Free LongLast scrubber, but lacks the smooth sponge side. The extra soapiness of this scrubber helped take grime off easily. Small size and nice flexibility.

RECOMMENDED	PERFORMANCE	TESTERS' COMMENTS
SCOTCH-BRITE Dobie Cleaning Pad PRICE: $2.39 for 3	PERFORMANCE: ★★★ NO-SCRATCH TEST: ★★★	The Dobie's nylon mesh covering removed sticky gunk in just 73 strokes. It was easy to maneuver, especially into tight corners. However, the lack of durability and mildly uncomfortable design (some testers thought it was rough on the skin) put it just slightly below our winners.

RECOMMENDED WITH RESERVATIONS	PERFORMANCE	TESTERS' COMMENTS
SCOTCH-BRITE Delicate Duty Scrub Sponge PRICE: $4.79 for 3	PERFORMANCE: ★★ NO-SCRATCH TEST: ★★★	This sponge performed fairly well, but the thickness made it harder to maneuver into corners. The scouring side of the sponge wore down significantly after 500 strokes. Testers found the "wave-like" shape awkward with repeated scrubbing.
O-CEL-O No-Scratch Scrub Sponge PRICE: $2.29 for 2	PERFORMANCE: ★★ NO-SCRATCH TEST: ★★★	This sponge performed fairly well, but the colorful designs that were printed onto the scouring surface almost completely wore off after 500 strokes, revealing this scrubber's lack of durability. Its curved sides made it difficult to clean edges and corners.
CLOROX S.O.S All-Purpose Scrub Sponge PRICE: $2.67 for 3	PERFORMANCE: ★★ NO-SCRATCH TEST: ★★★	Though this scrubber achieved a fair performance rating, tiny nylon fibers from the scouring material peppered the foam of the soapy water after just a few strokes. The bulky sponge made this scrubber feel "heavy" and "tedious to work with."

NOT RECOMMENDED	PERFORMANCE	TESTERS' COMMENTS
CHORE BOY All-Purpose Scrubbing Sponge PRICE: $2.99 for 3	PERFORMANCE: ★ NO-SCRATCH TEST: ★★★	For all of its durability—it emerged from a battery of tests looking completely untouched—this scrubber was the poorest performer. Although the tightly woven nylon fibers of the scouring material may have increased the scrubber's durability, we suspect they also created too smooth a scouring surface to be effective.
SCOTCH-BRITE No-Scratch Scrub Sponge PRICE: $4.79 for 3	PERFORMANCE: ★★ NO-SCRATCH TEST: ★	Though this scrubber cleaned fairly well and looked fresh after multiple scrubbings, it was the only sponge to fail the no-scratch test outright, leaving gray marks on the nonstick skillet after repeated scrubbing. We would not trust this scrubber on our good nonstick pans.

PAPER PLATES

Some paper plates are so flimsy you have to use several stacked together. Others become sodden or even rip when you cut into barbecued chicken or grilled steak. We wanted one large enough to hold food without crowding, strong enough to not buckle, substantial enough to keep moisture and grease at bay, and tough enough to prevent knives from shredding it. We put seven brands to the test. Our testing showed that the right material (hint: not paper) is the key to excellence. Our top two performers were Vanity Fair Dinner Premium, made from crushed stone and polypropylene plastic, and Solo Heavy Duty, made from paperboard coated with clay, printed with water-based inks, and finished with a food-safe plastic soak-proof shield. Both were sturdy enough to handle themselves with aplomb in any outdoor social situation. Plates are listed in order of preference.

HIGHLY RECOMMENDED		PERFORMANCE	TESTERS' COMMENTS
VANITY FAIR Dinner Premium, 11 inches USABLE SIZE : 8⅛ inches PRICE: $3.79 for 14 plates (27 cents each)		WEIGHT BEARING: ★★★ CUT RESISTANCE: ★★★ SPILL PREVENTION: ★★ SOGGINESS PROTECTION: ★★★	Made from crushed stone and plastic, this plate was the sturdiest of the lot, but also the most expensive. Loaded with food, it didn't bend or crack, and with the largest surface area, it would be welcome at a buffet. Given its standout performance, we'd spend the extra money.
SOLO Heavy Duty, 10 inches USABLE SIZE: 7½ inches PRICE: $3.19 for 22 plates (15 cents each)		WEIGHT BEARING: ★★ CUT RESISTANCE: ★★★ SPILL PREVENTION: ★★★ SOGGINESS PROTECTION: ★★★	Sturdy enough to hold a pound of food easily, this plate began to bend with the press of a fork. Made from paperboard covered with clay and coated with a food-safe plastic varnish, it stopped knife cuts at the surface. We particularly liked a shallow well at the plate's perimeter, which stopped moist foods from sloshing out.

RECOMMENDED WITH RESERVATIONS		PERFORMANCE	TESTERS' COMMENTS
DIXIE Ultra, 10 inches USABLE SIZE: 7⁹⁄₁₆ inches PRICE: $3.99 for 40 plates (10 cents each)		WEIGHT BEARING: ★★ CUT RESISTANCE: ★★ SPILL PREVENTION: ★★★ SOGGINESS PROTECTION: ★	This plate bent slightly under weight, and a steak knife made inroads. Pizza grease soaked through fast, especially after the slice was reheated on the plate. Steeply angled sides prevented spills.

NOT RECOMMENDED		PERFORMANCE	TESTERS' COMMENTS
DIXIE 10¼ inches USABLE SIZE: 7¾ inches PRICE: $2.99 for 24 plates (13 cents each)		WEIGHT BEARING: ★ CUT RESISTANCE: ★★ SPILL PREVENTION: ★ SOGGINESS PROTECTION: ★	Dixie's cheaper, flimsier plate did not perform as well as Dixie Ultra. When we did our lap around the test kitchen holding a loaded plate, it buckled. Also, we blame the angle of the plate's lip, as well as the slick coating, for the pizza slice that fell to the floor.
STALKMARKET Heavy Duty, 10 inches USABLE SIZE: 7⅞ inches PRICE: $2.60 for 15 plates (17 cents each)		WEIGHT BEARING: ★ CUT RESISTANCE: ★★ SPILL PREVENTION: ★ SOGGINESS PROTECTION: ★	Engineered from the cellulose fibers of processed sugarcane, these plates are completely biodegradable. But they leaked and tore, buckled under hot food, and soaked through with pizza grease.
CHINET Dinner, 10⅜ inches USABLE SIZE: 7¾ inches PRICES: $3.49 for 15 plates (23 cents each)		WEIGHT BEARING: ★ CUT RESISTANCE: ★ SPILL PREVENTION: ★ SOGGINESS PROTECTION: ★★	Made from 100 percent unused milk-carton stock, this plate held coleslaw and potato salad with ease, but as soon as we introduced hot food, it buckled. Knives and forks stressed the plate, and bits of paper stuck to the tines of the fork.
EARTHSHELL Premium Strength, 9 inches USABLE SIZE: 6¼ inches PRICE: $4.25 for 25 plates (17 cents each)		WEIGHT BEARING: ★ CUT RESISTANCE: ★★ SPILL PREVENTION: ★ SOGGINESS PROTECTION: ★	Made from potatoes, corn, and limestone, this plate—the smallest in our lineup—was designed to biodegrade. But it was so brittle it started disintegrating the minute we put food on it.

INEXPENSIVE FOUR-SLICE TOASTERS

We bought eight 4-slot toasters priced under $50 and put them through their paces, toasting bread, frozen waffles, bagels, and Pop-Tarts. All toasters included a mechanism to control the degree of toasting. The models that toasted the most evenly had a similar number (between nine and ten) of evenly spaced heating elements on each side of the slot. To see how the toasters performed with heavy use, we did a rapid-fire test, making three consecutive rounds of toast on the medium setting. As the toasters heated up, the toasting times got shorter—and the toast progressively lighter. Only one showed minimal differences between the rounds. Testers preferred toasters with clear and intuitive controls, and slots that were long enough to accommodate oversized sandwich bread. Toasters are listed in order of preference.

HIGHLY RECOMMENDED	PERFORMANCE	TESTERS' COMMENTS
MICHAEL GRAVES DESIGN HAMILTON BEACH 4-Slice Toaster, Model 24301 PRICE: $34.99 FEATURES: Browning control, Bagel, Defrost, Reheat, Cancel	TOAST: ★★★ BAGELS/PASTRIES: ★★★ DESIGN: ★★★	This toaster simply outperformed the others, producing evenly golden toast in test after test. The toaster's carriage held all foods securely and prevented any possibility of items falling through or getting caught.

RECOMMENDED	PERFORMANCE	TESTERS' COMMENTS
KENMORE 4-Slice Toaster, Model 81004 PRICE: $49.99 FEATURES: Browning control, Bagel, Defrost, Reheat, Cancel	TOAST: ★★ BAGELS/PASTRIES: ★★★ DESIGN: ★★★	The controls on this toaster were well marked and intuitive. There was minor inconsistency in the color between the two sides of the toast, but not enough for a serious downgrade.
OSTER Inspire 4-Slice Brushed Stainless Steel Toaster, Model 6330 PRICE: $49.99 FEATURES: Browning control, Toast, Bagel, Frozen, Warm, Cancel	TOAST: ★★★ BAGELS/PASTRIES: ★★ DESIGN: ★★	This toaster produced some of the best toast. Its drawbacks were in the design. Billed as a four-slice toaster, the two slots were too short to fit four pieces of large sandwich bread, and there were no visual cues for which way to orient a cut bagel. Lacked separate controls for the slots.
CUISINART Electronic Cool-Touch 4-Slice Toaster, Model CPT-140 PRICE: $49.99 FEATURES: Browning control, Bagel, Defrost, Reheat, Cancel	TOAST: ★★ BAGELS/PASTRIES: ★★ DESIGN: ★★★	This toaster performed admirably in the rapid-fire test, but there was some minor inconsistency between the sides of the toast. Intuitive and easy to clean. There was no visual cue for which way to orient a cut bagel.
BLACK & DECKER 4-Slice Toaster, Model T4560B PRICE: $24.88 FEATURES: Browning control, Bagel, Frozen, Cancel	TOAST: ★★ BAGELS/PASTRIES: ★★★ DESIGN: ★★	This toaster had minor problems toasting both sides of bread evenly. On the bagel setting, however, this model was a champ, nicely browning the cut side while gently warming the exterior. The crumb trays were too shallow and thus messy to empty.

NOT RECOMMENDED	PERFORMANCE	TESTERS' COMMENTS
SUNBEAM 4-Slice Toaster, Model 3823-100 PRICE: $22.99 FEATURES: Browning control, Bagel, Stop	TOAST: ★★ BAGELS/PASTRIES: ★★ DESIGN: ★★	The slots on this toaster were too short for large sandwich bread. With 11 wires on one side and 14 on the other, the toaster produced inconsistent toast. The "cancel" button was hard to see, and the toaster's crumb tray was too shallow.
FARBERWARE Millennium 4-Slice Toaster, Model FACT450T PRICE: $49.99 FEATURES: Browning control, Cancel, Bagel, Defrost; switch for 2- or 4-slice toasting	TOAST: ★★ BAGELS/PASTRIES: ★★ DESIGN: ★	Because it has controls on both the front and side, we needed to shift the toaster to access the different features. Top-heavy pastries tipped over and toasted unevenly in the angled slots. Even with bread, toasting was spotty and almost the same at light and medium settings.
TOASTMASTER Dual Control 4-Slice Toaster, Model T2040W PRICE: $27.00 FEATURES: Browning control	TOAST: ★ BAGELS/PASTRIES: ★★ DESIGN: ★	Bread had to be run through this toaster a few times before it was adequately toasted; the exterior of the toaster became dangerously hot. The bread guides inside the toaster didn't hold any of the food securely and actually tilted one side of the item closer to the heating element.

CONVERSIONS & EQUIVALENCIES

SOME SAY COOKING IS A SCIENCE AND AN ART. We would say that geography has a hand in it, too. Flour milled in the United Kingdom and elsewhere will feel and taste different from flour milled in the United States. So, while we cannot promise that the loaf of bread you bake in Canada or England will taste the same as a loaf baked in the States, we can offer guidelines for converting weights and measures. We also recommend that you rely on your instincts when making our recipes. Refer to the visual cues provided. If the bread dough hasn't "come together in a ball," as

described, you may need to add more flour—even if the recipe doesn't tell you so. You be the judge.

The recipes in this book were developed using standard U.S. measures following U.S. government guidelines. The charts below offer equivalents for U.S., metric, and Imperial (U.K.) measures. All conversions are approximate and have been rounded up or down to the nearest whole number. For example:

1 teaspoon = 4.929 milliliters, rounded up to 5 milliliters
1 ounce = 28.349 grams, rounded down to 28 grams

VOLUME CONVERSIONS

U.S.	METRIC
1 teaspoon	5 milliliters
2 teaspoons	10 milliliters
1 tablespoon	15 milliliters
2 tablespoons	30 milliliters
¼ cup	59 milliliters
⅓ cup	79 milliliters
½ cup	118 milliliters
¾ cup	177 milliliters
1 cup	237 milliliters
1¼ cups	296 milliliters
1½ cups	355 milliliters
2 cups	473 milliliters
2½ cups	592 milliliters
3 cups	710 milliliters
4 cups (1 quart)	0.946 liter
1.06 quarts	1 liter
4 quarts (1 gallon)	3.8 liters

WEIGHT CONVERSIONS

OUNCES	GRAMS
½	14
¾	21
1	28
1½	43
2	57
2½	71
3	85
3½	99
4	113
4½	128
5	142
6	170
7	198
8	227
9	255
10	283
12	340
16 (1 pound)	454

CONVERSIONS FOR INGREDIENTS COMMONLY USED IN BAKING

Baking is an exacting science. Because measuring by weight is far more accurate than measuring by volume, and thus more likely to achieve reliable results, in our recipes we provide ounce measures in addition to cup measures for many ingredients. Refer to the chart below to convert these measures into grams.

INGREDIENT	OUNCES	GRAMS
Flour		
1 cup all-purpose flour*	5	142
1 cup cake flour	4	113
1 cup whole wheat flour	5½	156
Sugar		
1 cup granulated (white) sugar	7	198
1 cup packed brown sugar (light or dark)	7	198
1 cup confectioners' sugar	4	113
Cocoa Powder		
1 cup cocoa powder	3	85
Butter†		
4 tablespoons (½ stick, or ¼ cup)	2	57
8 tablespoons (1 stick, or ½ cup)	4	113
16 tablespoons (2 sticks, or 1 cup)	8	227

* U.S. all-purpose flour, the most frequently used flour in this book, does not contain leaveners, as some European flours do. These leavened flours are called self-rising or self-raising. If you are using self-rising flour, take this into consideration before adding leavening to a recipe.

† In the United States, butter is sold both salted and unsalted. We generally recommend unsalted butter. If you are using salted butter, take this into consideration before adding salt to a recipe.

OVEN TEMPERATURES

FAHRENHEIT	CELSIUS	GAS MARK (imperial)
225	105	¼
250	120	½
275	130	1
300	150	2
325	165	3
350	180	4
375	190	5
400	200	6
425	220	7
450	230	8
475	245	9

CONVERTING TEMPERATURES FROM AN INSTANT-READ THERMOMETER

We include doneness temperatures in many of our recipes, such as those for poultry, meat, and bread. We recommend an instant-read thermometer for the job. Refer to the table above to convert Fahrenheit degrees to Celsius. Or, for temperatures not represented in the chart, use this simple formula:

Subtract 32 degrees from the Fahrenheit reading, then divide the result by 1.8 to find the Celsius reading.

EXAMPLE:

"Roast until the thickest part of a chicken thigh registers 175 degrees on an instant-read thermometer." To convert:

$$175° \text{ F } - 32 = 143°$$
$$143° \div 1.8 = 79° \text{ C (rounded down from 79.44)}$$

INDEX

A

Aligot (Garlic and Cheese Mashed Potatoes), 45–48, *46*
Almond(s)
  -Cherry Cobbler, Skillet, 242
  Crunch Topping, Blueberry Muffins with, 86
  Honey-Raisin Baked Goat Cheese Salad, 14
  and Red Grapes, Waldorf Salad with, 17
  and Smoked Paprika, Sautéed Green Beans with, 52
  Vinaigrette, Grilled Salmon Fillets with, 208–10
Appetizers
  Boneless Buffalo Chicken
      with Blue Cheese Dressing, *8,* 9–10
  Caponata, 4–7, *5*
  Crispy Bacon-Cheddar Potato Skins, 7
Apple(s)
  buying and storing, 245
  chopping, 15
  Pie, Skillet, 242–44, *243*
  sliced, preventing browning of, 15
  Waldorf Salad, 14–17, *15*
    Curried, with Green Grapes and Peanuts, 17
    with Dried Cranberries and Pecans, 17
    with Red Grapes and Almonds, 17
Arugula, Fontina, and Prosciutto, Skillet Pizza with, 107
Asparagus, storing, 283
Atomic Ribs, 168–70
Au Gratin Potatoes, 48–50, *49*
Automatic drip coffee makers, ratings of, 302

B

Bacon
  applewood, taste tests on, 296
  artisanal, taste tests on, 81
  -Cheddar Potato Skins, Crispy, 7
  Eggs Benedict, 72–75
  German Potato Salad, 17–19, *18*
  and Onion, Savory Bread Pudding with, 84
  Quiche Lorraine, 79–82, *80*
  Ricotta, and Scallions, Skillet Pizza with, *106,* 107
  Scallions, and Cheddar, Quiche with, 82
Baked Goat Cheese Salads, 12–14
Baked Ziti, *114,* 115–16
Baking powder, shelf life for, 287
Baking soda, shelf life for, 287
Baltimore Pit Beef, 155–56
Barbecued Beef, Shredded, 148–49
Barbecued Beef Brisket, Slow-Cooker, 149–52, *150*
Barbecued Chicken Wings, 180–81
Barbecued Pan-Fried Pork Chops, 166
Barbecue Shrimp, New Orleans, 217–18
Bars, Dream, 233–35, *234*

Basil
  and Fresh Mozzarella, Cherry Tomato Salad with, 11
  and Roasted Red Peppers, Sautéed Green Beans with, 52
Bean(s)
  baked, canned, taste tests on, 301
  Green
    Casserole, Make-Ahead, 62–64, *63*
    Sautéed, with Garlic and Herbs, 51
    Sautéed, with Ginger and Sesame, 52
    Sautéed, with Roasted Red Peppers and Basil, 52
    Sautéed, with Smoked Paprika and Almonds, 52
  Kentucky Burgoo, 35–38, *36*
  Slow-Cooker Cassoulet, 40–41
Beef
  Baltimore Pit Beef, 155–56
  Barbecued, Shredded, 148–49
  brisket, buying, 152
  Brisket, Slow-Cooker Barbecued, 149–52, *150*
  checking for doneness, 139
  en Cocotte with Caramelized Onions, 159–60
  Glazed Meat Loaf, 163–64
  Green Chile Cheeseburgers, 128–30, *129*
  marinating, 288–89
  Reuben Sandwiches, 134
  Ribs
    buying, 155
    short, bone-in versus boneless, 136
    short, boning, 136
    Short, Braised, 135–37
    Short, Braised, with Guinness and Prunes, 137
    Texas Barbecued, 152–55, *153*
  Roast, and Gravy, Classic, 160–62, *161*
  roast, top sirloin, tying, 160
  Slow-Cooker Meatballs in Marinara Sauce, 124–25
  Steak
    Chicken-Fried, 139–42, *140*
    flank, slicing, 123
    flap meat (sirloin tips), buying, 147
    Shiitakes, and Spinach, Skillet Ramen with, 123–24
    Strip, Pan-Seared, with Crispy Potatoes and Salsa Verde, 137–39
    Tacos with Sweet and Spicy Pickled Onions, 130–32, *133*
    Teriyaki, Grilled, 144–47, *145*
  Stew, Hungarian, 33–34
  Stuffed Cabbage Rolls, 64–67, *66*
  Swedish Meatballs with Pickled Cucumbers, 142–44
  Tenderloin, Roast, 157–59
Beer
  -Battered Onion Rings, 55–56
  Cheddar Soup, Wisconsin, 26–28, *27*
Berries
  Blueberry Muffins, 85–86
    with Almond Crunch Topping, 86
    with Frozen Blueberries, 86
    with Orange Glaze, 86

Berries *(cont.)*
  Blueberry Pie, 245–47, *248*
  storing, 283
  Waldorf Salad with Dried Cranberries and Pecans, 17
  washing, 283
Biscuits, Cornmeal, 94–96, *95*
Black peppercorns, taste tests on, 291
Blenders, upright, ratings of, 22, 308
Blueberry
  Muffins, 85–86
    with Almond Crunch Topping, 86
    with Frozen Blueberries, 86
    with Orange Glaze, 86
  Pie, 245–47, *248*
Blue Cheese
  Dressing, *8,* 9–10
  and Tarragon, Cherry Tomato Salad with, 11
Bold and Spicy Gingerbread Cake, 258–60, *259*
Boneless Buffalo Chicken
        with Blue Cheese Dressing, *8,* 9–10
Bourbon Whipped Cream, 250
Braised Beef Short Ribs, 135–37
Braised Beef Short Ribs
        with Guinness and Prunes, 137
Bread(s)
  Blueberry Muffins, 85–86
    with Almond Crunch Topping, 86
    with Frozen Blueberries, 86
    with Orange Glaze, 86
  Cornmeal Biscuits, 94–96, *95*
  English muffins, taste tests on, 72
  Popovers, 96–97
  Pudding, Chocolate, 238–39
  Pudding, Savory, 82–84
    with Bacon and Onion, 84
    with Spinach and Feta, *83,* 84
  Rustic Dinner Rolls, *98,* 99–100
  Ultimate Cinnamon Buns, 88–91, *89*
  see also Pizza
Breakfast and brunch
  Blueberry Muffins, 85–86
    with Almond Crunch Topping, 86
    with Frozen Blueberries, 86
    with Orange Glaze, 86
  Bread Pudding, Savory, 82–84
    with Bacon and Onion, 84
    with Spinach and Feta, *83,* 84
  Cinnamon Buns, Ultimate, 88–91, *89*
  Eggs Benedict, 72–75
  Eggs en Cocotte, 77–79
    with Mushroom Cream, 79
    with Parmesan Cream, 79
  French Omelets, *74,* 75–77
  Gooey Butter Cake
    Butterscotch, 93–94
    Chocolate, 94
    St. Louis, 91–93, *92*

Breakfast and brunch *(cont.)*
  Pancake Mix, Homemade, 87–88
  Quiche Lorraine, 79–82, *80*
  Quiche with Bacon, Scallions, and Cheddar, 82
Broccoli and Rice Casserole, Cheesy, 67–68, *69*
Brownie mixes, boxed, taste tests on, 298
Buns, Ultimate Cinnamon, 88–91, *89*
Burgers
  Green Chile Cheeseburgers, 128–30, *129*
  Shrimp, Southern, 218–20
Burgoo, Kentucky, 35–38, *36*
Butter, Shallot-Parsley, 158
Butter, storing, 286
Butterscotch Gooey Butter Cake, 93–94

C

Cabbage
  Reuben Sandwiches, 134
  Rolls, Stuffed, 64–67, *66*
  sauerkraut, taste tests on, 135
Cakes
  Caramel, Easy, 260–63, *262*
  Chocolate, Emergency, 257–58
  Gingerbread, Bold and Spicy, 258–60, *259*
  Gooey Butter
    Butterscotch, 93–94
    Chocolate, 94
    St. Louis, 91–93, *92*
  Pound, 7UP, 263–65, *264*
  Triple Chocolate Mousse, 269–71
Canadian bacon
  Eggs Benedict, 72–75
Can openers, safety, ratings of, 111, 310
Caponata, 4–7, *5*
Caramel Cake, Easy, 260–63, *262*
Carne Adovada, 38–40, *39*
Carrots
  bagged, storage tip, 276
  buying and storing, 279
  dicing, 279
Casseroles
  Baked Ziti, *114,* 115–16
  Broccoli and Rice, Cheesy, 67–68, *69*
  Green Bean, Make-Ahead, 62–64, *63*
  Make-Ahead Creamy Macaroni
        and Cheese, 120–23, *121*
  Summer Squash, 61–62
  Summer Vegetable Gratin, 58–61, *59*
  Summer Vegetable Gratin
        with Roasted Peppers and Smoked Mozzarella, 61
Cassoulet, Slow-Cooker, 40–41
Celery
  buying and storing, 279
  dicing, 279
  and Orange, Salmon en Cocotte with, 212

Celery *(cont.)*
  Waldorf Salad, 14–17, *15*
    Curried, with Green Grapes and Peanuts, 17
    with Dried Cranberries and Pecans, 17
    with Red Grapes and Almonds, 17
Cheddar cheese
  Au Gratin Potatoes, 48–50, *49*
  Bacon, and Scallions, Quiche with, 82
  -Bacon Potato Skins, Crispy, 7
  Beer Soup, Wisconsin, 26–28, *27*
  Cheesy Broccoli and Rice Casserole, 67–68, *69*
  Make-Ahead Creamy Macaroni and Cheese, 120–23, *121*
  Skillet Shrimp and Grits, 215–17, *216*
  Summer Squash Casserole, 61–62
Cheese
  Au Gratin Potatoes, 48–50, *49*
  Baked Ziti, *114,* 115–16
  Blue, and Tarragon, Cherry Tomato Salad with, 11
  Blue, Dressing, *8,* 9–10
  Cheddar
    Bacon, and Scallions, Quiche with, 82
    -Bacon Potato Skins, Crispy, 7
    Beer Soup, Wisconsin, 26–28, *27*
  Cheesy Broccoli and Rice Casserole, 67–68, *69*
  Cherry Tomato and Watermelon Salad, 11–12
  cottage cheese, taste tests on, 116
  Enchiladas Verdes, 184–87, *186*
  Feta and Spinach, Savory Bread Pudding with, *83,* 84
  Fontina, Arugula, and Prosciutto, Skillet Pizza with, 107
  Fontina, Tomatoes, and Sausage, Pizza Bianca with, 104
  and Garlic Mashed Potatoes (Aligot), 45–48, *46*
  Goat
    Baked, Herbed, Salad, 12–14, *13*
    Baked, Honey-Raisin, Salad, 14
    Baked, Sun-Dried Tomato, Salad, 14
    Olives, and Spicy Garlic Oil, Skillet Pizza with, 107
    taste tests on, 14
  Greek Cherry Tomato Salad, 10–11
  Green Chile Cheeseburgers, 128–30, *129*
  Macaroni and, Creamy Make-Ahead, 120–23, *121*
  Mozzarella
    Fresh, and Basil, Cherry Tomato Salad with, 11
    Smoked, and Roasted Peppers,
      Summer Vegetable Gratin with, 61
    and Tomatoes, Pizza Bianca with, 104
  Parmesan Cream, Eggs en Cocotte with, 79
  Pizza, Skillet, 105–7
  Quiche Lorraine, 79–82, *80*
  Reuben Sandwiches, 134
  Ricotta, Bacon, and Scallions, Skillet Pizza with, *106,* 107
  Savory Bread Pudding, 82–84
  Savory Bread Pudding with Bacon and Onion, 84
  Skillet Pasta with Peas and Prosciutto, 117–18
  Skillet Phyllo Pie with Chicken, 187–89
  Skillet Shrimp and Grits, 215–17, *216*
  Summer Squash Casserole, 61–62
  Summer Vegetable Gratin, 58–61, *59*

Cherry
  -Almond Cobbler, Skillet, 242
  Cobbler, Skillet, 239–41, *240*
  Red Wine, and Cinnamon Cobbler, 242
  Stuffing, Holiday Roast Pork with, 174
Cherry Tomato Salad
  with Basil and Fresh Mozzarella, 11
  Greek, 10–11
  with Mango and Lime Curry Vinaigrette, 12
  with Tarragon and Blue Cheese, 11
  Watermelon and, 11–12
Chewy Chocolate Cookies, 228–31, *229*
Chicken
  Boneless Buffalo, with Blue Cheese Dressing, *8,* 9–10
  checking for doneness, 139
  Cornell, *192,* 193–94
  cutlets, preparing, 183
  Cutlets, Sautéed, with Porcini Sauce, 181–84, *182*
  Enchiladas Verdes, 184–87, *186*
  Huli Huli, 199–202, *200*
  Kentucky Burgoo, 35–38, *36*
  Noodle Soup, Hearty, *30,* 31–33
  Roast, Glazed, 197–99
  Roast Lemon, 194–97, *195*
  Skillet Phyllo Pie with, 187–89
  Slow-Cooker Cassoulet, 40–41
  Spiedies, 189–91, *190*
  whole, cutting in half, 194
  Wings, Barbecued, 180–81
  wings, cutting up, 180
Chicken-Fried Steak, 139–42, *140*
Chile(s)
  Atomic Ribs, 168–70
  Enchiladas Verdes, 184–87, *186*
  Green, Cheeseburgers, 128–30, *129*
  Steak Tacos with Sweet and Spicy
    Pickled Onions, 130–32, *133*
Chili, New Mexico Pork
  (Carne Adovada), 38–40, *39*
Chimney starters, ratings of, 155
Chives, chopping, 275
Chocolate
  Bread Pudding, 238–39
  Cake, Emergency, 257–58
  Chip Cookies, Perfect, 226–28
  chips, taste tests on, 228, 294
  cocoa mixes, taste tests on, 299
  Cookies, Chewy, 228–31, *229*
  dark, taste tests on, 258
  Gooey Butter Cake, 94
  Ice Cream, Easy, 235–36, *237*
  -Orange Soufflé, Skillet, 268
  Pie, French Silk, 251–53, *252*
  shelf life, 287
  storing, 287
  Triple, Mousse Cake, 269–71
  white, taste tests on, 271

Chocolate chippers, ratings of, 230
Chowder, Corn, 23–24, *25*
Cinnamon Buns, Ultimate, 88–91, *89*
Clam juice, taste tests on, 120
Classic Roast Beef and Gravy, 160–62, *161*
Cobbler, Skillet
    Cherry, 239–41, *240*
    Cherry, Red Wine, and Cinnamon, 242
    Cherry-Almond, 242
Cocoa mixes, taste tests on, 299
Coconut
    cream of, taste tests on, 233
    Dream Bars, 233–35, *234*
Coffee makers, drip, ratings of, 302
Cookies and bars
    Chewy Chocolate Cookies, 228–31, *229*
    Dream Bars, 233–35, *234*
    Hermits, 231–33
    Perfect Chocolate Chip Cookies, 226–28
Cooking temperature guides, 274
Cookware sets, ratings of, 309
Corn
    canned, taste tests on, 24
    Chowder, 23–24, *25*
    on the cob, buttering, 277
    cutting kernels from the cob, 54
    fresh, storing, 283
    Individual Spoonbreads, 54
    Kentucky Burgoo, 35–38, *36*
    Sweet, Spoonbread, 52–54, *53*
Cornell Chicken, *192*, 193–94
Cornmeal
    Biscuits, 94–96, *95*
    Individual Spoonbreads, 54
    removing dough from hands with, 276
    shelf life, 287
    storing, 287
    Sweet Corn Spoonbread, 52–54, *53*
Cottage cheese
    Baked Ziti, *114*, 115–16
    taste tests on, 116
Cranberries, Dried, and Pecans,
    Waldorf Salad with, 17
Creamless Creamy Tomato Soup, 22–23
Cream of coconut
    Dream Bars, 233–35, *234*
    taste tests on, 233
Crispy Bacon-Cheddar Potato Skins, 7
Cucumbers
    American, notes about, 19
    English, notes about, 19
    German Potato Salad, 17–19, *18*
    Greek Cherry Tomato Salad, 10–11
    Pickled, 143–44
Curried Waldorf Salad
    with Green Grapes and Peanuts, 17
Cutting boards, ratings of, 279

D

Dates
    Jefferson Davis Pie, 249–50
Desserts
    Cakes
        Caramel, Easy, 260–63, *262*
        Chocolate, Emergency, 257–58
        Gingerbread, Bold and Spicy, 258–60, *259*
        Pound, 7UP, 263–65, *264*
        Triple Chocolate Mousse, 269–71
    Chocolate Bread Pudding, 238–39
    Cobbler, Skillet
        Cherry, 239–41, *240*
        Cherry, Red Wine, and Cinnamon, 242
        Cherry-Almond, 242
    Cookies
        Chocolate, Chewy, 228–31, *229*
        Chocolate Chip, Perfect, 226–28
        Hermits, 231–33
    Dream Bars, 233–35, *234*
    Easy Chocolate Ice Cream, 235–36, *237*
    Pies
        Apple, Skillet, 242–44, *243*
        Blueberry, 245–47, *248*
        French Silk Chocolate, 251–53, *252*
        Jefferson Davis, 249–50
        Pumpkin, 253–56, *255*
    Skillet Soufflé
        Chocolate-Orange, 268
        Lemon, 265–68, *267*
Dips and spreads
    Blue Cheese Dressing, *8,* 9–10
    Caponata, 4–7, *5*
    Ginger-Soy Dipping Sauce, 222
Dish-drying space, tip for, 276
Dough, sticky, washing off hands, 276
Dream Bars, 233–35, *234*
Duck, checking for doneness, 139
Dutch ovens, ratings of, 223

E

Easy Caramel Cake, 260–63, *262*
Easy Chocolate Ice Cream, 235–36, *237*
Eggplant
    Caponata, 4–7, *5*
    Skillet Ratatouille, 56–58
Egg(s)
    Benedict, 72–75
    checking for freshness, 286
    en Cocotte, 77–79
        with Mushroom Cream, 79
        with Parmesan Cream, 79
    French Omelets, *74,* 75–77
    poaching, by the dozen, 72

Egg(s) *(cont.)*

poaching, tip for, 72

separating, tip for, 275

storing, 286

whites, whipping, 54

see also Skillet Soufflé

Emergency Chocolate Cake, 257–58

Enchiladas Verdes, 184–87, *186*

English muffins

Eggs Benedict, 72–75

taste tests on, 72

Equipment, ratings of

automatic drip coffee makers, 302

blenders, upright, 22, 308

can openers, safety, 111

chimney starters, 155

chocolate chippers, 230

cookware sets, 309

cutting boards, 279

dry measuring cups, 10

Dutch ovens, 223

four-slice toasters, 313

gratin dishes, 58

gripper mats, 57

knife sharpeners, 280

knives

chef's, 279, 280

paring, 279

slicing, 156, 305

mixing bowls, innovative, 228

omelet pans, 76

paper plates, 312

peelers, 279

pie plates, 250, 306

plastic wrap, 162, 307

popover pans, 97

potato mashers, 45

rasp graters, 268

safety can openers, 310

scrubbers, nonscratch, 52, 311

silicone spatulas, 304

skillets, nonstick, 117

skillets, traditional, 215, 303

spatulas, heatproof rubber, 131

storage containers, 287

vertical roasters, 198

F

Feta cheese

Cherry Tomato and Watermelon Salad, 11–12

Greek Cherry Tomato Salad, 10–11

Skillet Phyllo Pie with Chicken, 187–89

and Spinach, Savory Bread Pudding with, *83, 84*

Fish

Grilled Salmon Fillets

with Almond Vinaigrette, 208–10

Salmon en Cocotte with Celery and Orange, 212

Salmon en Cocotte

with Leeks and White Wine, 210–12, *211*

salmon fillets, skinning, 212

Skillet Salmon and Leek Pot Pie, 213–14

see also Shrimp

Flour, storing, 287

Foil rack, creating, 78

Foil sling, creating, 93

Fontina cheese

Arugula, and Prosciutto, Skillet Pizza with, 107

Tomatoes, and Sausage, Pizza Bianca with, 104

Foolproof Double-Crust Pie Dough, 247–49

Foolproof Single-Crust Pie Dough, 249

French Omelets, *74,* **75–77**

French Silk Chocolate Pie, 251–53, *252*

Fruit

storing, 282–83

see also specific fruits

Fruit flies, trapping, 276

G

Garlic

buying and storing, 278

and Cheese Mashed Potatoes (Aligot), 45–48, *46*

Garlicky Shrimp Pasta, 118–20

Mashed Potatoes, 44–45

preparing, for cooking, 278

preparing paste with, 278

removing skin from, 278

German Potato Salad, 17–19, *18*

Ginger

Bold and Spicy Gingerbread Cake, 258–60, *259*

freshly grated, freezing, 276

Hermits, 231–33

and Sesame, Sautéed Green Beans with, 52

-Soy Dipping Sauce, 222

Gingerbread Cake, Bold and Spicy, 258–60, *259*

Glazed Meat Loaf, 163–64

Glazed Roast Chicken, 197–99

Goat Cheese

Baked, Herbed, Salad, 12–14, *13*

Baked, Honey-Raisin, Salad, 14

Baked, Sun-Dried Tomato, Salad, 14

Olives, and Spicy Garlic Oil, Skillet Pizza with, 107

taste tests on, 14

Grains

Cheesy Broccoli and Rice Casserole, 67–68, *69*

Cornmeal Biscuits, 94–96, *95*

Individual Spoonbreads, 54

Skillet Shrimp and Grits, 215–17, *216*

Sweet Corn Spoonbread, 52–54, *53*

Grapes
    Green, and Peanuts, Curried Waldorf Salad with, 17
    Red, and Almonds, Waldorf Salad with, 17
Graters, rasp, ratings of, 268
Gratin dishes, ratings of, 58
Gratins
    Summer Vegetable, 58–61, *59*
    Summer Vegetable, with Roasted Peppers
        and Smoked Mozzarella, 61
Greek Cherry Tomato Salad, 10–11
Green Bean(s)
    Casserole, Make-Ahead, 62–64, *63*
    Sautéed, with Garlic and Herbs, 51
    Sautéed, with Ginger and Sesame, 52
    Sautéed, with Roasted Red Peppers and Basil, 52
    Sautéed, with Smoked Paprika and Almonds, 52
Green Chile Cheeseburgers, 128–30, *129*
Greens
    Baked Goat Cheese Salad
        Herbed, 12–14, *13*
        Honey-Raisin, 14
        Sun-Dried Tomato, 14
    fresh, storage tip, 276
    lettuce, storing, 283
    Savory Bread Pudding with Spinach and Feta, *83, 84*
    Skillet Pizza with Fontina, Arugula, and Prosciutto, 107
    Skillet Ramen with Beef,
        Shiitakes, and Spinach, 123–24
    see also Cabbage
Grilled dishes
    Atomic Ribs, 168–70
    Baltimore Pit Beef, 155–56
    Barbecued Chicken Wings, 180–81
    Cornell Chicken, *192,* 193–94
    Green Chile Cheeseburgers, 128–30, *129*
    Grilled Beef Teriyaki, 144–47, *145*
    Grilled Rack of Lamb, 174–76, *175*
    Grilled Rack of Lamb
        with Sweet Mustard Glaze, 176
    Grilled Salmon Fillets
        with Almond Vinaigrette, 208–10
    Grill-Roasted Ham, 170–72, *171*
    Huli Huli Chicken, 199–202, *200*
    Shredded Barbecued Beef, 148–49
    Shrimp Tempura with
        Ginger-Soy Dipping Sauce, 220–23, *221*
    Spiedies, 189–91, *190*
    Texas Beef Ribs, 152–55, *153*
Grills
    cleaning grate, 177
    determining heat level, 130
    gas, turning off, tip for, 277
Gripper mats, ratings of, 57
Grits and Shrimp, Skillet, 215–17, *216*
Gruyère cheese
    Aligot (Garlic and Cheese Mashed Potatoes), 45–48, *46*
    Quiche Lorraine, 79–82, *80*

H

Ham
Grill-Roasted, 170–72, *171*
    Skillet Pasta with Peas and Prosciutto, 117–18
    Skillet Pizza with Fontina, Arugula, and Prosciutto, 107
Hearty Chicken Noodle Soup, *30,* 31–33
Hearty Root Vegetable and Mushroom Stew, 28–29
Herbed Baked Goat Cheese Salad, 12–14, *13*
Herbed Pan-Fried Pork Chops, 166
Herb(s)
    dried, checking for freshness, 286
    dried, storing, 286
    fresh, storing, 283
Hermits, 231–33
Holiday Roast Pork with Cherry Stuffing, 174
Holiday Stuffed Roast Pork, 172–74
Hollandaise Sauce, 72–75
Homemade Pancake Mix, 87–88
Honey
    -Raisin Baked Goat Cheese Salad, 14
    shelf life for, 287
Horseradish
    Baltimore Pit Beef Sauce, 156
Hot cocoa mixes, taste tests on, 299
Huli Huli Chicken, 199–202, *200*
Hungarian Beef Stew, 33–34

I

Ice Cream, Easy Chocolate, 235–36, *237*
Individual Spoonbreads, 54
Ingredients, tastings of
    bacon, applewood, 296
    bacon, artisanal, 81
    baked beans, canned, 301
    beef brisket, 152
    beef ribs, 155
    black peppercorns, 219, 291
    boxed brownie mixes, 298
    chocolate, dark, 258
    chocolate chips, 228, 294
    clam juice, 120
    corn, canned, 24
    cottage cheese, 116
    cream of coconut, 233
    cucumbers, 19
    elbow macaroni, 122, 295
    English muffins, 72
    goat cheese, 14
    hot cocoa mixes, 299
    kielbasa sausages, 41
    lamb, domestic versus imported, 177
    lamb chops, 37
    maple syrup, 88, 293
    microwave popcorn, 297

Ingredients, tastings of (cont.)

mirin, 147

molasses, 232

mustard, coarse-grain, 19

olive oil, extra-virgin, 212, 290

pancake syrups, 293

peas, frozen, 117

sauerkraut, 135

strawberry yogurt, low-fat, 300

sweet paprika, 35

tomato paste, 113

vanilla extract, 241, 292

J

Jefferson Davis Pie, 249–50

K

Kentucky Burgoo, 35–38, *36*

Kitchen twine, storage tip, 274

Knife sharpeners, ratings of, 280

Knives

chef's

anatomy of, 280

blade maintenance, 280

cutting with, 281

ratings of, 279, 280

safety basics, 281

paring, ratings of, 279

slicing, ratings of, 156, 305

L

Lamb

checking for doneness, 139

chops, taste tests on, 37

domestic versus imported, 177

Kentucky Burgoo, 35–38, *36*

Rack of, Grilled, 174–76, *175*

Rack of, Grilled, with Sweet Mustard Glaze, 176

rack of, trimming, 177

Leek(s)

buying and storing, 279

cleaning, 279

preparing, 213, 279

and Salmon Pot Pie, Skillet, 213–14

when to use in recipes, 279

and White Wine, Salmon en Cocotte with, 210–12, *211*

Lemon(s)

Chicken, Roast, 194–97, *195*

juicing, tip for, 277

7UP Pound Cake, 263–65, *264*

Lemon(s) *(cont.)*

Soufflé, Skillet, 265–68, *267*

zesting, tip for, 277

Limes

7UP Pound Cake, 263–65, *264*

zesting, tip for, 277

M

Macaroni

and Cheese, Creamy Make-Ahead, 120–23, *121*

taste tests on, 122, 295

Main dishes (beef)

Baltimore Pit Beef, 155–56

Beef en Cocotte with Caramelized Onions, 159–60

Braised Beef Short Ribs, 135–37

Braised Beef Short Ribs with Guinness and Prunes, 137

Chicken-Fried Steak, 139–42, *140*

Classic Roast Beef and Gravy, 160–62, *161*

Glazed Meat Loaf, 163–64

Green Chile Cheeseburgers, 128–30, *129*

Grilled Beef Teriyaki, 144–47, *145*

Hungarian Beef Stew, 33–34

Pan-Seared Strip Steak

with Crispy Potatoes and Salsa Verde, 137–39

Reuben Sandwiches, 134

Roast Beef Tenderloin, 157–59

Shredded Barbecued Beef, 148–49

Slow-Cooker Barbecued Beef Brisket, 149–52, *150*

Steak Tacos with Sweet

and Spicy Pickled Onions, 130–32, *133*

Stuffed Cabbage Rolls, 64–67, *66*

Swedish Meatballs with Pickled Cucumbers, 142–44

Texas Beef Ribs, 152–55, *153*

Main dishes (pasta)

Baked Ziti, *114,* 115–16

Garlicky Shrimp Pasta, 118–20

Make-Ahead Creamy Macaroni and Cheese, 120–23, *121*

Quick Tomato Sauce, *110,* 111–12

Skillet Pasta with Peas and Prosciutto, 117–18

Skillet Penne alla Vodka, 112–13

Skillet Ramen with Beef, Shiitakes, and Spinach, 123–24

Slow-Cooker Meatballs in Marinara Sauce, 124–25

Main dishes (pizza and vegetables)

Hearty Root Vegetable and Mushroom Stew, 28–29

Pizza Bianca with Tomatoes, Sausage, and Fontina, 104

Pizza Bianca with Tomatoes and Mozzarella, 104

Skillet Pizza

Cheese, 105–7

with Fontina, Arugula, and Prosciutto, 107

with Goat Cheese, Olives, and Spicy Garlic Oil, 107

with Ricotta, Bacon, and Scallions, *106,* 107

Main dishes (pork and lamb)

Atomic Ribs, 168–70

Carne Adovada, 38–40, *39*

Grilled Rack of Lamb, 174–76, *175*

Main dishes (pork and lamb) *(cont.)*
   Grilled Rack of Lamb with Sweet Mustard Glaze, 176
   Grill-Roasted Ham, 170–72, *171*
   Holiday Roast Pork with Cherry Stuffing, 174
   Holiday Stuffed Roast Pork, 172–74
   Pan-Fried Pork Chops, 164–66, *165*
      Barbecued, 166
      Herbed, 166
   Slow-Cooker Cassoulet, 40–41
   Spiced Pork Tenderloin with Potato Rösti, 167–68
   Swedish Meatballs with Pickled Cucumbers, 142–44
Main dishes (poultry)
   Barbecued Chicken Wings, 180–81
   Cornell Chicken, *192,* 193–94
   Enchiladas Verdes, 184–87, *186*
   Glazed Roast Chicken, 197–99
   Huli Huli Chicken, 199–202, *200*
   Kentucky Burgoo, 35–38, *36*
   Old-Fashioned Roast Turkey and Gravy, 202–5, *203*
   Roast Lemon Chicken, 194–97, *195*
   Sautéed Chicken Cutlets
      with Porcini Sauce, 181–84, *182*
   Skillet Phyllo Pie with Chicken, 187–89
   Spiedies, 189–91, *190*
Main dishes (seafood)
   Grilled Salmon Fillets with Almond Vinaigrette, 208–10
   New Orleans Barbecue Shrimp, 217–18
   Salmon en Cocotte with Celery and Orange, 212
   Salmon en Cocotte
      with Leeks and White Wine, 210–12, *211*
   Shrimp Tempura
      with Ginger-Soy Dipping Sauce, 220–23, *221*
   Skillet Salmon and Leek Pot Pie, 213–14
   Skillet Shrimp and Grits, 215–17, *216*
   Southern Shrimp Burgers, 218–20
Make-Ahead Creamy
      Macaroni and Cheese, 120–23, *121*
Make-Ahead Green Bean Casserole, 62–64, *63*
Mango and Lime Curry Vinaigrette,
      Cherry Tomato Salad with, 12
Maple syrup
   shelf life for, 287
   taste tests on, 88, 293
Marinating foods
   effect of salt in marinades, 288
   marinade ingredients, 289
   myths about, 288
   tips for success, 289
Mashed Potatoes
   Garlic, 44–45
   Garlic and Cheese (Aligot), 45–48, *46*
Measuring cups, dry, ratings of, 10
Meat
   checking for doneness, 139
   ground, cooking tip, 274
   marinating, 288–89
   see also Beef; Lamb; Pork

Meatballs
   Slow-Cooker, in Marinara Sauce, 124–25
   Swedish, with Pickled Cucumbers, 142–44
Meat Loaf, Glazed, 163–64
Melon. *See* Watermelon
Melon ballers, uses for, 276
Microwave splatters, preventing, 274
Mirin, taste tests on, 147
Mixing bowls
   ratings of, 228
   stabilizing, 275, 276
Molasses
   Bold and Spicy Gingerbread Cake, 258–60, *259*
   Hermits, 231–33
   shelf life for, 287
   types of, 232
Monterey Jack cheese
   Au Gratin Potatoes, 48–50, *49*
   Crispy Bacon-Cheddar Potato Skins, 7
   Enchiladas Verdes, 184–87, *186*
Mozzarella cheese
   Aligot (Garlic and Cheese Mashed Potatoes), 45–48, *46*
   Baked Ziti, *114,* 115–16
   Fresh, and Basil, Cherry Tomato Salad with, 11
   Skillet Cheese Pizza, 105–7
   Skillet Pizza with Goat Cheese, Olives, and Spicy Garlic
      Oil, 107
   Skillet Pizza with Ricotta, Bacon, and Scallions, *106,* 107
   Smoked, and Roasted Peppers,
      Summer Vegetable Gratin with, 61
   and Tomatoes, Pizza Bianca with, 104
Muffins, Blueberry, 85–86
   with Almond Crunch Topping, 86
   with Frozen Blueberries, 86
   with Orange Glaze, 86
Mushroom(s)
   Cream, Eggs en Cocotte with, 79
   dried, buying and storing, 29, 284
   dried, handling, 284
   fresh, buying and storing, 284
   fresh, cleaning, 284
   Make-Ahead Green Bean Casserole, 62–64, *63*
   porcini, selecting, 183
   and Root Vegetable Stew, Hearty, 28–29
   Sautéed Chicken Cutlets
      with Porcini Sauce, 181–84, *182*
   Skillet Ramen with Beef, Shiitakes, and Spinach, 123–24
   varieties of, 285
Mustard
   coarse-grain, taste tests on, 19
   Glaze, Sweet, Grilled Rack of Lamb with, 176

N

New Mexico Pork Chili, 38–40, *39*
New Orleans Barbecue Shrimp, 217–18
Noodles
  Hearty Chicken Noodle Soup, *30,* 31–33
  Skillet Ramen with Beef, Shiitakes, and Spinach, 123–24
Nuts
  Curried Waldorf Salad with Green Grapes and Peanuts, 17
  Dream Bars, 233–35, *234*
  Herbed Baked Goat Cheese Salad, 12–14, *13*
  Jefferson Davis Pie, 249–50
  Sun-Dried Tomato Baked Goat Cheese Salad, 14
  toasting, 15
  Waldorf Salad, 14–17, *15*
  Waldorf Salad with Dried Cranberries and Pecans, 17
  see also Almond(s), Peanuts, Pecans, Walnuts

O

Oils, storing, 286
  see also Olive oil
Old-Fashioned Roast Turkey and Gravy, 202–5, *203*
Olive oil
  checking for freshness, 286
  extra-virgin, taste tests on, 212, 290
  storing, 286
Olives
  Goat Cheese, and Spicy Garlic Oil,
    Skillet Pizza with, 107
  Greek Cherry Tomato Salad, 10–11
  Skillet Phyllo Pie with Chicken, 187–89
Omelet pans, ratings of, 76
Omelets, French, *74,* 75–77
Onion(s)
  Caramelized, Beef en Cocotte with, 159–60
  dicing and mincing, 278
  Hungarian Beef Stew, 33–34
  Pickled, Sweet and Spicy, Steak Tacos with, 130–32, *133*
  Rings, Beer-Battered, 55–56
  storing, 278
Orange
  and Celery, Salmon en Cocotte with, 212
  -Chocolate Soufflé, Skillet, 268
  Glaze, Blueberry Muffins with, 86

P

Pancake Mix, Homemade, 87–88
Pancake syrups, taste tests on, 293
Pan-Fried Pork Chops, 164–66, *165*
  Barbecued, 166
  Herbed, 166
Pan-Seared Strip Steak with Crispy Potatoes
    and Salsa Verde, 137–39

Paper plates, ratings of, 312
Paprika, sweet, taste tests on, 35
Parmesan cheese
  Baked Ziti, *114,* 115–16
  Cheesy Broccoli and Rice Casserole, 67–68, *69*
  Cream, Eggs en Cocotte with, 79
  Savory Bread Pudding, 82–84
  Savory Bread Pudding with Bacon and Onion, 84
  Summer Vegetable Gratin, 58–61, *59*
Parsley
  Salsa Verde, 137–39
  -Shallot Butter, 158
Pasta
  Baked Ziti, *114,* 115–16
  Garlicky Shrimp, 118–20
  macaroni, taste tests on, 122, 295
  Make-Ahead Creamy Macaroni
    and Cheese, 120–23, *121*
  measuring, weight-to-cup equivalents, 113
  Quick Tomato Sauce, *110,* 111–12
  Skillet, with Peas and Prosciutto, 117–18
  Skillet Penne alla Vodka, 112–13
  Slow-Cooker Meatballs in Marinara Sauce, 124–25
  see also Noodles
Pastry cutter, improvising, 275
Peanuts and Green Grapes,
    Curried Waldorf Salad with, 17
Peas
  frozen, taste tests on, 117
  and Prosciutto, Skillet Pasta with, 117–18
Pecans
  Dream Bars, 233–35, *234*
  and Dried Cranberries, Waldorf Salad with, 17
  Herbed Baked Goat Cheese Salad, 12–14, *13*
  Jefferson Davis Pie, 249–50
Peelers, ratings of, 279
Penne alla Vodka, Skillet, 112–13
Peppercorns, black, taste tests on, 219, 291
Pepper jack cheese
  Enchiladas Verdes, 184–87, *186*
Peppers
  Roasted, and Smoked Mozzarella,
    Summer Vegetable Gratin with, 61
  Roasted Red, and Basil,
    Sautéed Green Beans with, 52
  Skillet Ratatouille, 56–58
  see also Chile(s)
Perfect Chocolate Chip Cookies, 226–28
Phyllo Pie, Skillet, with Chicken, 187–89
Pickled Cucumbers, 143–44
Pickled Onions, Sweet and Spicy,
    Steak Tacos with, 130–32, *133*
Pie Dough
  Foolproof Double-Crust, 247–49
  Foolproof Single-Crust, 249
  rolling out, tip for, 276
Pie plates, ratings of, 250, 306

Pies (dessert)
  Apple, Skillet, 242–44, *243*
  Blueberry, 245–47, *248*
  French Silk Chocolate, 251–53, *252*
  Jefferson Davis, 249–50
  Pumpkin, 253–56, *255*
  slicing, tip for, 277
Pies (savory)
  Skillet Phyllo, with Chicken, 187–89
  Skillet Salmon and Leek Pot Pie, 213–14
  see also Pizza
Pizza
  Bianca, 101–4, *103*
    with Tomatoes, Sausage, and Fontina, 104
    with Tomatoes and Mozzarella, 104
  Skillet
    Cheese, 105–7
    with Fontina, Arugula, and Prosciutto, 107
    with Goat Cheese, Olives, and Spicy Garlic Oil, 107
    with Ricotta, Bacon, and Scallions, *106,* 107
Plastic bags, storage tip, 274
Plastic wrap, ratings of, 162, 307
Popcorn, microwave, taste tests on, 297
Popover pans, ratings of, 97
Popovers, 96–97
Pork
  Boston butt, butterflying, 173
  Carne Adovada, 38–40, *39*
  checking for doneness, 139
  Chops
    cooking tips, 166
    Pan-Fried, 164–66, *165*
    Pan-Fried Barbecued, 166
    Pan-Fried Herbed, 166
  Glazed Meat Loaf, 163–64
  Grill-Roasted Ham, 170–72, *171*
  marinating, 288–89
  Ribs
    Atomic, 168–70
    removing membrane from, 169
    St. Louis–style, about, 169
  Roast, Holiday, with Cherry Stuffing, 174
  Roast, Holiday Stuffed, 172–74
  salt pork, about, 204
  Skillet Pasta with Peas and Prosciutto, 117–18
  Skillet Pizza with Fontina, Arugula, and Prosciutto, 107
  Slow-Cooker Cassoulet, 40–41
  Swedish Meatballs with Pickled Cucumbers, 142–44
  tenderloin, removing silver skin from, 167
  Tenderloin, Spiced, with Potato Rösti, 167–68
  see also Bacon; Sausage(s)
Potato(es)
  Au Gratin, 48–50, *49*
  Corn Chowder, 23–24, *25*
  Crispy, and Salsa Verde,
    Pan-Seared Strip Steak with, 137–39
  Garlic and Cheese Mashed (Aligot), 45–48, *46*

Potato(es) *(cont.)*
  Garlic Mashed, 44–45
  Hearty Root Vegetable and Mushroom Stew, 28–29
  Kentucky Burgoo, 35–38, *36*
  Rösti, Spiced Pork Tenderloin with, 167–68
  Salad, German, 17–19, *18*
  Skins, Crispy Bacon-Cheddar, 7
Potato mashers, ratings of, 45
Pot Pie, Skillet Salmon and Leek, 213–14
Poultry
  checking for doneness, 139
  marinating, 288–89
  see also Chicken; Turkey
Pound Cake, 7UP, 263–65, *264*
Prosciutto
  Arugula, and Fontina, Skillet Pizza with, 107
  and Peas, Skillet Pasta with, 117–18
Prunes and Guinness, Braised Beef Short Ribs with, 137
Pudding, Bread
  Chocolate, 238–39
  Savory, 82–84
    with Bacon and Onion, 84
    with Spinach and Feta, *83,* 84
Pumpkin Pie, 253–56, *255*

Q

Quiche Lorraine, 79–82, *80*
Quiche with Bacon, Scallions, and Cheddar, 82
Quick Tomato Sauce, *110,* 111–12

R

Raisins
  Hermits, 231–33
  Jefferson Davis Pie, 249–50
  Waldorf Salad, 14–17, *15*
Ramen, Skillet, with Beef,
    Shiitakes, and Spinach, 123–24
Rasp graters, ratings of, 268
Ratatouille, Skillet, 56–58
Red Wine, Cherry, and Cinnamon Cobbler, Skillet, 242
Refrigerator zones, 282
Reuben Sandwiches, 134
Rice and Broccoli Casserole, Cheesy, 67–68, *69*
Ricotta
  Bacon, and Scallions, Skillet Pizza with, *106,* 107
  Skillet Pasta with Peas and Prosciutto, 117–18
Roast Beef Tenderloin, 157–59
Roasters, vertical, ratings of, 198
Roasting rack, improvising, 274
Roast Lemon Chicken, 194–97, *195*
Rolls, Rustic Dinner, *98,* 99–100
Rulers, uses for, 275
Rustic Dinner Rolls, *98,* 99–100

S

Safety can openers, ratings of, 111

Salads
  Baked Goat Cheese
    Herbed, 12–14, *13*
    Honey-Raisin, 14
    Sun-Dried Tomato, 14
  Cherry Tomato
    with Basil and Fresh Mozzarella, 11
    Greek, 10–11
    with Mango and Lime Curry Vinaigrette, 12
    with Tarragon and Blue Cheese, 11
    and Watermelon, 11–12
  Potato, German, 17–19, *18*
  Waldorf, 14–17, *15*
    Curried, with Green Grapes and Peanuts, 17
    with Dried Cranberries and Pecans, 17
    with Red Grapes and Almonds, 17

Salmon
  en Cocotte with Celery and Orange, 212
  en Cocotte with Leeks and White Wine, 210–12, *211*
  Fillets, Grilled, with Almond Vinaigrette, 208–10
  fillets, skinning, 212
  and Leek Pot Pie, Skillet, 213–14

Salsa Verde, 137–39

Salt pork, about, 204

Sandwiches
  Reuben, 134
  Spiedies, 189–91, *190*

Sauces
  Dipping, Ginger-Soy, 222
  Hollandaise, 72–75
  Salsa Verde, 137–39
  Tartar, 219
  Tomato, Quick, *110,* 111–12

Sauerkraut
  Reuben Sandwiches, 134
  taste tests on, 135

Sausage(s)
  cooking tip, 274
  hard, removing white casing from, 276
  kielbasa, taste tests on, 41
  Slow-Cooker Cassoulet, 40–41
  Stuffed Cabbage Rolls, 64–67, *66*
  Tomatoes, and Fontina, Pizza Bianca with, 104

Sautéed Chicken Cutlets with Porcini Sauce, 181–84, *182*

Sautéed Green Beans
  with Garlic and Herbs, 51
  with Ginger and Sesame, 52
  with Roasted Red Peppers and Basil, 52
  with Smoked Paprika and Almonds, 52

Savory Bread Pudding, 82–84
  with Bacon and Onion, 84
  with Spinach and Feta, *83,* 84

Scrubbers, nonscratch, ratings of, 52, 311

Seafood. *See* Fish; Shrimp

Seeds, toasting, 15

7UP Pound Cake, 263–65, *264*

Shallot(s)
  mincing, 279
  -Parsley Butter, 158
  shopping for, 11
  when to use in recipes, 279

Shellfish. *See* Shrimp

Shredded Barbecued Beef, 148–49

Shrimp
  Burgers, Southern, 218–20
  defrosted, storing, 120
  deveining, 219
  and Grits, Skillet, 215–17, *216*
  New Orleans Barbecue, 217–18
  Pasta, Garlicky, 118–20
  Tempura with Ginger-Soy Dipping Sauce, 220–23, *221*

Side dishes
  Broccoli and Rice Casserole, Cheesy, 67–68, *69*
  Cabbage Rolls, Stuffed, 64–67, *66*
  Green Bean Casserole, Make-Ahead, 62–64, *63*
  Green Beans, Sautéed
    with Garlic and Herbs, 51
    with Ginger and Sesame, 52
    with Roasted Red Peppers and Basil, 52
    with Smoked Paprika and Almonds, 52
  Macaroni and Cheese,
    Creamy Make-Ahead, 120–23, *121*
  Onion Rings, Beer-Battered, 55–56
  Potatoes
    Au Gratin, 48–50, *49*
    Garlic and Cheese Mashed (Aligot), 45–48, *46*
    Garlic Mashed, 44–45
  Ratatouille, Skillet, 56–58
  Spoonbread, Sweet Corn, 52–54, *53*
  Spoonbreads, Individual, 54
  Summer Squash Casserole, 61–62
  Summer Vegetable Gratin, 58–61, *59*
  Summer Vegetable Gratin
    with Roasted Peppers and Smoked Mozzarella, 61
  see also Salads

Silicone spatulas, ratings of, 304

Skillet Apple Pie, 242–44, *243*

Skillet Cobbler
  Cherry, 239–41, *240*
  Cherry, Red Wine, and Cinnamon, 242
  Cherry-Almond, 242

Skillet Pasta with Peas and Prosciutto, 117–18

Skillet Penne alla Vodka, 112–13

Skillet Phyllo Pie with Chicken, 187–89

Skillet Pizza
  Cheese, 105–7
  with Fontina, Arugula, and Prosciutto, 107
  with Goat Cheese, Olives, and Spicy Garlic Oil, 107
  with Ricotta, Bacon, and Scallions, *106,* 107

Skillet Ramen with Beef, Shiitakes, and Spinach, 123–24

Skillet Ratatouille, 56–58
Skillets
  nonstick, ratings of, 117
  nonstick "omelet," ratings of, 76
  storing, tip for, 274
  traditional, ratings of, 215, 303
Skillet Salmon and Leek Pot Pie, 213–14
Skillet Shrimp and Grits, 215–17, *216*
Skillet Soufflé
  Chocolate-Orange, 268
  Lemon, 265–68, *267*
Slow-Cooker Barbecued Beef Brisket, 149–52, *150*
Slow-Cooker Cassoulet, 40–41
Slow-Cooker Meatballs in Marinara Sauce, 124–25
Soufflé, Skillet
  Chocolate-Orange, 268
  Lemon, 265–68, *267*
Soups
  Chicken Noodle, Hearty, *30,* 31–33
  Corn Chowder, 23–24, *25*
  Tomato, Creamless Creamy, 22–23
  Wisconsin Cheddar Beer, 26–28, *27*
  see also Stews
Southern Shrimp Burgers, 218–20
Soy-Ginger Dipping Sauce, 222
Spatulas, heatproof rubber, ratings of, 131
Spatulas, silicone, ratings of, 304
Spiced Pork Tenderloin with Potato Rösti, 167–68
Spices, storing, 286
Spinach
  Beef, and Shiitakes, Skillet Ramen with, 123–24
  and Feta, Savory Bread Pudding with, *83,* 84
Sponges, kitchen, 277
Spoonbread(s)
  Individual, 54
  Sweet Corn, 52–54, *53*
Squash
  Pumpkin Pie, 253–56, *255*
  Skillet Ratatouille, 56–58
  Summer, Casserole, 61–62
  Summer Vegetable Gratin, 58–61, *59*
  Summer Vegetable Gratin with Roasted Peppers and
    Smoked Mozzarella, 61
St. Louis Gooey Butter Cake, 91–93, *92*
Starters
  Boneless Buffalo Chicken
    with Blue Cheese Dressing, *8,* 9–10
  Caponata, 4–7, *5*
  Crispy Bacon-Cheddar Potato Skins, 7
Steak, beef. *See under* Beef
Stews
  Beef, Hungarian, 33–34
  Carne Adovada, 38–40, *39*
  Kentucky Burgoo, 35–38, *36*
  Root Vegetable and Mushroom, Hearty, 28–29
  Slow-Cooker Cassoulet, 40–41
Storage containers, ratings of, 287

Strawberry yogurt, low-fat, taste tests on, 300
Stuffed Cabbage Rolls, 64–67, *66*
Stuffing, baking in muffin tins, 275
Sugar, storing, 287
Summer Squash
  Casserole, 61–62
  Skillet Ratatouille, 56–58
  Summer Vegetable Gratin, 58–61, *59*
  Summer Vegetable Gratin with Roasted Peppers and
    Smoked Mozzarella, 61
Summer Vegetable Gratin, 58–61, *59*
Summer Vegetable Gratin with
    Roasted Peppers and Smoked Mozzarella, 61
Sun-Dried Tomato Baked Goat Cheese Salad, 14
Swedish Meatballs with Pickled Cucumbers,
    142–44
Sweet Corn Spoonbread, 52–54, *53*
Sweet paprika, taste tests on, 35
Swiss cheese
  Aligot (Garlic and Cheese Mashed Potatoes), 45–48, *46*
  Quiche Lorraine, 79–82, *80*
  Reuben Sandwiches, 134

T

Tacos, Steak, with
    Sweet and Spicy Pickled Onions, 130–32, *133*
Tartar Sauce, 219
Techniques, illustrated
  anatomy of a chef's knife, 280
  buying, storing, and cleaning mushrooms, 284
  chef's knife cuts and safety basics, 281
  keeping kitchen staples fresh, 286–87
  keeping produce fresh, 282–83
  maintaining chef's knife blade, 280
  marinating meat and poultry, 288–89
  mushroom varieties, 285
  preparing vegetables, 278–79
  working with dried mushrooms, 284
Teriyaki, Grilled Beef, 144–47, *145*
Texas Barbecued Beef Ribs, 152–55, *153*
Thermometer, attaching to pot, 274
Tips, quick kitchen, 274–77
Toasters, four-slice, ratings of, 313
Tomatillos
  Enchiladas Verdes, 184–87, *186*
  shopping for, 187
Tomato(es)
  Baked Ziti, *114,* 115–16
  Caponata, 4–7, *5*
  Cherry
    Salad, Greek, 10–11
    Salad, Watermelon and, 11–12
    Salad with Basil and Fresh Mozzarella, 11
    Salad with Mango and Lime Curry Vinaigrette, 12
    Salad with Tarragon and Blue Cheese, 11

Tomato(es) *(cont.)*
and Mozzarella, Pizza Bianca with, 104
Sauce, Quick, *110,* 111–12
Sausage, and Fontina, Pizza Bianca with, 104
Skillet Penne alla Vodka, 112–13
Skillet Ratatouille, 56–58
Slow-Cooker Meatballs in Marinara Sauce, 124–25
Soup, Creamless Creamy, 22–23
Stuffed Cabbage Rolls, 64–67, *66*
Summer Vegetable Gratin, 58–61, *59*
Summer Vegetable Gratin with Roasted Peppers and
    Smoked Mozzarella, 61
Sun-Dried, Baked Goat Cheese Salad, 14
Tomato paste, taste tests on, 113
Tortillas
buying, tips for, 131
Enchiladas Verdes, 184–87, *186*
Steak Tacos with Sweet and Spicy Pickled Onions,
    130–32, *133*
warming, 131
Triple Chocolate Mousse Cake, 269–71
Trivets, makeshift, 275
Turkey
leftover, reheating, 274
Roast, and Gravy, Old-Fashioned, 202–5, *203*

U

Ultimate Cinnamon Buns, 88–91, *89*

V

Vanilla extract
aged versus fresh, flavor of, 258
shelf life, 258, 287
storing, 287
taste tests on, 241, 292
Vegetable(s)
bagged, storage tip, 276
Root, and Mushroom Stew, Hearty, 28–29
storing, 282–83
Summer, Gratin, 58–61, *59*
Summer, Gratin with
    Roasted Peppers and Smoked Mozzarella, 61
see also specific vegetables
Vertical roasters, ratings of, 198
Vinegar, storing, 286
Vodka, Skillet Penne alla, 112–13

W

Waldorf Salad, 14–17, *15*
Curried, with Green Grapes and Peanuts, 17
with Dried Cranberries and Pecans, 17
with Red Grapes and Almonds, 17
Walnut(s)
Sun-Dried Tomato Baked Goat Cheese Salad, 14
Waldorf Salad, 14–17, *15*
Watermelon and Cherry Tomato Salad, 11–12
Whipped Cream
Bourbon, 250
preparing, tip for, 275
White chocolate
taste tests on, 271
Triple Chocolate Mousse Cake, 269–71
Wisconsin Cheddar Beer Soup, 26–28, *27*

Y

Yeast, storing, 287
Yogurt, low-fat strawberry, taste tests on, 300

Z

Ziti, Baked, *114,* 115–16
Zucchini
Skillet Ratatouille, 56–58
Summer Vegetable Gratin, 58–61, *59*
Summer Vegetable Gratin with
    Roasted Peppers and Smoked Mozzarella, 61